Catholicism and Politics in Communist Societies

CATHOLICISM AND POLITICS IN COMMUNIST SOCIETIES

Edited by Pedro Ramet

CHRISTIANITY UNDER STRESS
Volume II

Duke University Press Durham and London 1990

Printed in the United States of America
on acid-free paper ∞

Library of Congress Cataloging-in-Publication Data
Catholicism and politics in communist societies / edited by Pedro Ramet.
— (Christianity under stress ; 2)
Includes bibliographical references.
ISBN 0-8223-1010-4
ISBN 0-8223-1047-3 (pbk.)
1. Communism and Christianity—Catholic Church. 2. Christianity and politics—History—20th century. 3. Catholic Church—Communist countries. 4. Church and state—Communist countries. 5. Communist countries—Church history. I. Ramet, Pedro, 1949– . II. Series.
BX1396.4.C367 1990
282'.09171'7—dc20 89-39178

To

PETER F. SUGAR,

my trusted friend . . .

Contents

Preface ix

PART I INTRODUCTION

1 Catholic Tradition, Hierarchy, and the Politics of Coexistence Under Communism: An Introduction *Pedro Ramet* 3

2 Catholic Social Teachings: A Brief History *Arthur F. McGovern, S. J.* 28

PART II CATHOLICISM UNDER EUROPEAN COMMUNISM

3 The Catholic Church in the Soviet Union *Roman Solchanyk and Ivan Hvat* 49

4 The Catholic Church in East Germany *Robert F. Goeckel* 93

5 The Catholic Church in 1944–1989 Poland *Vincent C. Chrypinski* 117

6 The Catholic Church in Czechoslovakia *Milan J. Reban* 142

7 The Catholic Church in Hungary *Leslie László* 156

8 The Catholic Church in Yugoslavia, 1945–1989 *Pedro Ramet* 181

9 The Catholic Church in Romania *Janice Broun* 207

10 The Catholic Church in Albania *Janice Broun* 232

PART III CATHOLIC-COMMUNIST ENCOUNTERS ON OTHER CONTINENTS

11 The Catholic Church in China *Eric O. Hanson* 253

12 The Catholic Church in Vietnam *Stephen Denney* 270

13 The Catholic Church in Cuba *Thomas E. Quigley* 296

14 The Catholic Church in Sandinista Nicaragua *Humberto Belli* 313

PART IV PAPAL POLICY

15 Papal Eastern Diplomacy and the Vatican Apparatus *Hansjakob Stehle* 341

16 Karol Wojtyła and Marxism *George H. Williams* 356

Notes 383

Index 441

Contributors 451

Preface

This is the second volume in a three-volume series, Christianity under Stress, on the experiences of Christian churches in communist-ruled societies. The first volume, *Eastern Christianity and Politics in the Twentieth Century*, which included a discussion of precommunist politics as well as of Orthodox church life in noncommunist Finland and Greece, was published in February 1988. The third volume, *Protestantism and Politics in Eastern Europe and the Soviet Union*, is nearing completion.

A number of scholars generously took time to read the chapters in this book and offer suggestions for improvement. In particular I thank Enrique Baloyra, Ivo Banac, Fr. Vincent Minh, Earl Pope, Thomas Quigley, Nicholas Riasanovsky, Grazyna Sikorska, Peter F. Sugar, and Otto Ulč for their insightful comments on individual chapters. We are all also indebted to the two anonymous readers contracted by Duke University Press, who provided invaluable feedback and criticism.

George H. Williams's chapter is based on an earlier study which originally appeared in the *Pope John Paul II Lecture Series* in honor of the College of St. Thomas Centennial. I am grateful to the college for permission to publish a revised and updated version of this study.

I also wish to thank the Graduate School of the University of Washington for its generosity in providing a publication subsidy for this book.

And finally, I express my continuing gratitude to Reynolds Smith of Duke University Press, whose patience, interest, good humor, intelligent feedback, and sheer hard work have helped to make work on this book a pleasure.

Pedro Ramet
Seattle, September 18, 1989

I

INTRODUCTION

1

Catholic Tradition, Hierarchy, and the Politics of Coexistence Under Communism: An Introduction

Pedro Ramet

There is a curious duality in Catholic tradition. On the one hand, terrestrial life is treated as having distinctly secondary and instrumental importance, and Catholics are exhorted to endure present sufferings patiently, in hopes of heavenly reward. On the other hand, the church long ago developed a tradition ascribing great value to the earthly institutions of the church and a concomitant interest in any temporal matters that affect its institutional interests.[1] This duality provides the backdrop against which there has been perennial change. For as societies change, their religious institutions change too in their doctrines, their structures, and their styles. Despite the myth of ecclesiastical changelessness, carefully nurtured by the Roman Curia from the sixteenth to the mid-twentieth centuries,[2] the Catholic church has evolved over the centuries and has proven itself open to adaptation to local and national conditions. Hence, as Hans Küng once observed, "there is not, and never was in fact, an essence of the Church by itself, separate, chemically pure, distilled from the stream of historical forms."[3]

The recollected past that emerges out of the stream of historical forms is known as *tradition,* and the aspiration for continuity with ecclesiastical tradition is an important hallmark of Catholicism. Hence Catholicism is inseparable from the lodestar of tradition. For conservatives, the question has been how to preserve and insulate authentic tradition from the pressures of modernity and political vicissitudes. For reformers seeking to legitimize their innovations in terms of earlier tradition, the question has been variously how to *restore* authentic tradition and strip away the corruptive accretions of time, how to reconceptualize tradition as a dynamic force (as Cardinal Newman and Abbé Alfred Loisy held),[4] or how to adapt what is contingent in tradition to the extent necessary while preserving what is essential (as Avery Dulles outlines his own position). Bearing that in mind, this book is organized around the themes of tradition versus modernity, hierarchy versus lower clergy, and institutional structure versus grass-roots organizations. These themes, I would argue, are important not only in the life of the church per se, but also more specifically in shaping church-state relations under communism.

No less an authority than theologian Richard P. McBrien has suggested that the sole characteristic that distinguishes the Roman Catholic church from *all* other Christian churches is the so-called Petrine doctrine, i.e., the belief that the authority of the pope derives directly from Christ's elevation of Saint Peter to primacy among the apostles.[5] Until the Second Vatican Council (1962–65) this doctrine lay at the heart of the church's claim to be the one, true church, and indeed, until then the other Christian communities were—with the exception of the Orthodox church—never dignified with the name "church" by Catholic spokesmen. This has changed now, and for the mainstream of postconciliar Catholicism, the "church" embraces all of Christianity, though the Catholic church still claims a special place for itself in the ecclesiastical order.[6] Thus the Catholic church now contains more people open to ecumenical dialogue than ever before, and some, especially in Latin America, who are open to dialogue with communists.

The Catholic church that confronted communism from the Bolshevik Revolution in 1917 until Vatican II presented a different face. Its ranks were more unified; it believed strongly in the unchanging nature of its truth and tradition; it stood resolutely opposed to communism. Neoscholastic philosophy reigned supreme. This school of thought took its bearings from the scholastic philosophy formulated in the Middle Ages by Saint Thomas Aquinas and others who explained church teachings in Aristotelian categories.[7] Although it was acknowledged—e.g., by the Jesuit Thomist Josef Kleutgen (1811–83)—that scholasticism per se could not be said to predate the twelfth century, it was argued with some conviction that scholasticism was the legitimate heir to the Aristotelian scientific method, which had been adopted in Christian form by the early church fathers and reached maturity in the Middle Ages.[8] Hence, in its confrontation with communism, the Catholic church tended to emphasize the continuity of its tradition rather than its syncretic growth and adaptation. In this regard, the spirit of Vatican II has been slow to penetrate Eastern Europe. The Polish church in particular has drawn greater inspiration from Polish history and the legacy of the past than from Vatican II, and has stressed vigorous authority rather than conciliar collegiality.[9] In the context of a repudiation of the changes brought about by the Second Vatican Council, a Catholic scholar recently gave spirited expression to this idea: "Either Truth is important, and doesn't change, or it changes and then is of no importance."[10]

On the communist side of the ledger, Khrushchev's de-Stalinization campaign of the latter 1950s marked a dramatic watershed in the evolution of communism. But the limited liberalization it spawned did not extend to the religious sphere, and the Vatican's first meeting with a communist leader was with maverick Yugoslav president Josip Broz Tito in 1971.

Catholic-communist encounters display considerable diversity because they are affected by a number of factors, including local traditions and legacies (e.g., in differences between Eastern Europe and Latin America), specific personalities, and whether or not the communist government in question is subservient to the Kremlin.

Authority, Tradition, and Modernity

Catholicism has embraced at least five major currents of thought about authority and tradition in the period since the early eighteenth century. *Traditionalists* such as Joseph de Maistre, Louis de Bonald, and Louis Bautain adopted an organic model of society specifically rejecting the individualistic, mechanistic model favored by Enlightenment philosophers. For the traditionalists, it is misleading to speak of "human reason" as if it had a validity or universality that transcends social forms and cultural institutions. Hence it followed, for de Maistre, that reason has no independent capacity to inquire into revelation. Suspicious of individual reason, de Maistre was politically promonarchist and ecclesiastically ultramontane. De Bonald likewise stressed the primacy of society in the formation of thought, but he went further than de Maistre in arguing that society is also the source of moral ideas and conventions. For de Bonald, the Protestant commitment to private conscience paralleled the Cartesian commitment to individual reason and led to the rejection of tradition and authority, upon which alone revelation could be preserved untarnished. Bautain, too, underlined the centrality of tradition in the transmission and development of revelation.[11]

Neoscholastics and *conservatives* are less wedded to monarchism, though they frequently display a distrust of democracy, which is seen as inimical to both authority and tradition. Theologian Joachim Salaverri is representative of the conservative school. His *Sacrae Theologiae Summa* (5th ed., 1962) argues that the church is inherently hierarchical and monarchical, claims that the hierarchical structure is necessary if the church is to carry out Christ's work, and dismisses all other churches as "false churches."[12] Again, Josef Cardinal Ratzinger, head of the Congregation for the Doctrine of the Faith, has argued that insofar as Truth is a fixed given, it is, at least in theory, beyond debate and cannot be made subject to the outcome of a vote.[13] This interpretation tends in the direction of excluding democracy from Catholic tradition. As Rocco Buttiglione, a leading thinker of Communione e Liberazione (a group strongly supportive of Pope John Paul II), recently put it, "Democracy is a wonderful formula for political society, but the Church is not a democracy."[14] Again, in 1937 Pope Pius XI (1857–1939, pope 1922–39) wrote, "It is not true that all have equal rights in civil society. It is not true that there exists no lawful social hierarchy."[15] For conservatives, distrust of authority is characteristic of Protestants, who are seen as more likely to refer doubts to their own private (subjective) conscience, while Catholics should be taught to distrust subjectivity and to refer doubts to established authority. This means that authority, or more specifically ecclesiastical authority, becomes the benchmark of moral and political Truth, and individual judgment comes to have validity *only* insofar as it chooses obedience to church positions. In the process, where Protestantism accepts relativism as a given, Catholicism aspires to rise above relativism. Peter Nichols drew the obvious consequences when he commented, "One of the finest of Catholic defects seems to me to be excessive loyalty."[16]

Conservatives are wary of reform because, as Joseph A. Komonchak has phrased it, they reflect on the fact that what may qualify as "reform" in theological terms may be "revolutionary" in sociological terms.[17] Conservatives tend to see themselves as moderates occupying the theological and political "center" between integralists and liberals, and to stress continuity with the past. For Pope John Paul II, the documents of Vatican II must be interpreted, above all, within the context of Catholic tradition, i.e., in terms of their continuity with and affirmation of preexisting principles.[18] Cardinal Ratzinger, the bête noire of the liberals, likewise positions himself at the ideological center, criticizing integralists for rejecting the Second Vatican Council and liberals for allegedly rejecting everything prior to the Second Vatican Council.

Whereas conservatives insist on the divine character of the church, *liberals* are, at least at times, prepared to argue that the church should be viewed as a *human* institution.[19] Ecclesiastical liberals are apt to be pluralists in both theological and political terms, and to accept diversity as a fact of life, if not as an outright boon. In assuming an ecumenist posture and adopting its Declaration on Religious Freedom in 1965,[20] the Second Vatican Council may be seen as liberalizing. As McBrien noted, adoption of the declaration ended the double standard under which the Catholic church had long "demand[ed] freedom for itself when in a minority position but refuse[d] to grant freedom to other religions when they are in the minority."[21]

In the early years of this century, Alfred Loisy figured in some ways as a forerunner of contemporary ecclesiastical liberalism when he wrote that important church doctrines are historically relative and derivative (e.g., the doctrine of the Trinity, which Loisy traced to the ancient Greek Olympian religion).[22] Loisy argued forcefully that "the Church, as a living organism, was destined to develop far beyond all that Jesus had foreseen and all that the apostles had believed. In Loisy's theology, Christianity was portrayed as a movement that took its departure, and even its inspiration, from Jesus and the apostles, but was not governed by them as its norm."[23]

In the 1940s French theologians Henri de Lubac and Henri Bouillard noted that religious doctrines arise in contingent cultural contexts, from which they concluded that doctrines of the faith should be open to reconceptualization.[24] More recently, Avery Dulles has urged that the reinterpretation and reshaping of the Magisterium is a healthy and necessary process, and he argued that while church teaching is in some sense infallible, it is nonetheless susceptible to reform. Like conservative Ratzinger, liberal Dulles views himself as occupying the ideological "center."[25]

Further to the left, but still within the "liberal" camp, are Hans Küng, Hermann Häring, and Norbert Greinacher. In an embittered and highly polemical article originally written for the Toronto *Globe and Mail*, Küng misrepresented Cardinal Ratzinger's position on Vatican II, claiming that Ratzinger finds almost nothing good in the council. Küng charged that Ratzinger and the conservatives are more at home with totalitarian regimes than with democratic systems, and characterized the German prelate as "anti-modernist."[26] In a similarly polemical attack on Ratzinger, Häring charged that "Ratzinger has lost his bearings" and stressed Ratzinger's alleged distrust of democracy at the outset, as if this were the central theme of Ratzinger's book.[27] By contrast, Greinacher attacked Ratzinger not for an alleged affinity for totalitarianism but for the very opposite, viz., Ratzinger's supposed desire to defend the free-market system. Greinacher's "proof" for this portrayal is an extract in which Ratzinger condemned the practice of using Scripture to support *any* sociopolitical order.[28] The difference in spirit between conservatives and liberals is aptly captured in Küng's plea for exalting faith *over* the institutional church—in contradistinction to Ratzinger's greater solicitude for the latter.[29]

Radicals are sometimes lumped together with liberals, but actually they are quite different. Radicals are, in general, characterized by a much more developed this-worldly orientation. Langdon Gilkey, Schubert Ogden, and David Tracy, for instance, have pleaded for the church to make the present world its *exclusive* concern, with Gilkey arguing that the hierarchy has "no special competence" in interpreting the gospel and that "personal judgment and conscience take priority over every form of authority."[30] A similar conviction animated Camilo Torres, a Colombian clergyman who left the priesthood in June 1965 to join a guerrilla movement, only to be killed in action in early 1966. According to Torres, "When circumstances impede men from devoting themselves to Christ, the priest's proper duty is to combat these circumstances. . . . The revolutionary struggle is a Christian and priestly struggle."[31] Again in 1972 a group of American Jesuits drew up a document advocating "the construction of a revolutionary social strategy for the Society of Jesus which is explicitly neo-Marxist and Maoist." The document continued:

> The Society of Jesus must purge itself of its bourgeois consciousness and identify itself with the proletariat, acknowledging that only the proletariat, as the living negation of advanced monopoly capitalism and as the subject of history, can achieve correct and objective social knowledge—the proletariat simultaneously knows and constitutes society. It is at this point that we are very close to understanding the mystery of Jesus' own proletarian background.[32]

Ivan Illich was only slightly less activist in writing:

> The specific task of the Church in the modern world is the Christian celebration of the experience of change. . . . The new era of constant development must not only be enjoyed, it must be brought about. What is the task of the Church in the gestation of the new world? The Church can accelerate time by celebrating its advent, but it is not the Church's task to engineer its shape. She must resist that temptation. Otherwise she cannot celebrate the wondrous surprise of the coming, the advent.[33]

Liberation theology, an outgrowth of this current, holds that Christ explicitly advocated social and political transformation for the purpose of saving people "as whole persons in all dimensions."[34]

On August 6, 1984, the Sacred Congregation for the Doctrine of the Faith issued the *Instruction on Certain Aspects of the "Theology of Liberation."* The *Instruction* criticized liberation theology for giving an overly political reading of the Bible and for shifting priority from liberation from sin—a spiritual task—to liberation from political and economic injustice—a political task. Among the consequences which Ratzinger, primary author of the *Instruction*, traced to liberation theology were the relativization of Truth (because there is only the truth of one class versus the truth of another class), the confusion of Christian concern for the poor with Marxist mobilization of the "proletariat," and the subordination of theological criteria to the imperatives of class struggle. As a result, "*orthodoxy*, or the right rule of faith, is substituted by the notion of *orthopraxy* as the criterion of the truth."[35] The radical camp also includes Bishop Francis Simons and Leslie Dewart, who argue that there is no such thing as infallible teaching and that further reform of dogma is always possible.[36]

To these currents of thought one may add also the *integralists* (a modern version of the traditionalists), once powerful but now marginal, who sought to maximize the authority of the pope, minimize the room for free theological discussion, and prevent any change in the theological or ecclesiological positions of the church. Integralists are ideologically close to conservatives in the high value they place on tradition, institutional structures, and inherited laws, but differ from conservatives in treating intraecclesiastical currents as reducible to two basic camps (all others being "liberals") in their greater affection for a monarchical papacy, in their greater emphasis on the changelessness of Truth, and in their concern that the Second Vatican Council has had basically destructive effects. James Hitchcock, for instance, regrets that the Second Vatican Council produced a change in values and, with it, changes in the attitudes and behaviors of Catholics.[37] Hitchcock believes that Vatican II stimulated a "headlong flight from the Absolute" and in 1979 warned that "the danger now is that having settled for a comfortably this-worldly religion, the religiously tone-deaf, as it were, will come to dominate the life of the Church."[38] Hitchcock added that the ecology movement is a form of modern "paganism,"[39] that the advocacy of intraecclesiastical democracy and the encouragement of sex education will alike promote the growth of totalitarianism,[40] and criticized the humanization of Christ.[41] In a similar spirit, Romano Guardini warned that the withering away of dogma and the attendant relativization and attenuation of tradition will result in the moral atomization of the individual.[42]

The high priest of integralism is probably Archbishop Marcel Léfebvre, luxuriously ensconced in Ecône, Switzerland. From the very start Léfebvre rejected the Second Vatican Council because of its endorsement of religious liberty, its embrace of lay participation, and its demystification of the hierarchy. He also rejected Vatican II's call for improving relations with other churches. Léfebvre said that the council had been infected with "neo-Modernism and neo-Protestantism," and went into opposition. Distrustful of all forms of *aggiornamento*, he and his followers continued to say the Mass in Latin according to its preconciliar form. In 1970 he established the ultraconservative "Pius X Brotherhood," and in 1974 he established his own institute and seminary at Ecône, which was soon bankrolled by wealthy supporters. Although suspended from sacerdotal duties in June 1976, he continued to ordain priests into his brotherhood.[43] Gerard Noel called Léfebvre's Pius X Brotherhood "the nearest thing imaginable to a clerical 'black-shirt' party in today's Church."[44] That assessment notwithstanding, Archbishop Léfebvre had a two-hour meeting with the newly elected Pope John Paul II on November 18, 1978, and met with Cardinal Ratzinger for an hour in October 1987. Following that meeting, the Vatican announced its intention to restore Léfebvre's legal standing and to investigate his priestly order with an eye to establishing regulations for it.[45] By mid-1988 this ostensible rapprochement had collapsed. Léfebvre announced that the pope was "the anti-Christ," condemned the Catholic church for its "modernism," and in defiance of papal stricture consecrated a number of bishops, thus signaling a schism. The Vatican replied by excommunicating Léfebvre.[46]

Rama Coomaraswamy is another adherent of this integralist school. In Coomaraswamy's view, Truth is a fixed given, and it cannot change: "That truth can change is against the doctrine of the indefectibility of the Church."[47] Coomaraswamy concluded from this that Vatican II "destroyed" the Christian tradition. The distrust of innovation extends to ritual and religious language, and, for that matter, "conservative" Cardinal Ratzinger held that change in religious language is "always dangerous."[48] In this spirit the Catholic church has tended to present the proclamation of doctrines (e.g., of papal infallibility in 1870, and of the Immaculate Conception, by Pius IX) as the clarification, or "rediscovery," of earlier tradition.

Unchanging tradition signifies the weight and stability of the past. Hence the Catholic assertion of the primacy of tradition over Scripture signified in the pre-Vatican II era the rejection of the possibility of a reinterpretation of Scripture, which was held to be a subjective and individual exercise, in favor of the authority of church and tradition; in the post-Vatican II era it signified an openness to critical biblical exegesis.[49] Ratzinger himself bewailed the modern tendency for faith to be experienced as "a personal event" rather than as subordination to God's will through communion with and in the church.[50] There are pressures for change in this respect welling up within the Catholic church itself, and there are divisions. Integralists and moderates by and large continue to accept the notion of the primacy of tradition over Scripture, with all its consequences. Partisans of liberation theology do not, and they have encouraged Catholic laity to study the Bible on their own.[51] Liberation theologians preach the right of every Christian to interpret the Scripture for herself or himself. In fact, Bible study among Catholics in the base communities of Latin America has become so popular that, according to the general secretary of the Latin American Theology Fraternity, the United Bible Society now sells more Bibles through Catholic churches than through Protestant churches in several Latin American countries—a reversal of the earlier trend.[52]

Recent survey data collected by George Gallup in the United States reinforce the view that Catholics are less inclined than Protestants to look to Scripture for guidance. In a 1984 survey 21 percent of Catholics, 52 percent of Protestants generally, and 85 percent of Evangelicals said that reading the Bible was "very important" to them. By contrast, 28 percent of Catholics, 12 percent of Protestants, and only 2 percent of Evangelicals said it was "not very important."[53] Catholics were, on the other hand, more inclined than Protestants to experience religion as a communal phenomenon and less likely to feel they had a "personal relationship" with God.[54]

Insofar as there is a Catholic political tradition, it is not only incompatible with communism but also critically distant from capitalism. The papal "Syllabus" of 1864, for instance, condemned communism, socialism, liberalism, freemasonry, and Bible-study societies alike as "pestilences."[55] Seventy years later, the Vatican paper, *L'Osservatore Romano*, declared that "Protestantism, schism, laicism and Bolshevism are basically the same thing."[56] Since then, the Vatican has shown a greater sensitivity to the differences among these diverse "pestilences," but its choice as to which constitutes the greatest threat has been neither static nor uniform at any given time among different currents within the church. In March 1937 the Holy See issued back-to-back encyclicals condemning first fascism and then communism, viewing them as equally dangerous.[57] In the latter, Pope Pius XI condemned "bolshevistic and atheistic communism, which aims at upsetting the social order and at undermining the very foundations of Christian civilization," but added that "the way had been already prepared for it by the religious and moral destitution in which wage-earners had been left by liberal economics."[58] During World War II, however, the Vatican, while abhorring the specter of communist inroads into postwar Europe, considered Nazism and fascism to be the greater evil, and in 1941 passed word discreetly that the anticommunist encyclical *Divini redemptoris* "is *not* to be applied to the present moment of armed conflict."[59] And while Pope Pius XII (1876–1958; pope 1939–58) declared a virtual crusade against communism after the war, and in 1949 declared the excommunication of all members and supporters of communist parties, his successors have tended to view both the individualism and consumerism associated with liberalism on the one hand, and communist collectivism on the other hand, as sources of threat, albeit in different ways and with different levels of gravity. Pope Paul VI's (1897–1978; pope 1963–78) mournful warning to the Sacred College of Cardinals in his 1977 Christmas address seems aimed more at Western consumerist society than at communist collectivism:

> Dark shadows are pressing down on mankind's destiny—blind violence; threats to human life, even in the mother's womb; cruel terror-

> ism which is heaping hatred on ruin with the utopian aim of rebuilding anew on the ashes of a total destruction; fresh outbreaks of delinquency; discriminations and injustices on an international scale; the deprivation of religious liberty; the ideology of hatred; the frenzied apology of the lowest instincts for the pornography of the mass media which, beneath false cultural claims, are concealing a degrading thirst for money and a shameless exploitation of the human person; the constant seductions and threats to children and the young, which are undermining and sterilizing the fresh creative energies of their minds and hearts: all these things indicate that there has been a fearful drop in the appreciation of moral values, now the victim of the hidden and organized action of vice and hatred.[60]

Catholic political thinking has traditionally rejected both the individualism of Western liberalism and the anti-individualism of Eastern collectivism. Liberal individualism errs, in the church's thinking, in failing to comprehend the organic link between human rights and duties, and in ignoring the responsibility of the state to promote the common good (preferring to restrict itself to maintaining order and allowing the "invisible hand" of free enterprise to produce what is fondly called the "greatest good for the greatest number").[61] Bishop Thomas C. Kelly, general secretary of the National Episcopal Conference of the United States, put it in these terms in 1980:

> The primary responsibility of the state is to serve the common good. It has a responsibility to adopt economic policies to ensure that the essential needs of all its people are met. These needs include adequate income, employment, food, shelter, health care, education and access to the necessary social services. All persons have the right to these basic necessities; and the government as the provider of last resort has the responsibility to ensure that they be made available to all.[62]

Collectivism errs in the opposite direction by denying basic human rights, including the right to religious freedom, which, according to the Second Vatican Council, has its foundations in "rational principles."[63]

Hence, John Paul II's radical critique of both Western liberalism and Eastern collectivism is consonant with earlier teachings of the church. And yet, in his seventh encyclical, *Sollicitudo rei socialis* (February 19, 1988), even while applying moral criteria to criticize both liberalism and Marxist collectivism the pope reserved some of his sharpest language for the failure of the latter:

> In today's world, among other rights, the right of economic initiative is often suppressed. Yet it is a right which is important not only

> for the individual but also for the common good. Experience shows us that the denial of this right, or its limitation in the name of an alleged "equality" of everyone in society, diminishes, or in practice absolutely destroys, the spirit of initiative, that is to say the creative subjectivity of the citizen. As a consequence, there arises, not so much a true equality as a "leveling down." In the place of creative initiative, there appear passivity, dependence, and submission to the bureaucratic apparatus, which, as the only "ordering" and "decision-making" body—if not also the "owner"—of the entire totality of goods and the means of production, puts everyone in a position of almost absolute dependence, which is similar to the traditional dependence of the worker-proletarian in capitalism. This provokes a sense of frustration [and] desperation and predisposes people to opt out of national life, impelling them to emigrate and also favoring a form of "psychological" emigration.[64]

Catholic thought has presumed the intrinsic value of political community and has urged that politics be an arena of rationality and moral responsibility.[65] The intrinsic value placed on political community has consequences for the orientation traditionally adopted by the church toward civil authority, as we shall see in the next section. At this stage, suffice it to note that the positive orientation toward political community, in tandem with the church's awareness of its own autocratic structure, has often been reflected, especially prior to the Second World War, in a fondness for monarchical forms of civil government. Even as late as 1945, József Cardinal Mindszenty (1892–1975), the prince-primate of Hungary, protested against the dissolution of the thousand-year-old Hungarian monarchy and the proclamation of a republic.[66]

The high value the church places on tradition is also a clue to the source and nature of the church's "nationalism." As Yugoslav theologian Tomislav Šagi-Bunić pointed out, the church's nationalism does not consist in the endorsement of the claims of one nation against another (at least not in theory) but in the desire to conserve the national heritage and tradition in the belief that the identity and moral life of a national community is indissolubly bound up with and expressed in its culture.[67] It is in this sense, I believe, that one should understand the words uttered by Pope John Paul II (born 1920; elected pope 1978) at Częstochowa during his second papal visit to Poland in June 1983:

> The nation is truly free when it can mould itself as a community determined by the unity of culture, language and history. The State is really sovereign if it governs the community serving at the same time the common good of society, and allows the nation to realize its own

> subjectivity, its own identity. Among other things this involves the creation of suitable conditions of development in the fields of culture, economic and other spheres of life of the social community. The sovereignty of the State is closely linked with its capacity to promote the freedom of the nation, that is to create conditions which will enable it to express the whole of its own historical and cultural identity, that means conditions which will allow it to be sovereign to the State.[68]

The church is, by the admission of its own prelates, wary of modernism, which is associated in its collective mind with materialism and moral permissiveness, though it views Protestantism as "wide open to modern thought, . . . [which] constitutes both its opportunity and its danger."[69]

Although Communist parties have generally claimed to be "modernizing," communism has not proven uniformly supportive of modernity and modernization. Its "modern" attitudes toward industrialization, urbanization, and education have been offset by rather backward-looking attitudes about political participation, the use of force, and the nonseparation of church and state. And whereas the church, sometimes with exaggeration,[70] has claimed to preserve the unchanged Truth of the apostles (the Magisterium) and champions the conservation of national tradition, ruling Communist parties have tended, in most national contexts (at least in the mobilization phase of revolutionary political development), to be hostile to national traditions and have insisted, largely without exception, that rather than conserving the heritage of the past, political control should be exploited to expunge the collective memory and to transform society in accordance with collectivist thought. The inception of authentic dialogue between Catholic church and communist state thus presumes either that the Catholic church must cease to be "traditional" or that the particular Communist party must give up its project of transforming society. The relatively more propitious environment in which the Yugoslav Catholic church is able to operate is unmistakably a dimension of the League of Communists of Yugoslavia's abandonment of any serious program to transform society.

Finally, where ecclesiastical tradition is concerned, the Communist party's attitude has often been overtly manipulative. In Cuba, for instance, there were attempts to eliminate the Three Wise Men from Christmas imagery and to replace them with the figures of Cuban revolutionary *comandantes*.[71] And in Nicaragua after the Sandinistas took power in 1979, there were efforts to redesign religious celebrations, and thousands of posters were printed portraying Christmas as a celebration of the dawn of the communist "new man."[72] And again, in the Soviet Union, churches were at one time pressured to portray Christ as a worker, and to emphasize his proletarian origins and antipathy for moneylenders, etc.[73] The Vatican disapproves of such portrayals, and Pope John Paul II expressly told the Episcopal Conference at Puebla (1979) that it was wrong to portray Christ as a revolutionary figure.[74]

The Hierarchical Church and the Relationship Between the Episcopate and the Lower Clergy

The concept of hierarchy is inseparable from the concept of obedience: hierarchy entails authority, which is empty without subordination. Ignatius of Loyola, founder of the Jesuit order, impressed upon his adherents the stricture "to believe that the white that I see is black, if the hierarchical Church so decides."[75] Private judgment is suspect,[76] and, extrapolated to the civil sphere, any sovereign who does not attack the institutional church or flout its central values is said to deserve obedience, while oaths take on a value that competes with other moral imperatives. Interestingly, Pope Pius XII fretted that the adoption of too voluble a posture against the Nazis could create a crisis of conscience for German Catholics: "Do not forget, there are millions of Catholics in the German army! Should I throw them into a conflict of conscience? They have taken an oath; they owe obedience."[77] And later, this same pope would boast to Romanian communist authorities that Catholics "are second to none in respect for civil authority and in obedience to the laws, insofar as these do not demand anything that contradicts natural law, the law of God and the Church."[78]

The functions and responsibilities of the earliest popes remain shrouded in obscurity, though it is clear that St. Clement (pope c. 91–c. 101) enjoyed considerable prestige as a leading spokesman of the Christian community in Rome. By the reigns of St. Telesphorus (pope c. 125–c. 136) and St. Hyginus (pope c. 138–c. 142), collegial episcopacy was gradually giving way to papal monarchy, and by the reign of St. Pius I (pope c. 142–c. 155) the bishop of Rome exercised autocratic authority. Rome claimed priority over all other patriarchal sees from the beginning, and in A.D. 180 Irenaeus codified this in the doctrine of *potentior principalitas*, said to be an attribute of the Roman See.[79] Prior to the middle of the third century no one thought of the papacy as a permanent office,[80] but between the middle of the third century and the middle of the fifth century the office gradually became institutionalized. In the high Middle Ages St. Gregory VII (c. 1020–85; pope 1073–85) declared that all Christians were subject to his authority and asserted the exclusive prerogative of the pope to depose or reinstate bishops and the right of the pope to transfer bishops or depose emperors. He declared that no one could judge the pope, that no synod could be called "general" without papal authority, and that "the Roman Church has never erred, nor ever, by the witness of Scripture, shall err to all eternity."[81] This was a bold claim for papal and ecclesiastical authority.

Innocent III (1160/61–1216; pope 1198–1216) raised the papacy to its apogee, using the *False Decretals* of Pseudo-Isidore (c. 847–52) and other documents to claim monarchical status for the papal office and calling himself the Vicar of Christ—the first time this title had been ascribed to the pope. Some historians believe that he aspired to world *political* dominion, and Innocent certainly felt that all Christian princes were his subjects.[82] In the *Patrologia latina* Innocent III expressed himself thus: "The Pope is the meeting point between God and man . . . who can judge all things and be judged by no one."[83] As McBrien noted, Pope "Boniface VIII carried the claim even further, insisting on absolute power over the whole world, temporal as well as religious."[84] Later, the anonymous papalist author of a pamphlet entitled *Determinatio compendiosa* (1342) claimed that:

> Especially is he, the pope, above every council and statute. . . ; he it is, too, who has no superior on earth; he, the pope, gives dispensations from every law. . . . Again, it is he who possesses the plenitude of power on earth and holds the place and office of the Most High. . . . He it is who alters the substance of a thing, making legitimate what was illegitimate. . . . He it is who by absolving on earth absolves [also] in heaven, and by binding on earth binds [also] in heaven. . . . Again, it is to him that nobody may say: "Why do you do that?" . . . He it is for whom the will is reason enough, since that which pleases him has the force of law (*ei quod placet, legis vigorem habet*); . . . he is not bound by the laws . . . *etc.* (*solutus est legibus*). Indeed, the pope is the law itself and a living law (*lex viva*), to resist which is impermissible. This then is the Catholic and orthodox faith, approved and canonized by the holy fathers of old, from which all justice, religion, sanctity and discipline have emanated. If anyone does not believe it faithfully and firmly, he cannot be saved, and without doubt will perish eternally.[85]

In the thirteenth, fourteenth, and fifteenth centuries the cardinals (who in 1179 had become the sole electors of the pope) tried to reduce the powers of the pope, often obtaining "capitulations" during the election process. The popes were by and large not inclined to honor such capitulations, however, and several decrees were issued banning capitulations, beginning in 1274.[86] In the course of the fifteenth century, Pontifex maximus, the pagan title claimed by the Roman emperors until Gratian and Theodosius dropped it in 382, was revived and came to be applied to the popes—on coins, in their official biographies, in discourses addressed to them, and on their funeral inscriptions. From the sixteenth century onward there was a steady tendency toward a purely monarchical concept of the papacy, a concept which survived even the dismantlement of the Papal States.

On December 8, 1854, Pope Pius IX (1792–1878; pope 1846–78) solemnly pronounced the new doctrine of the Immaculate Conception of Mary. Although he had sought and obtained the approbation of the bishops prior to doing so, he made no reference in the celebration to the assent of the bishops, thus demonstrating papal authority in matters of doctrine.[87] Later in his reign, after a furious debate which presaged the withdrawal of a small number of clergy to form a new "Old Catholic Church," the First Vatican Council (1869–70) issued a decree defining the doctrine of papal infallibility:

> If any one, therefore, shall say that Blessed Peter the Apostle was not appointed Prince of all the Apostles and the visible head of the whole Church Militant; or that he directly and immediately received from the same Lord Jesus Christ a primacy of honor only, and not of true and proper jurisdiction—*let him be anathema.* . . .
>
> We teach and define that it is a dogma divinely revealed: that the Roman Pontiff, when he speaks *ex cathedra,* that is, when in discharge of the office of Pastor and Doctor of all Christians, by virtue of his supreme apostolic authority, defines a doctrine regarding faith or morals to be held by the Universal Church, by the divine assistance promised him in Blessed Peter, is possessed of that infallibility with which the Divine Redeemer willed that his Church should be endowed for defining doctrine regarding faith or morals: and that therefore such definitions of the Roman Pontiff are irreformable of themselves and not from the consent of the Church. But if anyone, which God forbid, presume to contradict this Our definition—*let him be anathema.*[88]

This tendency was partly reversed at the Second Vatican Council (1962–65). Where Vatican I had emphasized the infallibility and autocratic authority of the pope, Vatican II stressed the collegial authority of the episcopacy. The councils differed in other ways, too. Vatican I had emphasized the unchanging identity of the church; Vatican II displayed sensitivity to change and cultural diversity. Vatican I had been inclined to abstract and metaphysical concepts, while Vatican II preferred the concrete. And where Vatican I had accented the role of the hierarchy, Vatican II highlighted the role of the laity.[89] The council did not, of course, adopt any measures which might undermine the authority of the pope as such, but it underlined the apostolic succession of bishops and stressed the organic link between their authority and the authority of the pope. The relationship might even be described as symbiotic. Hence, as Pope John Paul II once put it, "the Church is also a communion of the churches—*communio Ecclesiarum*—constituted by the communion of bishop-pastors."[90]

This implies a degree of autonomy of judgment on the part of the bishops—an autonomy that is unavoidable if the church is to function at all. By contrast, Rome would consider it heretical to claim that the church is a communion of local parishes if that meant that local priests and pastors were authorized to make autonomous decisions affecting policy, relations with civil authorities, religious instruction, or the presentation of doctrine. Under communism, however, priests have often been pressured to take actions which tend in just such a direction. The threat of division between hierarchy and lower clergy (or local hierarchy and Rome) has taken four chief forms.

First, communists in China[91] and most of the East European countries[92] attempted to persuade local hierarchs to break ties with Rome and reconstitute the church as nationally self-governing. In the 1980s the Soviet regime likewise offered to relegalize the suppressed Ukrainian Greek Rite church, provided that its head-designate agreed to sever relations with Rome: He refused.[93] Only in China did this strategy bear fruit: There, under pressure from the government, five of the twenty-eight bishops joined the government-sponsored Chinese Catholic Patriotic Association and agreed to administer a church cut off from contact with Rome. These bishops subsequently ordained other bishops without Rome's approval.[94]

Second, communist regimes in a number of countries have lent their backing to proregime clerical associations, often called "patriotic priests' associations." The Czechoslovak version, Pacem in Terris, inspired a papal ban in March 1982, after which membership plunged. In Hungary, Archbishop József Grősz, chairman of the Hungarian episcopate, adopted a different tactic in the endeavor to neutralize the Priests of Peace organization: He and his bishops joined the organization in May 1957.[95] In Yugoslavia, on the other hand, the sundry priests' associations (one per republic) faded in importance as church-state relations thawed, and they are fairly marginal today. Elsewhere, neutralization on either the Hungarian or the Yugoslav model has not been possible. Similarly, in North Vietnam the Liaison Committee of Patriotic and Peace-Loving Catholics was created in 1955, only to be condemned by the apostolic delegate and the bishops of the major dioceses the day after its establishment.[96] And in Nicaragua the regime has naturally been pleased that some priests have concluded not only that it is *possible* to be a devout Christian and be actively engaged in support of the revolution—which is already denied by the mainstream of the church[97]—but that it is a Christian *duty* to work for the revolution.[98] Some "patriotic priests" in Nicaragua have even allowed their political loyalties to inspire innovations in rites.[99]

Third, the Second Vatican Council itself created fissures within the church and spawned currents which communists have tried to exploit. The example that comes most readily to mind is the Theological Society

Christianity Today, based in the Yugoslav city of Zagreb. Created by the archbishop of Zagreb in 1968, the organization became a center of theologically progressive thought and was already at odds with more conservative prelates in the country when, in 1977, it reorganized itself in line with Yugoslav self-management in order to gain preferential tax treatment. Since then, the organization has been under fire from local bishops for insubordination and at the same time has enjoyed a certain favor in regime circles.[100]

And fourth, as a function of heightened lay awareness and interest, local clergy have taken the initiative, most prominently in Hungary, in organizing grass-roots discussion groups. This is discussed below.

Where divisions appear naturally from within the church or in those cases where they are fomented by the regime, they offer the possibility of serving as pressure points for a regime strategy of *divide et impera*. In Cuba, interestingly enough, the Castro regime never adopted this approach.

Grass-roots Organizations and Groups

In turning to the subject of grass-roots organizations, it is critical to understand that such organizations have no automatic political aspect: Their activity is not necessarily in the interest or contrary to the interest of either church or state. And indeed, while the hierarchy has tolerated some grass-roots groups, it has volubly opposed the activity of others.

The difficulty lies in the fact that grass-roots organizations often rise and function outside the control of the hierarchy. As such, they present potential difficulties in several respects. First, they afford contexts in which devout Catholics sometimes discuss the Scriptures in an open-ended fashion that may at times ignore the Magisterium. Once people read the Bible and interpret it for themselves, there is an immediate risk that the church's authority may be diminished, circumscribed, and compromised. This is what Cardinal Ratzinger meant when he spoke of the danger that "the bond between the Bible and Church" might be broken in cases where appropriate supervision is not exercised.[101] Second, insofar as such groups downplay the Magisterium and emphasize instead the religious experience as such, there is a risk that the subjective experience may claim priority in the individual's faith. It is for this reason that the American Bishops' Conference warned as early as 1969 that such groups had to be properly supervised: "Proper supervision can be effectively exercised only if the bishops keep in mind their pastoral responsibility to oversee and guide this movement in the Church. We must be on guard that they avoid the mistakes of classic Pentecostalism. It must be recognized that in our culture there is a tendency to substitute religious experience for religious doctrine."[102] Third, where these groups function in defiance of the bishops (as with some communities in Hungary), a question of discipline may be involved. And fourth, in Latin America at least, base communities sometimes have been drawn to liberation theology, arguing that the church should support revolutionary change in the interests of the poor. Pope John Paul II addressed this subject while on tour in Chile in April 1987, warning against the "politicization" of the base communities and advising them to stick to religion.[103] Earlier, the Third General Conference of Latin American Bishops (Puebla, 1979) had urged "disengagement from direct, partisan politics in favor of a more general stress on highlighting and denouncing injustice," and thus returned to the traditional view that the clergy should not get directly involved in politics.[104]

Grass-roots groups have often been controversial.[105] In Hungary, for instance, so-called base communities sprang up and flourished in the course of the 1970s. There are currently some five thousand such groups in Hungary, with 70,000–100,000 members in all. These communities have operated at the parish level and have been highly critical of the Hungarian episcopate for what they interpret as a "servile attitude toward the state."[106] In their view, the Hungarian episcopate has adopted a policy of extreme self-censorship, avoiding any discussion of social problems in Hungary, human rights violations, or limitations on religious freedom, while praising governmental measures beyond the bounds of what would be proper. These base communities have attracted young people and intellectuals especially. The young priests who lead them have been clearly antihierarchical and have repudiated the notion of absolute obedience to the episcopate.[107] There are five important currents within the Hungarian base community movement: the Charismatic, Focolari, Taisei, Regum Marianum, and Bush networks. The first four have essentially untroubled relations with both hierarchy and the state. But the Bush, also called the Bulányists after their founder, Fr. György Bulányi, have successfully defied both the hierarchy and the state. In June 1982 the bishops released Bulányi from his priestly duties—in a nugatory move that was also welcome to the state. Bulányi refused to back down and replied that individual conscience must take priority over regime orders channeled through the episcopate. Bishop József Cserháti, secretary of the Hungarian Bishops' Conference, called this "Protestant" thinking.[108]

The pope called on Bulányi to obey his bishops—but without effect. Later, Agostino Cardinal Casaroli sent a letter to Hungarian primate László Cardinal Lékai making it clear that base communities, "in order to call themselves truly ecclesial, must above all be firmly united to the local Churches . . . and through them to the Universal Church, working always in communion with and under the guidance of their respective bishops."[109]

Eventually, in September 1986, Cardinal Ratzinger drafted a letter to Bulányi, charging him with error in four areas: his rejection of the doctrine of apostolic continuity, his failure to maintain a clear distinction between clergy and laity (for example, letting laypersons serve as spiritual leaders in his base communities), his argument that private conscience may override church authority, and his support for the ordination of women. This letter was published in the Catholic weekly *Új Ember* after a nine-month delay, along with a statement by Lékai's successor as primate, László Paskai, warning of the "political dangers" of Bulányi's views.[110]

Base communities also have arisen throughout Latin America, where, according to Lawrence Cunningham, they have tended to take on a marked political character.[111] Greil and Kowalewski noted that "Nicaraguans became most politically radical in those locales where the liberation-theology base communities were operating."[112] A leading figure in the movement, and one who has captured the media's attention, is the charismatic priest Fr. Uriel Molina, who speaks of a link between Christianity and revolution and is supportive of the Sandinista program.[113] In the now-defunct Solentiname community, members read and studied the Bible together with the speeches of Fidel Castro and Ernesto "Che" Guevara.[114] Some leading figures in the base communities saw a fusion between revolutionary praxis and authentic Christianity. Juan Hernández Pico of Nicaragua, for example, spoke of developing a Christian strategy to support the revolutionary regime: "There is no place in this Christian strategy for saying that religion and revolutionary politics are incompatible." On the contrary, "the revolution was able to become the highest value for authentic Christians. . . . The revolutionary process could now become the maximum Christian value because it represented the one and only approximation to the maximum, absolute value of the kingdom."[115]

Pope John Paul II had addressed this theme earlier, in his speech to the Puebla Conference on January 28, 1979: "[Some] people purport to depict Jesus as a political activist, as a fighter against Roman domination and the authorities, and even as someone involved in the class struggle. This conception of Christ as a political figure, a revolutionary, as the subversive from Nazareth, does not tally with the Church's catechesis."[116]

But not all base communities in Nicaragua are pro-Sandinista. Some are said to be hostile to the Sandinistas; others are either nonpolitical or uncomfortable with a black-and-white approach in either direction.

But from the hierarchy's standpoint, the major issue is not the base communities' attitude toward the Sandinista regime but their attitude toward the hierarchy itself. Here, interestingly enough, one of their more enthusiastic supporters praised the base communities by calling them "remarkably Protestant"—an intended compliment that only confirms Ratzinger's fears

—adding that, "like Luther, they speak scathingly against the Catholic church's lofty view of the hierarchy because they believe it goes against scriptural teaching."[117] Michael Dodson confirmed this appraisal, noting that the mushrooming of base communities in Nicaragua, *independent of the hierarchy,* sowed deep division within the Nicaraguan church, threatening the hierarchy with what he called the emergence of a "parallel Church."[118] In fact, at the Puebla Conference the assembled bishops had already declared: "It is lamentable that visibly political interests intend to manipulate them [the base communities] and separate them, in some places, from authentic communion with their bishops. . . . Attracted by purely lay institutions and ideologically radicalized, they are losing the authentic ecclesial sense."[119]

Czechoslovakia witnessed a much more severe development in the 1970s. Here a psychologically unbalanced priest named Felix Davidek, who had been consecrated a bishop in the 1960s without Vatican approval, was trying to build up an underground church outside the hierarchical framework. According to one informant,[120] Davidek ordained probably hundreds of priests, including married men and women. The Prague regime knew about Davidek but tolerated his organization in the hope that it could stimulate schismatic fissures within the clergy.

But in other national contexts grass-roots groups have been welcome to the hierarchy. In Lithuania, for instance, the Catholic Committee for the Defense of the Rights of Believers was created in 1978 by five Catholic priests in order to heighten public awareness of abuses and to gather petitions. The committee succeeded in reducing government interference in the seminary at Kaunas, and the seminary was even able to grow somewhat. During the six years of its existence (before its ultimate suppression by the KGB), the committee was supportive rather than critical of the Lithuanian church hierarchy.[121] Again, in Czechoslovakia the Oasis Movement has functioned with the blessing of Cardinal Tomášek. Base communities also have developed in Poland and Romania.

In Poland, in fact, the episcopate seems to have wanted to organize lay associations to discuss social and economic issues. In a move probably designed to test the waters, Rev. Alojzy Orszulik, director of the church's press office and thus chief spokesman of the episcopate, wrote an article for a Catholic weekly, contending that Polish law permitted people to organize grass-roots associations independent of Communist party control. He urged believers to take advantage of this "freedom" to create associations to take part in a national discussion of social and economic subjects. The censors prevented the article's publication. Jerzy Urban, a government spokesman, explained, "The government cannot accept any Church program which would allow the Church to create its own organizations in every field of life."[122]

The Vatican Factor in the Church-State Equation

State relations with the Catholic church are distinguished from relations with Orthodox and Protestant churches by the role played by the Vatican; hence, where Catholicism is concerned, church-state relations are not a bilateral relationship but a trilateral one involving the local church hierarchy, the regime, and the Vatican. This means that the Catholic church has resources and strengths not available to other church organizations. It also means that the regimes are tempted at times either to try to play the Vatican against the local episcopate or to pursue dialogue with whichever ecclesiastical partner seems more forthcoming.

The individual bishops enjoy administrative but not theological autonomy, and they are responsible for the day-to-day decisions in their respective dioceses.[123] In any country where there is a formally designated primate, the officeholder functions essentially as the head of that nation's church. Vatican II strengthened both the national and the collegial dimension of the episcopacy by providing for the establishment of national episcopal conferences. In *Ecclesiae sanctae* (1966), Pope Paul VI encouraged "bishops of countries or territories which have not yet established an episcopal conference . . . [to] take steps as quickly as possible to do so and draw up its statutes which are to be approved by the Apostolic See."[124]

The Vatican and the local episcopate maintain direct contact, of course, through letters and other communications and direct visits. In addition, the Holy See often appoints pontifical representatives (nuncios, or papal ambassadors) to represent the wishes of the Vatican to the local hierarchy and to provide an additional channel for information to the Vatican. Pope Paul VI explained the duties of the pontifical representative in these terms:

> The primary and specific purpose of the mission of the Pontifical Representative is to render even closer and more operative the ties that bind the Apostolic See and the local Churches.
>
> He furthermore interprets the solicitude of the Roman Pontiff for the good of the country in which he exercises his mission. . . .
>
> Upon the Pontifical Representative also falls the duty of safeguarding, in cooperation with the Bishops, among the civil authorities of the territory in which he exercises his office, the mission of the Church and the Holy See.
>
> This is also the task of those Pontifical Representatives who have

no diplomatic character; they will take care, however, to entertain friendly relations with these same authorities.

In his capacity as envoy of the Supreme Shepherd of Souls, the Pontifical Representative will promote, in accordance with the instructions he receives from the competent offices of the Holy See and in agreement with the local Bishops and particularly with the Patriarchs in eastern territories, opportune contacts between the Catholic Church and the other Christian communities and will favor cordial relations with the non-Christian religions.[125]

The Holy See reserves to itself the right to appoint archbishops and to elevate archbishops to the college of cardinals; but as a rule, the Holy See has negotiated with the communist regimes to obtain their approval of such appointments, thus continuing a practice prevalent in east-central Europe since precommunist times.[126] (The Holy See has not, however, negotiated with either the Cuban or the Nicaraguan regime.) It is the prerogative of archbishops and bishops to consecrate other bishops, but as a rule, the specific approval of the Vatican is required. At times, however, the Holy See has authorized local bishops to select apostolic administrators and consecrate additional bishops without seeking Rome's permission. Bishop Pie Eugen Neveu was granted these and other plenary powers in the Soviet Union in 1926, as was August Cardinal-Primate Hlond in Poland in 1945.[127]

At times the Holy See has played an obstructive role, as, for instance, in Romania in 1948, when the apostolic nuncio dispatched to Bucharest vetoed a statute which the local bishops had worked out with the government and which would have provided some legal guarantees to the church.[128] At other times the Holy See has simply bypassed the local bishops, as, for example, in 1966, when the Vatican negotiated a protocol with Belgrade while barely informing the Yugoslav bishops.[129] And on still other occasions the local hierarchs have by-passed the Vatican, as happened in Hungary in August 1950 when Archbishop Grősz signed an agreement with state authorities promising episcopal support for the state's internal and foreign policies in exchange for a guarantee of freedom of worship, the return of eight of the more than three thousand Catholic schools that had been seized by the regime, and the grant of a state financial subsidy. The agreement made no reference to the Holy See or to the bishops' right of contact with the Vatican.[130]

The same pattern was played out in Poland in April 1950 when, after hard negotiations, Stefan Cardinal Wyszyński (1901–81) signed an agreement with the state which, among other things, included a promise on the part of the authorities to respect the independent Catholic University in Lublin, the existing Catholic associations, the free activity of religious orders, and so forth. The pope was shocked by the agreement, above all because he had not been informed in advance, and he subjected Wyszyński to cool treatment when the latter came to Rome in April 1951.[131] Despite this, Wyszyński again negotiated an agreement unilaterally in December 1956, obtaining government agreement to the installation of five titular bishops in the Oder-Neisse region while pledging "full support for the work undertaken by the [newly installed Gomułka] government aimed at the strengthening and development of People's Poland."[132] Pope Pius XII remained unreconciled to the idea of coexistence with communism, and when Wyszyński came to Rome in May 1957 for the formal conferral of his cardinal's hat, the pope found a series of means by which to communicate his displeasure: sending a low-ranking Vatican representative to meet Wyszyński at the airport, making Wyszyński wait an unusually long period for his audience, and finally rushing in just ten minutes through a ceremony that normally takes two days.[133]

In the mid-1960s the Gomułka regime considered normalizing relations with the Holy See with the idea that this would lead to the installation of an apostolic delegate in Warsaw who could be used to undercut the authority of Wyszyński. Agostino Cardinal Casaroli, secretary of state for the Vatican, was given royal treatment during three visits to Poland in 1967 and was permitted to travel freely throughout the country. The regime hoped that Casaroli would find fault with Wyszyński, and that these trips would constitute the opening wedge that would set Vatican and episcopate at odds. When, on the contrary, it turned out that Casaroli was favorably impressed with what he saw, Gomułka abruptly terminated contacts with the Vatican.[134]

Subsequent efforts by Gomułka's successor as party secretary, Edvard Gierek, bore greater fruit: By then, Pope Paul VI was pursuing a policy of Ostpolitik, and he was coming to perceive Wyszyński as an intransigent hard-liner who was interested in safeguarding his personal power and was excessively skeptical of détente—an odd charge in view of Wyszyński's agreements in 1950 and 1956. Despite this, the Vatican declined to install an apostolic delegate in Warsaw, precisely because it realized that the regime would inevitably try to play the apostolic office against the episcopal office.[135]

Against Rome, Wyszyński would regularly use the argument that he understood the Polish situation better than the Holy See possibly could, and that he understood communism from firsthand experience. With these arguments he tried to maintain maximum flexibility for himself in dealing with the regime. With the election of Karol Cardinal Wojtyła of Kraków as pope, neither of these arguments were relevant any longer, and Wojtyła's election has meant in general a stronger, more dynamic posture on the part of the Vatican vis-à-vis Eastern Europe in particular, and on the world stage more broadly. He may well be, as British writer Paul Johnson calls him, the pope of the "Catholic Restoration."[136]

Conclusion

The central values of both Catholicism and communism have proven impervious to change. Catholicism continues to center its values on supernatural legitimation, belief in a system of rewards and punishments in the afterlife, hierarchy, obedience to legitimate authority, the family, the community (bound by love and mutual respect), and fair distribution of the world's wealth. Communism—until the dramatic changes unleashed in the USSR and Eastern Europe in the late 1980s—by and large emphasized maintaining its organizational monopoly, suppressing sources of conflicts of interest, creating a new value system in which political authority commands the highest loyalty, and vesting the hopes and aspirations of its subjects in the present life rather than in an afterlife.

Yet the strategies and tactics of both church and Communist parties have proven remarkably adaptable and flexible. It was Pope John XXIII's (1881–1963; pope 1958–63) encyclicals *Pacem in terris* and *Mater et magistra* that opened the door to Catholic acceptance of religious and political pluralism in the world. Pope Paul VI took this further through his policy of Ostpolitik, which explored grounds for mutual understanding with communist governments. Paul VI thus approached the issue diplomatically, as something to be negotiated between sovereigns. Pope John Paul II has brought a new vision and a new strategy to the Vatican. His frequent travels are the clearest indication that he bases his strategy above all on direct appeals to the people. His elevation of cardinals in the USSR, Angola, Nicaragua, Ethiopia, Poland, and Yugoslavia reflects his desire to strengthen the hands of bishops facing communist governments. The present pope seems to hope that the communist governments will lose the will or the ability to continue their restrictive policies and eventually will consign them to the past.

Among ruling communist parties—with the exception of the Yugoslav and Hungarian parties and, arguably, the East German regime[137]—the basic strategy seems to be split the church; to draw more pliable clerics into a cooperative relationship, imprisoning, exiling, or sometimes liquidating clerics (such as Popiełuszko) who show themselves irreconcilably critical of the regime; and to sap the church's base through incremental but steady atheization. In some countries the resulting cooperative relationship has reached extremes. Hansjakob Stehle, a veteran observer of Vatican politics, recalled, "When in 1960, on a visit to the archepiscopal palace in Prague, I mistakenly opened the wrong door, I discovered that the diocesan administration was a department of the Ministry of Culture, with party pictures decorating the office. Timid, powerless vicars capitular, often discredited ecclesiastically as well as morally, maintained hardly more than an outward appearance."[138] Consistent with this, Władysław Gomułka's comment in 1966—"If [the bishops] wish to express their opinions on political problems, they should be able to do so. But, let their remarks be consistent with the policy of the government"[139]—expresses what would surely be the ideal of any communist head of state.

There have always been differences in the contours of church-state relations across the communist world, extending to church access to media, church retention of schools and hospitals, discrimination against believers, church ability to obtain permits for the construction and repair of church buildings, harassment and assault of clergy, and the interference of the regime in the screening of candidates for seminaries. Since 1987 the pace of change has quickened. In Hungary the old Office for Religious Affairs has been abolished, and the same thing has been proposed in Poland. Commissions have been put to work drafting new laws on religious associations in Poland, Hungary, and the USSR. Poland and Hungary have recognized the Vatican and exchanged diplomatic representatives.[140] In Slovenia and Lithuania, Christmas is now a state holiday. Finally, in December 1989 Gorbachev traveled to Rome to meet the pope amid reports that the Greek Rite Catholic Church in Ukraine, banned in 1946, would soon be made legal again.

Communism reached the point of crisis in the course of the 1980s and has been confronted with the challenge of democraticization or decay. Inevitably, church-state relations will be affected by these larger political processes.

2

Catholic Social Teachings: A Brief History

Arthur F. McGovern, S.J.

Nearly a century has passed since Leo XIII's *Rerum novarum* (1891) ushered in a new era of church teachings focused on socioeconomic problems in the world. I have been asked to present a summary of the history of these Catholic social teachings and to note also some currents of Catholic social thought that have diverged from official lines. To meet this objective I have had to be selective, treating central themes in the major social encyclicals and focusing later in the chapter on liberation theology as an illustration of a somewhat divergent political theology. Readers also can find other works, often reflecting quite different political perspectives, that offer more lengthy studies of church social doctrines.[1] To give unity to the chapter I have focused on a perspective of continuity and change, choosing themes in each section that reflect the changes especially.

Anyone familiar with the history of the Catholic church will expect continuity in its teachings. The Catholic church stresses fidelity to its tradition, and every major papal encyclical since *Rerum novarum* has made reference to "what our predecessors have said." Though the language may change, the elements of continuity in Catholic social teachings can be rather easily discerned; for example: the right and duty of the church to speak out on social issues, a fundamental concern for the human dignity of every person, concern for community or the common good, principles of justice, warnings about false solutions (collectivist socialism, individualistic capitalism), and recognition of the need for state intervention balanced with a concern to limit state control.

Giving some perspective on change requires a more difficult discernment, one which unavoidably involves some interpretation and narrowing of points chosen for emphasis. To develop such a perspective I have divided this history into three periods, selecting themes that I feel best characterize each period. In the period of the great foundational encyclicals of Leo XIII and Pius XI, "restoring the moral order" is presented as a dominant theme. In the era of Vatican II, "transforming the world" is suggested as a major theme. The present age is represented by the theme "promoting true Christian liberation," because this reflects Pope John Paul II's great concern to ground promotion of justice on truly authentic church teachings. This heading seems also appropriate for discussing the challenge raised by liberation theology.

Some brief reflections on the situation of the church prior to *Rerum novarum* may be a useful introduction to this history. Some historians have questioned and attempted to explain why the church waited until nearly the end of the nineteenth century to speak out about the social unrest caused by the Industrial Revolution. After all, socialist thinkers—novelists such as Charles Dickens and Victor Hugo, and numerous Catholic reformers—had drawn attention in preceding decades to the plight of the working class.[2] One might simply reply that a few decades do not constitute a significant time lag, especially because the church viewed its primary mission as the salvation of souls, not solving temporal problems. But several other factors appear to have contributed to the church's delay in responding. The French Revolution of the late eighteenth century left deep scars in the psyche of the Catholic church. Remembering the violence done to priests and religious and the expropriation of church property, church leaders tended to distrust and resist any movements which championed social change. Defense of temporal authority over the Papal States in Italy also preoccupied the popes of the nineteenth century and led them to react against liberal movements, many of which were anticlerical.

In addition to these specific fears, an overriding view of modern history also influenced church attitudes. While many secular thinkers in the nineteenth century glorified the "march of progress" in history, church leaders viewed the same history as one of tragic decline from the days of medieval Catholic Christendom. The Reformation had challenged church authority; the Enlightenment introduced pernicious secularized values; the French Revolution subordinated the church to the state; capitalism had destroyed the harmony of guild structures; and now socialism seemed bent on carrying these disruptive ideas and tendencies to their radical conclusion—the destruction of all that was sacred, holy, and "natural." Contrasted with this negative view of modern history, an idealized view of medieval society as a harmonious, organic community seems clearly to have influenced Leo XIII's reflections on social issues.

Restoring the Moral Order: Leo XIII and Pius XI

The papacy of Leo XIII marked a decisive turning point in the Catholic church's stance toward the world. Leo XIII was already sixty-eight years old and besieged by a host of problems when he became pope in 1878. The French church wanted a return to monarchy and clashed with the French republic over education and other issues; the German church was still locked in battle with Bismarck and his *Kulturkampf*; in Italy the recent loss of the Papal States was a festering wound. Yet Leo not only dealt with these problems but also turned his attention to the great social question of the day. Influenced by the progressive work of Bishop Wilhelm Emmanuel von Ketteler (1811–77) and by the efforts of Catholic theorists in the Freiburg Union, Pope Leo commissioned Francesco Cardinal Zigliari to draw up the first draft on an encyclical on the condition of the workers (best known by its Latin title, *Rerum novarum*).

Leo XIII: Rerum Novarum *(1891).* The problem Leo addressed was the disturbing disparity between "the enormous fortunes of individuals and the poverty of the masses," with all the conflict this disparity was causing.[3] "Some remedy must be found," Leo insisted, "for the misery and wretchedness which press so heavily at this moment on the large majority of the very poor."[4] Marxists attributed the problem to private ownership and control of the means of production, and consequently called for the overthrow of the private property system. Leo XIII viewed the problem quite differently: "No practical solution will ever be found without the assistance of religion and the Church."[5] Nothing is more powerful than religion in bringing rich and poor together.[6] History proves what religion has done to achieve harmony, as in the age of medieval Christendom. "Of these things there cannot be the shadow of doubt; for instance, that civil society was renovated in every part by the teachings of Christianity . . . the human race was lifted up to better things . . . to so excellent a life that nothing more perfect had been known before or will come to pass in the ages that are yet to be."[7] Restoring respect for Christian morality and restoring associations like the guilds in ages past held the key to resolving problems of the present.[8] "And, if Society is to be cured now, in no other way can it be cured but by a return to the Christian life and Christian institutions. When a Society is perishing, the true advice to give to those who would restore it is, to recall the principles from which it sprung."[9]

Given this analysis of the problem, the church's mission was to call men and women back to principles of Christian morality. "It calls men to virtue and forms them in practice"; Christian morality "powerfully restrains the lust of possession," and it inspires charity in support of the needy.[10] Religion reminds each class of its duties to the other. Workers should carry out honestly agreements they have made, never employing violence or engaging in disorders; the rich (employers) should treat workers with dignity, not like "chattels to make money by," and they should not tax workers beyond their strength.[11]

Since the encyclical was written a full century ago, it not surprisingly contains assumptions that some modern readers might find objectionable. Thus, for example, when the encyclical stresses the restoration of "harmony" in society, it assumes as natural a certain order and priority of different spheres in society: the spiritual over the temporal, church over state, owners over workers, husbands over wives.[12] So while the call to conversion is strong, acceptance of one's state and priorities in life is also strong. "God has not created us for the perishable and transitory things of earth, but for things heavenly and everlasting; He has given us this world as a place of exile, and not as our true country."[13] Poverty is no disgrace, nor is seeking one's bread by labor. The division of employers and workers is natural: "It is ordained by nature that these two classes should exist in harmony and agreement."[14] If each class observed its duties and the rights of the other, strife would cease quickly.[15]

The correct principles of natural law and religion, principles more evident in medieval Christendom, were brought to judgment in *Rerum novarum* on two prevalent ideologies of the day. Socialists, Pope Leo asserted, base their doctrines on false principles. They want to take away the natural right to private property.[16] They propose solutions which are "clearly futile," believing that all inequalities can be overcome and the hardships of work eliminated.[17] They assume that hostilities between classes are natural and inevitable.[18] Finally, they want to bring the state into a sphere not its own, making rights come from the state, letting civil government penetrate into the family, and risking the complete absorption of the individual and the family by the state.[19]

Socialism is wrong in principle because "every man has by nature the right to possess property as his own."[20] The encyclical gave several reasons, drawn from St. Thomas Aquinas's writings, in defense of private property: It is a means of providing for the future; it is the worker's right to "what his own labor has produced"; and it is a means for a father to provide for his family.[21]

If Pope Leo defended private property in principle, he castigated capitalism as it manifested itself in practice. He denounced the "callousness of employers," "the greed of unrestrained competition," and the dealings of "avaricious and grasping men."[22] More important, Leo attacked the underlying principle of "laissez-faire" capitalism, that the free-market system should be allowed to function unrestrained. The principal obligation of an employer is to give every worker a "just wage."[23] But the laissez-faire view that "wages are fixed by free consent" is not convincing, for every person has a right to procure what is required in order to live, and the poor can procure this only through wages.[24] Workers also have the right to form unions,[25] thus changing the "market" in wage negotiations. Contrary to the principle of laissez-faire capitalism, the state also has a critical role to play. It must recognize justice for all and step in when the general interest or any particular class suffers.[26] The state has a right and a duty to protect workers against degrading work conditions, work that is too hard or too long, and insufficient wages. It also should protect women and children from being placed in unsuitable work conditions.[27]

"Restoring the moral order," in *Rerum novarum*, implied primarily a call for moral conversion and the end of strife. Order would be restored, conflicts would cease, and inequities would be overcome if all members of society would heed the voice of the church and guide their actions by moral principles of the natural law. The adequacy of moral appeals to effect social change has been challenged by contemporary commentators on the social encyclicals,[28] and few today would look back to the Middle Ages, with its hierarchical divisions, as a model for modern society. But whatever the limits we may see from our present-day vantage point, the impact of *Rerum novarum* should not be underestimated. Many of Leo's proposals were considered bold and daring in their day. They directly challenged liberal capitalism's contention that there should be no interference with the laws of the free market. The very approval of labor unions, independent of the patronage of employers or the tutelage of church authorities, placed Leo among the avant-garde thinkers in the church. The insistence on a just wage made justice, and not simply charity, a focus of church concern. The church's entry challenged socialism as the sole or major defender of the workers' cause. *Rerum novarum* gave great moral support to the working class and made social issues, for the first time, an important part of the church's agenda.

Pius XI: Quadragesimo Anno *(1931)*. Forty years passed before another major social encyclical was published, but the forty years witnessed a significant growth and development of the principles of *Rerum novarum*. Heinrich Pesch, Oswald Nell-Breuning, John A. Ryan, and numerous other scholars promulgated and refined the new church social teachings on just wages, rights of workers to unionize, the duties of the state, and so on.[29] Thus Pius XI's new encyclical took root in a soil already cultivated.

Quadragesimo anno reaffirmed most of the premises and principles set down by Leo XIII. It stressed again that natural law provides the general principles needed for determining social doctrines and practices. It retained the right to private property as a fundamental principle of natural law.[30] It again rejected both collectivist socialism and liberal capitalism.[31] It reemphasized the importance of renewing morals and the spirit of the Gospel, and even held out again the ideal of reconstructing the social order along lines that once prevailed in medieval Christendom.[32]

But more notable shifts, at least in emphasis, can also be discerned in Pius XI's encyclical. While retaining the "right to private property," Pius also insisted that the rights of the individual must be balanced by the common good of the whole human race,[33] and he recognized that immense numbers of wage earners were in fact propertyless.[34] He also came down more harshly on capitalism, using the strongest language one finds in any of the social encyclicals. Thus he noted that "immense power and despotic economic domination is concentrated in the hands of a few."[35] "Free competition is dead; economic dictatorship has taken its place"; the whole economic life "has become hard, cruel and relentless in a ghastly manner."[36] Pius's most often quoted statement about socialism, that "no one can be at the same time a sincere Catholic and a true Socialist,"[37] seems to suggest an even stronger position than was taken by Pope Leo. But Pius made a distinction between "true" socialism, an ideology which subordinated people and human dignity to material gain,[38] and "mitigated" socialism with its rejection of violence and more moderate views on class warfare and abolishing private property. The programs of mitigated socialism, the pope noted, often strikingly resemble the demands of Christian social reform. "If these changes continue," Pius XI concluded, "it may well come about that gradually the tenets of mitigated Socialism will no longer be different from the program of those who seek to reform human society according to Christian principles."[39]

The major thrust of Pius XI's encyclical was the search for a "middle course" between the individualism of laissez-faire capitalism and the collectivism of socialism.[40] Leo XIII had discussed the idea of associations enriching both owners and workers, but the practical impact of his encyclical had been the defense of labor unions and specific worker demands. Pius XI wanted to propose a new, long-range vision and plan for reconstructing the social order. The basic plan was to reconstruct the whole economic system gradually through the creation of corporations based on vocational or professional groupings.[41] Workers would have a share in the ownership of these corporations and a voice in their management.[42] Owners would have to belong to these corporations and would no longer have complete control over investment, work, and distribution of wages and profits. The common good, not the profit motive, would serve as a governing principle in decisions about automation, plant location, and production goals. These corporations would not be state-owned. The state would serve to encourage and protect them but would not take over the operation of the economy. Pius insisted on the "principle of subsidiarity" (one of the most significant principles in Catholic social thought): "[A]s it is wrong to withdraw from the individual and commit to the community at large what private enterprise and industry can accomplish so, too, it is an injustice . . . for a larger and higher organization to arrogate to itself functions which can be performed efficiently by smaller and lower bodies."[43]

This vision of a corporate society served as a bridge between past and future church teachings on the economic order. By calling for a "reconstruction of society," Pius XI anticipated the stress on transforming society and changing structures that would characterize much of post–Vatican II social thought. The misuse of corporatist ideas by Nazi Germany and Fascist Italy brought the term "corporatist" into disrepute. But the underlying ideas of corporatism—for example, workers sharing in ownership and in some decision-making—would be reemphasized by later popes.

The concept of "social justice"[44] played perhaps an even greater role in anticipating later stresses on "changing structures" in society. Social justice went beyond commutative and distributive justice by stressing the political obligation of individuals and groups to aid in the creation of structures, or patterns of social organizations, needed for the protection of human dignity and the promotion of the common good.[45]

In the years following *Quadragesimo anno*, the threat of communism became an ever-greater focus of Catholic social thought. In France, Jacques Maritain and Emmanuel Mounier worked to develop sociopolitical viewpoints which acknowledged Marxist criticisms of capitalism but avoided atheistic communist solutions. Pius XI took a stronger stand in his encyclical *Divini redemptoris* (1937), condemning "the principles of Atheistic Communism as they are manifested chiefly in Bolshevism."[46] He attacked the principles and ideology of communism on many scores: its false messianic promises, its materialism, its violence and hatred, its rejection of the right to property, its undermining of marriage and the family, the unlimited power it gives over to the state, etc.[47] Pius's unqualified condemnation of bolshevik communism would characterize Catholic anticommunism for many years to come. "Communism is intrinsically wrong, and no one who would save Christian civilization may collaborate with it in any undertaking whatsoever."[48]

Pius XII: Fundamental Social Values. Pius XII did not promulgate any major social encyclicals during his twenty-year reign, but his many addresses and letters on social issues merit some attention because they served as the link between the foundational encyclicals of Leo XIII and Pius XI and the new era inaugurated by John XXIII and Vatican II. Throughout the World War II years and into the postwar era of reconstruction Pius XII spoke repeatedly of the need for a "new social order," an order built upon fundamental Christian values.

The pope first articulated these values in an address (1941) commemorating the fiftieth anniversary of *Rerum novarum.* As his predecessors had done, Pius XII warned of the dangers of collectivist Marxist socialism and the fatal consequences of individualistic economic liberalism. To offset these the pontiff set forth directives based on three interrelated "fundamental values." The first value related to the use of material goods: The goods of the earth, created for all persons, should flow equally to all, according to the principles of justice and charity. "Every man, as a living being gifted with reason, has in fact from nature the fundamental right to make use of the material goods of the earth."[49] This right also demands private property and the free exchange of goods with the state as a control over both these institutions. But all these are subordinate to the right to make "use" of goods, a right which is intimately linked to the dignity and other rights of the human person. As Fr. Jean-Yves Calvez has noted, this stress on "use" marked a significant shift away from Leo XIII's emphasis on "ownership" of private property as a natural right.[50]

Pius XII's second fundamental value was "labor," which is both personal and necessary as a means to achieve the use of material goods.[51] Pope John Paul II later made "labor over capital" a cardinal principle of his social thought, but concern for protection of the "personal" character of work was a dominant concern for Pius XII as well. He was concerned that the worker could too easily be treated as a depersonalized cog in the machinery of modern productive forces, given the growth of large corporations, state power, and increasingly mechanized modes of production.[52]

The third value noted by Pius XII in his 1941 address was the family. Society must seek to protect and strengthen the bond of the family. The stability and security of the family can be strengthened through the ownership of *land,* which serves both as a homestead and as a holding from which products of subsistence can be drawn.[53] This concern for the family was a recurrent theme in Pius XII's speeches and writings. Thus he called on German Catholics to cherish and to defend first of all the Christian life of the family.[54] In another address he listed defense of social unity in the family as one of the basic points for ordering a new society.[55]

To these three fundamental values, articulated in his 1941 address and repeated in other talks, a fourth and unifying value should be added: the organic cooperation and unity of all parts of society: "The Church never ceases to labor so that the apparent conflict between capital and labor, between employer and worker, be transformed into a higher unity . . . into that organic cooperation of both parties which is indicated by their very nature and which consists in the collaboration of both according to their activity in the economic sector and professions."[56]

In proposing means for realizing these values, Pius XII sought to reform and transform existing socioeconomic relations. But he felt compelled also to confront strongly the Marxists' appeals to workers in postwar Europe. Thus, while he viewed the right of private property as subordinate to use, he felt called upon to defend private property against those (Marxists, in particular) who sought to eliminate it: "One of the essential points of Christian social doctrine has always been the affirmation of the private enterprise as compared to the subsidiary function of state enterprise."[57] The pope believed that more extensive social planning undoubtedly was necessary in modern society, but not the almost-absolute directed planning called for by Marxists. This cannot be, because "the independence of the family and the freedom of the citizen are naturally bound up with a sound functioning of private property as a stabilizing social function."[58] He recognized the licitness of some nationalizations but warned French activists that such nationalizations could accentuate control *over* workers.[59]

Throughout his tenure as pope, Pius XII warned repeatedly about the dangers of Marxism, telling workers that "evolution in concord," not social revolution, was the correct path to social change.[60] Troubled by the threat of communism in Italy, Pius XII issued a decree in July 1949 forbidding Catholics to join the Communist party or to encourage it in any way. The decree forbade the faithful, moreover, to publish, distribute, or even read books and papers which upheld communist doctrine.[61]

How, then, should society be restructured to avoid the evils of both communism and economic liberalism? Like his predecessor Pius XI, the pope viewed the development of a "corporative" society as the best way to achieve the values needed for a new social order. It should be a society which retains private enterprise but gives workers a share in profits and a voice in decision-making (though he did not consider this voice a natural right of workers). Solidarity, cooperation, and organic unity were all expressions of the "higher unity" Pope Pius XII hoped could be embodied in the new social order.[62]

Transforming the World: John XXIII and Vatican II

The Catholic church underwent a succession of dramatic changes in the 1960s. Pope John XXIII and the Second Vatican Council adopted new attitudes which profoundly affected the Catholic church and its relationship to the world. The changes began with seemingly contained goals. The pope wanted the church to exert positive leadership in addressing world problems, and Vatican II sought to reexamine the nature of the church and its relation to the world. Both wished to make the church more effective in transmitting the gospel message in modern times. But the changes that ensued proved far greater and more difficult to control than ever were anticipated.

Pope John's two major social encyclicals, *Mater et magistra* (1961) and *Pacem in terris* (1963), retained natural law as the basic source of church social teachings.[63] On that score they reaffirmed continuity. But the pope's own personal spirit gave a new tone to church social teachings. The encyclicals were more positive, more optimistic, more pastoral, and more future oriented than any previous papal encyclicals. They spent little time on correcting false ideologies and sought to promote practical, creative responses to the world's problems. *Pacem in terris,* moreover, was addressed not just to Catholics but to the whole world; it sought to find common principles related to the value of human dignity to which all people of good will might respond. Previous encyclicals had also tended to "deduce" social doctrines from principles. John XXIII proceeded more inductively. Thus *Mater et magistra* analyzed "trends" and characteristics of modern society, and *Pacem in terris* began with "signs of the times." Pope John also addressed new issues such as the problems of rural populations and the poor of underdeveloped nations.

Given the universal popularity of John XXIII, commentators on church social teachings all manage to find some aspect of his teaching that supports their own perspective. Thus Michael Novak rejoiced in Pope John's defense of private property, his emphasis on production (not just distribution), and the value he placed on work done for the common good by individuals and groups over state actions.[64] From a very different perspective, Donal Dorr saw and welcomed a "shift to the left" in John XXIII, in the pope's recognition that increased "socialization" calls for *more* state intervention.[65]

From my own perspective, I view Pope John's extension of the notion of human rights to include socioeconomic rights as his most important and far-reaching contribution. Thus, in speaking about human dignity, Pope John claimed that all have the right to the means necessary for a truly dignified life: food, shelter, medical care, and necessary social services.[66] Also, while he continued to reaffirm the "right to private property,"[67] Pope John affirmed Pius XII's declaration that this right is subordinate to the right of every person to use needed material goods.[68] Vatican II's *Gaudium et spes* carried this change still further, making no mention of the right to property and stressing instead "the universal purpose of created goods" as the most basic principle.[69]

Vatican II: Gaudium et Spes. Quite possibly no document in church history has ever influenced the church's understanding of its role in the world as much as did Vatican II's *Gaudium et spes* ("On the church in the modern world"). The statements of the document itself seemed careful and balanced enough, as one would expect from a council of bishops trained in respect for tradition. But their effects went far beyond what was intended. If earlier encyclicals had tended to view the church as "above" the world, *Gaudium et spes* placed the church very much "in" the world. The church, it said, identifies itself with the joys, hopes, griefs, and aspirations of humanity, especially of the poor. The church is "intimately linked" with humanity and its history.[70] The church serves humanity[71] and is a "kind of soul for human society," which is to be transformed into God's family.[72] Moreover Jesus was crucified and rose to break the power of evil "so that this world might be fashioned anew according to God's design and reach its fulfillment."[73] Vatican II acknowledged the growing consciousness of men and women "that they themselves are the artisans and authors of the culture of their community."[74] It affirmed the importance of human activity in transforming the world and viewed human achievement as a sign of God's greatness.[75] It offered a new eschatology which spoke not only of eternal salvation but of "a new earth where justice will abide."[76]

All of these statements about transforming the world were balanced with qualifiers. Human destiny is not bound up with this world alone; it transcends the world.[77] The primary mission of the Church is religious, not political and economic,[78] and Christians who take political stands should not claim to do so in the name of the church.[79] While earthly progress is of "vital concern" to the Kingdom, it cannot be equated with the fulfillment of the Kingdom, which can only come from God.[80] For many, however, efforts to transform the world became *the* most important mission. While Vatican II certainly did not intend this, it did place far more emphasis on "this world." It viewed the spiritual and temporal not as separate spheres but as a single unit integrating man's Christian and human natures.[81]

Gaudium et spes covered a range of other topics, including the fostering of marriage, the proper development of culture, work and all its related social issues, political participation, and the fostering of peace. But the truly new dimension involved the church's mission to the world, defined in terms that bound the church inseparably to the good of humanity (intimately linked, the very soul of humanity). Of very great significance also was the reliance on Scripture and the Gospel message, rather than natural law, as a new primary source for reflection on social issues.

The strongest statement of commitment to justice and to transforming the world came later, however, in a document entitled "Justice in the World" by the 1971 Synod of Bishops. The bishops asserted that "action on behalf of justice and participation in the transforming of the world fully appear to us as a constitutive dimension of the preaching of the Gospel, or, in other words, of the Church's mission for the redemption of the human race and its liberation from every oppressive situation."[82]

The Years of Paul VI. The 1971 synod statement on transforming the world as a "constitutive dimension" of the church's mission, and its use of "liberation" to express this, provide a lead to the discussion of a dramatic new impulse in Catholic social thought, the advent of liberation theology. But for the sake of historical continuity, as well as to indicate how "official" teachings prepared the way for it, some reflections should be included about the contributions of Pope Paul VI. Some viewed his *Populorum progressio* (1967) as the most "leftist" of the papal social encyclicals. The *Wall Street Journal* called it "warmed over Marxism,"[83] presumably because of the pope's criticism of rich nations in their relation to poorer developing nations. In analyzing the causes of poverty in underdeveloped nations, Paul VI cited colonialism as partially responsible because it left countries dependent on one-crop economies,[84] and he criticized the disparity of power in trade relations between rich and poor nations.[85] He angered some as well with disparaging remarks about a system (presumably capitalism) "which considers profit as the key motive for economic progress, competition as the supreme law of economics," and private ownership as an absolute right without limits.[86] The major thrust of the encyclical was an appeal to rich nations to lend aid to poor ones and to rectify inequitable trade relations.

An even stronger voice on behalf of the poor in developing nations was raised by the Second General Conference of Latin American Bishops (CELAM) meeting in Medellín, Colombia, in 1968. The bishops denounced the misery of large masses in Latin America as an "injustice which cries to the heavens"[87] and committed themselves to solidarity with the poor. In addressing the problem they used "liberation" in the double sense soon to be popularized by liberation theologians. Politically, liberation signified freeing Latin American countries from their dependence on the North (the United States and Europe). Theologically, liberation referred to God acting in history to free people from oppression. The bishops suggested the political sense when they placed the "principal guilt" for Latin American economic "dependence" on foreign monopolistic powers.[88] They adopted the theological sense when they affirmed that God had sent his Son "that he might liberate" all people from the slavery to which sin had subjected them and from hunger, misery, and oppression.[89]

The Medellín conference appeared to offer a green light to the new liberation theology and at least some support for its leftist critiques. Pope Paul VI's *Octogesima adveniens* (1971) gave a very cautious "yellow light" to movements or issues where red lights by the church in the past had signaled only danger. Thus Paul VI drew distinctions between different expressions of socialism (its aspirations, its historical movements, its ideology) and between different meanings of Marxism (as class struggle, as one-party rule, as a materialist ideology, and as a scientific method). He also warned, however, that these different aspects of Marxism are usually linked, and that their linkage has led to violence and totalitarian societies.[90]

It helped the cause of liberation theologians to be able to cite passages from Vatican II, Medellín, and Paul VI's writings to support their views. They found considerable affirmation in this regard in "Justice in the World," the 1971 Synod of Bishops' document cited earlier in which the language of "liberation" was used repeatedly.[91] Numerous points stressed in liberation theology were stressed in the synod document as well: violence and oppression caused by "unjust systems and structures"; the failure of "development" policies; "international systems of domination"; "the obstacles social structures place in the way of conversion of hearts"; the need for self-determination by poor nations; "the intervention of God's justice on behalf of the needy and the oppressed"; a mission of preaching *and witnessing* to justice as proper to the church's mission; the need for justice "within" the church itself; education for justice (raising consciousness); and hope in the coming Kingdom and "the radical transformation of the world."[92]

Liberation Theology. Gustavo Gutierrez's *A Theology of Liberation* was published in 1971 (1973 in English), and it set down the foundations of this new theological movement.[93] Gutierrez stressed that theological reflections should be based on "praxis," active involvement with and commitment to the poor, based on an understanding of the conditions in which they live and their struggles to overcome these conditions. From the Bible he drew upon the Exodus story as a paradigm of God's acting in history to liberate the poor from oppression, on the denunciation of injustice by the prophets of the Old Testament, and upon Jesus' identification with the poor and the political conflict engendered by his speaking out against their oppressors. From the social sciences he drew upon dependency theories and elements of Marxist analysis (its ideas of "praxis," its critique of capitalism, its ideas on class struggle, and its critique of religion). He argued that the church must "opt for and with the poor" in their struggles against oppression.

This new theology, all too briefly summarized above, quickly became a source of controversy. The first major confrontation with church authorities did not involve liberation theology directly, but it did involve a movement which drew many of its ideas from the new theology, the Christians for Socialism in Chile (CFS). In 1973 the Chilean bishops criticized the CFS movement on points that would later be directed at liberation theology: (1) it reduced faith to politics, (2) it treated Marxism as an "indisputable science" and viewed all social change in terms of class struggle, and (3) it was attempting to create its own church and its own magisterium.[94] In 1976 Paul VI promulgated a letter on evangelization (*Evangelii nuntiandi*) which included some similar "reservations" about possible misuses of the concept of "liberation." Donal Dorr, in his commentary, listed these reservations under five headings: reductionism, politicization, limitations (in attempting to achieve earthly liberation), violence, and attitudinal change (giving the impression that change of structures alone is sufficient to bring about human liberation).[95] The issue of liberation theology divided the church in Latin America. Many bishops supported it; many others (led by Bishop Alfonso Lopez Trujillo) opposed it, as the history of the Puebla conference (Mexico, 1979) demonstrates.[96] For the Vatican under Pope John Paul II, liberation theology became an issue of grave importance.

Promoting True Christian Liberation: John Paul II

Pope John Paul II's views on social change do not fit neatly into any one classification. He clearly rejects communism and classical Marxist analysis, but he uses Marxist concepts to criticize capitalism and consumerism in the Western world. He criticizes liberation theology but embraces the cause of the poor and accepts "liberation" as a legitimate theological concept. He warns priests and religious about political involvement, but his own speeches contain strong and clear political messages. One can discern, however, a consistency in all these positions. Pope John Paul II seems quite clearly to have two important objectives or priorities in mind: to build social principles and a vision of what society should be, not on any secular basis but on truly authentic Christian doctrines; and to make the "official," hierarchical church the guiding force in establishing the social mission of the church. If this observation is accurate, it suggests that Pope John Paul II combines the concern first raised by Leo XIII, to "restore" Christian principles of morality, with Vatican II's stress on transforming society by seeking to integrate more fully the spiritual and the temporal in a "true" liberation theology.

In *Laborem exercens* (1981), written to commemorate the ninetieth anniversary of *Rerum novarum*, John Paul II did a very striking thing. He took up themes and employed categories usually associated with Marxism, but he gave them distinctively Christian, person-based meanings. Marx wrote about the primacy of work in understanding society, work as the main way in which humans "realize" their nature, alienated work under capitalism, and class conflict. Each of these themes is taken up by *Laborem exercens*. The encyclical begins with assertions about the centrality of work in human life: "Work is one of the characteristics that distinguishes man from the rest of creatures. . . . Thus work bears a particular mark of man and of humanity, the mark of a person operating within a community of persons."[97] Then, building on these statements, the pope concluded that "human work is a key, perhaps the essential key, to the whole social question."[98] Work, the pope continued, is the primary way in which humans develop their capacities and gain a sense of their own dignity.[99] Work is not just a useful pursuit, it is "something that corresponds to man's dignity, that expresses this dignity and increases it."[100] Thus work must be judged by the measure of dignity it brings to those who perform it.[101] From this the pope derived the central principle of the whole encyclical: the priority of labor over capital.[102]

Laborem exercens does not attribute alienation in work to the very nature of capitalism, as Marx did. But it does recognize that early-nineteenth-century capitalism did invert the priority of labor over capital, and the danger of treating workers as a kind of "merchandise" or cost factor still persists.[103] The encyclical certainly does not speak of class struggle in Marxist terms as the driving force of history, but it does recognize the reality of class conflict in history. Moreover, the encyclical unequivocally blames "capital" for the conflict: Capitalists exploited workers by keeping their wages at the lowest possible minimum so that their own profits would be maximized.[104]

If these points parallel Marxist thought, what makes *Laborem exercens* distinctively Christian? First, the primacy of work and work as self-realization are rooted in the biblical notion of humans as sharers in God's creativity.[105] Also, the pope did not restrict the notion of "labor" to factory workers (the "proletariat") but included all humans as potential subjects of work.[106] Second, given the broad sense of labor, workers are not viewed as a "class" struggling to obtain power. Here also the pope made a very useful distinction between morally acceptable struggles and Marxist class struggles. A struggle "for" the just needs of workers is commendable; a struggle "against" others is not. Struggle on behalf of justice is praiseworthy; struggle to eliminate the opposition and bring one class into power is wrong.[107] Third, while the encyclical accepts "truly socialized" forms of ownership as valid,[108] for example, shared ownership and shared decision-making, it sharply rejects collectivist (Marxist) socialism. Collectivist socialism only shifts control from an elite comprising private owners to the control of a bureaucratic party elite who run the state and society.[109] Fourth, the pope recognized the need for centralized planning, for example, in dealing with unemployment.[110] But he rejected total state control and insisted on the need for decentralized power structures (e.g., unions, different types of ownership, intermediate bodies). Finally, *Laborem exercens* sees Marxist dialectical materialism as a philosophy that reduces humans to objects, or "resultants," of a deterministic process of production.[111] But this runs counter to the central message of the encyclical: that humans are creative "subjects" of work; hence the "priority of labor over capital." An economic system should be judged on whether it truly treats humans as subjects.

The Vatican on Liberation Theology. The Vatican has been clearly disturbed by the liberation theology movement in Latin America. In his *Instruction on Certain Aspects of the Theology of Liberation* (1984), Joseph

Cardinal Ratzinger, speaking for the Congregation of the Faith, charged liberation theology—or at least some forms of it—with the same kind of errors attributed to the Christians for Socialism eleven years before: (1) the reduction of faith to politics (neglecting eternal salvation; neglecting personal sin in favor of social, structural sin; treating the Kingdom of God as achievable by human efforts alone); (2) the uncritical use of Marxism (treating it as a science; making class struggle the driving law of history); and (3) creating a "popular" church in opposition to the hierarchical church (disdain for church teachings; treating church authorities who disagree with liberation theology as bourgeois enemies; promoting ideas in base communities which the poor are not trained to handle).[112] Some commentators questioned the fairness of Ratzinger's description of liberation theology. At times he seems to "read into" liberation theologians far more than they state (for example, none of them, to my knowledge, equates the Kingdom of God with earthly progress, denies the seriousness of personal sin, or claims that "class struggle is the driving force of history"). Some also questioned how much Cardinal Ratzinger's statements reflect the views of Pope John Paul II, though they certainly share the same concerns.

The more recent *Instruction on Christian Freedom and Liberation* (1986) does not treat liberation theology directly, but almost every point it makes seems intended to counter tendencies that the earlier instruction attributed to liberation theology. The fact that some leading liberation theologians (Gutierrez, Boff) applauded this newer instruction suggests, however, that they do not consider it a condemnation of their views. Whatever degree of "official" standing one should assign to the *Instruction*, it frequently cites John Paul II and again appears to reflect some of his chief concerns.

The *Instruction* clearly wants to establish any discussion of liberation on a truly Christian basis, guided by the Magisterium of the church, which the *Instruction* defends against criticisms.[113] Freedom and liberation must flow from the truth, a truth that comes from God through faith in Jesus.[114] As I read it, the truth the *Instruction* most strongly wishes to emphasize is that freedom, which is primarily personal and spiritual, is more fundamental than any social, earthly liberation. This fundamental thesis expresses itself in various ways in the course of the document.

Liberation movements, while they have at times helped to create new conditions of freedom, have often proved delusionary and have led to new forms of servitude.[115] Temporal liberation can only create better conditions for authentic freedom; it does not create freedom itself. Even under conditions of servitude humans never lose their spiritual freedom.[116] The Exodus of the Israelites out of Egyptian bondage (a frequently used paradigm in liberation theology) was not just a this-worldly liberation—justice flowed from obedience to the laws of the Covenant.[117] The poor find their freedom in communion with Yahweh.[118] Through grace and the sacraments we gain true freedom by being released from sin and restored to communion with God.[119]

Thus the *Instruction* stresses that "the Church's essential mission . . . is a mission of evangelization and salvation."[120] The primacy of the spiritual is clear: "The Church desires the good of man in all his dimensions, first of all as a member of the city of God, and then as a member of the earthly city."[121] Promotion of justice does not go beyond the church's mission, but its mission should not be absorbed by or reduced to temporal preoccupations.[122]

The relationship between conversion from personal sin and changing structures also is addressed in the *Instruction*. Inner conversion is essential for social changes to become truly human; giving priority to structures over persons runs counter to human dignity. Personal sin is the root cause of evil; "social sin," in reference to structures, is sin only in a derived, secondary sense.[123]

The *Instruction* changes the language of Medellín and Puebla from an "option for the poor" to the poor as "the object of a love of preference on the part of the Church."[124] One reason for this is clear: The Vatican does not wish "option for the poor" to be taken as a partisan political commitment, and most especially not as an option to enter into class struggle.[125] But the word *object* and the language used to discuss the poor unfortunately seem to suggest that the poor are indeed viewed as "objects" of compassion rather than as "subjects called to shape their own destiny," as stressed in *Laborem exercens*. The poor are referred to often as "the little ones" who "endure poverty and affliction" by placing their trust in Yahweh.[126] Response to them is put primarily in terms of relief and charity, with little sense of working *with* them to help them overcome injustices.

The *Instruction* does, however, make some allowance for changing structures and offers at least one statement about an active part the poor might themselves play. Thus, after a reference to works of charity, the *Instruction* continues: "In addition . . . [the church] has sought to promote structural changes in society so as to secure conditions of life worthy of the human person."[127] The church does condemn unjust situations and make judgments about the values of structures and systems. And while appeals for inner conversion should be given priority, this "in no way eliminates the need for unjust structures to be changed."[128] Most important, the *Instruction* also says that it is legitimate "that those who suffer oppression on the part of the wealthy or the politically powerful should take action, through morally licit means, in order to secure structures and institutions in which their rights will be truly respected."[129] Even armed struggle could be justified as a last resort where prolonged tyranny gravely damages basic rights.[130]

Conclusion

A century of church social teachings has provided a rich heritage and resource for Christians concerned about creating a world in which both freedom and justice might prevail. In communist countries of the world authoritarian rule has made it difficult, at times almost impossible, for any mobilization of Christian efforts to achieve the freedom and true justice championed in church documents. One can only hope that moments of potential change will emerge again, as happened with the Solidarity movement in Poland, which found support in Pope John Paul II's defense of worker solidarity in *Laborem exercens*.

In his most recent social encyclical, *Sollicitudo rei socialis*, John Paul II not only reaffirmed the importance of solidarity but made it the central ethical norm in his letter. We live interdependent lives; human development requires mutual responsibility and solidarity. The nations of the world are likewise interdependent, and the pope criticized the superpower blocs in both the West and the East of neglecting and impeding the development of poorer, weaker nations. The race to win military superiority diverts funds needed for basic human needs. Marxist regimes marked by ambition for power and capitalist regimes driven by profit and consumerism both subordinate the common good of all people to their own interests.[131]

A more promising relationship finally has developed between the hierarchical church and liberation theology. While continuing to stress the warnings voiced in the Vatican instructions about liberation, the pope nevertheless wrote to the bishops of Brazil in 1986 that the theology of liberation "is not only opportune, but useful and necessary," and a spokesperson for CELAM declared in early 1988 that "the problem with liberation theology has passed for Latin Americans," and true dialogue had begun.[132]

In a deeply divided world one can only hope and pray that Christians might take the lead in resolving their own differences and come together to work for the ideals proposed in the church's social teachings. Beyond that lies the even greater task of achieving freedom, peace, and justice among peoples of widely different faiths, ideologies, and cultures. We still live by hope, but it is a hope God has expressed as a promise: "Now I am making the whole of creation new" (Revelation 21:4–5).

II

CATHOLICISM UNDER EUROPEAN COMMUNISM

3

The Catholic Church in the Soviet Union

Roman Solchanyk and Ivan Hvat

Catholicism in the Soviet Union is a minority religion. Several years ago, in an interview with a Polish journalist, Konstantin Kharchev, former chairman of the governmental Council for Religious Affairs, claimed that the number of Catholics in the Soviet Union was about five million.[1] Western estimates are considerably higher, particularly if the recently legalized Ukrainian Catholics of the Byzantine Rite (Greek Catholics, or Uniates) are taken into consideration. Thus, *L'Unita*'s Vatican correspondent has placed the number of Soviet Catholics at ten million, the majority concentrated in the Soviet west: Lithuania, Latvia, western Ukraine, and western Belorussia.[2] According to Soviet sources, the Catholic church is active in ten of the fifteen Soviet Union republics. In 1986 there were 1,099 Roman Catholic communities. The number of functioning churches is said to be 1,100, about half of which are in Lithuania. The only Catholic seminaries are in Lithuania (Kaunas and Telsiai) and Latvia (Riga).[3]

Catholic communities in the Soviet Union are characterized by a high degree of diversity with regard to historical development, ethnic affiliation, rite, and numbers. The spectrum ranges from the officially recognized and perhaps most important Lithuanian Catholic church to the numerically greater but long outlawed Ukrainian Uniates, and includes the diaspora parishes of Poles, Belorussians, Germans, and Hungarians scattered throughout various republics. The isolation of these Catholic communities is, of course, in the interest of the Soviet regime. Unlike the Russian Orthodox church or the Union of Evangelical Christians-Baptists, the Catholic church in the Soviet Union has not been permitted to establish a countrywide, centralized ecclesiastical authority led by a conference of bishops, and the only established hierarchies are in Lithuania and Latvia. This differentiated approach in Soviet religious policy, which also is evident in areas other than the internal organization of church life, underlines the persistently hostile attitude of the authorities toward Catholicism, which has been conditioned by a number of specific factors, both internal and external.

Communism, Catholicism, and Nationalism

Perhaps the most important factor shaping Moscow's view of the Catholic church has been the confluence of religion and nationality. In Russia and in the Soviet Union Catholicism has been identified largely with specific national groups that are characterized by a predominantly Western cultural orientation. For the majority of Lithuanians, Poles, and western Ukrainians, the concepts of faith and nation are easily interchangeable, which testifies to the important role the church has played in the process of nation-building. Thus in Lithuania the link between religion and nationalism is such that Lithuanians, like Poles, are commonly perceived as a "Catholic nation." The result often has been that Moscow's antireligious policies in these areas are seen as an attack on the nation itself, which serves only to deepen the conflict.[4] This is perhaps best illustrated by the liquidation of the Ukrainian Catholic church in 1946 and the forced "reunion" of its clergy and believers with Russian Orthodoxy.

Another element that must be taken into account is the centuries-old tradition of anti-Catholicism rooted in Russian political culture, which was inherited by the Bolsheviks in 1917 and subsequently utilized as the occasion demanded. The political and ideological relationships between church and state in Muscovy and the Russian Empire were complex and multifaceted. For our purposes, suffice it to say that Christianity was introduced into Kievan Rus' at the end of the tenth century in its Orthodox form, which carried with it the hostility of the Byzantine East to the Roman West. Over the centuries Russian Orthodoxy became closely intertwined with the state and increasingly served its expansionist interests. The symbiosis between the two found its clearest expression in the messianic religious-political ideology of "Moscow, the third Rome" that was formulated in the early sixteenth century. By the first half of the nineteenth century Russian Orthodoxy had emerged as one of the mainstays of "official nationality," the modern Russian nationalist ideology based on the principles of "Orthodoxy, autocracy, and nationality." The legacy bequeathed by Russian Orthodoxy—on the one hand, aversion to the "heretical Catholic West" and, on the other, faithful service to the state—fell on fertile Soviet ground.

Finally, Soviet ideologists have correctly recognized that Catholicism, with its universalist teachings and a global organization to match, represents a formidable opponent in the international arena. In purely ideological terms, the Kremlin consistently perceived the Vatican as an ally of capitalism and world reaction that poses a concrete challenge to its own no less universalist aspirations. In practice, relations between Moscow and the Holy See have varied as the demands of political expediency required. An entirely new element in these relations emerged with the election in October 1978 of a Polish cardinal as the first Slavic pope.

The First Confrontation: 1917–39

In the 1890s there were slightly more than 10.5 million Roman Catholics in the Russian Empire, concentrated for the most part in the western provinces of the country. But in the aftermath of the Polish-Soviet War (1919–21) and the formation of the independent states of Lithuania, Latvia, and Estonia, the Roman Catholic population of the Soviet republics was reduced to only about 1.6 million.[5] By 1923 the church was organized into six dioceses: the Mogilev Archdiocese under Archbishop Eduard von der Ropp, and the Kamianets'-Podil's'kyi, Minsk, Zhytomyr, Tiraspol', and Vladivostok dioceses. There was also the Apostolic Vicariate of Siberia, the Apostolic Vicariate of the Caucasus and Crimea, and the Apostolic Administration for Catholics of the Armenian Rite. In addition, in May 1917 Metropolitan Andrei Sheptyts'kyi, archbishop of Lvov, named Fr. Leonid Fedorov exarch of the Russian Catholic church of the Byzantine Rite in Petrograd.[6]

During the first five years of Bolshevik rule,[7] the Catholic church was in a relatively more favorable position than Russian Orthodoxy, which was perceived as the more dangerous and immediate enemy. Moreover, the new Soviet regime initially hoped to obtain recognition from the Vatican, which served to moderate its policies toward the church. Nonetheless, like other religions, Catholicism was subjected to the discriminatory policies pursued by the atheistic state. Thus the Catholic Theological Academy in Petrograd, the diocesan seminaries, and all parochial schools were closed, and church properties were confiscated. The first direct blow to the church hierarchy came in April 1919 with the arrest of Archbishop von der Ropp, who eventually was freed and sent to Poland in exchange for the imprisoned communist leader Karl Radek. Still, throughout 1921 and early 1922 the interests of both church and state dictated a pragmatic relationship, which was reflected in the Vatican's contribution to the Soviet famine relief effort and diplomatic contacts at the Rapallo Conference.

The first major crisis developed in the aftermath of the Soviet government's decision in February 1922 to seize church valuables, ostensibly for famine relief. This was resisted by the church hierarchy and the clergy, now headed by Jan Cieplak, leading to serious conflicts and the closing down of churches in Petrograd. In November Archbishop Cieplak was served with a statement of charges and informed that he would be tried for antigovernment propaganda, inciting the overthrow of the regime, and counterrevolution. The trial of Cieplak, his assistant Msgr. Constantine Budkiewicz, Exarch Fedorov, twelve other priests, and a Catholic layman was held in Petrograd on March 21–25, 1923, resulting in death sentences for Cieplak and Budkiewicz and terms ranging from six months to ten years for the remainder of the defendants. Cieplak's sentence was soon commuted, and the following year he was released and expelled from Russia; Budkiewicz was executed. In the meantime, all of the remaining bishops except the aged Bishop Zerr of Tiraspol' had been arrested. The Vatican withdrew its relief mission in 1924. At that time there were still about 1.6 million Catholics in the Soviet Union but only 127 priests, sixteen of whom were imprisoned.

The Soviet initiative to conduct talks with the Vatican in early 1925 resulted in three visits to the Soviet Union by the Vatican emissary Michel d'Herbigny, a French Jesuit who was secretly consecrated a bishop and charged with the task of reestablishing a church hierarchy. On his second trip, in April–May 1926, d'Herbigny clandestinely consecrated three bishops: Pie Eugen Neveu for Moscow, Boleslavs Sloskans for Mogilev and Minsk, and Alexander Frison for Odessa. On his final trip, in August 1926, d'Herbigny completed the reorganization of the clandestine church hierarchy in the Soviet Union.[8] The state security organs were, of course, aware of d'Herbigny's activities, and in early September he was expelled from the country. There followed a series of arrests, trials, incarcerations, and, in some cases, executions, resulting in the liquidation of the hierarchy in 1929–32. According to one source, during this period 114 priests were either imprisoned or deported, and barely fifty priests remained at liberty in the entire country.[9]

This coincided with the strengthening of antireligious propaganda, which was centered in the newly reorganized League of Militant Godless in 1929, and more restrictive antireligious legislation.[10] Increased hostility toward the church and violent persecution of its clergy accompanied the mobilization of the party and Soviet society for the collectivization and industrialization drive launched by Stalin. The Vatican's response came in the form of Pope Pius XI's well-known letter of February 1930 calling for a ceremonial "mass of atonement for Russia" and condemning the persecution of Christianity in the Soviet Union. The Kremlin responded by denying any religious persecution and accusing the Vatican of launching a crusade as part of a general capitalist onslaught on the workers' state. Throughout the remainder of the 1930s there was no improvement in the church's situation in the Soviet Union nor in relations between the Vatican and Moscow. Although contacts between the two sides were maintained and the Popular Front policy moderated Soviet behavior in the international arena, Catholicism, like other religions, ranked high among the "enemies of the people." The seemingly irreconcilable conflict between church and state was accurately reflected in Pius XI's 1937 encyclical *Divini redemptoris*, which condemned both communism as an ideology and the Soviet Union as its source.

By 1937 the number of functioning priests was reduced to ten and the number of churches to eleven. In 1939, on the eve of World War II, all of the churches had been closed except the Church of St. Louis des Français in Moscow and the Notre Dame de France in Leningrad.[11]

The Soviet West: Incorporation and Aftermath

Between 1939 and 1945 Soviet territorial expansion in the west resulted in the incorporation of significant Catholic populations in western Ukraine, western Belorussia, Lithuania, and Latvia. The occupation of eastern Poland in September 1939 placed approximately 10 million Catholics under Soviet rule (6.5 million Roman Catholics, between 3.2 and 3.9 Ukrainian Byzantine Rite Catholics, and between 20,000 and 30,000 Belorussian Byzantine Rite Catholics). In June 1940 the Baltic states were annexed, adding another 3 million Roman Catholics (2.5 million in Lithuania and 500,000 in Latvia), and in June 1945 Transcarpathia was ceded to the Soviet Union by Czechoslovakia, which accounted for almost 462,000 Ukrainian Byzantine Rite Catholics.[12]

Initial Soviet policy in the newly acquired territories was relatively restrained, with a view toward promoting the political integration of the local population. This was reflected in the optimistic reports from the Latin Rite dioceses in western Ukraine at the end of 1939. Nonetheless, church properties were nationalized and heavy taxes were imposed; Catholic schools, monasteries, and other religious organizations and the press were closed; and priests were arrested. The authorities also displayed caution in their policies toward the Ukrainian Uniate church, permitting Metropolitan Sheptyts'kyi to convene an archdiocesan synod in May 1940. An important factor was Sheptyts'kyi's enormous popularity and authority both at home and abroad. Accordingly, an attempt was made to undermine his position and launch a schismatic movement within the church aimed ultimately at its separation from Rome. These plans were interrupted by the German invasion in June 1941. Still, almost two years of Soviet occupation had taken its toll. Sheptyts'kyi reported in a letter to the Vatican that more than thirty priests had died while incarcerated and that another thirty-three had been deported to Siberia from the Lvov Archdiocese alone.[13] Arrests and persecution of priests were also carried out in western Belorussia.[14]

The policies pursued by the authorities in the Baltic states during the first Soviet occupation between June 1940 and June 1941 were similar to those that had been implemented in western Ukraine and western Belorussia. Already by August 1940 the concordats between the Vatican and Lithuania and Latvia had been renounced and the papal nuncios in both countries expelled. Full-scale repression did not begin until mid-June 1941, and it was interrupted by the German invasion. In spite of the relative tolerance displayed toward the church, in Lithuania thirty-nine priests were imprisoned and twenty-one were killed during this period. In Latvia eleven priests were either executed or deported. Estonia's small Catholic community of about two thousand was dealt a severe blow by the arrest of the apostolic administrator, Msgr. Edward Profittlich, who was never heard from again. Of the fourteen Estonian priests before the war, only four remained; most of the others had been expelled.[15]

After the reoccupation of the Baltic states in 1944, the Soviet regime directed its energies toward the destruction of the church hierarchy and organization. An unsuccessful attempt was made in Lithuania to establish a "national" Catholic church cut off from the Vatican. Between 1946 and 1947 four Lithuanian bishops were arrested, tried, and deported, leaving only the aged Bishop Kazimieras Paltarokas at liberty.[16] During the first postwar years 357 priests (one-third of the total) were deported. According to Paltarokas, in early 1954 there were 741 priests in Lithuania. Thus this represented a loss of about half of the clergy since 1940. Of the 1,202 churches, 688 remained. Of the four existing seminaries in 1944, only the seminary at Kaunas remained in 1946, with 75 students as compared to 300 in 1944. No Catholic literature was legally published until 1956.[17]

When the Soviets returned to Latvia in 1944, the only remaining bishop was Archbishop Antonijs Springovics of Riga. In 1947 he consecrated two bishops, Kazimirs Dulbinskis and Peteris Strods. Dulbinskis was arrested in 1949 and deported. Springovics himself was expelled and took refuge in Aglona, the spiritual center of Latvian Catholicism. After his death in 1958 he was succeeded by Strods. Dulbinskis was able to return to Latvia permanently only in 1964 but was not permitted to assume his ecclesiastical duties. In 1948, according to a Soviet source, there were 214 "registered Catholic communities [parishes]" in the country.[18] In Estonia there were only four priests at the end of 1944; the following year their number was reduced to two.[19]

The reoccupation of western Ukraine in 1944 at first witnessed considerable restraint on the part of the authorities. Freedom of worship was not seriously interfered with, and the seminaries remained open. Indeed, when Metropolitan Sheptyts'kyi died in November 1944, the authorities permitted an elaborate funeral that was attended by Nikita Khrushchev, at that time first secretary of the Communist Party of Ukraine. Nor did they interfere with the enthronement of his successor, Metropolitan Iosyf Slipyi. The situation changed radically in the spring of 1945, signaled by the publication of an article in the Lvov newspaper *Vil'na Ukraina* on April 6, 1945, attacking the deceased metropolitan. Shortly thereafter, on April 11, five Ukrainian bishops were arrested for "collaboration" with the Nazis: Metropolitan Slipyi, Bishop Mykyta Budka, Bishop Mykola Charnets'kyi (apostolic visitator of Volhynia), Bishop Hryhorii Khomyshyn of Stanyslaviv, and Bishop Ivan Liatyshevs'kyi. In June Msgr. Petro Verhun, apostolic administrator for Ukrainians in Germany, was arrested in Berlin. An *in camera* trial was held in Kiev in 1946 resulting in five-to-ten-year terms for the defendants. In June of that year Polish authorities arrested Bishop Iosafat Kotsylovs'kyi of Peremyshl' and his auxiliary, Bishop Hryhorii Lakota, and delivered them to Kiev for trial.[20]

The planned destruction of the Ukrainian Catholic church was not, however, to be accomplished through the annihilation of the hierarchy and clergy, although such methods certainly promoted this aim. Instead, acting in concert with the Russian Orthodox church, Moscow decided on the "self-liquidation" of the church and its "reunion" with Russian Orthodoxy. At the end of May 1945 the Initiative Group for the Reunion of the Greek Catholic Church with the Russian Orthodox Church emerged, headed by the Lvov priest Hryhorii Kostel'nyk. It proclaimed itself the only legal administrative organ of the church and was recognized as such by the authorities. Simultaneously, the Moscow Patriarachate urged Ukrainian Catholics in "Galician Russia" to break with the Vatican and "return" to Russian Orthodoxy. What followed was a "reeducation" campaign of the clergy and repression of recalcitrant priests. It is estimated that by early 1946 about 740 clerics either had been arrested and deported or were in hiding. Finally, on March 8–10, 1946, a bogus church sobor met in Lvov, neither convoked nor attended by any of the bishops, and proclaimed the annulment of the union with Rome and the return to the Orthodox faith and the Russian Orthodox church. The sobor's decisions also applied to the Belorussian Uniates, who are said to have had thirty-six churches and about twenty thousand adherents in western Belorussia in the early 1930s.[21] The proceedings of the church sobor were published in Lvov in 1946 as *Diiannia Soboru hreko-katolyts'koi Tserkvy u L'vovi 8–10 bereznia 1946*. It is interesting to note that the materials in this publication are so compromising that in the second edition, issued by the Moscow Patriarchate in 1982, the relevant passages were omitted.[22]

The liquidation of the Ukrainian Uniate church in Transcarpathia was considerably less formal. The campaign for conversion began with the seizure of churches and a propaganda assault on Catholicism and the Vatican. In October 1945 a synod of the Russian Orthodox church in Moscow appointed Bishop Nestor as bishop of Mukachiv-Presov to supplant Bishop Teodor Romzha of the Mukachiv Diocese. An article in the local press stated that the new Orthodox bishop would assume control of the Catholic cathedral in Uzhhorod and the entire Mukachiv Diocese and that Bishop Romzha's jurisdiction had ended. By mid-1947 the Russian Orthodox church had taken over seventy-three Catholic churches; in the process, fifteen priests were deported. Bishop Romzha died in November 1947 after what appears to have been a deliberately staged road "accident."[23] His secretly consecrated successor, Bishop Oleksander Khira, was immediately arrested and sentenced to a ten-year prison term. In February 1949 the cathedral in Uzhhorod was confiscated, all Uniate churches were closed, and the Uniate clergy were forbidden to celebrate the liturgy on the grounds that the church was not officially registered. In August of that year the "reunion" with Russian Orthodoxy was simply proclaimed at a church ceremony.

Soviet policy in western Ukraine—i.e., the forcible "self-liquidation" of the Ukrainian Catholic church and its "reunion" with Russian Orthodoxy—makes it difficult to avoid the conclusion that Moscow's intentions went beyond purely religious matters. By eliminating the church, the regime also hoped to eliminate a national institution that had played an exceptionally important role in defining national consciousness in western Ukraine. This link to national identity is more or less openly admitted by Soviet spokesmen. Addressing the all-Union conference on national relations in Riga in 1982, the ideological secretary of the Communist Party of Ukraine, Oleksandr Kapto, warned that "foreign clerical-nationalist propaganda has set itself the task of reviving the Uniate church in Ukraine and utilizing it in the capacity of a religious-nationalist opposition." Furthermore: "Ideologists of clericalism attempt to portray everything religious as national and to render the processes of atheistic upbringing as 'denationalization of the people.' Hostile propaganda forcibly imposes upon our people the stereotype of clerical ideologists that every 'Ukrainian is Greek Catholic,' every 'Uzbek is Muslim,' every 'Lithuanian is Catholic,' [and] every 'Jew is Judaist.' "[24] Similar arguments have been made by leading party officials in Moscow, most recently by Central Committee secretary Egor Ligachev. In his speech at an all-Union gathering of social scientists in Moscow in October 1986, Ligachev argued that "at times bourgeois nationalists disguise themselves in religious clothing." Among others, he cited the example of the "reactionary segment of the Uniate clergy."[25]

The Post-Stalin Period

Stalin's death in 1953 and the ensuing de-Stalinization campaign initiated by Khrushchev could not leave religious policy unaffected. Initially, however, there was a marked absence of a clearly defined and consistent approach to religious matters, which probably reflected the vicissitudes of the post-Stalin struggle for power in the Kremlin. Thus in July 1954 the party Central Committee issued a resolution, "On Major Shortcomings in Scientific-Atheistic Propaganda and on Measures to Improve It," which was made public only in 1961. It ordered a resumption of the antireligion campaign by party and government agencies and criticized their neglect and passivity with regard to religious activities. Not long after, in November, this position was somewhat moderated by another Central Committee resolution, "On Errors in the Conduct of Scientific-Atheistic Propaganda among the Population," calling for the elimination of administrative measures, brutality, and force in the conduct of atheistic work. Believers, it argued, were not necessarily enemies of the state; they were people who needed to be reeducated.[26] By 1959, however, in the aftermath of the defeat of the so-called antiparty group, Khrushchev's campaign against religion went into full swing and continued until his ouster at the end of 1964. After the November 1958 plenum of the CPSU Central Committee, the regime mounted an ideological campaign supplemented by legislative and administrative measures subjecting all religious groups to persistent media attacks, harassment, and restrictions on the permissible scope of their activities. An important turning point was the June 1963 ideological plenum of the CPSU Central Committee. Shortly afterward, in November, an enlarged session of the party's Ideological Commission resolved to increase atheist propaganda, and its decisions formed the basis for the new Central Committee resolution entitled "On Measures to Strengthen the Atheistic Upbringing of the Population," adopted in January 1964. During this period the Institute of Scientific Atheism was established in the Central Committee's Academy of Social Sciences for purposes of coordinating the party's efforts in this area.[27] The sudden removal of Khrushchev broke the momentum of the antireligion campaign without bringing it to a halt, leading to a critical reappraisal of the regime's approach to the struggle against religion and a moderation of its policies in some areas.[28]

In spite of the losses suffered by the churches in the course of the antireligion campaign, the abandonment of organized terror as a political weapon after Stalin's death resulted in a relative improvement of conditions for the development of religious life in the Soviet Union. Perhaps the single most important by-product of de-Stalinization was the return of deported clergy from the camps following the amnesties of 1954 and 1955. In Lithuania about 130 priests who survived and did not remain in the RSFSR for missionary work returned home. Among them were two bishops, Teofilius Matulionis and Pranas Ramanauskas, who were released in 1956 but not permitted to resume their duties.[29] During this period the authorities also permitted a partial replenishment of the Lithuanian episcopate. In 1955 two Vatican appointees, Julijonas Steponavicius and Petras Mazelis, were consecrated bishops. Two years later another bishop, Vincentas Sladkevicius, was consecrated, apparently without Moscow's approval. For the first time since the war a prayer book and church calendar were published. In an interview in 1956 Bishop Mazelis was optimistic about the prospects of the Lithuanian church, announcing that plans had been approved for the construction of a new church in the port city of Klaipeda. Permission to build the Queen of Peace Church in Klaipeda had indeed been granted in 1954, and construction was completed by 1960.[30]

By early 1958, however, it was apparent that Mazelis's optimism was unfounded. The newly consecrated Bishop Sladkevicius was banned from his diocese and exiled to a small town near the Latvian border. At the same time the authorities also exiled Bishop Matulionis, who had consecrated Sladkevicius. The same treatment was accorded in 1961 to Steponavicius, who was removed by decision of the Lithuanian Council of Ministers. Restrictions also were placed on the remaining bishops, and the quota of students at the only remaining seminary in Kaunas was reduced from eighty in 1958–59 to twenty-eight in the last year of Khrushchev's rule.[31] Furthermore, claiming that the church in Klaipeda had been built illegally, the authorities refused to allow it to open and confiscated it for use as a concert hall. In early 1961 two parish priests from Klaipeda and five laymen were arrested and subsequently tried and sentenced on charges of "economic speculation." These moves were accompanied by increased atheistic indoctrination and harassment of clergy and faithful in line with the general policy of combating "remnants of religious superstition."

Although Khrushchev's ouster in October 1964 brought some relief, it did not fundamentally change the church's position or the regime's view of its activities. Even before Khrushchev was removed, a church delegation from Lithuania was permitted to attend the Second Vatican Council (1962–65) in Rome. In November 1965, while in Rome, Msgr. Juozapas Matulaitis-Labukas was appointed administrator of the Kaunas Archdiocese, and in December he was consecrated a bishop without opposition from Moscow. Further consecrations followed in Lithuania in February 1968 (Juozas Pletkus) and December 1969 (Liudvikas Povilonis and Romualdas Kriksciunas) in agreement with the authorities. And in 1966–68 the regime allowed several religious publications to be issued in Vilnius. Nonetheless, harassment of priests and believers and restrictions on the church's activities continued. In mid-1966 the Lithuanian republic, following the lead of the RSFSR, adopted new legislation affecting its Criminal Code that delineated proscribed religious activities more specifically and provided for harsher sentences. By the late 1960s continued pressure on the church gave rise to organized protests that initially took the form of petitions to the authorities. In the summer of 1968 a priest from the Telsiai Diocese wrote to the chairman of the USSR Council of Ministers, Aleksei Kosygin, protesting restrictions on the church. By the end of the year a collective grievance from sixty-three priests of the same diocese was addressed to Kosygin. More mass petitions followed in 1969–72, including the well-known memorandum of December 1971–January 1972 on the situation of the Lithuanian Catholic church addressed to CPSU General Secretary Leonid Brezhnev and sent to the United Nations with over 17,000 signatures. The authorities responded with arrests and trials. In the short space of sixteen months, between September 1970 and January 1972, four major trials were held in Lithuania. By early 1972, with the appearance of the first issue of the clandestine *Chronicle of the Catholic Church in Lithuania*, a full-fledged religious dissident movement had come into being.[32]

In Latvia, Bishop Dulbinskis returned from Siberia for a second time in 1958 but was soon exiled again, this time to Belorussia. He was finally able to return in 1964 but was not permitted to resume his duties. Bishop Strods died in August 1960, leaving the Catholic church in Latvia without a functioning bishop for the next four years. At the end of the 1950s Latvia's approximately 500,000 Catholic faithful, concentrated for the most part in the southeastern province of Latgale, were served by 126 priests. By 1964, according to a Soviet source, the number of churches had been reduced from 214 (1948) to 179. The number of students at the Riga seminary, which stood at sixty at the beginning of the Soviet occupation, was reduced to thirteen by 1961.[33] In November 1964, however, while in Rome for the Second Vatican Council, Julijans Vaivods was consecrated a bishop and named apostolic administrator of the Riga Archdiocese and the Liepaja Diocese, thereby restoring the church hierarchy in Latvia. This was followed in November 1972 by the consecration of Valerijans Zondaks as auxiliary bishop to Vaivods.[34]

The "self-liquidation" of the Ukrainian Catholic church did not, of course, make it disappear. The clergy and faithful reacted in several ways. Some simply boycotted the new "reunited" churches and attended the remaining Roman Catholic churches, of which 132 were reported to be still functioning in Ukraine in 1961.[35] In other cases churches remained closed because the faithful refused to admit Orthodox priests; in the Ivano-Frankivs'k (formerly Stanyslaviv, or Stanislav) Diocese alone there were at least 175 such parishes between 1946 and 1956.[36] Perhaps the most common response was to accept Orthodoxy in name only while remaining Catholic. Writing in 1961, Walter Kolarz noted that "the Orthodox Church in Eastern Galicia [western Ukraine] has remained very largely a crypto-Catholic Church."[37] Still others, the "recalcitrants," preferred to go underground, giving rise to the so-called Ukrainian Catholic church in the catacombs. This process was aided by the return of deported priests who had either served their terms or were amnestied; these included Bishops Liatyshevs'kyi and Charnets'kyi, who were prohibited from performing their duties. Metropolitan Slipyi was released and allowed to leave for Rome in February 1963 after American and Vatican intervention. In the early 1970s the number of underground Ukrainian Uniate priests was conservatively estimated at between 300 and 350 led by at least three bishops.[38]

Soviet publications as well as samizdat sources provide ample illustration of the church's clandestine activities. In 1964, for example, a Kiev youth newspaper claimed that Bishop Charnets'kyi, who died in 1959, had engaged in illegal pastoral duties, including the ordination of new Uniate priests.[39] Perhaps the best-known case is that of Bishop Vasyl' Velychkovs'kyi, who is said to have been secretly consecrated by Slipyi. Velychkovs'kyi was arrested in January 1969 along with two priests, sentenced to a three-year term, and then allowed to leave for the West in early 1972. A recent Soviet source concedes that Velychkovs'kyi and his group "attempted to establish their illegal episcopate in the Lvov region," adding that they made use of an underground printing press and photo laboratory for publication of "anti-Soviet falsifications and libels."[40] Velychkovs'kyi's arrest coincided with a perceptible increase in Uniate activity, which may have been stimulated by the legalization of the Ukrainian Uniate church in neighboring Czechoslovakia. According to a Ukrainian samizdat source,

> religious persecution increased severely in western Ukraine as of October 1968. Among Greek Catholics it is being said—one doesn't know how true it is—that the initiator of these repressions is the Kievan Orthodox Metropolitan. Supposedly, at a congress of clergy in Pochaiv in 1968 some Orthodox priests from Western Ukraine complained about the competition of the Greek Catholics, and the Metropolitan promised to approach the Party and government (Shelest personally, supposedly) with a request to intervene.[41]

A Soviet publication has written that in the same year exiled Cardinal Slipyi demanded from the Supreme Soviet of the Ukrainian SSR that the ban on the church be lifted.[42]

Another illegal religious group based in western Ukraine, the Penitents, or Pokutnyky, evolved as a dissident element within the Ukrainian Uniate church. The group traces its origins to the village of Serednia, where in 1954 the Virgin Mary is said to have appeared to a local woman. The "miracle of Serednia" quickly attracted pilgrims to the site, and a local Marian cult soon developed.[43] The movement was promoted by three underground Ukrainian Catholic priests. It repudiated the Soviet regime, the Vatican, and the underground Ukrainian Catholic church, which it blamed for having compromised with the regime, and preached an eschatological doctrine infused with a heavy dose of Ukrainian nationalism. Their first leader, Ihnatii Soltys, proclaimed himself the "true pope." He was imprisoned and succeeded by another itinerant priest, Antin Potochniak. According to the samizdat *Chronicle of the Catholic Church in Ukraine*, Potochniak joined the cult for the express purpose of bringing its membership back to the Uniate fold, which he is said to have largely accomplished. By 1982, according to the *Chronicle*, there were only about 130 "true believers" left. In October 1983 Potochniak was arrested for the fifth time and sentenced to a one-year term in a Lvov camp where he died the following year at the age of seventy-two.[44]

The Catholic Minorities

Information on Catholic communities outside of Lithuania and Latvia usually has been haphazard and sketchy. However, the latest register of the Riga Metropolitanate, which was compiled in the fall of 1987, provides detailed statistics on the number of parishes and priests in nine republics (see table 3.1).[45]

In 1958 Walter Kolarz was told by the Orthodox metropolitan of Minsk, Pitirim, that 30 percent of the Belorussian population (about 2.5 million people) were Catholics. Twenty years later, the representative of the Council for Religious Affairs in Minsk estimated the number to be about 2.2

Table 3.1 Active Parishes and Priests in the Soviet Union.

Republic	Parishes	Priests
Belorussia	107	56
Ukraine	93	49
Moldavia	4	2
Georgia	2	3
Estonia	2	1
Kazakhstan	31	8
Tadzhikistan	3	2
Kirghizia	2	1
RSFSR	12	5
Total	256	127

Source: "Administratio Metropoliae Rigensis," typescript, Riga, September 1987, pp. 15–20.

million, accounting for almost 25 percent of the republic's population. The current figure is said to be about 1.8 million.[46] The majority of these are in western Belorussia, that is, in areas that formed part of Poland prior to World War II, where there is also a sizable Polish minority (for example, the Grodno Oblast' accounts for almost 75 percent of Belorussia's 403,169 Poles). The efficiency of the Stalinist and post-Stalinist policies of religious repression in Belorussia may be gauged by the fact that until 1981 there was not a single Catholic church in the eastern oblasts of the republic, namely, in those areas that had been part of the Soviet Union since 1921. The first church to open there was in Minsk, and it was reported to be functioning in 1986.[47] In 1979 there were 112 registered churches in Belorussia, compared with 349 in 1944.[48] In early 1987 *L'Unita*'s Vatican correspondent reported that there were 104 parishes in Belorussia with as many as eighty priests, and a Soviet source now places the number of churches at 110. According to the register of the Riga Metropolitanate, at the end of 1987 there were 107 Catholic parishes in Belorussia served by fifty-six priests.[49] A recent Soviet study has reported that up to 80 percent of the priests in Belorussia are over sixty years old.[50] In 1973, after representations in Moscow regarding the shortage of priests, permission was granted for Belorussian candidates for the priesthood to study in Riga, but it was not until 1975 that the first student actually was enrolled. However, a petition in 1979 to republican authorities from twenty-seven priests requesting a theological seminary and a bishop was rejected.[51]

The situation of the Lithuanian minority in Belorussia is particularly difficult. Most Lithuanian Catholic churches there were closed after the war. According to a 1978 samizdat report, although there were thirty thousand Lithuanians in the republic, churches are not permitted to hold services in Lithuanian. Only Polish is used, which is also a problem for the younger generation of Belorussian Catholics.[52] The plight of the Lithuanian Catholics in Belorussia is documented in the Lithuanian *Chronicle*, particularly the various petitions that have been sent to the authorities requesting the return of confiscated churches and the need for Lithuanian priests.[53]

In spite of the existing problems, a recent Soviet report on survey research conducted among Catholics in Belorussia notes the "strong tenacity of [Catholic] traditions" in the western regions of the republic.[54] Previous studies have defined the proportion of believers among young people (aged 16–25) in western Belorussia in the range of 8–10 percent. The recent findings registered "no significant increase" in this category as gauged by such indicators as church attendance. The survey, which encompassed a cohort of five hundred Catholics and 40 percent of the clergy and "church *aktiv*" in the Grodno, Minsk, and Brest oblasts, yielded the following results with regard to participation in religious services and rites:[55]

Systematic church attendance, 37.5 percent
Regular prayers, 34.0 percent
Regular confession, 38.8 percent
Observance of all holy days, 50.0 percent
Baptism and burial rites, 100.0 percent

There are clear indications that the new political course initiated by party and state leader Mikhail Gorbachev, which also encompasses religious policy, is beginning to have an impact on Catholics in Belorussia. In September 1988 TASS reported that three Catholic churches had recently been reopened in Grodno Oblast' at the request of parishioners. Altogether, according to Keston College, six churches were reopened and returned in 1988.[56] An important development, particularly for Belorussia's Polish minority, was the September 1988 visit of Cardinal Glemp to Catholic centers in the republic at the invitation of Metropolitan Filaret of Minsk. The Polish press characterized the visit as "historic," the first by a Polish bishop to former Polish territories incorporated into the Soviet Union after the war.[57] The "new thinking" represented by the policies of glasnost, perestroika, and democratization also has resulted in the widespread grass-roots activity of so-called informal groups, which are posing demands, particularly in the non-Russian republics, that have long been anathema to the authorities. One of the most active informal groups in Belorussia is the Talaka Historical-Cultural Association, which has included the demand for the restoration of the Belorussian Autocephalous Orthodox church and the Belorussian Greek Catholic (Uniate) church in one of its programmatic documents.[58] The most significant development, however, came in July 1989, when the Catholic faithful in Belorussia were provided with a bishop for the first time in more than sixty years. On July 25 the Vatican announced the appointment of Rev. Tadeusz Kondrusiewicz as Apostolic Administrator of the Minsk Diocese and titular Bishop of Hippo, with pastoral care for all Roman Catholics in the republic. The Vatican press office noted that Soviet authorities were informed of the appointment and offered no objections, emphasizing that "this may be a *first step* towards the complete restructuring of the Catholic hierarchy in Belorussia." In an interview with the Turin daily *La Stampa* shortly thereafter, Bishop Kondrusiewicz noted the "very dynamic process" currently experienced by Catholicism in Belorussia, with thirty churches restored to worship since 1988 and imminent prospects for the return of the Minsk cathedral. He added, however, that there was a great disproportion between the approximately 140 churches that were open for worship and the sixty-two or sixty-three available priests, stressing the need for a Catholic seminary in Belorussia.[59]

Fifteen years ago a leading expert on Soviet religious affairs estimated that possibly as many as half of the 132 Roman Catholic churches officially reported in Ukraine in 1961 had been closed.[60] According to a recent Soviet source, there are now more than one hundred churches in the republic, a figure borne out by Polish sources.[61] In the early 1970s the Hungarian minority in the Zakarpattia Oblast' was said to include about eighty thousand Catholics served by twenty-six churches and twenty-two priests; they have a vicariate in Uzhhorod.[62] The Soviet press has reported that there are now almost seventy thousand Catholics in Zakarpattia and forty-one functioning churches.[63] According to the Hungarian Catholic weekly *Új Ember*, however, only about thirty-one parishes are actually operating. There are ten priests, but only one is under seventy. Recently a young priest from the Riga seminary arrived in the region, the first since 1944. Several churches also have been renovated. Interestingly, *Új Ember* noted that the Hungarian Catholic church could provide assistance to its brethren across the border.[64] This assistance came in May 1989 in the form of a week-long visit by László Cardinal Paskai to the Catholic community in Zakarpattia, the first by a member of the Hungarian hierarchy to the region since it came under Soviet rule after the Second World War. Cardinal Paskai celebrated mass in various cities and villages and delivered several thousand copies of Hungarian-language prayerbooks and five hundred copies of the scriptures. At a press conference in Uzhhorod at the conclusion of his visit, the Hungarian primate reported that as a result of official talks priests from Hungary would now be able to carry out pastoral duties in the region, local seminarians would be permitted to study in Hungary, and that the Hungarian Catholic weekly *Új Ember* would be available to readers in Zakarpattia. He also said that Hungarian Catholics had requested to have their own bishop "as soon as possible," and that this request would be conveyed to the pope.[65]

Roman Catholics in Moldavia are for the most part Germans, Poles, and Ukrainians. In a letter to Pope Paul VI in January 1978 that reached the West through samizdat channels, their number was given as approximately fifteen thousand.[66] At the end of 1977 the Moscow *Chronicle of Current Events* reported that all Catholic churches in Moldavia had been closed with the exception of a small cemetery chapel in Kishinev.[67] In 1973 the only Catholic priest in the republic, Bronislaw Chodanenko, died. He was replaced in mid-1974 by Vladyslav Zaval'niuk, a graduate of the Riga seminary, who was initially permitted to carry out his pastoral duties throughout the republic. This permission was later withdrawn, and Zaval'niuk was restricted to the city of Kishinev. An autobiographical samizdat document describes the various forms of official harassment that he was subjected to, ultimately resulting in his banishment from Moldavia in December 1979.[68]

Several sources refer to the existence of only one church in Moldavia, in Kishinev.[69] However, a recent report by the Moldavian representative of the Council for Religious Affairs, Ivan Vichku, refers to four functioning Catholic churches in the republic, which is confirmed by the register of the Riga Metropolitanate.[70] The process of *perestroika* has not left Moldavia unaffected. In April 1989 Vichku told a TASS correspondent that since 1988 more than 300 religious communities had been registered in the republic, including two Catholic parishes.[71] This would bring the total number of Roman Catholic parishes in the republic to six.

The Georgian human rights activists Tengiz and Eduard Gudava, who were given early releases from labor camp in April 1987 and subsequently emigrated to the West, reported that there are about ten thousand Catholics in Georgia but only two churches (in Tbilisi and Akhaltsikhe) and a single priest. Now, according to a recent TASS report, there are three priests serving in the Tbilisi church alone.[72]

In the late 1960s and throughout the 1970s Soviet sources listed two Catholic congregations in Estonia. The small Catholic community, estimated at between three and four thousand, was served by two priests from Latvia conducting pastoral work in Tallinn and Tartu. Since 1965 there has been only one priest working in the republic.[73]

Moscow and Leningrad continue to have one church each, and there are an additional ten parishes in the RSFSR in cities like Novosibirsk, Chelyabinsk, Omsk, Tomsk, and Saratov.[74] Catholics in these areas, as in central Asia, are mostly Poles, Germans, and Lithuanians who were deported by Stalin. The Catholic community in Novosibirsk benefited from the pastoral work of Fr. Jozef Swidnicki, who arrived in 1983 after working among various congregations in central Asia. In December 1984, however, he was arrested and subsequently sentenced to a three-year term in the camps, most likely because of his activity in the Christian Ecumenical Group founded by Aleksandr Riga. Swidnicki was released in March 1987 prior to the expiration of his term.[75]

It was only at the end of the 1960s that permission was granted to register two Catholic congregations in Kazakhstan, in Alma-Ata and in Kustanai. They were later disbanded but then registered once again. In March 1977 the German Catholic community in Karaganda was allowed to proceed with the construction of a church. Local officials in Kirghizia were somewhat more tolerant; permission to open a church in Frunze was granted in 1965.[76] In early 1984 the Lithuanian *Chronicle* reported that there were ten priests working in Kazakhstan, two in Kirghizia, and that the three Catholic congregations in Tadzhikistan were without priests. The Catholics in Tashkent and in Uzbekistan as a whole are said to be unorganized and without priests as well.[77]

The Vatican has given jurisdiction over all priests and parishes in the Soviet Union outside of Lithuania to the archdiocese of Riga. The Riga seminary is also responsible for the training of priests from locations throughout the USSR, again with the exception of Lithuania, and some two-thirds of its students are from outside Latvia.[78]

The Catholic Church in Lithuania and Latvia

The crystallization by early 1972 of an organized protest movement with its own journal must be seen as a turning point in the postwar history of the Catholic church in Lithuania. The petitions of the clergy and laymen generally focused on the regime's discriminatory practices against the church, which often violated existing Soviet legislation on religion. Specific issues included demands that the internal banishment of Bishops Steponavicius and Sladkevicius be lifted; protests against restrictions on the activities of the bishops and clergy; criticism of the authorities' interference in the functioning of the Kaunas Seminary, particularly the imposition of deliberately low quotas on the contingent of students, the recruitment of informers, and restrictions on the religious education of children; complaints regarding the routine refusals to permit construction of new and repair of old churches, discriminatory taxation, and lack of adequate religious publications; and, increasingly, the Vatican's Ostpolitik. With the appearance of the first issue of the *Chronicle* on March 19, 1972, the Catholic protest movement established a vehicle for the systematic documentation of violations of religious rights and the regular dissemination of its views. A characteristic feature of this movement has been the mass support that it enjoys. The 1971–72 memorandum noted earlier gathered more than 17,000 signatures; a 1979 petition to the former chairman of the Council for Religious Affairs, Vladimir Kuroedov, was able to mobilize over 10,000 supporters; and in the same year more than 148,000 petitioned General Secretary Leonid Brezhnev for the return of the confiscated church in Klaipeda.[79]

The regime responded with a combination of repression, administrative pressure, and concessionary gestures. Three priests were sentenced in 1970 and 1971 for violating the laws on religion. Furthermore, in April 1972 the functioning Lithuanian bishops and diocesan administrators were forced to issue a pastoral letter criticizing the 1971–72 memorandum. On the other hand, at the end of 1972 a small edition of a new Lithuanian translation of the New Testament was issued, and the following year the Book of Psalms was published.[80] An indication of official dissatisfaction with developments in Lithuania was the removal of the local representative of the Council for Religious Affairs in February 1973. His replacement was seen by the

Chronicle as an attempt by the authorities to deal with the church in a more tactful manner. Finally, it should be pointed out that although harassment in the form of house searches, imposition of fines, and press attacks continued unabated, it was not until 1983 that the authorities resorted once again to arresting priests and putting them on trial. Instead, energies were directed at liquidating the *Chronicle*, eight issues of which appeared in 1972–73. The campaign was launched in November 1973, and during the next two years ten collaborators of the *Chronicle* were sentenced in four separate trials. These initial trials coincided with a general crackdown on national rights activists in Lithuania as well as in other non-Russian republics. By 1980 a total of fourteen individuals had been convicted for involvement in distributing the *Chronicle*.[81]

Not only was the *Chronicle* not liquidated, but from the end of 1975 it was joined by a host of other underground journals. Several of these are clearly intended for a Catholic audience, while others, although not specifically Catholic in orientation, devote their pages to issues concerning the church.[82] Indeed, in November 1978 the Catholic protest movement was augmented by the formally constituted Catholic Committee for the Defense of the Rights of Believers, which was established by five priests. The emergence of the Catholic Committee may have been partly inspired by the election several weeks earlier of Kraków's Karol Cardinal Wojtyła to the throne of Saint Peter in the Vatican. The committee addressed Pope John Paul II, stating, "we priests of Lithuania have decided to speak up and to defend the sacred rights of the Church and the believers, as our silence and inaction provide the atheists with the best conditions for destroying the Church from without and demoralizing it from within."[83] In the course of its activities the committee issued more than fifty documents in line with its stated objective to work against discrimination of the faithful. One of its most important initiatives was the protest against the 1976 Statutes on Religious Associations of the Lithuanian SSR, which was detailed in its document no. 5 issued in December 1978. Within three months the committee's stand gained the support of 522 priests, representing about 75 percent of Lithuania's clergy, as well as both exiled bishops, who announced their intention to disregard the regulations. According to the *Chronicle*, the number of priests who signed petitions supporting the committee is said to have been even larger, with only 8–9 percent of the clergy refusing to join in the protest.[84]

Clearly, the committee's apparent ability to mobilize broad support posed a serious challenge to the authorities. In July 1979 the Lithuanian representative of the Council for Religious Affairs, Petras Anilionis, denounced the committee's activities at a meeting with Lithuanian bishops and diocesan administrators, and in September two of the committee's founding members, Alfonsas Svarinskas and Sigitas Tamkevicius, were given formal warnings by the Lithuanian prosecutor's office that were publicized in the press. The following year one of the founding members, Juozas Zdebskis, withdrew from membership after he was badly beaten by unknown assailants, but at the same time four new members joined, including an imprisoned layman. Surprisingly, the authorities did not move against the committee until January 1983, when Svarinskas was arrested. At his trial in May, which resulted in a sentence of seven years in strict-regime camps followed by three years of internal exile, Tamkevicius was summoned to the courtroom and arrested on the spot. His trial in November–December 1983 resulted in a term of six years in strict-regime camps followed by four years of internal exile. In the meantime, two other committee members resigned under pressure from authorities, thereby effectively putting an end to the committee's activities.[85] Opposition to the state's religious policies also came from Lithuania's bishops and diocesan administrators, who have generally avoided open confrontation with the authorities. The occasion was the officially sponsored "debate" on the new Lithuanian constitution announced in the spring of 1978, which resulted in a critical commentary focusing on several articles of the constitution that was submitted to the Presidium of the USSR Supreme Soviet by the church's leadership. The criticisms were, of course, ignored.[86]

Nonetheless, by the early 1980s several developments indicated a general improvement of the church's situation, especially from the standpoint of its leadership. Against the background of mutual interest on the part of the Vatican and the Kremlin to continue their dialogue, perhaps most important were the steps taken to regularize the church's hierarchichal structure. Certainly one factor that must be taken into consideration is the vigorous support extended by the new pope to all Catholics in Eastern Europe and the Soviet Union, which was dramatically illustrated during the pope's first visit to his native Poland in the summer of 1979. John Paul II has been criticized and, on occasion, vilified in the Soviet media, but it is fairly clear that the Soviet leadership realized that the challenge that he posed could not be countered by primitive propaganda. Very soon, a more immediate challenge came from Poland in the form of the Solidarity workers' movement, which enjoyed the support of the Polish Catholic church. Thus it was probably not entirely fortuitous that at the end of 1982 a branch of the Institute of Scientific Atheism of Moscow's Academy of Social Sciences was established in Vilnius, with one of its tasks being the coordination of atheistic research in Estonia, Latvia, and Belorussia.[87]

In July 1982 the Vatican announced that Bishop Sladkevicius had been appointed apostolic administrator of Kaisiadorys Diocese, thereby ending more than two decades of an official ban on his activities. At the same time Antanas Vaicius was consecrated a bishop and appointed apostolic administrator of Telsiai Diocese and the Klaipeda Prelature. Both bishops are popular, and their appointments were applauded by the *Chronicle*.[88] In April 1983 all four officially sanctioned Lithuanian bishops (Povilonis, Sladkevicius, Kriksciunas, and Vaicius) were permitted an *ad limina apostolarum* visit to the Vatican, the first since the country's incorporation into the Soviet Union, during which the pope emphasized his intention to fully reestablish the Lithuanian church hierarchy. Also during this visit Bishop Povilonis invited the pope to visit Lithuania the following year for the celebrations marking the five hundredth anniversary of Saint Casimir, Lithuania's patron saint. Shortly thereafter, the Vatican announced the resignation of Bishop Kriksciunas as apostolic administrator of Panevezys Diocese. Kriksciunas, it should be noted, had been singled out for criticism by militant priests and the *Chronicle*, and his departure may be viewed as a sign of the Vatican's deference to these quarters. Further changes in the church hierarchy were made in November 1984, when the Vatican announced that Povilonis had been raised to the titular rank of archbishop of Arcavica (not of Kaunas, where he is the apostolic administrator), and that Juozas Preiksas had been consecrated an auxiliary bishop to Povilonis. In August and October 1986 Pope John Paul II appointed Sladkevicius, Vaicius, and Povilonis to posts in the Vatican Curia, and in December Vladas Michelevicius was consecrated a bishop, raising the total number of Lithuanian bishops to seven.[89]

A very positive development with important long-term implications has been the increase in the number of students permitted to train for the clergy. In 1973 there were only forty-three students at the Kaunas seminary. By 1982 the number had risen to ninety-three, and in that year eighteen new priests were ordained, the largest single contingent since the early 1960s. In 1985 there were 122 seminarians, with the first-year contingent set at a maximum of thirty per year.[90] In May 1988 twenty-seven new priests were ordained, the greatest number since 1948. Moreover, the seminary accepted forty-six new students in 1988, about fifteen more than in previous years. Still, the number of priests ordained each year is not sufficient to replace those who have died. Between 1973 and 1988 only 183 graduates of the Kaunas seminary were ordained, while 308 priests died. As of September 1988 the average age of Lithuania's 674 priests had fallen to fifty-seven, although more than half were at least sixty.[91] It should be pointed out, however, that the increase in the number of seminarians is due in part to the regime's desire to counteract the underground seminary founded in the early 1970s. In 1985 the *Chronicle* published several confidential government documents, including a report by the Lithuanian representative of the Council for Religious Affairs that named ten "illegal" priests who were presumably products of the clandestine seminary.[92]

During the last several years there has been an increase in religious publications. In 1980 the catechism was published, and in 1982 three books of the Roman missal and liturgical prayer books; and, for the first time since 1939, a church calendar has appeared regularly on an annual basis. At the end of 1985 it was announced that the fourth volume of the projected eleven-volume missal would appear shortly along with a new edition of the New Testament, all in Lithuanian translation. A prayer book in an edition of 160,000 copies is also to be issued.[93] A major concession, announced by the authorities in mid-1987, was the promise to return the Klaipeda church to its parishioners within the next two years. This followed numerous petitions, the latest gathering 76,000 signatures by January 1987.[94]

The Catholic church in Lithuania also has suffered its setbacks, some of them quite serious. Perhaps the greatest of these was the decimation of the Catholic Committee for the Defense of the Rights of Believers in 1983. The following year, in November, authorities arrested Jonas Kastytis Matulionis, a graduate of the underground seminary, for organizing a religious procession; he was sentenced to three years in the camps. In 1980 and 1981 three priests died violent deaths under circumstances that, according to Lithuanian samizdat journals, point an accusing finger at the Soviet security organs; one of them, Bronius Laurinavicius, had joined the Lithuanian Helsinki Group in 1979. The suspicious death of Juozas Zdebskis, the well-known activist and founding member of the Catholic Committee for the Defense of the Rights of Believers, occurred in early 1986.[95] Throughout this time clergy and laymen continued to flood the authorities with appeals and protests, among them a petition for the release of the three imprisoned priests (Svarinskas, Tamkevicius, and Matulionis) and the return of Bishop Steponavicius to his diocese that was reported to have been signed by more than 46,000 Lithuanians by mid-1987.[96]

A visit to Lithuania by Pope John Paul II for the anniversary of the country's patron saint in 1984 would have been a major source of inspiration for Lithuanian Catholics. No doubt precisely for this very reason—particularly so soon after what was euphemistically referred to in the Soviet press as the "events in Poland"—the Soviet leadership decided that such a visit was fraught with too many dangers. The pontiff had made clear his concern for Catholics in the East on various occasions since his investiture at the end of 1978. The invitation from the Lithuanian bishops had already been extended in 1983, and at an audience with reporters on January 27 of the following year the pope said he would visit the Soviet Union if invited.[97] When the visit was denied, the Vatican took the unusual step of publicizing the affair by releasing the pope's message to Povilonis explaining that he had been deprived of the possibility of attending the celebrations in Vilnius. Several days later the pope reaffirmed his continued interest in visiting Lithuania's Catholics.[98] Nor was it possible for a church delegation from Lithuania to attend the celebrations in the Vatican. The whole affair, which received wide coverage in the world press, could only have been an embarrassment for the Soviet authorities. The pope, in turn, kept the issue alive by intermittently underlining his solidarity with the Soviet Union's Catholics, particularly in Lithuania. As the six hundredth anniversary of Lithuania's Christianization (1987) and the millennial anniversary of the introduction of Christianity in the Kievan state (1988) drew closer, speculation about a papal visit increased. In November 1986, during his Asian tour, the pontiff once again expressed his desire to visit Lithuania, and a Vatican spokesman subsequently explained that there would be no papal visit to Moscow in 1988 unless the pope was permitted to travel to Lithuania and Ukraine.[99] What followed was a repetition of the 1984 scenario. While in Poland in June 1987 the pope announced publicly that he was still unable to participate in the Lithuanian commemorations: "It has not been given to me to be among them in this jubilee year, to be able to pray on their soil and in their language."[100] The anniversary celebrations were held in Vilnius in June without the pope's participation, although a Lithuanian church delegation headed by Bishop Vaicius took part in the ceremonies at the Vatican.[101] Kharchev subsequently explained that a papal visit to Lithuania had not been possible because of the Vatican's nonrecognition of the Soviet Union's borders, that is, the incorporation of the Baltic states in 1940.[102] Later, Gennadii Gerasimov, the USSR Foreign Ministry spokesman, told a news conference in Warsaw that the decision not to invite the pope to Lithuania had been made "by the local authorities of the Catholic Church in Lithuania," not in Moscow, adding that the pope had not expressed a desire to visit the Soviet capital.[103] Perhaps the most definitive response to the speculation about a papal visit to the Soviet Union came from Metropolitan Filaret, the Ukrainian exarch, who told a press conference in Kiev in October 1987 that conditions for such a visit were not ripe. The reasons, he maintained, were purely religious—specifically, the pope's position on the Ukrainian Catholic church.[104]

How have Lithuania's Catholics fared after more than forty years of incessant struggle between church and state? Or, stated differently, how Catholic is Catholic Lithuania today? Posing the question in this way is perhaps not as flippant as it may first appear. Based on a study of Soviet survey data, Kestutis Girnius, a leading Western expert on Catholicism in Lithuania, has suggested that

> perhaps a fifth of all Lithuanians are relatively firm believers, another fifth convinced atheists, while the majority who are undecided contains many individuals, even nominal atheists, who retain a sufficiently large residue of religious sentiments that they attempt to con-

> secrate in a religious fashion in the more important moments of their lives. From such people the Church can often find sympathy, if not open support.[105]

Some Western estimates have placed the number of Catholics in Lithuania as high as 83.5 percent of the total population.[106] At the end of 1982 a Lithuanian priest participating in an official Soviet exhibition in the Federal Republic of Germany stated that 70 percent of the 2.7 million Lithuanians were Catholic and that 30 percent attended church services regularly.[107] Soviet sources have consistently reported lower figures. Data for 1977 indicate that 44 percent of children were baptized, slightly more than 25 percent of marriages were administered by priests, and almost 44 percent of burials were conducted with religious rites. The same data show that there have been significant declines in all three categories since the late 1950s, while also indicating that the situation has remained rather stable during the period 1972–77.[108] But is participation in religious services a genuine indicator of religiosity? Girnius has pointed out that "being a religious person is a complex of experiences in which attitudes, beliefs, and behavior patterns are intertwined in a multitude of ways. Because of this, it is difficult to determine what are necessary and sufficient conditions for stating that anyone is a Catholic."[109] The problem is further complicated by the specific conditions under which survey research is conducted in the Soviet Union. Yet even with these caveats in mind, the Soviet data reveal the remarkable tenacity of religiosity among Lithuania's Catholics under decidedly hostile conditions. This is borne out by a more recent Soviet study of the republic's adult population that recorded "religious" attitudes in 62 percent of rural workers, 41.5 percent of urban manual workers, and 18.6 percent of students.[110]

"The most influential church organization on the territory of Latvia is Catholicism." This conclusion was reached by a recent Soviet analysis of survey research conducted in the republic. Although in terms of the number of parishes the Catholics rank behind the Lutherans, the more rapid abandonment of religion on the part of Lutherans has led to the disintegration of their congregations, while the number of Catholic parishes has remained practically unchanged since the 1964 figure of 179. Two-thirds of the parishes are in the strongly Catholic Latgale region.[111] This general trend was confirmed by former Latvian party first secretary Boriss Pugo at a news conference in Moscow during the the Twenty-seventh Party Congress in February and March 1986. Pugo referred to figures from Latvian church sources that gave the number of Christian believers as about 40 percent of the republic's population of 2.5 million. According to the Latvian party leader, 50 percent, or approximately 500,000, of these were

Catholics; 30 percent were Lutherans; and the rest were Russian Orthodox and a small number of Baptists.[112] In early 1985 *L'Osservatore Romano* reported that there were about 130 priests in Latvia and fifty-nine students at the Riga seminary (thirty-one from Latvia, twelve from Belorussia, eight from Ukraine, four from Kazakhstan, and one each from Estonia, Kirghizia, Tadzhikistan, and the RSFSR). At the end of 1987 Latvian Catholic parishes were served by 105 priests, but the number of seminarians had risen to eighty-one.[113]

Unlike Lithuania, there is no visible rights movement among Latvian Catholics, although in 1975 a document signed by 5,043 residents of Daugavpils, Latvia's second-largest city and the center of the Latgale region, reached the West warning that officials intended to tear down a local Catholic church.[114] There also have been cases in recent years of priests found murdered under circumstances that have given rise to suspicions that security organs were involved.[115] Priests have been harassed and have suffered repressive measures at the hands of the authorities. The best-known case is that of Vladyslav Zaval'niuk, who was forced out of Moldavia at the end of 1979 but continued to work in Latvia. In November 1980 he was forcibly placed into a psychiatric hospital in Riga, where he remained until early summer of the following year.[116]

The leadership of the Latvian church has consistently pursued a nonconfrontational policy of "quiet diplomacy" aimed at winning incremental concessions from the regime, an approach viewed in some quarters as bordering on "collaborationism." The Lithuanian *Chronicle*, for example, wrote in 1977 that Latvian Catholics "are accustomed to accommodating themselves to the demands of the government."[117] In any case, Vaivods's policy has shown certain results. The catechism has been published in Latvian (1978) and in the Latgale dialect (1981), and a five-volume lectionary prepared by the Latvian Catholic Liturgical Commission also has been issued.[118] In 1980 authorities permitted construction of a new building for the seminary in Riga, which was completed in the fall of 1982. The number of seminarians has doubled since the 1970s.[119] In November 1982 Janis Cakuls was consecrated a bishop and named an auxiliary in the Riga Archdiocese and the Liepaja Diocese—the first senior Vatican appointment in Latvia in a decade.[120] With the death of Bishop Zondaks in September 1986, however, the Latvian church hierarchy was, in effect, left with only Cakuls to assist Vaivods, who is over ninety.

Certainly the most important development in recent years was Pope John Paul II's naming of Vaivods to the college of cardinals in January 1983. This was an unexpected and unprecedented development. A spokesman for the Council for Religious Affairs in Moscow claimed that the Vatican had not informed Soviet authorities of its intentions in advance.

"This was something of a surprise for the Soviet Union," he said. "We were not officially informed about this by the Vatican."[121] The spokesman noted, however, that the appointment of a cardinal did not require prior consultation and approval from Moscow. This was the first time that a resident Soviet prelate had been publicly elevated to the rank of cardinal. In an interview with a Western news agency in Rome, Vaivods speculated that he had been chosen by the pope to serve as "a bridge between the Holy See and Moscow."[122]

In 1986 Latvian Catholics celebrated the eight hundredth anniversary of their Christianization. According to Radio Vatican, 150,000 Catholics participated in the various celebrations, which culminated in a service at the Marian shrine in Aglona on August 15. The service coincided with the annual pilgrimage during the Feast of the Assumption, in which an estimated 50,000–60,000 Catholics took part.[123] A recent issue of the Lithuanian *Chronicle* notes that more pilgrims took part in the Aglona ceremonies in 1986 than in the past, citing the participation of converts from Lutheranism.[124] One Western expert, confirming the growth of the Latvian Catholic Church in recent years, maintains that it is the result of "mass conversions" from Russian Orthodoxy.[125] This appears unlikely in view of the overall small numbers of Orthodox. Moreover, there are clear indications of growing dissatisfaction among Lutherans with their church, which was manifested by the recent establishment of the unofficial Rebirth and Renewal Group by fourteen Lutheran pastors and a layman. The members of the group maintain that the diminishing prestige of the Lutheran church among the Latvian people led them to form their organization.[126] Interestingly, a recent Soviet study also has alluded to the drawing power of the Latvian Catholic church and the corresponding "crisis" in Lutheranism, citing the former's "activism" and the policies of Pope John Paul II as factors that have led to an "increase in the authority of the Church in the eyes of Catholic believers in Latvia."[127]

As noted earlier, survey research on religious attitudes conducted in Latvia has concluded that Catholicism presently leads the field of religious groups in the republic, which also includes Lutherans, Russian Orthodox, and Old Believers. The majority of confessions, baptisms, and burial rites, for example, are conducted among Catholics. Indeed, between 1970 and 1983 the Catholic share increased from 87.2 percent to 94.2 percent for confession; from 58.5 percent to 62.5 percent for baptism; and from 46.3 percent to 57.5 percent for burial rites.[128] A slightly higher percentage of Catholic children are baptized than the total percentage in all religions (86 compared to 82 percent). Although decreases in the number of baptisms were registered in all the churches between 1970 and 1983, they have been greater among Lutherans and Russian Orthodox than among Catholics.[129] There are also more young and middle-aged churchgoers among Catholics.[130] Perhaps the most interesting indicator is the predominance of Catholics among those who have "become religious" and "become more religious" during the 1970s.[131] All of these signs are said to reflect the "relative stability" of Latvian Catholicism—no mean achievement in the face of almost fifty years of Soviet antireligion policies.

Ferment Among Ukrainian Catholics

The central issue for Ukrainian Catholics is the legalization of their church. The Lithuanian *Chronicle* has reported that various Catholic communities in western Ukraine had been petitioning the authorities in Lvov, Kiev, and Moscow for decades to officially register their churches. Such requests were routinely rejected and often followed by increased repression.[132] Detailed information about the efforts of Ukrainian Catholics to secure recognition from authorities is also contained in a lengthy samizdat text dated January 1980 and entitled "From the Life of the Ukrainian Catholic Church."[133] The anonymous author describes, for example, the desecration of the local church in the village of Mshana in the Lvov region, which prompted more than a hundred petitions to the authorities and eleven delegations to Moscow, all without success.

The struggle for legalization took a new turn in September 1982 with the organization of the Initiative Group for the Defense of the Rights of Believers and the Church by three underground priests and two laymen. Its first chairman, layman Iosyp Terelia, announced the group's formation in a declaration to the Central Committee of the Communist Party of Ukraine, identifying its membership and explaining that the decision to organize was in response to increased repression. "As of today," wrote Terelia, "all information [about] the Ukrainian Catholic Church will be submitted for examination by world public opinion; Catholics of the world must know and remember under what conditions we live. We have one aim—*legalization.*"[134] At the same time, the Initiative Group forwarded a statement to the Ukrainian government with specific demands that would have to be met as part of the legalization process.[135] Still another document from members of the group announced that its leadership expected arrest, and referred to the existence of a Central Committee of Ukrainian Catholics, also headed by Terelia. And indeed, several months later, in December, Terelia was arrested and sentenced to a one-year term in the camps for "parasitism."[136] His place was taken temporarily by another layman, Vasyl' Kobryn, who became chairman of the group in March 1984.[137] Terelia was released in December 1983 and resumed his activities in defense of Ukrainian Catholics, and in early 1984 the group began issuing the *Chronicle of the Catholic Church in Ukraine*.[138] Threatened once again with arrest, he went underground in November 1984. At the same time, on November 11, Kobryn was arrested and subsequently sentenced to a three-year term in the camps. Not long after, in February 1985, the authorities were able to catch up with Terelia, who was arrested again and sentenced to a term of seven years in the camps followed by five years of internal exile.[139] In spite of the crackdown the Ukrainian *Chronicle* continued to be compiled and disseminated; number 30 was issued in September 1987.[140]

Certainly a major factor in the decisive stand taken by Ukrainian Catholics in the early 1980s was the election of a Slavic pope who very quickly demonstrated his intention to speak out in defense of the rights of Catholics in the Soviet Union and Eastern Europe. Within several weeks of his investiture, on November 20, 1978, he met for the first time with the head of the Ukrainian church, Cardinal Iosyf Slipyi, who often had been an outspoken and bitter critic of the Vatican's Ostpolitik, specifically its reluctance to publicly defend the Ukrainian church.[141] Earlier, on November 3, Slipyi had expressed the hope that the new pope would "revise" the dialogue with the Russian Orthodox church and form a Ukrainian patriarchate.[142] Pope John Paul II responded in a letter to Slipyi dated March 19, 1979, the full text of which was published in *L'Osservatore Romano* in mid-June, in which he recalled the persecution of Slipyi and the church and reaffirmed the principle of "every believing person to profess his own faith and also to be a participant of the community of the Church to which he belongs." Religious freedom, said the pope, "demands that the rights of the Church to live and to function be acknowledged for the vicinity to which the individual inhabitants of any state belong."[143] The pope's letter was viewed by Vatican observers as representing a possible shift in the Holy See's Ostpolitik and a challenge to the Kremlin to recognize the Ukrainian church.[144] This is also how it was interpreted by the leadership of the Russian Orthodox church. In September 1979 Metropolitan Iuvenalii, head of the Department for External Church Relations of the Moscow Patriarchate, sent what was in effect a letter of protest to the president of the Roman Curia's Secretariat for Promoting Church Unity, Cardinal Johannes Willebrands, asking for an explanation of the Vatican's ecumenical policy. Willebrands responded that the policies of the Second Vatican Council would be continued in this regard, but at the same time expressed regret that some circles within the Russian Orthodox church tended to judge the Uniate Catholic churches in a negative light.[145] A "responsible worker" of the Central Committee of the Communist Party of Ukraine saw the pope's letter as having a "political meaning," namely, "to support the Uniate church and its claims to speak in the name of the Ukrainian people."[146]

In March 1980 the pope convened an extraordinary synod of Ukrainian bishops, giving the Ukrainian church more independence, including the right to call future synods on its own initiative, albeit with papal approval. This move fell short of the patriarchate that the Ukrainian bishops have often called for, although it could be seen as a first step in that direction. The pope also selected Archbishop Myroslav Ivan Lubachivs'kyi as coadjutor with the right of succession to the Lvov Metropolitan See, thereby assuring the continuity of the Ukrainian Catholic church's leadership. In November of the same year Slipyi summoned his first synod, which rejected the dissolution of the Ukrainian church at the Lvov Sobor of 1946 as uncanonical, stating that it "never took place." This resulted in another letter from Moscow, this time from Patriarch Pimen to the pope, arguing that the declaration of the Ukrainian bishops threatened relations between the two churches and asking that it be renounced by the Holy See. In his reply Pope John Paul II distanced himself from the declaration, maintaining that it had no official status, but at the same time he affirmed his strong support for the rights of Ukrainian Catholics. Slipyi in turn issued a statement on the correspondence justifying the synod's position.[147] In the meantime, *Spotkania*, an unofficial journal issued by young Catholics in Poland, published an open letter from Catholics in Ukraine to Pope John Paul II with a copy to Soviet party leader Brezhnev, expressing their joy that the new pope comes "from the family of long-suffering Slavic nations" and therefore knows their needs and expectations. The authors reaffirmed the hope that their church would be legalized and appealed to the pope to intervene on their behalf.[148]

For the authorities in Ukraine, the policies of the Vatican and the visible ferment among Ukrainian Catholics meant further complication of an already difficult situation. Overall, more than half of the functioning Orthodox and Protestant congregations in the Soviet Union are in Ukraine.[149] Several studies of religion conducted in the republic in the latter half of the 1960s found that the greatest number of believers were in the western oblasts—that is, in the traditional stronghold of Catholicism—and that religiosity in this area was twice as great as in other regions. In some villages of the Zakarpattia, Ivano-Frankivs'k, Ternopil', and Chernivtsi oblasts, believers constituted 50–60 percent of the population.[150] Without undue concern for the niceties of logic, propagandists have been struggling against the ostensibly "nonexistent" Uniate phenomenon for more than four decades. Soviet data show that 23 percent of all atheist propaganda in western Ukrainian newspapers, which is described as the "main thrust," is devoted to Catholicism and the Uniates. A breakdown by individual newspapers yields the following results: *Vil'na Ukraina*, 47.7 percent; *Prykarpats'ka pravda*, 31.7 percent; *Vil'ne zhyttia*, 25.5 percent; *Zakarpats'ka pravda*, 23.3 percent.[151] By comparison, the proportion of materials devoted to Orthodoxy in the seven western Ukrainian oblast newspapers is 13.3 percent, or about half the amount for the Catholics and Uniates. Although verifiable statistics are unavailable, Bishop Josef Stimpfle of Augsburg reported after a recent trip to Ukraine that the Ukrainian Catholic church is led by nine bishops and that one thousand priests serve about five million faithful.[152] During the past decade there have been reports, some confirmed in the Soviet press, of arrests, trials, and other forms of harassment of Ukrainian Catholic priests; there also have been cases of unexplained murders, as in Lithuania and Latvia. In January 1975, for example, authorities arrested the underground priest Mykhailo Vinnyts'kyi, and in July of that year he was sentenced to a five-year term in the camps followed by three years of internal exile. Vinnyts'kyi had been jailed twice previously, in 1950–55 and 1964–68.[153] His trial was subsequently reported in the Lithuanian *Chronicle*, which also referred to the murder of the Redemptorist priest Ievhen Vosykevych in Lvov in May 1980.[154] The *Chronicle* also reported the arrests of two other Ukrainian priests, Vasyl' Kavatsiv and Roman Iesyp, in March 1981; both were tried in October of that year and sentenced to camp terms of five years and three years of exile.[155] The samizdat bulletin *+ 26* reported that Vinnyts'kyi was arrested for the fourth time in June 1985; he was subsequently sentenced to a term of five years in a strict-regime camp and three years of internal exile.[156]

The new pope's obvious determination to support the strivings of Catholics in the Soviet Union and Eastern Europe, which could not be lost on Soviet ideologists after the first papal visit to Poland in June 1979, injected a fundamentally new factor into the picture. Barely a month after his Polish trip, Vatican policies were discussed at a meeting of secretaries of the Soviet bloc parties that gathered in Berlin to examine international and ideological matters. This was not mentioned in the official communiqué, but later a functionary of the Central Committee of the Communist Party of Ukraine revealed that the participants had agreed that "the Vatican's policies with regard to the socialist countries has entered a new phase that is characterized by a sharp increase in the activity of the Roman Catholic church and the desire to turn it into a political opposition in the socialist countries." The Ukrainian SSR, he wrote, was being attentively watched by the Vatican: "It is attempting to utilize the still existing formidable *aktiv* of the Catholic Church [in Ukraine] as a base for the broadening of religious influence on the population of the republic."[157] One of the more sophisticated Soviet studies of Catholicism in Eastern Europe, published in 1982, pointed out that "it is absolutely clear that the activity of the new Pope, who has devoted a great deal of attention to East European Catholicism, introduces a new element in the politics of the national churches and in their relations with the socialist states. This, in turn, cannot but have an impact, to one degree or another, on the mind-sets of believers in the individual countries of socialism."[158] The author went on to note that although the Vatican intended to continue the ecumenical dialogue with Orthodoxy, it was "simultaneously attempting to revive ties with the Uniates and stimulate their activity."[159]

Soviet sources concede that this policy has proved successful. Addressing the conference on national relations held in Riga in 1982, the head of the Central Committee's Propaganda and Agitation Department in Kiev, Leonid Kravchuk, said:

> We have information that in the republic, especially in its western oblasts, the propaganda of the Vatican and other bourgeois clerical and clerical nationalist centers is finding a response among certain circles of listeners. Among them are Catholics, former Uniate priests and monks, and nationalistically inclined individuals. There is also a certain revival of religious activity within several of the registered communities of sects. The Catholic clergy has become more active under the influence of hostile propaganda. The former Uniate clergy has tried to promote the psychological preparedness of believers with a view toward putting forth demands for the resumption of the activity of the Uniate Church.[160]

The first secretary of the Lvov Oblast' Komsomol, writing in early 1985, made a similar observation: "In recent years the representatives of the Uniates and former Uniate priests have become more active, and one can even hear demands that the activities of this Church be resumed."[161] The regime's response, in addition to a massive propaganda campaign in the media, was to organize conferences of experts on Ukrainian Catholicism to study the problem and prepare recommendations for atheistic work.[162] Increasing attention was devoted to the relationship between the ethnic factor and religion in Ukraine, particularly in view of the millennium celebrations in 1988. Oleksii Shuba, who has written several pamphlets on the subject, cites survey research showing that in Ivano-Frankivs'k Oblast' in western Ukraine 29.8 percent of those who waver between religion and atheism and 14.3 percent of believers explain their participation in religious rituals inter alia, because they view them in national terms. "Sometimes," wrote Shuba, "even non-believers, as they themselves explain, celebrate religious holidays ostensibly because of their national overtones."[163] At the aforementioned conference in Riga, the Ukrainian agitprop chief, referring to the problems posed by propaganda from abroad, maintained that "one can distinctly see the tendency of merging of religion and nationalism: Nationalist forces increasingly act under the banner of religion, and a new variety of nationalism has made its appearance—religious nationalism."[164] Similarly, Kapto, then the Ukrainian ideological secretary, told participants in the all-Union ideological conference in Moscow in December 1984 that in the future nationalistic prejudices in the Soviet Union would be largely of a "religious-ethnic character," and that clerical nationalism would be the main form of bourgeois nationalism abroad. What was necessary, he argued, was to "develop theoretical problems and practical ways of counteracting this phenomenon."[165]

If there have been any breakthroughs in this area, conceptual or otherwise, they are difficult to detect in Soviet publications. The defining characteristic of Soviet writing on Ukrainian Catholicism has been its hopelessly primitive level. Books bearing such titles as *The Criminal Alliance: On the Union of the Uniates with Ukrainian Bourgeois Nationalism* (Moscow, 1985) and *Uniatism in the Service of Anti-communism* (Lvov, 1988) continue to be issued. Soviet television viewers are told by experts on Ukrainian Catholicism that "the so-called catacomb church exists only in the diseased imagination of Ukrainian Catholic Church dignitaries [abroad]."[166] Similarly, the former chairman of the Council for Religious Affairs, when asked by a Polish interviewer in early 1986 if the Uniate church is functioning in the Soviet Union, answered that it is not, that it was dissolved in 1946, and that "today there is no problem of the Uniate church on the territory of the Soviet Union."[167] Several years earlier a first deputy chairman of the all-Union KGB wrote in *Kommunist* that "Ukrainian bourgeois nationalists" are "supporting illegal Uniate groups" in Ukraine, and leading Soviet ideologists are struggling to find better ways of dealing with the problem.[168]

In the meantime, the demands of Ukrainian Catholics that their church be legalized and Pope John Paul II's consistent defense of their right of religious freedom have made the Uniate issue a major stumbling block in relations between the Vatican, on the one hand, and the Kremlin and the Moscow Patriarchate, on the other. Although no details were made available at the time, it is likely that the question of Ukrainian Catholics was discussed during the second meeting between Foreign Minister Andrei Gromyko and the pope on February 27, 1985. According to Vatican sources, the situation of Catholics in the Soviet Union was on the agenda of the talks.[169] In any case, in an interview with *L'Unita* conducted on February 21 but published in the newspaper several weeks after Gromyko's audience with the pope, the Orthodox exarch of Ukraine, Metropolitan Filaret of Kiev and Halych, referred specifically to the Vatican's positive attitude toward the Uniate church as an impediment to better relations with Orthodoxy.[170] The Vatican's position, however, has not been modified. In May 1985 Slipyi's successor as head of the Ukrainian church, Archbishop Major Lubachivs'kyi, was raised to the rank of cardinal, and in July the Vatican representative at the tenth anniversary meeting marking the signing of the Helsinki Final Act once again alluded to the Ukrainian Catholics by recalling his speech at the Belgrade review conference in 1977. "Is it possible," he asked, "that the commitment now included in the Madrid document can open a ray of hope for the hundreds of thousands of faithful who, with their bishops and priests, are prevented by civil laws from belonging to the Church to which they feel bound by a profound conviction of their conscience?"[171] In October 1985 Pope John Paul II, addressing the synod of Ukrainian bishops in their language, once again referred to the suffering of the Ukrainian Catholics, maintaining that "your religious community should also enjoy religious freedom to which it has a right the same as any other religious faith."[172]

The Moscow Patriarchate has continued to view the Ukrainian Catholics as a major obstacle in its relations with the Vatican. This was pointed out by *L'Unita*'s Vatican correspondent, who cited "authoritative political sources" to that effect in a dispatch from Riga in early September 1986.[173] The Uniate issue was raised again by Metropolitan Filaret of Minsk and Belorussia in an interview in the Bologna fortnightly *Il Regno* in January 1987, maintaining that the Ukrainian Catholics were "a nationalistic, not a religious problem."[174] At the same time representatives of the Russian Orthodox church and the Soviet government showed no signs that the "nonexistent" status of the Ukrainian church was subject to revision. In the spring of 1986 the fortieth anniversary of the Lvov Sobor was celebrated with the appropriate pomp and circumstance, thereby sending an unmistakable political message.[175] In this connection, Archbishop Makarii of Ivano-Frankivs'k and Kolomyia stated plainly in an article entitled "Once and for All": "Our believers recall the Church Union as dark days in history, as an insult that can be neither pardoned nor forgotten. The return of the Union is out of the question."[176] This stand was reiterated by Kharchev in the course of Soviet-American discussions on human rights in April 1987. According to a U.S. State Department official, the former chairman of the Council for Religious Affairs indicated that the Ukrainian Catholic church would not be legalized because it is viewed as a vehicle for Ukrainian nationalism.[177]

The Uniate question has remained largely intractable despite the fact that the twin policies of glasnost and perestroika have registered successes in other areas touching on religious life in the Soviet Union.[178] An important indication that religion might benefit from the "new thinking" in the Kremlin came from remarks made by Kharchev at the end of 1987 while in the United States, saying that mistakes had been made in the past with regard to religious policy and that changes were under way: "Both religion and the churches will live free under socialism, and that is the objective reality."[179] He also said that twelve new Catholic churches would be opened shortly. The fact that in early 1987 *Literaturnaia gazeta*, one of the most widely read newspapers in the Soviet Union, published an interview with the Polish primate, Cardinal Glemp, certainly must have been a hopeful sign for many Soviet Catholics.[180] Moreover, a number of religious rights activists were among the political prisoners granted early releases from imprisonment or exile. Included in this group was Terelia, head of the Central Committee of Ukrainian Catholics, who was freed in February 1987 and later was allowed to emigrate.[181] The campaign for glasnost also touched on Ukrainian Catholic matters. Soviet readers were no doubt astonished to see that *Sobesednik*, the popular monthly supplement to *Komsomol'skaia pravda*, had published a letter from a young Ukrainian Catholic challenging his opponents to "cross swords" with him on religious matters. The young man wrote:

> I am twenty-two years old. I would like, with your help, to initiate a correspondence with anyone from among the Komsomol. I myself am faithful to the Ukrainian Catholic Church, and it would be interesting for me to "cross swords." Although I am already convinced that I am right, and I think that today's Komsomol members are not the same as, for example, those in the 1920s. In short, they are weaklings. Well then, are you ready to take me on? If you ignore me and do not respond, I will conclude that you are afraid of a dialogue and have lost.[182]

He went on to describe meetings of his congregation where members sing religious songs, read from the Bible, and listen to Radio Vatican. Religious literature is brought in from abroad by tourists and relatives. "If someone told me that I must die or suffer for my faith," he said, "I would not hesitate for a moment to put my head on the altar, indeed, not only I but every one of us would do the same. Do you have people among you who are so devoted to the ideas of the Komsomol?"

Equally surprising was the fact that both *Literaturnaia gazeta* and *Moskovskie novosti* devoted articles to the mass pilgrimages in the spring and summer of 1987 to the village of Hrushiv in the Lvov region, where local inhabitants claimed to have seen an apparition of the Virgin Mary. The Writers' Union weekly reported that in one month alone over 100,000 people came to the village, and then criticized local authorities for harassing the visitors. *Moskovskie novosti* ascribed the "explosion of religious fervor this summer" to the poor handling of the matter by local authorities and the Ukrainian Council for Religious Affairs, who "apparently think that they can 'defend' atheist positions only by violating the law and trampling on the rights of believers." The newspaper also criticized the authorities for rejecting petitions that churches be opened. Without specifying which religious groups were involved, it revealed that 120 such requests had been made in 1986 in Ternopil' Oblast' alone. The "miracle in Hrushiv" led one Kiev journal to comment: "Just as Chernobyl' reminded us how poorly we know the atomic nucleus, so too Hrushiv reminds us that we do not know our society as we should, that we are only guessing about people's moral condition, their psychology, attitudes, and interests."[183]

The more liberal policies being pursued by the present Soviet leadership found an echo among Ukrainian Catholics in the Soviet Union. In June 1987 Ukrainian church sources in the Vatican released a document addressed to Gorbachev and signed by Terelia and twenty others; it expressed the hope that relations between Ukrainian Catholics and the state could be improved in the context of "the new political policy of the Soviet government."[184] Not long after, the Western press reported a statement addressed to Pope John Paul II and signed by two Ukrainian underground bishops, a group of priests, monks, and nuns, and 174 laymen announcing their decision to henceforth conduct their activities in the open. The statement, dated August 4, declared that "in connection with the restructuring in the USSR and the more favorable conditions that have developed, and also in connection with the 1,000 anniversary of Christianity in Ukraine, we consider it useless to remain underground and therefore ask Your Holiness to promote by all possible means the legalization of the Ukrainian Catholic Church in the USSR."[185] On August 12 Terelia delivered a copy of the document to the USSR Supreme Soviet.

It also is interesting to note that the campaign for legalization has been joined by Ukrainian rights activists and former political prisoners who have not been previously identified with the underground church. In June 1987 Stepan Khmara, who edited issues 7–8 and 9 of the samizdat journal *Ukrains'kyi visnyk* in the early 1970s, wrote to Patriarch Pimen requesting that he support the suppressed Ukrainian Catholics. A similar petition, in the form of a letter to *Izvestiia*, was made by Vitalii Shevchenko, who also worked with the *Ukrains'kyi visnyk*.[186] After Terelia emigrated in September 1987, the Initiative Group for the Defense of the Rights of Believers and the Church was reorganized as the Committee in Defense of the Ukrainian Catholic Church, composed of four priests and five laymen and headed by another former political prisoner, Ivan Hel'.[187] In early 1988 the committee began issuing its journal, *Khrystyians'kyi holos*, as a continuation of the *Chronicle*.

In spite of the new atmosphere in church-state relations ushered in by Gorbachev, neither the authorities nor the Russian Orthodox church gave any indication that a change in the status of the Ukrainian Catholics was imminent. The August 4 appeal was rejected after negotiations with church leaders in Kiev. Subsequently, a Radio Kiev broadcast attacked Terelia and claimed that the signatures on the "pseudo-document" had been falsified.[188] In early December Hel' and three other activists from Ukraine were prevented from attending an unofficial human rights seminar in Moscow organized by the Press Club Glasnost'. Several weeks later, he and two Ukrainian Catholic priests managed to reach the Soviet capital with a petition for the legalization of their church bearing more than 1,500 signatures; 500 additional signatures were mailed to Moscow. According to *Khrystyians'kyi holos*, the Committee in Defense of the Ukrainian Catholic Church intended to gather 100,000 signatures demanding legalization.[189] The journal also reported that the committee had invited Pope John Paul II to Kiev for the millennium celebrations and requested that the authorities facilitate the pontiff's trip to the Ukrainian capital. Presumably in response to these initiatives, the government newspaper *Izvestiia* carried a lengthy article at the end of December denouncing the Ukrainian Catholic church for its alleged collaboration with the Nazis during the war and claiming that "in our country there is no 'Ukrainian Catholic Church' (UCC) as a religious community." Two weeks later, *Sotsialisticheskaia industriia* followed with another broadside.[190] A third petition for legalization with over 5,400 signatures was brought to Moscow in mid-February 1988, but it was not accepted at the offices of the Presidium of the Supreme Soviet.[191]

In the meantime, the leadership of the Russian Orthodox church reiterated its opposition to a papal visit to the Soviet Union in conjunction with the millennium celebrations, once again singling out the Ukrainian Catholics as the main problem. During the synod of Ukrainian bishops in Rome in September 1987, the pope renewed his call for "full liberty" for the Ukrainian church and expressed his desire to visit Ukraine, describing himself as "a Slav like you who wants to be together with his brothers."[192] The negative response came from Metropolitan Filaret, the Ukrainian exarch, during a press conference in Kiev in October. The pope returned to the issue in January 1988 during his visit to the Foreign Press Association of Italy in Rome, emphasizing that in addition to Lithuania and Latvia, he wished to meet with Catholics in Ukraine, Belorussia, and Kazakhstan. He also noted that the ban on Ukrainian Catholics remained a serious obstacle. Filaret responded at a press conference in Moscow on March 2, repeating that the pope would not be invited to the Soviet Union and categorically rejecting the notion that the Ukrainian Catholic church could be recognized. "The problem was solved in 1946," said Filaret.[193] At the same time a group of deputies of the Ukrainian Supreme Soviet—including a number of prominent academic and cultural figures—issued a statement protesting a draft resolution of the U.S. Congress on the religious situation in Ukraine, describing it as "flagrant interference" and "an attempt to falsify the policies of the Soviet state with regard to the church and believers." According to *Radians'ka Ukraina*, the protest was prompted by "the provocative calls of the Congressmen for the legalization of churches in Ukraine that had discredited themselves before the people and, having lost [their] believers, ceased to exist. This refers to the Greek Catholic (Uniate) and Ukrainian (Autocephalous) Orthodox Churches."[194] Similar protests concerning the

Ukrainian Catholics were made by Metropolitan Filaret of Minsk and the Ukrainian exarch in the aftermath of the pope's letter "Magnum baptismi donum," which addressed the Ukrainian Catholics on the occasion of the millennium. The letter, made public in April, expressed the hope that the rights of the Ukrainian Catholic church would be restored.[195]

Thus, on the eve of the millennium the outlook for about five million Ukrainian Catholics in the Soviet Union remained essentially unchanged. Neither the Vatican nor the Moscow Patriarchate showed any inclination to abandon their stated positions. Ukrainian Catholic priests and faithful, increasingly conducting their activities in the open, continued to be harassed, particularly by the imposition of heavy fines, while specialists on atheism were still meeting at conferences to work out better solutions to the Uniate problem. Indeed, one such gathering held March 21–25, 1988, in Ivano-Frankivs'k in western Ukraine, which was attended by more than 240 participants, aptly reflected the existing state of affairs in the title of its proceedings—"The Problem of Counteracting Foreign Uniate-Nationalist Propaganda and Surmounting Pro-Uniate Manifestations among Believers."[196]

Soviet Catholics and Perestroika

By the end of 1988 the outlook for Catholics in the Soviet Union was probably better than at any other time during the more than seventy years of difficult coexistence with the atheist state. Conditions varied, of course, from region to region, but the overall situation had shifted in the direction of positive change. This was perhaps best reflected in the June 13 meeting in the Kremlin between Vatican Secretary of State Agostino Cardinal Casaroli and General Secretary Gorbachev, the first such meeting of its kind. Casaroli, in Moscow for the millennium celebrations, gave Gorbachev a personal letter from the pope with an addendum outlining the Vatican's concerns about the religious freedom of Catholics in the Soviet Union and expressing the desire for regular contacts with the Soviet government.[197] Although its contents have not been made public, the memorandum is understood to address three main topics: normalization of ecclesiastical life in Lithuania and Latvia, pastoral care for Roman Catholics in Belorussia and other parts of the Soviet Union, and legitimization of the Ukrainian Catholic church.[198] Casaroli's talks with the Soviet party leader have been seen by observers as opening a new chapter in the Vatican-Kremlin dialogue.

But high-level diplomacy has not been the sole factor responsible for the recent changes. A crucial role has been played by the mobilizing power of national sentiment unleashed by the policies of perestroika. Nowhere is this in greater evidence than in Lithuania. In mid-September 1987 the Lithuanian party and government took an unprecedented step by inviting leaders of the Catholic church to discussions at the Supreme Soviet. The meeting, which was reported in the press, witnessed authorities admitting that mistakes had been made in the state's attitude toward the church and promising to be more responsive in the future. Moreover, party officials noted that such meetings should be conducted on a regular basis, indicating a willingness to seek a modus vivendi with the church. And indeed, subsequent meetings were held on February 9 and May 13, 1988.[199] The party's new approach to the Catholic church was very likely influenced by the demonstrations that were held in Lithuania (and in Estonia and Latvia) in August, the first of several that ultimately gave rise to the mass national mobilization of Lithuanians in the Sajudis popular front movement.

In April 1988 all of the Lithuanian bishops except the internally exiled Bishop Steponavicius and the retired Bishop Kriksciunas made an *ad limina* visit to the Vatican. During the visit Bishop Sladkevicius was named head of the Lithuanian Conference of Bishops in place of Archbishop Povilonis. Not long after, on May 29, Pope John Paul II announced that Sladkevicius had been made a cardinal, the first publicly named Lithuanian cardinal in modern times. *Sovetskaia Litva*'s July 29 interview with Sladkevicius entitled "We Wish to Understand Each Other" was a sign of the times. In the summer of 1988 the last two imprisoned Lithuanian priests, Frs. Svarinskas and Tamkevicius, were granted early releases; Svarinskas was permitted to leave for West Germany, and Tamkevicius returned to Lithuania in early November. A major turning point in relations with the church was the reversal of the regime's position on Bishop Steponavicius, the long-standing symbol of the uneven struggle of Lithuania's Catholics. Steponavicius was permitted to travel to Rome at the end of September, and three months later—after more than a quarter century of internal exile—he was allowed to resume his duties as apostolic administrator of the archdiocese of Vilnius. Steponavicius's reinstatement removed the last major impediment to the improvement of church-state relations.[200] Before the year ended the authorities had returned both Saint Casimir's Church in Vilnius and the Vilnius cathedral to worshipers. As late as mid-October the party was arguing that the return of the cathedral was a "complicated question" that required "careful analysis," thereby making a "quick decision impossible."[201] Within two weeks, as the Lithuanian popular front Sajudis gathered for its inaugural congress on October 22–23, the leadership of the Lithuanian party changed hands, the two churches were relinquished by the state, and the first mass celebrated at the cathedral in forty years was broadcast live by state television.

In the spring of 1989 the Vatican announced a major restructuring of the Lithuanian church hierarchy. For the first time since Lithuania came under Soviet rule all six of the church's dioceses were placed either under resident bishops or apostolic administrators. At the same time the pope appointed two new bishops, Juozapas Matulaitis and Juozas Zemaitis, bringing the total number of Lithuanian bishops to nine.[202] In early January 1989 it was announced that plans were under way to convene the founding congress of a Catholic youth organization called Ateitis, and in February Lithuanian Catholics saw the premier issue of the first legal Catholic periodical in the Soviet Union, the fortnightly *Kataliku pasaulis* (Catholic World), which was issued in an edition of 100,000 copies.[203] By the end of the year the Lithuanian Supreme Soviet amended its constitution, granting "the church and other religious organizations" the status of juridical entities, and the ministry of education introduced religious instruction into the republic's general education schools.[204]

The changes in Latvia have been no less important, albeit perhaps not as dramatic. At the end of November 1987 the pope named a new Latvian bishop, Wilhelms Nukss, to assist Cardinal Vaivods. Bishop Dulbinskis, who for decades has been prevented from carrying out his duties, was given special permission by the authorities to assist in the consecration. Little more than a year later, in January 1989, Vatican sources reported that the restrictions on Dulbinskis had been officially lifted. At the same time it was announced that permission had been granted for the publication of the Latvian Catholic journal *Katolu dzeive* (Catholic Life), a monthly with a circulation of fifty thousand copies.[205]

For Ukrainians, Casaroli's visit to Moscow had special significance. On June 10, prior to his meeting with Gorbachev, the Vatican secretary of state together with a delegation of church dignitaries that included Cardinal Willebrands met with two Ukrainian bishops and three priests in a Moscow hotel for the first high-level official contact between representatives of the Vatican and the Ukrainian Catholic church. No details were released, but the talks obviously centered on the issue of legalization.[206] Great hopes were raised when Metropolitan Filaret of Kiev told reporters at a Moscow news conference on June 4 that the Vatican and the Russian Orthodox church would soon be discussing the Ukrainian Catholic issue at a meeting in Finland. As it turned out, however, that meeting, held June 19–27, was simply another in the series of sessions of the Mixed Vatican-Orthodox Theological Commission, which limited itself to establishing a subcommittee concerned with all of the Uniate churches.[207] In essence, the leadership of the Russian Orthodox church remained adamant in its opposition to legalization. This was reiterated in 1988 by several high-ranking prelates, including Patriarch Pimen on the pages of *Izvestiia*,[208] and was reaffirmed in early 1989 by Metropolitan Filaret of Minsk, who stated flatly: "We view the Union as a non-church way to unity." Filaret added that "we would nonetheless like to be honest in solving this problem" and "begin discussing this question at the forthcoming session of the Orthodox-Catholic dialogue."[209]

In contrast to the Moscow Patriarchate, a number of Russian Orthodox activists (Alexander Ogorodnikov, Fr. Georgii Edel'shtein, Vladimir Poresh, Gleb Yakunin) and human rights campaigners (Andrei Sakharov, Valerii Senderov) recently have declared their support for the Ukrainian Catholics. Indeed, during his visit to Italy in February 1989, Sakharov met with Cardinal Lubachivs'kyi and once again urged the Soviet leadership to end the discrimination, pointing out that the main obstacle was the Russian Orthodox church.[210] Moreover, in the latter half of 1988 the first sympathetic statements about the plight of the Ukrainian church, including the desirability of its legalization, began to appear in the Moscow press (but not in Kiev).[211] Leading the field was *Moskovskie novosti*, which published several such articles in 1989, including an interview with the "illegal" but de facto head of the church in Ukraine, Archbishop Volodymyr Sterniuk, and *Ogonek*, which printed a groundbreaking article in September that exposed the Lvov Sobor in 1946 as an NKVD operation.[212] Ukrainian officials and publications became relatively more forthcoming as well, admitting that Ukrainian Catholic priests and faithful existed and that they were active. At the end of 1987 the head of the Propaganda and Agitation Department of the Lvov Oblast' party committee wrote that "there are more than 300 former priests and monks who live and work in the oblast, a part of them are trying to revive the Uniate Church, and they perform rites at home." Several months later the chairman of the Council for Religious Affairs in Ukraine, Mykola Kolesnyk, told readers of a Kiev Komsomol newspaper that "Uniates, it is true, exist. They are few." And two experts on atheism even revealed some statistical data on the proportion of Ukrainian Catholics among believers in parts of Ternopil' Oblast', referring to the petitions requesting registration that currently circulate in western Ukraine.[213] Although it had no immediate or direct impact on the Ukrainian Catholic issue, an article published in February 1988 in the Ukrainian atheistic journal *Liudyna i svit* signaled an important ideological turning point in the official attitude towards religion in the republic. Written by Volodymyr Tancher, a leading expert on religious affairs, the article called for a total restructuring of atheist propaganda, admitting that it had largely been a failure, and argued the need for a comprehensive new law on religion that would grant churches juridical status.[214]

The problem of the Ukrainian Catholics, however, remained unresolved and, indeed, grew more serious as the overall situation in Ukraine, and especially in the western regions, became more politicized in the course of 1989. Previous efforts at a compromise had failed. It had been suggested that something like an autocephalous Ukrainian Catholic church that is not linked to the Vatican might be recognized. Another proposal was that the Ukrainian church subordinate itself to Cardinal Vaivods in Riga. Both variations were rejected.[215] In the face of increasing pressure for legalization, the authorities began promoting the mass registration of Russian Orthodox communities and the opening of Orthodox churches in the traditionally Catholic western Ukrainian regions. Thus, in an interview in *Izvestiia*, Kolesnyk revealed that more than 430 Russian Orthodox churches were consecrated in Ukraine in 1988, and that the "overwhelming majority of the new Orthodox parishes have been opened in the western oblasts of the republic, above all in the Lvov, Ternopil', Ivano-Frankivs'k, and Zakarpattia oblasts, that is, in the areas that were formerly a stronghold of the Uniates." According to Metropolitan Nikodim, over two hundred parishes were opened in the Lvov Ternopil' Diocese, and another two hundred were planned for 1989. Indeed, it has been reported that in order to expedite this campaign, party activists were mobilized to gather petitions with the twenty signatures required to open new parishes.[216] The degree to which Ukraine has recently been "flooded" with new Russian Orthodox parishes is reflected in the statistics provided by Soviet sources. Overall, of the more than 3,000 Orthodox parishes that were newly registered in the Soviet Union in 1988–89, 2,050, or about two-thirds, were in Ukraine.[217] Instead of drawing Ukrainian Catholics away from their church, this approach has served only to exacerbate conflicts with the Orthodox in some areas. Moreover, the drive for legalization was stepped up, with Ukrainian Catholics staging demonstrations and hunger strikes in Moscow's Arbat and mass rallies in western Ukrainian cities. On September 17, 1989, the anniversary of the Soviet occupation of western Ukraine, an estimated 150,000 people demonstrated in Lvov to press their demand for legalization, and a march through the city on November 26 is reported to have attracted some 200,000 supporters—the largest mass gathering in Ukraine thus far.[218] Ukrainian Catholics also began forcibly taking over churches that were formerly theirs but that had been handed over to the Orthodox in 1946. The Church of the Transfiguration, the second largest in Lvov, was seized on October 29, and two months later the newly appointed head of the Moscow Patriarchate's department of External Church Affairs, Archbishop Kirill of Smolensk and Kaliningrad, told a press conference in Moscow that fifteen of the nineteen Orthodox churches in Lvov were in the hands of the Ukrainian Catholics.[219]

It was against this background of growing confrontation with the Orthodox, and with Gorbachev's scheduled visit to the Vatican drawing closer, that the authorities decided, on November 24, to allow Ukrainian Catholics to register their parishes. An announcement to that effect was issued by the Council for Religious Affairs in Kiev on December 1, presumably timed to coincide with Gorbachev's meeting with the pope on the same day.[220] The decision was almost certainly made in Moscow and in opposition to the Russian Orthodox church hierarchy. In July 1989 Metropolitan Filaret had once again insisted that "the Eastern Rite Greek Catholic (or

Uniate) church in Ukraine has not existed for more than forty years," and as late as October and November he was still maintaining that "we are not going to reanimate the Union [Ukrainian Catholic church] in Ukraine."[221] Indeed, the Ukrainian exarch revealed that in recent discussions with the Vatican the Orthodox side remained intransigent, offering the following "proposal": "The pope recommends to all Uniates that they become members of the Orthodox Church (this is easy to do because both rites overlap). Those inhabitants of Ukraine who are more devoted to the dogmas of the Catholic church could attend [Roman] Catholic churches."[222] A much more flexible position has become apparent within the Ukrainian party, with some leaders arguing publicly that the problem of Ukrainian Catholics can no longer be ignored.[223] On the other hand, little more than three months before he announced its "legalization," the chairman of the Ukrainian Council for Religious Affairs told a Kiev newspaper that "there is no room for the activities of the initiators of forming the Ukrainian Greek Catholic church and their active supporters within the framework of the Constitution of the Ukrainian SSR."[224]

The reaction of Ukrainian church activists to the December 1 announcement has been something short of euphoric. While welcoming the permission to register their communities, they have emphasized that this falls short of genuine legalization, demanding that the Lvov Sobor be disavowed, their church rehabilitated as a victim of Stalinism, and its confiscated property returned. The authorities in Kiev concede that legalization is a matter for the courts to decide, but have rejected the Catholics' demands as an "absurd ultimatum." The Russian Orthodox church, in turn, has declared its opposition to "state interference" in the matter, maintaining that the Ukrainian Catholic problem is an issue that can only be resolved through "inter-church dialogue" with the Vatican. This was the position taken by Archbishop Kirill in an interview on Soviet television two weeks after the Ukrainian Catholics were told that they could register their parishes. The Moscow Patriarchate's uncompromising position is explained in large part by the material losses that it is likely to suffer if the rights of the Ukrainian Catholics are fully restored. Of the total of approximately 10,000 Russian Orthodox parishes in the Soviet Union at the end of 1989, about 5,700, or 60 percent, were in Ukraine; of these, about 3,000, or more than half, were in western Ukraine.[225] In short, the full legalization of the Ukrainian Catholic church confronts the Moscow Patriarchate with the possibility of losing about one-third of all its parishes as well as the revenue that goes with them.

As 1989 came to a close, prospects for the Catholic church in the Soviet Union looked better than at any time since the early 1920s. Significant improvements in the church's position had been made in Lithuania, Belorussia, and Ukraine, the three areas singled out by the Vatican only little more than a year earlier. And on December 1 Mikhail Gorbachev met with John Paul II in the Vatican, the first such visit by a Soviet party leader, opening the way for further contacts that are expected to result in the establishment of formal diplomatic relations between the Holy See and the Kremlin.

FACT SHEET

The Catholic Church in the Soviet Union

Given the fact that there is no all-Union Catholic church hierarchy in the Soviet Union and that the government of the Soviet Union claims not to be interested in such things as the number of believers ("it is a private matter"), it is impossible to provide any kind of official data on the Catholic church—i.e., "official" in the sense that it is published in statistical handbooks or comparable publications. However, from time to time Soviet officials do provide some general information along the lines "there are about," "there are almost," etc. More or less the same is true about information provided by church sources. Moreover, the figures for churches, priests, seminarians, etc., are constantly changing, particularly as a result of the Gorbachev reforms. In short, the data given below, valid for the end of 1988 and early 1989, represents the best available estimates.

Current strength of the church

Between 5 and 10 million faithful	
1,906 priests	
a. Lithuania	674
b. Latvia	105
c. Ukraine	1,000
d. Other	127
22 bishops	
a. Lithuania	9
b. Latvia	4
c. Ukraine	9
0 monks (underground?)	
0 nuns (underground?)	
238 seminarians	
a. Lithuania	157
b. Latvia	81

Number of churches and church facilities

- 1,100 churches (Soviet sources)
- 3 seminaries

- o convents
- o monasteries
- o hospitals
- o theological faculties

Chief news organs (official)

Kataliku pasaulis (Catholic World) (fortnightly; 20,000–100,000 copies; Vilnius; Lithuanian)

Katolu dzeive (Catholic Life) (monthly; 50,000 copies; Vilani; Latvian and Latgallian)

Underground religious periodicals

Chronicle of the Catholic Church in Lithuania (1972–present)

Chronicle of the Catholic Church in Ukraine (1984–87)

Khrystyians'kyi holos (1988–present)

Primates or archbishops of capitals

Lithuania

Juozapas Skvireckas (1926–53)—Metropolitan; forced out of Lithuania by German occupation forces in 1944

Chairmen of College of Diocesan Ordinaries (est. 1965)

Petras Mazelis (1965–66)

Juozas Matulaitis-Labukas (1966–79)

Liudvikas Povilonis—chairman of Conference of Bishops (1979–88)

Vincentas Sladkevicius (April 1988–present)

Latvia

Antonijs Springovics (1937–58)—Metropolitan

Peteris Strods (1958–60)—Bishop (Riga)

1960–64—no functioning bishops

Julijans Vaivods (1964–present)—church hierarchy restored in 1964 with his consecration as bishop and apostolic administrator of Riga Archdiocese and Liepaja Diocese

Ukraine

Andrei Sheptyts'kyi (1901–44)—Metropolitan

Iosyf Slipyi (1944–84)—Metropolitan; arrested in 1945 and imprisoned; released in 1963 and permitted to leave for Rome

Myroslav Ivan Lubachivs'kyi (1984–present)—Metropolitan

Belorussia

Tadeusz Kondrusiewicz (1989–present)—Bishop (Minsk)

4

The Catholic Church in East Germany

Robert F. Goeckel

The East German Catholic church represents a unique case among Catholic churches in communist Europe in two salient respects. First, it is the only church to exist in the context of a divided nation. The postwar division of Germany along East-West lines has weighed heavily in the calculations of the church and in its relationship with the state. Conserving tradition, to the extent that this is rooted in German national tradition, has been more problematic than in other Eastern bloc settings due to the international implications. Second, the East German Catholic church is the only one to confront a dominant Protestant (Lutheran) church and a largely Protestant cultural milieu. This has had the effect not only of lowering the attention paid by the state to Catholics but also of providing an alternative model for internal structuring of the church and for dealing with the communist state.

Despite these dimensions which distinguish the East German church from its counterparts in the bloc, like them it has faced the challenge from a communist regime pursuing the revolutionary transformation of society. Employing atheistic propaganda and policies aimed at curtailing the church's role in social life, particularly in education, the GDR followed a bloc-wide trend during the Stalinist period. The GDR also sought to fragment the church by creating organizations of "progressives," as in other bloc settings. Like elsewhere, the modernizing GDR regime confronted an essentially traditional institution in the Catholic church. Thus a study of the East German Catholic church will allow analysis of the differential effects of the inter-German factor and the Protestant culture on the relationship between church and state as well as on political choice of the actors involved.

In this chapter I will develop and expand on several themes. First, the story of the East German Catholic church, like that of the Lutheran church, has been one dominated by the division of the nation and the church's gradual accommodation to the reality of this division. Unlike the predominant Lutheran church, which has sometimes managed to bridge the political chasm between East and West Germany, the weaker Catholic church has depended on ties to its stronger West German brothers and has been slower to accept its socialist environment.

Second, the church's integration into the world Catholic church has allowed the Vatican to affect the church-state relationship in the GDR. At times, such as the 1950s, the Vatican's role has accentuated the church's antagonism with the regime; at other times (as in the 1960s and 1970s) it has moderated the relationship with the regime. In any case the Vatican as a global transnational actor has different interests from those of the regional actor, West Germany, raising the question of which external actor is more likely to pursue a consistent policy vis-à-vis the local East German Catholic church in the 1980s and beyond.

A third theme is the basically conservative nature of East German Catholicism, both doctrinally and organizationally. Though in the heartland of the Protestant Reformation, the East German church is infused with tradition. The onset of communism has stunted modernization efforts compared with the West German Catholic church.

A final theme flowing out of this study concerns the sources of change in the church: Internal church dissent has increased in the last fifteen years, but neither grass-roots organizations nor state-steered "progressive" groups have been influential. Rather, external sources of change, for example, broad changes in society, the activism of the Evangelical-Lutheran church, and the prompting of the Vatican, have been more significant in promoting greater political activism by the church.

Transition: 1945–49

The early postwar period in the Soviet occupation zone saw a relatively mild policy toward the churches. The Soviet military administration demonstrated considerable interest in a cooperative relationship with both churches. With the collapse of order in 1945, the Soviets relied on clergy to restore normal conditions, going so far as to ask Catholic leaders to "take care that the Berliners believe in God again."[1] Catholic priests were even recruited into civil administrative posts.[2]

A major figure in facilitating this cooperation was the emissary of the

German Bishops' Conference (or Fulda Conference), Heinrich Wienken. The circumstances of the collapse in 1945 thrust him into the spotlight: There was no papal nuncio in Berlin; the chair of the Fulda Conference, Cardinal Bertram, was stranded in Czechoslovakia; and Bishop Preysing of Berlin assumed a low profile, shell-shocked by the arrival of the Soviets. Wienken was a particularly appropriate choice to play the role of intermediary with the new authorities. He was basically pragmatic in orientation, having come from a background in Caritas, the Catholic social welfare agency. His patient diplomacy with the Nazis demonstrated an inclination to appeal to the humanity in his opponent. Wienken was also a Slavophile by nature, and apparently he developed a certain personal rapport with the Soviet commanders in Berlin.[3] During the heyday of the Allied Control Council in administering occupied Germany, the Vatican relied on Wienken in making policy for Germany; with the declining viability of the Allied Control Council in 1947–48, Wienken's role became limited to the Soviet zone.

The policies of the Soviet authorities, and later the GDR government, soon tested Wienken's pragmatism. As in other so-called people's democracies in Eastern Europe, public policy in the transition period aimed at removing the church from its traditionally prominent role in society, with the goal of eventually limiting the church to a purely cultic role similar to that assigned successfully by the Soviet regime to the Russian Orthodox church. Thus, under the rubric of separation of church and state, the zonal authorities eliminated the confessional schools and introduced so-called unified schools. Bishop Preysing of Berlin protested vigorously that "the areligious school necessarily provides an education antithetical to faith" and scorned it as a "school of the Nazi past and hopefully not the school of the future."[4] Seeing the battle for confessional schools as hopeless, Wienken negotiated to retain the right of religious instruction in the schools in the 1949 GDR Constitution.[5]

The zonal authorities also acted to curtail the church's public role by forbidding church youth groups, not wishing any competition with the newly created Central Youth Committee (by 1946 renamed Free German Youth, or FDJ). The FDJ initially recruited religious youth to its leadership but ousted and arrested them in 1947.[6] Soviet authorities also rejected the church's request in 1945 to license a weekly newspaper in their zone and later forbade the circulation of the West Berlin *Petrusblatt*.[7] Now-Cardinal Preysing attacked this process of curtailing the church's social presence, charging that "the limiting of religious life to the purely cultic, in conjunction with the molding of public and private life in the spirit of materialism, constitutes a recipe for liquidation of religious life entirely."[8]

In the context of the sharpening church-state conflict and the creation of separate German states in 1949, the different orientations of Wienken and Preysing were bound to have an impact on their mutual relationship. Wienken's conciliatory approach can be summarized by his view that the church has no fundamental qualms about discussions with representatives of the GDR, since, unlike politicians, it is not required to ask about the diplomatic recognition of the state or form of government, but rather to deal with the realities under which it lives.[9] This contrasted dramatically with Preysing's views which accused the Communists of seeking, "under the misuse of the Germans' desire to restore unity to their fatherland, to extend their power position to all of Germany."[10] In his so-called Preysing Decree, he forbade political participation by priests, a position that was reconfirmed by his successors, Cardinals Doepfner and Bengsch. He pointedly rejected participation in the People's Congress (1948) and National Front (1950), initiatives by the regime to increase its popular support based on generalized opposition to the growing division of Germany.[11] In the context of increasing East-West polarization, Preysing asked Wienken to resign his commission from the Fulda Conference. Shortly thereafter, in accommodation to these realities, Wienken was relieved of his responsibilities by the Fulda Conference, and Pope Pius XII formed an East German Bishops' Conference subordinate to the umbrella Fulda Conference. Thereafter, responsibility for negotiating with the regime would be centralized under the aegis of the chairman of the new East German Bishops' Conference (soon to be designated the Berlin Ordinarien Conference).[12]

Despite his displacement as a key intermediary with the government and the increasing chill in church-state relations, Wienken is credited with several achievements that served to anchor the presence of the Catholic church in society for years to come. After years of negotiations he was able to gain the state's approval for two weekly church newspapers: *Tag des Herrn*, published in Leipzig since 1951; and *St. Hedwigsblatt*, published in Berlin since 1953.[13] In addition, in 1951 the state licensed a Catholic publishing company, St. Benno Verlag, after repeated petitions by Wienken that "satisfying the religious needs of the population for religious publications is impossible without one." Again in the area of church communications, he proved instrumental in the state's decision in 1954 to include Catholic services in its Sunday radio broadcasts on a monthly basis (weekly Protestant services had been included since 1945). The state's motive for these concessions was hardly altruistic: It wanted to compete with Western media sources that were being illegally imported from West Germany. As one director of the State Radio Committee put it, "Of importance are the political commentaries which follow the radio worship services. These discuss certain developments in society, inform about church-political developments, and help raise the consciousness of Christians in the socialist society."[14]

Even more crucial to the institutional autonomy of the church has been its ability to train priests and make personnel decisions in conjunction with the Vatican. Lacking local institutions for training priests, the Catholic church in prewar eastern Germany had relied on priests trained in western Germany. After the war the church essentially continued to rely on external sources of priests. However, by 1951 the regime made such supply increasingly tenuous. Wienken's negotiations, particularly with leading Christian Democratic Union (East) (CDU) officials such as Otto Nuschke, bore fruit in 1952 when the state agreed to the founding of a new seminary in Erfurt. By insisting upon its location in Erfurt and its direct subordination to the Vatican rather than the Fulda Conference, the GDR underscored its independence from the West German church.[15] Although the state certainly hoped thereby to influence the new clergy in the GDR, the Erfurt seminary has permitted the Catholic church greater autonomy than the Protestant churches, which rely heavily on the state universities for theological education.

Wienken was thus able to gain certain concessions from the state in areas of church institutional interests, even as the state sought to curtail the churches' role in society. Wienken's pragmatism is best captured in his comment to the director of the GDR's Information Office: "The Catholic church is already very old, has existed for a long time and will long continue to exist. The GDR is still young, but wants to exist a long time. Thus we must find a way of coming to terms with each other and existing together."[16] Wienken was thus able to use the regime's growing interest in self-assertion vis-à-vis West Germany to meet certain church institutional interests.

Ideological Conflict: 1949–60

In the 1950s this pragmatic approach fell victim to the heightened campaign against the churches and religion and the conservative Western orientation of Preysing and his eventual successor, Julius Doepfner. Following the formation of the GDR in 1949, the regime pursued a policy of more rapid socialist transformation of the economy and society, a process which logically entailed conflict with the churches, both Protestant and Catholic.

During this period the state repeatedly sought to curtail the church's social presence and limit it to a purely cultic role. For example, in May 1953 the state confiscated certain church orphanages, charging that they were guilty of child abuse and "currency violations." Although these actions, organized largely by the FDJ, were rescinded in the context of the June 1953 unrest, pressure on the orphanages increased again in 1958–59 as the state eliminated monetary support for children in such orphanages.[17]

The state also sought to impede church meetings and events. For example, the state introduced a legal requirement that certain church events be registered with the local police. In 1952–53 the state applied this law narrowly, exempting only traditional worship services. Fines were levied for the failure to register church retreats and pilgrimages; in some cases church activities were disrupted or banned.[18] Another tactic involved the use of administrative measures such as withholding logistical support for church conventions (*Katholikentag*), harassing West German visitors to the *Katholikentag*, and confiscating materials from participants.[19]

The state also intensified its pressure on the youth, emphasizing atheistic indoctrination in particular. In a pastoral letter in 1949 and a letter to the government in 1950, Preysing already had protested the "godless materialism" pervading the schools.[20] After some relaxation in strictures following the June 1953 upheaval, the atheistic campaign escalated in 1954 with the introduction of the youth consecration ceremony, or *Jugendweihe*.[21] This ersatz rite was meant to supplant the confirmation ceremony and was supplemented by other ceremonies such as the socialist name-giving ceremony, socialist marriage ceremony, etc. Moreover, the preparatory instruction for the *Jugendweihe* was clearly atheistic in nature. Although participation in the *Jugendweihe* was officially voluntary, youth and their parents were subject to considerable pressure to participate by educators and managers, respectively. By 1959 participation was practically universal.

The Catholic church, like the Lutheran church, took an early stand opposing the *Jugendweihe* as "irreconcilable with faith."[22] In a 1958 Lenten pastoral letter the East German bishops described the socialist rites as "broken cisterns, from which no good can come" and declared "no Catholic Christian can complete [the socialist rites] without denying his holy faith."[23] The bishops called on Catholics to insist upon their constitutional right to freedom of conscience and exhorted them to remain steadfast in the face of threats and pressure by reminding them of earlier persecution of Christians.

Responding to this challenge from the Catholic church, the regime launched ever-greater assaults on the church's leaders. In 1955 Walter Ulbricht, first secretary of the Socialist Unity (Communist) party (SED), vilified them as "justifiers of rule of the imperialistic bourgeoisie, defenders of aggressive enemies of the people and purveyors of hatred against the workers' and peasants' power."[24] In 1956 Prime Minister Otto Grotewohl accused the church of misuse of the Constitution to "interfere in the state's internal affairs in a negative, even malicious sense."[25]

By 1957–58 the conflict had become even more intense, as Ulbricht pressed the socialization of the economy (collectivization) and escalated pressure on West Berlin. Increasing numbers of Catholics were arrested, tried, and convicted of spying for a "West Berlin headquarters." Cardinal Doepfner's protests were dismissed as "political clericalism." Indeed, the state rejected petitions from Doepfner, a resident of West Berlin, as coming from a "noncitizen of the GDR."[26] A 1958 decree issued by the Education Ministry proscribed extracurricular instruction in schools within two hours of the conclusion of normal instruction, in effect preventing religious instruction after school hours and limiting it to church facilities.

During this period the Bishops' Ordinarien Conference issued repeated pastoral letters to the laity and appeals to the government reiterating its position and calling for adherence to the Constitution. The regime censored church publication of these pastoral letters, going so far as to require that the church newspapers print state rebuttals. Doepfner was accused of "protecting agents of Western security services" and charged with seeking "special" rights of conscience and faith beyond those granted in the Constitution.[27] Like the all-German Lutheran church, the Catholic church became increasingly subject after 1958 to the charge of being a fifth column for West German CDU policy.

This worsening relationship between church and state in the late 1950s was reflected in bureaucratic changes by the state. In 1957 responsibility for the relationship with the churches was shifted from the office of the deputy prime minister, occupied by Otto Nuschke (CDU-East), to the current office, the State Secretariat for Church Questions, headed initially by Werner Eggerath (SED). The displacement of Nuschke, who had demonstrated some sympathy for the churches' position, further signaled the harsher line.[28]

"Socialist Human Community" and the Conflict over Inter-German Church Ties: 1961–1975

The erection of the Berlin Wall in 1961 marks a watershed in the church-state relationship because it resulted in attenuated ties to West German Catholics and gave impetus to the slow process of reconsideration of the church's proper role in the GDR. The 1960s also saw a significant shift in the state's approach toward the churches: Internally, the state articulated a more conciliatory policy, at least rhetorically; externally, the state sought to curtail church ties with the West German churches.

The state shifted from direct assaults on the church and religion to an indirect approach combining public overtures with criticism of reactionary church leaders. Ulbricht heralded this new orientation in October 1960, claiming that "Christianity and the humanistic goals of socialism are not contradictory." He also began a series of "selective dialogues" with certain "progressive" forces, largely in the Lutheran church, and criticized the Catholics for rejecting such dialogue with the state "due to influence of military-tinged clericalism steered by the influence of Bonn."[29] The deemphasis on ideological struggle eventually was codified in the inclusionary cache of the late Ulbricht period, "socialist human community," and its guiding dictum, the "political-moral unity of the people." This new emphasis on inclusion did not, however, signal an end to the struggle against religion, merely a shift from actively promoting its demise via atheistic propaganda to reliance on the forces of secularization to erode the churches' base.[30]

This tactical maneuver derived from the increasing primacy given by the state to its goal of breaking the inter-German church ties. Although this campaign was directed primarily at the larger Lutheran church, the Catholic church also found it increasingly difficult to maintain its links with the West.[31] Already in 1958 Cardinal Doepfner had been denied access to the eastern portion of his Berlin diocese. Due to his residence in West Berlin he had been rejected as a negotiating partner by the GDR. Likewise, the papal nuncio to Germany was forbidden access to East Berlin. The *Katholikentag* in 1958 was the last all-German Catholic event of any import. These problems proved harbingers of the greater rupture to come in 1961 with the building of the Berlin Wall.

Personnel changes by the church in 1961 left it better positioned to deal with the escalating pressures in the 1960s. Because of the low ebb of his relations with the regime and his vulnerability as a resident of West Berlin, Cardinal Doepfner was reassigned by the Vatican to the diocese of Munich. Shortly after the wall was constructed, the Vatican named his successor, Alfred Bengsch, a resident of East Berlin. The GDR permitted Bengsch to visit the West Berlin section of the diocese several days per month, an arrangement it has continued and expanded over time. The regime found the so-called Bengsch solution conducive to its claim that West Berlin properly belonged to the jurisdiction of the GDR.

Although the Bengsch solution defused the situation regarding Berlin, it did not satisfy the state's demands on issues regarding wider inter-German ties, such as diocesan borders and the role of the Fulda Conference. Unlike the Lutheran provincial churches, whose borders were roughly coincident with those of the GDR, the diocesan borders in the Catholic church transcended the GDR boundary. Only in the case of Berlin and Dresden-Meissen did the bulk of the diocese lie in GDR territory. Reflecting the weakness of the Catholic church in this traditionally Lutheran region, the remaining areas of the GDR were subject to dioceses centered outside the GDR.[32] These areas were headed by consecrated bishops or bishops' commissars. Although members of the East German Bishops' Conference and, de facto, responsible for church matters in their jurisdictions, these officials were designated by their respective West German bishops and nominally accountable to them. Moreover, the Fulda Conference, with its balance of power and head in West Germany, also represented West German organizational influence in the GDR. Thus, with Ulbricht's heightened efforts to curtail such Western influence in the GDR in the 1960s, it is not surprising that the regime should bring pressure and propaganda to bear on such ties.

This campaign intensified particularly after 1966. The tentative steps toward Ostpolitik by the "Grand Coalition" government in Bonn produced an allergic reaction in East Berlin, which is fearful of any compromise in its position on the German question. In the particular case of the Catholic church, the exchange of letters between the Fulda Conference and the Polish episcopate in 1965, designed to foster reconciliation between the two peoples, prompted the GDR to accuse Bengsch of a "political action in the spirit of revanchism of Bonn."[33] The regime criticized the letter as "directed against the peace policy of our government and against the Catholic population in the GDR also." The state also criticized the 1966 decision to rename the Fulda Conference the German Bishops' Conference, comparing it to the West German government's claim to be the sole representative of Germans, East and West.[34] The state sought to impede ties with the German Bishops' Conference and demanded an end to the naming of GDR bishops' representatives by the West German bishops.[35]

Compared with the Lutherans, the Catholic church found itself in a stronger position to withstand the state's demands not only because of the Bengsch solution but also because of the key role played by the Vatican. As a juridically sovereign state, the Vatican could offer international legal recognition to the legitimacy-starved GDR. Moreover, in the centralized Catholic church the Vatican held the keys to the jurisdictional changes demanded by the GDR. However, the Vatican was reluctant to grant diplomatic recognition to the GDR or make the demanded jurisdictional changes because the West German government, episcopate, and laity threatened that such action would invalidate the concordat between Hitler and the Vatican, which the FRG had continued to recognize.[36] The Vatican's interest in maintaining the status quo regarding the concordat left the GDR in a disadvantageous position.

The GDR now moderated its posture and responded positively to some Vatican pronouncements. The SED hailed Pope John XXIII's encyclical *Pacem in terris* as an endorsement of the peaceful coexistence policy of the Soviet bloc and a rebuff to "West German military-political clericalism."

A leading SED Politburo member praised the Catholic social doctrine reflected in the encyclical *Popularum progressio*.[37] As a result of the role of the Vatican, the campaign against the Catholic church's inter-German ties began later and was milder than the campaign against the Lutheran church. Indeed, East German Catholic contacts with the Vatican were never interrupted during this period of conflict, in contrast to Lutheran ecumenical contacts.[38]

Strengthening the GDR's position, however, was the newfound interest of Pope Paul VI and his lieutenant, Agostino Cardinal Casaroli, in pursuing his own Ostpolitik in Eastern Europe, a trend which seemed to bode well for the GDR's demands for accommodation to political realities.[39] Using back-channel diplomacy in Belgrade and the Conference on Security and Cooperation in Europe (CSCE) in Helsinki, the Vatican undertook partial measures which were clearly timed with and linked to the developing process of West German Ostpolitik. In March 1970 the consecrated bishops in Magdeburg and Schwerin were upgraded to the status of adjutor-bishops, a newly created title. In June 1972, following the ratification of the Warsaw Treaty, the bishop's commissar of Goerlitz was designated an apostolic administrator, an office directly subordinate to the Vatican rather than to the local, now-Polish, bishop of Wrocław. After the ratification of the Basic Treaty between the FRG and GDR in 1973, apostolic administrators were designated in Erfurt/Meiningen, Magdeburg, and Schwerin.[40]

Publicly the state criticized these compromise measures as "first steps," yet privately the state had limited expectation of change. In the press and in meetings with Bengsch the state insisted upon independent bishoprics for the GDR and attacked the East German bishops for "inadequate state consciousness" and "service to the West German hierarchy."[41] But in 1970 the SED privately acknowledged that the creation of a separate bishops' conference for the GDR was a "distant goal."[42] After considerable negotiation, including a visit by Casaroli to the GDR in 1975, the Vatican in fact did move to transform the Berlin Ordinarien Conference into the separate Berlin Bishops' Conference in October 1976. However, it issued the caveat that this action had "no effect on the German question," following the lead of the West German interpretation of the Basic Treaty.[43] Opposition by Bengsch and the West German episcopate precluded the more extensive move of diplomatic recognition or the delegation of a papal nuncio. General Secretary Honecker had shown himself increasingly solicitous of the Vatican, in 1979 selecting Klaus Gysi, former ambassador to Rome, as state secretary for church questions and meeting with Pope John Paul II in 1985. However, the state now seems more interested in general aspects of peace than in changes in the diocesan structure.[44]

Thus the partial solution regarding its inter-German ties promulgated by the Catholic church reveals both the preferential treatment accorded the Catholic church and the impact of Honecker's succession to power in 1971. Because of the key role of the Vatican, the regime has tolerated greater legal bonds between the Catholics in the two Germanies than between Lutherans. Moreover, the ascension of Honecker and his relatively pragmatic policy toward inter-German relations in recent years allowed both Lutherans and Catholics to maintain and further develop closer inter-German ties.

The Church's Role in Socialism

The state's campaign against religion and the church's influence on society, compounded by its campaign against inter-German ties, left the church with the impression of living in an ideological diaspora. This ideological diaspora reinforced the traditional sense of living in a religious diaspora surrounded by Lutherans. This sense of double diaspora was captured most vividly in the "alien house" metaphor employed by Bishop Otto Spülbeck (Meissen) in 1956: "We live in a house, whose structure we have not built, whose basic foundation we even consider false. We gladly contribute, living worthy and Christian lives. But we cannot build a new story on this house, since we consider its foundation false. This house remains an alien house. We thus live in a diaspora not only in terms of our church, but also in terms of our state."[45]

For much of the 1960s and 1970s this sense of double diaspora led the church to assume a stance of political abstinence toward the regime and a standoffish attitude toward the Lutheran church. This stance was most strongly identified with Cardinal Bengsch of Berlin, chair of the Berlin Ordinarien Conference throughout this period and leading spokesman of the church. Bengsch's operative principle was that when in the den of lions, like Daniel, one should neither pet the lions nor pull their tails.[46] Consequently, the Bengsch years involved limited political protests on narrowly religious concerns such as the *Jugendweihe*, abortion, and the new law on the socialist education system. On more political issues such as military service, discrimination in education and career, the invasion of Czechoslovakia, and détente, the Catholic church remained mostly silent, unlike the Lutheran church. Bengsch emphasized a conservative, nonpolitical theology. At Vatican II he rejected Western criticism of "churches of silence" and anticommunist slogans as producing only more repression of the church in communist countries.[47] His fear of liberal Western Catholic influence seems to have made the limited measures of separation from the West German church more palatable.[48]

Reflecting this conservative line, the church emphasized preaching and liturgy as well as outreach to the young. The rhetorical opposition to the *Jugendweihe* was reiterated, but the penalties for participation in it were reduced in a tacit admission of the failure of the church's opposition.[49]

Bengsch also endorsed the Preysing Decree banning political participation by priests. In the context of limited but increasing Lutheran participation in mass organizations such as the CDU and the National Front, as well as increasing voting by Lutheran ministers in the 1970s, the significantly lower voting levels among Catholic priests demonstrate the effect of Bengsch's emphasis on abstinence. In the 1960s, electoral participation by priests in Berlin actually declined from the levels of the 1950s, averaging one-half of the level for Catholic priests in the GDR as a whole in 1967 (32.5 percent versus 60 percent).[50] Bengsch's behavior matched his beliefs: he was the only bishop not to vote in the referendum on the new 1968 constitution, and he rejected the state's suggestion in 1972 that he, "like Pope Paul VI has done many times," make a public declaration in support of the CSCE.[51]

Not surprisingly, during the Bengsch era the relations with the Lutheran church were cool. Bengsch's conservative political abstinence contrasted with the Lutherans' growing acceptance of the GDR and articulation of an active role as a "church in socialism." This was dramatized best in the cardinal's critical reaction to the summit between Honecker and the Lutheran leadership in 1978.[52]

New Voices: Progressive and Grass-roots Dissent

The fundamentally conservative religious orientation of the church and its political abstinence under Bengsch were bound to lead to challenges to the leadership, particularly in the context of Vatican II. One source of challenge stemmed from the "progressive" Catholics mobilized by the SED in certain front organizations.

The broadest of these movements is the Christian Democratic Union of East Germany. Licensed as a political party in 1945 and victim of SED *Gleichschaltung* by 1949, it aims to mobilize Christians, including Catholics, in support of the SED and socialism. The CDU has had little luck, however, in mobilizing Catholic clergy; for example, in 1974 only twenty priests were members of the CDU.[53] The CDU has thus been dominated by Protestants and has focused primarily on issues affecting the Lutheran church.

Partly in order to overcome the failure of the CDU and the Prague-based Christian Peace Conference as transmission belts, the regime formed a new organization in 1964 designed to appeal specifically to Catholics, the Berlin Conference of European Christians (BCEC). The BCEC sees itself as a "forum of peace forces from all of Europe for consultation and activizing the peace service on the basis of the doctrine of our church."[54] It holds meetings every two years in Berlin, bringing together "progressive" Catholics from East and West to discuss peace and the international situation, and issues a communiqué which usually supports Soviet foreign policy positions. For example, it criticized "nationalistic and extremist forces in the FRG" and demanded a "distancing from revanchism" by the West German government in 1970 and lobbied the Dresden pastoral synod in 1973 for greater separation from the West German church.[55]

The BCEC has been singularly unsuccessful in mobilizing any significant support in East Germany, and is carried largely by Western leftist Catholics and peace priests from other socialist countries. For example, despite the participation of two hundred delegates from eighteen countries at the 1966 meeting, no priests from the GDR participated.[56] Unlike other East European countries, the Berlin Bishops' Conference has not participated in the BCEC, and Bengsch castigated "progressives" as "emigrants from the communion."[57] The lack of a domestic base in the GDR and its foreign policy orientation strongly suggest that the BCEC was created to promote the GDR's role in the world community. Moreover, it would appear that the CDU, jealous of the lead role played by the Czechs in the Christian Peace Conference, sees the BCEC as a means of competing with this umbrella peace organization.

Despite their criticism of the church hierarchy on political grounds, the "progressive" Catholics in the CDU and BCEC (and their organ, *Begegnung*) distinguish themselves from other dissenting voices in terms of their views on internal church matters. Paradoxically, the "progressives" have traditionally followed a very conservative line on questions of theology and church practice. For example, Otto Hartmut Fuchs, founder of the BCEC and longtime editor of *Begegnung*, supported the pope's position on celibacy and birth control, declaring that those "who gather under the flag of 'critical Catholicism' have nothing to do with the church, at least with Catholicism."[58]

Fuchs was referring to a group of Catholic intellectuals who began to dissent from the ghetto mentality of the hierarchy in the mid-1960s. Meeting on an informal basis and centered in the Halle area, they came to be known as the Action Group Halle (AGH). Their criticism of monolithic church structures and undemocratic processes is captured in their 1966 manifesto: "We ponder our church in the GDR which, appearing unified to the outside, maintains this unity only through manipulated activities and initiatives of church officials; largely clerical, it has not yet discovered the potential of pluralism which rests in the responsible activity of the laity. How much potential of authentic democratization of relations among bishops, priests, and laity, how much potential of Christian impact never imagined by church officials could be released!"[59] The AGH criticized, among other things, the lack of information provided to the laity by church publications, the prohibition against all forms of church work by priests who have left the priesthood, and denial of ecumenical travel to internal church dissidents.[60]

The response of the church leadership to the new dissidents was predictably negative, although discreet. Insinuations were made that the Halle-based dissenters were linked to radical Catholics in the West and were being used by the East German State Security Service in an effort to weaken the unified front of the church. Ironically, it was simultaneously alleged that they were disturbing the improving relationship between church and state in the GDR.[61]

Despite this negative response, the church leadership did seem to venture from its rigid ghetto in the early 1970s. In a marked departure from Spülbeck's 1956 description of the GDR as an "alien house," Bengsch had words of praise for the GDR on the occasion of the twentieth anniversary of its founding in 1969. He admitted that "we are ready to recognize all that which is done for the true welfare of the people, because everywhere Christians have also contributed. . . . We are able to say with thanks to God that it is possible for the church to work for the spiritual needs of people and, if we are truly honest, the church has had more chances than it has been able to use."[62]

A major opportunity to demonstrate forthcomingness toward the democratizing agenda of the AGH presented itself with the first pastoral synod of laity and clergy in 1973–75. This initiative stemmed from the mandate of Vatican II and was preceded by a diocesan synod in Meissen in 1969–70. The synod had issued resolutions calling for Christian activity for peace and opposing "the raising of children to hate other worldviews, races, and political systems." Moreover, it called for "partnerlike cooperation" and appropriate structures in the church.[63] The working papers for the 1973 Dresden Synod were even more activist than the Meissen resolutions. The working paper on service in the world called for an "intellectual-spiritual analysis of the socialist doctrine of society," a dialogue with nonbelievers, a rethinking of the position on the *Jugendweihe,* approval of certain types of political-social participation, and reduction of hierarchical power structures in the church.[64]

The working papers of the Dresden Synod were subject to criticism from both progressives and the AGH. The progressives attacked the working paper's rejection of the atheistic basis of GDR society and activity in the SED. They offered advice regarding the "societal position-finding and new orientation" of the church, calling for the synod to endorse the CSCE and national independence for the GDR church. The Halle group also sought to influence the synod with an open letter criticizing the narrow framing of questions for the synod and calling for more flexibility regarding treatment of former priests.[65]

These attempts to influence the synod were invoked by Bengsch and the Berlin Ordinarien Conference to justify limiting the content and format of the synod. The working paper on "service in the world" was eliminated, and the agenda was narrowed to focus primarily on the individual and the parish. The Vatican set conditions on the synod—no more than 50 percent laity and no outside influence—and the bishops retained veto power over any resolutions passed. These limitations, as well as sessions closed to the public, resulted in a synod which did not realize its potential for democratizing the church.[66] Regarding political issues, the synod also avoided any significant departure from the Bengsch line by employing diplomatic and vague language. Although 40 percent of the synod desired strong criticism of the *Jugendweihe* and discrimination in education, the synod's resolution merely called for Christians to "help young Christians when making these responsible decisions." Similar mild language was used in reference to the question of military service. Regarding the church's role in the GDR, it was content to note that "we live in a socialist social order, which is characterized by atheism."[67]

Despite the status quo outcome of the 1973 Dresden Synod, the concerns of the lay Catholics regarding discrimination did eventually evoke a response by Bengsch. Penalties for youth and their parents for participation in the *Jugendweihe* were reduced, even while the episcopate affirmed its rejection of the rite. More pointedly than the Lutherans, Bengsch protested the new youth law of 1973, which posited "socialist personality" as the state's goal. Finally, in 1974 a pastoral letter was issued demanding tolerance of Christians in education and decrying an education system informed by a "materialistic understanding of mankind stamped by the worldview of dialectical materialism." Responding to increased lay pressure as well as the heightened emphasis on ideology during the early Honecker years, Bengsch began to pull on the lion's tail, albeit gently.

This criticism notwithstanding, the 1970s saw the Catholic church continue to emphasize its status as a diaspora church and pursue political abstinence, in marked contrast to the vigorous debate in the Lutheran church regarding its role in socialism and its self-definition as a "church within socialism." The primary factors responsible for the absence of such a debate in the Catholic church include the delayed and partial accommodation to the division of Germany, the diaspora tradition, the hierarchical internal structures, and the preeminent role of Bengsch.

The Peace Movement and the Catholic Church

Since the late 1970s, however, foreign and domestic developments have challenged the Catholic church to assume a more activist posture. Widespread popular opposition to heightened militarization in the GDR and the deployment of missiles in Europe, in the context of worsening East-West relations internationally, led to the development of an indigenous, independent peace movement in the GDR.[68] Because of the SED's monopoly on legitimate political organization, the activists in this movement have often turned to the church, in particular the Lutheran church, as a forum and umbrella for their activities. Given its stance of political abstinence, the Catholic church did not prove to be a hospitable venue for these peace activists; nor did it offer the lay Catholics much spiritual support and counsel on this issue until recently. Consistent with its past record for greater political activism, the Evangelical-Lutheran church has been more vocal on the issue of peace.

Prior to 1982, the few East German Catholic statements on peace and the military had been informed by traditional Catholic social doctrine and focused on individual and parental rights. For example, responding to the 1962 law on military service, the church basically concluded that the military obligation was compatible with Catholic doctrine and sanctioned the taking of the oath to defend the GDR.[69] The working paper for the 1973 Dresden Synod was quite activist in support of those opting for alternative service (called *Bausoldaten*), a little-publicized alternative for conscientious objectors. But the final resolutions of Dresden reiterated the support for military obligation, making only scant reference to the law covering the *Bausoldat* service.[70] The introduction of military training in the high schools in 1978 signaled an escalation of militarization in the GDR and brought forth critical responses from both Lutheran and Catholic churches.[71] However, unlike the high-visibility chancel statement of the Lutherans, the Catholic response took the form of a letter from Bengsch to State Secretary for Church Questions Seigewasser, a letter which later was made public. In it Bengsch criticized the friend-foe dichotomy as irreconcilable with peace education and emphasized the primary right of parents regarding the education of their children. The Catholic response was diplomatic and worded in traditional terms, in contrast to the Lutheran response, which spoke more directly to the inconsistency of the GDR's peace policy. The limited circulation of Catholic pronouncements—largely in the form of advisories to priests and letters to the government—left the laity out of the picture.

With the rise of the peace movement in the early 1980s, criticism of the Catholic church's response to the issue mounted. The AGH opined that "many Christians perceive with disgust the deafening silence of the Catholic church regarding the present threats to peace." They regretted that "since Dresden, no public discussion of the tasks of peace has taken place in the Catholic church in the GDR" and bemoaned the absence of an office in the church, such as in the Lutheran headquarters, to deal with this question. As a result, the church remains an "impassive observer" of the developments, and the youth are left in an "ethical vacuum."[72]

In the early 1980s, however, the church began to respond to the pressure from society and the laity, and it addressed the issue more directly. A first indication of this was the bishops' criticism (in a pastoral letter) of the "inculcation of hate as destructive of the desire for peace and peace itself."[73] An important stimulus for the church rethinking was the series of lectures by Bishop Wanke of Erfurt in 1982.[74] These lectures, which represent the first systematic treatment of the subject, were circulated widely throughout the GDR and have served as the basis for the church's current position. In them Wanke acknowledged the people's heightened fears of war. He inveighed against "the penetrating defense education" and the pressure upon young people to commit themselves to extended military service in order to gain admission to the university. However, Wanke struck a balanced view rejecting total pacifism and endorsing a balance of military forces as necessary for maintaining the peace. Last, but certainly not least, was the impetus to greater outspokenness given by Pope John Paul II. During an *ad limina* visit to Rome, the GDR bishops were urged to "answer the questions of peace posed by the youth" and engage in greater exchange of views with the Evangelical churches.[75]

The pope's advice was heeded by the GDR bishops. In November 1982 they issued guidelines to the parishes for dealing with the issue. In January 1983 they issued a major pastoral letter on peace.[76] Prefacing their position by encouraging the faithful that "peace is possible, that war is not inevitable," the bishops reiterated the pope's call for mutual and controlled disarmament and rejected as immoral the use of weapons of mass destruction. They questioned the notion of just war in the era of nuclear weapons but did not reject war outright, particularly "when the rights of the weak must be protected." Regarding specific problems facing the youth in the GDR, they expressed understanding for the "crisis of conscience" facing the youth, and they expressed support for those rejecting military service and respect for those opting for such service. Again they criticized military training in the high schools and the discrimination against those refusing to participate. Although somewhat less critical than the Lutheran church, particularly regarding pacifism and military service, this expression represented a dramatic departure from the Bengsch era: In a public pronouncement the church addressed concerns of society and expressed itself critically on a major political issue.

The reaction of the state was predictably negative.[77] In an attack reminiscent of the 1950s, the official news agency accused "certain officials in the GDR" of "being steered from Rome" and delivering propaganda to the West German media. The state also treated the church coolly in terms of protocol, for example, barely recognizing the naming of Bishop Joachim Meisner of Berlin as cardinal. Indirectly, of course, the GDR, like other bloc states, was attacking the more critical role of Pope John Paul II in the wake of the rise of the Solidarity movement in Poland. In the late 1960s and early 1970s the SED had defined Social Democratic Party (SPD)-led West German détente as the major threat, equating the SPD with "political clericalism," and looked hopefully toward the prospects of the papal Ostpolitik; ironically, by the 1980s the Honecker regime had come full circle to see the Catholic church and Rome as the greater danger.

Modernization in the Catholic Church in the 1980s

The church's newfound voice on the issue of peace reflects a general trend away from the ghetto orientation characteristic of the Bengsch era. The church has begun to define itself in terms of its immediate environment—the socialist society of the GDR—rather than in terms of merely surviving this environment as part of some larger, all-German entity.

This trend was manifest most clearly in the landmark 1986 pastoral letter entitled "Catholic Church in the Socialist State."[78] The letter clearly reflects the mark of Bishop Wanke and his efforts "to spell the gospel in middle-German" in a "secularized, materialist environment."[79] Continuing the "house" metaphor of Spülbeck and Bengsch but altering its import, the bishops described the GDR as a "livable house." More recently, Cardinal Meisner of Berlin went so far as to describe the GDR as a "home for us Christians because Christ lives in it."[80] This clear accent on the GDR not as a hostile environment to be survived but as an opportunity to grow reflects the new, more positive orientation of the church. In this trend it follows, some years later, the reorientation of the Lutheran church.

Despite this new orientation toward their immediate environment, the East German bishops sounded a strong cautionary note regarding relations with the state. In a pastoral letter in 1986 they rejected the idea of "real partnership between church and state" embraced by some leaders in the Lutheran church. The bishops asserted the independence of the church from secular power, which "alien interests" might wish to compromise. The letter highlighted areas of conflict with the state, for example, discrimination against Christians ("Christians do not want a foundation of Christian cement, but equal rights in the house"), conflicts of worldview, and state efforts to recruit Christians. Although the bishops reiterated some familiar stands, such as rejection of membership in the SED and participation in the *Jugendweihe*, they advocated an openness to dialogue with the state on the issues separating them and admitted that the church has a "political dimension."

An extremely important factor in the church's reorientation is a new recognition that "practical materialism" is a greater threat in the modern GDR than the double diaspora of the regime's atheistic orientation and the Protestant majority. Bishop Wanke particularly has emphasized the need to "express solidarity" with those inside and outside the church and to employ innovative approaches to reach the common man. Pope John Paul II gave this view added credibility during the recent *ad limina* visit of the GDR bishops to Rome. During that visit he criticized scientific atheism but focused most attention on the need to combat the generic, daily materialism of modern society.[81]

Another dimension of modernization in the church has been greater interest in ecumenical ties with the Lutheran church in the GDR. To be sure, pragmatic cooperation (e.g., sharing of churches in the wake of wartime destruction) has long been practiced at the grass-roots level. In the wake of Vatican II certain bureaucratic interfaces with the Protestants had been introduced. But at the highest levels of the episcopate there was little interest in closer ties, reflecting the double diaspora orientation. Indeed, the episcopate had squelched a grass-roots newsletter promoting ecumenical communication in the GDR.[82] However, with the encouragement of the pope, the bishops have recently stressed a new openness to Protestants in the face of the practical materialism they both confront.[83] Again, Bishop Wanke has been at the forefront of this new openness. Logistical cooperation has deepened, as demonstrated during the 1983 Luther year and the 1987 *Katholikentag* in Dresden. Despite this rapprochement, the Catholics do not seem inclined to seek the same "partnership" with the state that the Lutherans have attempted. For example, the episcopate has held only one summit with Honecker, in 1981, in contrast with the Lutheran meetings with Honecker in 1978, 1985, and 1988; the low visibility accorded it by the church indicates a continued ambivalence about the benefits of such public summitry.

Another manifestation of the modernization is greater interest in public assemblies with high visibility.[84] In 1987 the church held its first *Katholikentag* in the GDR; it was attended by 100,000 persons. Although the entire event was controlled closely by the Berlin Bishops' Conference, and the laity played a greatly reduced role when compared with Protestant church conventions or West German Catholic conventions, it represents a major breakthrough when measured against the tradition of the ghetto church. By downplaying the West German presence, the *Katholikentag* demonstrated a new self-confidence in the East German Catholic community. On a limited scale, such activities as the press conference of bishops and Cardinal Ratzinger's question-and-answer session offered greater opportunities for the expression of opinion in the church.

Regarding the role of priests in the church, however, the church remains quite conservative. It has maintained strong opposition to altering the celibacy requirement and has criticized other churches, such as the Dutch church, which have supported such liberalization. Bengsch, responding to the shortage of priests, did engineer a reform introducing lay deacons in the 1960s.[85] Bengsch's sanction against voting participation by priests has been lifted, resulting in greater political participation. The hierarchical structures, however, remain largely intact.

Finally, on social issues such as abortion and birth control the church retains its traditional opposition. It sharply criticized the liberalization of abortion laws in 1965 and 1971, arguing that "when a society eliminates the legal protection of developing life, it makes unbelievable its efforts for a true humanism."[86] Given the large numbers of letters by individual Catholics protesting the state's liberalization policy, it is likely that the bishops were speaking authoritatively for their parishioners. The Berlin Ordinarien Conference even criticized the Fulda Bishops' Conference for its soft support for the papal encyclical *Humanae vitae* in 1968![87]

Sources of Change in the Church-Regime Relationship

The foregoing description and analysis of the Catholic relationship with the GDR regime reveal a conflictual relationship during the late 1940s and throughout the 1950s resulting from the claims of the regime upon society and goals of social transformation. As a result of the modus operandi between Bengsch and the regime in the 1960s, direct conflict was reduced somewhat internally. Externally, however, conflict increased as a result of the GDR's efforts to attenuate ties between the two Germanys, although the church's link to the Vatican served to moderate this conflict. The 1970s saw reduced pressure on the church following a partial resolution of the inter-German question. In the post-Bengsch era of the 1980s the church has modernized to a certain extent, accepting the socialist environment and becoming more active politically but altering internal structures little.

What factors seem to be responsible for the changing relationship? One factor that does *not* explain these changes is any collapse in church adherence. Unlike the Lutheran church, which suffered dramatic declines in membership and the consequent financial and morale problems, adherence to the Catholic church has remained relatively strong. Roughly 25 percent of members attend church, much higher than the 1–2 percent in the Lutheran church.[88] Since it was never a *Volkskirche* (people's church, or national church) like the Lutheran church, it has not suffered the same loss of prestige.

The present analysis indicates that another factor with little impact on the changed relationship is the grass-roots dissenters, whether "progressives" or "critical Catholics." The progressive associations, such as the Berlin Conference of European Christians, the Christian Democratic Union, and the National Front, have had little success in attracting Catholic support and cannot be compared in their role or effectiveness with the "patriotic priests' associations" in other socialist bloc countries. Dissenters in such grass-roots groups as the Action Group Halle have likewise enjoyed little resonance in the church. The tight control of the hierarchy and the sense of diaspora have limited the appeal of these critics of the hierarchy. They have remained largely a phenomenon of intellectuals. Comparisons with the "basis groups" in Hungary are inaccurate.

Several factors seem to explain the changes in the relationship. First, changing priorities of the regime seem to have dictated varying policies. The primacy of delimitation from West Germany, for example, has varied over time. Honecker's accommodation of relatively intense inter-German ties played an important role in the decline of diocesan borders as an issue of conflict with the church. As a consequence of this accommodation, Honecker sought greater accord with the churches, both Lutheran and Catholic, in order to limit the regime's vulnerability to the increased exposure to the West. Thus the Honecker regime by and large ceased its efforts begun in the 1950s and 1960s to curtail the social presence of the churches.

Another factor explaining the changes is the example set by the Lutheran church in its process of accommodation to the GDR as environment. Although the Catholic church still accentuates the differences in approach to the regime, the fact is that the Lutherans' internal church debate about their role in socialism served as an ersatz debate for the Catholics as well. The current positions of Wanke and the other bishops regarding the "GDR as home" reveal striking similarity to those of the Lutherans, such as Bishops Schönherr and Krusche.

Of course, a generational change in leadership was necessary for these arguments to become authoritative in the Catholic church. In the centralized Catholic church, the effect of the passing of individual church leaders cannot be underestimated, particularly one such as Cardinal Bengsch, whose death in 1979 ended an almost twenty-year tenure. The current leadership has matured under conditions of socialism, and its more system-immanent orientation flows from this experience with the system.

The centralized nature of the Catholic church suggests another significant factor in the changing relationship: the Vatican. The anticommunist stance of the Vatican in the 1950s certainly reinforced the attitude of the local hierarchy in the GDR. The more conciliatory approach of Pope John XXIII, and particularly the Ostpolitik under Pope Paul VI, significantly affected the relationship, particularly on foreign policy. Unlike in other Eastern bloc countries, the Ostpolitik of the Vatican in the early 1970s cannot be said to have come at the expense of the East German church. Indeed, given the liberal currents in the Western church, the greater separation from the West German hierarchy may have been desirable from the perspective of the conservative episcopate in the 1970s. It certainly met with opposition in the West German church, and this opposition was strong enough to limit the concessions made by the Vatican. The evidence strongly suggests that the ties to the Vatican have strengthened the position of the East German church, particularly in comparison with the Lutheran church.

Finally, the church's recent emergence from political hibernation seems to reflect the broader forces at work in GDR society, forces beyond the control of either the church or the regime. The rise of the peace movement was a function of international developments and an increasing disaffection in GDR society, particularly among the youth. State policy and the political structures inhibiting dissent have led disaffected elements to seek other forums for expressing such dissent. Given the lack of glasnost in the GDR until recently, it is no surprise that the Catholic church should be challenged to reevaluate its traditional inner-directed orientation and political abstinence.

Despite the changes that have occurred in the Catholic stance toward the communist regime, the church still represents a largely traditional value system. If modern structures are defined by self-regulating mechanisms and feedback channels, the structures of the church are relatively unmodern. Exits by Catholics to Lutheran forums, although modest in dimension, seem to have been more effective than internal dissent in bringing about revision in the church's stance. This has hardly been a hindrance to developing a modus vivendi with a regime which claims to arrogate modernism for itself. Indeed, the very contrast between modern and traditional may have facilitated this accommodation; as the case of Czechoslovakia attests, the Christian-Marxist dialogue is hardly an automatic prescription for harmonious church-state relations. This arrangement might have continued undisturbed had it not been for changes affecting both church and state, including increasing disaffection, generational changes in the hierarchy, and a more critical line from the Vatican. Whether the church will modernize internally by facilitating greater input from the grass roots or rely on the appeal of tradition and authority in an era of uncertainty and flux in the Soviet bloc remains an intriguing question that future developments will answer.

FACT SHEET

The Catholic Church in East Germany

Current strength of the church

- 1.05 million faithful (1987)
- 1,300 priests (130 in orders)
- 6 bishops (two full bishops, four apostolic administrators)
- 2,500 nuns
- 7,347 total employees

Number of churches and church facilities

- 1,037 churches
- 11 seminaries/retreat houses
- 330 convents and monasteries
- 34 church hospitals
- 11 nursing homes
- 107 old-age homes
- 44 orphanages/homes for the handicapped
- 80 kindergartens
- 1 theological faculty (seminary in Erfurt)

Chief news organs

- *Tag des Herrn*, Leipzig (established 1951; 100,000 copies)
- *St. Hedwigsblatt*, East Berlin (established 1953; 25,000 copies)

Underground religious publications

- *Action Group Halle* (irregular papers since 1966)

"Progressive" organizations

- Berlin Conference of European Christians, since 1964
- *Begegnung*, monthly journal for "progressive" Catholics

Primates since 1945

- Bishop Konrad Cardinal von Preysing (1945–50)
- Bishop Wilhelm Weskamm (1951–56)

Bishop Julius Cardinal Doepfner (1957–61)
Bishop Alfred Cardinal Bengsch (1961–79)
Bishop Joachim Cardinal Meisner (1980–88)
Bishop Georg Sterzinsky (1989–present)

Sources: Eugen Voss, ed., *Die Religionsfreiheit in Osteuropa* (Zollikon, Switz.: Glaube in der Zweiten Welt Verlag, 1984), p. 84; *Keston News Service*, no. 279 (July 9, 1987), p. 19; and *Frankfurter Allgemeine* (May 11, 1989), p. 14.

5

The Catholic Church in Poland, 1944–1989

Vincent C. Chrypinski

The end of World War II brought Poland's Roman Catholic church face to face with a new challenge fraught with direct and oblique dangers—the encounter of Catholicism with Marxism in a state ruled by the Communist party and within a society undergoing rapid socioeconomic changes. Examination of the situation after over forty years of enforced coexistence reveals three main areas that have affected the fortunes of the church: the support of the Catholic community, the institutional strength of the church, and relations with the state. This chapter starts with a review of the last topic, though it should not be taken as an indication of the predominant importance of that issue.

The Church and the State

There is little doubt that Poland's conversion to Christianity in 966 was greatly motivated by the political considerations of the Polanian ruler, Prince Mieszko.[1] Yet Polish Catholicism did not become the state religion, and by the Middle Ages the Roman Catholic church—undoubtedly reflecting the reformist trend that reached its apex under Gregory VII (1073–85)—was starting to emancipate itself from political power and become a sort of moral check on autocratic rulers. Saint Stanisław of Szczepanów, who defied the king in the name of moral law and suffered death for his sense of duty in 1079,[2] set a model of behavior to be emulated by church leaders.

Thus, despite the church's proclivity to seek the state's protection against the forces of pagan reaction and German attempts to subject the young Polish ecclesiastical organization to the archbishopric of Magdeburg, a distance was established between the spiritual and secular realms. Though the relative position of the church vis-à-vis the state was not uniformly maintained, they remained in equilibrium throughout the ensuing centuries until the partitions in the last decades of the eighteenth century. The balance survived mainly due to external determinants, which, on the whole, favored the independence of the church: first, it was Poland's division into small principalities in the twelfth and thirteenth centuries; later, the peculiarities of the Polish political system, particularized by the elective monarchy and the legislative supremacy of the nobility, helped the church maintain its autonomy. Besides, Polish kings, whose Catholic subjects in the Polish-Lithuanian domain numbered only about half of the total population,[3] were not always inclined to identify themselves or the state with Catholicism.

The loss of Poland's independence caused a fundamental change in the position of the church. Although the situation differed between the sectors of the partitioned country, all three occupying powers, including Catholic Austria (motivated by Josephinism), were anxious to subject the church to governmental controls, and they openly intervened in ecclesiastical affairs. As might be expected, these policies were generally resented, and the hiatus between the church and the state became deeper and more pronounced,[4] notwithstanding papal instructions of 1795 that ordered the hierarchy to cooperate with the occupiers[5] and despite not a few cases of ultraloyal behavior of individual bishops.

In reborn Poland (1918–39) the church enjoyed a privileged position guaranteed by the Constitutions of 1921 and 1935 and by the concordat with the Apostolic See of 1925.[6] Yet there continued to be distance between church and state, and—as some historians who cannot be suspected of pro-church views admit[7]—the relations between the two entities were not always amicable. The reasons for this situation were many, but the "markedly anticlerical temper of the ruling elite"[8] and the support given by Catholics, including many priests and several bishops, to the main opposition force, the National Democratic party,[9] significantly influenced reciprocal attitudes.

There were no Quislings in Poland during World War II, and the occupiers used the same methods of terror and extermination on the clergy that they used against the entire Polish intelligentsia, which was treated as the leadership group of national resistance. Out of 10,017 priests in 1939, no less than 2,647 perished at the hands of Nazi and Soviet executioners or as a result of military operations. It should be noted that Poland was the only German-occupied country where residential bishops were arrested and sent to concentration camps.[10]

It comes as no surprise that the Communists' acquisition of governmental powers in Poland at the end of World War II did not help to close the distance between the church and the state. In fact, the entire postwar period was marked by continuous and mutual tension. Of course, the intensity varied, and spans of sharp and dramatic encounters were followed by spells of tranquility and apparent truce. Characteristically, it was the state's behavior toward Catholicism and the church that determined the nature of each stage. Frequent and abrupt policy changes make it difficult to distinguish aspects basic to the long-term communist strategy from those which expressed only tactical modifications. Under these circumstances, and keeping in mind the hidden input into the state's policy by the Kremlin and other members of the Soviet bloc, long-term policy predictions are very risky, if not entirely impossible.

The tension in church-state relations was by no means accidental; it was the result of several heterogeneous causes, among which two had basic significance. One was the desire of the ruling elite to subordinate Polish society to the exclusive influence of the Communist party (PUWP). Motivated by monistic ambitions and political calculations, the party leaders were bent on the destruction of all autonomous organizations that were obstacles to the realization of their goal. The church, which enjoyed massive popular authority in Poland, was the main object of the communist offensive.

The other important source of strained relations was deeply rooted in the conflicting philosophical doctrines that form the very core as well as the legitimacy of both Catholicism and Marxism-Leninism. Atheism is an inherent part of the materialist worldview, and Polish disciples of Marx and Lenin continue to treat religion as a false and obscurantist ideology which acts as "the opium of the people" and prevents Polish masses from taking part in building socialism.[11] In that context, it was considered the right, even the duty, of the communist leadership to eliminate religion from the people's lives.[12] Attaining this goal was impossible, however, unless the church was either subordinated or its influence undermined, and unless the Communist party became the sole focus of all societal activities. Having at their disposal the entire apparatus of the totalitarian state and enriched by the experience of Soviet mentors, Polish Communists were determined to achieve their goal by resorting to a variety of available methods.

Officially, the religious policy of the Polish state was governed by two highly acclaimed principles:[13] freedom of conscience and religion (*wolność sumienia i wyznania*), and the separation of church and state.[14] Unfortunately, both tenets received in Poland, as they had before in the Soviet Union, an application quite different from the traditional and widely accepted views which ascribed to the state a neutral role in matters of conscience and religion. As might be expected, this peculiar interpretation had far-reaching social and political consequences. In short, the state assumed the right not only to control activities, external as well as domestic, of all confessional organizations and to eliminate religious content from public life, but also to secularize the Polish society.[15] The state's monopolization of mass media, organization of special secularizing machinery, legal regulations, and social policy greatly facilitated the spread of materialistic ideas and antireligious patterns of behavior. Strict censorship and other restrictions imposed on religious publications drastically limited the ability of the church to propagate its own creed, combat the spread of official ideology, and resist communist attempts to secure conversions to a rival way of life.

The hostility of the ruling communists manifested itself throughout the postwar era, even at times when circumstances forced them to abstain from direct assaults on the church. Thus, between 1945 and 1947, when the international situation and awareness of the unfriendly populace compelled the provisional government to adopt amicable pretenses,[16] the church was assailed by the abrogation of the 1925 Concordat, various legislative and administrative measures, bureaucratic chicanery, and naked abuses of power accompanied by virulent attacks in the mass media. It was during this period that the communists started to nurture Catholic splinter groups among the clergy and the laity, of which the most notorious was the Pax Association led by Bolesław Piasecki (1915–79).[17] Similarly, after the 1956, 1970, 1976, and 1980 upheavals, when popular unrest forced the communist leadership to seek the church's help, the authorities did not abandon their hostile posture. It is true that they stopped resorting to open acts of repression, but they continued administrative chicaneries, especially toward priests on the blacklist of activists, and they intensified the policy of financial harassment.[18]

In addition, the regime persisted in its proselytizing efforts by introducing into school programs antireligious subjects disguised under the euphemistic name of "religious knowledge" (*religioznawstwo*). No less significant were steps taken against the Catholic press affiliated with the episcopate. Of 2,776 newspapers and magazines published in Poland in 1986, only thirty-three were Catholic; of fifty-six dailies, none were Catholic because one cannot consider periodicals published by the proregime Pax and Christian Social Association as Catholic. While the average number of issues of all Polish periodicals amounted to 48,871,000 copies, the Catholic share for an average month totaled only 1,200,000 copies. The seriousness of the problem was aggravated by discrimination in the allocation of printing paper. Out of 250,000 tons for all 1986 publications in the country, Catholic publishers received only 3,000 tons, i.e., only 1.2 percent of the total. This amounted to 80 percent of the 1985 allocation, which was already inadequate and, on top of this, not fully delivered. As a result, even *Przegląd*

Katolicki, an organ published by the Warsaw Archdiocese and close to the primate, was faced with the prospect of cutting the number of copies to 38,000, reducing the volume by half, and hoping that the allocated thirty-two tons would allow the publication of thirty issues.[19]

The discussion to this point may now be briefly summarized. The ruling Communists were using the state for the realization of their philosophical, socioeconomic, and political goals. The religious policy of the state was therefore aimed at the total secularization of the Polish society. Since the church was the main obstacle to the achievement of this goal, the authorities were determined to undercut its influence and activities by all means appropriate at the moment. The state's unceasing hostility was most openly expressed, as late as 1978, by a former head of the Office for Religious Affairs, Kazimierz Kąkol, who said: "If we cannot destroy the Church, we shall at least stop it from causing harm."[20] The depth of the rulers' hostility and its pervading influence on the apparatus of the state were brutally demonstrated in 1984 by the grisly murder of Fr. Jerzy Popiełuszko. Proclamations of "outstretched hands" and promises of "normalization" of state-church relations were but tactical turns in long-term strategy. Casual courtesies (e.g., Gierek's visit with Pope Paul VI), compliments (e.g., sending flowers to Cardinal Wyszyński on his seventy-fifth birthday), or public praises (e.g., Jaruzelski's recognition of the church's role in Polish history) did not indicate any change in the fundamental posture of hostility but rather an excuse *pro domo sua* for a temporary abandonment of frontal attacks. It is worth noting that the election of a Polish pope, while decisively tipping the scale in the church's favor, had no visible impact on basically adverse state-church relations, which essentially were determined by society's acceptance of the regime. The weaker the popular support, the more lenient were the attitudes toward the church, and vice versa.

This interpretation of communist religious policy in postwar Poland requires a complementary addendum on the behavior of the church. What was the attitude of bishops and priests toward the new regime? What issues were of special significance for the church? What considerations prompted the church to adopt a particular posture?

Meaningful answers to these questions are possible only when we understand the nature of Catholic doctrine, remember the thousand years of the church's presence in Poland, and take into account the consciousness of the church's leaders, who are fully aware of the role they play in the Polish national life. In addition, of course, we also have to keep in mind the pre-Vatican II position of the church in regard to its role in the contemporary world.

There can be little doubt that the great majority of Catholic clergymen, like their countrymen, regarded the communist regime with reserve and anxiety. Yet, undoubtedly for pragmatic reasons, the church leaders did not refuse business contacts with representatives of the provisional government who started to officiate within their dioceses.[21] Perhaps—as some writers suggest—they preferred a country run by Polish communists to the incorporation of Poland into the Soviet Union.[22] Anyway, in general state officials reported no signs of "reactionary postures" of the clergy, whose main attention was directed toward pastoral and charitable activities and rebuilding war-torn churches.[23]

Preoccupation with daily tasks and a growing awareness of the unfavorable international situation did not prevent the bishops from expressing their concern for domestic developments. Not unexpectedly, some of the episcopate's pronouncements were treated by the ruling communists as overstepping religious bounds and as political partisanship. In particular, party spokesmen raised the issue in connection with two acts of the church hierarchy. The first was Cardinal Hlond's refusal to postpone the reading of a letter from Pope Pius XII. This was to be read in Polish churches on the eve of a national referendum scheduled for June 30, 1946. The referendum was treated by the communists as a test of strength. The papal message was critical of the regime's unilateral abrogation of the 1925 Concordat and called it proof of the communists' hostility to the church. The other act was the episcopate's appeal on September 10, 1946, on the eve of elections to the national parliament (Sejm), urging the people to exercise their duty and vote "only for such persons, lists and election programs which do not oppose Catholic teaching and morality."[24] Clearly, the voters were instructed to cast their ballots for the anticommunist opposition led by Stanisław Mikołajczyk, though neither his nor his party's name was openly mentioned.

A similar, perhaps even more virulent, outcry was raised by the communists in December 1965 after the Polish bishops participating in the last session of the Second Vatican Council sent a letter to the German episcopate inviting its members to take part in the celebrations, in 1966, of Poland's Christian millennium. The courageous message of forgiveness formed the first attempt to bridge the chasm between the two neighboring nations and quell the historical antagonism fed by official propaganda.

While strict separationists might find some justification for communists' accusations in these incidents, one must remember that each fundamental issue raised by the church could be observed from the perspectives of religion and politics, because for the church, politics means "concern for the common good" (*Laborem exercens*, 1981). Clearly, all three cases belong to this category. Clear as well is the fact that the Polish episcopate was unwilling to abandon the Catholics or, indeed, the entire Polish nation, to false guidance and to resign from voicing the moral principles that should permeate not only the life of an individual but of the society as well. Numerous interventions on behalf of exploited workers or political prisoners—some of them in the form of confidential protests to and interventions with the authorities, others in the form of public sermons and pastoral letters—provide manifest indication of the church's "involvement in politics." The solicitude of the episcopate was demonstrated even for Marxists who fell out of favor because they abandoned their former creed or refused to conform to the leadership's dictates.

At the same time, however, the church most emphatically separated itself from direct participation in political battles for the control of the government. Consequently, the bishops ordered their priests not to run for elective offices in the parliament and in local councils and not to accept nominations to administrative positions. While this decision might have been motivated by considerations of the specifically Polish situation, it was a forerunner of later canonical changes of the universal church adopted since Vatican II. Paradoxically, the early decision of the Polish episcopate prohibiting political activities by the priests was interpreted by the communist authorities as a sign of antigovernment posture.[25] Obviously, the communists desired not disengagement of the church from politics but a full endorsement of their political and socioeconomic program and the approval of their day-to-day operations.

As might be expected, the church consistently refused to oblige and give the communists its blessing. However, the church never rejected cooperation when "the common good" was involved. The case of the "recovered territories" as well as the episcopate's stand in the recurrent social crises prove that beyond any doubt.

The refusal of the episcopate to engage actively and openly in political life was not a resignation from exercising the church's prophetic critical role and from expressing the bishops' views on current events, especially when governmental actions impinged on "the dignity and rights of man, in particular on his right to be a subject, to form his own destiny."[26] Because there was no other institution or association in postwar Poland that could perform as a censor of the regime, the church became ipso facto a quasi-political opposition. But the episcopate always insisted that direct political activities belonged to laymen, and as soon as a trace of an independent social force appeared in the shape of the Solidarity movement, the church assumed the position of an intermediary between the society and the government. During the period 1982–May 1989, when Solidarity was banned, the church persisted in its endeavors to be a link between the rulers and the ruled. By the nature of things, the posture of political neutrality was open to partisan interpretation, seldom appreciated, and often bitterly criticized.

While political neutrality did not indicate the church's weakness, the posture of the episcopate vis-à-vis the state was markedly defensive. The strategy resulted, above all, from a deep desire for peace, which was badly needed for the nation and for the church, with both just emerging from the bloodbath of the war and occupations. The search for social harmony was deeply ingrained in the minds of the bishops, whose spiritual formation was shaped by the teaching of the church and its history, which often manifested a willingness to make compromises and concessions. At the same time the episcopate's position gave evidence of the political wisdom and foresight of the bishops, who were able to combine firmness on principles with flexibility on temporal matters. Last, but not least, the strategy was based on hopeful expectations that developments in Poland might follow a different course from that followed in the Soviet Union, Hungary, and Czechoslovakia.[27]

Looking back at the postwar era, one cannot overlook the dominant role of Stefan Cardinal Wyszyński in guiding the course of the church's policy toward the state. He led the church for thirty-two difficult years (1949–81) as the primate of Poland and the chairman of the Conference of the Polish Episcopate. A determined and tenacious man with great faith and courage, he was able to keep the church on the track that was crucial in maintaining its independence, unity, and vitality, and in securing some freedoms for the Poles. Although not all of his actions—from the 1950 agreement to the Jasna Góra sermon of August 1980, in which he appealed to the workers for moderation—gained him general acclaim, ultimately not only his protagonists (e.g., Micewski)[28] but his ideological foes as well (e.g., Kąkol)[29] recognized his greatness and paid him glowing tributes.

Wyszyński's attitude toward the socialist state was not antagonistic, and he wanted to establish some sort of modus vivendi with the communist regime. For this reason, just a few months after assuming the leadership of the church, he approved discussions on a future accord and was the main driving force among the bishops toward its conclusion.[30] Such a stance was not simply tactical ingenuity but also the outcome of a deep conviction—not unlike that of Saint Augustine—that social peace was the necessary precondition for the advancement of religion and the promotion of national interests. Love of the church and love of his homeland were the guiding beacons of all his actions. The Polish people perceived it, and in return bestowed upon the church their faithful affection. And this was the strongest line of the church's defense.

The Church and the Nation

It is a well-recognized fact that a strong bond exists between the Catholic church and the Polish nation. The tie resulted from complex sociocultural and political developments that accompanied the inception and growth of Christianity in Poland. Catholicism sanctioned the country's independence and unity, greatly motivated Polish foreign policy, and injected Polish culture with decidedly universal values—cognitive, aesthetic, and ethical. The close link of Catholicism with the nation and its culture led to the convergence of religious and national consciousnesses, to a unique phenomenon of identifying Polishness through Catholicism.

The church's subordination to three foreign sovereigns in the era of the partitions (1795–1918) and their efforts to undermine the prestige of the church among the masses had little visible effect. The religious life of the people centered on their parishes and their pastors. As before, for peasants, craftsmen, and petty and even middle nobility, religion remained an important element of daily life, and the authority of the priest was, in general, undiminished.

The traditional bond between the church and the Polish people was further strengthened during the nineteenth-century struggles for national liberation and social justice, ideals that found ardent apostles among the clergy, especially the lower ranks. The absence of a "union of the altar with the throne" undoubtedly played an important and beneficial role in unifying lay and clerical elements in the popular resistance against the foreign domination.

The religious sanction accorded the fight for independence, the personal participation of numerous priests in conspiratorial and insurgent activities, and the governmental repressions, particularly severe in the Russian sector, which affected thousands of clergymen (including several bishops), greatly contributed to the creation of a symbiotic "union of the Church and the nation."[31]

In reborn Poland (1918–39), while the church enjoyed a privileged position, an emergent anticlericalism threatened to weaken the unity of the church with the Polish masses.[32] The process, instigated by the spread of liberalism and socialism, was observed also among the villagers, who were greatly influenced by peasant political parties, which, including the right-wing Piast under Wincenty Witos, demonstrated a high degree of anticlerical attitudes. Paradoxically, these postures were rooted in the nineteenth-century involvement of the church in the struggles for independence that gradually drew Polish priests into various cultural and social activities, and eventually into party politics in liberated Poland. Unfortunately, many clergymen saw fit to extend their authority in the religious field to other areas as well. Not unexpectedly, this paternalism met with resistance and caused most of the animosity. The church's opposition to submitting its land estates to the needed agrarian reform added another, and highly emotional, dimension to the anticlerical feelings among the peasantry, especially its younger members. Significantly, the phenomenon almost never had antireligious or anti-Catholic traits.

The outbreak of World War II arrested this ominous development and once again, more than ever before, brought the church and the nation together. Once again the people turned to the church as the source of moral strength, and once again the church demonstrated its outstanding ability to rise to popular expectations.

The era of communist rule over Poland created a situation which the Polish Catholic philosopher Józef Tischner has called "the coercion of choice,"[33] a choice between giving in to secularization or remaining with the church. The great, continuously increasing majority decided to remain faithful to the church.

It is hard to obtain an overall view of the complex mosaic of factors that have helped the church to achieve victory. Mentioning them, one has to keep in mind that in postwar Poland about 95 percent of the people were christened Roman Catholics, and, according to an official 1987 study, 78 percent of those questioned expressed full confidence in the church, putting it above any other institution.

I am inclined to share the view of a noted Polish sociologist, Józef Majka,[34] who ascribed the success of Polish Catholicism in retaining the loyalty of the people to its religious authenticity and its union with national culture. Polish Catholicism has not swerved from preaching the gospel and from announcing the evangelical message of transcendent hope. Avoiding all anathemas and polemics, it gave a constructive presentation of faith by demonstrating the readiness for solidarity and cooperation with all men of goodwill. While not indifferent to changes in the political environment and to socioeconomic transformations, the church never lost sight of the demarcation between the sacred and the profane, and it never became a carrier of political or social ideologies.

In past ages Catholicism acted as a powerful agent in forming the national culture, and it inspired many works in the fields of plastic arts, literature, and music. The church as an institution continuously performed the beneficial role of a patron of cultural endeavors. In the time of the partitions, churches provided a refuge for the Polish language and for Polish cultural traditions, and thus made possible their survival despite hostile attempts at Russification and Germanization.

Under communist rule the church again became the defender of the national culture against attacks aiming at eliminating, especially from history and literature, all references to Catholicism and the church. By falsifying Polish history and pillaging Polish literature, the authorities expected to clear the ground for an easier acceptance of a secular culture cleansed of all religious attributes. These attempts found eager executors among official religiologists bent on undermining the church's prestige among the masses.[35]

As might be expected, the church fought openly and courageously against Marxist aims and stressed the need for the continuation of cultural endeavors of past generations. The argumentation, not new for Catholic circles,[36] took into consideration not only the unbroken sequence of Catholic tradition in Poland but of the entire Polish cultural heritage as well.

The church's resistance to the wholesale repudiation of traditional values in all cultural matters gained support from the group of nonbelievers, some of them professed atheists, for whom—as Leszek Kołakowski expressed it later—"this rationalist ideal may seem not only naïve but dangerous as well."[37] Afterward, when this cluster became attracted to Catholicism by the church's defense of freedom, many of its members became practicing Catholics.

While taking a stand on the issue of human rights, the church remained on its "own age-long terrain of Christianity,"[38] and the Polish episcopate has been active in the defense of civil liberties since the early years of communist rule over Poland.[39] The posture of the hierarchy became especially strong in the 1970s and 1980s with the spontaneous growth of popular opposition to the regime. Characteristically, the bishops supported not only the struggle for religious freedom but the fight against all forms of coercion imposed by individuals, social groups, or governments. This position, hailed also by the secular Left,[40] undoubtedly increased the prestige of the church and further cemented its close bonds with the masses.

Nor is that all. There were other sources of the people's growing allegiance to the church. Some of them are very evident and easy to identify, others are less visible, and their effects have grown gradually over time.

The election of the Polish pope and his pilgrimages to Poland certainly belong in the first category. The unexpected elevation of a countryman to the throne of Saint Peter became for Poles not only a source of pride and satisfaction but also a powerful stimulant of religious renewal that was especially manifest among the young,[41] and also noticeable even among members of the Communist party. The three papal journeys to Poland (1979, 1983, and 1987), though different in scope and consequences, were in all cases like national plebiscites in which the people overwhelmingly demonstrated their loyalty and dedication to the church.

Another momentous factor in mobilizing the masses for the church was the pastoral care of the clergy and the religious orders. More on this subject will be said later, but I should say here that the shape of Polish religiosity and the affinity of the Polish people with the church would be much weaker if not for the activities of priests, monks, and nuns. Their resolve and diligence not only animated traditional parish-centered devotionalism but also led to the increased involvement of individuals in the life and work of the entire church.

There is no doubt that the personal attitude of Cardinal Wyszyński and his ecclesiological concept of the "church of the nation" exercised a powerful influence on the direction of religious activities. Although in his mind the church and the nation were not identical, there existed between them a relationship similar to the one between body and soul.[42] He saw the role of the church as serving the nation, but he readily admitted that the church was also a beneficiary of the close relationship with the nation.[43]

Last, the influence of the Catholic intelligentsia also should be underlined here. The backbone of the group was formed by members and sympathizers of the Znak movement, a loose federation of five clubs of Catholic intelligentsia (Warsaw, Kraków, Wrocław, Toruń, and Poznań),[44] editorial boards of three Catholic periodicals (*Tygodnik Powszechny*,[45] *Znak*, and *Więź*) and, between 1967 and 1976, the Center for Documentation and Social Studies (ODISS). Znak originated during the "Polish October" of 1956 and gained the endorsement of both church and communist authorities, who gave it a small parliamentary representation of five deputies (out of 458).

Znak was not a homogeneous body, and, despite the concurrence of views on basic issues of Christian ethics, there existed marked differences with regard to ideology, aspirations, and modes of behavior. The diversities were crystallized around three centers, namely *Tygodnik Powszechny*, *Więź*, and ODISS. The most visible distinctions manifested themselves in divergent attitudes toward political involvement, with *Tygodnik Powszechny* retaining a "minimalist" position, while the other two clusters expressed more willingness for working side by side with the communists in the mainstream of national life.

In matters of religion, Znak promoted "open Catholicism" with its freer and deeper search for an adequate perception of the Christian message for the contemporary world. During Vatican II the group displayed enthusiasm for the conciliar concept of *aggiornamento* and, disregarding the actual situation, urged the prompt reform of the "conservative" church in Poland. The contributions of Znak members to the intellectual foundations of Faith had a visible effect on slowing down secularization and attracting to the church a substantial segment of Polish intellectuals who in the early postwar era cherished illusions about the blessings of the new political system.

The account presented above would be incomplete without mention of the impact exercised by the declining appeal of communist claims. The basic assumptions of Marxist ideology, such as "equality," "end of exploitation," "social control," etc., which originally did mobilize some support for the regime, fell victims to the despotic whims of the rulers and the soulless officiating of the bureaucracy. The outcome was a pervasive blow to the expectations of abundance, happiness, and freedom that the communists promised on assuming political control over Poland. Quite obviously, the failures contributed to the perseverance of what Marxists call "religiogenic conditions"[46] for the increase of religious beliefs and for the strengthening of the church.

The enumeration of the strong bonds between the church and the nation in Poland makes it necessary to consider their implications for Polish Catholicism. Without attempting a sociological analysis of the phenomenon, which would be out of place here, one can summarize at least the highlights and indicate their effects. Recall that the invigoration of traditional ties occurred under the conditions of communist assault on the "common good" of the nation, of which religion and the church were considered by most Poles inseparable elements. In order to defend these values, Poles participated en masse in religious practices,[47] openly demonstrated by symbols and rituals their allegiance to the church, and made generous contributions for the needs of the church, especially for the construction of new church buildings.

The situation led to increased manifestations of Christian morality, such as brotherhood, compassion, forbearance, and cooperation among the people. It also contributed to fuller awareness of and greater respect for human dignity, civil rights, social justice, and solidarity among all countrymen. In order not to be misleading, however, I must point out the "other side of the coin," as evidenced by the plague of alcoholism, the high level of abortions and divorces, as well as the abhorrent lack of labor discipline. While many of these manifestations can be ascribed to prevailing socioeconomic conditions, their existence indicates a very urgent need for greater involvement of the church in combating these problems, which bear grave consequences for the national well-being.

In addition, there also exist certain less apparent undercurrents whose developments might have a great impact on the future relationship of the church with the people in Poland. It is not at all surprising that these trends manifest themselves mostly among young intellectuals. One tendency, fairly strong and dangerous, discloses itself in the form of "selective religiosity." Its essence consists of an individual scrutiny of the entire doctrine of Catholicism as conveyed by tradition and supported by the authority of the church. Only some dogmas and some moral principles are accepted, while others are ignored or rejected. Religious practices are neglected, and those performed are chosen on the basis of personal preferences and without any consistency. The authority of the church is replaced by personal legitimization of Faith and by individual justification of the professed worldview. Religion becomes a matter of private selection.[48]

Another trend, of great promise for the qualitative betterment of Polish Catholicism, remains closely associated with the church and follows the Catholic theological creed for both hereafter and here and now. Those within this category have a dynamic relationship with the church and are vitally interested in its religious and social activities. However, they do not hesitate to express their criticism of certain traditions and current practices. They seek to deepen their knowledge about the teaching of the church and treat religion as a value which not only enriches subjective experiences but also regulates human behavior. Their view of religious practices is determined by their effects on the deepening of the relationship with God and with other men, and by the ways religious practices contribute to ennobling men's conduct in daily affairs.

While this current tendency encompasses only about 30 percent of all believers,[49] it found expression in some very effective coordinated actions of such groups as the Oasis (Light and Life), the charismatic movement, and other assemblies of religious renewal. The first, in particular, has become an integral part of Polish Catholic vitality. Initiated in the mid-1950s by Fr. Franciszek Blachnicki, Oasis conducts a great variety of activities such as prayer meetings, retreats, and summer camps which, despite governmental harrassment, have attracted thousands of participants, mainly high-school seniors and university students. As a result of their growing perception of doctrinal matters as well as their increasing awareness of the problems of the church, they are becoming a Catholic intellectual elite with a great potential for enriching Polish Catholicism and improving its ability to meet the challenges presented by the unknown future to the traditionally monolithic relationship between the church and the nation.

The existence of the two trends mentioned above warrants an inference. Despite the likelihood of their equal growth, it may be assumed that the dynamism and the missionary zeal of the second current, as compared with the rather withdrawn and closeted nature of the first, will exercise a greater impact on the complex processes by which the new relationships between the church, the nation, and the state will be shaped. Of course, a significant role, perhaps decisive, in the formation of future dispositions will be played by the church as an ecclesiastical organization.

The Institutional Church

On the whole, it seems that the church in Poland is equal to the challenges that the future might bring. Its organizational structure is broad and strong and well adapted to the expansion of the country in the west and north.[50] Poland is divided into twenty-seven dioceses, of which two —Gniezno and Warsaw—although not physically contiguous, are joined in a personal union under the primate of Poland, who resides in Warsaw. Dioceses come in all shapes and sizes. At present the biggest in territorial extent is the diocese of Warmia, which embraces 7.8 percent of the area of the country (24,519 square kilometers), while the smallest is that of Lubaczów, with only 1,810 square kilometers, i.e., 0.6 percent of Poland's territory. The archdiocese of Kraków contains 2,315,000 Catholics, while at the other extreme again lies Lubaczów with only 90,000 believers. The proportion of Catholics to the rest of the population ranges from 100 percent in Lubaczów to 52.3 percent in Drohiczyn, while in seventeen dioceses it reaches over 95 percent.

The contours, sizes, and contents of Polish dioceses were formed by accidents of history and the military vicissitudes of World War II, which moved the Polish borders to the west, causing the loss of about 94,000 square kilometers in the east and the gain of half that area in the west and north. As a result, some new dioceses were added, some were lost, and some were partitioned. This situation, only partially rectified in the "recovered territories," calls for reorganization, which is still justified by the huge postwar population movement. Although not much is known on the subject, recently Bishop Ignacy Tokarczuk of Przemyśl suggested an increase to forty dioceses.[51]

Each diocese is subdivided into a number of deaneries and parishes. Most of these units are found in the Wrocław Archdiocese, which contains 48 deaneries and 587 parishes. It is worth noting that the organizational network underwent considerable expansion not only in the "recovered territories," where before World War II the Catholic church was rather weak and the influx of the Polish believers very strong, but also in old Polish dioceses that between the two world wars already had witnessed dramatic improvements of their organizational structure. Thus, for instance, the Przemyśl Diocese increased the number of parishes from 352 in 1938 to 522 in 1982, and that in Katowice from 197 to 358.

The total number of Polish parishes in 1980 amounted to 7,167, of which 5,843 were located in villages and towns with less than 10,000 inhabitants. Only 1,324 parishes were found in cities with over 10,000 inhabitants.[52] Since the majority of the Polish population now lives in cities (18,034,000 compared to 17,014,000 in villages and towns), the distribution of parishes is highly disproportionate (18.46 percent versus 81.54 percent). The imbalance is accentuated still more by the structural relocation of people from villages and small towns into bigger urban areas. Since the cities could not accommodate all newcomers within their old borders (where churches built in past centuries were located), the massive overflow was directed to new housing complexes constructed in suburban fields where no sacral buildings existed.

On the average, a parish in 1980 served 4,890 people, but the regional differences were very substantial, ranging from 2,296 in Przemyśl Diocese to 16,800 in Łódź Diocese. In addition to Łódź, an urgent need for readaptation of the parish network to the redistribution of the population existed also in the dioceses of Warsaw and Lublin. In Łódź, Lublin, and Białystok one parish provided care for 26,000 people on the average. In Warsaw the situation was somewhat better, and the average figure was 20,000. But the averages did not reflect the huge diversity amongst big-city parishes. For instance, in Warsaw the smallest parish (Saint Vincent Pallotti) served only 2,000 people, while the biggest (Saint Michael's) served 90,000 inhabitants.

It was estimated in 1980[53] that it would be necessary to create 734 new parishes in urban centers with over 10,000 dwellers; 76 of them should be located in Warsaw and 52 in Łódź, the two biggest Polish cities. At the present population level, the additions would increase the percentage of parishes in this category to 26.06 percent. The project envisaged the accomplishment of this goal within ten years. But the creation of new parishes required the building of new churches.

The necessity for construction of new temples was aggravated by the fact that many of the existing parishes were using provisional structures such as former movie houses, meeting halls, cemetery chapels, workshops, private homes, and even beer halls (Saint Gerard in Gliwice). Although it was not known how many parishes were in this unfortunate situation, it was not a rare phenomenon. For instance, in the city of Sosnowiec seven of sixteen parishes did not have real churches. The fast-developing town of Stalowa Wola in the Przemyśl Diocese had one small wooden church transported from the Sandomierz Forest. Altogether over one hundred sacral buildings in this diocese were of a temporary nature.[54]

The painful delay in the construction program was caused primarily by the hostile attitude of the government, whose permission was needed to establish new parishes and build churches. The well-known case of Nowa Huta—which had been built as a "new socialist" (i.e., churchless) city, but where local Catholics simply built a church themselves—clearly demonstrates the unwillingness of the authorities to recognize the legitimate requests of the church. As a result of such a negative posture, between 1945 and 1970 only 327 churches were built and another twenty-five started. Some of them, especially in the Przemyśl Diocese, were erected without officially required permits. Under the pressure of social tensions in the Gierek era, the situation improved somewhat, and between 1971 and 1980 the government issued 741 authorizations for construction or renovation of churches and chapels. In 1981 another 331 licenses were granted; and in 1982 the authorities accepted the four-year plan calling for the construction of 304 big objects (over 600 square meters) and 300 smaller ones.[55] Among these, only 283 were permits for new churches, while the rest applied to catechetic points, cloisters, and living quarters.

The growth, especially since 1976, was truly uncommon and it went some way toward meeting the objectives of the church. Undoubtedly the moderation of governmental attitudes was due to a highly explosive tension in the country, which forced the regime to make concessions to the church in order to get the church's help in calming the political storm. Not surprisingly, the bishops were not reluctant to accept the permits, which they had sought in vain in previous years.

Unfortunately, it seems that the rulers had second thoughts about their largess. A disquieting indicator of their change of heart was an article published in 1985 in a weekly reflecting the attitudes of the ruling circle.[56] Its author argued that the expansion was not only higher than in the rest of Europe and went beyond Polish needs, but he also imputed that its moral and economic consequences were detrimental to national interests. According to him, behind the church's drive lurk nonreligious, secular, often political aspirations to reach areas of social life beyond the traditional scope of the church's activities. He bemoaned the trend and indicated that the extension of pastoral care into professional, cultural, artistic, recreational, and other fields will lead to the desacralization of churches. In addition to his apprehension about the danger of ethical deviation, the critic deplored the financial burden imposed by the building of churches. The burden rests not on the believers alone, mostly the poorest citizens, but on the entire society, which—it may be assumed—has to suffer housing shortages because building resources are directed toward the construction of temples.[57] While admitting that some sacral buildings were realized thanks to hard currency aid from abroad, he concentrated on the assistance rendered by the Catholic organizations in West Germany, which, he claimed, were motivated by anticommunist and revanchist intentions. He ended with an ominous warning that further development of the infrastructure of pastoral care will create a hazard of new conflicts that might equal those of the turbulent past.

Anybody who reads the hazy and truth-stretching argumentation of the article is bound to come to two conclusions. The first is that some Communists were greatly concerned with the future of planned secularization, whose crawling tempo was unlikely to increase when confronted with an expansive growth of pastoral activities. Obviously, they were still toying with the idea of pushing the church back within four walls. The second is that these people were not averse to the notion of a new confrontation with the church and were possibly already giving serious consideration to the pros and cons of a renewed offensive. One of the factors they had to take into account was the posture of the Polish clergy.

The apex of the Polish clergy is formed by the episcopate composed of three cardinals (Józef Glemp, the primate of Poland and the archbishop metropolitan of Gniezno and Warsaw; Franciszek Macharski, archbishop metropolitan of Kraków; and Henryk Gulbinowicz, archbishop metropolitan of Wrocław), three archbishops (Jerzy Stroba, archbishop metropolitan of Poznań; Bronisław Dąbrowski, secretary of the Polish episcopate; and Jerzy Ablewicz, ordinary of the Tarnów Diocese), and almost one hundred bishops, of whom twenty-two are in charge of individual dioceses, the rest serving as their auxiliaries. The average age of the prelates is a little over sixty, with Jan Czerniak, auxiliary bishop of Gniezno, born in 1906, at one end of the scale, and Piotr Skucha, auxiliary bishop of Kielce, born in 1946, at the other. The average age of diocesan bishops is slightly higher than sixty.

While more than thirty of these prelates were consecrated and eleven were appointed to head dioceses since Cardinal Glemp became the primate of Poland in 1981, more than one-half of all hierarchs and more than one-half of diocesan bishops were inducted when the church's leadership rested with the late Cardinal Wyszyński. Interestingly, all of them were nominated after 1956, i.e., after the primate's imprisonment (1953–56), during which he critically evaluated the behavior of his contemporary confreres who—he believed—had "forsaken" him.[58] In these circumstances it may not be unusual that Wyszyński sought above all else unblemished reputation and steadfastness in matters of Faith and allegiance in candidates for high offices. It is also highly probable that they shared his view on the perils menacing the church, an assumption that some critics[59] have described as the source of the "besieged fortress" mentality that left hurtful imprints on the Polish church in the form of authoritarianism, poor personnel selection, and distrust of intellectuals.

Every criticism contains a grain of truth, and an observer inclined to look for faults can surely find some in the stewardship of Cardinal Wyszyński. At the same time, however, one cannot overlook facts that put a fuller light on the accusations mentioned above. Despite the besieged fortress mentality, every major problem facing the church was debated at the episcopate's plenary conferences, in which all bishops participated and freely expressed their opinions. Decisions always reflected the majority views, and there was no case of the primate overriding the majority. As to the personnel, it is enough to recall the words of John Paul II, who publicly stated that there would be no Polish pope without Cardinal Wyszyński.

Although Cardinal Glemp is sometimes criticized for his behavior, the future will certainly show that Wyszyński's choice for his successor was fully justified. Finally, Wyszyński kept lay intellectuals at bay not because of some innate loathing but because he was afraid that their uncritical eagerness to introduce Vatican II reforms would bring a crisis to the traditional religiosity of the Polish masses. The primate did not fear highly educated bishops. A great majority of the prelates consecrated during his term of office had, like himself, doctorates from Polish or foreign universities. Also, his efforts on behalf of the Catholic University of Lublin speak eloquently against the insinuations of anti-intellectual bias.

There is little doubt that in terms of moral and educational standards elevations to the episcopate are currently following the pattern established under Cardinal Wyszyński. It seems, however, that most of the recent promotions have been given to professors of seminaries who have been instrumental in shaping the postures of the lower clergy and who enjoy the respect of their former pupils.

As of October 1987[60] there were 17,726 diocesan and 5,706 monastic priests in Poland. Their distribution throughout the country is not even, ranging from between 8 and 9.6 priests per ten thousand population in the southeast corner of the country (dioceses of Tarnów and Przemyśl) down to 2.8 in the voivodship of Zielona Góra (diocese of Górzow, located on the western Polish border), and 2.9 in the city of Łódź. The ages of priests range from below twenty-five years to over seventy years (circa 9 percent), with the largest group between thirty-one and thirty-five years (circa 23 percent), followed closely by priests between thirty-six and forty (over 21 percent).[61] The annual loss of about three hundred priests,[62] as well as the growing size of the population and of pastoral activities, are met by the constant influx of new candidates for the priesthood, whose number grew from 803 in 1971 to 1,755 in 1982.[63] The trend appears unchanged, and the number of first-year students in diocesan seminaries in October 1987 amounted to 1,231, and in monastic seminaries to 645.[64]

Unfortunately, the growth of priestly vocations in Poland, a phenomenon unique when compared to other Catholic countries, has not received enough scholarly attention, and there is a marked dearth of recent and comprehensive studies on the subject. The pioneering attempts of Rev. Józef Majka, then the head of the Institute of Sociology of Religion at the Catholic University of Lublin, and of Dr. Tadeusz M. Jaroszewski from the Institute of Religiology at the WSNS (a sort of party university) found very few followers.

Available information indicates the existence of several basic factors influencing vocations.[65] Here belong such elements as family and social environment, the influence of active Catholic groups, and the personality and deportment of known priests. The inducement of social advancement, which played a very important role in attracting village boys before World War II, is now negligible. Yet the rural areas, especially along the Carpathian Mountains, still provide the majority of young seminarians, while the sons of workers, mostly from traditionally religious families of the Silesia, Opole, and Częstochowa regions, form another 30 percent plus of the new generation of priests, thus putting a question mark on the Marxist thesis that only peasantry can assure the inflow of vocations. On the other hand, the offspring of intelligentsia comprise only about 13.5 percent of the candidates for priesthood.

The alumni of Polish seminaries are faithful to the church and appreciate the organizational authority and hierarchy, which they learn to respect as a natural arrangement of the brotherly community. The education serves them well, and attempts, planned or spontaneous, to disrupt the bond of unity between the lower clergy and the episcopate have proved fruitless. Admittedly, during the Stalinist period the regime used "carrot and stick" tactics to create a cluster of "patriotic priests" who were to act as a Trojan horse within the Catholic community. While the government-controlled press boasted of three to four thousand members of the group, a careful Radio Free Europe count revealed only seventy-seven activists in 1953.[66] The rest were passive, and the whole scheme proved to be a failure. It is true that some remnants of the regime's machinations still congregate around a charitable organization, Caritas (taken over by the regime in 1950 and only returned to the church in 1989), published a weekly newspaper (*Myśl Społeczna*), and periodically bring before the public melancholy recollections,[67] but their influence on other priests is practically nil. The same can be said about the monthly *Ancora*, issued since 1973 by the secretive Polish Movement for Conciliar Renewal with the transparent purpose of slandering the Polish episcopate for delaying the *aggiornamento* of the church.

Unlike the fraudulent and coerced actions of the "patriotic priests," an incident that took place at a meeting of clergy of the Warsaw Archdiocese appears to have been genuine. On December 7, 1982, in the presence of about three hundred priests, several participants questioned Cardinal Glemp's behavior in the wake of the military coup of 1981. One of them expressed anxiety that the episcopate concluded a pact with General Jaruzelski;[68] another accused the primate of acting "against the nation." Cardinal Glemp reacted to the charges with visible bitterness and suggested that priests should not be swayed like "journalists and politicians" by occasional statements, but that they should always keep in mind the spiritual role of the church and remember that the church is not an instrument "to change political systems."

Against the background of this controversy it is timely to recall that the Polish church has never lacked priests who dared to stand up against the authority of bishops and question the specific applications of moral principles made by the hierarchy. Piotr Ściegienny (1801–99) and Stanisław Stojałowski (1845–1911), both radical social reformers, are cases in point.[69] It is doubtful, however, whether these stances represented the views of many in the priestly community. In any case, a great majority of Polish clergymen preferred to hold to the traditional discipline of their calling. In addition, and especially in the present circumstances, even the least-sophisticated priests appreciate the importance of unity. Hence, perhaps agonizing between impulses of the heart and dictates of reason, they follow the line determined by the episcopate.

Pastoral care, like all other activities of the church in Poland, is coordinated by the Conference of the Episcopate, which created for this purpose a special commission, headed by an auxiliary of the Warsaw Archdiocese Bishop Władysław Miziołek.[70] This body cooperates with other related committees such as those for the family, mass media, ecumenism, students, farmers, etc. It is composed of bishops and priests, diocesan and monastic, and is systematically assisted by the pastoral institutes existing at the Catholic University of Lublin and at the Papal Theological Faculty in Wrocław. Laymen are employed by the commission only occasionally as experts for particular problems, but they are on the staff of both institutes.

As might be expected, the liturgical and sacramental ministry forms the main concern of Polish priests, who devote about 40 percent of their time to these activities. Next on their list is religious education of schoolchildren, which is conducted in 22,218 catechetical points. In this work, which occupies about one-fifth of their pastoral work (400–500 hours annually), priests are aided by almost three thousand nuns and over two thousand lay instructors.[71] The rest of their time is consumed by visitations of hospitals, nursing homes, and abodes of parishioners (traditional after-Christmas *kolenda*), organization of mass pilgrimages, and work with small communities, which range from disabled children (*muminki*) to the creative intelligentsia. And priests, of course, especially pastors, are extensively concerned with building churches and with massive charitable and protective functions.

It appears reasonable to expect that in these circumstances the priests would bring more laypersons into their activities. This has not been the case, however, although the process of change is already noticeable. The reasons for the small amount of progress are complex. On one hand, there exist legitimate causes for the reticence of the priests. They are overworked and afraid that, at least in the beginning, involvement of outsiders will invoke additional burden of instruction and supervision. Especially in the cities they do not know their parishioners well, and hostile attempts at infiltration put them on guard and restrict their initiatives. The fact that almost all laypersons are employed by the state also acts as a restrictive factor. On the other hand, even some priests—and this is greatly to their credit—ascribed the low participation of laymen to the sui generis "clericalism" of the clergy, who are unwilling to grant laypeople greater participation and wider autonomy in the affairs of the church.[72] Undoubtedly the critics hope that through their views the problem can be better understood and appropriate measures taken.

Be that as it may, there is still considerable demand, even in industrialized areas, for the pastoral services of priests. At the same time, there appeared in the wake of Solidarity a significant interest in the Catholic social doctrines, and many laymen are calling on the clergy to provide them with pertinent information.

The strengthening of the church's position, the intensification of its dynamism, and the deepening of Polish religiosity were to a great extent the work of numerous orders, especially nuns. In 1982 there were 44 male orders with 9,797 members and 102 female orders (of which 11 were closed) with 23,711 members in Poland.[73] All of them were engaged in the apostolate of the church and significantly contributed to its vitality and its close bonds with the people.

The enumeration of the church's assets would be incomplete without at least a short mention of the "Weeks of Christian Culture" that now reach even remote parishes and of the efficient network of charitable activities coordinated by a committee of the episcopate, headed by Bishop Czesław Domin, auxiliary of the Katowice Diocese. And, of course, one must not overlook higher institutions of Catholic learning. The Catholic University of Lublin, in existence since 1918, is a private school supported by the church and donations of the faithful. It provides education for over three thousand students, about 60 percent of them lay. The Academy of Catholic Theology in Warsaw, founded in 1954, is financed by the state. It has about eight hundred students, of whom about 50 percent are priests. In addition, there are four papal theological faculties (Kraków, Warsaw, Wrocław, and Poznań) that also play an important role in furthering the education of priests, supplying teachers for seminaries, and disseminating scholarly Catholic writing.

Conclusion

The Catholic church of Poland is usually classified as a "folk Church," in which religious values and models of behavior are passed from generation to generation as part of the total cultural heritage. This fact, as well as historical and contemporary concern for Polish national interests, assures the church broad possibilities of influencing the Polish people. Conflicts with the communist regime, still considered by many Poles as an alien body, only increased the church's authority within the society, which manifested its political defiance by massive participation in seemingly purely religious activities.

Thus it may be assumed that in spite of recognized weaknesses of Polish "folk Catholicism," and regardless of the process of secularization, the church will maintain its high status for a long time to come. There are, however, certain factors that must persist in order to make the assurance safe.[74]

Above all, the church must continue to stay in close contact with the people, their problems and their aspirations. In other words, besides evangelization the church has to perform other functions, including the patriotic. In the present situation, marked by a political and ideological realignment in the wake of the Communist party's embarrassing defeat in the June 1989 elections, the church is trying once again to maintain the stance of an impartial critic of sociopolitical relations, to keep a distance from the partisan strife, and to courageously defend the people against injustice, violations of human rights, economic exploitation, and other abuses of power.

It appears that the church should be able to play a significant role in shaping future developments. Its enhanced legal status, resulting from the May 17, 1989, statute on relations with the state and the July 1989 decision of Pope John Paul II to establish a nunciature in Warsaw, should strengthen the position of the church even more and increase its organizational means for effective interventions. At the same time, however, one cannot overlook the existence of some disturbing circumstances.

Perhaps, the most ominous is the emergence of a political coalition incorporating the leaders of the opposition affiliated with the "secular Left" and the senior reformists of the Communist party. At this writing, it seems certain that the new "social-democratic" formation will control the newly elected parliament and set up a new government. It is less certain that the new ruling elite would give up its secularist inclinations, purge the bureaucratic apparatus from militant atheists, and steer the state along the road of ideological neutrality.

One can reasonably surmise that the upholding of the leftist preponderance in Polish politics, though unexpected by and shocking to many opposition activists, did not catch the church by surprise. Polish bishops are too close to the political arena to be unaware of main undercurrents. Almost certainly they were informed of the preparations for the emerging socialist bloc and decided, perhaps with misgivings, not to oppose these plans. Their acceptance may have two sources. First, there is the realization that the founders of the new coalition are the same people who were the architects of the roundtable agreement. The church's mediation brought them together, and the episcopate welcomed the fruit of their labors. Second, there is the awareness that the Polish example could exercise a greater impact on the neighboring countries of the Soviet bloc if at the helm of the reformist movement stood leaders not identified with the church. Thus, for the "common good" of all these nations, the Polish bishops were willing to accept domestic risks and face inevitable difficulties.

Tensions already manifested themselves in connection with a new church-sponsored bill protecting the rights of unborn children. A forthcoming parliamentary debate of the draft law and its passage or defeat might further intensify mutual apprehensions.

But the final test will come when the government starts dealing with grave economic problems. Unavoidable radical reforms will certainly call for additional hardships and sacrifices by the working masses and lead, very likely, to renewed outbursts of public protest. The methods that the new leadership will apply in handling the crisis will determine the church's attitude.

FACT SHEET

The Catholic Church in Poland

Current strength of the church (1988)

- 34,843,665 faithful (94.6 percent of the population)
- 17,726 diocesan and 5,706 monastic priests
- 98 bishops
- 23,711 nuns
- 9,792 monks
- 9,038 seminarians

Number of churches and church facilities

- 10,719 churches
- 1,835 chapels
- 46 higher seminaries
- 11 lower seminaries
- 2,506 convents
- 447 monasteries
- 1 university (Catholic University of Lublin)
- 12 high schools (1 exclusively for nuns training to become registered nurses)

Chief news organs

Przegląd Katolicki, Warsaw (est. 1984 by metropolitan curia; 38,000 copies)

Gość Niedzielny, Katowice (est. 1923 by local curia; 2,000,000 copies)

Tygodnik Powszechny, Kraków (est. 1945 by lay Catholic group Znak; 75,000 copies)

Primates since 1926

August Cardinal Hlond (1926–48)

Stefan Cardinal Wyszyński (1948–81)

Józef Cardinal Glemp (1981–present)

6

The Catholic Church in Czechoslovakia

Milan J. Reban

Since 1948 the Catholic church in Czechoslovakia has been subjected almost incessantly to severe pressures designed to forge a pattern of church-state relations acceptable to the communist leadership. Although there have been discernible stages in church-state interactions through the years, the position of the church has remained difficult since the communist takeover in February 1948. The basic pattern was forged in those early years, especially in 1949.

Historical antecedents shaped the confrontation, particularly the complex events of the post-White Mountain period, in which it is difficult to determine whether the Catholic church served the Czech nation or a foreign power, the Habsburg state. A process of *etatization* accelerated from the eighteenth century onward, and with it came Germanization, especially among the higher levels of the church hierarchy. The Czech elements were inexorably pushed into the background. Together these forces resulted, especially in the Czech lands, in a strong aversion to Catholicism that extended into the post-1918 period of the Czechoslovak Republic and beyond. Although the antagonisms were profound, resulting, for example, in the emergence of the Czechoslovak church, the interwar years produced significant growth in Czechoslovak Catholicism.[1] No longer subjected to the pressures of the Habsburg state, the church witnessed the emergence of significant intellectual forces and a desire to maintain a suprapolitical stance.

But above all else it was the course of World War II that influenced the post-1948 confrontation between church and communist state. World

War II altered the demographic profile of the church, among both the rank and file and the clergy. According to the last authoritative census on religious affiliation in 1930, of the 14,729,536 people living in Czechoslovakia, 73.54 percent were Roman Catholics; Greek Catholics and Armenian Catholics accounted for 3.97 percent of the total.[2] Reliable figures are not readily available for the religious groupings after 1930, though at the time of the communist takeover the Catholic church claimed 75 percent of the 12,339,000 inhabitants. Between 1930 and 1948 there were substantial shifts in religious affiliation. Around 600,000 ethnic Germans had emigrated from Czechoslovakia during the war, and approximately 2.5 million were expelled immediately following the war. The Soviet annexation of Subcarpathian Ruthenia in late 1944, with the concurrent loss of nearly 1 million, and the population transfer between Hungary and Slovakia also altered the profile of religious affiliation. There were other consequences. The expulsion of the German ethnics, a predominantly Roman Catholic group, meant the ranks of the clergy likewise were affected. The clergy in the Litoměřice Diocese, for example, declined by 78.82 percent.[3] Similar declines occurred in other Czechoslovak regions with large German populations. It is estimated that between 1,400 and 1,500 priests were deported.

The war had a major impact on Slovakia. The complex developments in this eastern part of Czechoslovakia produced a surge of nationalism, which was linked closely with the process of modernization during the interwar period and culminated in the creation of a truncated Slovak Republic in the wake of the dismemberment of the country. Even as a Nazi German vassal Slovakia evinced elements of strong nationalism. As such, it came to be closely tied to the Roman Catholic church. After the war, punitive measures were taken against the leaders of the Slovak state, including several prominent Catholics, notably the ex-president, Msgr. Tiso, who was executed. Charges against Slovak clerico-fascism were heard. These measures fueled Slovak resentment of the Czechs, exacerbating the problems between the two nationalities and facilitating the exploitation of the rift by the communists in the post-1945 provisional Czechoslovak government and beyond. These were among the reasons why the various demands for Slovak autonomy, agreed upon during the last stages of World War II and formulated into the Košice Program, were not implemented until 1968, producing the only positive attainment of that momentous year.[4]

The developments associated with World War II resulted in a number of measures against the church, despite the provisional government's promise of religious freedom. All church schools in Slovakia were nationalized in May 1945; various restrictions were placed on church publications; and a number of leading Catholic clergy were arrested. As Pedro Ramet has observed, "It is clear, thus, that Czechoslovakia was susceptible to anti-clerical programs, quite independent of the communist takeover in 1948."[5]

Relations After 1948

After the communist takeover in February 1948, the pattern of politico-religious relations materialized quickly. Seeking to maintain its newly won position, the leadership, at least until June 1949, sought to confine the influence of the Catholic church while attempting to reach an agreement with it. The leadership viewed the relationship in terms of power: The church was above all a political force in competition with the Communist party. Indeed, both the chairman of the Communist party, Klement Gottwald, and Rudolf Slanský, the general secretary, viewed the church as the last and most dangerous threat to the new regime.[6]

The new and still insecure leadership saw the church as a force with a potential for undermining the party's monopoly in the system. The church assumed a defensive posture, groping for a modus operandi that would permit it to continue its mission. The party leadership, on the other hand, sought agreements demanding submission, with the distinct possibility of the church's liquidation as an alternative. In a protracted conflict the adversaries come to behave similarly; in fact, sociologists of conflict note that an actor failing to do so will be at a disadvantage.[7] Since the initiative came from the Communist party, and its basic approach assumed a power-political nature, the Roman Catholic church found itself compelled to respond accordingly in political terms. The ensuing struggles have not produced a clear outcome. The organizational dimensions of the church have been severely impaired, but its influence remains and is seen by some as ascendant.

The church's linkage to the Vatican was especially objectionable to the communist leadership. The Vatican represented one of the most dangerous elements of world imperialism, seeking as it did to undermine the authority of the new regimes in the socialist bloc. In accord with this view, the policy of the Czechoslovak leadership sought to separate the Roman Catholic church from the Vatican and make it independent. For some eight years this policy was pursued inexorably. The complex strategy that emerged called for the isolation and replacement of the hierarchy of the church.

The negotiations began shortly after February 1948. The principal demand of the Communists was an unequivocal expression of loyalty, whereas the church proclaimed its service to the nation and loyalty to the state but refused to give allegiance to any particular political and state form. The church sought respect for religious freedom and an explication of conditions for its continued functioning. When a priest, Josef Plojhar, became a political candidate for the upcoming elections, an action proscribed by the church, the conflict, now revolving around the issue of the candidature, resulted in the termination of the negotiations. In the latter half of 1948 the bishops sought a resumption of talks, but these and those that followed in early 1949 did not produce concrete results. The tension escalated, especially after the January 1949 meetings between the episcopate and the party leaders. The directions of the conflict were determined after that time, but they were not unilinear at the outset.[8]

Several institutional developments were pertinent to the conflict. On March 18, 1948, the Commission for Religious Affairs, an entity linked with the National Front, had been formed, supplementing an advisory body consisting of six members functioning under the Presidium of the Central Committee of the Communist party. The candidacy of Plojhar was especially significant because he had been named minister of health in a step designed to broaden the legitimacy of the regime. The church, on the other hand, did not wish to endorse this step, reaffirming instead the episcopate's stand of November 1947 and January 1948 against political activity of priests. The encounters that followed revealed divisions within the episcopate, which, according to the party's evaluation, divided into three groups: (1) the most reactionary, who refused to collaborate at all; this group included the bishops of Slovakia and the Czech bishop Picha; (2) Beran's group (Archbishop Josef Beran of Prague), which was well aware of the forthcoming conflict; and (3) the "progressive" bishops Trochta and Hlouch.[9]

These divisions played an important role in shaping the government's strategy for the future. In the short run, however, the leadership was concerned about the upcoming elections, and the negotiations at that time sought above all to limit the potential damage that might be done by the church. The election outcome was deemed satisfactory by the party, worsening the position for the church in the dealings that followed; the results led to the view that the church had been effectively neutralized.

The Czechoslovak church hierarchy encountered pressures from the Vatican, for whereas the Czechoslovaks called for Plojhar's suspension, the Vatican sought excommunication, with sanctions against priests cooperating with the regime. Archbishop Beran and the episcopate refused to soften the stand of the church, leading to open conflict with the government.

Extant agreements between the church and the communist leaders were quickly abrogated, publications were limited, some church organizations were dissolved, many priests and lay leaders were tried, and pressure was applied to secure collaboration from the priests. The formula for the struggle was formulated during the summer of 1948. Its principal objectives were to isolate the Catholic church from the Vatican—transforming it into a national church separate from other churches—to win over the lower clergy, and to neutralize the episcopate.[10]

The strategy for securing these objectives called for the depiction of the top hierarchy as an instrumentality of the Vatican and the formulation of laws prohibiting activities against the government. Additionally, new organizations, the Associations of Czech and Slovak Catholics, with the participation of the clergy, were to be created to represent the church. A break with the Vatican would follow, and a national Catholic church would emerge.

It appears that the communist leadership had not yet formulated a fully developed church policy, but the general line had been set. According to Karel Kaplan, the line had received the endorsement of the Soviet leaders at the Cominform meeting in June 1948.[11] Various contacts continued, and there were some differences within the episcopate, fitting the communist strategy of developing a conflict within the clergy. The conflict escalated in April 1949. The political measures sought to (1) forge a Catholic movement of priests and laypeople supporting a modus vivendi between church and state; (2) emphasize the pan-Slavonic heritage of Saints Cyril and Methodius, in an attempt to forge links to Russian Orthodoxy; and (3) demand the Czech and Slovak language in religious services. These basic political steps were accompanied by numerous administrative measures designed to secure the state's complete legal control over the church. These included the termination of religious associations, schools, and publication activities that went beyond those considered strictly religious, as well as the formation of a party network attending to religious affairs.

An important element of the strategy for dividing the clergy was the creation of an organization of "progressive priests." Their initial gathering occurred April 28. Though their numbers at the outset were miniscule, they proclaimed support for the Presidium's church policy. The conflict escalated with the formation of Catholic Action on June 10. The bishops responded to its founding with a pastoral letter condemning the organization as a divisive act and subjecting its supporters to church sanctions. The letter was to be read in all churches on June 19. The communists forbade that and arranged for a provocation against Archbishop Beran at the Cathedral of Saint Vitus in Prague, preventing him from reading the letter and forcing his departure, presumably in order to ensure his safety. After that day, and until his departure from Prague, Beran never left the archbishop's palace.

Prior to June 19, some 240 clergy signed a declaration favoring agreement between church and state. According to the National Front, after one week the campaign had resulted in 16 percent of all clergy signing, 11 percent wholly opposed, and 16.2 percent giving verbal consent.[12] The church responded decisively, though the specifics of the conflict remained fluid relative to both actors. Within the church, for example, there was the vexing problem of the sanctions against the cooperative priests. However, with the formation of Catholic Action even the leaders inclined to negotiate and compromise with the state came to resist, and soon after its birth the Catholic Action effort began to fail. Kaplan's analysis of this initial failure may be correct: The party leadership dealt with the church in a manner suitable to dealing with a political party; the analogy was faulty.[13]

The Pattern of Relations Emerges

This critical stage in the evolution of church-state relations ended in October 1949 with the promulgation of a number of laws intended to regulate religious life in the state.

Law 217/49 of October 14, 1949, established the government Office of Church Affairs, which was to be responsible for all church and religious matters. Its current name is the Secretariat for Church Affairs of the Government Presidium. In Prague and in the Slovak capital of Bratislava respective Czech and Slovak regional Church Secretariats were created, with inferior organs down to the county level. This bureaucracy controls church life, proscribing activities extending beyond "cultic" (worship-related) acts. Only masses, baptisms, weddings, and church burials do not require advance approval. Various forms of associational activity are not permitted, including religious education and the like. Significant commemorative activities are discouraged, and visits of foreign delegates are forbidden.

The titles of law 218/49 and the related government regulation 219/49, both of October 14, 1949, convey the intent to secure full control of the church. They are (law and government regulation, respectively) the Law to Ensure the Economic Security of Churches and Religious Groups, and the Law to Ensure the Economic Security of the Catholic Church. Both circumscribe the activities of the clergy. The most important provisions demand the state's approval to serve in a pastoral role. A priest must serve in a parish for which he has been approved, and this rule applies to the bishops as well. The scope of the law is reflected in the result that in Czechoslovakia today, only three of thirteen dioceses have their own bishops: Prague, Nitra, and Banska Bystrica. Two dioceses are administered by an administrator apostolicus with bishop's rank (Olomouc and Trnava), and the remaining dioceses are under the leadership of "elected chapter vicars," that is, individuals chosen by the church Secretariat. Indeed, the status of the episcopate is a source of ongoing conflict, and will be considered later.[14]

The inevitable consequence of the state paying priests a salary and the nationalization of church property was more effective control, magnified by the fact that the Penal Code provides for punishment of pastoral activity lacking state sanction.

Other regulations affecting the functioning of the church followed. Government regulation 112/20 of July 14, 1950, reorganized theological studies in the country, permitting only two seminaries to function, one in Litoměřice and one in Bratislava, and by placing them under the jurisdiction of the church Secretariat removed them from university jurisdiction. With severely restricted enrollments, the numbers of priests have been diminishing, and many parishes throughout Czechoslovakia are without priests, though the picture has been more favorable in Slovakia.

Policies designed to isolate the church, inhibit its activity, and limit its influence as much as possible accelerated in the early 1950s. These included abolition of religious orders and the Greek Catholic (Uniate) church.

After coming to power, the ruling elite attempted to sever the links between the Greek Catholic church and Rome, just as it sought to break the ties between Rome and the Roman Catholic church. Unlike the Roman Catholic church, the Greek Catholic church had dual loyalties: toward the Vatican and toward fellow believers, especially the roughly 4 million residing in the Ukrainian SSR. These believers, who lived along the line dividing western and eastern Christianity, had adopted policies in the late sixteenth and seventeenth centuries which accepted the primacy of pope, but they were allowed to retain some traditions such as the use of the Slavonic language in liturgy and the right for priests to marry.

When Czechoslovakia was created in 1918, there were approximately 555,000 Greek Catholics. In Subcarpathian Ruthenia, annexed to the Soviet Union in late 1944, the Greek Catholic church was abolished in 1947. Some one-fifth of the parishes that traditionally belonged to the Mukacevo-Uzhorod eparchy remained active in southeastern Slovakia. In 1948 there were about 300,000 Greek Catholics in all of Czechoslovakia.[15] The effort to replace the Greek Catholic church with the Russian Orthodox church surfaced in August 1948 with an attempt to create a movement among the clergy in support of the policy and with numerous steps in late 1949 and early 1950 to implement it. It appears that some, including Gustáv Husák, at the time in charge of Communist party policy toward the church, objected to the speed of the process. Despite lack of success, and in part due to the failure of the Catholic Action effort, those favoring speed prevailed, and the formal decision to liquidate the Greek Catholic church was taken on April 29, 1950. There was much resistance, and many were arrested, including Bishops Gojdic and Hopko. For the next eighteen years the church ceased to function formally, but evidence in 1968 suggested that considerable secret activity continued.

Actions to liquidate religious orders began in fall 1949, with preparatory steps to arrest and try suitable leaders. The campaign escalated in early 1950, and the plan of action called for the concentration of male members of the monasteries at two locations, a move that was to take place in one night. The plan also called for the outright termination of two orders, the Jesuits and the Knights of the Cross. The Brothers of Mercy were to be exempted. Similar measures were to take place against women's orders. In the first political show trial in Czechoslovakia ten superiors were tried, ostensibly to show the hostile intent of the religious orders as well as the nefarious links to the Vatican, and they were sentenced to up to twenty-five years.

As planned, on the night of April 13/14, 1950, all monasteries and other residences were seized by police and military forces, all properties were confiscated, and the members were moved to detention monasteries in Zeliv and Bec. There they were to undergo reeducation. Action against female religious orders had been planned for October, with 4,073 of 11,896 nuns to be dealt with in a manner like that applied to the male orders. Some had been moved before in order to turn their facilities over to the military, and many (9,748) continued to work in health, social institutions, and industry, mostly jobs difficult to staff. Several proposals to liquidate them outright were not carried out, and a decision favoring a gradual ten-year liquidation was finally adopted.[16] Catholic nuns are now permitted to work only with the aged and with handicapped young.

The church's holdings, from buildings to art items, many destroyed in the process of transfer, constituted a vast property transfer. All orders have been forbidden from accepting new members, and their extinction therefore is inevitable.

Organizing Priestly Support

Given the failure of Catholic Action as a vehicle for creating a pliant church, policy concern shifted from the priests to an organization outside the church that would realize the twin goals of separation from the Vatican and separation from the episcopate.

The Office of Religious Affairs reached within the Patriotic Priests, of whom there were around fifty in late 1949, using them not only in a consultative capacity but elevating them to positions of power within the church. According to Kaplan, by March 1951 they held the posts of canon, vicar-capitular, and vicar general in most diocesan organizations, thereby assuming key administrative positions.[17] The authorities sought to expand priestly participation by creating a group of 500 supportive individuals. Around 1,750 priests were publicly noncommittal on church-state matters, and another 700 remained openly hostile. Still, the leadership admitted that except for the first group, all priests adhered to the pope and his inferiors. Attempts to take advantage of the declaration of four bishops supportive of the Association of Catholic Clergy encountered difficulties. Among the decisions taken was one to favor the use of house arrest over criminal proceedings. Emphasizing the regime's intent to push the peace issue, the group became known officially as the Peace Committee of the Catholic Clergy in Czechoslovakia, changed at the end of 1966 to the Peace Movement of the Catholic Clergy, headed by Josef Plojhar. He remained in his post until 1968, though he had been removed by the church from the ministry. In 1968 the movement dissolved.

Particularly vexing was the challenge of the continuing power of the episcopate; the goal of dividing and curbing it as an institution remained in place. The repressive measures of 1950 resulted in the isolation of bishops and suffragans. Still, the ruling elite sought the cooperation of at least some bishops to ordain new priests and ecclesiastical leaders.[18] While the episcopate, as such, ceased to exist, and the bishops were under house arrest or in prison, the principal goal—severing their ties with the Vatican, —had not been achieved.[19] Indeed, the Office of Religious Affairs had to admit that despite its successful neutralization of most priests, it had failed to win them over and sever their links to the Vatican.[20]

The coercive measures of the late 1940s and early 1950s set the tone for control of all aspects of religious life in Czechoslovakia. Despite the concordats between Hungary and Poland and the Vatican, and despite changes in the international setting in the aftermath of the Twentieth Congress of the CPSU, there were no significant changes in policy toward the organized church until 1968. This was in part due to the belated and incomplete process of de-Stalinization.

Still, several important events occurred during this time. In Czechoslovakia the reduced international tensions, with their somewhat diminished ideological tensions, coincided with the release of a number of high-ranking clergy from prisons and a modest increase in monitored contacts with the Vatican. Archbishop Beran was formally released in 1963 and permitted to depart for the Vatican in 1965. Still, as late as August 1967 the Novotný leadership ceased negotiations pertaining to the administration of eight of the twenty dioceses because the church would not agree to the regime's demand that at least some of the vacancies be filled by priests loyal to the regime.[21]

1968

In the pluralistic and participatory ferment of 1968, religious matters did not enjoy high priority, and indeed, the leading documents of that year, such as the Action Program of April 1968, failed to address the issues of religion and church. Nonetheless, religious groups benefited from the evolving liberalization of debate and social life, gaining in self-confidence. Entwined with the call for rectification of the status of Slovakia within the system was the question of the Greek Catholic church. The Czechoslovak government took up the problem on June 13, 1968, promising to deal with the attendant issues in the coming six months. After receiving both moral and financial support, religious activity had revived in some 248 parishes by September 1969, though the process encountered many obstacles owing to the decimation of the clergy and restrictions in the aftermath of August 21, 1968.

Some saw Alexander Dubček's steps as inadequate for dealing with the religious issues. Yet charity homes were permitted to manage themselves after April 1968, and religious processions celebrating Corpus Christi Day were held again in such traditional sites as Levoca and Stare Hory. *Katolické noviny* (Catholic gazette) enjoyed renewed popularity, several new churches were founded, and expectations in religious matters were rising.[22]

The foremost thrust of the ruling elite after Dubček's fall was a program of forced emergency resocialization of the Communist party membership and society as a whole to curb the ferment of 1968. The program of consolidation and "normalization" affected all areas of life. The party leadership attempted to create a successor to the Peace Movement of the Catholic Clergy among the clergy. Called the Union of Catholic Clergy Pacem in Terris of Czechoslovakia, the organization was designed to carry out the will of the political leadership. However, a declaration enunciated on March 6, 1982, upon papal instructions placed sanctions on this organization.

As a major component of the socialization process the Husák platform emphasized the need to intensify efforts to reduce the religiosity of the population, focusing on the continuing, if diminishing, popularity of religious education, especially in Slovakia, where 70 percent of the population showed strong religious convictions.[23] June 1, 1970, witnessed the initial steps, with the issuance of directives aimed at strengthening the proper scientific outlook by depressing the numbers of pupils receiving religious instruction. Surveys revealed its persistence even among the members of the power establishment. Steps were taken to discourage the teachers themselves from seeking religious instruction for their own children, and to enlist their active support in the cause of atheism. While not prohibiting it altogether, the various regulations were designed to make religious education more difficult to secure. For instance, the application has to be signed by both parents, instructional personnel must be approved by political authorities, and hours of instruction are limited. All religious instruction outside the officially sanctioned programs is proscribed. These programs have produced the results desired; many communities have no instruction whatever, and the numbers of students involved have decreased since the late 1960s.

The Current Status of the Church

Despite the many signs of religious revival in Czechoslovakia, the fear expressed by the aging Czechoslovak primate and archbishop of Prague, František Cardinal Tomášek, that if the West fails to take more notice of the conditions in Czechoslovakia, the Church "will die," could be realized. A speech given by Karel Hrůza, former head of the Secretariat for Church Affairs, presented pertinent data that suggested an overall decline. In the 1950 census 94.6 percent of all Czechs and Slovaks claimed to be believers; the current figure stands at about 30 percent.[24] Though official registration ceased in 1954, about four to five million are believers. Major rites attest to the persistence of religious orientation. Hrůza claimed that in 1984, 71.6 percent of the children born in Slovakia were baptized, whereas in the Czech lands it was 31.2 percent. Church funerals stood at 80.5 percent in Slovakia and 50.6 percent in the Czech lands. Fifty-three percent of weddings were held in churches, though in Czech parts it was only 15.8 percent.

In his advancing years František Cardinal Tomášek has become a visible symbol of the church's position vis-à-vis the regime. Now ninety years old, he has given many interviews in recent years that characterized current relations as poor. In an interview with a Viennese newspaper he held that the Czechoslovak leadership sought to enslave the church. Noting that church and state were separate entities in Poland and in Hungary, he suggested the same for Czechoslovakia: "We are able to pay our priests ourselves; our congregations are also willing to maintain their churches."[25] Tomášek characterized the situation of the church in Czechoslovakia as the most difficult of any in the East European countries. On a positive note, in 1985 there was a modest increase in enrollment in the two church seminaries, and there were rumors that 100,000 Bibles would be made available in 1987. The Czech seminary in Litoměřice had fifty-five entrants, and the Slovak institution in Bratislava had fifty-eight.[26] Still, the situation remains that of a church with more self-confidence but fewer priests.

In the struggle for a degree of autonomy for the church, the key issue after nearly forty years is still symbolized by the appointment of the bishops. Tomášek noted that "the government wants bishops from the ranks of the Pacem in Terris association, which is close to the regime, but we want bishops who are loyal to the Pope."[27] Tomášek noted that eight of the thirteen Czechoslovak dioceses were without bishops. Vladimir Janku, the new head of the Office for Religious Affairs, along with CPCS Presidium secretary Vasil Bilák, reiterated the position that any new bishops must have positive relations with the state, and that the Vatican continues to make unreasonable demands. Bilák also stated that an agreement would require that the Vatican no longer tolerate what he called the "secret church" in Czechoslovakia.[28]

As of early 1987, despite Tomášek's strong views, the episcopate appeared to be riven with dissension, and it was possible to divide Czechoslovak bishops and ordinaries into two groups, those maintaining orthodox views (Tomášek, Gabris, Garaj, and Hirka) and those who were loyally bound to the regime (Feranec, Pasztor, and Vrana). Tomášek remained uncompromising.[29] These divisions prevent an effective response to the Vatican's policy in Eastern Europe.

Recently the government of strongly Catholic Slovakia proposed to liberalize the already liberal law on abortion, evoking protests, with more than thirteen thousand Czechs and Slovaks signing protest petitions. Cardinal Tomášek rose to support the protesters.[30] This and other developments resulted in acrimonious exchanges, criticism of the pope and his stand on abortion, and continued claims that the Vatican remains a supporter of "imperialist" designs against Czechoslovakia. The Vatican apex allegedly sought to forge out of the Roman Catholic church a "potential center of antisocialist opposition," and continued to support "aggressive imperialist circles."[31]

Cardinal Tomášek attempted to invite Pope John Paul II to visit Czechoslovakia in 1987 to participate in the canonization of Blessed Agnes of Bohemia, but as with his failure to obtain the assent of the authorities for the pope's presence to commemorate the 1,100th anniversary of the death of Saint Methodius, so too he failed in this effort.

In recent years there have been many instances of repressive measures against all religious activities not undertaken within the strictly defined limits. Arrests of Catholic activists and priests and other forms of harassment have abounded in the 1980s and have been noted by others abroad, including the Vatican. The religious press appears to be under strong pressure, and some see the restrictions of the 1980s exceeding those of the 1950s. Whereas atheistic writings abounded, the official Catholic publications could not engage in polemics.

The authorities continued to defend their policies, including in the international forums. Summarizing the general status of relations from the official perspective, Dr. Karel Hrůza defended the official policy. He pointed out that the clergy received regular monthly salaries from the state, and the salaries were raised in 1981 "to a level corresponding to average wages of Czechoslovak citizens." Citing the state's support for church facilities, Hrůza argued that the church on its own would be unable to maintain them. As an example of state support for publications he cited the printing of *Katolické noviny* in 1982 in 120,000 copies in its Czech-language version and 130,000 copies in the Slovak edition. Hrůza offered the official defense of the Pacem in Terris, blaming the émigré churchmen and even President Reagan for the continued Vatican opposition toward such groups, noting that the ban extends to priestly activism in Latin America, clearly in support of imperialism there. Hrůza, who participated in various negotiations with the Vatican, defended the record of the state regarding its willingness to negotiate. He expressed resentment over the appointment of several secret Catholic bishops. Regarding the basic struggle, Hrůza once again reiterated that the larger forces "in a great contest between the forces of socialism and capitalism in the present-day world" cannot be avoided.[32]

This overview of church-state relations in Czechoslovakia reveals that despite the changing international context, and perhaps in part because of it, the political leadership was able to pursue a coercive policy for nearly forty years. The changing conditions in neighboring countries notwithstanding (especially the impact of the upheaval in Poland in the early 1980s), the leadership has been at least partly successful in isolating the impact of their echoes in Czechoslovakia. They have succeeded in part due to the weaknesses of Catholicism in Czechoslovakia, which are rooted deeply in history and political culture.

Thus far the Czechoslovak leaders have failed to realize their paramount objective of effecting a complete break with the Vatican culminating in the creation of a separate church. They certainly have not succeeded in eradicating important elements of the Catholic subculture. Indeed, recent years have witnessed many signs of revival and, as a result, an escalation of official efforts at the eradication of religious education. The unprecedented pilgrimages of recent years, the signs of an extensive underground religious, and the surge of interest among the intellectuals and the young all attest to remarkable resilience.[33] Admittedly, there seems to be more activity in Slovakia than in the Czech section of the country. Still, the Roman Catholic church may today be more significant for a larger portion of the population than at any time in this century.

The current reformist thrust in the Soviet Union, with its complex consequences for Eastern Europe, combined with the coming of a new leadership in Czechoslovakia may be important variables in future church-state relations. The dynamic policy of the Vatican in Eastern Europe, shaped to some degree by prominent Slovak and Czech clergy at the Vatican, constitutes another critical variable.[34] The ultimate direction, however, will be influenced above all by conditions that are specific to Czechoslovakia.

FACT SHEET

The Catholic Church in Czechoslovakia

Current strength of the church

- 5 million faithful (1981)
- 3,260 priests (1982)
- 3 bishops (February 1988)
- 10 apostolic administrators (February 1988)
- 7,247 nuns (1972) (7,169 Latin-rite; 78 Greek-rite)
- 284 seminarians (1980)
- 470 theological students (1977)
- approx. 100 priests and religious activists in prison (1986)

Number of churches and church facilities

- 5,002 churches (1982)
- 332 convents (1972)
- 0 monasteries (1988)
- 2 seminaries (Bratislava, Litoměřice) (1988)
- 0 church-run schools
- 13 charitable institutions (1980)

Chief official news organs (circulation figures as of 1982)

- *Katolické noviny* (120,000 copies in Czech; 130,000 in Slovak)
- *Duchovní pastýř*, journal

Underground religious periodicals

- *Informače o cirkví* (est. 1980)
- *Naboženstvo a Sučasnost* (est. 19??)
- *Vzkršeni* (est. 1980)
- *Una Sancta Cattolica-Advent* (est. 1983)
- *Teologičke texty* (est. 1980)

Archbishops of Prague since 1948

- Josef Cardinal Beran (1946–65; died in Rome 1969)
- František Cardinal Tomášek (apostolic administrator of Prague, 1965–78; archbishop since 1978)

7

The Catholic Church in Hungary

Leslie László

What happened to the *aggiornamento* so insistently demanded by the Second Vatican Council some twenty years ago? This question should provoke passionate debate among Catholics, but more often than not it is met by embarrassed silence. In this chapter this very question will be asked about the church in Hungary, a country whose professedly Marxist-Leninist rulers claim that they have granted full religious freedom to their subjects and boast that they have achieved an ideal relationship with the churches that could serve as an example to other socialist countries.

Is it true that the churches of Hungary—and here we are concerned first of all with the predominant Roman Catholic church—have abandoned their futile resistance to communism and are now following the road of cooperation, accepting their assigned places in the great task of "building socialism"? Did they indeed undergo internal renewal by joining the "progressive forces" of society and thus becoming respected building blocks of the socialist system? Or is all this but window dressing designed to camouflage the servile subordination of the church to the state after years of pressure and outright persecution?

For a better understanding of the state of the church and of the peculiar character of church-state relations in Hungary today, a brief review of the post-World War II developments is in order. This will be followed by a discussion of the tasks and challenges the church is facing in Hungary today.

New Wine into Old Bottles

As the semifeudal, "neo-baroque" edifice of Horthy's Hungary came tumbling down under the blows of Nazi Germany and the Red Army, the thousand-year-old Hungarian Catholic church was confronted with a radically new situation.[1] For centuries the influence of the church has been very great indeed: The archbishop of Esztergom, as prince primate of Hungary, was the second dignitary of the realm after the king; the bishops were ex-officio members of the upper house of Parliament; the clergy's civil status was that of public officials. Moreover, the church owned immense landholdings and supported numerous schools and institutions. Thus it was able to exert considerable influence on public life. All this came to an end at the end of World War II, albeit not without bitter resistance.

The first measure of the new order which hit the church hard was drastic land reform. This was enacted on direct orders from the Red Army via the Provisional Government of Debrecen on March 15, 1945, when large areas were still under Nazi rule.[2] While the land reform was long overdue, it was done for political ends with scant regard for economic rationality. The land was divided into uneconomical small parcels, providing good conditions for future collectivization. Moreover, it was carried out in a vindictive spirit, with neither compensation for former owners nor provision for the continuing existence of those institutions which were dependent on revenues from the confiscated church properties.

In the ensuing three years Hungary lived in the twilight of a democratic multiparty system under a coalition government in which the Communists were pushing inexorably toward a monopoly of power. Parallel to the ruthless struggle in the political arena there developed a bitter contest between the Catholic church and the communists.

What made this conflict even fiercer in Hungary than elsewhere in Eastern Europe was the character and beliefs, or illusions, of the principal antagonists. On the one hand, the leaders of the church, above all the prince primate, József Cardinal Mindszenty, expected the Soviet occupation and the resulting communist ascendancy in Hungary to last only until the impending conclusion of the peace treaty between the Allied Powers and Hungary.[3] This hope strengthened Mindszenty's resolve not to yield an iota to secularism and atheism and to defend Hungary's traditions and the rights of the church. He was sure of the support of the overwhelming majority of the people, who were anti-Soviet and anticommunist in their sentiments. But if Cardinal Mindszenty acquired worldwide fame as a fearless champion of his church and an unbending maximalist in his insistence on preserving from the past all that was good, his sterling character was matched on the opposite side by a most fanatic and ruthless communist warrior, Mátyás Rákosi, who was totally committed to the destruction of the old Hungary and its replacement with a revolutionary new system of Marxist-Leninist-Stalinist socialism. Moreover, Rákosi and his comrades in the ruling Quadriga—Ernő Gerő, Mihály Farkas, and Zoltán Vas—were singularly insensitive toward Catholic beliefs and needs. Hungarian Jews by birth, all four had spent much of their adult life in Moscow, where they received the training for their future leadership careers. They regarded the subservient Orthodox church of Russia as the model to which the Hungarian Catholic church should conform.[4]

Mindszenty fought with all the means at his disposal, through pastoral letters, inspired newspaper articles, speeches at mass rallies, going so far as to excommunicate all deputies of Parliament who voted for the nationalization of denominational schools. In the end all this was in vain. The communist-dominated government proceeded to dissolve all Catholic social organizations, including the 500,000-member agrarian youth league KALOT, nationalized all Catholic schools (over 3,000 in number: 2,900 elementary and 184 secondary schools), suppressed nearly all Catholic publications, and expropriated the publishing houses and their assets, thus largely eliminating the church from public life. These repressive policies went hand in hand with an increasing persecution of priests and believers, who were accused of disloyalty and antistate activities. This period of uneven struggle culminated in the arrest and show trial of Cardinal Mindszenty in early 1949.

The Agreement of 1950

The principal obstacle thus removed with the conviction of Cardinal Mindszenty, the government pressed the bishops for a public declaration of loyalty and submission to the communist regime in the form of an agreement between church and state similar to those which had already been signed by representatives of Hungary's main Protestant churches.[5] Since the document included statements of a sensitive political nature hardly reconcilable with the traditional independence of the church, the bishops balked at the demand, declaring that only the Holy See would be competent to deal with such issues. Rákosi had no intention of having anything to do with the pope; in fact, relations with the Vatican had been severed in 1945. He decided on other means to extort compliance. On the one hand, the Priests for Peace movement was launched on the initiative and with the active support of the government. The participants, dubbed "peace priests" by the populace, parroted government slogans, defied the church hierarchy, and confused the faithful, posing thereby a direct threat to the unity of the church. On the other hand, thousands of members of religious orders, male and female, were arrested in nightly raids on monasteries and convents and taken to designated detention centers, their ultimate fate uncertain. Under such duress the bishops signed the agreement on August 30, 1950.[6] In return for their cooperation, the members of the religious orders were released from custody, although they were not permitted to return to their previous homes and occupations. The church was allowed to reopen eight secondary schools, six for boys and two for girls. Four religious orders were given permission to retain just enough staff to service these schools. The other religious orders were suppressed. Of 2,500 priests in the orders, only 460 were allowed to do pastoral work as secular priests within the framework of the dioceses. Furthermore, as part of the agreement the church had to hand over its remaining lands—namely, those owned by the rural parishes—as well as all the buildings and assets of the disbanded religious orders. In return the state promised to grant financial aid in the form of subsidies complementing the lower clergy's salary. This aid was to continue for eighteen years, after which the church was expected to be financially self-supporting.[7] As the most important point of the agreement the bishops were obliged to exhort the clergy and the faithful to support the policies of the government, especially the collectivization of agriculture, and to punish those who opposed or tried to sabotage them.

Contrary to expectations, signing the agreement did little to improve the situation; the campaign against the church continued. Four bishops and an auxiliary bishop were placed under house arrest. Archbishop József Grősz of Kalocsa, president of the Hungarian Bishops' Conference at the time and a signatory of the agreement, was tried on trumped-up charges and sentenced to fifteen years' imprisonment for counterrevolutionary activities. Indeed, the following years, 1951–53, marked the nadir in the spoliation and debasement of the church.[8] The bishops, under the leadership of the more malleable Gyula Czapik, archbishop of Eger, were forced to issue a condemnation of Grősz and his high-ranking clerical "accomplices." Then, on July 21, 1951, all bishops, diocesan vicars, and the superiors of the remaining religious orders had to repair to the presidential hall of Parliament, where in the presence of the highest state dignitaries and the clicking of cameras they had to swear an oath on the Constitution of the People's Republic. Instead of the genuine separation between church and state proclaimed in the 1949 Constitution, the church was placed under the strictest government control. To this end a special department, the State Office of Church Affairs, was created.[9] Government officials ("mustached bishops") were placed in every chancery. They opened the bishops' mail, checked their visitors, and were in possession of the diocesan seals. In a decree issued on July 3, 1951, appointments to bishoprics and all other church offices of importance were made subject to government approval.[10] The bishops were forced to assign members of the Priests for Peace movement as their chancellors and to fill all other influential positions in their dioceses from among the ranks of these priests. Moreover, the government ordered all minor seminaries and seven of the thirteen major seminaries disbanded.

The regime did not stop with crippling the authority of the duly constituted church hierarchy; neither was it satisfied with having reduced the activities of the church to worship within the confines of the church buildings. As soon as the state succeeded in silencing the church as a voice of opposition, new pressures were applied to turn the church into an instrument in the service of the communist cause. Prelates and priests were forced to support the Soviet-sponsored peace campaign with its anti-Western slogans. The pastoral letters issued by the bishops' chancery, instead of teaching the gospel, praised the government's domestic and foreign policies, pleading for the fulfillment of the production quotas in industry and giving instructions to the peasants on how best to perform the agricultural tasks of the season. The people dubbed these the "manuring pastoral letters" (*ganajozó pásztorlevelek*).[11]

This pitiful degradation of all that was sacred in the eyes of believers was alleviated somewhat with the death of Stalin in 1953 and the new course that was imposed by his successors. Cardinal Mindszenty was transferred from prison to less severe confinement, where he was joined by Archbishop Grősz. The latter, however, was soon permitted to move to a parish in his archdiocese, and when Archbishop Czapik died in May 1956, Grősz was allowed to return to his see of Kalocsa and to resume the presidency of the Hungarian Bishops' Conference.

During the October 1956 Revolution Cardinal Mindszenty was freed by a detachment of the Hungarian army and returned to Budapest. He promptly suppressed the Priests for Peace movement and cleansed the chanceries of government stooges. Within a week, on November 4, Soviet forces intervened anew, ending the hope for a neutral, democratic Hungary. Cardinal Mindszenty took refuge in the U.S. legation while the new regime of János Kádár proceeded to assert its power. Disassociating himself from the hated Stalinist dictatorship of Rákosi, Kádár claimed to lead a "revolutionary workers-peasants government." To demonstrate his willingness for reforms in church policies, he dissolved the State Office for Church Affairs. For their part, the Hungarian Bishops' Conference, once again presided over by Archbishop Grősz, established the Opus Pacis movement, which replaced the "peace priests" organization. But the same people who had controlled the "peace priests" organization now took the same positions in Opus Pacis, which was, however, under the aegis of the official church. Moreover, in 1959 the State Office for Church Affairs was reestablished, and the "peace priests" reoccupied their strategic positions in the church administration. Only the "mustached bishops," i.e., the civilian administrators of the dioceses, disappeared from the chanceries for good. The Holy See, which had already in the spring of 1956 placed the press organ of the "peace priests" on the Index, in 1958 struck three prominent members of the movement with excommunication because, as deputies in Parliament, they had accepted political office without Rome's permission. However, the government forbade the bishops to enforce the decrees issued by the Vatican.

Toward Normalization of Church-State Relations

The first rays of sunshine entered this bleak picture of irreconcilable church-state antagonism with Pope John XXIII's overtures to the East. His successor, Pope Paul VI, sent an emissary, Archbishop Agostino Casaroli, to Budapest in 1963 to open talks. These negotiations between the Vatican and the Hungarian government culminated in the signing on September 15, 1964, of a "partial agreement," the first of its kind in all of Eastern Europe.[12] By mutual consent only a part of the document was made public. This included, first of all, the appointment of new bishops—an all-important matter because at the time only three of the eleven dioceses had ordinaries (the rest were governed by apostolic administrators). Second, the section of the Hungarian Academy in Rome housing the Hungarian Papal Institute was once again placed under the jurisdiction of the Hungarian bishops, enabling eight priests each year to continue their education in Rome. The unpublished part of the document contained a list of problems to be discussed in the future. Both sides agreed to meet twice a year, alternately in Rome and in Budapest.

In the follow-up negotiations the Hungarian side continued to insist on giving priority to questions of personnel in the apparent hope that the new appointees selected jointly by Rome and Budapest would more willingly cooperate with the government than the older prelates. Between 1964 and 1980 twenty-six persons were appointed bishops or auxiliary bishops. In spite of the fact that some of the appointments were the result of compromise, insisted upon by the state authorities, the Vatican regarded the restoration of the hierarchical leadership in the church as a step forward. Similarly, the participation of several Hungarian bishops in the closing session of the Second Vatican Council in 1965 was greeted as a sign of the reintegration of the Hungarian Catholic church into the mainstream of the universal church. On the other hand, most of the pastoral problems are still unresolved and remain on the agenda of the seemingly unending series of meetings.

In concluding the partial agreement of 1964, the most sensitive issue of all—the fate of Cardinal Mindszenty—was prudently sidestepped. At the age of eighty he was still living at the U.S. legation, unable to exercise his office but still the primate of Hungary. Not always in the best health, he was a cause of worry to his hosts for fifteen long years and also an irritant in Hungarian-U.S. relations. Pope Paul VI finally persuaded him to leave Hungary, which he did in September 1971, and, after a short stay in Rome, he settled in Vienna. Soon afterward, however, the Hungarian government launched a strong protest with the Vatican, charging that Mindszenty, with his pastoral travels among the two million Hungarians in the West and the impending publication of his memoirs, had violated the conditions accepted by the Holy See at the time of his departure. They demanded that Rome impose silence on the cardinal or remove him. When Mindszenty refused to be muzzled, the pope, on February 5, 1974, declared the see of Esztergom vacant. The following year, on May 6, 1975, Cardinal Mindszenty died. Pope Paul VI then appointed László Lékai archbishop of Esztergom and primate of Hungary.[13] Shortly afterward he also received the red hat of a cardinal.[14]

Through a series of episcopal appointments in 1975 and early 1976 the Hungarian hierarchy was now complete; for the first time since World War II, each diocese was governed by a resident bishop. In April 1977 Cardinal Primate Lékai could lead the full complement of Hungarian bishops to Rome to pay their obligatory five-yearly *ad limina* visit to the Holy Father, after some forty years of absence. Then, in June of the same year, János Kádár, the first secretary of the Hungarian Workers' party, was received together with his wife by His Holiness in a private audience.

Hungary as a Model?

Spokesmen of the Hungarian government maintained throughout the 1970s and 1980s that church-state relations in Hungary were mutually satisfactory and could serve as a model for other socialist states.[15] However, this view represented wishful thinking rather than reality.

Ever since the much-heralded partial agreement of 1964 with the Vatican, there has been confusion and a certain disorientation in the ranks of party functionaries. Their task has not been made easier by the contradictory demands to welcome a reconciliation with the church and at the same time to continue to fight against religion in all spheres of life. They were bound to err through excessive zeal in one or the other direction. An editorial entitled "The Ideological Offensive of Marxism" in the monthly *Társadalmi Szemle* (Social review) expressed the party's concern over the situation:

> Recently there has been confusion in some of the party organizations. . . . This happened because in some places—where they can conceive the fight against religion only in a simplistic fashion—they misunderstand the normalization of relations between the State and the Churches, certain changes in the Vatican's stand, the recently concluded agreement between our State and the Vatican. . . . This is why the conference on ideology deemed it necessary to recall to attention: religion remains a retrograde worldview, . . . and the ideological fight against religion continues to be the daily task in our ideological work.[16]

In fact, there was no relaxation of party control over the church, nor was there any lull in the repressive measures adopted against the clergy and the believers. The first signs of a subtle change in attitudes appeared only in the mid-1970s. By then the communists of Hungary apparently had discovered that religion is not only an annoying habit cum superstition of the elderly and ignorant, who, incidentally, can be quite decent people and good workers, but that religion might provide man with a code of ethics based on moral values that are sorely needed in present-day Hungary. Thus, for example, in a widely distributed study State Secretary Imre Miklós, chairman of the State Office for Church Affairs, admitted that

> the church can also carry out a positive role within socialistic society, such as in the defense of peace, in the promotion and encouragement of national unity with socialist content—for which the development of trust is especially important—in defining societal and personal property, in spreading the ideas of humanism, in love for the people, in the fight against crime, in the promotion of the progressive traditions of the national inheritance and of cultural values.

Moreover, it would be wrong to underestimate the influence of religious faith "in the private life of individuals, in interpersonal relationships, in the defence of certain moral norms and critical view of other norms."[17]

One might suspect, although tangible proof is lacking, that this change in perception and attitude toward religion might be due at least in part to some cold statistics that were brought to light by the new breed of sociologists in Hungary, who grow bolder every year in their research.

The first thing confirmed by statistical findings is that religion has retained a strong hold on Hungarian society despite nearly forty years of communist domination.[18] In fact, there are still more Christian believers in Hungary than Marxist-Leninists. To be sure, the worldwide trend of secularization also has affected Hungary, and as a result, the number of believers had greatly declined. While church spokesmen maintain that the number of Catholics is as high as 5 to 6 million in the overall population of some 10 million, statistics based on churchgoing, practicing Catholics estimate their number as 1.5 million, i.e., about 15 percent of the population.[19] This is still a respectable figure, one which would compare favorably with many Western societies and, even without adding the practicing Protestant Christians, it still exceeds the membership of the Hungarian Socialist Workers' party, which numbers some 800,000.

Realization of this continuing hold of religion on a large segment of the population must have contributed to the ideological formula arrived at by the second colloquium organized by the East European practitioners of the sociology of religion at Prague in 1968. The participants concluded that religiosity is a social phenomenon which survives even in socialist societies, and that therefore the believing masses and their churches should be included in the program of building socialism.[20]

The Social Ills of a Consumer Society

What lent special urgency to the call for a united effort to build socialism was the realization that there were, indeed, great obstacles on the road toward a better society. Beginning in the late 1960s, when Kádár's Hungary finally entered a period of prosperity, when many of the shackles restricting the acquisition of private property were removed by the New Economic Mechanism (NEM), and when religion began to decline, a vulgar materialism increasingly took hold of large segments of the populace, whose chief goals in life became material possessions and la dolce vita. Few of them, however, have striven to realize their dreams by hard work. Popular belief, based on observation of easy-to-find notorious examples, says that there are better and quicker ways to success and riches. Corruption, bribery, cheating on the job, embezzling, and the stealing of public property have become so widespread that it is almost accepted as normal behavior for smart folk. At the same time those who cannot make it sink into the stupor of alcohol, absent themselves from work, and often end up on skid row or commit suicide. The picture that the newly emancipated sociologists are showing to the public in journals and even in the daily newspapers is truly shocking and certainly beyond anything the party and the government care to admit, even to themselves. After all, no country, and even less one which calls itself socialist, would want to brag about such sorry records as having the lowest birthrate and the highest suicide rate in the world, and probably the worst problem of alcoholism. It is said that between 500,000 and 1 million men and women are severely affected by alcohol, while about 150,000 can be regarded as alcoholics proper, among whom the male-female ration is 5:3. Work discipline is almost nonexistent, and productivity is abysmally low. These are the symptoms of a seriously ill society, even if to the outside world Hungary presents the picture of the showcase of the communist world, with its happy-go-lucky people, considerable degree of individual and artistic freedoms, and fully stocked magazine shelves. Even its critics describe Hungary as "the merriest barracks in the Soviet camp."[21]

This, then, was the somber background to the remarkable dialogue which took place in 1975–76 between the party's chief ideologue and cultural czar, Deputy Premier György Aczél, and the bishop of Pécs, Msgr. József Cserháti. There is no space here to go into details of their widely publicized exchanges; suffice it to say that to Aczél's invitation to the believers to join in the task of defending world peace and building socialism, Bishop Cserháti replied that if the regime wanted sincere cooperation, it should stop offending the feelings of the believers by its constant attacks on their most sacred convictions. Why not end the deeply humiliating treatment of the believers as "second-class" citizens subject to various kinds of harassment and discrimination? Instead, the government should aim at restoring their pride and self-esteem, so necessary for the good performance of any job, by openly acknowledging the positive values of ethics and morality that Christian believers contribute to society. This would, of course, also necessitate granting greater freedom to the church in its mission to strengthen those values among the adults and inculcate them in the children by teaching them the catechism of Christian faith and morality.[22]

It is interesting to note that Bishop Cserháti's challenge was not ignored or rejected outright, as it would have been in the past. In fact, the authorities seemed to have come around, at least halfway, to accepting his suggestion. As we have seen, Secretary of State Imre Miklós now talked about the churches' role "in the defense of certain moral norms," their positive role within socialist society "in their love for the people," "in defending societal and personal property," "in the fight against crime," etc. In a similar vein, Professor József Lukács, the foremost philosopher of atheism in Hungary and editor of *Világosság*, lecturing on "Churches and Religiousness in Socialist Hungary" at the Political Academy of the Hungarian Socialist Workers' party, conceded that religion could perform a useful social function. It is by no means a negligible social force, and it "preserves certain moral principles," especially in the realm of human and family relations.[23]

For a long time this change of attitude, while significant, seemed half-hearted and could not be regarded as unequivocally sincere. A big stumbling block lay in the way of true reconciliation and fruitful cooperation between church and state, and this was the question of the youth.

The Youth

The overwhelming majority of all studies done by the Hungarian sociologists have focused on Hungary's young people. Their data show that the most rapid secularization—the steepest decline in religiosity—has been registered among the young, especially the students.[24] The party takes a certain satisfaction in these results. It even claims credit for weaning the youth away from religion, which it identifies with false consciousness and unreal idealism, attitudes that are positively harmful to the development of the new socialist man. In reality, the communists have little reason for jubilation and self-congratulation. The very same data show that the youth which abandoned its religious heritage did not automatically turn to the officially propagated Marxist-Leninist belief system. Far from it: While the number of Marxist atheistic youth is estimated to be 10–15 percent at the maximum, the vast majority of young people in Hungary today, well over 60 percent in all polls that have been published, are found to be totally indifferent, without any belief whatsoever. If they call themselves "materialists," that term has nothing to do with Marxist philosophy:[25] It simply means that they are interested only in money and what money can buy—comfort, pleasure, and sex—in other words, what Marxists disdainfully describe as "vulgar materialism."

This is hardly an intellectual attitude or passing fad. The sober truth is that it is both the symptom and a self-perpetuating cause of the grave societal ills already mentioned: low work discipline, alcoholism, disintegration of the family, widespread corruption, theft of public property, and so on. Of course, these are not new phenomena (they have been deplored and castigated by the party for years), but now it turns out that these failings—once said to have been the remnants of bourgeois-capitalistic society—are to a great degree characteristic of the young generation that has been educated and shaped by the socialistic system. That this is so has been demonstrated again by the data collected by sociologists and by the merciless figures on growing juvenile delinquency.[26]

These are not secrets any more: The Hungarian public is bombarded by articles appearing in periodicals and in the daily press, roundtable discussions on the radio, and dramatic television shows depicting the nihilistic, cynical, hedonistic young people wearing jeans, playing rock music, and dancing in discos—young people whose only goal in life is to own a motorbike or an automobile and live the sweet life.

Although János Kádár, addressing the Twelfth Congress of the Hungarian Socialist Workers' party in 1980, himself complained about those young people who have "negative attitudes, such as indifference, in the case of some people even cynicism, and the tendency to seek an easy life,"[27] there was no admission of failure, nor a call for help addressed to the churches. The communists stubbornly and desperately cling to their faith that it is they alone who should mold young minds. They still hope against all evidence that they will succeed in educating the youth in the Marxist-Leninist ideology and imbue them with the supposedly superior morality of communism. In this case there seems to be no room left for compromise with the churches, which also insist on their mission to win the souls of the young. If anything, the shackles on religious instruction have been tightened even further while communist indoctrination has intensified. Thus, in spite of the official assurances about the satisfactory church-state relations in Hungary, a muted tug-of-war for the young continues.

Reform or Stagnation

Let us suppose that the regime would relax its control over the church, allowing it free pastoral activity, including work among the youth. Would the church then be in a position to catch up with years of enforced inactivity, to fill the existing void in religious-moral knowledge and practice among the people? The answer to this question is anything but encouraging.

The average age of the active clergy in Hungary today is near sixty and getting older every year. The number of young men entering the priesthood remains far below the number of priests who die.[28] The church does not have adequate training programs, nor does it have the research facilities in the social sciences that are indispensable for the understanding and effective treatment of the ills in contemporary society. Moreover, the church in Hungary in its struggle for survival has tried to hang on to what it could preserve from the past rather than getting involved in new experiments. In this defensive posture traditions became emphasized, while reforms and the dynamic inner renewal heralded by Vatican II had little chance to take root. To be sure, the liturgical reforms of the council have been gradually implemented in Hungary, and a handful of theological tracts dealing with the teachings of Vatican II have been published. By and large, however, the church in Hungary remains quite untouched by the ideas of collegiality in church government and participation of the laity as full members of the "people of God" in all aspects of church life.

The fact that the late Primate Cardinal Lékai[29] took a seat on the Presidium of the People's Patriotic Front and exhorted the faithful to participate conscientiously in the building of socialism does not mean that he was a progressive leftist in the Western sense. In fact, he was to the end a profoundly conservative man, as are, to a varying degree, all the other members of the Hungarian Bishops' Conference. Lékai's cooperation with the regime was in tune with the old Josephinist doctrine of the unity and harmony between throne and altar,[30] and thus an aspect of his conservative makeup. The same can be said of other manifestations of active church participation in politics; for example, the spectacle of Catholic priests—and Protestant ministers—sitting in Parliament. At a time when the pope had been forbidding the clergy to stand for election in the Western democracies and in Latin America, in Hungary a handful of priests are regularly nominated by the party and take their seats in the legislature.[31] To outside observers this may seem incongruous indeed, but in Hungary this has always been the case, and the Communists are merely continuing an age-old practice. Not that it matters much one way or the other: Parliament has had no real power, and until recently the public has shown little interest in its deliberations.

But if the church leadership can be regarded as basically of a conservative bent, what about the "peace priests" who were the first to demand a break with the past, a greater democratization within the church, and the cheerful acceptance and cooperation with progress, defined in Marxist terms as the inevitable march of history toward a socialist future. The trouble is, of course, that the "peace priests" are a discredited lot, comprising intimidated or corrupt careerist individuals who are despised or totally ignored by the faithful, who consider them "collaborators" with the enemies of religion. They were, and are, still used, but they are never really trusted or respected by their communist masters.[32] While their role in church administration remains a sore point, their influence on the religious life of the people is negligible. Moreover, since their movement was reintegrated into the framework of the official church with the creation of Opus Pacis in 1957, while the regime simultaneously showed a growing interest and willingness to seek accommodation with the Hungarian Bishops' Conference and the Vatican, the importance of the "peace priests" has declined sharply, so that today—unlike the problems caused by Pacem in Terris in neighboring Czechoslovakia—in Hungary the "peace priests" are no longer an important issue.

The Base Communities

In contrast to the "peace priests," whose progressivism consisted of supporting government policies and the Soviet anti-imperialist peace drive, there are priests and small groups of lay Christians genuinely committed to realizing the teaching of the Gospels in their own lives; many of them also advocate general nuclear disarmament and peace. Most of these people belong to the so-called base, or basic, communities. Such small communities of Christians—Catholics and Protestants—have sprung up all over the world since World War II with the aim of practicing the faith together in prayer and charity in a more intensive way than people who, though baptized and registered, do not participate in their parish communities.

In Hungary the impulse for the creation of such small communities came in the late 1940s when the government suppressed the various religious orders and lay associations. Some of their members continued to meet in private, usually under the guidance of a zealous priest or former monk, in order to preserve and deepen their religious life. Unauthorized by the government, these associations and meetings had to be clandestine. Participants were placed under police surveillance and often were severely persecuted and imprisoned, charged with "political subversion." This continued until 1975 when, ostensibly to gain good points as a signatory of the Helsinki Accords, the Hungarian government ceased to harass people meeting in private for Bible reading, prayer, and discussion of purely religious topics. With the dramatic changes of 1988–89, the base communities have ceased to be an issue for church-state relations. On the contrary, they are now the focus of renewal in the church.

It would be difficult to categorize these base communities as representatives of either traditional or progressive Catholicism. Their aim is to return to the sincerity, simplicity, and total dedication to God of the early Christians and thus to contribute to their own and the world's salvation. To this end they make use of the traditional means of conscientious work, prayer, penance, and the sacraments, and they engage in charitable activities. However, they have scant regard for the bureaucratic institutions and power of the church, and they take the teaching of the Second Vatican Council about the "people of God" more literally than the bishops. Moreover, ideas that are regarded as progressive even among Catholics in the West, such as advocacy of women's ministry, refusal to bear arms, and universal disarmament, are gaining ground among the more radical of the Hungarian base communities. On the other hand, the "theology of liberation," with its Marxist overtones, is rejected outright. Advocates of liberation theology in Latin America want the church to be intensely involved in politics, to become an agent of the revolution. In Hungary, however, the most important reason for joining the base communities was, and still is, the believers' deep resentment over the use and manipulation of their church by the Marxists for their political ends, i.e., for building socialism.

The Legacy of the Past

László Cardinal Lékai died in July 1986 after almost exactly ten years in office as primate of Hungary. János Kádár, who had presided over the fate of Hungary since 1956, resigned his post of first secretary of the Hungarian Socialist Workers' party in May 1988. Before embarking on a discussion about the developments in church-state relations under the new leadership, it seems appropriate to draw up a balance sheet of the last decades.

Looking back, one can see that the Kádár regime was caught on the horns of a dilemma: It wanted the church's help to restore the moral fiber of the nation, but at the same time, unable to free itself from the ideological straitjacket of Marxism-Leninism, it abhorred the prospect of a genuine religious revival. This was well illustrated in its Janus-faced policies. On the one hand, the state continued to deal courteously with the Vatican, and it permitted Cardinal Primate Lékai to pursue his cautious policy of "small steps" forward, one at a time, granting him permission to open a house of retreat, build a Catholic retirement home for a few old people, start correspondence theology courses for laymen, and construct a handful of new churches—even a chapel in the crypt of Saint Peter's in Rome.[33] At the same time he was obliged to accept all the painful restrictions on church activity and the severe limitations on religious instruction of youth, and, on top of all this, he was ordered to put a brake on the intense religious revival manifest in the spread of the base communities.[34] The dirty job of harassing and silencing the most fervent believers, in the past a reserve of the political police, was handed over to the cardinal primate himself. In this game the regime was the winner in more than one sense; it succeeded in making Cardinal Lékai a "collaborator" in the eyes of the most zealous clergy and believers, while the base communities, regarded with intense suspicion by the regime, were crippled without the need to resort to unpopular "administrative measures."

Among these communities, the thousands of followers of the charismatic Father György Bulányi are regarded as the most dangerous because they live the lives of early Christians, reject the values of the consumer society around them, and frown upon the subservience of the church hierarchy vis-à-vis the state authorities. They are contracting out, so to speak, of the secular world of the twentieth century. Their greatest crime, however, is the commitment to follow the example of the Prince of Peace and refuse to bear arms. In Hungary conscientious objection to military service is equated with treason. The government requested and received the support of the primate in condemning the conscientious objectors and their mentor, Father Bulányi. Rome at first hesitated to take sides, patiently advising negotiation and compromise, but in the end gave its backing to Lékai and admonished Bulányi and his followers to submit to their bishops.[35] It is hard to see what other stand the Vatican could have taken without undermining the authority of the primate. Nevertheless, this affair is bound to remain a sad chapter in the history of the Hungarian Catholic church.

To sum up, the severe persecution of the church in the first fifteen years of communist rule, deplored today even by regime publications,[36] left the church debilitated, and deep psychological scars remain on both sides, making adjustment and adoption of new attitudes an extremely difficult and long process. There have been definite changes for the better. Communion with Rome has been restored, the hierarchy of the church has been reestablished, and police persecution of clergy and believers has all but disappeared. One also could mention the modest but very real growth of the Catholic press,[37] the permission by state authorities for the employment of lay graduates of the theological academy's correspondence courses to assist the priests in their duties, the authorization of a new order of nuns to work in the charitable institutions of the church, etc. On the other hand, the freedom of the church remains severely curtailed: The state continues to interfere with the appointments to church offices, imposes severe limitations on religious instruction of children, and prohibits any autonomous religious association or activity outside the authorized institutional framework of the church.

For the Communists, whose basic frame of reference in church-state relations remains the 1950 agreement, the church today represents an accepted though legally well-circumscribed and strictly regulated entity within the socialist state. Far from being persecuted, it has been invited to participate constructively in the Patriotic People's Front in the common task of fighting for peace and building socialism. The regime regards the status quo as satisfactory, though they admit that there is room for further improvement. Government spokesmen claim that there is freedom of religion in Hungary: Nobody is arrested for praying to God or going to church. The official leaders of the Hungarian Catholics, Protestants, and Jews echo these sentiments when they talk about great improvements in their lot; some even express complete satisfaction with the present state of church-state relations.[38] Of course, those who paint such a rosy picture do not tell about the state monopoly of the media and education whereby atheism and the materialistic worldview are virtually forced upon the entire population. Nor do they mention the continuing harassment and discrimination against believers at school and in the workplace, or the denial to them of university admission, job promotion, etc.

One also should mention the little-publicized but very serious tensions within the church, which are directly attributable to government policies. Apart from the old and still-festering issue of the "peace priests," which continues to poison relationships among the clergy, there was the 1975 decree establishing strict state control over and severely limiting religious instruction on church premises, which was accepted by the bishops but bitterly resisted by the lower clergy. The latter considered the deal a cowardly sellout by a hierarchy unable to break the old habit of Josephinist subservience to the state. Then there is the problem of the base communities mentioned above, which not only have caused widespread alienation of many priests and believers from the church leadership as it was represented by Cardinal Lékai, but also have caused cracks to appear even in the ranks of the hierarchy. By no means did all the bishops share the primate's crusading zeal against the Bulányists, whom Lékai regarded as little short of schismatics. In fact, a number of prelates and leading theologians rushed to the defense of the base communities and encouraged their activities.[39] In the process the unity and cohesion of the church have been weakened, not to mention the damage done to Lékai's image and authority.

The church requires genuine freedom to fulfill its mission. This was made amply clear by Pope John Paul II in his allocution to the Hungarian bishops at the close of their *ad limina* visit in October 1982. The Holy Father expressed grave concern over the moral decline in Hungary, especially the destruction of the ideal of the Christian family. He exhorted the bishops to do everything possible to expand evangelization—especially the religious instruction of the youth—reestablish the religious orders, and integrate the base communities into the hierarchical structure. Without mentioning the existence of discord or tension within the Hungarian church, the pope stressed the need for collegiality, mutual trust, and cooperation among the bishops, and also between them and their priests and between the clergy and the laity.[40]

Following the papal audience, Cardinal Lékai and Bishop Cserháti made statements to the press. While emphasizing the positive achievements of the last years, both admitted that serious problems have yet to be overcome if the church is to exercise its mission in freedom.[41]

The Dawn of a New Era?

Even before General Secretary of the CPSU Mikhail Gorbachev proclaimed perestroika, glasnost, and democratization as his program for the Soviet Union, Hungary was already moving toward greater openness, economic reform, and a certain restructuring of society. The need for change on all fronts, including the party and government structure, was widely recognized, and steps were taken to involve the churches in remodeling and revitalizing the stagnant society. The National Assembly devoted several hours of its winter session in December 1987 to an unprecedented discussion of the government's church policy, including the activities of the State Office for Church Affairs.[42] The head of that office, Secretary of State Imre Miklós, delivered a much-publicized and lengthy report to the assembly.[43] In it he repeated past declarations about the harmonious cooperation between the state and the churches in Hungary. He indicated that the government wished to see this cooperation widened and strengthened. He did not elaborate on how this should be done; however, in a press conference in Vienna on February 2, 1988, he suggested that the range of issues open for negotiations with the churches should be broadened. Among these issues he mentioned the possible increase in the number of church-operated schools, the expansion of the churches' network of charitable services, and the possible legalization of some of the monastic orders outlawed in 1950. On the other hand, he made it clear that regular religious broadcasts on television would not be allowed due to "organizational questions" and "limited time" in the television schedule.[44]

An indication that a significant improvement in church-state relations was indeed in sight was the invitation to the leaders of Hungary's churches from Prime Minister Károly Grósz to meet with him on March 14, 1988, at his office in the National Assembly for a discussion concerning the new legislation on church policy that his government was preparing.[45] During a three-hour discussion with the prime minister, Primate László Paskai, successor to Cardinal Lékai in the see of Esztergom,[46] recommended that the projected bill be of a regulative, not a restrictive, character. Furthermore, he asked the state to ensure the freedom for the churches necessary for them to function according to their nature. This ability to function includes all that the church needs to exercise its mission; i.e., freedom of worship, teaching, and association (including religious orders); maintaining schools, publishing houses, and press organs; and access to radio, television, and other media. He also asked the prime minister for legislation to permit conscientious objectors to perform an alternative service instead of bearing arms.[47] Bishop József Szendi of Veszprém was more outspoken. He reminded the prime minister that the existing agreements with the state were signed by an intimidated hierarchy under duress. He called for new, equitable legislation, for the removal of all restrictions on religious instruction, and for the freedom to reestablish all the religious orders which were dissolved by government decree. Furthermore, he demanded unrestricted opportunity for the church to work with the youth and for Catholic youth organizations to function and to have their own journals. This interjection by Bishop Szendi was published only in samizdat form, but it quickly spread all over the country, and not just among Catholics.[48]

Shortly after his historic meeting with the church representatives, Károly Grósz was elected on May 23, 1988, by a special party conference of the

Hungarian Socialist Workers' party to replace János Kádár as general secretary of the party. Thus he became the leader of both the party and the government.[49] By autumn 1989 Grósz was out of power and Rezsö Nyers headed the party. Meanwhile, as in August 1988, Primate Paskai, who received the cardinal's hat from Pope John Paul II on June 28, 1988, was notified via a letter from the government of all the salient features included in the law on church policy being drafted.[50]

The letter said that the government's aim was "regulation" rather than "restriction" of religious life, and it asked for "active participation of the Churches" in preparing the draft, stating that "only a Church that functions properly can be effective in helping us realize our social goals." The letter holds out the prospect for "legal guarantees for the autonomous activity of the Churches" and the elimination of "all discrimination on account of religious belief," including discrimination against teachers for their religious convictions. As a further concession, the churches would no longer be required to request state permission to hold religious instruction for the young or to report the names of those taking part to the authorities. Moreover, religious instruction would no longer be restricted to Sundays. The proposed law would lift the present limit on the number of pupils in church schools, including those run by Catholic monastic orders. Teachers in church schools would no longer have to reapply for a new work permit each year but would receive a one-time, unlimited permit.

According to the letter, the government plans to "reduce the number of Church positions requiring state approval" and ease restrictions on building and repairing church buildings and on receiving gifts from abroad. Churches would no longer need permission to organize public religious festivities and processions, but would only have to notify the authorities of the dates and places. Bishops would no longer be required to submit their circulars to state censors. The government also indicated that it was prepared to allow clergymen wider access to minister in hospitals and convalescent homes and possibly in prisons and reformatories.

In two important areas the government showed itself less willing to make concessions. First, the letter made it clear that some of the monastic orders outlawed in 1950 would not be relegalized, although they did not rule out the possibility of reestablishing some others. Second, the letter also did not promise to fulfill the churches' long-standing wish to increase their publishing activities, but said that the question would be examined.

There is a limit to the newfound generosity of the government. This was demonstrated in the repercussions to an article written by Bishop Endre Gyulay of Szeged-Csanád entitled "With Understanding and Patience," published in the government daily *Magyar Hirlap* on July 13, 1988. In it Gyulay challenged the authorities to "speak about the mistakes, abuses, and wrongdoings of their 'predecessors,'" and to "acknowledge publicly that they need a living church able to do its work." Only this would guarantee that the authorities' words would not be "tactical tricks." Gyulay also demanded the rehabilitation of church figures condemned in show trials, writing that such a gesture "would help heal the wounds that the Church still bears." He ended his article with an emphatic plea for an end of discrimination, especially in the hiring practices toward religious believers. Gyulay's article drew a public rebuke from the chairman of the State Office for Church Affairs, Imre Miklós. At the reception in honor of Primate Paskai's elevation to cardinal, Miklós broke into a tirade against a "bishop, who sought popularity by publishing in a newspaper some pathetic and rhetorical questions that do not speak well of his leadership qualities."[51] Gyulay's answer to Miklós's personal attack was not long in coming. In a speech at a birthday celebration the bishop repeated his conviction that "the era of blind subservience toward the authorities" was over. "The spirit of the new age bids us to speak out," he said. "We all have this responsibility."[52]

There is evidently a new era dawning in church-state relations in Hungary, affecting not only the Catholic church but also the Protestant churches, which are reclaiming some of their "nationalized" schools. The new spirit of greater tolerance and even cooperation in a growing number of issues also is reflected in a plethora of scholarly conferences and celebrations organized jointly by church and state organs, as well as in the way the media report these events. Apart from such international gatherings as the Congress of the Lutheran World Federation in 1984, the International Symposium of Marxist and Catholic Scholars in 1986, the meeting of the Executive of the World Jewish Congress in 1987, the General Assembly meeting of the World Federation of Bible Societies in 1988—all held in Budapest, a city vying to become an international convention center—there also have been symposia on Hungarian subjects which had been either neglected previously or given an unabashedly biased Marxist interpretation.

An example of the reevaluation of the church's role in Hungary's past was the Péter Pázmány Symposium organized jointly by the Hungarian Bishops' Conference, the Academy of Sciences, and the University of Budapest, February 29–March 12, 1988. Péter Cardinal Pázmány, who died 350 years ago, was the leader of the Counterreformation in seventeenth-century Hungary. Founder of Budapest University and numerous other schools, he was a great patriot, politician, orator, and writer. More than anyone else in his time, he helped to transform the archaic structure of medieval Hungarian to an easily flowing modern idiom. After World War II, the name of this Catholic prelate, a giant in Hungarian history, was barely mentioned, while his great contributions to Hungarian culture were minimized if not altogether ignored. Now, however, Cardinal Pázmány was rehabilitated by the Marxist and non-Marxist participants in the symposium, and, figuratively speaking, he was restored to his pedestal.[53] Shortly after this event, and perhaps inspired by it, the Workshop of Church History was created with the participation of Marxist, non-Marxist, Catholic, and Protestant historians.

In April 1989 Hungarian authorities made a dramatic announcement: the State Office for Church Affairs would be abolished and replaced with a new institution that would respect the independence of the churches. Hungarian authorities have already permitted the establishment of an independent ecumenical association of Catholics and Protestants. In July 1989 the ruling party decided that henceforth it would allow religious believers to join its ranks.[54]

The year 1988 held a special significance for the Hungarian church. In addition to the celebration of the worldwide Marian Year, proclaimed by Pope John Paul II, Hungarian Catholics remembered the fiftieth anniversary of the Thirty-fourth Eucharistic World Congress of 1938 in Budapest, and also the 950th anniversary of the death of Saint Stephen, the founder of the Christian Kingdom of Hungary. A symposium devoted to the memory of the holy king was held jointly by the Hungarian Bishops' Conference and the Hungarian Academy of Sciences on June 21–22, 1988. "Feudal King Stephen I," whose role as builder of the state was belittled in the history books of the last forty years, had again regained his title "Saint," as he is called now even by the Marxist historians and in the government media. He is highly praised for his statecraft and his accomplishments, which have been of lasting significance for the Hungarian nation. This rehabilitation process reached its high-water mark when on August 20, the feast day of Saint Stephen—renamed Constitution Day since the communist takeover—Politburo member János Berecz, the HSWP's central committee secretary for ideology, hailed Stephen as "the first among the great Hungarians and great ancestors whose memory and work is sacred to all decent patriots." Furthermore, he assured the public that the present government was willing to act "in the spirit of Saint Stephen's continually valid message."[55] Religious celebrations of Saint Stephen's Year, as 1988 was named by the Catholic Bishops' Conference, were organized countrywide. At specific dates the ornate reliquary with the Holy Right—the preserved right hand of Saint Stephen—was transported by an armored car of the state police to each of the episcopal sees, and there it was exposed to veneration in the cathedral and/or the largest public square. On August 19 at Székesfehérvár, the city where the holy king was buried, Brúnó Straub, the president of the Hungarian People's Republic, gave the festive address. In the presence of the special papal legate, Archbishop Francesco Colasuonno, and other distinguished guests, Straub praised Saint Stephen for his wisdom in learning about the world surrounding his country and for recognizing the necessity of timely constitutional changes in order to survive. Applying this wisdom to today's situation, he declared that the key to Hungary's further development was "the respect for democracy." This was unimaginable "without constitutional arrangements of the relations between the state and the citizen and also between the state power and the Church."[56]

On the feast day of Saint Stephen an outdoor mass was celebrated by Cardinal Primate Paskai on the steps of the Saint Stephen Basilica in Budapest before a crowd estimated at forty thousand.[57] Before the mass the cardinal read a letter from Pope John Paul II addressed to Hungarian Catholics, and then he repeated Saint Stephen's prayer offering the country to the Holy Virgin, the Magna Domina Hungarorum. At the end of the ceremonies he announced that the government and the bishops had invited His Holiness John Paul II to visit Hungary.[58] The entire event was broadcast live by Hungarian state television.

It should be mentioned that there has been a dramatic increase in media coverage of religious events since the Christmas mass was first broadcast on television in 1987. There have been interviews in the press, on radio, and on television with Catholic and Protestant bishops and clergymen, and even roundtable discussions on religious topics have been broadcast. The treatment is generally sympathetic. In recent months several newspaper articles paid tribute to Hungary's Christian heritage, whose value they freely acknowledged. When considering all the official speeches and writings celebrating the first king, it is interesting to note that Hungary is at a difficult turning point, just as it was during Saint Stephen's time. The leadership thus needs the support of a united people in facing the arduous task of a complete overhaul of the socioeconomic structure.[59]

Unanswered Questions

As we approach the end of the 1980s, questions inevitably rise as to the scope and direction that future developments might take. Suppose the present trend of liberalization continues, even accelerates, and that new legislation is going to free the church from the rusty shackles forged in the better-to-be-forgotten Stalinist period; would the hope for reconciliation between church and state become a reality? Would this have the desired impact on society? These are questions difficult to answer.

First of all, it is doubtful that the long-ingrained suspicion and distrust on both sides could be overcome enough to allow sincere respect for each other and cooperation to take root and grow. Is it not too much to expect the communists to tone down their atheist propaganda and to rescind the monopoly of "scientific materialist" orientation in teaching and thus allow the church a true and equal partnership in education and in the socialization of the youth? Would it not be more accurate to assume that as long as communist ideology remains what it is, i.e., diametrically opposed to religious belief, harmonious cooperation must remain just wishful thinking?

Bishop József Cserháti of Pécs, secretary of the Hungarian Bishops' Conference, published a lengthy article entitled "Dialogue without Prejudice" in a special edition of the government daily *Magyar Nemzet* on August 20, 1988, calling for a renewed effort on both sides to overcome old prejudices and new ones that, according to him, have surfaced recently. While acknowledging the sincerity of the government's efforts at rapprochement with the churches, Cserháti complained about a "certain stagnation" which seems to have set in in the dialogue, holding back the implementation of needed reforms.

There is, of course, a question whether the church would, or could, fulfill the promise expected from it even if it regained complete freedom of action. That is, to give effective assistance toward revitalizing and curing the sick society. Suppose the law now in preparation created such ideal conditions. How many schools, for example, would the church be able to staff and sustain financially? How many young men would choose to become monks or friars? How many girls would want to don the nun's habit? Let us not forget that the majority of religious orders were banned forty years ago, and their youngest surviving members are over sixty, while the younger generation of Hungarians grew up without any acquaintance with monastic life in a thoroughly secularized milieu, often without the most elementary knowledge about religion. Under such circumstances it is very likely that the church would not be in a position to do much more than it is doing now—at least, not in the foreseeable future.[60] In any case, it would take time and effort to build new cadres in order to replace the aged clergy, religious, and laity and to rebuild the many associations and clubs, the press, etc., which would be needed as instruments of evangelization. Will the church succeed better than the communist propaganda machine did in winning the allegiance of the broad masses? This is the ultimate question.

While it is impossible to answer these questions, there are encouraging signs on both sides pointing toward a better future. On the one hand, the political leadership in Hungary is committed to radical economic and social reforms which necessitate a far-reaching democratization and respect for human rights and liberties, including freedom of religion. This time it has little to fear from Big Brother, since Gorbachev's Soviet Union is struggling along the same path of perestroika, glasnost, and democratization. On the other hand, the recent episcopal appointments have given the

Catholic church a top-quality leadership.[61] Inspired and encouraged by the Polish-born pope, who cares deeply for Hungary, these relatively young, intellectually gifted, zealous pastors, ably led by Cardinal Primate Paskai, will certainly strive to do their best not only for the cause of the Kingdom of God but also for the earthly welfare of their compatriots and for their country.[62]

Finally, one should note also the many signs among the population at large, and particularly among the young students, that people are searching for the meaning of life and are determined to create a better, freer, and more pluralistic Hungary.[63] Taking everything into account, it is perhaps not just an idle dream to hope that there will be a revitalization of the church in the near future, a church as "the people of God," in the parlance of the Second Vatican Council, and that this people would, in the spirit of the council, work in harmony with their fellow men—regardless of religion or the lack of it, and including the Communists—in justice and brotherly love for the common good of all. The ideal of harmonious church-state relations and sincere cooperation, an empty propaganda slogan today, might yet become tomorrow's reality.

FACT SHEET

The Catholic Church in Hungary

Current strength of the church (1984)
- 6,464,000 faithful (62 percent of the population)
- 3,128 priests (2,517 in active service)
- 24 bishops (11 diocesan and 13 auxiliary)
- 65 nuns
- 247 seminarians

Number of churches and church facilities
- 4,268 churches
- 6 seminaries
- 8 convents
- 1 monastery
- 8 high schools (6 for boys, 2 for girls)
- 1 spiritual retreat home
- 4 old-age homes for priests (86-person capacity)
- 1 old-age home for former members of male religious orders (100-person capacity)
- 10 old-age homes for former nuns (630-person capacity)
- 2 old-age homes for lay persons (165-person capacity)
- 7 rest homes for priests

In the Saint Francis of Assisi Hospital in Budapest, formerly owned by nuns and the only hospital in Hungary still having a chapel, 30 medical beds and 10 surgical beds are reserved for church personnel.

Publishing houses

2 church-owned publishing houses

Chief news organs

Új Ember (New Man) (weekly since 1945; 90,000 copies)

Katolikus Szó (Catholic Word) (organ of the Catholic Priests for Peace Movement; biweekly since 1957; 14,000 copies)

Vigilia (monthly since 1935; 12,000 copies)

Primates since 1945

József Cardinal Mindszenty, archbishop of Esztergom, prince primate of Hungary (1945–74). During Cardinal Mindszenty's impediment, due to imprisonment and exile, the Conference of the Hungarian Catholic Bishops was chaired by:

József Grősz, archbishop of Kalocsa (1949–51) (imprisoned 1951–56)

Gyula Czapik, archbishop of Eger (1951–56)

József Grősz, archbishop of Kalocsa (1956–61)

Endre Hamvas, bishop of Csanád (1961–69), from 1964 archbishop of Kalocsa

József Ijjas, archbishop of Kalocsa (1969–76)

László Cardinal Lékai, archbishop of Esztergom, primate of Hungary (1976–86)

László Paskai, archbishop of Esztergom, primate of Hungary (1986–present)

8

The Catholic Church in Yugoslavia, 1945–1989

Pedro Ramet

Relations between the Catholic church in Yugoslavia and the regime are colored by three central symbols: Josip Strossmayer, Alojzije Stepinac, and the Second Vatican Council. For the regime, Bishop Josip Juraj Strossmayer of Djakovo (1815–1905) represents the spirit of "Yugoslavism" (promoting the cultural and political unity of Serbs, Croats, Slovenes, and Macedonians) and cooperation between church and state, while Alojzije Cardinal Stepinac (1898–1960) symbolizes exclusivist Croatian nationalism and the spirit of defiance. For the church, on the other hand, Strossmayer is remembered also as an active missionary, an ecclesiastical "liberal" who opposed introduction of the principle of papal infallibility, and a champion of Slavic (vernacular) liturgy in Catholic churches in Croatia; Stepinac is associated with heroic efforts to protect Serbs and Gypsies from slaughter by the Ustaše fascists during World War II, with defiant outspoken criticism of both the Ustaše and the communists, and with unflinching loyalty to the church. Thus in certain ways—for both regime and church—twentieth-century Stepinac symbolizes the church's traditional pastoral care for the nation, while nineteenth-century Strossmayer symbolizes adaptability, liberality, and modernity. It is worth noting, however, that through his progressive social programs and his use of church funds for charitable programs, Stepinac may be said to have anticipated the "church of the poor" of the Vatican II period.

The Second Vatican Council (1962–65) was a watershed for the church. More particularly, it was the point at which modernizing currents within the church received strong encouragement, in certain aspects, from the Holy See. The results for the church were a new impetus to self-assertion, a new direction in its social presence, and a deepening of the division between traditionalists and modernizers. Interestingly enough, while the Belgrade regime expresses enthusiasm for the "modernizing" Strossmayer, it has felt threatened, according to Zlatko Markus, by the reformist wing of the church, which it views as "dangerously" active.[1] Far more to the liking of at least some elements in the regime is the opinion once expressed by Archbishop Frane Franić of Split (retired in 1988) to the effect that the church is called upon "to administer the sacraments and to conduct Church services, but political and social revolution should be left to others. That is not our calling."[2] The result is that theological conservatives in the church (including the mixed conservative Franić and the generally conservative onetime archbishop of Sarajevo, Smiljan Čekada) have enjoyed better relations than have some of their theologically more liberal colleagues with those elements in the regime who have sought to constrict church activity.

In Yugoslavia, as elsewhere, the traditional/modern dichotomy manifests itself against the backdrop of another—partly reinforcing, partly crosscutting—dichotomy between hierarchy and lower clergy. In the early postwar years, tensions between hierarchy and lower clergy centered on the establishment of priests' associations, a move encouraged and supported by the regime. More recently, tensions have developed between the episcopal conference and the Christianity Today Theological Society over the latter's unilateral 1977 decision to reorganize itself as a self-managing enterprise and thereby obtain certain tax exemptions. The society is responsible for running a formidable publishing house and for issuing the *AKSA Bulletin*.

The Dawn of Communist Rule

In April 1941 the Nazis invaded Yugoslavia and partitioned it into several zones of occupation. The Croatian fascist movement known as the *Ustaše*, under the leadership of Ante Pavelić, set up a puppet state in Croatia, under Nazi protection. Communist "partisans," led by Josip Broz Tito, organized guerrilla resistance against the Nazis and the *Ustaše*. Although the communist regime would later try to portray the Catholic church's role during World War II monochromatically as the advocacy of Croatian independence and Ustaše rule, a rather substantial number of Catholic clergymen actually cooperated with or fought on the side of the Partisans, including Archbishop Kuzma Jedretić, Fr. Franjo Pos from Prezid, Franciscans Bosiljko Ljevar and Viktor Sakić, and the pastor of Saint Mark's Church in Zagreb, Msgr. Svetozar Rittig, lauded by one Yugoslav author as "the most important figure in the people's liberation struggle, among Catholic priests."[3] Rittig, who joined the Partisans in 1943 and later became first president of the Croatian Commission for Religious Affairs, remaining active on the political scene until his death in July 1961, is said to have been devoted to the ideas of Bishop Strossmayer. By contrast, according to Ćiril Petešić, "only a part of the clergy, and a small part at that," mostly young priests, actually endorsed the Ustaše program, while most of the older clergy are said to have been pro-Yugoslav.[4]

From the beginning of partisan warfare, the Partisans needed priests to cater to their combatants, and this led to the establishment of the Religious Department of the AVNOJ[5] Executive Committee in December 1942. Where religious schools were concerned, the Partisans were eager for instructors to teach about Cyril and Methodius (who created the Glagolitic alphabet), Sava Nemanjić (founder of the autocephalous Serbian Orthodox archdiocese), and Bishop Strossmayer.[6]

After the trying experiences under the Kingdom of Yugoslavia in which Croats had failed to achieve the autonomy they had sought,[7] the Croatian Catholic hierarchy initially welcomed the establishment of a separate Croatian state.[8] Some clergy, such as Archbishop Ivan Šarić of Sarajevo, remained sympathetic to the Ustaše until the very end. Other hierarchs were more critical. Bishop Alojzije Mišić of Mostar, for instance, began condemning Ustaše oppression of Serbs as early as 1941.[9] Similarly, Zagreb's Archbishop Stepinac repeatedly contacted Minister of the Interior Andrija Artuković (e.g., in letters dated May 22, 1941, and May 30, 1941) to register his objection to the new legislation affecting Catholics of Jewish descent (which required them to wear the Star of David). He declared membership in the lay activist movement Catholic Action and the Ustaše movement to be incompatible (in December 1941), worked quietly to obtain the release of Orthodox believers from prison, and spoke out in his sermons against racism, genocide, and Ustaše policies (for example, in his sermon of October 25, 1943).[10]

But if the local clergy were divided in their attitudes toward the Ustaše, and if some were frankly ambivalent about the Croatian state, the Vatican had a clear line where *communism* was concerned. The difficulties experienced by the church in the USSR provided a troubling precedent, and Pope Pius XII adopted a forcefully anticommunist stance. *Katolički list* (April 24, 1937) put it this way: "Communism is in its very essence evil. Therefore, the person who values Christian culture will not cooperate with [communists] in a single thing. If some are seduced into error and on their part help communism to grow stronger, they will be the first to be punished for that error."[11] Thus there was no basis at that time for a relationship of trust between the Vatican and the emerging Communist parties in Eastern Europe.

Meanwhile, as the Partisans captured districts of Croatia they massacred both civilians and priests, including more than two dozen unarmed Franciscans at the monastery of Široki Brijeg.[12] The independent state of Croatia collapsed in May 1945, and the Communist party set up its administration in the remaining parts of the country.

On June 2, 1945, Communist party General Secretary Josip Broz Tito, Croatian President Vladimir Bakarić, and Msgr. Rittig held a meeting with Catholic bishops Franjo Salis-Seewis and Josip Lach. Tito's statement on that occasion has given rise to so much subsequent controversy that it is worth quoting at length. Replying to a statement presented by Bishop Salis, Tito said:

> As I have already explained to Msgr. Rittig, I would like to see a proposal worked out, as you see fit, as to how to solve the question of the Church in Croatia, the Catholic Church, because we shall be discussing the same thing also with the Orthodox Church. On my own part, I would say that our Church needs to be national [*nacionalna*], that it be more responsive to the [Croatian] nation. Perhaps that will seem a bit strange to you when I so strongly support nationality. . . . I must say openly that I do not want to undertake the right to condemn Rome, your supreme Roman jurisdiction, and I will not. But I must say that I look at it critically, because [church policy] has always been attuned more to Italy than to our people. I would like to see that the Catholic church in Croatia now, when we have all the preconditions there, would have more independence. I would like that. That is the basic question. That is the question which we want to see resolved, and all other questions are secondary questions which will be easy to work out.[13]

Given the consistency with which communists in other East European countries were pressing Catholic hierarchs to break with the Vatican,[14] it seems reasonable to interpret this statement along the same lines (though Tito later denied that that was his intention). After all, the so-called Old Catholic church in Croatia had already provided a precedent. Indeed, this church, which had formed in reaction to the proclamation of the doctrine of papal infallibility in 1870, was able to set up additional independent organizations after World War II in Slovenia, Serbia, and Vojvodina.[15]

The following day, Tito and Bakarić received the papal delegate, Abbot Ramiro Marcone, together with his secretary, Don Giuseppe Masucci, who complained that the communist media were relentlessly attacking the clergy and the Vatican, even claiming that the Vatican had wanted a Nazi victory, and that the children were being taught in the schools that there is no God and trained to sing, "We will fight against God! There is no God!"[16]

On June 4 Tito and Bakarić received Stepinac, and on this occasion Tito praised Pope Leo XIII for having backed Strossmayer in a dispute with the court of Vienna about Russia and asked Stepinac to support Belgrade in its dispute with Italy in Istria. Stepinac in turn urged Tito to meet with representatives of the Croatian Peasant party and even those of the Ustaše movement, to try to heal the emotional wounds of the war.[17] In spite of this meeting, the communist government continued to arrest Catholic priests and believers, including the bishops of Križevci, Split, and Krk.

Archbishop Stepinac was receiving hundreds of appeals from Croats asking him to intercede with the new authorities on behalf of imprisoned relatives. On June 28, 1945, he took up the matter with the president of the Croatian government and urged the authorities to drop the campaign against "collaborators" because eventually it would be necessary to imprison ordinary workers, peasants, and so forth. But one reason for the campaign was sheer opportunism on the part of particular individuals in the party, many of whom wanted to settle old scores.[18] Stepinac also criticized the secret trials being conducted at the time, calling it inconsistent with the regime's claim to be a "people's" government.

Meanwhile, the regime decided to abolish all private high schools following completion of the 1945–46 school year and moved to eliminate religious instruction from the curriculum of state elementary schools. In late summer 1945 the authorities began bulldozing the cemeteries in which combatants from other sides were buried, stirring protests from believers in the areas affected. Within a month of the war's end, the communist authorities also began forcible confiscations of church property in Križevci, Zagreb, Remete, and elsewhere, seized Caritas property and property of the Zagreb archbishopric, and outlined a more extensive program of agrarian land reform, which promised to produce further confiscations. When Stepinac complained about these developments in a letter to Tito, the latter replied by alluding to his interest in receiving a reply from the Catholic bishops with respect to "the possibility of coming to an agreement about certain matters between church and state."[19]

In these circumstances the first episcopal conference in Yugoslavia in six years was convened by Stepinac, on September 17–22, to discuss the new situation in which the church found itself. Immediately upon convening, the episcopal conference sent a letter to Tito asking for withdrawal of the law on agrarian reform, respect for Christian marriage, respect for continuation of religious instruction in elementary schools, and respect for Catholic cemeteries, and offering to consult with the state on a new law on agrarian reform. The following day, after further discussions, the conference sent a second letter to Tito, this time asking for the release from detention of Bishop Janko Simrak, freedom of the press, continuation of the private schools, and the return of confiscated property to the church.[20] At the close of the conference the assembled bishops issued a joint pastoral letter recounting the hardships suffered by the church at the hands of the communists (243 priests and 4 nuns killed over four years, 169 priests still in prison, and 89 unaccounted for) and demanding complete freedom for church activities, institutions, and press. This pastoral letter was read in the churches, with copies sent to the commissions for religious affairs in each of the federal units.[21]

The letter convinced the communist authorities that Archbishop Stepinac would be as much a thorn to them as he had been to Ustaše leader Ante Pavelić. They therefore reached a decision, shortly after the letter was issued, that a case would be prepared against him and he would be put away in prison.[22]

The Trial of Archbishop Stepinac

The authorities continued to try to persuade Archbishop Stepinac to break relations with Rome; instead, Stepinac denounced the proposal in yet another pastoral letter.[23] The authorities then tried to persuade the Vatican to remove Stepinac from his seat in Zagreb; the Vatican refused.[24] The archbishop was arrested on September 18 and put on trial together with fifteen other persons who were being tried on criminal charges connected with the excesses of the Ustaše Independent State of Croatia (*Nezavisna Država Hrvatska*, or NDH). On September 30 the charges against Stepinac were read in court. Specifically, he was accused of collaborating with the Ustaše in the calculated hope of enriching the church and the upper clergy, allowing the Križari (Crusaders) and Catholic Action to work for fascism, using traditional religious celebrations as political manifestations in support of the Ustaše, encouraging the coercive conversion of Orthodox Serbs to Catholicism, serving as a rallying point for enemies of the communist state after the war, and concealing Ustaše archives and materials of the Croatian Foreign Ministry under an agreement concluded with Ante Pavelić.[25]

The *official* (edited) record of the trial shows Stepinac refusing to cooperate with his interrogators:

> *Presiding judge: Nedjelja* no. 15 of April 27, 1941, carries a report with the following content: "Archbishop Dr. Alojzije Stepinac, as representative of the Catholic Church and Croatian metropolitan, visited General Slavko Kvaternik as deputy of the Poglavnik in the homeland and conducted a lengthy conversation with him. In that way, as Radio Zagreb reports, the most cordial relations were estab-

lished between the Catholic Church and the Independent State of Croatia."

Why did you consider it necessary, only two days after the establishment of the Independent State of Croatia and the occupation of our country by the enemy, to hurry to visit the Ustaše commander, Slavko Kvaternik?

The accused: I have nothing to say.

Presiding judge: Did you visit Pavelić on April 16, 1941, four days after the occupation of our country but two days before the capitulation of the Yugoslav army, which was at war with the enemy?

The accused: I decline to answer. . . .

Presiding judge: Did you, immediately in the first days of the occupation, i.e., in mid-April or early May, take part in a meeting to which you invited Ustaše emigrants, returnees?

The accused: I have nothing to say. If necessary, the defense lawyers appointed for me can answer that.[26]

The prosecution made use of a string of citations from the Catholic and Ustaše presses to try to incriminate the archbishop. But most of the Catholic periodicals cited by the prosecution in substantiation of its charges were published in dioceses lying outside Stepinac's jurisdiction; in particular, the Franciscan publication *Andjeo čuvar*, the Jesuit publication *Glasnik Srca Isusova*, the Sarajevo weekly *Katolički tjednik*, and the Sarajevo publication *Glasnik sv. Antuna*.[27] The prosecution claimed that Stepinac and other clergy had received decorations from the Croatian government in gratitude for their political support and produced pictures showing the archbishop together with Ustaše ministers on official occasions and at official receptions.[28]

Chief prosecutor Jakov Blažević dwelled at length on the church's cooperation with the Ustaše in carrying out forced conversions of Orthodox believers. The archbishop defended himself by insisting that the church had exerted no pressure on the Orthodox and could not be held responsible for coercion applied by others, and by pointing out that a large number of Catholics had converted to Orthodoxy, under pressure, during the period of the Yugoslav kingdom.[29] Against the archbishop's denials, Blažević insisted that between 1943 and 1944 Archbishop Stepinac became involved in vaguely defined "conspiratorial work" with Pavelić and Croatian Peasant party leader Vladko Maček, and—in a bizarre turn—charged the archbishop with having sent Christmas wishes to Croatian prison laborers in Germany.[30]

L'Osservatore Romano, the Vatican newspaper, scoffed at the charges and held that the real reason for the trial was the pastoral letter of September 22, 1945.[31] By continually returning to the subject of this letter, the authorities seemed to confirm this interpretation:

Presiding judge: In the pastoral letter of last year, of 1945, one finds, among other things, the claim that the Franciscans at Široki Brijeg were well-known antifascists. Here is a photograph, taken at Široki Brijeg, showing Ustaše colonel Jure Frančetić with Fr. Bonaventura Jelačić, an "antifascist" from Široki Brijeg. Also in the photograph are [other] Franciscans of Široki Brijeg together with Ustaše and Italian officers. Is this the famous antifascist stance of the Franciscans from Široki Brijeg?

The accused: I have nothing to say.

Presiding judge: You could correct your declaration in the pastoral letter—were they not, maybe, fascists?

The accused: I think that we have nothing to correct.[32]

Blažević later returned to this subject in order to assail the idea of freedom of the press:

J. Blažević: Defendant Stepinac, in connection with the facts which have been revealed and established in this trial, I ask you please, for what purpose did you convene the episcopal conference in September 1945 and for what purpose did you write the pastoral letter?

The accused: I have nothing to say.

J. Blažević: I will cite some passages from the pastoral letter to you and then I will ask you some questions about it. Speaking of the persecutions of priests etc., . . . you say this: "And when we explain all this to you dearest believers, we do not do so in the hope of provoking a battle with the state authorities. We neither desire such battles nor do we seek them." Defendant, you say that you have always sought peace and stable political life and you say, "That peace is so necessary to everyone today, but we are deeply convinced that that peace can only be founded on the pacification of relations between church and state." What do you say to that, defendant Stepinac?

The accused: I have nothing to say.

J. Blažević: You have nothing to say, because you are ashamed. In the pastoral letter, in order to realize the principles that you stress, you seek complete freedom for the Catholic press. Is that freedom for the press we have been reading? . . .

The accused: I have nothing to say.

J. Blažević: You have nothing to say. In the pastoral letter you write, "Only under those conditions can circumstances be put in order in our state and can lasting internal peace be achieved." So, you

> demand freedom for your press, that is, the Catholic press which you commanded and which you converted completely into an instrument of fascism. That press could only return if fascism would return, if the Ustaše were to return. . . . It's clear that you seek to introduce fascism in our country anew, that you seek [foreign] intervention in the country.[33]

The court rejected most of the witnesses proposed by the defense; on the other hand, most of the fifty-eight witnesses summoned by the prosecution to testify against Stepinac were not from his archdiocese. The trial ended on October 11 when the court found all but three of the defendants guilty[34] and sentenced Archbishop Stepinac to sixteen years at hard labor followed by five years' deprivation of civil and political rights. *L'Osservatore Romano* condemned the proceedings as a complete sham whose outcome had been determined in advance and whose script had been drafted to serve political ends, and challenged the authenticity of some of the documents produced by the prosecution.[35]

Some time after the trial, Milovan Djilas—at that time still a prominent member of the political establishment—admitted in private conversation that the real problem with Stepinac was not his politics vis-à-vis the Ustaše but his politics vis-à-vis the communists themselves, and in particular his fidelity to Rome. "If he had only proclaimed [the creation of] a Croatian Church, separate from Rome," said Djilas, "we would have raised him to the clouds!"[36] More recently, in February 1985, Blažević himself admitted this in an interview with the Croatian youth weekly *Polet*. Admitting that Tito had wanted Stepinac to cut the Croatian church's ties with Rome, Blažević commented, "That trial of Stepinac was forced on us. If Stepinac had only been more flexible, there would have been no need of a trial."[37]

The Priests' Associations

Since it had proved impossible to co-opt the church hierarchy, the authorities quickly pursued an alternative policy of trying to sow divisions and discord within the church and win over *portions* of the clergy into a cooperative relationship. One token of this was the regime's response to the pastoral letter of September 22, 1945. *Borba*, for example, reported that many Catholic priests in Bosnia-Herzegovina refused to read the letter in their churches,[38] while other papers carried a story claiming that Archbishop Nikola Dobrecić of Bar had criticized those bishops who had signed the pastoral letter.[39]

A more tangible symptom of this strategy was the promotion of priests' associations that would lie outside the authority of the bishops. However, after the controversial trial and imprisonment of Archbishop Stepinac, the clergy, especially in Croatia, were ill disposed to cooperate with the regime. All the same, the first Catholic priests' association was created in Istria in 1948, under the presidency of Dr. Božo Milanović, and most Istrian priests joined. That same year an attempt was made to set up an association in Slovenia. The first attempt failed, however, and the matter had to be taken up again the following year. These first two associations were more or less spontaneous on the part of the priests, though actively encouraged by the government.

A third priests' association was set up in January 1950 in Bosnia-Herzegovina. The government set up health insurance for members and pressured priests to join, for example, by making permission to give religious instruction contingent on membership (a policy adopted in 1952 but eventually abandoned). By the end of 1952 nearly all the priests in Istria were association members, along with 80 percent of priests in Bosnia-Herzegovina and 60 percent of priests in Slovenia.[40]

The bishops were opposed to these associations and, in a statement dated April 26, 1950, declared them "inexpedient." Two and a half years later, after consulting the Vatican, the bishops issued a decision forbidding the clergy to join the associations. This move provoked a crisis in church-state relations when the Yugoslav government sent a note of protest to the Holy See on November 1, 1952. The Holy See replied on December 15, detailing the troubles being experienced by the church, but this note was returned unopened. On December 17 the Yugoslav government terminated diplomatic relations with the Vatican.[41]

By the end of 1953 three more priests' associations for Catholic clergy were created, in Croatia, Serbia, and Montenegro. The associations thus paralleled the federal structure of the political system, with one association per republic. These associations served as conduits for state subsidies—which were welcome given the destruction caused by the war. The Bosnian Franciscan province, for example, began receiving state subsidies through this source in 1952, and in the period 1952–64, received a total of 63 million old dinars in subsidies (estimated as equivalent to DM 315,000).[42] Nor were the Franciscans the only ones to receive state aid. Other institutions of the Catholic church also received aid, including the theological faculty in Ljubljana, which received several state subventions; the diocese of Djakovo (where Strossmayer once presided), which received a subsidy to restore the cathedral; and the diocese of Senj, which received a state subsidy to restore the episcopal palace.

In addition to health insurance, subsidies, and better relations with the bureaucracy, the priests' associations also enjoyed preferential treatment where publications were concerned. Thus Dobri pastir, the Bosnian association, has been able to publish a religious periodical and a calendar since 1950, that is, even at a time when almost all of the rest of the church press was suppressed.[43]

The priests' associations are integrated into the structure of the Socialist Alliance of Working People of Yugoslavia (SAWPY) and are officially viewed as a means for clergymen to protect and realize their "professional interests." Despite claims by various observers that the associations have benefited the church, the hierarchy has remained deeply suspicious.[44] In 1970, for example, Archbishop Frane Franić of Split wrote that the Franciscans, insofar as they constitute three quarters of Dobri pastir's membership, were "true collaborators with the people's authorities."[45] A meeting of representatives of clergymen's associations in 1978 showed that the antagonism felt by the hierarchy toward the associations was working against the latter. Vinko Weber, secretary of the Society of Catholic Priests of Croatia, told that meeting that his once-vibrant organization was "now in its last gasp," that it had not been allowed to distribute its publications on church premises, and that it had subsequently even lost its printing facilities. Weber continued,

> Unfortunately, the days of *non licet non exedi* are still with us. This ban has remained in force right up to the present day. And let me tell you why this is so! Our society has its own statutes, and these statutes include the famous article 3, which, inter alia, states that members of the Society of Catholic Priests shall promote the brotherhood and unity of our peoples, defend the achievements of the national liberation struggle, promote ecumenism, and so on. And this is the crux of the matter, that is, they cannot forgive us for incorporating this article into our statutes, and this is why they keep trying to foil us in everything we do. Things have finally reached the point where even certain Catholic societies in other republics are starting to refuse to have anything to do with us, thinking that we are some kind of black sheep, and this is only because they have been misinformed. But the upshot of all this is that nowadays our society is barely managing to keep itself together.[46]

Similarly, the Association of Catholic Priests of Montenegro, which attracted more than twenty of the thirty Catholic priests serving in that republic in 1954, could count only six members as of 1978—and all of them were *retired* priests. Thus, far from being able to serve as an effective intermediary between church and state, the priests' associations are at the most a useful mechanism for health insurance and other material benefits, or, on the other hand, irrelevant vestiges of a failed strategy. In Slovenia, by contrast, the Catholic priests' association has always been weak and marginal, and it figures today chiefly as the publication outlet for a quarterly newsletter and for a series of religious books for children.

Phases in Church-State Relations

The years 1945–53 were the most difficult period for the church. The Catholic press shriveled, and where there had been about 100 periodical publications prior to the war, the church could now count only 3: *Blagovest* (in Belgrade and Skopje), *Dobri pastir* (in Bosnia), and *Oznanilo* (in Slovenia), which appeared as a two-page (front-and-back) bulletin from 1945 to 1946, and as a four-page bulletin from 1946 to 1952. (As of 1987, by contrast, the Catholic church was publishing 134 periodicals in Croatia alone.[47]) Catholic hospitals, orphanages, and homes for the aged were seized and closed, and Catholic secondary schools were nationalized. Seminaries were likewise confiscated; for example, in Zagreb, Split, Travnik, Sent Vid, Ljubljana, Maribor, and Sinj.[48] Some six hundred Slovenian priests were imprisoned. The faculties of theology of the Universities of Ljubljana and Zagreb were separated from the universities by governmental decree in 1952.

The passage of the Law on the Legal Status of Religious Communities on April 27, 1953, stirred hope for change insofar as it guaranteed freedom of conscience and religious belief. Perhaps as important was Tito's call, in a speech at Ruma that same year, for a "halt to physical assaults on the clergy,"[49] although this was partly a concession to Western public opinion, now that Tito's Yugoslavia had broken with the Soviet bloc. The years 1953–64 saw some reduction in the pressures against believers, though as Paul Mojzes noted, "excesses—such as torture, imprisonment on false charges, and even murder by the secret police—were still practised from time to time, more in some parts of the country than in others."[50] Both church and state were clearly groping toward a modus vivendi during this period. And hence when Yugoslavia's bishops submitted a memorandum in September 1960 detailing their complaints and demands (including the unhindered prerogative to build and repair churches), they also included a calculated invitation to dialogue, noting that "the Constitution guarantees freedom of faith and conscience to all citizens, while the Law on the Legal Status of Religious Communities [gives form to] and defines this constitutional provision more closely. These legal provisions contain the nucleus of all that is necessary for relations between the church and the state to develop in line with the principle of a free church in a free State."[51] By early 1964 there were unmistakable signs of a new atmosphere in church-state relations; by 1965 Belgrade and the Holy See were engaged in negotiations; and on June 25, 1966, Belgrade and the Vatican signed a protocol and exchanged governmental representatives. In the protocol Belgrade guaranteed the Roman Catholic church "free conduct of religious affairs and rites," confirmed the Vatican's authority over Catholic clergy in Yugoslavia in religious matters, and guaranteed the bishops the right to maintain contact with the Vatican. On the other side, the Vatican undertook to ensure that priests in the country would respect Yugoslavia's laws and that the clergy "cannot misuse their religious and church functions for aims which would have a political character."[52]

The hierarchy in Yugoslavia welcomed the protocol. Archbishop Franić saw in it the promise of "a new era for our Church,"[53] while Franjo Cardinal Šeper, then archbishop of Zagreb, commented in 1967:

> The Catholic community cannot escape being engaged. But that presumes a greater amount of freedom. We hope that that freedom will steadily increase for the Catholic Church as well as for other social communities. . . . In the Belgrade Protocol, the Catholic Church accepted the existing legislation of Yugoslavia as a starting point. That at least presumes the possibility of legislative development in religious questions, so that [religious policy] would not lag behind the development of reality and become an anachronism.[54]

Four years later, Yugoslavia reestablished full diplomatic relations with the Vatican, and in March 1971 Tito paid an official visit to the Vatican.

The general liberalization in Yugoslavia in the late 1960s permitted the launching of a series of church periodicals, including the fortnightly newspaper (now weekly) *Glas koncila*, which has become an important organ for church opinion. The church also began to revive its social programs for youth, not only in Croatia and Slovenia but also in Bosnia, where the authorities showed especial misgivings at the church's new self-confidence.[55] Catholic clergy in Rijeka, Split, Zadar, and Zagreb responded enthusiastically to the Croatian liberal-nationalist groundswell of 1967–71, and in Bosnia-Herzegovina Franciscan priests gathered data on the number of Croats occupying administrative posts in that republic.[56]

It was this renewed self-assertion of the church, combined with the purge of the liberal faction in the party in 1971–73, rather than the protocol and exchange of emissaries that colored church-state relations at the outset of their fourth postwar phase, from 1970 to today. On the church's part, the tenth anniversary (in 1970) of the death of Cardinal Stepinac was commemorated as demands emerged for his canonization.[57] For the regime, however, the rehabilitation of Stepinac seemed fraught with danger because his trial had converted him into something of a Croatian mythological hero. Accordingly, Croatian sociologist Srdjan Vrcan warned a seminar at Krapinske Toplice in January 1973 that "viewpoints, completely political and totally nonreligious in spirit, have again been revived as the widest ideological base, viz., viewpoints that the Croats and Serbs are two completely separate worlds between which no kind of stable and positive form of unity can be established."[58] Stepinac has become the focal point for the self-defense of the Croatian Catholic church (as witnessed in Franjo Cardinal Kuharić's annual sermons in defense of Stepinac) and his trial remains the foundation of the attempted self-legitimation of the regime.

In this most recent period at least six issue areas have complicated the church-state relationship.

First, the church has never reconciled itself to the inclusion of courses in atheism and Marxism in the school curricula and has repeatedly asked for equal time or, alternatively, the removal of these courses from the schools. The point of view of the League of Communists of Yugoslavia (LCY) was summarized by *Nedjeljna Dalmacija* in 1972: "The LC cannot accept the concept of an ideologically neutral school nor a school pluralism based on the individual right of each parent, because the educational system is the social obligation and affair of a social institution."[59] The church, however, complains that it is dissatisfied "with the method [of teaching], with the content, with the textbooks, with the sundry provocations through which believing children . . . are indoctrinated and atheized."[60] In late 1987 the Episcopal Conference of Yugoslavia issued a statement calling on the government to respect the right of parents to obtain a religious education for their children.[61]

In autumn 1987 the episcopal office set up a theological institute in Mostar, Herzegovina, in cooperation with the Franciscan province in Mostar. The institute planned to offer a three-year theological program to laypersons and quickly registered forty-five students for the 1987–88 academic year. Despite the fact that there were precedents for such an institute (in Zagreb, Split, Ljubljana, and Maribor), republic authorities closed it down in November 1987. The Yugoslav news agency TANJUG explained that the establishment of the institute was "directly opposed to the law on the legal position of religious communities in the Socialist Republic of Bosnia-Herzegovina which, in article 20, states emphatically that religious communities can form religious schools only for the training of religious officials. Scientific and educational treatment of believers outside the church itself is, therefore, not in conformity with the law."[62] *Glas koncila* issued a strong protest of this action.[63]

Second, the church has from time to time questioned the legitimacy of excluding believers from the ranks of the LCY. In 1971, for instance, the Slovenian Catholic weekly *Družina* published an article complaining that the opportunities provided by SAWPY to Christians were inadequate and that their exclusion from the party was a token of political inequality.[64] Again, in 1987, Cardinal Kuharić raised this issue in an interview with the Catholic journal *Veritas*, adding that believers are excluded from high posts in various sectors of public life.[65] The party has repeatedly repudiated this interpretation, however, and has even urged party members to eschew marriage with believers and to stay away from church ceremonies.[66] On the other hand, a 1988 article about religious life in Serbia found that only a third of party members in Serbia called themselves atheists, with most giving a positive description of religion.[67]

Third, the church has repeatedly challenged the regime over human rights—whether civil, national, or even the human rights of believers qua believers. In a public statement Kuharić used his 1987 Easter sermon to plead on behalf of a twenty-six-year-old Croatian dissident named Dobroslav Paraga. Paraga had been charged with "slandering the state" after he gave an interview to the Slovenian youth magazine *Mladina* in which he discussed the treatment he had received during a three-year prison sentence for antistate activity.[68] The defenselessness of believers in the face of slander by the secular press has also preoccupied the church, which has deplored the lack of objectivity and fairness in the mass media and the inability of those calumniated to reply in the same forum.[69] *Glas koncila* is probably the church's single most important vehicle for self-defense against insinuations and distortions in the secular press.

Fourth, the church continues to complain that believers are in other ways treated as second-class citizens and that religious belief is treated as an *alienable* right. In particular, the church complains that military personnel are not allowed to attend church services in uniform or to receive church newspapers or religious books in the barracks. The church also has long sought to obtain access to incarcerated believers, regardless of the crime for which they are in prison.[70] The church also has been concerned about continued discrimination against believers in hiring practices in the public sector. This issue was raised by the Split archdiocesan journal, *Crkva u svijetu*, in late 1987 and by a special commission of the Provincial Episcopal Conference of Slovenia in 1988.[71]

Fifth, some elements in the political establishment continue to try to foster and aggravate internal divisions within the church. Recently, the Christianity Today publishing house has seemed to some to be the beneficiary of official favor because of its "liberal defiance" of the hierarchs. Earlier, *Glas koncila* expressed concern that *Nedjeljna Dalmacija* was seeking to drive a wedge between the archbishop of Zagreb and the archbishop of Split, manipulating the latter's statements to suggest opposition to or divergence from the policy of the Zagreb archbishopric.[72] This strategy is epitomized by the rival formula that recurrently praises the "vast majority" of the clergy while condemning the "political extremism" of a "reactionary minority."

And sixth, the legislation governing religious practice has itself been an important bone of contention between church and state, both in the preparatory stage and in discussions about the execution of policy. With the passage of the 1974 Constitution, the religious law of 1953 was suspended and the republics were entrusted with the task of passing their own legislation in this domain. The new religious laws took effect in Slovenia on May 26, 1976, and in Bosnia-Herzegovina on January 4, 1977. After a vocal debate, Croatia was the last of the eight federal units to pass a new law; it took effect on April 17, 1978. Among the issues in contention were the ban on church sponsorship of recreational activities, the absence of legal sanction for church access to radio and television, and an article requiring the consent of the minor before parents could enroll him in religious instruction. *Glas koncila* objected, saying that "many citizens who are believers quite properly observe that neither they nor their minor children are asked for consent to be introduced in the course of their schooling to Marxism in its emphatically atheistic form."[73] The authorities compromised on the last point mentioned, and the final version of the Croatian law requires the child's consent from age fourteen on, rather than from age seven, as specified in the draft.

Internal Divisions

In an earlier study I described the presence of three opinion groupings within the political establishment where religious questions are concerned: (1) orthodox Marxists, who have no interest in genuine dialogue with the churches and believe that they should disappear under communism; (2) passive contract Marxists, who are willing to adopt a passive attitude toward religion provided that the churches adopt a passive posture toward society and politics; and (3) liberals, who are interested in dialogue and believe the churches can make a positive contribution to society.[74] In consequence, Catholic clergy note an increasing diversity among secular newspapers in their treatment of the church. Fr. Živko Kustić, chief editor of *Glas koncila* since 1973, has said that most of the secular newspapers are interested in dialogue, and in particular that the widely read Croatian daily *Večernji list* has an increasingly positive content. *Politika ekspres*, by contrast, is less serious in its treatment of the church, according to Kustić, while a few papers (specifically *Dnevnik* of Novi Sad and *Večernje novosti* of Belgrade) are overtly hostile to the church.[75] Some papers are strangely inconsistent, doubtless reflecting serious differences of approach among those to whom they are beholden. The best example of this tendency may be *Vjesnik*, which has run conciliatory articles in the past but also presented Pope John Paul II's 1987 trip to Chile in a highly distorted fashion, obscuring the pope's searing criticism of the Pinochet regime and his call on Chilean believers to work toward a better future and portraying him instead as supportive of the oppressive Pinochet.[76] Thus factionalism on the part of the regime is as important as factionalism within the church in shaping church-state interaction.

It might be noted parenthetically that factionalism is far less pronounced in Slovenia, where, aside from the very prosocialist theologian Vekoslav Grmič of Maribor, the church is by and large very harmonious, while liberals clearly predominate in the establishment. The result is that church-state relations in Slovenia are more tranquil and less marked by controversy than relations in Croatia and Bosnia.

In this section I propose to focus on three sources of internal discord within the Catholic church in Yugoslavia: the heterogeneity of responses to the Second Vatican Council, the controversy surrounding Christianity Today, and the rivalry in Herzegovina between the secular bishop and the Franciscan order.

Twenty-five of Yugoslavia's twenty-nine Catholic bishops (at the time) participated in the Second Vatican Council. Four Yugoslav bishops also participated in the work of the commissions, namely, Archbishop Franjo Šeper of Zagreb and Archbishop Frane Franić of Split in the Theological Commission, Archbishop Gabrijel Bukatko of Belgrade in the Commission for Eastern Churches, and Bishop Alfred Pichler of Banja Luka in the Liturgical Commission.

Two things quickly became clear: first, that the more general division between theological traditionalists and theological progressives was replicated within the ranks of Yugoslavia's bishops; and second, that certain bishops espoused a mix of "traditional" and "progressive" views. On the whole, Šeper figured as a progressive, Archbishop Smiljan Čekada of Sarajevo as a traditionalist, and Franić as a mixture. In fact, Franić himself conceded that while he took a traditional stance on some issues, on others he was innovative and prepared to try new approaches.[77]

Šeper and Franić favored introduction of the vernacular for Holy Mass, for example, with Franić favoring use of the vernacular for all church rituals; Čekada preferred to retain Latin as the universal language of liturgy. Šeper and Franić also both supported ecumenism and efforts to patch up old conflicts with particular churches. But when a specific application of the ecumenical spirit came up—namely, a proposal to build a cathedral in

Skopje for joint use by Catholics and Orthodox—Čekada resisted, calling this "an infantile and romantic ecumenism." Šeper and Franić split on the proposed introduction of married deacons, on the other hand, with Šeper favoring it but Franić and fifteen other Yugoslav bishops opposed. Franić also found himself among the traditionalists in defending the notion of the personal primacy of the pope, and he proposed that the vow of poverty, hitherto taken only by orders, also be extended to secular clergy. Much of the discussion during the council centered on proposals to expand the role of the laity in the church generally and in the liturgy in particular. Predictably, Čekada spoke out against laicization.[78]

Vatican II ended in a compromise between the traditionalist and progressive wings, but not without strengthening the latter current and reinforcing the self-awareness of the former. The result has been a reinforcement, within Yugoslavia, of a polarization of opinion among clergy that goes back well over a hundred years.[79]

In some ways the Theological Society Christianity Today is a product of Vatican II.[80] Founded in 1968 as a research and publishing center, Christianity Today soon became a haven for theologically progressive clergymen. In May 1977 the society reorganized itself as a self-managing association in order to free itself from the rather overwhelming tax burden to which it had been liable previously. Several of the bishops condemned this move, arguing that it had not been cleared by an episcopal authority and that it opened the prospect for the society to come under Communist party supervision and thus figure as a Trojan horse.[81] Archbishop Franić became one of the most vocal critics of Christianity Today; he banned priests in his archdiocese from having any contacts with the association and told *Glas koncila*, in an interview in 1981:

> Some of our theologians tell us that the Church has in its history adapted to all social systems, and that it can and must adapt today, say, to self-managing socialism. . . . It is also said that this is in fact the doctrine of the Second Vatican Council.
>
> I hold that this is an altogether mistaken interpretation of the council and of Church history. The Church has, to be sure, adapted to all social systems, for example, even to slave-owning society and feudal society, and today to capitalist and socialist society. . . . However, the Church did not introduce into its structures either the slave-owning system or the feudal system or the capitalist system. So, accordingly, it cannot introduce the system of self-managing socialism into its structures either. In this sense, neither the Church nor its theology nor its pastoral work can be based on the principles of self-managing socialism, nor can they enter into self-managing socialism as a part

> or branch, since this socialism of ours, although it is a more humanist form of Marxism and of the dictatorship of the proletariat, is still essentially aimed at creating a new civilization which is supposed to be atheist.[82]

Priests in Croatia and Bosnia-Herzegovina have been divided over this decision by Christianity Today, with the Jesuits tending to be among the most critical. Moreover, with the issuance of the encyclical *Quidam episcopi* on March 8, 1982, directed against the Czechoslovak priests' association Pacem in Terris, the episcopal conference has wielded yet another weapon in its battle with the progressive theologians of Christianity Today.[83] The danger as the bishops see it is that the publishing house will carry out its tasks "outside Church structures," and open up channels for LCY influence in the church.[84] The danger as the Christianity Today theologians see it is that a traditionalist view of episcopal authority will result in the strangulation of a perfectly pragmatic adjustment to fiscal realities. And thus the controversy surrounding Christianity Today is simultaneously a controversy between traditionalist and theologically progressive points of view, a controversy between hierarchy and theologians, and a controversy about possible channels of regime penetration of church institutions.

The third and final focus of internal church discord to be treated here is the long-standing rivalry between the diocesan clergy in Bosnia-Herzegovina (most particularly the bishop of Mostar) and the Franciscan order. The Franciscans are the largest order in Yugoslavia (1,094 members in 1978), far ahead of the next largest order—the Salesians (103 members in 1978).[85] For centuries the Franciscans enjoyed a complete monopoly within the Catholic church where Bosnia-Herzegovina was concerned, based on an understanding reached with the Ottoman sultan. The Franciscans of Herzegovina separated from the Bosnian Franciscan province in 1852 and established a separate administrative province forty years later. The regular diocesan clergy entered Bosnia-Herzegovina only in 1881, in the wake of the Austrian occupation, but even so, for the next sixty years the bishop of Mostar was almost always a Franciscan. The Franciscan–diocesan church relationship became seriously troubled only in the wake of non-Franciscan Petar Čule's appointment as bishop of Mostar in 1944.[86] In particular, the Catholic church in Yugoslavia was receiving aid from Catholic agencies in the United States after World War II, but a decision was made to withhold all of it from the Franciscans.[87]

A delicate balance prevailed in Franciscan-diocesan relations. Hence, in the period 1945–78, of the seventeen new parishes established within Bosnia-Herzegovina, eight were entrusted to the Franciscans, seven to the diocesan clergy, and two were split between them.[88] Beginning in the mid-

1960s, there were repeated clashes between pro-Franciscan parishioners and diocesan clergy over efforts to place Franciscan parishes in the hands of diocesan clergy or to redraw parish boundaries.[89]

Starting in 1976, the present bishop of Mostar, Pavao Žanić, has pressed hard to roll back Franciscan jurisdiction. In early 1981 two young Franciscans—Ivica Vego and Ivan Prusina—refused to relinquish their posts in Mostar and became the center of considerable strife and controversy. Bishop Žanić declared them suspended and initiated action to obtain their expulsion from the order. Shortly thereafter, six youngsters whom these two Franciscans had been counseling began to report apparitions of the Madonna, who, they said, was endorsing the Franciscans and blaming the bishop of Mostar for his "severity."[90] The apparitions continued on a daily basis for more than five years, with Franciscans taking the lead in ministering to the many thousands of pilgrims who have been flocking to the site of the apparitions in the Herzegovinan village of Medjugorje. (Beginning on January 8, 1987, the appearances were reported only every twenty-five days.)[91] These circumstances made it inopportune for the bishop to take any further steps against the Franciscans for the time being. Žanić, thus frustrated by the Franciscans, referred to the apparition as the "Franciscan miracle" and was said to have stacked the initial investigative commission with skeptics in order to defuse the miracle as fast as possible.

Even this brief elaboration of three important sources of internal discord should make it clear that the Catholic church in Yugoslavia cannot be considered a monolith, and that church-state relations are accordingly diffracted by political complexity.

Belief and Unbelief

In the years since the communist takeover of Yugoslavia, religiosity has declined overall. This decline has been sharpest among the traditionally Orthodox[92] and least noticeable among the Muslims, while the smaller neo-Protestant sects such as Seventh-Day Adventists and Jehovah's Witnesses have probably grown in membership. In varying degrees, as the figures in table 8.1 make clear, the trend has been unmistakably toward the secularization of society, especially in urban areas.

A 1960 survey conducted among youth found that Croats recorded the greatest proportion of believers, followed by Slovenes and Muslims (both ten percentage points behind the Croats), Macedonians, Serbs, and Montenegrins.[93] A 1985–86 survey among more than 6,500 Yugoslav young people found similar results. Of those from Catholic families, 62.3 percent said they were religious, as compared with 43.8 percent of those from Muslim families and only 26.2 percent of those from Orthodox families.[94]

Table 8.1 Believers and Nonbelievers in Yugoslavia, 1953–84 (in percentages)

	1953	1964	1969*	1984*	1984**
Believers	87	70.3	53.1	45	51.9
Indifferent or undecided	—	0.5	32.1	37	27.4
Atheists	13	29.2	14.2	18	18.6
No answer	—	—	0.6	—	2.1

* Zagreb region

** secondary-school children in Split

Sources: Zlatko Frid, *Religija u samoupravnom socijalizmu* (Zagreb: Centar za društvena djelatnosti omladine RK SOH, 1971), p. 33; Branko Bošnjak and Štefica Bahtijarević, *Socijalstičko društvo, crkva i religija* (Zagreb: Institut za društvena istraživanja Sveučilišta u Zagrebu, 1969), p. 29; *Nedeljni vjesnik,* April 1, 1984; and *Slobodna Dalmacija* (Split), March 2, 1987.

Among the traditionally Catholic republics of Croatia and Slovenia, moreover, while the 1970s and 1980s have seen a continued decline in religiosity in Slovenia, the same period (1968–85) recorded an increase in religious observance in Dalmatia: Where 32 percent of Dalmatian youth declared themselves religious in 1968, 52 percent did so in 1985.[95] A 1985 survey of obituary notices in the press confirmed these results, showing 46 percent religiosity and 54 percent indifference or atheism.[96]

Following a pattern typical of transitional societies, urban residents and young people are less likely to be religious. The difference between city and village is reflected, for example, in the recent report that while 95 percent of young Catholics in Yugoslav villages obtain religious instruction, only 10 percent of those in cities do so, averaging 60 percent for the country as a whole.[97] And for reasons still not clear, a 1986 survey in Belgrade showed that the proportions of *both* atheists and believers were shrinking, with an increasing number of people reporting themselves to be "agnostics."[98] By 1975 a group of Zagreb sociologists had found that 40 percent of respondents had no definite or clear worldview.[99] The persistence and even increase of agnosticism may be related to the more general failures of Yugoslav ideology and socialization.

For all that, party members have tended, at least until recently, to see religion as an unwelcome social phenomenon. Branko Bošnjak and Štefica Bahtijarević conducted an extremely comprehensive survey of attitudes toward religion among residents of Zagreb and its immediate vicinity in 1969. Their results showed that 28.7 percent of LCY members viewed religion as actually "damaging," as compared with 18.7 percent of government functionaries, 15.8 percent of World War II veterans, 10.3 percent of members of administrative organs, and 8.5 percent of SAWPY members.[100]

Other results show a clear relationship between atheization and social-

Table 8.2 Responses to the Question "Do You Accept Marxism?" (1969; in percentages)

	Yes	No	Partly	Not acquainted with it
Believers	18.5	2.3	10.7	66.0
Undecided	32.8	0.0	23.8	41.9
Nonbelievers	61.1	0.0	15.0	23.9
Atheists	82.7	0.0	4.7	12.6

Source: Bošnjak and Bahtijarević, *Socijalističko društvo*, p. 122.

Table 8.3 Responses to the Question "How Often Do You Participate in Public Meetings?" (1969; in percentages)

	Regularly or very often	Sometimes	Never
Believers	17.5	40.0	40.9
Undecided	30.6	48.6	19.5
Nonbelievers	39.5	47.2	13.3
Atheists	51.7	37.4	10.9

Source: Bošnjak and Bahtijarević, *Socijalističko društvo*, p. 101.

ization to accept Marxism and respond positively to Yugoslav politics, thus confirming LCY suspicions of religion, though perhaps only with circular logic. In table 8.2, for example, three times as many nonbelievers as believers are shown to accept Marxism, while believers were the most likely to report nonacquaintance with the Marxist creed. Table 8.3 shows a clear inverse correlation between religious belief and participation in public meetings. When asked if church teachings influenced their participation in public life, 33.2 percent answered in the affirmative.[101]

Other questions touched on the practice of religion in Yugoslavia. Of the sample polled, 46.8 percent said they felt that they could practice their faith freely in Yugoslavia, versus 6 percent who felt they could not (7.8 percent answered with a qualified "yes," adding that they avoided conversations about religion, while 37.8 percent were not believers, and 1.6 percent declined to answer).[102] Asked if they considered it easy to safeguard their faith in an atheistic environment, 25.1 percent of the sample replied in the negative, with an additional 16.4 percent replying merely that they did not reveal their religious belief to others. This makes for a composite negative reply of 41.5 percent.[103]

And finally, when asked if believers are more moral than nonbelievers, 1.6 percent of party members answered in the affirmative—indicating that not all LCY members are convinced atheists.[104] A more recent poll, conducted anonymously in 1987, found that 7.7 percent of party members

Table 8.4 Population Reporting Religious Belief (November 1985), by federal unit

Federal unit	Percentage
Kosovo	44
Croatia	33
Slovenia	26
Macedonia	19
Bosnia-Herzegovina	17
Serbia	11
Vojvodina	10
Montenegro	10

Source: Intervju, March 28, 1986, as reported in AKSA (April 4, 1986), in *AKSA Bulletin*, August 5, 1986, p. 8.

surveyed (in the Zagreb region) were believers, and that 12.5 percent admitted that they were sending their children to religious instruction.[105] Table 8.4 shows the proportion of Yugoslavs reporting religious belief in 1985.

Yugoslav society is a partly secularized and partly secularizing society, and not merely because of LCY rule. In this context the Catholic church has had to adapt to changed circumstances and to discover new strategies for maintaining and propagating the faith. Many clergymen have called for coexistence, such as Croatian theologian Tomislav Šagi-Bunić, who wrote in his *Ali drugog puta nema* (1969): "The political community and the Church are independent and autonomous of each other, each in its own sphere. Both stand in service, although for different reasons, at the personal and social summons of the very same people. Thus, . . . appropriate cooperation between them is necessary, so that they can better carry out their service toward people."[106]

Conclusion

In his report to the Tenth Congress of the League of Communists of Croatia (LCC) in May 1986, Mika Spiljak, president of the LCC Central Committee, devoted a few lines to the Catholic church. These were interesting only for the claim that the Croatian party had adopted a "comprehensive program" in summer 1985 specifically to uproot dogmatic antireligious attitudes from the ranks of the LCC.[107]

One is entitled to be skeptical of the success with which such a program can be carried out. Not that there are no sincere people working for a reevaluation of the church-state relationship. Shortly after Branimir Stanojević's doctrinaire book *Alojzije Stepinac, zločinac ili svetac?* (Alojzije Stepinac, criminal or saint?) went to press, *Književne novine*, the organ of the Serbian Writers' Association, published an article by Branislav Petrović urging abandonment of the saint-criminal dichotomous approach to Stepinac, commending Cardinal Kuharić for discussing the Stepinac case, and calling for a new, posthumous "trial" to reassess the controversial case.[108] This plea was not taken up, and in May 1986 Croatian authorities put sociologist Ivan Cvitković to work defaming Stepinac with comments which *Glas koncila* termed completely false.[109]

Ironically, while the Catholic church has persisted in calling for the posthumous rehabilitation of Stepinac, the weekly magazine *Danas* expressed hopes in July 1985 that the projected commemorative celebrations in Djakovo of Saint Methodius (whose fame had been boosted partly through Strossmayer's efforts) would "lead to the rehabilitation of Strossmayer in the eyes of the [Croatian Catholic] Church, as 'one of the most significant personalities of her history.'"[110] This is foolishness, of course, because Strossmayer has never been condemned by the church and cannot therefore be rehabilitated.

One may well wonder why it is that church and state in Yugoslavia should expend so much energy debating the merits of two long-dead hierarchs. Clearly it is not the individual historical person who is of concern here but rather the currents and meanings which each is taken to symbolize and personify. Strossmayer, among other things, is useful as evidence that there are, from the regime's point of view, "good" clergymen as well as "bad" clergymen. Stepinac is much more central to the church-state relationship in Yugoslavia, however, for he is a key part of the lens through which the past *and the present* are viewed. To restore Stepinac's good name would be to place church-state relations on a new footing and to open the door to the possibility of liberalization. The association of the two was reflected in the cautiously positive comments made by Ivan Lalić, longtime chair of the Croatian Office for Religious Affairs, about the Catholic church's ecclesiastical congress at Marija Bistrica in 1984, adding praise for Kuharić's public defense of Stepinac. Soon after, the decision was taken to remove Lalić from his post.[111] He was replaced by the relatively hard-line Zdenko Svete, a former Yugoslav ambassador to the Holy See.

Not surprisingly, it is in Slovenia—where both Strossmayer and Stepinac are largely irrelevant—that church-state relations have acquired a somewhat friendlier tone. This was signaled in December 1986 when Ljubljana's Archbishop Šuštar became the first Yugoslav hierarch in the postwar period to be allowed to wish his flock a Merry Christmas over public radio.[112] The decision sparked a lively national debate, but in September 1989 the Slovenian Assembly passed a law on holidays, which declared Christmas a public holiday in the Republic of Slovenia.[113] Šuštar's Christmas greetings were once again broadcast in December 1987, but only amid massive controversy and discussion in the press. Meanwhile, Mitja Ribičič, a prominent Slovenian politician, suggested that rather than engaging in endless debate about the rectitude of broadcasting the prelate's Christmas greetings, it would be better to discuss how to improve the access of believers to jobs in both local and federal governmental agencies.[114] Could all this be a sign of impending liberalization? Perhaps. One suggestive piece of evidence is the announcement in 1988 that the Catholic Faculty of Theology in Ljubljana, which was forced to separate from the university shortly after the war, would shortly be reincorporated into the University of Ljubljana.[115] On the other hand, the resolutions of the Thirteenth Party Congress in June 1986, insofar as they concerned religion, showed no sign of such a liberalizing inclination.[116] Moreover, with party and government alike divided into competing power centers in the eight federal units, church-state relations assume a distinctly regional character in this multiconfessional society.

FACT SHEET

The Catholic Church in Yugoslavia

Current strength of the church (1985)
- 7,293,000 faithful (1984)
- 4,077 priests (2,645 diocesan; 1,432 secular)
- 36 bishops
- 6,029 nuns
- 269 monks (68 diocesan; 201 secular)
- 853 seminarians (504 university level; 349 secondary level)

Number of churches and church facilities (1985)
- 2,778 parishes (2,375 diocesan; 403 secular)
- 7 theological faculties (2 higher schools at Zagreb and Ljubljana; 3 diocesan schools at Makarska, Rijeka, and Sarajevo; 1 Franciscan at Sarajevo; 1 faculty at Split)
- 1 philosophical-theological institute (Jesuit institute in Zagreb)
- 34 seminaries (10 diocesan university level; 14 diocesan secondary level; 7 secular university level; 3 secular secondary level)
- 283 monasteries (124 operated by Franciscans)
- 415 convents
- 528,457 children attending catechism classes (1974)

Chief news organs (circulation figures for 1987)
- *Glas Koncila* (Croatian-language weekly, since 1962 as bulletin, since September 1963 as newspaper; 100,000 copies)

Družina (Slovenian-language weekly, 1952–73 as biweekly; 100,000 copies)
Kana (Croatian-language family monthly since 1970; 40,000 copies)

Important institutional structures
Kršćanska Sadašnjost (Christianity Today), publishing house, created in Zagreb, 1968
Interdiocesan Conference for Youth, created in Ljubljana, 1971

Archbishops of Zagreb (since 1945)
Alojzije Cardinal Stepinac (1937–60)
Franjo Cardinal Šeper (1960–70), coadjutor from 1954
Franjo Cardinal Kuharić (1970–present)

Archbishops of Ljubljana (since 1945)
Gregorij Rožman (1930–45/59), fled his post in 1945
Anton Vovk (1945/59–63)
Jozef Pogačnik (1963–80)
Alojzij Šuštar (1980–present)

9

The Catholic Church in Romania

Janice Broun

Catholicism in Romania is dominated by two factors: the church's own national diversity and the state's particularly antagonistic policy. There are between 2 and 3 million Catholics in Romania, belonging to two churches. One is the Roman, or Latin Rite, church; its members, primarily national minorities, have increased in numbers from fewer than 1.2 million in 1945 to approximately 1.4 million, about 60 percent of whom are Hungarians, the rest mainly Germans and Romanians. This church has an ambiguous legal status and therefore has to function under even greater handicaps than the recognized religious bodies. The Eastern Rite Catholic church is in an even worse situation because it officially ceased to exist in 1948. At that time it had a membership of more than 1.5 million. It was Romanian in nationality and fully accepted by most Romanians. It now functions clandestinely and seems to have retained the allegiance of over two-thirds of its original membership, making it the largest, most flourishing, and best organized underground church in Eastern Europe.

Catholics have been victimized by the state on several counts: as a Christian denomination facing a hard-line communist government with an aggressive atheist policy; as a church that owes ultimate allegiance to a "foreign ruler," the pope; as far as the Latin Rite church is concerned, as a church of national minorities and therefore subject to the chauvinism of a government that specializes in playing off one national minority against another; and as far as the Eastern Rite church is concerned, paradoxically, because it is thoroughly Romanian, it is regarded by the state and certain church leaders as a potential threat to the "national" Orthodox church. Romania is by tradition an Orthodox country, with 80 percent of its population of 23 million people Orthodox at least in name.

Many Catholics are hardly aware of the existence of their church in Romania. This is partly because of its division into two churches and its national diversity, which have made united action difficult, and partly because the state has generally blocked its communication with the West. Survival has been the basic concern for both Catholic churches, a fact which makes the usual criteria applied in this volume almost completely irrelevant.

Historical Background

In order to understand the unique situation which faces Catholics in Romania we are compelled to examine Romania's history and geography, and thus to see how the separate branches of the church originated, developed, and reached their respective statuses during Romania's period of independence between the two world wars.[1]

Romania comprises three provinces: Wallachia, which lies south of the great arc of the Carpathian Mountains; Moldavia to the northeast and east; and Transylvania, a triangle bounded by Wallachia, Moldavia, and Hungary. Wallachia and Moldavia were vassals of the Turks from 1504 to 1714 but remained Orthodox. After various vicissitudes they achieved independence in 1859. The two together are known as the Old Kingdom. Transylvania has been, and still is, the most controversial part of the land. It is a region of national, religious, linguistic, and cultural diversity, and it is of key importance with regard to the Catholic church. Although the majority of its population of over 7 million are Romanians (about 5 million), almost indubitably the longest-settled group, Transylvania did not become part of Romania until 1918. Its fertile valleys and mineral resources have long attracted other settlers, notably Hungarians (1.7–2 million today). The Hungarians settled the area between the late ninth century and the thirteenth century. Their kings installed Saxons (Germans) and Czekels (other Magyars speaking a Hungarian dialect) to protect Hungary from Turkish invasion, using the Carpathians as a bulwark, and, after the disastrous Hungarian defeat at Mohács in 1526, as a refuge. (It is possible that the Czekels, who settled in the eastern Carpathians around Mercurea-Cinc, may have penetrated the Carpathians directly from the east. The Hungarians had a high regard for them.) Transylvania thus became a dependency of Hungary.

The three "nations"—Hungarians, Saxons, and Czekels—their rights carefully defined, enjoyed feudal, and in the case of the Germans (mostly town dwellers) civic privileges, including religious freedom, along with economic and social supremacy, largely at the expense of the native Wallachs (Romanians), who were regarded merely as "plebs," and not as a nation. Although in the majority, the Wallachs were kept in a state of illiteracy, poverty, and servitude (serfdom and its attendant abuses were not abolished until the late eighteenth century). Transylvania indeed might be described as a classic example of European colonialism. Whether the Wallachs or Hungarians were the original settlers is still a hotly disputed issue.

Because the Hungarians and Germans were originally Catholics, the Latin Rite Catholic church has been long established, though alien to the Romanians. The settlement of Swabians, mostly Catholics, in the Banat after the Turks were driven out in the eighteenth century added yet another foreign group. The Reformation, however, made considerable inroads in Transylvania, and Catholics eventually were outnumbered by Calvinists and Lutherans.[2] Thus the diets, the ruling bodies, became predominantly Protestant. Zealous Protestants put the Orthodox peasantry under considerable pressure to convert. They translated the Bible and catechisms into Romanian; even their bishops were appointed by the Protestant rulers. The Orthodox church in the Old Kingdom, severely crippled through circumstances beyond its control, was in no position to help.

When the Austrian victory over the Turks in 1683 brought Transylvania into the Habsburg Empire, Emperor Leopold I wanted to reestablish Catholicism. Finding Protestantism too firmly entrenched among the Hungarians and Germans, he turned to the Orthodox Romanians, offering them the same rights as Catholics if they would accept papal supremacy, purgatory, the *filioque* in the creed, and the use of unleavened bread at mass, while they would be allowed to retain their own liturgy and married priesthood. A synod at Alba Iulia in 1698, led by Bishop Athanasius with thirty-eight senior clergy, accepted the proposed union as the best way of escaping from Calvinist proselytizing; the agreement was signed by 2,772 representatives of the church.[3] Thus the Eastern Rite Catholic church came into existence, though not until 1738 did it have its own bishopric, at Blaj. Though denounced by the patriarch of Constantinople and other Orthodox, this despised union became a major means whereby the Romanian people rediscovered their national identity and culture. Priests and seminarians sent to Rome to complete their studies came to realize how much their distinctive language and culture owed to Latin and to the Roman settlement of the lower Danube dating from the empire under Trajan and Hadrian in the second century. Romanians in this way came to see themselves as descendants of the Roman colonists and true heirs of Roman civilization, which proved a vital psychological breakthrough for a people who had ceased to value themselves.

These beliefs spread through the medium of the "schools of Blaj" from 1754 onward.[4] These schools functioned at every level; they taught Orthodox and Catholic alike, brought literacy, and pioneered the resurgence of national culture and scholarship that inspired the independence movement. The Orthodox in the Old Kingdom, who had used mainly Slavonic, and Greek, in their liturgy, experienced a similar cultural resurgence, and by the eighteenth century had replaced Greek with Romanian.

The promised equality with the Latin Rite Catholics failed to materialize, as Bishop John Innocent Micu (Klein), spokesman for the Romanians of Transylvania, repeatedly pointed out in the Diet—to such an extent that he was eventually driven into exile.[5] At last, in 1744, the church was given the status of a "received religion," putting it on a par with Lutherans, Reformed, Unitarians, and Latin Rite Catholics. By 1750 Transylvania could claim 1,704 Eastern Rite Catholic parishes (543,657 members) and only fourteen Orthodox parishes (25,065 members). Soon after, however, a wave of disenchantment with the Catholic union led to secessions, and a Serbian Orthodox bishop was installed in Brasov as a result of desperate requests from the Orthodox; in 1762 the imperial patent recognized the Orthodox community, although it was not granted "received religion" status.

Under an increasingly tolerant imperial policy, well over half the Eastern Rite parishes reverted to Orthodoxy. Despite this, once the religious situation stabilized there was generally little ill feeling between members of the two churches, who were mostly peasants living side by side with practically identical services.

Leaders of considerable stature emerged in the Eastern Rite church. They reformed the alphabet, which had been Slav, published a new Romanian-language Bible (used by all the churches), and helped establish a Romanian literary tradition. In the nineteenth century they countered the Magyarization brought on by an upsurge in Hungarian nationalism.[6] Blaj was given metropolitan status in 1853; ten years later, the Romanians of Transylvania received the same rights as other nationals, and the Orthodox church was put on an equal footing with Catholics and Protestants. The leaders of both the Eastern Rite church and the Orthodox church continued to cooperate, particularly in the promotion of Romanian independence. Significantly, in 1918 an Orthodox bishop, Miron Cristea, and a young Catholic bishop, Iulius Hossu, journeyed to Bucharest together to announce to Emperor Ferdinand their Diet's decision to unite Transylvania with the Old Kingdom to form modern Romania.

The Catholic Churches in Romania, 1918–45

With the entry of Transylvania into the new Romania the two Catholic churches faced a change in status. Whereas previously the Latin Rite church had shared the privileged position of its Hungarian and German members, now it found itself in a country to some extent hostile to them. By contrast, the Eastern Rite church, by the Constitutions of 1923 and 1938, was placed second only to the Orthodox church; the latter was the "church of the majority," the former received "priority over other cults."[7] Relations between the Orthodox and the Eastern Rite Catholics were close, in many ways closer than those between the two Catholic churches. Both regarded the Latin Rite church as foreign rather than truly Romanian. Their clergy could stand in for each other in emergencies. Mixed marriages were common, and a workable compromise led to sons usually joining their father's church, daughters their mother's. The atmosphere of harmony and mutual respect at the grass-roots level still exists today, despite the communists' attempts to destroy it.

Both Catholic churches were adversely affected by the nationalization of all primary schools in 1921, but they were still able to maintain their many secondary schools,[8] over 100 aid and welfare institutions, 140 monasteries and convents with about 2,100 religious, and 7 seminaries. Attempts to have united seminaries were foiled by the opposition of certain Orthodox in the government. There were thiry religious publications catering to a wide range of readers. The 1927 Concordat gave the churches ample scope for their activities and considerable rights; the state insisted, however, that all bishops be Romanian citizens.

In 1930 the diocesan structures of both churches were redefined. The Eastern Rite church now had six dioceses: Fagarus and Alba Iulia (with the seat of the metropolitanate at Blaj), Cluj-Gherla, Lugoj, Oradea, Maramures, and a new auxiliary diocese of Bucharest to serve the 100,000 or so members who had migrated to the capital. In 1945 there were 1,561,000 members in 1,807 parishes served by 1,906 priests.[9]

Whereas the Eastern Rite church was fairly compact and homogeneous, its sister church was nationally divided and geographically scattered, and its members spoke several different languages. The Hungarians, who formed 75 percent of the membership, were mainly found in the Transylvanian dioceses of Oradea, Satu-Mare, and Alba Iulia; the Germans (21 percent) lived mostly in the Banat in Timoşoara Diocese, where there were also Bulgarians, Slovaks, and Croats; the remainder, mostly in Moldavia (diocese of Iaşi), were Romanians, though their origin is a matter of controversy.[10] Hungarians claim that these people are descendants of Czekels who fled from Transylvania in the eighteenth century, but the government regards them as Romanians from Transylvania who were forcibly Magyarized and converted to Catholicism before they fled. They are known as Changos, and some still speak a Hungarian dialect. It is significant that in the 1977 census fewer than 6,000 registered themselves as Hungarian, though this could be in response to pressure to become more Romanian. Certainly the members of the Catholic church in Moldavia seem to regard themselves as Romanians with little in common with Hungarians. The archdiocese was in Bucharest, ministering to those who had migrated there. In numbers they were fewer in 1945 than the Eastern Rite church, with 1,182,000 members in 683 parishes with 1,107 priests.

On the eve of the communist takeover both churches were flourishing, the Eastern Rite church especially so, with clergy and religious of high caliber, something that would stand them in good stead under future persecution and clandestine existence. Moreover, 95 percent of country people and 75 percent of city dwellers received the sacraments regularly; indeed many communicated weekly or even daily, far more often than the Orthodox.[11] The "double" clergy system was working well, with most married priests coming from and working in the villages, while the celibates came from the towns and worked as administrators, teachers, and mission priests, and, of course, provided the hierarchy.

The Catholic Church under Attack: The First Phase

When they came to power in 1947 the Communists realized that religious faith was far too deeply rooted in Romania's largely peasant population (still 23 percent illiterate) to be easily eradicated. They adopted the policy, still in force, of subjecting every religious body to strict control and demanding complete cooperation from their leaders. As a precondition to their legal recognition, each body had to produce a charter acceptable to the state. Fourteen groups received recognition, including Jews and Muslims, but not the Catholics, nor the Lord's Army, an Evangelical renewal movement in the Orthodox church with at least 500,000 members.

The two branches of the Catholic church were treated differently. In 1944 the thousand members of the Romanian Communist party were predominantly Hungarian and Jewish—a reflection of the dissatisfaction some members of national minorities had felt toward the somewhat nationalistic Romanian government policy between the wars—and Hungarian churches in general were given slightly more leeway than Romanian ones.

The fate of the Eastern Rite church was dictated by Stalin's policy of complete suppression and absorption of such churches into the Orthodox church and his desire that Romania should stress its Slavic origins at the expense of its Latin elements.[12] It may be significant that the first attack on Catholics coincided with the visit of Patriarch Alexis of Moscow in 1947 (May 30–June 12).

The attack began with discriminatory measures against graduates of the Blaj schools and some harassment of priests.[13] Then, in February 1948,

Party Secretary Gheorghe Gheorghiu-Dej declared that the sole obstacle to democracy was the "imperialist Catholic Church." In June the state unilaterally renounced the concordat, and on August 4 decree no. 177, on religious cults, showed how drastically the state intended to curb their rights. Article 51 declared that "the Ministry of Cults has unlimited power over Church administration and instruction." Articles 40 and 47 effectively cut off the church's contact with the Vatican: "No religious community, nor any of its officials, may have relations with religious communities abroad, except with permission of the Ministry of Cults and through the Ministry of External Affairs" (Article 40); and "foreign religious cults may not exercise jurisdiction on Romanian state territory" (Article 47). This enabled the state to close or nationalize most Catholic institutions, which it proceeded to do.

At this time, too, the number of dioceses was reduced from ten to four, two for each branch of the church, owing to an arbitrary new regulation stating that the minimum number of members for a diocese was 750,000. Registration of all local religious associations was introduced, and limitations were put on their activities: "Assemblies other than for worship . . . may be convened only with the approval of the authorities." All church circulars, including pastoral letters, had to be first submitted to a censor, and all church budgets came under state inspection and control. In the following year, 1949, by decree no. 810 of August 1, the religious orders of the Latin Rite church were dissolved except for a token handful of religious houses, which were left open but forbidden to take novices, to "prove" that the religious life was dying out!

On August 27, 1948, the combined Catholic episcopate protested strongly to the minister of cults against the new laws, finding them completely unacceptable; and in a later protest (October) they said that "three million citizens are being treated as enemies of the people." Foreseeing impending persecution, Pope Pius XII ordered his nuncio in Romania, American Archbishop Gerald O'Hara, to consecrate secret bishops and appoint twenty apostolic administrators, drawing up a list of replacements to succeed those who might be imprisoned, as all, in fact, were. The names became known to the authorities, and all were imprisoned; none ever became a diocesan; O'Hara himself was declared persona non grata in 1950 and left Romania.[14]

The Eastern Rite Church Suppressed

Meanwhile, the scheme for the ultimate suppression of the Eastern Rite church had been set in motion. It required the collusion of the Orthodox church. In the new patriarch, Justinian Marina, an able and ambitious man, the government found the ideal instrument for its policy. He represented the minority of Orthodox who regarded Eastern Rite Catholics as victims of a forced conversion. Now, after two and a half centuries, they could be free to return to the church to which, in his view, they really belonged. Enforced retirement removed other Orthodox bishops who would have opposed this policy, and the hierarchy, now totally subservient to the state, fell into line with Justinian.

Despite threats, deceit, blackmail, and even torture in some cases, neither the clergy nor the laity showed any enthusiasm for reunion with the Orthodox church. Of more than 1,800 priests, only 430 signed a formulary approving it. (Some of them claimed that they had not signed it, but their signatures had been forged.) On October 1, 1948, thirty-eight delegates (symbolically, the same number as the original proponents of the union with Rome) demanded reunion with the Orthodox church at a (canonically invalid) synod at Cluj. The delegates were kept, literally, underground and were in a pitiful state; several later recanted.

On October 8 the whole Catholic hierarchy protested, but on the twenty-first, at Alba Iulia, without the presence of a single Catholic bishop, the patriarch and other Orthodox bishops signed a new "synodal declaration confirming the end of the union with Rome." This action set a precedent for compromise with the state which damaged the credibility of the Orthodox hierarchy among many Romanians—both Catholic and Orthodox—and also broke the long tradition of cooperation between the two hierarchies.

From December 1, 1948, the Eastern Rite Catholic church officially ceased to exist; most of its confiscated property went to the Orthodox church. All six bishops, who had carried out an energetic mission to their people during the preceding months to strengthen them for the trials ahead, were first deposed, then arrested (October 28–29) along with about six hundred priests and many dissentient laity. Half of the priests and three of the six bishops died in prison; forty-six-year-old Vasile Aftenie, bishop of Bucharest, died in 1950; Traian Frentiu of Oradea in 1952, and the church's young and dynamic leader, Ion Suciu—scholar, ascetic, fine preacher, and bishop of Blaj—in 1953. Some prominent Orthodox priests who had the courage to speak out against the reunion or who refused to take over Catholic congregations were also imprisoned. The heroic conduct of Catholics in prison, including a lesser number from the Latin Rite church, won the admiration of thousands of their fellow prisoners and only increased the sympathy for the suppressed church.

Resistance to the takeover was initially almost total. Lugoj Cathedral was packed when the Securitate (secret police) arrived; the congregation were ejected and the doors were sealed. Someone cried out: "Go on, comrades, seal them, just as the Jews sealed Christ's tomb, but he rose on the third day!"[15] Brutal coercion was backed by blatant dishonesty; thousands of names were forged to "prove" that Catholics were in favor of the reunion.

During the temporary lull following Stalin's death, many of the imprisoned clergy were released on the condition that they not resume priestly duties. The surviving bishops, who were still under house arrest, presented a memorandum to the government on April 22, 1956, calling for the rehabilitation of their church. Within a month this was backed by a petition signed by half a million people (about a third of the membership). The government's response was renewed suppression. In 1957 Alexandre Rusu, bishop of Maramures, was sentenced to twenty-five years, and the other two bishops, Ion Balan of Lugoj and Iulius Hossu of Cluj, to ten years. Rusu died in prison in 1960, Balan in 1963; only Hossu survived his sentence.

At first, parishioners boycotted churches whose priests had signed, but this near-total opposition proved impossible to maintain in face of determined and arbitrary government measures. Many of the priests were married men, and eventually about a thousand (along with great numbers of their parishioners) had to join the Orthodox church rather than see their families starve. The result in practice was that most Catholics continued to attend the same churches with the same priests and more or less the same services, all now officially Orthodox, but tacitly understood that if and when the opportunity arose, they would revert to their allegiance to Rome. Some convents were transferred en masse to Orthodoxy, and their nuns apparently made such an impression with their fervor, that they were removed and sent home to live, at least outwardly, secular lives.

The surviving bishop, Hossu, was confined to an Orthodox monastery after his release from prison. When offered his freedom if he would take part in the fiftieth anniversary celebrations of full Romanian independence, which he himself had helped to negotiate, he refused unless his church was rehabilitated. Created cardinal *in pectore* by the pope on May 5, 1968, the first in his church's history, he accepted the secret honor on behalf of his whole suffering church; it became public only in 1973, three years after his death on May 28, 1970. Although he died in obscurity in Bucharest, his tomb soon became a place of pilgrimage (and not only for Catholics), much to the annoyance of the government.

The whole Catholic church suffered grievous losses, particularly during the period ending in 1953, when of 3,331 priests and religious, 1,405 were dead, 250 had been abducted—their fate unknown—and 400 were in prison or labor camp. Every Catholic bishop was imprisoned. Many of those who survived their prison sentences (often more than one term) emerged broken in health, physically and sometimes psychologically.

What Has Happened to the Eastern Rite Catholics?

No one knows how many Eastern Rite Catholics there are in Romania today. The already confused situation is muddied further by a state policy which reflects the erratic personality of President Nicolae Ceauşescu—full of inconsistencies and ever ready to play off one nationality or church against another. Some have become Orthodox; some attend Latin Rite churches; others have managed to retain their identity by organizing an efficient catacomb church; some attend both legal and catacomb churches. Catholics lost most ground to the Orthodox in the villages, especially in areas of Transylvania bordering the Old Kingdom, and in Bucharest. In previously Catholic parishes the Orthodox bishops, acting on state instructions, tried without success to fill vacancies with priests hostile to Rome. Today possibly only twenty "Orthodox" parishes are really still Catholic. Since 1976, relics of their Catholic past have been removed or deliberately desecrated.[16] Between 1978 and 1980 the parish clergy were interrogated in an attempt to unearth crypto-Catholics, and they were asked to provide detailed information on all former Eastern Rite members resident in the parish, including their occupations, their attitudes toward the Orthodox and the reunion, and particulars of any suspicious activities in which they might be involved.[17]

Paradoxically, several thousand Ukrainian Eastern Rite Catholics, now fairly widely scattered, are not under pressure. They get favored treatment, are allowed to keep their churches and liturgy—in which they pray openly for the pope (and did for Cardinal Slipyi when he was alive)—and they are even supplied with Ukrainian-language service books. Orthodox bishop Ion Picura, who was assigned to them, is regarded as an upright and caring spiritual father.[18]

The identities of the secret bishops of the catacomb church are usually known to the authorities, and these men have been subjected to continuous pressure. As one appeal put it in 1978, they "run the risk of losing their minds and health."[19] Nevertheless, they continue to maintain unofficial residence in the dissolved dioceses to which they hold canonic titles: Blaj, Cluj-Gherla, Lugoj, Baia Mare, and Oradea.

About three hundred of the original priests who remained Catholic are still alive, and the church owes much to their dedication. They secretly train new priests because no former Eastern Rite Catholic is permitted by the regime to enter the Latin Rite seminary. New nuns are also professed. However, they must live in tiny groups and have secular jobs; instructing the young is their special task. Retreats are even arranged. The exiled priest Fr. Petru Mareş compared their life to a "beehive. From outside you can't convey to outsiders what it is like inside, where Christians are working constantly."

There are thought to be about six hundred active priests, many of them married men. They may be highly qualified professional people or unskilled workers. Some are pensioners, and some are vagrants moving from place to place. Each priest visits a number of families regularly, saying mass in private houses and performing baptisms, weddings, and funerals for his parishioners. Some Catholics who attended Orthodox services were in the habit of getting a secret priest to "duplicate" these rites, though this has not been strictly necessary since 1969, when the Vatican gave Catholics official dispensation to receive Orthodox sacraments. As a result of this, apparently marriages are no longer solemnized in Eastern Rite "house churches." On the local level, close friendship and intermarriage between Orthodox and Eastern Rite Catholics continue as they did before the advent of communism, and there is often no clear line of demarcation between them. Those involved in underground activities run considerable risks in the face of laws which forbid assisting at private masses or "social activity that could intensify religious life." Many were arrested. Since 1974, however, there has been no news of the arrest of any priest. As long as only the family and immediate friends of the celebrant are present at a house mass, local authorities nowadays usually turn a blind eye. There is no underground press to attract unwanted attention.

Some Eastern Rite Catholics joined the Latin Rite church, but since its language in most places was Hungarian, and most Eastern Rite Catholics were peasants and workers who spoke only Romanian, it was an alien church. Until 1978 the Hungarian dioceses were forbidden to say mass in Romanian. Then, however, for reasons which remain unclear but were probably opportunist and pragmatic, the authorities tried to pressure the Eastern Rite bishops into a union with the Latin Rite church. This they refused; they had little in common with it and would accept nothing less than full restoration.[20]

However, the increasing provision of Romanian masses in certain towns, intended to help the growing number of migrant Moldavians, created an opportunity for Eastern Rite members to worship in a Catholic church and was appreciated particularly by intellectuals who had given up hope of the restoration of their own rite. By the mid-1980s it had become obvious that having mass in Romanian was actually helping to revitalize the Eastern Rite church. The authorities therefore executed another *volte-face* and tried to ban it, skilfully exploiting the continuing hostility between Romanians and Hungarians.[21]

The Struggle for Recognition

Pope Paul VI offended Ceauşescu by making Hossu (by then freed from prison but secluded in an Orthodox monastery) a cardinal. Romania was the only Eastern bloc country that did not send a representative to the investiture of John Paul II. He has supported the bishops in their repeated demands for *restitutio in integrum* and nothing less. Their various memoranda to the government base their claim on Article 37 of the Constitution, which automatically allows a church to change its denomination if over half of its members wish it.[22]

On June 29, 1977, the Committee for the Restoration of the Church was formed, claiming that there were still 600 priests and between 700,000 and 1 million members.[23] It was backed by the Committee for the Defense of Religious Rights (ALRC). This active body, founded basically by Baptists and soon ecumenical, made the restoration of the Eastern Rite church and the Lord's Army one of its fundamental demands, a testimony to the widespread respect in which they were held. The ALRC (which also had demanded the full recognition of the Latin Rite church) was rapidly dismantled by punitive government action.

In 1980, after many fruitless appeals, three bishops—Ion Dragomir, Ioan Ploscariu, and Alexander Todea—appealed to the Madrid Conference, asking for full recognition, return of confiscated buildings, and freedom to hold services, train priests, publish literature, and enjoy a normal church life. "Here even the Muslims have more liberty than we have," they commented.[24]

A firm statement of support by the pope on January 2, 1982, and his appointment of émigré Traian Crisan as a titular archbishop and secretary to the Sacred Congregation for the Cause of the Saints, a post which involves historical research, produced a strong reaction from the Romanian Orthodox hierarchy. The pope's statement, they said, was an "intrusion into the internal affairs of the Romanian Church" and "contrary to the spirit of ecumenism." In June 1987 at a press conference in Vienna, Patriarch Teoçtist Arapãs claimed that Romania had "once and for all" solved the Uniate problem by reuniting the church with the Orthodox church in 1948, and that former priests and believers had been 100 percent integrated. The position of the church, therefore, remains precarious today—officially nonexistent but apparently alive and well, its membership is around a million strong, despite sporadic suppression.

The Vatican marked the death of Ion Dragomir in April 1985 in Maramures with honors that are normally accorded only to deceased bishops, and also let it be known that it continued to regard the ban on the church as legally invalid and in contravention of international conventions signed by the Romanian government.

The Latin Rite Church After the Communist Takeover

Unlike their Eastern Rite brethren, the Latin Rite Catholics were allowed to remain Catholics. They were cut off from contact with Rome, however, and the government set about trying to break down all resistance, just as they did with other churches, by arrests and torture. All the bishops were imprisoned, most of them after a show trial in 1951 at which they were forced to confess that they had tried to overthrow the government. There is an eyewitness account of how one of them, Anton Durcovici of Iaşi, was thrown naked into a crowded cell. No one recognized him until he said, "Sorry, brothers, I am your bishop." He was removed and never seen again, but a priest passing a cell heard the words "Antonius moribundus" and spoke the words of the last rites through the locked door.[25] Two hundred priests were also imprisoned, the latest arrests being in 1962 in Moldavia.

The text of the charter required by the government for recognition could not be agreed on (Pope Pius XII rejected what might have been a workable compromise),[26] and the Latin Rite church therefore did not receive official status. This did not prevent state interference. Under its new regulations only two dioceses were permitted, Alba Iulia and Bucharest. Aron Marton, bishop of Alba Iulia since 1939, was in prison from 1949 to 1955 and under house arrest for a further six years. For twenty years he was the only Latin Rite bishop functioning, and even so his ministry was long exercised under serious restrictions (he was not allowed to visit Rome until 1970). He was an incorruptible man whose outlook was so broadened by his prison experiences that he became widely revered by Romanians of both churches. He showed his concern for the Eastern Rite Catholics by instructing his priests to assist the banned Eastern Rite clergy when help was requested.

The archdiocese of Bucharest was entrusted by the state to Franz Augustin, a German, who became its provisional administrator from 1954 until his death in 1983. As a member of the Front for Social Democracy and Unity in Romania's parliament, the Grand National Assembly, and as chief church spokesman for the government, he was never trusted by the Vatican and so was never consecrated bishop.

Normalization of the Church's Position

Conditions in the 1960s gradually became less intolerable. In 1964 priests began to be released from prison, though many were not immediately allowed back into their parishes. After 1965 priests were allowed to visit families who dared to invite them, but seldom did, in order not to compromise them.[27] In 1967 the visit of Franz Cardinal König, archbishop of

Vienna, signaled the reopening of relations with the Vatican. Despite an increasing stream of church leaders to Rome in the 1970s and regular visits to Romania by Msgr. Luigi Poggi, a realist with few illusions, Vatican Ostpolitik achieved very little apart from arousing deep distrust among the faithful, who believed that it was impossible to negotiate with a regime that had killed more than 1,400 priests, monks, and nuns.[28]

However, in 1972 the Romanian Church Office allowed Hungarian Antal Jakab to be consecrated and appointed coadjutor to the ailing Marton. Marton retired in 1979 and died on October 2, 1980. In 1981 another Hungarian, Lajos Balint, was appointed auxiliary bishop of Alba Iulia, but an earlier attempt by the Vatican to occupy the see of Iaşi miscarried. While on a visit to Rome in 1965, Fr. Petru Plesca was consecrated bishop, and he did his best to run the diocese until his death in 1977. His efforts were largely nullified by the authorities, however, and in his later years he was interrogated almost daily by the Securitate.[29]

It is only in the last few years, after prolonged negotiations, that the former dioceses have been reconstituted with interim bishops. In 1978 Pope Paul VI appointed Petru Gherghel to Iaşi, whose priests had held out against being incorporated into Bucharest. In 1983 Pope John Paul II appointed sixty-one-year-old Sebastian Krauter for Timoşoara and sixty-four-year-old Stefan Daszkal for Oradea. Part of the Oradea Diocese, Satu-Mare, was detached by the state in 1982 and added to Bucharest, although it has no historical connection with it and is far away to the northwest.

When Augustin died in 1983, the clergy of Bucharest took the courageous step of designating a successor, forty-two-year-old Msgr. Ioan Robu. An ethnic Romanian from Moldavia, he had studied in Rome from 1973 to 1977, had been rector of the Iaşi seminary, and, unlike Augustin, had refused a seat in parliament; he was acceptable to the Vatican and was upgraded to apostolic administrator. Thus diocesan administration throughout the whole country is now more normal. Moreover, the working out of a charter has been left to the church by the Vatican, and a first draft appeared in 1979.

Other positive signs in the early 1980s included allowing Catholics to go on pilgrimage to Rome for the first time under communism, and, temporarily, a more favorable press image. Their morale was raised by the beatification of Jerome of Wallachia, who died in Naples in 1625, the first Romanian to be thus honored.[30]

Church Life Today

Even in its truncated form, the visible Catholic church is still Romania's second-largest religious body, comprising 8 percent of the population in

1978. Since it still lacks a charter it is denied some basic privileges permitted to "recognized" cults, but its unrecognized status prevents the state from exercising as much control and interfering as minutely in its affairs as it does with the other churches. Only a few approved leaders have been allowed to visit Rome; none have spoken with complete frankness about their church's problems. Some students may now go. Visitors to Romania find it equally hard to gather information, because there is much fear and all visits by a foreigner must be reported to the Securitate within twenty-four hours. Samizdat material is limited to a handful of complaints; that most of them are unsigned is another indication of the degree of fear within Romania. For many years such statistics as were available were out of date or full of discrepancies.[31]

All clerical ordinations and appointments have to be approved by the Department of Cults; transfers wanted by the church can be blocked, while priests with successful ministries may find themselves moved rapidly from parish to parish. Stipends are minimal, and they are subsidized (33 percent) by the state. There is no pension scheme, nor are there any homes for retired priests.[32] Clergy who prove themselves "loyal" or "efficient" in support of the government may, however, be given special salaries.

Largely through local initiative, two seminaries were reopened, Alba Iulia in 1952 and Iaşi in 1956. These have managed to produce a supply of fervent, dedicated, and, understandably, strongly conservative priests despite appalling difficulties caused by government infiltration and harassment, a total lack until 1981 of basic up-to-date textbooks,[33] and, at Alba Iulia, dreadful overcrowding and deplorably unhygienic conditions—the worst anywhere in Europe, with nearly two hundred students housed in buildings intended for sixty. Their success and good morale have been due largely to firm and uncompromising rectors; in this respect particularly they have been more fortunate than the Orthodox and Baptist seminaries in Bucharest.

The 1974 plan to modernize the Alba Iulia seminary with help from grants from Aid to the Church in Need, a Western Catholic charity, was held up by the state until the early 1980s, Iaşi, on the other hand, benefited indirectly from being damaged in the 1977 earthquake; it was rebuilt and enlarged in 1980 and can accommodate seventy to eighty students. Alba Iulia also started providing teaching in German and Romanian as well as Hungarian: German because Timoşoara diocese had no seminary, and Romanian because of the increasing number of Romanian Catholics having to move out of Moldavia to find work. There is no shortage of vocations in Iaşi diocese, where Catholic families are large and pious.

In 1982 the state suddenly imposed a drastic new *numerus clausus* on all seminaries. At Alba Iulia twenty of the 192 students were summarily ejected, and they are now allowed only thirty new senior seminarians and fifteen juniors each year. By 1986 numbers at Alba Iulia had dropped to 148 and at Iaşi to fifty. The claim by Vladimir Peterca, a professor at Iaşi, on a visit to Bonn—that the seminary took only twenty out of 120 candidates because that was a sufficient number for their needs—may represent the government line.[34] The result is that a church which had the highest ratio of priests to people in the Eastern bloc, Poland excepted, is now facing a rapid fall in the number of clergy; 60 percent are said to be over sixty, and its future pastoral care is jeopardized.

Restrictions on the activities of the clergy are severe, though often not apparent to the outsider. The Securitate tries to sow distrust and isolate clergy from each other, from their bishops, from intellectuals, and from the young. Presbyteries are often bugged, telephones tapped, and mail opened. Official clergy gatherings suffer from the inhibiting presence of a Department of Cults representative who often acts as unofficial chairman.[35] Among his parishioners each priest has four or five informers who report on his activities and the content of his sermons.

Priests may instruct children in church, in presbyteries, or in parish rooms. It is estimated that only 20–30 percent of Catholic children receive instruction because of job discrimination against parents who request it. In areas where Catholics are in a majority, however, as in many Hungarian parishes, there is less discrimination and more instruction. Much also depends on specific local authorities.

Teaching religion is made even more difficult because, not having a charter, the church is not allowed its own press or newspaper. The import of religious books is illegal without government permission, which usually is withheld. For years not a single Catholic publication, not even the texts of Vatican II, was available in Romania; only in the last few years has there been a slight improvement.

Until 1976 there were no prayer books or catechisms in Hungarian. The sporadic supplies permitted since then have been totally inadequate—an issue of catechisms in the early 1980s for the Alba-Iulia diocese, with its 500,000 Catholics, was limited to three thousand copies. Even church calendars were usually unobtainable.

The import and printing of Bibles is very limited, too, and Catholics got none until 1980, when ten thousand New Testaments were imported from Paris and a four-hundred-page prayer book was printed.[36] The first complete Romanian Bible is due in 1990. Theological books in any language are almost unobtainable. Hungarians and Germans could rely on some religious literature being smuggled over the border until the clampdown on Hungarians.

Building is strictly controlled, and the repair or enlargement of church premises is a constant source of friction for Catholics, as for all religious groups in Romania. Refusal of permits meant that many congregations, particularly those affected by the 1977 earthquake, had to worship in leaky or dangerous buildings, or ones too small for their growing numbers. This was a real problem in Moldavia, where some churches were filled by the elderly and nursing mothers, while the rest of the congregations stood outside. But in Timoşoara and Transylvania, due to recent German and Hungarian emigration, some churches are nearly empty.

Catholics have considerable grounds for resentment because, unlike the Orthodox, they have to pay a 17 percent tax on each person employed by the church. In many parishes, even in the Hungarian ones, this can pose a crippling burden.

Congregations dare not go ahead with repairs or improvements without the necessary permits, for reprisals can be drastic and include the possible closure of the church and harsh measures against those concerned. Sometimes in Moldavia the wait has lasted twenty years. Even to prepare for rebuilding in the hope of one day receiving a permit seems to be forbidden: sixty-seven-year-old Fr. Michael Godo was arrested in 1979 and given a six-year prison sentence after 75,000 lei had been discovered in his room, money he had collected for rebuilding his church. Even the facts that he had kept accurate accounts, lived in personal poverty, and that not one of thirty witnesses would say anything against his character did not save him, but protests following publicity in the West led to his release in 1981.[37]

The almost total ban on religious orders prevents hundreds of Catholics from testing their vocation;[38] it is especially resented because the Orthodox are allowed monastic life, albeit restricted and under close surveillance. Heavy sentences against priests deterred them from organizing secret orders but often groups of two or three people, mostly women, who found a priest they trusted, made their vows before him and lived together; they carried out a valuable ministry assisting overworked priests. Being in secular employment they had more contact with the laity, who often confided in them rather than in their closely watched clergy. They live so simply that they are able to help the poor, whereas organized charity by the church is forbidden. There is constant need because of the acute food shortages.

Discrimination was widespread against Catholics wanting to enter the professions, especially the army and teaching; in Moldavia, in Transylvania, and in Bucharest even teachers may attend mass with impunity.

The campaign against any religion is particularly strong in the schools: atheism is taught; compulsory events are timed to coincide with Sunday services; believers' children are ridiculed.[39] The general atmosphere is well summed up in the Eastern Rite Catholic bishops' appeal to the Madrid Conference: "When a whole people is poisoned spiritually by atheism, what can we do? They even stuff the brains of five-year-olds with it and try to wrest God from the hearts of the elderly. . . . We demand the right to give our people good bread and meat. If others prefer poison, they can drink it, but our hearts are torn. Traditions are dying; corruption penetrating to the depths of men's hearts; young people are disoriented and despondent; adults are tired and skeptical; the old are in despair."[40]

A Divided Church

Because of their division into three national groups, Latin Rite Catholics have been unable to present a united front against the state, unlike their Eastern Rite brethren. It is necessary to examine each group separately to see how the state has cleverly exploited these divisions, as well as to assess the differing degrees of survival, or even revival, in the various groups. For convenience the church may be divided into four groups: the Romanians in Moldavia (Iaşi Diocese); the Romanians, Hungarians, and Germans in the archdiocese of Bucharest; the Hungarians outside Bucharest (about 90 percent of whom live in Transylvania in the dioceses of Alba Iulia, Oradea, and Satu-Mare); and the Germans, most of whom live in the Banat (Timişoara Diocese) or in Transylvania. There has been a fairly recent shift in their relative proportions, with the Hungarian majority dropping from 80 percent to 60 percent, the Germans, once 21 percent, now in irreversible numerical decline owing to emigration, and the Romanian element becoming increasingly strong and trying hard to make their presence felt (as by appeals to the pope in the late 1970s). Catholics are at the mercy of a government which oppresses all sections of the community alike but shifts its attention at different times to different groups. Persecution has, if anything, intensified the nationalistic feelings of each local church. On the other hand, there is no evidence that the Romanian regime has ever created a patriotic priests' association for Catholic clergy, and the Catholic church in Romania has been relieved of that potential source of disunity.

Moldavia: Iaşi Diocese. The Romanians from Moldavia, numbering 262,650 according to the 1986 *Annuario Pontificio*, represent a highly promising element for the future of the Latin Rite church, both quantitatively and qualitatively—the former thanks to their high birthrate and rejection of abortion (now generally discouraged by the regime, Ceauşescu having reversed his population policy).

The main sources of information on Catholic life are, significantly, from

Moldavia, and come from two anonymous documents dating from 1978,[41] and from Fr. Petru Mares, the outspoken Catholic priest in exile since 1978. All come from the period when the human and religious rights movements were at their height, just before they were crushed. The documents emphasize the severe victimization that the Romanian part of the church suffered compared with the Hungarian and German parts and expose corruption among the leading personnel in the archdiocese of Bucharest. The authorities are accused of favoring these groups while regarding the Moldavian Catholics with particular dislike and suspicion because they are Romanian yet not Orthodox. The authors told how their religious life had been tried and purified in the fire of persecution and passed on within their close-knit families. Moldavians, they claimed, provide the state with a large, honest, and productive workforce. More enlightened officials recognize that the priests' control over the people, especially the young, is beneficial to society, yet they lose their jobs if they try to win better conditions for them. With increasing industrialization, many Catholics migrated to other parts of the country and found it hard to discover churches with mass in Romanian.

Bucharest. Objective information about the Bucharest Archdiocese was almost nonexistent before Augustin's death in 1983. One of the 1978 documents mentioned above refers to a generally low level of spiritual life; to inadequate pastoral care and rushed services provided by its priests, mostly Hungarian or German in origin, and many too old; and to two good priests whose attempt to expose dishonest practices in the running of the archdiocese resulted in suspension for one while the other left the priesthood. It also makes alarming accusations about the misappropriation of funds sent by Caritas through connivance between the Department of Cults and Augustin's clique. The allegations cannot be substantiated, but the document was addressed to the pope, and sending appeals is so risky a business that it should be taken seriously. Similar corruption is also alleged in Orthodox samizdat documents against certain Orthodox priests in Bucharest.[42]

The stand made by the priests of Bucharest in appointing Robu (described earlier) indicates that there is a significant nucleus of priests who are backed by the laity in their determination to reduce government interference and improve the pastoral situation. The 1986 *Annuario Pontificio* figures show fifty-two priests, fifty parishes, thirty-two seminarians, and 72,285 Catholics.

The Hungarians. Though the proportion of Hungarians in Transylvania has decreased, they still form about 30 percent of the population. Over half a million of Romania's Catholics are Hungarian. Visitors report well-attended churches with many children receiving instruction and a flourishing parish life. The three Hungarian dioceses are producing an encouraging number of candidates for the priesthood (123 in 1986, eighty-nine of them from Alba Iulia). They have benefited from the conscientious episcopate of Marton, who did everything he could to reduce state interference and tried to visit every parish. In 1986 Alba Iulia had 356 priests, 266 parishes, and 504,448 Catholics; Oradea had 68 priests, 55 parishes, and 111,285 Catholics; and Satu-Mare had 91 priests, 54 parishes, and 150,000 Catholics—the latter figure only approximate.

Transylvania is traditionally the richest, most advanced province, and generally Hungarians are reasonably prosperous. However, since the mid-1980s they too have experienced traumatic hunger, cold, and deteriorating economic conditions. Churchgoing is still much more an integral part of life in Transylvania than in their native Hungary, where it has dropped sharply. The main reason would seem to be that since becoming minorities, both the Germans and the Hungarians have regarded their religion along with their culture and language as part of their national identity. Unlike the situation in many of the Protestant churches, however, it has not usually degenerated into mere "folk religion," but has remained a living faith.

The plight of the Hungarian minority has received disproportionate attention abroad. Until recently the Hungarians probably received better treatment from the government than did Romanians. Since the early 1980s, however, their language and culture have come under attack: Hungarian-language publications are no longer imported; Hungarian is no longer even taught in schools. Repression led to an upsurge of Hungarian nationalism, leading to more repression, which has also affected the churches, both Protestant and Catholic. A most sinister manifestation of anti-Hungarian feeling has been a series of attacks on Hungarian priests. The popular Fr. Ion Ecsy died under suspicious circumstances in 1982. In a Christmas sermon in 1983 Fr. Géza Palfi protested it being a working day, when elsewhere, even in Hungary, it was a public holiday. This was considered a political remark, and he was arrested and beaten; he died about two months later in a hospital and is regarded by Catholics as a martyr. In 1985 Fr. János Csilik, aged twenty-nine, was unable to use his hands for weeks after refusing to cooperate with the Securitate: They were suspicious of his contacts with the family of Attila Ara-Kovács, a Catholic philosopher who had been active in support of Hungarian rights before emigrating to Hungary in 1983. Csilik was transferred from Oradea cathedral to a remote country parish, and a number of priests were interrogated about their contacts with him. Fr. János Csibi, after imprisonment, was forced to work on a collective farm and permitted to function as a priest only on Sundays. Another priest who was beaten up and imprisoned reportedly disappeared. Thus selected Hungarians are experiencing brutality similar to that inflicted on Romania's Evangelical Christians.

In this context of increasing Hungarian-Romanian tension in Transylvania, it is at least understandable that many Hungarian priests are unwilling to provide mass in Romanian for the growing number of Romanian-speaking Catholics there. By 1988 Romanians actually were being encouraged with cash bonuses to move into Transylvania to "dilute" the Hungarian presence.

The Germans and Timoşoara Diocese. In areas where there were large German minorities, notably the Banat (Timoşoara Diocese) and the previously Saxon areas of Transylvania, the church has suffered heavy losses through emigration. Life in Romania is so intolerable that most people who get the chance to leave and can afford to pay the heavy "tax" involved do so. In this respect the Germans are a favored group, and up to sixteen thousand have emigrated each year since 1975.

With the number of church members falling, the number of priests and seminarians is falling too. In 1967 Timoşoara had 210 priests for its 164 parishes; by 1978 the figure had declined to 153, with only 123 still active, and 25 seminarians. Since 1978 the decline has continued; then there were 320,000 Catholics, in 1986 they were down to 290,000. Only 10 percent of the priests are under forty. They experienced problems in the face of the increasing proportion of Bulgars, Slovaks, Slovenes, Croats, and Romanians resulting from emigration of the younger Germans. Some of the problems were ones of communication with these people, who did not speak German but were often Catholic. Meanwhile, as younger Germans emigrated and numbers plummeted, congregations became predominantly elderly. As, with decreasing numbers, cultural and national amenities were withdrawn, it became increasingly difficult for Germans to maintain their distinctive cultural and religious life.

Prospects for the Latin Rite Church

Despite persecution, restrictions, isolation, and internal divisions, the Latin Rite church has proved extremely resilient. The transmission of the faith owes much to devout, hardworking priests who preach good sermons (people take notes on them) and to a stable, close-knit family life. Bishop Jakab says that the prohibition of religious education in school has brought home to parents their responsibility. Church leaders have claimed that 80 percent of their membership attend mass on Sundays,[43] and attendance is, if anything, increasing in line with a general revival in religion since the mid-1970s. Ceauşescu's Romania today presents communism at rock bottom: Living standards are the lowest in the Soviet bloc, standards in every aspect of life are falling, and Christianity represents the only hope in an apparently hopeless situation. The continuous difficulties have focused the people's concern on basics: maintaining their faith and worship. Their faith is largely simple, joyful, secure, and unquestioning, and it is based on their trials and their experience.[44]

One of the surest testimonies to the quality of Catholic life in Romania today is that some converts are attracted even from Orthodoxy. With a discredited hierarchy giving no leadership, the Orthodox church has lost many members to the Evangelical churches, but some, especially town-dwelling intellectuals, are becoming Catholics. They are attracted by better, less politically subservient sermons; by the more thorough instruction and pastoral care; by the witness of Catholics under persecution; by the cleaner record of the bishops; by admiration of Pope John Paul II; and by hefty attendance at Sunday masses. Some of these converts, of course, may be former Eastern Rite Catholics who had temporarily accepted incorporation into the Orthodox church.

Relations between Ceauşescu and the pope continue to be strained. Clergy have great difficulty getting travel permits. In autumn 1985 not a single representative from Romania was allowed to attend the European Bishops' Conference. Such partial concessions as have been made to the church are long overdue and must be seen in the context of Vatican-Romanian relations as a whole. The Vatican's view is that as long as half of Romania's Catholics (the Eastern Rite church) are denied the right to exist, the situation cannot be considered normal.

Conclusion

The situation of both Catholic churches remains ambiguous, but in very different ways. The Latin Rite church shares the same internal problems as other Romanian churches, with a few additional ones thrown in because of its as yet undefined legal status. As with the other churches, the internal problems are to a great degree due to state interference. From all the evidence we have, there is no tension between tradition and modernity in the Romanian case: the Romanian church is wholly traditional. In a body that has suffered such constant undermining by the state, along with extreme isolation from the outside world, a strongly conservative attitude is hardly surprising. Moreover, theological conservatism is a feature of all Romanian churches; experimentation is a virtual nonstarter in such a repressive police state. Even in those parts of the church that might be expected to show signs of interest in modernist trends—the Hungarian and the German—there seem to be none (just as there is little interest within the Catholic churches in adjacent Hungary and the GDR, where there is far greater religious freedom).

Such friction as exists between the hierarchy and the lower clergy springs, as already noted, from discontent with particular individuals, not from any antipathy to the hierarchy as such. In any case, the hierarchy is not a properly constituted one and thus lacks a certain authority. The clergy, and the laity, too, are acutely aware of the disadvantages under which their acting bishops have to function and make allowances for them. There seems to be a considerable degree of unanimity within the church, except in the problem area of national divisions.

The Eastern Rite church has none of these difficulties. Its effective underground organization presupposes a very high degree of internal solidarity and mutual loyalty. Moreover, recent statements by outspoken Orthodox priests indicate that among Romanian Christians (Evangelicals perhaps excepted), it is still respectfully regarded as Romania's "second Church."[45]

During 1988 Ceauşescu's village relocation scheme, which involved the replacement of around 7,000 of Romania's 13,123 villages by 585 agro-industrial complexes, was started to the dismay of hundreds of thousands of peasants, regardless of ethnicity. This added to the insecurity of the minorities, whose distinctive cultural life was already threatened. Their living standards, meanwhile, continued to decline. The relocation scheme would have necessitated the destruction of most churches, even if they are hundreds of years old and of outstanding architectural value, and there was apparently no provision for helping the displaced communities erect new ones.

Increasing numbers of Hungarians fled across the border despite the risk of being shot. By the end of 1988 around forty thousand had arrived in Hungary, posing considerable problems for a government and people who were indignant at their treatment and deeply sympathetic toward their plight, so much so that the government even enlisted the willing assistance of the churches to feed, clothe, counsel, and find accommodation for the refugees. Among them, inevitably, a considerable proportion are Catholics. Jakab begged László Cardinal Paskai not to take a public stand on their problem because it could cause further deterioration in the situation of Hungarian Catholics in Romania. It has been reported that women and children as well as priests are being terrorized by the Securitate.

The Germans are luckier. The West German government can afford to buy them out. Conditions had deteriorated so badly that the German government decided to pull them out within five years, at a rate of thirty thousand a year. It is estimated that 90 percent of Germans want to leave. Most of the 10 percent who remain are elderly. Thus the end of the German presence and German church life in Romania is in sight.

FACT SHEET

The Catholic Church in Romania

Latin Rite Catholics

Current strength of the church

1,386,668 faithful
945 priests and monks
6 bishops (1 diocesan)
160 nuns (in addition, several hundred secret nuns)
230 seminarians

Number of churches and church facilities

654 parishes
2 seminaries
2 convents
1 monastery
0 church-run schools
0 church-run hospitals

Chief news organs

None

Underground religious periodicals

None

Primates since 1948

None

Eastern Rite Catholics

Current strength of the church

There are estimated to be around a million still basically Eastern Rite, but this is only a rough figure.
600 priests and monks (estimate)
5 or 6 bishops (identity of most not known)
probably several hundred secret nuns
0 seminarians, officially (as they are trained in secret, numbers are not known)

Number of churches and church facilities

None

Chief news organs
None

Underground religious periodicals
None

Primates since 1948
None

10

The Catholic Church in Albania

Janice Broun

Albanian believers have been victims of the most radical social experiment ever put into practice by a communist government. For twenty years there has been no visible church life; since 1967 all places of worship have been closed and all religious practices banned, under draconian penalties. The personality cult of the late Enver Hoxha seems to be the only form of worship allowed.

Although Albania lies only fifty miles across the Adriatic from Italy, it might be in another world—where there are statistical figures for other countries, there are only dashes in the *Annuario Pontificio*. The government has isolated Albanians so completely from the outside world that it is almost impossible to obtain information. The only sources are references in the official media, news from the few Albanians who have succeeded in escaping, and the observations of the occasional tourist or journalist. Those older people (the lower age limit for foreign travel was recently dropped from fifty to thirty by Ramiz Alia) permitted to visit relatives in Greece or in Kosovo in Yugoslavia have been too terrified to pass on information for fear of reprisals.

Albania is a very small country, only 13,000 square miles, with probably as effective a totalitarian regime as anywhere in the world. Of 1.8 million votes cast in the 1987 election, there was only one dissentient. People are "protected" from "contamination" by the outside world and have to obtain local party permits even for travel within Albania. The country is kept on a permanent military footing with all able-bodied adults obliged to do annual military service, and it is riddled with secret police and informers. From kindergarten onward children are indoctrinated with an aggressive form of atheism and trained to hate and distrust foreigners and to denounce parents who follow religious practices at home. From the age of fourteen (since June 1979) Albanians are liable to internal banishment or internment in labor camps merely on suspicion of being a danger to the system. There is no Ministry of Justice; there are no defense lawyers. Failure to denounce treachery to the state—and religion falls in that category—may be punished by ten years in prison. According to the Constitution of 1976 (Article 37), "The state does not recognize any religion at all and supports and develops atheistic propaganda in order to implant in mankind the scientific materialist worldview." Article 55 states: "The formation of any organization of a fascist, antidemocratic, religious, or antisocialist nature is forbidden. Fascist, religious, warmongerish, anti-socialist activity and propaganda are forbidden, as is incitement to hatred between peoples and races." The Penal Code of June 1977 specifies that "religious propaganda and also the production, storage, or distribution of literature" may be punished by sentences of between three and ten years. Since 1967 people have been sent to labor camps without trial merely for possessing religious objects such as prayer books, Bibles, crucifixes, or icons, or for taking part in "underground" religious services. On September 23, 1975, decree no. 5339 announced that "all citizens whose names do not conform to the political, ideological, and moral standards of the state are to change them as from 1976."[1] Amnesty International estimated in 1986 that there were still, despite amnesties, as many as 12,000 political prisoners, many of whom had been incarcerated for religious offenses. To maintain any religious practices in the face of such laws obviously requires a degree of heroism—though heroism has not been unknown in Albanian history.

All this means that any assessment of possible Catholic survival over the last two decades has to be based on a thorough examination of the events preceding the clampdown and rather fragmented reports of deaths and arrests, plus press attacks on religion, which rarely specify which religion is involved: Islam or the Orthodox or Catholic church. We also need to look at the rather peculiar historical nature of Albanian religion in general.

Religion in Albania is not merely complex; it is confusing, and not just to outsiders but to many Albanians themselves. Nowadays a typical Albanian is outwardly an atheist and a Communist, and can hardly profess to be otherwise. In 1945, according to the census, 73 percent of Albanians were Muslim. Albania was the only predominantly Muslim state in Europe, though since Islam was adopted only under duress or through material incentives under Ottoman rule, it rarely went deep, and relations with the Christians, who predated the Muslims, were generally close. Most of the Muslims were Sunni; but over a quarter, about 200,000, and those the most influential, were Bektashi, a very tolerant sect which originated in Asia Minor in the thirteenth century and incorporated Muslim, Christian, and pagan beliefs. In addition, there were an unknown number of Laramani, Christians who while outwardly conforming to Islam continued to say Christian prayers secretly at home; they were despised and unable to integrate properly into either the Muslim or the Christian community. When we come to the Christians, 17.1 percent, mainly in the south adjacent to Greece, were Orthodox, and 10.1 percent, in the north and probably representing the oldest nonpagan strand, were Catholic. However, for many Albanians, especially the clans in remote, almost inaccessible valleys in northern Albania and what is now Kosovo, both Islam and Christianity were merely a veneer overlying tenaciously held pagan beliefs and customs. Thus, if we strip our typical Albanian atheist communist we may find a layer of Islam underlain by a layer of Christianity, and within that a core of pre-christian religiosity which may be the dominant element. An Albanian Catholic highlander may be far removed from the conventional image of a Catholic; picturesque indeed, but often of dubious orthodoxy.

To understand the Albanian religious mentality, and also the motives behind the extraordinarily vicious government attack on religion, some background knowledge of Albanian history and tribal society is essential.

History

The Christian church is well rooted in Albania (ancient Illyricum in Roman times); indeed, it may have been visited by Saint Paul himself.[2] In 395 the province passed into the Byzantine Empire. However, Slav invasions from the seventh century onward destroyed almost all vestiges of Roman civilization. Many Illyrians withdrew to the almost impregnable mountains of the interior, where they reverted to primitive shepherds and nomads, a way of life which persisted almost unchanged well into this century, particularly in those areas of northern Albania among the Gheg tribes where the Catholic church has remained strong.[3] Illyricum became divided linguistically and ecclesiastically, with Latin used in the north and Greek in the south. Until 734 it belonged ecclesiastically to Rome; thereafter, Constantinople's hold was not strong, and by the fifteenth century, when the Turks arrived, most of it was virtually Roman Catholic. The resistance against the Turks from 1443 until 1468 was led by a great soldier, leader, and politician, Gjerje Kastrioti (Scanderbeg), a hostage of the Turks who reverted to Christianity and made heroic attempts to organize the Balkan and other Christian states in a crusade to halt further penetration by the Turks. He went in person to Rome to beg Pope Paul I for help and was acknowledged by two subsequent popes as having prevented the Turks from overrunning Christian Europe.[4] Even in Hoxha's Albania the religious allegiance and motivation of Albania's greatest national hero could not be concealed altogether.

By 1501 Albania was under Ottoman rule, though the Turks never really had control over some of the remoter Gheg clans. Until the eighteenth century the Orthodox church, stronger among the more prosperous and less isolated Tosk tribes of the south, enjoyed broad toleration because of their Greek connections and grew at the expense of the Catholic church, which suffered various disabilities and lost its hold on central Albania. The latter church, however, was in some ways more closely identified with Albanian culture and education; the first-known book in Albanian was a missal published in 1555. Even by 1616, according to the archbishop of Bar, only 10 percent of the population was Muslim, but during the seventeenth century the Turks began a policy of Islamization and imposed such crippling taxes on Christians that most apostatized—two-thirds of the northern Ghegs did so—though crypto-Christian practices persisted. Catholicism all but died out in the later seventeenth and eighteenth centuries when, deprived of adequate support from more fortunate Christian states and of its seminary, schools, and many churches and monasteries following fruitless risings, and discredited by the territorial squabbles of mainly expatriate bishops, pastoral care reached an all-time low. Church survival, as in Bosnia, owed much to the Franciscans, who had been in Albania since 1219 and did not desert their flocks.

It was not until the nineteenth century that institutional church life was properly reestablished and the church took on its modern form; this owed much to the help and guidance of members of mission orders from Italy, notably Jesuits and Franciscans. It also owed much to the protection of the Habsburg Empire. The Jesuits, whose province was established in 1848, opened a pontifical seminary in 1859 at Shkodra, and in 1866 the first five Albanian bishops of this new era were consecrated. In 1855 the Franciscans reopened elementary schools; from 1877 onward, Saint Xavier College in Shkodra, the first Albanian school providing higher education, played a crucial role in educating the future leaders in the Albanian struggle for independence. Catholics and Bektashi played a vital part in this struggle in the north.

The religious establishments themselves, unlike those in neighboring Balkan countries like Serbia, Montenegro, and Bulgaria, did not assume a leading role in championing the cause of independence. Islam, Orthodoxy, and Catholicism were still closely dependent on Turkey, Greece, and Italy, respectively, though it should be noted that the Italian missionaries included priests from the Arboresh, the Albanian community in Italy descended from refugees from the early days of the Turkish conquest.[5] Although most had been Orthodox, they were incorporated into the Catholic church as Eastern Rite Catholics. However, there was no worship in the vernacular. Muslims worshipped in Arabic, Orthodox in Greek, and Catholics in Latin. Indeed, Albanian Catholics have never worshiped in the vernacular; they were to be cut off from Vatican II. All this meant that some of the new leaders had little sympathy for religion. As the poet Vaso Pasha (1825–92), himself a Catholic, said, "The religion of Albania is Albanianism." Later, Hoxha was to use the divisiveness of religion as one pretext for getting rid of it, and he made full use of this adage in his antireligious campaign.

The Years of Independence

The long struggle against the Turks culminated in the Albanian declaration of independence on November 28, 1912, recognized by the Great Britain and France on July 29, 1913, though with the proviso that the government should remain under their supervision. Hence nearly half of the territory where Albanians were settled was allotted by the London Conference to the Montenegrins and Serbs to the north, becoming part of Yugoslavia and a future bone of contention. The country suffered occupation and partition during World War I, finally achieving independence in 1920.

Independence proved a period of thwarted hopes. Democracy was short-lived, and Albania continued to suffer from misrule. Under Ahmet Zogu, a tough clan chief who seized power in 1924 and became King Zog (though he was to some extent a captive of the Ottoman legacy he inherited), the country became increasingly dependent on fascist Italy, which was allowed to exploit it virtually as a colony. Almost all the money earned went to Italians, who occupied all key posts, and to Zog's court. Corruption was rife. Even by Balkan standards Albania was backward, at about the same level as the predominantly Albanian areas in Kosovo, Montenegro, and Macedonia under Yugoslav rule. There was not a single bank with domestic capital. Fifty-three percent of the peasants were landless; 80 percent of the population was illiterate; and only 36 percent of children received even elementary education. There was no university, no medical school. Poor hygiene and nutrition, due largely to the deplorable status in which the majority of women were held and an almost total lack of preventative medicine, left Albanians open to the ravages of disease and epidemics. Tuberculosis and, especially in the swampy plains, malaria were endemic. Probably half of the babies died in their first year. In other words, Albania was a classic Third World country.[6]

The War and Communist Victory

The Italian invasion in 1939, their replacement by the Germans in 1943, and a bitter civil war only made matters worse. Albania may have had the distinction of being the only East European country where the Red Army played no part in "liberation," but its new rulers were largely Tosks and heavily dependent on Yugoslav support. In northern Albania, where Serbs were hated possibly more than the Turks had been, the Communists were despised for having sold out to the Yugoslavs, and the government's constant stock accusations that Catholics were fascist and antinationalist rang hollow. The scene was set for a dramatic confrontation between the remarkable party secretary, Enver Hoxha, a French-educated intellectual from a Tosk Muslim background, and the Catholic church, a united body which drew on deep, traditional Gheg loyalties. Although few, if any, clergy were actively involved in the guerrilla resistance which smoldered on in the northern mountains until Kim Philby's betrayal in 1948, many lay Catholics died in the struggle. This is an aspect of church-state relations which should not be overlooked.

Religious Life before the Communist Takeover

How did the Christian churches fit into this scenario? They were neither privileged nor wealthy, and in a predominantly Muslim state they were a minority. The Orthodox church in 1939 comprised an archdiocese and three dioceses (about 220,000 members in 200 parishes) and was trying to shake off identification with the Greeks and introduce services in Albanian, primarily under the instigation of the nationalist bishop Fan Noli, an intellectual and moderate liberal who was briefly prime minister and whose government had the support of the Catholic clergy before its overthrow by Zog in 1924. Although the Albanian Orthodox church declared its autocephaly in 1922, it was not recognized by Constantinople until 1937. Orthodox priests were generally less well educated than the Catholic clergy, many of whom had had the advantage of some education and thus proved better equipped to lead the resistance to the subsequent onslaught against religion.[7]

The Catholic church in 1939 had two archdioceses (Shkodra and Durres), three dioceses (Pulti, Sappa, and Lezha), one abbey (Nullius in Mirdita), and one apostolic administration for central Albania.[8] One hundred and twenty-four thousand Catholics in 123 parishes were served by forty-two indigenous and sixty-two foreign priests and thirty-two lay monks, along with seventy-three indigenous and sixty foreign nuns in twenty-nine monasteries and convents.[9] The Shkodra seminary had about sixty-five students, and the Franciscans there also provided a good theological education for would-be friars.[10] The orders ran two seminaries and fifteen secondary, trade, and primary schools (almost the only schools in the north) that provided education for 3,320 children, thirteen orphanages, and ten charitable institutions. The sisters, who were involved in education, social, and cultural work, and in staffing hospitals, were greatly appreciated; they also made a start in trying to emancipate women. Jesuits and Franciscans directed presses that produced not only popular religious magazines but also literary and cultural ones dealing with contemporary topics.

The significance of the Catholic church in the life of northern Albania was out of proportion to its size. Some leading figures in Albanian politics and culture—poets, historians, novelists, translators, musicians, philosophers, and men of letters—were Catholic priests, some of them expatriates who had come to have a passionate love for Albania. Several were among the first victims of communism, accused of collaboration with Albania's fascist enemies. This was unfair. Inevitably in such a backward country with such a high rate of illiteracy, clergy had found themselves forced to assume leading roles. If any were convinced fascists, they were a small minority. Most combined deep patriotism with a desire to bring Albania into the mainstream of European civilization while preserving its best traditions.[11]

Though religious groups were largely autonomous, relations with the state were not all plain sailing. The Catholic church did not support Zog's government, though the concordat signed in 1927 did improve the situation somewhat. In 1933, in an attempt to shake off the Italian grip and despite protests from the bishops, Zog closed all Catholic and private schools.[12] They were reopened in 1936 after Mussolini applied leverage by suspending loans. Spiritual life generally flourished; hundreds participated in pilgrimages to Rome and Albanian holy sites in Italy.

An Anthropological Excursion

In general there was considerable enthusiasm for the church, although, particularly in the northern mountains and in Kosovo, superstition and the ancient Law of Lek (supposed to have been laid down by Prince Lek Dukahjini in the fifteenth century but obviously of earlier origin) had a far greater hold than any religion and stood in the way of the people understanding such concepts as the soul and sin, giving rise to daunting pastoral problems.

The most important values in society were honor—*besa*, the word of honor, was sacrosanct—and loyalty to kin. The demands of the clan were paramount, and the clan system provided justice (according to its rather peculiar criteria) and material and psychological security, for men at least. There was no loneliness. Kinship ties, though based on what to us seem irrational premises, were very strong. Justice was enforced by means of blood feuds, which gave rise to some very odd situations. Killing a blood enemy, even a minor son of one, was not regarded as a sin, whereas eating an egg on a Saturday was.[13] There was nothing wrong with taking a brother's widow as a second wife, or marrying a cousin if she was on the woman's side, since relationships through women did not count. Men could be under obligation to kill someone they personally liked. They did not fear death and went out to kill with the greatest composure. One-fifth of all male deaths before World War II were the result of blood feuds. Men left their guns—a gun is traditionally an Albanian's best friend, far closer than his wife—stacked up outside the church wall during mass while the priest sang "Et in terra pax hominibus." Priests were continually having to intervene to try and prevent bloodshed.

Yet the lot of women was far worse. The female death rate was higher than the male death rate. Marriages were often arranged before a girl was born, and the only way she could opt out was by taking a vow of lifelong virginity! Women were kept in a state of appalling ignorance; for example, babies were tightly swaddled (as they still are in Kosovo) and never washed. Women were no more than chattels, did almost all the manual work, had to obey all males whatever their age, and were not allowed to eat with them.

Superstition, the use of charms, and belief in the evil eye were strong. Women wore as many charms as possible. The cross was used as a charm, carved on bread, on every door, on gables. It was worn round the neck, tattooed on the hands, arms, and breasts. When we examine religious survival in Albania, we should not underestimate the tenacity of such pre-Christian practices, which are unparalleled elsewhere in Europe; nor, in assessing Catholicism, should we overlook the fact that it was in the partly Catholic areas that people were most isolated and primitive, traditional beliefs were most persistent, and the overall picture was most confused, though many villages had neither priest nor hodja (equivalent of imam), neither church nor mosque. Considerable areas of northern Albania were still virtually a mission area for the Catholics until the time of the communist takeover. In Yugoslav Kosovo, where people are not under pressure to conform to communism, it is widely acknowledged even in the Catholic press that to this day many ancient practices, including blood feuds, persist. The party in Albania claims to have stamped out blood feuds, though some of Hoxha's recurrent vicious purges were not unreminiscent of them.[14] The party press often laments the survival of traditional marriage customs in addition to what it categorizes as less harmful practices, and attributes them to religion. In fact, the fatalism and subordination of women in the predominant Islam were more akin to the Law of Lek than was the attitude of the Christian churches, which did their best to uproot them.

The Catholic clergy had no illusions about their daunting pastoral problems. Edith Durham in *High Albania* and Ann Bridge in her novel *Singing Waters*[15] provide moving and unbiased testimonies to the caliber of the priests, mostly Franciscans, who worked indefatigably, treating the sick during appalling epidemics and teaching rudimentary hygiene. Even if their primitive flocks did not always do what they were told, they loved and respected their priests very deeply.

The Attack on Religion

Between 1945 and 1951 the party set out to "nationalize" the churches (the term *church* is used here in its broadest sense to include Muslims) and to terrorize believers by its treatment of all who opposed its policy. After 1951, with the state in complete control over church life, persecution slackened, only to intensify again in preparation for the final attack in 1967, when all religion was banned.

First Persecution: 1945–51. On August 29, 1945, under the Agrarian Law, the state appropriated most church property, including monasteries, libraries, and seminaries. In the course of the next six years the state set out to limit the autonomy and freedom of action of the churches. It curtailed their sources of income and forbade religious education; all education became the responsibility of the state alone. Its priority was to concentrate on producing a literate young generation, girls as well as boys, fully imbued with an atheist and materialist worldview. All religious publications and communications, including sermons, had to be approved by the government. The seven Catholic periodicals were suppressed. The state exercised control over the appointment of personnel to all religious posts; it took hospitals and charitable institutions out of church control and prohibited all religious orders with headquarters outside Albania.[16]

The implementation of these measures curbed the influence of religion and in turn provoked much resistance on the part of the church leadership. The party responded by indicting, arresting, trying, and sentencing recalcitrant clergymen. In the case of the Orthodox church this resulted in the virtual elimination of the church leadership.[17] Later, this church suffered the indignity of losing its hard-won autonomy and was subordinated in practice to the Moscow Patriarchate. The Muslim establishment was split, with the Bektashis being recognized as separate, and their clergy also were purged.

As Hoxha had foreseen, the Catholic church proved a tougher obstacle. His campaign was aimed at discrediting it, branding its leaders as fascists and American or Vatican spies, and then eliminating it entirely. This period is well documented. In May 1945 Hoxha expelled the apostolic delegate, Archbishop Leone Nigris. He then summoned Gasper Thaçi, archbishop of Shkodra and primate, and Vincenz Prendushi, archbishop of Durres, and demanded that they separate from Rome, promising in return "a conciliatory attitude" and material help in maintaining church institutions. Both refused. Thaçi died at the hands of the Sigurini (security police) in 1946 while under house arrest. After his death a similar demand was made of Bishop Fran Gjini, acting nuncio.[18] He also refused, but he had an open letter to Hoxha read in all churches in which he urged Catholics to cooperate in the reconstruction of their ravaged country. Annoyed by this show of independence, Hoxha had him arrested on a charge of spreading antigovernment propaganda. Meanwhile, Prendushi had been sentenced to twenty years' hard labor and probably died just over a year later, after torture, in February 1949. Bishop Nikol Dedi and the youngest bishop, Gjergj Volaz, also perished at this time.[19] By 1949 the only bishop left alive was seventy-five-year-old Bernadin Shllaku, bishop of Pulti.

In January 1946 all foreign priests, monks, and nuns, numbering about 120, were expelled; to the anger of the authorities, a crowd of grateful Catholics and Muslims turned out to bid them farewell. Fr. Anton Harapi, a leading Franciscan, was executed early in 1946 for alleged collaboration with the Nazis. Fr. Jak Gardin and Professor Gjergj Vata were given long sentences after a public ideological discussion in which they had discomfited the communists. A number of leading priests, seminarians, and laymen were executed, ostensibly for printing leaflets criticizing the government on behalf of the Albanian Union, a broadly based legal political organization, prior to the first parliamentary elections. Leading Jesuits and Franciscans, especially lecturers, were, of course, prime targets, and they and a number of students were accused of political crimes such as planting or concealing weapons and were executed or imprisoned. Some died heroically, praying for their country and their enemies. Nuns were publicly humiliated, some stripped naked. The seminary was closed. A number of churches were converted into theaters, cafés, and dance halls.

It is estimated that thirty Franciscans, thirteen Jesuits, sixty parish priests, ten seminarians, and eight of forty-three nuns sentenced to labor camps actually died by execution or during their imprisonment; this was a crippling loss for such a small church. A number of leading laymen also were shot. In the appallingly primitive camps, mostly established to drain the malarial swamps, the death rate was exceedingly high.[20] An outstanding young Padua-trained lawyer, Mustafer Pipa, although a Muslim, undertook the defense of the Franciscans in the certain knowledge that it would cost him his life.[21]

Pressure against the churches lessened after 1948, for Hoxha was preoccupied with problems resulting from Yugoslavia's leaving the Cominform. When this occurred Albania ceased to be the satellite of a satellite and came more directly under Soviet control. Tut Jakova, Catholic-born minister of the interior, was the go-between in negotiations with the remaining clergy and blamed Yugoslavia for the brutality against Catholics; he reassured the clergy that such harsh treatment was not in the interest of the Albanian government.[22] In 1952 Jakova became a victim of one of Hoxha's recurrent purges, on the grounds that he had befriended the clergy.

From November 1948 onward the churches were required to present draft statutes. It took two and a half years of dogged negotiations before, in July 1951, Bishop Shllaku (who was beaten personally by Premier Mehmet Shehu) and thirty priests, the last surviving active clergy, agreed to accept a statute which nationalized their church. They held out far longer than the other churches. Shllaku was forced to be "head" of the church, and he was kept under close surveillance. The clergy remained adamant that, even if organizational and economic relations with Rome were cut, in no way would they renounce the spiritual sovereignty of the pope or their allegiance to Jesus Christ, the founder of their church. When the government falsified the text and stated that all ties with Rome would be cut, the seminary would not be reopened, and children would not be allowed to receive instruction in church, the clergy courageously denounced the betrayal from their pulpits. Catholics continued to demonstrate their solidarity by packing the churches. Nika Stajka, a refugee, reported that professors, teachers, and students were well in evidence up to the time he left in 1955.[23] Later visitors, even up to the time of church closures, were extremely impressed by church attendance. The clergy were only too well aware of the vulnerability of their position. Crude antireligious propaganda was increasing; the grip of the secret police and surveillance were becoming tighter. By 1953 the number of churches had been reduced from 253 to about 100.

Shllaku consecrated a number of titular bishops. Strictly speaking, this was uncanonical, but he was the only bishop left alive, and the new bishops were all specifically appointed by Pope Pius XII. Ernest Coba, beloved for his work among the sick, poor, and destitute, became apostolic administrator of Shkodra on January 21, 1952. He ensured that a basic church organization would continue by secretly ordaining about a dozen ex-seminarians.[24] Antonin Fishta, a Franciscan, appointed apostolic administrator of Pulti on December 17, 1956, seems to have died in 1973. On April 18, 1958, Nikoll Troshani was made apostolic administrator of Durres and Lezha. The church was putting up a determined resistance to ensure its survival in the face of great odds.

The result was renewed persecution, if on a reduced scale, between 1958 and 1965. More than a dozen priests and members of orders were shot, and most of the others were either imprisoned or sent to forced-labor camps. This was a time of crisis for Hoxha as he opposed Khrushchev's demand for a rapprochement with Yugoslavia, which would have cost him his party leadership and his life. He needed complete discipline within Albania. At a show trial in April 1959 two priests, Ded Malaj and Konrad Gjalaj, and five laymen were condemned to death by a court consisting of Muslims for allegedly betraying state secrets to Yugoslavia. Diocesan offices and parishes were harassed, services were impeded, and bishops and priests were forced to clean streets and public conveniences and to wear clown outfits and placards reading "I have sinned against the people."

The Abolition of Religion. What led the Albanian government to take Marxism-Leninism to its logical conclusion with the unprecedented step of banning religion completely? Following Stalin's death, Hoxha progressively removed Albania from the Soviet grip. In 1961 he was able to break away from Khrushchev, whom he regarded as a revisionist, and put Albania under the protection of a conveniently distant China. He and his fellow ideologists had an almost paranoiac attitude toward religion. They regarded it as an entirely negative factor in Albanian life that divided the nation and exposed it to foreign interference, instilled a fatalistic passivity and submissiveness which retarded material progress, and kept women in a state of wretched slavery. They maintained that Albanians were not naturally religious, but rather opportunists prepared to change their faith when it suited them.

As détente developed and the Soviet satellites were renewing contacts with the Vatican, the party saw what they regarded as an unholy trinity of imperialists, revisionists, and the Vatican—for which the Catholic church represented an ideological fifth column—bent on carrying out counterrevolution against themselves, the true proponents of Marxism-Leninism.[25] Albania and China launched cultural revolutions concurrently in 1966. Albania's carefully engineered campaign against religion, however, predated the Red Guards. It started in 1965 when students began to organize meetings explaining that religion was outdated and obstructed the development of a genuinely socialist Albania. Places of worship were redundant and should be closed or converted to more useful purposes.[26]

On February 6, 1967, Hoxha launched the final stage of the campaign, the only part of Albania's cultural revolution to rival the Chinese one for its hysteria and fanaticism. At countrywide mass meetings representatives of all sections of society publicly renounced all belief in God and the saints, reviled the clergy as parasites, exploiters, and frauds, and pledged themselves never again to engage in worship or observe religious festivals. "Thunder sheets" appeared in public places attacking parents who had named their children after saints, as was customary among Christians.[27] By

May 1967 all 2,169 places of worship, including about 600 Orthodox and 327 Catholic churches,[28] had been vandalized by young people or closed, or were in the process of being put to secular uses, which were often offensive to believers.[29] Clergy were exposed to public ridicule in order to pressure them into renouncing their "parasitic" past. Not a single Catholic priest recanted. According to the party daily *Zeri i Populit*, 217 clergy were sentenced to prison or labor camps for "reeducation." Fr. Zef Bici was executed for sabotage, antigovernment agitation, and spying for the Vatican. Four elderly Franciscans were burnt to death when their friary, which had not been closed, was set on fire by young vandals. Five thousand Christians underwent a six-month brainwashing course using Mao's *Little Red Book* and carrying out degrading manual jobs. Bishop Ernest Coba, a frail old man, was beaten unconscious when he refused to recant; he was later seen wheeling a dustcart. Other clergy were given manual jobs; the elderly were told to return to the place of their birth and refused ration cards. Fr. Benedict Dema and, in 1973, Fr. Mark Harapi died of starvation.

A priest who had converted his room into a secret chapel was arrested in 1973 for stealing corn cobs. Former nuns were given jobs like cleaning toilets—unless a party member's wife was ill and needed expert nursing. Inevitably the campaign met considerable opposition, in which some clergy were involved, especially as it was combined with the completion of the program of agricultural collectivization. Fr. Shtjefen Jak Kurti, who had already served eighteen years in prison, was sentenced to a further fourteen years for fighting off with his bare fists those who came to destroy his church. He was over seventy years old at the time. The priest of Saint Anthony's, Jac, presented a petition in the name of ten thousand persons asking that his church be left alone.[30]

On November 19 decree no. 4337 annulled all previous decrees dealing with organized religion, thus placing religious bodies outside the law and ending the subsidies which had become essential for their survival. The legal niceties were not tidied up until 1976, when under the new constitution religion officially became illegal. In 1971 only thirty-one Catholic priests survived, twelve of them in camps. The struggle between the state and religion, and especially the Catholic church, had apparently ended in the complete defeat, suppression, and disappearance of the churches.

But had it?

Before the clampdown some far-sighted clergy had been distributing religious literature to keen members—though a lot of literature was confiscated when the churches were closed—and teaching them services they could perform at home, emphasizing that a believer could do without a church and worship in secret, "provided he has religion in his heart."[31]

The Catholic Church since 1967

In 1970 there was still strong resistance to closing places of worship, and clergy were resorting to all kinds of subterfuge. The older generation and "former priests" were transmitting religious teaching to the young. A review of arrests and deaths, news of which may take years to seep out, gives some idea of what practices are continuing underground.

In March 1973 news reached the West that seventy-four-year-old Fr. Kurti, who had relatives there, had been executed in February 1972 for baptizing a baby at the request of the child's mother, a fellow prisoner. In 1974 the three remaining bishops were sentenced to camps for conducting services in private; Antonin Fishta died after much suffering. Bishop Coba celebrated a secret mass at Easter 1979 at the request of fellow prisoners, who made simple vestments and an altar. They were caught and beaten; Coba, nearly blind, died the next day. The only bishop possibly still alive is Nikoll Troshani, apparently serving a twenty-year sentence and now in a camp for older prisoners.[32] It is not known if they consecrated successors; they certainly secretly ordained some well-educated former laymen.

In 1977 Fr. Fran Mark Gjoni was sentenced to twelve years after Bibles and other religious literature were discovered in his attic. Under torture he admitted that he had found them in parks and on the seashore, and was storing them against the day when religion would once again be legal. He was obviously aware of the ingenious activities of foreign Christians who try to float in literature in plastic bags. Although the trial was not reported in the press, it aroused widespread interest.[33] In May 1980, after considerable hesitation, Fr. Ndoc Luli, former director of Xavier College, baptized the twin sons of his sister-in-law on the commune where he was a laborer. He was apparently shot, and his sister-in-law was given a sentence of eight years.[34] A Franciscan former music teacher, Fr. Filip Mazrreku, died in 1985 in Ballsh camp. He had been arrested in the early 1950s and was deeply loved by his fellow prisoners for his cheerfulness and compassion.

The most recent arrest of which we have news is that of Fr. Pjeter Meshkella, S.J. (born 1901), for celebrating Christmas mass in a house near Shkodra in 1985. He died in camp on July 28, 1988. A lecturer at Xavier College, he was sentenced in 1947 for "sabotage"—trying to get international relief for flood victims—and spent the next twenty-five years in prison and camps. He was arrested again in 1973 and sentenced to life but was amnestied in 1983 on account of his poor health. He was an outspoken critic of his government's antireligious policy.[35] In 1980 there were believed to be about thirty priests and religious lingering in camps and prisons.[36]

The nature of religious survival varies tremendously from place to place.

It appears that there are still priests not under arrest, some of them actually administering the sacraments at mortal risk.[37] Up to the early 1980s church life was occasionally well maintained, with laypeople taking the sacrament to others at great personal risk, but according to recent refugees, the few remaining priests are now reluctant to officiate at any religious service, however secret, or even to discuss religion.[38] They also confirm what was reported by ex-seminarian refugee Marc Ndocaj in 1980 (also reported by the Albanian press), that religious survival is strongest in the family.[39] In the enforced absence of a priest, parents or older relatives sometimes baptize babies, bless brides and grooms (with a prayer such as "May God grant you to see your children's children"), and recite funeral prayers; this squares with the evidence from other faiths. This is what we might expect. Rites of passage are of prime importance. But the highly emotional traditional public mourning rites have been suppressed. No separate Christian or Muslim cemeteries exist, and no religious symbols are permitted on gravestones. So prayer can only be made within the home, although on All Souls' Day graves of Christians are still adorned with candles and flowers.

There are some former Catholic families where the young do not even know what a priest is; parents are often too terrified to talk. However, according to the press, there are cases of believers meeting to worship in homes, gardens, forests, mountain caves, and even abandoned churches. The most widespread form of Catholic life, the simplest and most suited to Albanians under persecution, is the rosary. As the Albanian Catholic paper, *Drita*, published in Yugoslavia, testifies, the rosary kept the faith alive in difficult times, such as the Turkish persecution. Tourists have reported seeing women holding rosaries, sometimes huddled together in groups, praying. Families are known to employ considerable ingenuity in concealing religious medals, crucifixes, icons, pictures, prayer books, Bibles, and rosaries, despite the possibility of imprisonment if they are found.

A particularly interesting practice that has caused the government much concern is that of disguised pilgrimages to holy places, especially those noted for cures. The church at Rozafat on the edge of Shkodra was closed and then razed to the ground and cordoned off when the authorities discovered that even relatives of party functionaries were visiting it and that cures had occurred, including that of the son of the late premier, Mehmet Shehu. It is significant that the church was a national shrine.[40] Again and again press complaints indicate that antireligious propaganda is being acted on only in a halfhearted manner, and that religious practices are proving more tenacious than was originally expected. It is possible that many believers have overcome the initial shock of the antireligion campaign. An editorial in the theoretical monthly *Rruga e Partise* complained: "In practice the party's demands are sometimes ignored, which leads to overestimation of progress and self-satisfaction, even euphoria, as if . . . everyone behaved like a fully convinced atheist. This explains why some Communists from Kruja, Leshe, and Shkodra [centers of Catholicism] act as if they did not notice those people who continue holding deep beliefs and maintaining religious customs, and who even now go to pray in the former 'holy' places of Lec."[41]

Not surprisingly, there has been considerable resistance to the extraordinary name-changing campaign of 1975, as a result of which parents cannot officially give their children the names of Christian saints.[42] Muslim names appear to be acceptable. There have since been frequent complaints in the press that children from religious families use a secular name at school but a saint's name at home—perhaps reverting to a Laramani practice. Other religious practices reported include keeping fasts and celebrating some major feast days and name days.

In 1980 sociologists complained that 96 percent of young Albanians were marrying persons from a similar religious background, reversing a previous trend. The figures suggest that religious groups are deliberately insulating themselves in order to preserve their distinctive cultures from further atheist erosion.[43]

These survivals are not proof that there are considerable numbers of doctrinally orthodox believers, as the party, well aware of Albania's confusing religious past, is not slow to point out. It attributes these practices to superstition, and in many cases is probably right. We have only to examine some of the problems facing the active little Catholic church in Kosovo to realize that there are still undisciplined congregations there and that many Albanians are still very confused in their religious beliefs. Laramani survive around Peć and Prizren; they could well survive in Albania. Nevertheless, a substantial section of the Catholic community has been educated, and congregations before the closure contained a fair proportion of the intelligentsia. Religious publications are secretly circulated, and people listen to Vatican Radio.[44] One remark from a Catholic, "What we have suffered has purified our faith,"[45] suggests that Christians have a surer conception of their beliefs than they had twenty years ago.

No Modification of the Antireligion Policy

External factors such as the break with China in 1978 did not lead to any modification of the party's antireligion policy. Nor did the advent of Ramiz Alia, a Stalinist hard-liner who succeeded Hoxha in 1985. Although economic problems allied with population pressures have forced it into closer relations with its immediate neighbors, Albania is still ideologically isolated from the rest of the communist world.

Albania has largely ignored adverse publicity from the West. Nevertheless, Albanian history books carefully avoid all references to the violence and excesses of the 1967 campaign. When news of Kurti's 1972 execution briefly focused world attention on the country, the press angrily explained that he had collaborated with the Italians and Germans during the war, had spied for English and American intelligence, and had been working as a subversive agent for the Vatican. Nowadays, obviously in response to awkward questions from the increasing number of tourists, guides are prepared to say that people are permitted to believe in God, and old people even to carry out simple rites at home, but not to do anything which might arouse the interest of the young.

Although information from an unusual yet reliable source, the Czechoslovak samizdat journal *Informace o Cirkví* (1986),[46] said that Alia had declared that people would no longer be imprisoned or otherwise punished for praying at home, an article by leading ideologist Hulusi Haki in March 1986 pointed out that the party attitude to religion had not changed. He admitted that people still resort to religious practices at moments of difficulty or weakness, that many still use religious names, and that the family has remained a stronghold of religion.

Tourists in 1987 reported that conditions seemed less repressive than in previous years but were unable to identify or open up relationships with believers, who were still far too frightened to speak freely. By 1988 there were some reports of encounters with believers, but conditions are still so tense that any significant information they may have gained cannot be made public.

The Vatican's attitude has not always been helpful to the Catholic church in Albania. Paul VI took party claims at their face value and spoke in December 1972 of the "peace of death. . . . With the shepherds stricken and the flock dispersed one cannot see what human hope remains for the Church."[47] This was somewhat premature, but it set the precedent for an almost total lack of concern for Albania from the Catholic world, which even the efforts of Gjon Sinishta and the repeated pleas of John Paul II have not been able to counter. Sinishta, a refugee and ex-seminarian, first tried to draw attention to the plight of his church by collecting memoirs of the martyrs in *The Fulfilled Promise* in 1976. Since 1980 he and other Albanian exiles have compiled an annual *Albanian Catholic Bulletin* containing press reports on Albania and Kosovo. John Paul II has been much more aware than his predecessor of the need for continuing concern. In 1980, from Otranto, he tried to draw attention not just to the sufferings of Catholics but to those of all believers in Albania, Muslims included. For his efforts he was castigated as "the pope cursing the irreligious Albanians," and he has continued to draw crudely worded attacks from the Albanian media. Whenever Italian television shows him or a religious program, it is jammed in Albania. With the possibility of some rapprochement between the Vatican and the Soviet Union, the attacks have become more strident than ever. As far as most Western Catholics are concerned, his words seem to fall on deaf ears.

Since the 1970s dedicated Evangelicals have shown the most practical concern for Albanian believers. They have been responsible for beaming in radio broadcasts apparently better suited to Albanian needs than those of Radio Vatican, which has been severely criticized by some leading émigrés. Its programs are unimaginative and still broadcast mass in Latin (apart from the Bible readings) which, as one of the staff admitted to me, very few people understood in the old days, anyhow. Its policy seems to be dictated by a misplaced caution. Catholics must be among the recipients (for the prewar Evangelical church numbered under a thousand) of the 30,000 Gospels smuggled in between 1979 and 1982 by a small Evangelical church, prompting the response: "The church of Jesus Christ is alive and growing in Albania; please send us more literature."[48]

Conclusion

Ramiz Alia is a realist. Albania's participation in the Balkan Conference in Belgrade early in 1988 was a promising step. Changes are at hand; Albania is to be brought into the orbit of European culture. More languages are being taught and more books translated. Trade is to be promoted across the Yugoslav and Greek frontier zones. Shortcomings in Albanian society have been admitted. But not a word has been said about allowing religious practices.

The Catholic church has survived long periods of almost total isolation in the past, and it is strongly rooted among the northern Ghegs. Although the smallest of the three major religious groups, it has provided the most determined resistance to state policy, as the record of Catholic victims of persecution shows. Like the smaller Bulgarian Catholic church, it is an extremely united church whose clergy have done their utmost to maintain religious life. It is significant that in both these minority Catholic churches the majority of the clergy were members of religious orders, which presupposes a higher caliber and degree of commitment and discipline than would be expected of the average parish clergy. Recent refugee reports suggest that little of its hierarchical structure remains, but that a significant number of families have maintained their beliefs.

FACT SHEET

The Catholic Church in Albania

Current strength of the church

Figures are either guesswork or unknown and would refer to underground activity. It is believed that there are less than 30 priests and monks, and probably one bishop. There are no seminarians.

Number of churches and church facilities

There are no parishes, seminaries, convents, monasteries, church-run schools, or church-run hospitals.

Chief news organs

None

Underground religious periodicals

None

Primates since 1944

Gaspar Thaçi, metropolitan archbishop of Shkodra and head of the Albanian Catholic church (died May 25, 1946, while under house arrest)

Vincenz Prendushi, metropolitan archbishop of Durres (died in prison February 23, 1949)

III

CATHOLIC-COMMUNIST ENCOUNTERS ON OTHER CONTINENTS

11

The Catholic Church in China

Eric O. Hanson

Any discussion of the politics of the Catholic church in China necessarily introduces many complexities, but three are particularly relevant to this chapter. First, China is an enormous country with a population of over one billion. While the People's Republic of China (PRC) does not have the percentage of minority citizens that the Soviet Union does, regionalism among the Han Chinese has been reinforced by factors as diverse as geography, a history of regional military power, multiple dialects, and even cuisine. If a cosmopolitan Shanghai intellectual finds many things strange in the everyday life of Canton, a Shandong peasant experiences such disorientation to a much greater degree. Statements about China as a whole, therefore, must often be modified when applied to particular regions. Second, the Catholic church in China remains a culturally Western institution immersed in an Eastern political culture constituted by the unique combination of many elements, especially traditional neo-Confucian values and Chinese Marxism.[1] Therefore political culture is especially significant in assessing the politics of an "expressive"[2] institution like the Catholic church. Third, changes in Chinese politics have been particularly rapid since the beginning of the Great Leap Forward in 1957. The need to make some stable judgment about the political meaning of Mao resulted in the Chinese Communist party's (CCP) official interpretation of its history at the Sixth Plenum in June 1981.[3] Nevertheless, the startling rapidity of ideological change during the last thirty years has produced a "crisis of faith" among both cadres and the people.

The first section of this chapter comprises three parts. The first part presents conclusions about the relation of Chinese political culture to religion from my earlier work, *Catholic Politics in China and Korea* (1980).[4] This presentation is followed by an introduction to the Chinese context for the three main themes of this volume: tradition versus modernity, hierarchy versus lower clergy, and institutional structure versus grass-roots organizations. Considerations from these parts will then be discussed in the context of Chinese regionalism.

This chapter immediately follows the volume's section on Catholic politics in Eastern Europe. The significant difference between the political cultures of Eastern Europe and China is relevant in narrating, in the second section of this chapter, the most significant Chinese state–Catholic church conflict of the 1980s, the Deng Yiming affair. In this misunderstanding Vatican Secretary of State Agostino Cardinal Casaroli followed the moderately successful diplomatic methods of Ostpolitik that have been developed over decades in dealing with the Communist states of Eastern Europe. In China a diplomatic debacle resulted. The third section of this chapter discusses major changes in the Chinese political system during the 1980s and their relevance to the politics of the Catholic church. Finally, I present the conclusions of the chapter with some tentative predictions for the future.

Political Culture, Major Themes, and Regionalism

My earlier work has stressed that Chinese history and traditional political culture are more significant than Marxist ideology in explaining the style and outcome of church-state relations in the People's Republic of China. This statement is even truer at the end of 1988 than it was in 1980 because of the subsequent dilution of Marxist ideological influence. Independent religious institutions like the Catholic church have always held a tenuous place in Chinese political culture. This latter position can be stated under the following four propositions:

1. In times of a strong Chinese state, only a religion with deep rural sectarian roots can effectively resist national government pressure.
2. The Chinese elite have tolerated foreign religious influence only during periods of social, economic, and political crisis. Buddhism, Catholicism, and Protestantism all found their initial strong acceptance during such periods. The more the old legitimacy fails to provide security and sustenance, the more the people are disposed to accept both universal religions and heterodox sects.
3. The more organizationally cohesive and complex a religion, the better able it is to resist Chinese state penetration, regulation, and control.
4. A strong Chinese state does not tolerate an independent Catholic

> church. At such times the church has had to choose between the alternatives of state penetration, regulation, and control, or underground sectarianism. Penetration has ensured that national government loyalists held positions of ecclesiastical leadership. Regulation has limited the number of clerical ordinations and new members. Control has enabled the state to use the ecclesiastical organizations for political goals. It is especially in this last aspect of active social control through campaign mobilization that the PRC has differed from its predecessor governments.

State penetration, regulation, and control of the church organization became the crucial church-state issue at both national and local levels. The PRC won the national battle only when it successfully established the Chinese Catholic Patriotic Association (CCPA) in 1957 and forced consecration of government-sponsored bishops. Furthermore, the more radical the general orientation of Chinese state policy, the more strongly the national government has attacked the Catholic church. In other words, state policy toward the Catholic church has followed the alternations in general policy in the PRC. For example, state pressure mounted in both the Great Leap Forward and the Cultural Revolution, when party cadres attacked not only Catholics who emphasized union with Rome but also Catholics who stressed the independent legitimacy of the Chinese Catholic Patriotic Association. Radical politics brought with it radical state religious policy.

With regard to this volume's theme of tradition versus modernity, Mateo Ricci and the Beijing Jesuits constituted the world's most significant case of modern technological transfer prior to the mid-nineteenth century. Since the end of that experiment,[5] the Catholic church in China has generally been a force for tradition, especially when compared with Protestantism. During the period 1839–1949 Protestant missionaries built Western-style universities and hospitals, and generally represented the modernizing vision of Great Britain and the United States. Catholics sought to build up their own local communities, often located in rural areas.[6] Some Chinese Catholics became prominent among the business leaders of the great trading centers like Shanghai, but in doing so they followed the traditional business practices of maritime China.

At the present time both the Chinese state and local Catholic communities advocate and practice a very traditional pre–Vatican II Catholicism. Mainland Catholic bishops did not participate in Vatican II, whose ending coincided with the full fury of the Cultural Revolution. In such circumstances of radical state pressure it would have been politically imprudent for local Catholics to make any adaptations in organization or ritual, even if they had wished to do so. In addition, the vast majority of Catholics still live in rural villages, many of which have a majority Catholic population with a very traditional religious life.[7] Even now, Chinese state ideology foresees the consignment of the church to the museum and remains vigilant against strong influence from the international church. Ironically, ideological and organizational changes in the universal church since Vatican II have removed some of the obstacles to Catholic cooperation with an official Marxist state like the PRC. For example, the attitude toward communism articulated by Pope John XXIII in *Pacem in terris* (1963) narrowed the gap between Vatican and PRC ideological positions.

The chapters on Eastern Europe have detailed how states in that region have fostered groups of laity and lower clergy which have attacked bishops loyal to Rome. Such PRC campaigns against Chinese Christian leaders in the early 1950s, ecumenical before their time, were noticeably unsuccessful among Catholics. The government's major breakthrough against Catholics came in 1957 with the formation of the Chinese Catholic Patriotic Association under Archbishop Pi Shushi, a legitimately consecrated bishop who had the respect of the majority of Chinese Catholics. Archbishop Pi consecrated state-approved bishops in the next year. As chapter 1 has pointed out, the state's success in establishing an autonomous Catholic episcopate makes the Chinese case unique. However, the expanded role of national bishops' conferences since Vatican II has brought the international church closer to the Chinese Three Self Principles.[8] This does not solve the difficulty of the CCPA's explicit rejection of union with Rome, but it does make discussion easier.

With the Chinese episcopate pursuing a course independent of Rome, grass-roots organizations have tended to be pro-Vatican in the Chinese sectarian tradition. The resulting political dynamic has featured tension between the government-approved episcopate and some local groups of clergy and laity who do not recognize their legitimacy. For example, district public security officials raided and closed an underground pro-Vatican seminary in Qiaozhai, Hebei, on May 28, 1986. This secret seminary existed ten kilometers north of a government-approved seminary in Shijiazhuang. The thirty seminarians who graduated from this seminary[9] in 1988 should begin to close the gap between the national hierarchy and the lower clergy and laity in Hebei. In the 1980s international Catholicism has emphasized reconciliation between those Catholics who have suffered for their devotion to Rome and those Catholics who have chosen to cooperate with government-sponsored institutions.[10]

The most significant Catholic political struggles do not occur at the national level, then, but in regional confrontations with myriad differences. For example, Hebei contains nearly one-fourth of China's Catholics, followed by Shandong and Shanxi. My earlier work devoted a chapter to the Shanghai confrontation of the 1950s, the most significant regional church-state conflict of that period, but the chief academic challenge today is to develop a typology of Chinese state–Catholic church relations that would retain its validity across regions. Relevant variables include the missionary traditions that first formed the various churches, urban and rural percentages of Catholics, relation of Catholicism to regional traditions, and the effectiveness of church leadership. National policy does set the parameters for the various religious affairs bureaus,[11] but Chinese Catholic input will be most effective at the regional level.

Emphasis on Catholic regional politics comes not just from the importance of regionalism in Chinese politics in general but also from the fact that the Catholic church is truly insignificant in the national domestic politics of the PRC. At the national level, state Catholic policy follows general state policy. A later section of this chapter discusses major changes in Chinese domestic politics in the 1980s, then treats their effect on state Catholic policy. Regional deviations from that national policy will be even greater than in other policy areas, however, because: (1) the regional development of Chinese Catholicism, reenforced by state persecution and pressure, has produced truly regional churches; and (2) Catholic policy in itself is not an important consideration for the national government.

The Deng Yiming Affair

As China emerged from the Cultural Revolution, the Vatican began to look for a way to establish relations with the PRC. Rome deemphasized its diplomatic ties to Taiwan by replacing the apostolic nuncio there with a chargé d'affaires.[12] When John Paul II visited Manila in February 1981, he addressed an emotional appeal to all Chinese for reconciliation with Rome. The pope praised Chinese culture and expressed his "deep admiration of the testimonies of heroic faith that many of you have shown and are still showing today."[13] John Paul II omitted any denunciation of the CCPA and took a nonjudgmental approach to individual decisions about the degree of cooperation with state-sponsored institutions: "In those long years you have undoubtedly lived through other experiences which are still unknown, and at times you will have wondered in your consciences what was the right thing to do. For those who never had such experiences it is difficult to appreciate fully such situations." The pope turned down an invitation to visit Taiwan but expressed interest through Casaroli, the architect of Ostpolitik, in going to the PRC.

One of the crucial issues in Ostpolitik has been to find bishops acceptable to both the Vatican and the Marxist states. At the conclusion of the papal visit, Casaroli flew to Hong Kong to confer with Bishop Deng Yiming (Dominic Tang) of Guangzhou (Canton). The PRC had arrested him at the height of the Great Leap Forward in 1958. After twenty-two years in prison, this Jesuit and native of Hong Kong had been released in June 1980 and restored to his bishopric. He had subsequently been allowed to go to Hong Kong for medical treatment and to visit relatives.

Casaroli and Deng held a joint press conference that was intended as the beginning of the new relationship between the Vatican and the PRC as visualized in John Paul II's address. Deng articulated a formula that he hoped might be acceptable to both parties. The Chinese Catholic church, said the bishop, would support the Three Self Principles, but such autonomy did not constitute independence from Rome. What it did constitute was left purposely vague. Casaroli stressed the flexibility of the Vatican diplomatic position, including the issue of diplomatic recognition. The cardinal said that the Vatican "would attach no special conditions for the normalization of relations with the Chinese Church, such as the release of certain clergy." The most prominent ecclesiastic referred to by this latter statement was Bishop Ignatius Gong Pinmei of Shanghai, who had been in prison since 1955.

When the secretary of state returned to Rome on March 5, he seemed willing to accept the CCPA as "an association of a civil, and not of an ecclesiastical character," thus needing no Vatican approval. Casaroli added that he hoped "that Monsignor Dominic Deng may have the opportunity to come to Rome himself to fulfill not only his own desire but also that of the Pope, who wants to meet him and express to him his affection and gratitude, and at the same time to hear directly from him all that can be said about China."[14] Deng came, and on June 6, 1981, John Paul II elevated Deng from bishop to archbishop of Guangzhou. Although this act conferred no new powers on Deng, it did indicate the Vatican's esteem for the bishop personally and signaled Rome's wish that Deng play a prominent role in Sino-Vatican rapprochement.[15]

The Catholic church in the PRC bitterly denounced the appointment. Bishop Michael Yang Gaojian made the first of many excoriating statements, which soon were echoed by the Religious Affairs Bureau and clergy and laity throughout the country. According to Bishop Yang, "The Holy See's move rudely interferes in the sovereign affairs of the Chinese Church. This cannot be tolerated."[16] The Guangzhou Patriotic Catholic Association and Guangzhou Diocese dismissed Deng as bishop on June 22.

Since the elevation of Deng to archbishop was a question of status only, why did the Vatican, intent on improving relations with Beijing, commit such a diplomatic faux pas? Why was Chinese reaction so harsh? While no definitive answer is possible, several partial answers have been suggested.

First, the Vatican misjudged the extent of Chinese state support for Bishop Deng. In early May Bishop Deng had paid a courtesy call on the PRC embassy in Rome and had been cordially received. It would be easy for Europeans to see more content in Chinese courtesy than actually existed. Second, if Deng became the keystone of Sino-Vatican rapprochement, it would necessarily reorder the power among existing Chinese bishops in their existing organizations. Third, the Religious Affairs Bureau had become more alarmed about the strength of traditional piety. For example, in October 1979 some Shanghai Catholics on pilgrimage to the shrine of Our Lady of Zose reported that they had seen a shining light and heard a message that the light would reappear on March 15, 1980. Shanghai communist press denunciations of this "superstition" resulted in Catholics from all over eastern China thronging to the shrine in early March.

A fourth reason concerned the changed domestic and international political climate since January 1979. State domestic policy had become less liberal, and United States recognition had not produced any breakthrough in Asian politics. Fifth, one Chinese priest indicated that the "perspective" of Deng may have been a problem. Guangzhou had been made an archdiocese before communist rule, but when Deng was appointed to the city he was made only a bishop because the retired French archbishop was still alive. Communist cadres used to taunt him with the fact that he, a Chinese, had not been made an archbishop like foreigners had. Finally, the Vatican did not notify the government of the impending appointment. According to Fr. John Tong, director of the Holy Spirit Study Centre in Hong Kong, the Holy See moved too quickly and "failed to take into consideration the historical background and feeling of the Chinese." The CCPA, without waiting for Bishop Deng's explanation of the event, denounced the appointment.[17]

Chinese Politics in the 1980s

The tightening of Catholic policy reflected trends in general PRC policy on civil and political rights. The political victory of Deng Xiaoping at the Third Plenum of the Eleventh Central Committee in December 1978 caused many of his supporters to interpret his new political and economic clout as signaling an era of general liberalization following the oppressive years of the Gang of Four. The euphoria at the time resulted in Beijing's Democracy Wall, that shrine to "the Fifth Modernization" (democracy). Only gradually did these supporters realize that Deng's sponsorship of modernization in agriculture, industry, defense, science and technology did not entail a similar commitment to Western liberal democracy. By March 16 Deng was warning that the democracy movement had "gone too far," and was threatening the "stability, unity, and the Four Modernizations." Less than two weeks later the police arrested the movement's leading figure, Wei Jingsheng.[18]

The timing was similar for state Catholic policy.[19] During January and February 1979 those who had suffered during the Cultural Revolution presented their grievances against the old religious policy of the Gang of Four. The party first indicated its new religious policy in the *People's Daily* on March 15. The key to the new policy was a distinction between "superstition" and "proper" religious activities in which believers "must conform to the policies and laws of the government. The state organs therefore must strengthen the administration of religious organizations."[20]

Such a policy followed the CCP religious policy which preceded the Great Leap Forward. A "United Front" allowed for the practice of religion, providing it was supervised by party and state organs, especially the United Front Department and the RAB. These organs had disappeared during the preceding period of radical domestic politics. As in numerous other sections of the party and state bureaucracies under Deng, cadres who had lost their positions during the Cultural Revolution returned to reconstitute the leadership of the organizations. Ulanfu became head of the United Front Department. At the first meeting this former boss of Inner Mongolia announced that the former director of the United Front Department, Li Weihan, had been rehabilitated. The RAB came back under the control of its last director, Xiao Xianfa. These cadres immediately began to extend their bureaucracies for the reinstitution of "moderate" Chinese religious policy. This new policy permitted the opening of churches and theological schools, establishing religious research institutes, and appointing clergy.

The national focus for this policy was an approved association for each religion. The CCPA, which was founded in 1957, held its third national conference May 22–30, 1980. The fact that its last national conference had been in 1962 under the same Xiao Xianfa who was now director of the RAB emphasized the continuity of Chinese state religious policy with the pre-Cultural Revolution era.

The 1980 meeting differed, however, in some organizational improvements. During the previous "moderate" period, many Catholics objected to the leading role of the CCPA in determining ecclesiastical policy. Catholic tradition did not allow direction from such a body, many of whose members were lower clergy or laypersons. To meet this objection, two new Catholic organizations were established at a second meeting, May 31–June 2. The Chinese Catholic Bishops' Conference deals with "doctrine, regulations, and exchange." The Chinese Catholic Religious Affairs Committee deals with "religious affairs in the spirit of independence, self-government, and self-administration." The relationship between the CCPA and these two groups is still not clear, but the CCPA and the Chinese Catholic Bishops'

Conference issued a joint letter to all Chinese Catholics at the conclusion of the meeting. Jinan's Bishop Zong Huaide headed the CCPA, with Bishop Zhang Jiashu of Shanghai (eighty-eight at the time of his appointment) leading the other two groups.[21] The organizational flexibility of such associations held together by interlocking personnel should be familiar to students of Chinese politics.

The rise of Deng Xiaoping, capped by the extensive elite personnel changes of 1985 and 1987, meant a return to the "normal" state Catholic policy of penetration, regulation, and control that existed before the Cultural Revolution. The "normal" policy, however, exists in a national and international environment that has undergone four significant changes since the 1950s.

First, Chinese communism suffers from a "crisis of faith"[22] that makes Chinese Marxism a much less effective ideological competitor. Chinese youth are again examining "novel" doctrines and life-styles, probably more seriously than at any time since the May Fourth movement. Cadres intent on *quanxixue*[23] seem to have a much higher toleration for all forms of "deviation," including Catholicism. That such tolerance is limited, however, was proved by conservative reaction to the second democracy movement (November 1986–January 1987), which led to the downfall of CCP General Secretary Hu Yaobang.

In the waxing and waning of contemporary national politics, Chinese Catholics indirectly benefit from the victories of "reformers" like Deng Xiaoping, Hu Yaobang, and Zhao Ziyang. As the fall of Hu in January 1987 was cause for alarm, Zhao's triumph at the Thirteenth Party Congress (October 25–November 2, 1987)[24] signaled increased maneuverability for Catholics. Zhao met with Jaime Cardinal Sin of Manila on November 11, with the general secretary expressing his "happiness about this frank and cordial meeting." In the following days Sin met with RAB Director Ren Wuzhi, CCPA leaders, and Sheshan seminary rector Bishop Jin Luxian[25] and his seminarians. The same day as the Sheshan visit, Sin was received at a Shanghai banquet by all four Shanghai bishops, including the state-appointed Zhang Jiashu and the Rome-appointed Gong Pinmei, who had been arrested in 1955. These two men had long been the symbols of the tension between Catholics cooperating with the CCPA and those who refused. Sin even had an opportunity to talk privately with Gong after the reception. The next day the cardinal expressed his gratitude to Bishop Jin and Mr. Yang Zengnian[26] for making his visit to Shanghai such a memorable one. Sin then departed to the native city of his father, Xiamen in Fuzhou Province.

Second, Deng's emphasis on the Four Modernizations has placed a premium on good relations with the West, which is envisioned as the source of considerable modern technology. Many of those Westerners involved in technological transfer are Catholics.[27] The most ambitious of these projects was the attempt to found the Chinese Experimental University of Shenzhen, headed by Dr. Shu-Park Chan, professor of engineering at the Jesuit Santa Clara University in California. The attempt to found an independent Western-style university incorporating the latest technology from Silicon Valley proved a formidable technical and political challenge. It has been suspended due to the suspicion generated by the economic debacle resulting from special trading autonomy given to Hainan Island and the conservative bureaucratic political reaction to the situation. During the November 1987 visit of Cardinal Sin, the prelate brought and returned personal greetings from Philippine President Cory Aquino to Zhao and blessed Xiamen's new Bank of the Orient (Philippines) in full liturgical vestments before a host of local dignitaries that included the deputy governor of Fuzhou. Rapid development of the coastal provinces has been a major focus of Zhao Ziyang's economic plan.

Third, the smooth transfers of Hong Kong (1997) and Macao (1999) to Chinese rule have become major political issues for the PRC leadership. In addition, by showing "reasonableness" in its dealings with Hong Kong, Beijing also hopes to convince Taiwan to become another Special Autonomous Region (SAR) of the PRC. Deng Xiaoping's policy of "one country and two systems," embodied in the Sino-British Declaration of December 19, 1984, provides that socialism will not be introduced into Hong Kong until at least 2047, and that the city's chief executive officers are to be chosen from among "patriotic" local residents.

In March 1985 Bishop John Baptist Wu Cheng-chung of Hong Kong, who had expressed the desire to play the role of "bridge-builder" between the church in China and the universal church, visited Beijing and Shanghai, where he was assured that the 267,000 Hong Kong Catholics would not be subject to local interference, and that they would retain complete religious freedom, including contact with the Vatican, after 1997. The return visit to Hong Kong and Macao of eight Shanghai Catholics, led by then Auxiliary Bishop Jin Luxian, occurred in July. On July 3, just before the Hong Kong visit, the government released Bishop Gong. The New China News Agency (NCNA) claimed that Gong had "admitted his crime," but the news release did not include any direct evidence for this assertion.[28]

The Guangdong RAB invited Bishop John Wu to visit Guangdong Province in late January 1986. In addition to seeing his eighty-five-year-old mother, the bishop said that the trip was useful in letting him see how religious freedom is practiced in Guangdong, and also in letting the Chinese authorities "know better our universal Church and the religious freedom outside, particularly differences in religion." The bishop added, "Both sides knew that was the first contact and dialogue. We both thought it was a good start and will continue."[29] In April 1986 national RAB Director Ren Wuzhi made a ten-day visit to Hong Kong to reassure local Buddhists, Catholics, Confucianists, Muslims, Protestants, and Taoists.

On May 29, 1988, Pope John Paul II announced that he would elevate Bishop Wu, then sixty-three years old, to the cardinalate on June 28. The bishop, who had been born in Guangdong, studied in Hong Kong, and served as a priest in Taiwan, used his first reactions to stress that he would be pleased to help the pope in improving Vatican ties with the PRC.[30] Unlike the Deng Yiming fiasco, government comment was supportive of the appointment. On September 6, 1988, Yang Zengnien, deputy head of the Shanghai United Front Department, made a private visit to the cardinal. Religious policy in the neighboring province of Guangdong, of course, is a special concern of Hong Kong Catholics. In late September in Beijing the RAB deputy head, Cao Jinru, assured a Hong Kong delegation that the proposed PRC religious law would not apply to the Hong Kong SAR, which would operate under the principle of "one country and two systems." Despite this and many other assurances, however, Hong Kong Catholics retain significant concern about the recently promulgated "Stipulations on Administrative Management of Religious Activity Venues in Guangdong Province."[31] The Tiananmen massacre has greatly increased this concern.

Fourth, the accession of Mikhail Gorbachev in March 1985 has produced major changes in Soviet Asian policy, articulated in the Vladivostok speech of July 1986 and the Krasnoyarsk speech of September 1988. The INF agreement to withdraw the SS-20s in Asia, troop reductions on the Sino-Soviet border, Soviet military reductions in Afghanistan, and the Moscow-mediated change of Vietnamese policy toward Kampuchea have all removed obstacles to better Soviet relations with the PRC. The effect of strengthened Sino-Soviet relations on PRC Catholic policy is ambiguous, and certainly is not even a minor concern in those relations. Reduction of military and political tension around the Korean peninsula, of course, would be encouraging news to moderates in all major governments. And the growing Seoul-Beijing connection might be useful to the Catholic church. Soviet religious policy has been less severe under glasnost.

Conclusions and Dilemmas

Conclusions. Chinese political culture continues to be a significant influence on PRC Catholic policy. Religious freedom, like the "Fifth Modernization" of democracy, exists in a limited environment. The state still formulates law to control religious activity. In addition to regional variations like the Guangdong example above, in 1988 the RAB was drafting a new national law to govern religious organizations. On April 4 Zhao Puchu, president of the Chinese Buddhist Association since the early 1950s and vice chairman of the Chinese People's Political Consultative Congress (CPPCC), told participants at a CPPCC plenary meeting that "the focus of the law should be placed on protecting the legitimate rights and interests of religious believers, organizations and temples and churches." Compared with other policies, said Zhao, "the implementation of religious policy was slow in process, great in resistance, full of problems, and unbalanced in development."[32]

Despite continued state control, however, PRC religious policy was certainly more benign at the end of 1988 than it was at the end of 1981. In November 1981 the Shanghai police arrested four Jesuits, the most famous being Fr. Zhu Hongshen (Vincent Chu). The arrest followed Fr. Zhu's refusal to join the CCPA and his reception of foreign Catholic visitors. Zhu, who comes from an old Shanghai Catholic family,[33] had already spent many years in prison but had been released in the general liberalization of the two preceding years. At his April 1983 trial Zhu received the most severe sentence of the four Jesuits—fifteen years. The government charged the Jesuits with collusion with foreign countries, collecting intelligence, fabricating rumors, and subversion.[34]

Nineteen eighty-three also saw the promotion of the anti-Deng campaign against "spiritual pollution." While general Westernization was the main object of the campaign, it reflected a political environment hostile to Catholicism. Bishop Peter Joseph Fan Xueyuan of Baoding, midway between Shijiazhuang and Beijing, was also arrested in 1983, one year before the Shijiazhuang seminary was opened. The "spiritual pollution" campaign passed, however, and, as Whyte noted, the "next attempted [Vatican-PRC] *rapprochement* came in 1984."[35] From late 1984 there was a strong increase in international exchanges by PRC Catholics.

With regard to the general treatment of dissidents, it is instructive to compare the fates of the leading figures of the democracy movements of 1978–79 and 1986–87. Wei Jingsheng (1978–79) died in prison, while astrophysicist Fang Lizhi[36] lost his party membership but was even allowed to give a short interview to the *New York Times* in February 1988. Almost all Catholic dissidents have been released. Bishop Fan was released six days after Cardinal Sin met with General Secretary Zhao. Bishop Gong had his full civil rights restored in January 1988 and went to the United States to receive medical care and visit relatives the following May. Father Zhu was released once again in January 1985 and lives with family members.

China in the 1980s existed in a very different domestic and international political environment. Young Chinese were again seriously examining non-Marxist systems of thought. Local cadres were following Beijing's directives in emphasizing the Four Modernizations. The PRC wanted to avoid upsetting the smooth transfer of Hong Kong and Macao and antagonizing Western sources of technology. All these factors contributed to more "breathing room" for Catholics. While Zhao Ziyang suffered reverses in his economic policies (price decontrol, coastal development, stock in state-controlled enterprises, and devaluing currency) at the Third Plenum of September 25–30, 1988, all relevant decision makers desire to cut the bureaucracy, ensure a smooth transition in Hong Kong and Macao, and import Western technology. The current policy disagreements concern advisable risks in the face of urban economic chaos caused by inflation, bank runs, and work stoppages.

National policy sets the parameters for religious freedom, but it is largely dependent upon other policy issues and thus generally removed from Catholic influence. In addition, the Catholic church in the PRC is weak at the national level, reflecting its missionary history, its pre–Vatican II character, and the strong regionalism of China during the period 1839–1949. The most significant Catholic political interactions will continue to be at the regional and local levels.

Current Dilemmas. The current, more auspicious environment probably will continue until at least 1997. This judgment presupposes no major upheavals in East Asia and domestic political dominance by the "eclectic modernizers."[37] Should Deng's Leninist enemies prevail, it will not mean a return to the radical religious policy of the Maoist Cultural Revolution but less "elasticity" in moderate policy. The major temptation in the current circumstances, of course, would be for foreign Catholic leaders to try to use the diplomatic, even military, contacts of major Western powers to their advantage.[38] Use of ecclesiastics from major powers carries the risk of repeating the mistakes of the nineteenth century. Someone like Jaime Cardinal Sin of Manila, of Chinese ancestry and not from a major power, has made a much better representative of the international church. With even Pyongyang willing to host Vatican representatives since summer 1987, Korean Catholics might play a significant role. It is in a reformist north-south approach to international affairs that Vatican and PRC foreign policies most closely approximate each other.

Future church development will vary considerably by region. Most auspicious for international Catholicism would be the Hong Kong–Shanghai bridge under the current leadership of Cardinal Wu and Bishop Jin. Wu is a Chinese cardinal whose diocese will become part of the PRC in 1997. Jin is one of the three Catholic episcopal members of the CPPCC standing committee, and he is respected in the international church. It is not that Bishop Jin offers a "third way,"[39] i.e., of those cooperating with the CCPA but not belonging to it; instead, the favorable situation results from a combination of personal openness to outside developments and the dioceses that Wu and Jin represent.

The national capital has always been a poor place to develop relatively open religious policy, no matter what the ideology of the Chinese government. For example, Archbishop Paul Yu Bin of Nanking became very much identified with the Kuomintang under Chiang Kai-shek. Beijing's bishop Michael Fu Tieshan was passed over for chairmanship of the CCPA because it was common knowledge that he had been married, thus raising questions of legitimacy among the majority of Catholics. Fu's appointment to Beijing in 1979, which had been without a bishop since 1964, was widely interpreted as an instance where the party placed political reliability over conformity to the traditional Catholic criteria for religious legitimacy. It has been Bishop Fu's thankless task to articulate Catholic support for controversial government programs like "one child per family," which is opposed by the Vatican and very unpopular in rural China.

Reestablishment of ties between the Vatican and the Catholic church in China before 1997 is possible but not assured. It is possible because there are no insuperable obstacles, and because it is in the rational political interest of PRC and Vatican moderates. Both sides seemed optimistic following the Thirteenth Party Congress and the visit of Cardinal Sin to Zhao Ziyang. This optimism has been tempered recently by Chinese economic troubles and their political fallout. In fact, one optimistic high-ranking participant in the informal dialogues commented that recognition merely awaited the solution of current economic problems. Such a comment probably does not do justice to the staying power of certain sections of the Chinese and Vatican bureaucracies.

Vatican-PRC ties are not assured because doctrinaire anticommunists in the Vatican and doctrinaire Marxists in Beijing still see them as an ideological threat. And history, which bears a particular political weight in the Chinese tradition, has given both sides plenty of reasons to mistrust the other. The Catholic church benefited from its close political identification with French imperialism in the nineteenth century and Kuomintang nationalism in the twentieth.[40] The PRC did persecute Catholics during the first two decades of its rule. Open ties with the Vatican are difficult because of traditional Chinese political culture and the continued strength of the bureaucracy in the PRC.

Since 1980 the Chinese government has been much more sophisticated in its religious policy, and the Vatican has been more flexible in its approach to the Chinese political-religious organizations. Dividing the Chinese Catholic Bishops' Conference and the Chinese Catholic Religious Affairs Committee from the CCPA strengthened the PRC argument that the latter was not a religious organization, an argument accepted by the Vatican. Observers also were impressed by the moderate tone of the Fourth Congress of the CCPA in Beijing, November 18–29, 1986.[41] While the Chinese church's autonomy was reaffirmed, there was strong support for international exchanges and no attack on the pope. It seems obvious that the majority of Chinese Catholics accept the primacy of the pope, even if they belong to the CCPA as a compromise which "guarantees the separation of religious life from political life."[42] This is true even for state-appointed bishops like Dong Guangqing of Hankou, who told a reporter in July 1988 that all but a few mainland bishops accept the pope's primacy.[43]

What reasons, then, are given for the continued impasse? First, the Vatican still recognizes the Republic of China. Second, church canon law seems to have automatically excommunicated certain state-appointed bishops for being illicitly consecrated, and also has automatically excommunicated the bishops doing the consecrating. Third, the Vatican is secretly consecrating bishops and ordaining priests in China without the permission of the government. Bishop Jin, for example, has said that the Vatican should stop supporting the "underground activities" of between ten and twenty bishops and about two hundred priests.[44] Objections one and three will have to be part of any comprehensive negotiated settlement. Objection two may be overcome by a strict interpretation of the conditions for automatic excommunication. After all, the names of the first state-approved bishops to be consecrated were sent to Rome for approval. Not usually stated publicly but also necessary would be a negotiated model of church and communion with Rome, bishops acceptable to both sides, and the probable transfer of some hard-line RAB officials. It also would be very difficult at present for most Chinese Catholics to accept married bishops and clergy, thus necessitating some episcopal and sacerdotal retirements. The predominantly rural Catholic church in China remains very traditional in doctrine and liturgical practice.

Internationally, the Vatican seems ready to recognize Beijing and break relations with Taipei as part of a larger package. In fact, there have been intermittent rumors that the Holy See would do so unilaterally.[45] In an interview at the end of 1986 Cardinal Casaroli characterized progress in resolving differences between the Catholic church and PRC officials as "slow." The China problem, he added, is both "simple and complex." "Simple because it is enough that they accept the common hierarchy—and then not too many other things would be asked [of them]. The real problem is communion [with Rome]."[46]

The Vatican, for its part, maintains its general approach of seeking reconciliation between Catholics within China while exhibiting maximum flexibility in diplomatic relations. The latest Vatican document drawn up by the Secretariat of State and the Congregation for the Evangelization of Peoples recognizes an "intermediate level" of priests and faithful who remain tied to the pope but have had to accept the political reality of the CCPA.[47] Many Chinese Catholics, both outside and inside the PRC, genuinely hope for restored diplomatic relations because such relations would greatly assist the internal healing of the church. In fact, when in October 1988 a group of Chinese Catholics in Manila summarized a large number of letters received from and interviews conducted in official and unofficial Catholic communities within the PRC, the felt need first listed was "to begin as soon as possible OFFICIAL [emphasis in original] conversations between the Vatican and Beijing, the first step towards giving the Catholics a channel of communication with the Holy See."

FACT SHEET

The Catholic Church in China

Current strength of the church

- 3.5 million (CCPA figure) to 6 million (outside estimate) faithful
- about 1,200 priests
- about 60 bishops (including 53 state-approved bishops)
- 1,300 or more nuns
- 700 or more seminarians

Number of churches and church facilities

- about 1,000 churches
- about 1,000 chapels
- 20 or more seminaries (7 regional, 4 minor, some local)
- about 20 convents
- 0 church-run hospitals
- 0 theological faculties (only teachers at seminaries)

Chief news organs

- *Catholic Church in China*, Beijing (quarterly published by the National Patriotic Association since 1980; 7,000 copies)
- *Compilation of Catholic Research Materials*, Shanghai (published irregularly by Shanghai Catholic Guangxi Press since 1985; circulation unknown)

Underground religious periodicals

- Unknown

Bishops in China elected and consecrated since 1981

Name	Diocese	Province	Date of Consecration
Xu Zhenjiang[a]	Shenyang	Liaoning	July 24, 1981
Zhang Wenbing	Dali	Shaanxi	July 24, 1981
Zhao Jingnong	Tianshui	Gansu	July 24, 1981
Ma Longlin	Suzhou	Jiangsu	July 24, 1981
Qian Huimin	Nanjing	Jiangsu	July 24, 1981
Li Pansi	Jiangmen	Guangdong	September 27, 1981
Cai Tiyuan	Shantou	Guangdong	September 27, 1981
Ji Huairang[b]	Xi'an	Shaanxi	December 18, 1981
Zhang Xin	Taiyuan	Shaanxi	December 18, 1981
Fan Wenxing	Hengshui	Hebei	December 20, 1981
Liu Jinghe	Tangshan	Hebei	December 20, 1981
Liu Zongyu	Chongqing	Sichuan	December 21, 1981
Liu Dianchi[c]	Jilin	Jilin	October 10, 1982
Liu Dinghan	Xianxian	Hebei	October 10, 1982
Jin Luxian	Shanghai	—	January 27, 1985
Li Side	Shanghai	—	January 27, 1985
Chen Shizhong	Yibin	Sichuan	June 14, 1985
Li Xuesong	Jilin	Jilin	September 22, 1985
Yu Runshen	Hanzhong	Shaanxi	November 30, 1986
Zhu Huayu	Bengbu	Anhui	November 30, 1986
Huang Ziyu	Xiamen	Fujian	November 30, 1986
Zhang Shizhi	Mindong	Fujian	November 30, 1986
Ma Qi	Pingliang	Gansu	March 16, 1987
Li Du'an	Xi'an	Shaanxi	April 5, 1987
Xu Lishi	Huanhua	Hebei	May 31, 1987
Wu Shizhen	Nanchang	Jiangxi	September 6, 1987
Wang Zicheng	Lixian	Hunan	December 8, 1987
Qu Tianxi	Changsha	Hunan	December 8, 1987

a. Xu Zhenjiang died in 1984
b. Ji Huairang died in 1986
c. Liu Dianchi died in 1985
Source: Holy Spirit Study Centre, Hong Kong

12

The Catholic Church in Vietnam

Stephen Denney

The Catholic church in Vietnam is in a unique situation. With approximately four million Catholics, or 7 percent of the total population, it is the second-largest Catholic church in Asia, behind only the Philippines. It is a minority church. At times it has been severely persecuted, and at other times it has exercised influence far out of proportion to its population. Today it is a church moving toward reunification after twenty years of partition during which two churches—north and south—developed under highly different circumstances. It is a church that is struggling to adjust to life under a communist regime, attempting to conduct a dialogue with the Marxist leaders while maintaining the integrity of its faith in the face of government harassment and persecution.

Catholicism was brought to Vietnam toward the end of the sixteenth century and spread rapidly with the arrival of French Jesuit missionary Alexandre de Rhodes in 1627. By 1639 there were 100,000 Catholics in Tonkin (then a separate kingdom of what is now northern Vietnam); by 1663 there were 200,000, out of a total population of 2 million.[1] Fr. Rhodes founded Domus Dei, an organization of lay catechists that became instrumental in maintaining and expanding Catholicism.[2] A missionary society was begun in France to train native priests, and French missionaries arrived in 1660.

However, the missionaries and the Vatican could not adapt well to the Confucian values of Vietnamese society. Their uncompromising attitude toward the different culture, particularly regarding ancestor rites, led to conflict and waves of severe persecution for Vietnamese Catholics. As many as 100,000 are believed to have died in the eighteenth century, and between 100,000 and 300,000 died in the nineteenth century.[3] The French intervention and colonial occupation (1860–1954) allowed the church to flourish as an institution, but Catholics became associated in the minds of many Vietnamese with the French, contributing to more ostracism and suspicion and further concentration of Catholics in certain areas and villages, particularly in the coastal regions.

Catholics became active in the various nationalist movements, and many supported the Viet Minh when it proclaimed a new republic in Vietnam in August 1945. But the drive of the Viet Minh to eliminate noncommunist nationalist groups led to disaffection among Catholics. Bishop Le Huu Thu of Phat Diem Diocese, who briefly assumed the role of adviser to Ho Chi Minh in the Viet Minh regime, broke away, and he and Bishop Pham Ngoc Chi of Bui Chu Diocese formed their own army and administration —anti-French and anticommunist.

1954 Exodus

At the signing of the 1954 Geneva Agreements it was agreed that Vietnamese north and south of the seventeenth parallel would be allowed to move across this temporary demarcation over a three-hundred-day period. Of approximately 900,000 who fled the North, about 700,000 were Catholics, including 619 priests and 5 bishops (leaving about 375 priests and 4 Vietnamese and 2 foreign bishops in the North).[4] This exodus radically changed the proportion of Catholics in North and South—before 1954 Catholics constituted about 10 percent of the population in the North and 5 percent in the South; after 1954 these figures were reversed.

Why did so many Catholics flee the North at this time? Hanoi accounts portray the majority of Catholics as illiterate and simple-minded peasants and fishermen who followed their priests like faithful sheep, motivated by false rumors such as "the Virgin Mary had gone South and those who refused to follow her would oppose God's will and risk damnation"; the United States was about to drop atomic bombs on North Vietnam; or the "Viet Minh would forbid religious practice, arrest the priests, and drive Catholics into the forests."[5]

There was indeed an organized effort to spread such rumors, and there were also efforts by the Viet Minh to forcibly prevent Catholics from fleeing the North. But Catholic refugees told of hardships and persecution directed against them by the Viet Minh. The harsh land-reform campaign had already begun in areas controlled by the Viet Minh, and because the church held much land, it became a target. There were also reports of Catholic believers, and especially priests, tortured for attempting to exercise ordinary religious activities.[6] Furthermore, there was the danger that the Viet Minh would follow the example of their close ally at the time, China, which was in the process of establishing a "patriotic church" and severely persecuting priests and other Catholics still loyal to the Vatican. Added to this was the legacy of persecution directed against Catholics over previous centuries and the hope for a better life under the Catholic president Ngo Dinh Diem in the South.

With this exodus and the official partition of Vietnam at the seventeenth parallel, the church also was essentially partitioned, and it developed under highly different political conditions over the next twenty-one years. I will discuss first its development in North Vietnam from 1954 to 1975, and then proceed to the church in unified Vietnam since 1975.

The Church in the North

Catholicism was feared and distrusted by the Democratic Republic of Vietnam (DRV) authorities despite its minority status. They saw the legacy of the church as one of close association with the French, and essentially as feudalistic. Its ties to the Vatican, which the DRV regarded as an agent of imperialism, further enhanced this image of the church as a foreign power. The church was a highly organized force—far more so than any other religious or political group besides the Viet Minh themselves—and deeply anticommunist in its values. The 1954 exodus had already demonstrated the attitude of Catholics toward the Viet Minh, and there was no evidence that Catholics remaining in the North felt differently. Catholics in Vietnam were generally very devout—daily attendance at mass was normal—and the bond between believers and priests was quite strong. Although a minority in Vietnam, the geographical concentration of Catholics gave them a majority status in several villages and districts.

Finally, the attitude of the Vatican toward communism was at the time much more hostile than it is today. A November 9, 1951, joint letter from the ordinaries meeting of John Dooley, delegate apostolic in Indochina, and the leading bishops of Vietnam stated, "The Catholic Church and communism are so completely opposed that our Holy Father the Pope declared that it is absolutely impossible to be at the same time communist and Catholic and that all Catholics who adhere to the Communist party are ipso facto severed from the Church. Not only are you forbidden to join the Communist party, but you cannot cooperate with it or do anything which might lead to power."[7]

Thus the church was seen as a rival to the new regime, and while it would be counterproductive to outlaw the church, the authorities felt it necessary to reduce and contain its power in order to mobilize believers in support of the regime's policies. The DRV's long-range objective was to transform the church into an instrument of the state, loyal to the ideology and legislation of the regime. The more immediate objective was to eliminate "backward" ideas, isolate and arrest priests judged to be reactionary, support "progressive" priests and laity struggling against the conservative hierarchy, and remove all obstacles from participation of the people, particularly the youth, in mass organizations.[8]

To integrate Catholics into the national community the regime gave some positions of responsibility to "progressive" Catholics, particularly in the local branches of the Fatherland Front and the National Assembly. Catholics also were given positions in local administrative organs and cooperative managerial boards in areas of high Catholic concentration.[9]

The most important body of the progressive Catholics has been the Liaison Committee of Patriotic and Peace-loving Catholics (LCPPC), created in 1955. Over the next twenty-nine years, until it was superseded in 1984 by the Committee for Solidarity of Patriotic Vietnamese Catholics (CSPVC), it played the designated role in propagating the government's policy toward Catholics and mobilizing believers in support of the regime. The LCPPC and its successor, the CSPVC, belong to the Fatherland Front, the umbrella organization for all the mass organizations representing women, youth, farmers, and other strata of the national population. The committee is not a mass organization itself, but it encourages Catholics to join these mass organizations in order to integrate them into the nation and the regime's value system.

The LCPPC was established at a conference held in Hanoi March 8–11, 1955, at a time when Catholics were still fleeing the North in massive numbers. The Hanoi journal *Vietnam Courier* (November 1977) claimed that 191 delegates attended this meeting, including "46 priests, 8 friars and nuns, 137 heads and deputy heads of parochial committees and other church members." The congress elected an executive committee, headed by a small group of priests who supported the Viet Minh, including Fr. Vu Xuan Ky (age sixty-nine, from Nam Dinh Province) as president and Fr. Ho Thanh Bien (age sixty-five, from Soc Trang Province) as vice president. Other priests who assumed prominent roles in this committee included Fr. Nguyen The Vinh (Ninh Binh Province) and the regrouped southerner Fr. Vo Thanh Trinh. The purpose of this committee, as envisioned by the congress, was to aid in the building of socialism and to "free Vietnamese Catholics from the influence of imperialism in order to restore dignity to the Fatherland and the nation."[10] A weekly publication, *Chinh Nghia*, was established by the committee, communicating over the following three decades the views of "progressive" Catholics and criticizing bishops and priests judged too conservative.

The day after the committee was established, however, it was condemned in a letter dated March 12, 1955, by Delegate Apostolic John Dooley and bishops of the major dioceses (Hanoi, Hung Hoa, Bac Ninh, Vinh, and Bui Chu) in the North: "The Movement of Catholics Loving God, the Fatherland and Peace, launched in Hanoi by some priests completely outside the hierarchy, is a danger to the unity of the Church in Vietnam. The hierarchy does not approve that this movement concerns the priests and faithful."[11] The committee responded by stating in an April letter to the pope, "All we do is to fight resolutely against the enemies of our Fatherland and our sacred religion. We have never had the idea that we stand against the Church."[12]

There were varying degrees of repression in DRV religious policy during this period. Shortly after the creation of the LCPPC, the bishop and priests no longer were able to communicate with the Vatican by mail.[13] But it was also in 1955 that the DRV enacted, on June 14, the president's decree "on the protection of the freedom of conscience and worship."[14] The decree's various promises of religious liberty were almost all conditional to the point of meaninglessness, and the actual degree of religious freedom in subsequent years became far more restrictive. Nevertheless, there was, according to Vatican observer Pierro Gheddo, an apparent thaw in the DRV religious policy in 1955, with churches and seminaries opened and religious processions allowed in city streets, particularly Hanoi.[15]

On the other hand, the land-reform campaign begun in 1953 was reaching its worst stage during this period, which, until autumn 1956, involved "people's trials," public denuncations, executions, and imprisonment. Bernard Fall estimated that 50,000 Vietnamese were killed and 100,000 imprisoned during this campaign.[16] Catholic notables (members of the village parish councils), landlords, and priests often came under strong attack during this period, as the regime sent cadres to these areas to mobilize Catholic peasants to denounce the accused.

Some priests spoke out against the inhumanity of this campaign during mass. According to a DRV spokesman, these priests blurred the lines between peasants and landlords; urged Catholic villagers to distance themselves from the land-reform cadres; threatened to excommunicate Catholics who denounced priests during this campaign; and when the campaign to denounce landlords began, issued letters calling upon Catholics "to love other people just as oneself."[17] Bishop Trinh Nhu Khue of Hanoi was criticized by the LCPPC for a circular letter he issued in early 1956 (on the occasion of the Vietnamese New Year) urging brotherly love.[18] From the DRV perspective the land-reform campaign was an opportunity for Catholic peasants to unite with other peasants in denouncing their former oppressors. But from the perspective of most Catholics it was a divisive campaign causing much suffering to the Catholic community, as many priests and Catholic laymen were sentenced to prison or executed.

The campaign began to backfire on the regime as its overbearing repression sparked resistance in the countryside, particularly in Catholic-dominated areas. The best-known uprising occurred in November 1956, in Quynh Luu of Ho Chi Minh's Nghe An Province, with a rebellion that threatened to spread to surrounding areas. It was followed only a few days later by an announcement from Ho Chi Minh beginning a rectification of errors campaign—which lasted through the end of 1957—acknowledging excesses of the land-reform campaign and allowing considerably more dissent than before. Catholics were allowed more freedom to carry on activities during this period. Many priests were released from prison; priests were allowed to travel more freely to visit their congregations; seminaries were reopened; and a press operated by the church was allowed to print catechisms and prayer books freely.[19]

Some church leaders acted unilaterally to correct errors of the land-reform campaign, to the consternation of the authorities. A notable example was an October 15, 1956, letter from Bui Chu Diocese that presented guidelines on dealing with those who caused harm to others during this campaign. It called upon those who slandered priests or other believers to correct their mistakes before the public and to have their cases announced within the hamlets or at important masses, depending upon the gravity of the offense. It also urged Catholics who illegally seized or damaged the property of others to restore such properties and pay damages.[20]

In 1958 the DRV renewed a harsher policy toward the church. Twenty-one foreign missionaries remaining in the country were expelled, and in July 1959 the Apostolic Delegation in Hanoi was forced to leave (the foreign missionaries and the Apostolic Delegation had been under virtual house arrest since 1954). For the next several years, contact between the Vatican and the church in Vietnam was extremely limited. The church's only press was confiscated by the DRV, and circulation of religious books and pamphlets was forbidden.[21] Even the teaching of catechism was prohibited during this period because the lay catechists were viewed as potential political rivals of the regime.[22]

Also in 1958 the DRV began a major effort to group peasants into agricultural cooperatives. Progress toward this goal was slower in Catholic areas, and, judging from the Hanoi press, there appears to have been much resistance among priests and bishops. Some priests were severely criticized by the press for refusing the sacraments to peasants who joined cooperatives and suggesting they work on private plots instead. Few Catholics joined cooperatives during the early years of this campaign.[23]

Vatican II

On December 24, 1960, the Vatican established an ordinary ecclesiastical hierarchy in Vietnam. The church in Vietnam finally had made the transition from a "missionary regime" of vicariates apostolic to an ordinary church regime. (There are now three archdioceses and twenty-six dioceses in Vietnam.) However, this historic event was barely noticed in North Vietnam.

Because of the poor relations between the Vatican and the DRV during this time, with no bishops allowed to visit Rome (as is customary for the church throughout the world), the church in Vietnam was insulated from changes taking place within the Vatican. The DRV did not allow any bishops to attend the 1962 Second Vatican Council. A long article by The Hung in the September 1962 issue of *Hoc Tap*, on "The True Nature of the Second Vatican Ecumenical Council," accused the church of continuing to oppose society and said the purpose of the council was to unite Christian churches into a political force headed by the Vatican as part of an overall effort to use imperialists to conquer the world. The council was a wasted effort, he added, which would not have any decisive effect. Hanoi commentators today credit the council for liberalizing Catholics' attitudes toward communism and local customs, yet the hostile DRV attitude at the time it took place was a serious tactical error from their point of view. The insulation of the church during these years reinforced its conservatism and reluctance to cooperate with the DRV authorities.

On the other hand, Vatican II brought significant changes to the church in the South, although the church was criticized by some Western observers for not adapting quickly enough. Mass was now said in Vietnamese, and the priests now faced the congregation when saying mass, signifying the new role of the laity as participants rather than followers in the faith. New churches were built according to the Oriental rather than the Western style of architecture. Certain rituals and customs of Vietnam previously regarded by the church as pagan were integrated into the Catholic faith. Incense sticks, a symbol of purification in Vietnam and previously forbidden in the church, could now be used in ceremonies. Catholics could now bow to the altars of their ancestors. This was forbidden previously because it was regarded as a pagan religious act, but now it was seen as a national custom, a way of paying respect. Catholics also were encouraged to adopt a more cooperative attitude toward other religions in Vietnam. Although the church in the South remained strongly anticommunist, Vatican II also influenced some priests and laity to develop a more liberal approach to political and social affairs. Thus the overall effect of Vatican II in the South was to bring the church closer to the national customs of Vietnam and to erode somewhat the barriers between Catholics and other religious groups in the country. After 1975 it was to provide the basis for initiation within the church hierarchy of a church-state dialogue.

The War and Church-State Relations

As the DRV began to mobilize the population for the struggle to overthrow the South Vietnamese regime, another problem occurred. Many northern Catholics supported South Vietnamese president Ngo Dinh Diem, and some even hoped he might somehow lead a force north to liberate them. When the DRV began its military conscription campaigns, some priests were accused of urging Catholics not to join the army.[24] For most of this period, Catholic youth, particularly those who had relatives in the South, were not generally trusted enough by the DRV to be sent south. But the DRV apparently had changed its attitude by 1971, as it began a campaign to enlist Catholic youth in the army and send them to the South.

The U.S. bombing of the North beginning in 1965 is said by the DRV and some Western observers to have significantly changed attitudes of northern Catholics toward the United States and the war. According to DRV spokesman Phong Hien, 486 churches were destroyed by American bombs between 1965 and 1973.[25] A May 30, 1971, letter to the pope from the LCPPC described instances in which churches had been bombed and priests wounded or killed, including a bombing attack on Vinh in which Msgr. Nguyen Dinh Nhien, coadjutator of Vinh, and Fr. Tuong Van Lieu were mortally wounded.[26] Yet some church leaders were criticized for their lukewarm response at the time of the bombing. The authorities apparently saw this as an opportunity to mobilize Catholics into the war effort, but they felt at least some of the bishops were trying too hard to develop religious piety within the church while remaining aloof from the politics of the war.[27]

In its efforts to appeal to Western opposition to the war, the DRV invited correspondents, antiwar activists, and others to visit the North. Some met with LCPPC representatives but rarely with more authentic representatives of the church. This was true even for George Hussler, secretary general of Caritas, who visited Hanoi in 1967 but was not allowed to meet Hanoi's Archbishop Trinh Nhu Khue.[28] Some northern Catholics also traveled abroad to represent the regime's point of view, but here again they were representatives of the LCPPC. Thus contact between foreigners and northern Catholics was strictly controlled. Nevertheless, these contacts may have lessened the degree of repression against Catholics.

Hussler's visit was significant because it signaled a trend begun by Pope Paul VI in the mid-1960s to adopt a more neutral stance toward the Vietnam conflict while calling for an end to the war. The liberalizing changes in the Vatican in all probability led the DRV leaders to realize finally that it was in their interest to allow bishops to visit Rome and in other ways let the Vatican and the northern church develop closer ties, not only to improve the DRV diplomatic standing but also so that the insulated church could begin to experience some of the changes brought about by Vatican II. The bishops first visited Rome in 1974. In May 1976 Archbishop Trinh Nhu Khue (seventy-six years old at the time) was allowed to travel to Rome, where he was consecrated as the first cardinal of Vietnam. (He died on November 27, 1978, and was replaced by Cardinal Trinh Van Can).

With the signing of the Paris agreements in 1973, and as the war approached its end, relations between the church and state appeared on the surface to be significantly better than they were twenty years earlier. This was indicated by the changed attitude of Cardinal Khue, who seemed more cooperative with the regime after 1974.[29]

The regime also perceived progressive changes in the church's practices and theology. Phong Hien noted with approval the decline of prayers for Our Lady of Fatima, elaborate religious processions, and costly banquets and weddings; the reform of musical techniques and elimination of Western tunes; and the general conformity of Catholicism to social activities, "without harming production, studies, or fighting." Furthermore, he noted, the "choice of the responsible officers of parish communities is based on both religious and secular criteria."[30] However, these perceived changes were more a reflection of the regime's values and policy toward the church than genuine reform.

It is difficult to assess how much support the "patriotic" Catholics had among the clergy in Vietnam. By 1975 the LCPPC in the North had progressed not through popular support among priests or lay Catholics but through acting with the government in pressuring the church hierarchy. Overall, the church in the North remained relatively monolithic, with a conservative and generally uncooperative hierarchy, ordinary believers deeply religious and loyal to the priests and bishops, and a small group of "progressive" priests whose positions were determined by loyalty to the party and its ideology rather than a genuine theology.

The Church in the Socialist Republic of Vietnam

It has been said that Vietnamese communist leaders employ three languages in their discussion of religious policy—the language of tolerance, the language of pragmatism, and the language of legislation.[31] The 1955 DRV religious policy decree combined the language of tolerance with the language of legislation (vaguely worded legal language conditioning the various guarantees of religious freedom). The most detailed and significant example of the legislative language is Council of Ministers Resolution 297, enacted in November 1977, which requires government approval for virtually every form of religious activity.[32] The pragmatic language is the language intended primarily for internal party documents, rarely seen by the public, although we may occasionally glimpse the language in the party's theoretical journals. It is the language that instructs cadres and officials how they are actually to implement the policy of the government.

An internal document of the Vietnamese Communist party promulgated after 1975 provides an example of the language of pragmatism as it presents the overall perspective of the party on the church in the South and sets forth guidelines for cadres in implementing the policy. The document viewed the political divisions among the Catholics in the South as fairly complex in comparison to Catholics in the North after 1954.[33] It divided Catholics in the South into four categories: the "progressives," the "partisans of adaptation," the "indecisives" and the "reactionaries."

As the document acknowledged, the Catholic Left in the South was very small. It was led by no more than twenty priests with a loose following of intellectuals, several thousand students, parishioners, and workers.[34] The leaders of the group were mostly French-educated. They had influence in only two parishes, both in Saigon, the Vuon Xoai and Redemptorist parishes. They were not influential among the ordinary Catholics but instead directed their activities toward the West and Catholic intellectuals in South Vietnam. They were particularly active in publishing dissident magazines, often censored, organizing demonstrations against repression and for workers' rights, and issuing statements for a negotiated settlement to the war. These "progressives" were less orthodox in ideology but younger and more articulate than their counterparts in the North.

Among the progressives' main proponents were the priests Chan Tin, Nguyen Ngoc Lan, Truong Ba Can, Huynh Cong Minh, Phan Khac Tu, and Tran The Luan; prominent laymen such as philosophy professors Nguyen Van Trung, Ly Chanh Trung, and agronomist Chau Tam Luan; and politicians such as Congressmen Ho Ngoc Nhuan and Ngo Cong Duc, both involved in publishing the anti-Thieu (often censored, later banned) newspaper, *Tin Sang*. Following the fall of Saigon in 1975, Father Lan told a reporter that he and the other leaders of this group secretly met with National Liberation Front (NLF) leaders during the war and agreed to work for their victory while pretending to be proponents of the "third force."[35]

The second group, the "partisans of adaptation," consists of those who seek to adjust to the new regime in order to protect their religion by participating in the communal work of the new society; consolidating the beliefs and doctrine of the church, particularly among young people; and reinforcing the associations of the church. They are partisans of social justice but not proponents of communism. Archbishop Nguyen Van Binh of Saigon, and to some extent Archbishop Nguyen Kim Dien of Hue, as well as most other Vietnamese bishops, might be placed in this category.

The third group, the "indecisives," comprises the great majority of Catholics. These are the mass of believers who seek peace to practice their religion and protect their private interests. They do not defy the policies or laws of the state, but they are reluctant to follow the progressives or partisans of adaptation. They are suspicious of the regime but not defiant.

The final group described by the document is the "reactionaries," who are divided into two categories: the "inveterate reactionaries," who openly oppose communism, and other "reactionaries" who (from the document's perspective) use certain forms of adaptation to oppose the regime. Besides imprisonment, the state harasses uncooperative reactionary clergy through means such as assignments to work details, special ration card requirements, close surveillance, and limitations on attendance at certain meetings and conferences.[36]

With the military conquest of South Vietnam in April 1975, and the official reunification of the country into the Socialist Republic of Vietnam in 1976, the religious policy of the North was extended to the South. The new regime moved to eliminate the church as an autonomous force in southern society and contain its future growth. The vast network of social institutions of the church—including schools, hospitals, and orphanages—were turned over to the government, although some nuns continued working in these institutions. Associations such as the Assembly of Catholic Dioceses, the Catholic Mothers' Association, the Associations of the Virgin Mother's Children, and particularly the Thanh The Youth Association (which was seen as a rival to the regime's youth groups) were banned from participating in public activities and thus forced to work covertly in teaching catechism and Catholic dogma and carrying out their normal operations.[37] The future of these associations could be seen in the North, where by March 1975 many Catholic associations had been eliminated, and others were criticized by the "patriotic" Catholics as unnecessary.[38]

According to Fr. Sesto Quercetti, S.J., about seventy priests who had been army chaplains were sent to reeducation camps in 1975, and over the next year another two to three hundred priests "were gradually arrested for various reasons: 'collaboration' with the former regime, working with war refugees, denunciation of revolutionary agents in the past, etc."[39] By January 1987 approximately one hundred priests remained in reeducation camps, according to the archbishop of Ho Chi Minh City, Nguyen Van Binh.[40] In September 1987 twenty-two Catholic priests who had served as military chaplains in the South Vietnamese army were released from reeducation camps after twelve years' detention.[41]

The progressives, on the other hand, were quickly given positions of responsibility. Ngo Cong Duc was allowed to resume his daily newspaper in Ho Chi Minh City (Saigon), *Tin Sang*, which he continued under government auspices until 1981, when it was forced to close because it had become more popular than the official city newspaper. Fathers Chan Tin and Nguyen Ngoc Lan also were allowed to resume their journal, *Doi Dien*, which was published sporadically until 1979. Fr. Nguyen Dinh Thi returned from exile in Paris to become editor of *Cong Giao Van Dan Toc* (Catholics and the people), the "patriotic" Catholic weekly of the South, which continues to be published today.

The Approach of Archbishop Binh

The first major confrontation between the new regime and the church in the South occurred in June 1975 in Ho Chi Minh City, when Vatican envoy Henri Lemaitre appointed Msgr. Nguyen Van Thuan as coadjutor bishop of the city. Monsignor Thuan, former bishop of Nha Trang and nephew of South Vietnam's late president Ngo Diem, was well regarded among many Catholics as an intelligent and staunch opponent of communism. The prospect of him succeeding Archbishop Nguyen Van Binh (then sixty-five) was obviously not favored by the new authorities.

The result was a demonstration of "patriotic" students demanding Lemaitre's expulsion from the country and a counterdemonstration by conservative Catholics supporting him (the latter was suppressed by police). Lemaitre was expelled from the country and replaced by Sesto Quercetti, who was in turn expelled the following year along with other foreign priests. Bishop Thuan was forcibly banished from Saigon, placed under house arrest in Nha Trang, and later was moved to Hanoi. Although Msgr. Thuan is still recognized by the Vatican as coadjutor bishop of Ho Chi Minh City, he is, of course, unable to exercise his functions. Pham Van Nam, who was subsequently appointed as auxiliary bishop of the city, has proven to be more amenable to government authorities.

The arrest of Bishop Thuan and the expulsion of Vatican envoys and foreign priests were signals from Hanoi to the Vatican of the state's primacy over relations between the Vatican and the Vietnamese church. Resolution 297 of the SRV Council of Ministers requires the Vatican to obtain SRV approval before selecting a bishop and forbids the church from enforcing religious documents of the Vatican contrary to the laws and policies of the regime. The resolution also requires government approval before receiving documents from the Vatican or other religious organizations abroad.

Shortly after the Thuan incident, Msgr. Binh was criticized by Fr. Nguyen Ngoc Lan for his past cooperation with South Vietnamese regimes.[42] However, in notable contrast to the position of the Vatican and the northern bishops in the 1950s, Archbishops Binh and Nguyen Kim Dien of Hue sought early to establish good relations with the new regime. During the last days of the 1975 spring offensive, both urged Catholics not to flee the country but to remain and cooperate with the new regime in national defense and reconstruction.[43] A July 1976 episcopal conference of the Hue and Saigon ecclesiatical provinces launched an appeal to Vietnamese Catholics to commit themselves to participating in the construction of the new society.[44]

Monsignor Binh's general approach to church-state relations was outlined in a 1977 address to the Vatican. He began with the point that Vietnamese Catholics live in an environment controlled by the Communist party, which is constructing a society according to its ideals and building the "new socialist man." He emphasized the need for Catholics to be aware of this new situation and of the regime's highly negative view of the legacy of the church in Vietnam. Rather than living in a ghetto, on the fringes of society, Catholics should cooperate with the regime while maintaining the integrity of their faith, in the spirit of Vatican II.[45]

Although Msgr. Binh's very positive statements on church-state relations after 1975 may to some extent have been motivated by a desire to preserve the church in a hostile environment (and it should be noted that many Vietnamese Catholics felt that his posture was too conciliatory), one can also sense in his words a genuine desire to integrate Vietnamese Catholics into the national community and find common ground between the socialist values of the regime and the values of the church. These concerns were brought out in a 1978 retreat he led for clergy at the Cu Chi state farm near Saigon. Centered on the theme of collective labor and living the gospel in the socialist society, the retreat emphasized manual labor as a way of transforming the priests and their role in society. The loss of "privileges" (particularly the social institutions and landholdings of the church) was perceived as a blessing, a way for Vietnamese Catholics to become more evangelistic by living among the people and being good citizens of the socialist regime.[46]

It was in this spirit that the first episcopal conference of unified Vietnam was held in Hanoi from April 24 to May 1, 1980. It was attended by all bishops except Bishop Pham Ngoc Chi of Danang and the imprisoned Msgr. Nguyen Van Thuan. The conference elected a permanent council headed by Cardinal Trinh Van Can of Hanoi.[47]

The congress, which has been held annually in subsequent years, was a significant step toward unification of the church in Vietnam and in establishing the authority of the bishops in adapting the church to its Marxist environment. A circular letter of the bishops underlined their desire to adapt the church to the national tradition and present reality of the country and urged Catholics to contribute to national reconstruction and defense.[48] Following the conference, the bishops met with Prime Minister Pham Van Dong and Hoang Quoc Viet. Later in the year, nineteen of the bishops were allowed to visit the pope in Rome, who warmly welcomed the conference and the approach of the bishops' letter.[49]

Repression and Resistance

In discussing the role of the church in the socialist regime, Hanoi spokesmen emphasize that Vietnamese Catholics must be Vietnamese first and Catholics second. This patriotism is equated with fidelity to Marxist-Leninist socialism as interpreted by the Politburo of the Vietnamese Communist party.[50] A corollary to this is the call upon Catholics to oppose any act of opposition to the regime.

Although passive resistance among the Vietnamese seems widespread, a viable armed resistance movement is not likely to emerge soon, nor has the church supported such resistance. However, some priests and lay Catholics have been accused of resistance activities. One such group was the United Catholic Association for National Restoration, reported in 1978 to have a force of about one hundred men operating in the Tan Hiep district of Kien Giang Province (on the southern tip of Vietnam, bordering Cambodia), ambushing government troops in isolated areas.[51] On February 3, 1978, the Fatherland Front in Ho Chi Minh City organized a meeting of priests to denounce various activities among Catholics, including collaborating in antigovernment activities, maintaining illegal residences, and conserving books, journals, or reviews regarded as reactionary. It also accused a Redemptorist priest of leading a resistance organization.[52]

The most publicized act of resistance occurred on February 12–13, 1976, in a shootout between the government and a group of Catholics barricaded inside the Vinh Son Church of Ho Chi Minh City. They were accused of having formed a resistance group and printing counterfeit money and leaflets urging Vietnamese to take up arms against the regime. When police raided the church, five people, including a priest, were arrested, and three, including a security officer, were killed. They were later brought to trial, and two were executed in August 1978 while the others were given lengthy prison sentences. There were reports of similar Catholic demonstrations occurring elsewhere in South Vietnam in early 1976, including a demonstration in the Ho Nai settlement near Saigon of family members of reeducation camp prisoners and another demonstration in Phu Nhuan of Gia Dinh Province led by local priests protesting political repression.[53]

Immediately following the Vinh Son incident, the regime sponsored mass meetings in which religious leaders, including Archbishop Binh, denounced the incident. Both church and government leaders seemed alarmed at the problems this could cause in relations between the Catholics and the regime. It also was apparent in the official press accounts that the regime wished to make it emphatically clear that no resistance or dissent would be tolerated and that Catholics would be expected to work with other Vietnamese in suppressing such activities.

The underground activities within the church over the last decade have been primarily religious rather than political, resulting from government restrictions on ordinary activities of the church—underground activities such as circulating religious publications, organizing Bible-study groups, participating in associations of the church, teaching catechism to children, holding unauthorized masses, and ordaining priests without prior government approval.

There were signs in 1980 of a hardening in SRV religious policy. The example of the Polish demonstrations and the growing influence of the church with the youth apparently caused some concern within the regime. Cadres in Ho Chi Minh City organized "family meetings" in the fall of 1980 to disseminate the party line on "the lesson to be learned from Poland," namely, the danger of criticism from Catholics and other groups and the influence of religion in general.[54] At the end of the year, Tran Bach Dang, who had established good rapport with the "progressive" southern Catholics, was replaced by the hard-liner Dang Thanh Chon as head of the Bureau of Religious Affairs.[55]

A serious confrontation with the church occurred in December 1980 and January 1981 when the government closed the Jesuit Dac Lo Center in Ho Chi Minh City, which had become the most popular cathedral in the South, particularly with the youth, and arrested the priests affiliated with the parish, including the seven most senior Jesuits in Vietnam. Among them was Fr. Nguyen Cong Doan, the superior Jesuit of Vietnam, a distinguished Bible scholar and close associate of Msgr. Binh. He also was the leading author of the aforementioned 1980 circular letter of Vietnamese bishops.[56]

The priests were held in prison until June 29, 1983, and finally were brought before a two-day show trial. They were accused of circulating a religious journal, *Dao Nhap The* (Religion incarnate), which the prosecution claimed was designed to slander the government; and of association with a previously obscure lay Catholic, Nguyen Van Hien, allegedly involved in resistance activities. Hien, who seems to have been made the scapegoat, was sentenced to life imprisonment. Father Doan was sentenced to twelve years, and the others received sentences ranging from probation to fifteen years' imprisonment. But the evidence presented did not support the charges, and most observers believe this trial and the closure of Dac

Lo were motivated by a concern over the appeal of the center to youth.[57] Following the trial, the Jesuit community was singled out for repression and harsh criticism. The arrests and trial also may have strained relations between Archbishop Binh and the regime.

The Sixth Congress of the Vietnamese Communist party in December 1986 and the selection of Nguyen Van Linh as its secretary general have led the way to reforms and some degree of liberalization, with some hopeful indications that this policy would extend toward Catholics. In November 1986 Linh spoke at the provincial party congress of Ho Chi Minh City and stated that Catholics, Hoa Hao believers, and intellectuals of the old regime should no longer be treated as outsiders.[58] Following the Eighth Bishops' Congress in Hanoi in May 1987, Linh met with the bishops and claimed that the "unswerving policy" of the government was to respect freedom of religion, but he acknowledged "shortcomings and errors in the implementation of the policy" due to ignorance of the cadres and prejudices among some people.[59] In October 1987, while visiting Rome, the auxiliary bishop of Hanoi, François-Xavier Nguyen Van Sang, described the new government attitude toward Catholics as one of "détente and openness."[60] One year later, in another visit to Rome, he said religious congregations would be allowed to resume recruitment and training and that a new translation of the Bible had been printed.[61]

However, the policy as implemented remains unclear and continues to vary from one area to another. According to a statement made by a "progressive" priest at a Ho Chi Minh City meeting in March 1988, bishops continue to suffer restrictions in carrying out ordinary activities such as ordaining priests, assigning priests inside the diocese, celebrating confirmation, and writing annual letters to the parishes; priests often are forbidden from teaching catechism; and Catholic laity continue to be treated as second-class citizens, particularly when applying for higher education.[62]

Furthermore, the regime continued to resort to highly publicized trials as a means of silencing suspected dissidents. On May 15, 1987, security forces raided the Congregation of Mother Coredemptrix (Dong Cong) monastery in Thu Duc and arrested about sixty members, including forty priests and brothers. A detailed article in *Saigon Giai Phong* (Liberated Saigon), the government newspaper for Ho Chi Minh City, claimed that Fr. Tran Van Thu, the superior general of the congregation, had allowed his monastery to become a resistance base and said further that security forces had found many illegal residents, a large amount of stored rice, many "reactionary" documents, paper cutters, bookbinding tools, mimeograph machines, printing ink, and one Colt .45 pistol with some ammunition. Its most ominous accusation was the claim that Fr. Thu had trained more than "1,600 key cadres" and planted them "in all parishes of various cities and provinces," indicating that a major wave of arrests might be expected in the near future. Father Thu denied these charges and appealed for the release of those arrested in a letter smuggled out of the country.[63] Catholic leaders in Ho Chi Minh City deny that the congregation was involved in political activities and describe it as an ultraconservative group which fled from the North in 1954 and acts like an "underground church" because its leaders do not believe Catholics can live openly in a communist society.[64] Certainly it is hard to imagine an elderly priest starting a revolution with a single Colt .45 pistol in a country which has the third-largest army in the world.

Archbishop Dien and the "Patriotic" Catholics

On June 7, 1988, the archbishop of Hue, Philippe Nguyen Kim Dien, died at the age of sixty-seven. Pending the appointment of a new archbishop, Joseph-Marie Cardinal Trinh Van Can of Hanoi was appointed apostolic adminstrator of Hue.[65]

Monsignor Dien will be deeply missed by Vietnamese Catholics because he had assumed a unique role in his forthright defense of human rights and religious freedom in Vietnam. The highly regarded bishop was never considered a fervent anticommunist or one who sided with the rich and powerful, but rather as a priest of the people, who embraced the social reforms generated by Vatican II. His criticism of the government's policies was therefore all the more painful to the authorities.

His first public criticism of the regime's policies came in April 1977, when he was called upon at a meeting to join others in denouncing six leading monks of the Unified Buddhist church (An Quang pagoda) who had just been arrested. Instead, he expressed sympathy for their plight and complained of similar restrictions against Catholics. He protested that the Mass and other religious ceremonies were restricted, priests were forbidden to travel to New Economic Zones (remote areas of the country where many Catholics were being sent during this period), children were subject to anti-Catholic propaganda in the schools, and Catholics suffered discrimination in seeking employment and lost jobs in hospitals and charitable institutions.[66] Subsequently, Archbishop Dien was placed under surveillance, and two priests in his diocese were arrested for distributing his statement.[67]

The resolve of Msgr. Dien and other Vietnamese bishops to preserve the autonomy of the church from the government was brought to its most crucial test with the creation in 1983 of the Committee for Solidarity of Patriotic Vietnamese Catholics (CSPVC), succeeding the LCPPC of North Vietnam and bringing "progressive" Catholics into one national organization. The first step was the establishment in January 1980 of the Committee of Action of Catholics of Ho Chi Minh City for the National Reconstruction and Defense, chaired by Rev. Vo Thanh Trinh of the LCPPC. Hanoi press accounts claim that Msgr. Binh welcomed the new organization, but another report indicates that he expressed reluctance over the new group, noting that the LCPPC established in the North did not have widespread support among the Catholics, and particularly the hierarchy.[68] At an August 24, 1983, meeting of LCPPC delegates in Ho Chi Minh City he expressed concern that the important church-state dialogue would be in vain if it did not include authentic representatives of the church.[69]

The congress held to establish the new committee opened in Hanoi on November 7, 1983; it was attended by 299 delegates, including 142 priests, eleven religious, and 146 laity. Ho Chi Minh City had the largest delegation with thirty-eight delegates, including 28 priests; Hanoi had twenty-five delegates; but Hue had only twelve delegates—eleven laity and one priest who was suspended from his functions by Archbishop Dien for attending the congress. Delegates were apparently chosen by the local branches of the Fatherland Front.[70]

The goals of the committee, according to Article 2 of its statutes, are to mobilize Vietnamese Catholics to defend the socialist regime, fight against "imperialists and reactionaries" who use religion to oppose the regime, and unite with Christians around the world in support of "peace, justice, and social progress." A new weekly was established, *Nguoi Cong Giao Viet Nam* (Vietnamese Catholic), replacing the publication of the LCPPC, *Chinh Nghia*.

The committee is organized at the national level, with branches in the provinces, cities, and special regions. The national congress is to meet once every five years, while the regional congresses meet every three years. The national committee includes the Presidium and the Secretariat; the Presidium sets the basic tasks of the CSPVC, while the Secretariat aids the Presidium in managing its activities. In wards, districts, and local areas where there are many Catholics, CSPVC "action cells" can be set up with the approval and aid of the Fatherland Front.[71] As of 1986, the CSPVC had branches in all but two dioceses.

The Congress elected seventy-four members to the national committee; and from these, twenty-four were selected for the Presidium and Secretariat—seven from the South and the rest from the North. Only twenty-one of the seventy-four members were laity, and all but four of these laymen were from the North. The Presidium included the president and four vice presidents, only one of whom was from the South, the others having been active in the LCPPC. The president chosen was Fr. Nguyen The Vinh, National Assembly delegate and former president of the LCPPC, but he died in December 1983 at the age of seventy-nine. He was replaced by

Fr. Pham Quang Phuoc from Haiphong Province, who died in March 1984 at the age of seventy and was replaced by the second vice president, Fr. Vo Thanh Trinh, a regrouped southerner who had served in the DRV National Assembly and was active in the LCPPC. The two other vice presidents selected were Fr. Vuong Dinh Ai of Nghe Tinh Province and Fr. Huynh Cong Minh of Ho Chi Minh City. The ten other Presidium members included the southerners Fr. Truong Ba Can and former Saigon professor Ly Chanh Trung. Father Nguyen Thai Ba of Thanh Hoa Diocese in the North assumed the position of secretary general of the Secretariat, which had nine other members, including two from the South: Fr. Vuong Dinh Bich, editor of *Cong Giao Va Dan Toc*, and Fr. Phan Khac Tu.[72] The southern radical priests Chan Tin and Nguyen Ngoc Lan were notably absent in the committee listing and appear to have lost the prominence they once had.[73]

The new committee was not welcomed by the Vatican, and most bishops in Vietnam kept a distance from the CSPVC while not being openly critical.[74] Only one bishop and one auxiliary bishop attended the congress. Some bishops, including Nguyen Huy Mai of Ban Me Thuot, Nguyen Van Hoa of Nha Trang, Bui Tuan (coadjutator) of Long Xuyen, and Nguyen Van Lan of Xuan Loc, were interrogated by police after admonishing the priests in their dioceses who attended the congress and forbidding them to continue in the CSPVC.[75]

The strongest reprisal came against Archbishop Dien, who suspended from his functions Fr. Nguyen Van Binh, the only priest in his diocese who attended the congress. His suspension of Fr. Binh and his strong opposition against the organization was supported by almost all priests in his diocese because it lessened government pressure on other priests to join the CSPVC.[76]

In a letter written to the organizers of the congress on October 19, 1983, Msgr. Dien expressed concern that the new committee could lead to the establishment of a separate church from Rome and protested the manner in which the delegates were chosen, with priests invited to the congress without (in most cases) receiving approval from their bishops. He argued that the episcopal conference founded in 1980, which called upon Catholics to contribute to national defense and reconstruction and to adapt the church to the national traditions, was the proper organization for orienting all the activities of Catholics. The CSPVC, he said, could interfere with other commissions of the church and upset unity among Catholics.[77] Copies of this letter were sent to the Bureau of Religious Affairs, the Fatherland Front, and the other bishops of Vietnam. Clandestine copies also were made of the letter and circulated in the country and smuggled abroad.

SRV authorities responded to Msgr. Dien's actions by placing more pressure on him and arresting and interrogating priests and nuns closely associated with him. In December 1983 a Hue priest, Fr. Nguyen Van Ly, was brought to trial for having led an unauthorized procession to the statue of the Virgin Mary at La Vang in Binh Tri Thien Province near the seventeenth parallel. The statue is quite popular among Vietnamese Catholics but is regarded as a symbol of anticommunism by the government. Father Ly was sentenced to twelve years' imprisonment, but the court blamed Msgr. Dien for instigating Fr. Ly, and his activities were subsequently restricted, as were the activities of Msgr. Pham Ngoc Chi of Danang, who was blamed for influencing Msgr. Dien.

On April 11, 1984, Msgr. Dien wrote an open letter to Nguyen Huu Tho, president of the SRV National Assembly, complaining about the unfair nature of this trial and its repercussions against him.[78] From April to October Msgr. Dien was subjected to lengthy police interrogation sessions centering on his opposition to the CSPVC and his suspension of Fr. Binh. Archbishop Dien defended his action by citing the 1982 Vatican Declaration of the Sacred Congregation of Clergy forbidding priests from participating in such political organizations. His interrogators countered that SRV Resolution 297 forbade the church from enforcing Vatican documents which contradict SRV laws and policies. Monsignor Dien said he placed the law of God and the church above the law of the state and was willing to follow the example of past Christian martyrs.[79]

Another incident occurred in July 1985 when a Hue nun was arrested while traveling to Ho Chi Minh City and found to be carrying various documents, including letters from Msgr. Dien. In October the superior nun of the Hue congregation was arrested and accused of espionage. On November 23 Msgr. Dien's secretary, Fr. Tran Van Quy, was summoned by police and subjected to six weeks of interrogation sessions concerning the activities of Msgr. Dien since 1980. Monsignor Dien responded with another letter, appealing for the release of the two nuns and defending his right to communicate with the Vatican. He was reported in September 1986 to be under house arrest.[80]

In January 1987 Msgr. Dien lifted his suspension of Fr. Binh and was in turn given more freedom by the government, including the right to travel to the bishops' conference in May of that year.[81] However, shortly before his death, in a March 1988 appeal to Vietnamese Communist party leader Nguyen Van Linh, Msgr. Dien said he was still confined to his place of residence and could not travel outside Hue to carry out his pastoral duties.[82]

CSPVC spokesman Fr. Vo Thanh Trinh claimed in a letter to Msgr. Dien (April 28, 1984) that the committee is a civil rather than religious organization and that priests joining it do not violate the 1982 Vatican decree.[83]

However, it is clear from the language of the Vatican declaration that the CSPVC is precisely the kind of organization priests are prohibited from joining.

The CSPVC is not likely to lead to a separate church, as happened in China, but rather will continue the tradition of the LCPPC established in North Vietnam. It seems aimed at bringing southern "patriotic" priests into this national organization dominated by northern priests, establishing more uniform control over church-state relations, and pressuring the church to conform its doctrine and practice to the new society. How far this committee goes in pressuring the church hierarchy may depend partly on external factors such as the present transition in leadership of the Communist party in Vietnam.

It remains to be seen to what extent the more independent southern priests in the committee will submit to the conformist approach of their northern brethern. SRV authorities were reportedly dissatisfied with the opening CSPVC congress in November 1983, feeling that too much criticism was expressed and too many CSPVC priests took advantage of their status as delegates to increase the pastoral activities of visiting churches, preaching, and giving sacraments.[84] The position of these southern priests seems to have been strengthened since the liberalization following the Sixth Party Congress in December 1986. Father Phan Khac Tu from Ho Chi Minh City, elected to the National Assembly in April 1987, pledged that he would seek to pass a law that would provide more comprehensive protection to the rights of Catholics.[85]

The Shortage of Priests

The most serious and practical problem facing the church in Vietnam has been obtaining government approval for the training and ordination of priests. In North Vietnam, a serious shortage of priests resulted from the 1954 exodus of 619 (out of 1,000) priests to the South. The DRV claimed that one hundred priests had been ordained between 1954 and 1975, although this seems exaggerated. Official estimates from Hanoi on the number of priests by the mid-1970s ranged between 310 and 350 as compared to three hundred priests in the immediate aftermath of the 1954 exodus.

The effect of this shortage was documented in a study of the largely Catholic Hai Van Commune in North Vietnam by François Houtart and Genevieve Lemercinier, based upon research conducted in 1979–80 by Vietnamese students of the Institute of Sociology in Hanoi. They found that whereas before 1954 there were nearly 100 priests in the Hai Hau district of Bui Chu Diocese, there were now only 8 to serve 44 parishes—each priest serving an average of 5.5 parishes and 19.5 places of worship. Furthermore, several of the priests were very old. In Bui Chu Diocese there were only 31 priests for 143 parishes, i.e., 4.6 parishes and 11,290 Catholics per priest.[86] Thus the priests have to travel to different parishes to say mass, which therefore cannot be held as frequently as before. As the priest has less time to spend with members of his parish, it would seem that his social importance diminishes, while the government's organizations move in to assume a greater role in the Catholic community. This was indicated by Houtart and Lemercinier's description of a 1975 incident in which a priest who threatened ecclesiastical sanctions against dissident parishioners was denounced first by a meeting of one thousand parishioners, then by the parish council, and next by the committee of the commune; finally the party secretary intervened to tell the priest "that it was intolerable that he should refuse religious rites at funerals to the faithful who asked for them, adding to his arguments threats of sanctions such as the denial of the supply of rice if he did not submit to the wishes of the parishioners. The conflict then subsided."[87] Such a conflict would have been unheard of before 1954, and it seems strange that a communist cadre would demand that a priest not deny funeral rites to his parishioners. But this is the result of the policy of mobilizing Catholics in support of the regime and encouraging divisiveness within the Catholic community.

The shortage of priests also can influence the changing role of the parish council, which played a very important role in the traditional Catholic village, corresponding to the council of notables in non-Catholic villages. The president of the Hai Van Parish Council is no longer chosen by the parish priest but is elected by the people of the parish with the approval of the civil authorities. In the South the priest still chooses members of the parish council but is pressured by the local Fatherland Front to choose at least one or two "progressive" members, and these in turn become the most powerful and influential members of the council, sometimes playing the role of informer or monitor.

If the shortage of priests results in their declining social importance, then it would seem that this is in the regime's interests. But besides this is the goal to develop a more "patriotic" church by controlling the kind of Catholics who are allowed to become priests. During the early 1960s several articles in *Chinh Nghia* criticized the church hierarchy for allowing Catholics with a "bad family background" to enter the seminaries, while more "progressive" students were at times forced to leave the seminary before completing training.[88] However, the DRV could easily control the number of priests ordained and pressure seminaries to include a political curriculum. Some dioceses ordained priests illegally, without government approval, but the overall result of this conflict was to choke off the supply of priests.

Eventually, the shortage of priests in the South may reach a level similar to that of the North, where one priest may have to serve three to seven villages. Under Resolution 297 (Article 3) the church must seek government approval for every step in the training and ordination of priests, including the opening of classes, religious trainees admitted, teachers, and curricula. Candidates for seminaries must have a "patriotic" family background and are under the management of the Religious Affairs Bureau. If they are not judged flexible enough, they may lose their residency permit and become quasi citizens, ineligible for food and other social services.[89] In 1982 the government authorized two seminaries in each of the ecclesiastical provinces of Hanoi, Hue, and Ho Chi Minh City, but there was reportedly a conflict over the degree of state control of the seminary teaching and the teaching of Marxism-Leninism as well as theology.[90] As a result, most seminaries remained closed.

In 1975 there were thirty-six seminaries in South Vietnam with nearly six thousand students. However, an American church delegation visiting Vietnam in April 1986 was informed that only one Catholic seminary was operating in the country, apparently in Hanoi, attended by sixteen students.[91] Another seminary was approved by the Ho Chi Minh City People's Committee for reopening in November 1985, with Fr. Tran Thai Hiep as rector and Fr. Le Tan Thanh and Fr. Huynh Cong Minh as deputy rectors.[92] It was finally opened in February 1987 with forty seminarians from surrounding dioceses (forty-eight by September 1987) who were accepted as a group to go through the six-year course together. Only after they have completed this course will a new group be allowed to enter the seminary.[93] In October 1988 it was announced that four new seminaries would be opened in the Vinh, Thanh Hoa, Can Tho, and Long Xuyen dioceses.[94]

The number of priests allowed to be ordained is even smaller than the number of students allowed into seminaries. In Ho Chi Minh City Archdiocese, which has experienced less repression than most other dioceses in the country, only eleven priests were ordained between April 1975 and the end of 1985.[95] Some prospective priests have been pressured to act as government informers on the activities of other priests and the Catholic community as a condition for ordination.[96]

There was not a great shortage of priests in the South in the immediate aftermath of the war, but the shortage is felt in certain areas more than others. Priests who had served more than one parish in the South before 1975 were allowed to continue doing so. But in cases where priests have died or been arrested, new priests are not often allowed to replace them, nor are priests from other parishes allowed to travel there to say mass.[97] It all depends on approval from local authorities, as stipulated in Resolution 297, and approval in this situation is not common. With no priests, the churches in the more isolated areas cannot continue their religious services, and therefore, under Resolution 297, the government has the right to confiscate these buildings and use them for their own purposes.

With the prospect of an increasing shortage of priests, the laity will have to assume a more prominent role in church affairs, but the degree and manner in which this can be done will be subject to government intervention.

Vatican Relations

Relations between the Vatican and the SRV seemed to be recovering from a low in 1985, when only three bishops were allowed to make their *ad limina* visit to Rome, as compared to nineteen in 1980. However, hopes for improved relations were seriously set back when controversy arose over the Vatican's canonization (June 19, 1988) of 117 Catholics who were martyred for their faith in Vietnam between 1773 and 1863 (ninety-six Vietnamese, ten French, and eleven Spaniards). The pope saw this as an opportunity to reinforce the faith of Catholics in Vietnam and give the "heroic church" there examples to follow. Hanoi, on the other hand, saw the act as an intervention in Vietnam's internal affairs and accused some of the martyrs of being collaborators with the French colonizers.[98] The government launched a major campaign to mobilize Catholic opinion within Vietnam against the canonization, but these efforts, as predicted by dissident priest Fr. Chan Tin, only served to increase Vietnam's isolation in the world and create dissatisfaction among Vietnamese Catholics.[99] However, perhaps in part to recoup its losses, the government agreed to allow masses for the saints on September 4, and allowed a number of CPSVC members to travel overseas to attend meetings in France, Australia, and the Philippines.[100] The Vatican has maintained its opposition to priests' associations such as the CSPVC, and it firmly supported Msgr. Dien's outspoken criticism of this organization. On the other hand, the SRV has given greater prominence to the CSPVC and increased pressure on bishops and priests who oppose it. Another problem is the question of who will succeed Msgr. Dien as archbishop of Hue and Msgr. Binh (age seventy-seven in 1987) as the archbishop of Ho Chi Minh City. Monsignor Thuan, bishop coordinator of Ho Chi Minh City, was finally released from house arrest and allowed to visit Rome in May 1989, but he was not allowed to return to Saigon. There was speculation in 1985 that he would be forcibly expelled from the country or brought to trial in order to deprive him of his episcopal and priestly functions and thereby prevent him from succeeding Msgr.

Binh.[101] Bishop Nicholas Huynh Van Nghi (age sixty in 1987) of Phan Thiet Diocese was asked by SRV authorities in May 1987 to replace Msgr. Binh in the event of his death, but he refused, stating that it was not the government's prerogative to appoint bishops.[102]

On the positive side, Pope John Paul II has appealed for international relief to Vietnam in times of distress; and Cardinal Trinh Van Can informed the pope in 1985 that the SRV had authorized a church plan to print eighty thousand missals and eight thousand Bibles.[103] Pope John Paul II also expressed a desire to visit Vietnam to "get to know personally every one of my children so that I could express the love I have always felt towards them"; but SRV officials refused, stating, in the words of Dang Thanh Chon, "the pope and the Vatican still follow policies against Vietnam."[104] On the other hand, a Vatican delegation to visit Vietnam was expected to be commissioned by the end of 1988, a sign of improved relations between the Vatican and Hanoi.[105]

Despite restrictions, church attendance is reported by refugees and foreign visitors to be high, and the faith is more intense than before. As an organization, the Catholic church has experienced less repression than other religions in Vietnam and has managed to preserve its internal unity and ties with the Vatican, providing Vietnamese Catholics with a temporary sanctuary from the political proselytizing and mass movements of the regime.

Catholicism has survived centuries of brutal persecution in Vietnam, and it will continue to survive. However, the type of repression and control is more systematic and more threatening to the integrity of the church than in the past. Vietnamese Catholic leaders will continue their efforts to conduct a dialogue with the communist government in the spirit of Vatican II, but the meaningfulness of the dialogue will depend upon the degree to which they are allowed to speak freely.

FACT SHEET

The Catholic Church in Vietnam

Current strength of the church (November 1988)

3,800,000 faithful
1,900 priests
40 bishops
6,000 nuns
65 seminarians

All figures except that for bishops are estimates; no Vatican statistics are available. The number of monks is unknown.

Number of churches and church facilities

4 seminaries
0 church-run schools
0 church-run hospitals
Figures for churches, convents, and monasteries are unknown.

Chief news organs

Chinh Nghia (Just Cause), Hanoi (1955–84, weekly newspaper of Liaison Committee of Patriotic Vietnamese Catholics in North Vietnam)

Cong Giao Va Dan Toc (Catholics and the People), Ho Chi Minh City (est. 1975, weekly newspaper of "patriotic" Catholics in the South)

Nguoi Cong Giao Viet Nam (Vietnamese Catholic), Hanoi (est. 1984, weekly newspaper of Committee for Solidarity of Patriotic Vietnamese Catholics and the successor to *Chinh Nghia*)

Underground religious periodicals

None of which I am aware. However, statements of Archbishop Nguyen Kim Dien of Hue critical of the regime's religious policy have been circulated clandestinely within Vietnam and smuggled abroad, and priests and nuns have been arrested for allegedly distributing his statements.

Several Jesuit priests associated with the Dac Lo Cathedral in Ho Chi Minh City were brought to trial in 1983 for, among other things, publishing a religious journal, *Dao Nhap The* (Religion Incarnate). However, this journal was distributed openly, with the approval of Archbishop Binh, and was not regarded by observers as a dissident magazine.

Primates since Communization

Joseph-Marie Trinh Nhu Khue, Hanoi, cardinal (1950–78)

Joseph-Marie Trinh Van Can, Hanoi, cardinal (1978–present)

Philippe Nguyen Kim Dien, archbishop of Hue (1968–88); Joseph-Marie Cardinal Trinh Van Can of Hanoi appointed apostolic administrator, June 10, 1988, pending appointment of new archbishop of Hue

Paul Nguyen Van Binh, archbishop of Saigon (Ho Chi Minh City) (1960–present)

13

The Catholic Church in Cuba

Thomas E. Quigley

The most salient characteristic of the church-state relationship in present-day Cuba is the apparently dramatic change now underway. Beginning in 1985, this phenomenon of a new presence of religion, and specifically of the Catholic church, in the Cuban equation has been widely noticed. The first ever exchange of visits by official delegations of the U.S. and Cuban episcopal conferences in that year may serve as the visible gateway to the present period. Those visits (U.S. bishops to Cuba in January; Cuban bishops to the United States in September) have been followed by a number of other widely noted visits to Cuba by prominent churchmen.[1]

The publication that same year of Frei Betto's *Fidel y la Religión*,[2] the upgrading of the Office of Religious Affairs as an entity of the Communist party's Central Committee, and the start of a process of releasing prisoners to the U.S. Catholic Conference for resettlement in the United States have since been followed by other, still more significant, developments. Most notable among these have been the 1986 National Meeting of the Cuban church (Encuentro Nacional Eclesial Cubano, ENEC),[3] the granting of visas to some thirty foreign priests and twenty women religious to enter the country,[4] and the permission for the bishops to import an offset printing facility. Moreover, few journalistic accounts of these events fail to speculate on the intriguing matter of the forthcoming papal visit to Cuba.

This chapter will situate the status of today's relative détente in the context of the previous thirty years, a period in which the church-state relationship moved rapidly from initial warmth through mutual mistrust to outright confrontation, resulting by the early 1960s in the total privatization of religion and the near suppression of the church. If the present rapprochement continues to prosper, we may soon hope to see some of the same kind of salutary reexamination of the recent past that other socialist societies have lately exhibited.

Several church-state issues that merit an honest and thorough revisiting are examined in this chapter. There are others, however, including the role of the politically progressive sectors of the Catholic lay associations; the near dominance of the anti-Batista movement (and thus of the insurrection that triumphed with the dictator's abdication) by the Catholic-led Revolutionary Directorate; the extraordinary number of priests collaborating with the "other" main opposition group, Fidel Castro's July 26 movement (hardly limited, as official hagiography would have it, to but a single "revolutionary priest," Father Guillermo Sardiñas who, after the triumph, wore his campaign ribbons on his olive-drab cassock); and even the attitudes of those pre–Vatican II bishops toward such matters as land reform, distributive justice, and the rights of workers—all these and more are themes demanding an unbiased reexamination.

This chapter's goal is more modest, viz. to touch on a few of the disparate themes involved in the postrevolution church-state conflict—both those that supposedly led to the confrontation between church and state and those that helped lead to the present modus vivendi—and it concludes with a tentative assessment of the present détente. Since this chapter deals exclusively with the Roman Catholic church, all references to "church" will pertain only to that entity.

The Standard Interpretation

The standard interpretation of the church-state conflict after the revolution can be told quite succinctly. The bishops, imagining an influence they did not possess, began to criticize the successive reforms implemented by the new government, some of which had adverse effects on entities of the church. An unusually high percentage of the men and women religious, in addition to being foreign-born, were engaged in teaching; when the schools were nationalized, most moved elsewhere. The bishops' ever-stronger pastoral letters and the growing militancy of the Catholic lay associations set in motion a dynamic of conflict that culminated in the 1961 expulsion of 132 priests and religious (including a bishop).

The church had come to be seen as the center of the counterrevolution. Its most faithful adherents were predominantly middle class and urban, and large numbers were leaving for their "true home" in Miami; its clergy were heavily Spanish and intensely anticommunist (if not *franquista*); and its pastoral theology exemplified all that Vatican II set out to reform. Other purely political opponents of the regime, especially the high bourgeoisie, succeeded in manipulating the church for their own counterrevolutionary purposes.

Finally, the regime, beset by enemies abroad and at home and determined to consolidate a social and economic (not just political) revolution as quickly as possible, felt it could brook no dissent. The church would have to leave the stage, and, by the end of 1962, four years after Castro's triumph, it had effectively done so.

The rest of the story, again according to the standard interpretation, is one of the gradual rehabilitation of a much-chastened, greatly reduced, but finally reformed Cuban church, which has, since roughly the mid-1980s, come to be seen as playing an increasingly positive and even important role.

The principal distortion represented by the above synopsis lies in its incompleteness. Scholarly as well as popular writing on the period has tended to so emphasize the limitations and failings of the Cuban church as virtually to ignore its equally relevant strengths and accomplishments, and to assign to the limitations a significance greater than the evidence seems to warrant. A tendency as well, especially among foreign visitors to the island (again with notable exceptions), has been to read from the book of the revolution, even if skeptically, while rejecting as too self-interested the voices of Cubans opposed to the regime.

We will look briefly at three of the elements that loom large in standard explanations for the church's failed relationship with the revolution: that its pastoral agents were predominantly Spanish; that the church's presence was almost entirely urban; and that its pastoral mode was elitist, exemplified by its major commitment to an educational system of Catholic schools.

The Spanish Clergy

A particularly high percentage of the Cuban clergy and religious in 1959 were of Spanish birth, a point referred to by Castro in early denunciations of the counterrevolutionary clergy and routinely mentioned in subsequent commentary as one of the church's special weaknesses. Latin American countries historically have depended to greater or lesser degrees on European and North American clergy to supplement low vocation rates, but Cuba did present a particularly high ratio.

The exact figures of the Spanish-born clergy are difficult to ascertain. Leslie Dewart set the mark at 75–80 percent;[5] Mecham held for "more than two-thirds,"[6] and most subsequent authors accept one or the other.

As in other national churches with large numbers of foreign-born clergy, relative advantages and disadvantages have long been debated, mostly within the church but also among those states concerned for whatever reasons about the activities of resident foreigners. In Cuba there is little evidence prior to 1959 of either official or popular hostility toward the Spanish clergy. On the contrary, according to the survey conducted by the *Agrupación Católica Universitaria* at the end of 1953, outside of a few isolated cases of middle- and upper-class individuals, "no one in Cuba criticized the church because some of its representatives had not been born here."[7]

And the clergy, it should be noted, were far from the only Spaniards in republican Cuba. According to Hugh Thomas, "over a million and a quarter immigrants, mostly Spanish, had entered the island between 1902 and 1930."[8] Indeed, in the first quarter of this century more Spaniards came to Cuba than in all the four preceding centuries.[9]

While the Cuban clergy in 1959 may have been generally conservative on theological and, perhaps to a lesser extent, social issues, the evidence of sizable numbers of them being either rabidly pro-Franco or unalterably opposed to the winds of change sweeping the island in the 1950s is lacking. The charge, however, is often made, as for example Herbert Matthews's summation: "What trouble occurred during the Revolution was not due to Marxism-Leninism but the fact that the chronic shortage of clergymen had led to the introduction of many Spanish priests who could not accommodate themselves to the radical revolution."[10] Raul Gómez Treto, a lay activist living in Cuba, asserts that "most of the Spanish clergy and religious" were sympathizers of the Franco regime,[11] and Canadian scholar John Kirk holds that "[f]or many priests trained in Franco's Spain . . . the radical reforms introduced by the revolutionary government were absolutely unacceptable."[12] If by "radical reforms" is meant the state's arbitrary and exclusive assumption of all education, for example, and the takeover of religious schools, it would not have been necessary to be a falangist or even Spanish to protest such reforms.

There is no doubt that the Spanish Civil War, to take another often-cited reason for clerical hostility to the revolution, did have a searing effect on those Cuban churchmen who had experienced it either firsthand or through their families and confreres. Castro's recollection of the Jesuit community at the Colegio Belén when he studied there was that their outlook was "derechista, franquista, reaccionaria . . . sin una sola excepción."[13] How these traits were manifested to the young student is not clear, but it is questionable that these Jesuits, or the rest of the Spanish-born clergy, were strongly outspoken advocates of either Franco or fascism. One can imagine that they spoke of the then-concluded Civil War, but had they praised Franco's friendship with the Axis powers, we would likely have heard such damning detail. Much of Castro's schooling coincided with World War II, in which Cuba, and public opinion, joined with the Allies.

It seems more likely that so-called *franquista* sentiments dealt mainly with the bloody persecution of the church, where, in both Spain in the 1930s and Mexico in the 1920s, churches and convents had been sacked and burned, and hundreds of priests and religious killed. Pope Pius XI's 1937 encyclical on communism, *Divini redemptoris*, drew heavily upon those recent conflicts and would very likely have been a frequent reference point in the Catholic social teaching of the time.

How much the Spanishness of the Cuban clergy merits the blame assigned to it for the church's difficulties with the state is likely to remain an open question. Scholars such as Harvard's Jorge Dominguez consider that many of the Spanish were as Cuban as anyone else, perhaps even more so, "because they chose to be Cubans in their life's experience well beyond an accident of birth."[14] Havana's auxiliary bishop, Eduardo Boza Masvidal, only months before his own expulsion, wrote that Cuba owed a debt of gratitude "to those priests whom we do not call foreigners, since they are Cuban by virtue of their love for this land in whose benefit they have come to work."[15] And Manuel Maza, Cuban-born Jesuit historian, in his thorough and frequently critical study of the Spanish clergy during the republican era, credits them with having laid the foundation for a truly Cuban Catholic church. He cites with approval Georgetown dean Jose Hernandez's view that although the earlier Spanish clergy were responsible for the ruinous state of the church at the beginning of the twentieth century, it was the later Spanish clerics whose "spirit of sacrifice, apostolic zeal and capacity for adaptation" rescued Cuban Catholicism from its penury.[16]

The Urban Church

It also is charged that the church was predominantly urban with little presence in the countryside. "There was very little religious outreach to the countryside," notes Harvey Cox, "where 70 percent of the people lived."[17] That is at least half true (the figure is wrong), although it is probably no truer than in other countries of Latin America, and hardly remarkable for the time.

That the church should concentrate its limited resources and personnel in areas of greatest potential effectiveness and in response to the needs of larger numbers of the faithful who lived in population centers was generally accepted pastoral practice. After Medellín, after the great influx in the 1960s and 1970s of several thousand North American and European priests and religious to supplement the meager resources of the Latin American churches, many of whom moved into the highlands of Peru and Guatemala and other semievangelized parts of the continent, the older practices gradually gave way to new forms of mission and evangelization. It may be only in Cuba that the earlier practitioners are held up to such scorn.

Cuba in the 1950s, moreover, was the fifth most urbanized country in all of Latin America, exceeded only by Argentina, Chile, Uruguay, and Venezuela.[18] According to the national census of 1953, 58 percent of the population lived in urban centers, which is where most of the churches and religious schools were naturally concentrated. Since the early 1930s a majority of Cubans had lived in towns or villages, and Cuba had ceased being primarily an agricultural country; "nor, in terms of workers, had it been so since the beginning of the century."[19]

Today, the trend toward increasing urbanization has been checked and even reversed. According to a World Bank study in 1986, the urban population has fallen from one-half to one-third of the total population since 1960. This is the result of deliberate policies to provide employment and social amenities to all provinces and avoid excessive rural-to-urban migration.[20] That Cuba in 1959 was at least a no more urban society than it is today, and with a less equitable distribution of the nation's resources, does not make a very telling argument regarding church indifference to the rural sectors.

The Elitist Schools

One of the first acts of the new government affected private education. The so-called Ley Once (Law 11, enacted January 11, 1959) disadvantaged Cuba's Catholic university, Saint Thomas of Villanova, by nullifying all degrees granted during the previous two years when the state universities were in recess. A temporary suspension of classes called for in November 1956 by the Havana University Student Council in support of the rebels then fighting in Oriente extended until the triumph and became a symbol of adherence to the revolution. Under the direction of the American and Spanish provinces of the Augustinian friars, Villanova suspended classes for days at a time in political protest but essentially remained functioning.

Ley Once was the first blow directed at the educational efforts of the church; it would be followed in a little over two years by the complete elimination of all Catholic schools except centers of religious and priestly formation.

The law promulgated on May 6, 1961, nationalizing all private education was a decisive blow to the church; it took place in the immediate aftermath and within the dramatic context of the Bay of Pigs invasion. During those days anyone suspected of sympathy with the invaders was detained, churches and schools were occupied, and priests and bishops were effectively put under house arrest. The presence of three chaplains among the captured forces, one of whom carried with him a very questionable proclamation reflecting an uncompromising "holy war" mindset, provided the occasion for the state's strongest denunciation of the church.[21] The apparent manipulation of religion by the invading forces gave Castro sufficient pretext to neutralize virtually all the institutions of the church.

Were the schools hotbeds of subversion and counterrevolution as charged? There is as yet little specific, even anecdotal, data that they were, other than in the sense in which much of the church still sought to be critical of certain aspects of the revolutionary process. It is a claim that is still made,[22] however, and one that clearly merits further research. In his discussions with Frei Betto, President Castro insisted that it was only because of the conflicts between the schools and the government that they had to be nationalized, "because it was precisely in those schools, especially the Catholic ones, that you found the children of the wealthy who opposed the Revolution, schools that became centers of counterrevolutionary activity."[23] Without those conflicts, he suggested, "we would not have needed to nationalize the schools." More surprisingly, Castro allowed that there might again today be room for private schools, as long as they do not conflict with the revolution.

The presumed counterrevolutionary character of the Catholic schools is usually explained by the class bias of the students, or at least of their parents. In their final joint statement of this era of confrontation, the "Open Letter to the Prime Minister" of December 4, 1960, the bishops firmly rejected the charge that the schools were havens of the privileged. The bishops asserted that many thousands of children and young people from very modest families received an education in these schools, that many of the schools charged little or no tuition, and that "in all the rest a very high percentage of students enjoy total or partial scholarships."[24] Schools of the very privileged there certainly were, but they were but a fraction of the Catholic schools.

Even the prestigious Jesuit schools that Fidel Castro attended in Santiago and Havana were able to keep their fees low because, as Castro noted admiringly to Betto, the teaching staff was composed of "austere, religious, self-sacrificing and hard-working" men who received no salary for themselves.[25] In addition, the Jesuit and Salesian vocational schools catered mainly to the poor, as did most of the schools run by the Cuban-founded Hermanas de la Caridad.[26]

Some 245 Catholic schools belonging to both religious orders and parishes were confiscated in 1961.[27] The greater part of these were engaged in primary education and thus even less likely than the high schools to represent more than an imagined counterrevolutionary challenge. What they did represent was the visible embodiment of the church's well-known insistence on the priority of parental rights in matters of educating their children, and thus a potential challenge down the road as the revolution eventually undertook its sweeping educational reforms.

Education in Cuba before the revolution, like health care, was both far superior to that of the island's most immediate neighbors—the countries of the Caribbean and Central America—and at the same time grossly inequitable. Rural Cuba, while not, as sometimes alleged, encompassing the vast majority of the population, was home to a substantial part of it and was extremely poorly served by the state, never mind the church, in the areas of health and education.

During the entire half-century of the republic there was little improvement in the percentage of school-age children actually matriculating in primary schools (just over 50 percent) or secondary schools (about 12 percent), but the disparity between urban and rural was indeed dramatic.[28]

The reversal of the trend toward increasing urbanization, especially in the education and health fields, is one of the most often-noted accomplishments of the revolution. Today, over 75 percent of the relevant-age population is in secondary schools, and some 60 percent of these students attend the rural *escuelas secundarias basicas*, learning basic agricultural skills in a mixed work-study program.[29]

The Catholic schools were located mostly in the towns and cities because only in population centers were there people enough to pay even the modest fees that were essential, together with the contributed labor of the teachers, to keep such schools open. Given existing resources, the alternative of establishing church schools in the countryside was simply not conceivable. The revolution, however, envisioning the thorough restructuring of public education that was eventually carried out, evidently considered the total elimination of all private schooling a necessary first step.

Today, the church in Cuba does not hesitate to acknowledge "the great effort carried out by the state to see to it that free schooling is available to all."[30] Indeed, on the twin accomplishments of extending the provisions of schooling and health care far beyond the prerevolutionary reaches the bishops are at one with the government. They object, of course, to the offensive stress on atheism in the schools, said to be less aggressive today than before, and they continue to find merit in some form of church-based independent schooling.

Finally, by way of evaluating the now-dismantled Catholic *colegios*, the ENEC document judges that they played no small role in the unquestioned religious renewal that was taking place before the revolution, especially among the young, and that they had much to do with the increased presence and participation of males in the life of the church.[31]

Divisions Within the Church

Since the church was characterized early in the process as counterrevolutionary, there is little record of the divisions that doubtless existed between the more conservative old-guard clergy and laity on the one hand, and the progressive, even revolutionary, and mostly younger priests, religious, and lay leaders of the Catholic Action cadres on the other. It was these latter who came to be, for a brief time, the most visible and outspoken representatives of the church.

With the official church's expressed opposition to the growing influence of the Communist party[32] (which, unlike many Christians, had basically sat out, even opposed, the insurrection), conservative Catholics came to identify more closely with the positions of their bishops, at least on selected issues. With the possible exception of their final joint statement before lapsing into silence (the December 1960 open letter), all their previous letters, no matter how critical, carried words of praise and encouragement for the revolution and its social reforms, which could not have pleased those on the far right.

The appearance in 1960 of a leftist group called Con la cruz y por la patria,[33] and later another called Avanzada Radical Cristiana, caused some limited division in church unity. Highly confrontational and intemperate in their rhetoric, these groups never found a popular base and soon disappeared.[34] Again, in the 1970s groups identifying with the continent-wide Christians for Socialism movements issued occasional statements critical of the rest of the church, but their significance was confined largely to similar groups in other countries. Both sets of leftist Christians sought to reconcile the church with the revolution, or, more accurately, to enlist and integrate the church fully into the revolution. The annual ecumenical meeting called the Jornada Camilo Torres, begun in 1971, had the ostensible goal of providing a forum for dialogue between believers and Marxists, but it too became little more than a platform for decrying the continued shortcomings of the church.[35]

A small group of Catholic intellectuals (Raul Gómez Treto is the best known) sought to move the bishops leftward. They sent statements to the Roman Synod of 1974 and to the Third General Conference of Latin American Episcopates (Puebla, 1979). Gómez Treto has recently written an account of the church-state relationship since the revolution that, while clearly avoiding criticism of the state, manages to put the church's more recent behavior in a generally favorable light.

If there is dissent today among Catholics opposed to the church's two-decade-long effort at dialogue with the state, it has remained private, and the ENEC document hints at no real fissures. Conceivably some individuals associated with the various human rights groups that began appearing in the late 1980s may represent a sector dissatisfied with the church's very quiet (though partially effective) diplomacy in the human rights area.

After the complete silencing of the church by 1963, the only possible contact with the government was through the representative of the Holy See, for a dozen years the able but controversial Vatican diplomat Msgr. (later Archbishop) Cesare Zacchi. Zacchi was the lead figure, indeed the only visible churchman, identified with the policy of détente and dialogue. Those Catholics for whom the idea of conducting a dialogue with the devil was anathema, and who considered the two bishops' pastorals of 1969 (the first in nine years) the final capitulation to the state and the definitive closing of the book on church-sanctioned confrontation, denounced Zacchi and moved into dissent. Some, most of them former members of the Catholic student and worker movements, organized the Revolutionary Popular Action Movement (MRAP) in May 1971. While its intent was sociopolitical education, not sabotage, it was quickly put down. Some thirty-two members were convicted on December 30, 1971, and sentenced to terms of from two to twenty years.[36]

After 1971 the principal locus of dissident Catholicism was likely to be the prisons.

The Vatican Role

Cuba is the only officially communist government that has maintained full and unbroken diplomatic representation at the Holy See. Indeed, its longtime ambassador, Luis Amado Blanco, became by virtue of seniority the dean of the Vatican diplomatic corps. The Holy See is never the one to sever relations with any government, but from 1962 to 1974 it reduced its representation in Havana to a mission headed by a chargé d'affaires, and reinstated it to full nunciature status only during the final month of tenure of Cesare Zacchi, who thus became apostolic pro-nuncio.

Monsignor Zacchi came to the Havana nunciature in 1961 as secretary to the aging and soon to retire Archbishop Luigi Centoz. Having served in Vienna and in Belgrade (whence he was reportedly expelled),[37] and thus experienced in the socialist world, Zacchi arrived in Cuba at a time when Vatican relations with the Eastern bloc countries were undergoing changes that others, though never the Holy See, would term its Ostpolitik. Appointed chargé in 1962, his instructions were said to be principally to stem the exodus of priests and prevent the total pull-out of religious, whose departure had accelerated with the confiscation of the schools.[38]

With the Cuban bishops thoroughly pushed to the sidelines, it fell to Zacchi to become the exclusive church interlocutor with the state. He skillfully used his access to government, and personally to Fidel Castro, to achieve two goals: to urge certain specific measures or to intervene on behalf of particular individuals (usually clergy) where the local church was impotent; and, on the longer term, to keep open the door to church-state dialogue, awaiting a better day.

His intervention is credited with stopping plans to send all the priests to the shameful UMAP camps, a short-lived (1965–67) experiment in concentrating what were generally called the "social scum" (chiefly clergy, Jehovah's Witnesses, and homosexuals) into forced-labor groups.[39] He succeeded in securing the eventual release of the four priests imprisoned in 1961,[40] including the three Spaniards from the Bay of Pigs, as well as of Fr. Miguel Angel Loredo, O.F.M., whose case provides one of the relatively few classic instances of specifically religious repression.[41]

His detractors, who are numerous in the exile community, consider that his diplomacy—getting a few priests out of jail but conveying legitimacy to the Castro regime—amounted to little more than betrayal. As judicious an observer as Fernandez faults Zacchi for never using his influence to press for the nonclerical political prisoners, many of whom were in fact socially progressive Catholic lay leaders who had run afoul of the new regime.[42] And Dominguez, acknowledging that Zacchi succeeded in diminishing (though not ending) the repression of the church and enabled it once more to receive personnel and material resources from abroad, considers that his policy delayed the Cuban church's reassertion of its own proper autonomy.[43]

This is probably true; the state dealt with the church only as the agent of a foreign entity, the Vatican, and Zacchi enabled that to happen. One would have to question, however, given the absolute power of the state and its evident determination to ignore the local church, that the Vatican chargé had any alternative course of action.

The policy of quiet diplomacy took a public turn in 1969 as the bishops, with Zacchi's encouragement, issued two joint communiqués, each containing conciliatory gestures toward the regime.[44] The April 10 communiqué called on the United States to end its economic embargo against Cuba, thereby enraging those who until then had considered the church's silence a form of protest. Although not generally known at the time, the circular was accompanied by a private letter to Castro critical of abuses of human rights, apparently never acknowledged.[45]

Outwardly, little changed in the following five years, at the end of which (May 1974) Zacchi was made archbishop (he had been ordained bishop, in Cuba, in 1967) and apostolic pro-nuncio with the rank of ambassador. More years of near invisibility were to pass, and two more pro-nuncios (Mario Tagliaferri and Giuseppe Laigueglia) came and went before the present era of increasingly active church-state relations dawned. The representative of the Holy See for most of this present era (1980–88) was Giulio Einaudi, now nuncio to Chile and credited with bringing the Zacchi efforts forward to, if not yet a successful conclusion, at least a major improvement.

Why Détente? Why Now?

There are several reasons for the widely noted improvement in the church-state relationship. Some, which could be termed "officialist" (whether coming directly from government sources or not), may be inadequate in themselves to explain a complex phenomenon, but neither can they simply be dismissed out of hand. These explanations tend to stress changes occurring in the church, not the state, noting various progressive developments within the other local churches of Latin America which have also, presumably in a derivative way, wrought improvements within the church in Cuba. As a consequence of these changes, therefore, the state has been able to alter its policy toward the church. In this view, because the Catholic church has experienced the Second Vatican Council (1962–65), the episcopal assemblies at Medellín (1968) and Puebla (1979), the development of liberation theology, the evolution of the base ecclesial communities, and the adoption of a preferential option for the poor, it has, in effect, "got religion" and may no longer be the bulwark of reaction it once seemed.

That is a caricature, of course, but it does seem that Fidel Castro has been personally and seriously affected by these ecclesial developments. What meaning they have for him and how they factor into policy decisions is far less clear. It is doubtful that this is a question of Fidel Castro's "faith" or that his attitude toward religion has undergone any kind of conversion. In his foreword to the Cuban edition of Frei Betto's book, Minister of Culture Armando Hart finds Castro's present views on religion as expressed in the book fully consistent with those he has held throughout his revolutionary life. Hart cites as examples "the talks with the Catholics in Chile in 1971, the meeting with the religious in Jamaica in 1977, and that phrase of his from the first years of the Revolution: 'Who betrays the poor, betrays Christ.'"[46] Ironically, all three were instances in which Castro denounced the bishops and the nonradical majority of the church, finding truly Christian only such revolutionary believers as the Christians for Socialism in Chile. For many years the Jornada Camilo Torres had the principal effect of underscoring the inadequacies of the local church, so lacking in what Castro still refers to as "honest Christians." Homage to religion by atheist states tends to convey more than one message; religion that "fits," or fits in, is often welcome.

Today, however, Fidel Castro speaks glowingly of the pope, lauds the bishops of the United States, and assiduously avoids all public criticism of the church. A journalist from *Granma*, the official party paper, quoted Cardinal O'Connor as saying he had "never heard anyone praise the Pope more highly than the President."[47] In his lengthy conversations with Frei Betto and with Italian journalist Gianni Miná, who did a similar book-length interview with Castro two years after Betto,[48] Castro deftly rejected the repeated opportunities both questioners offered him to criticize policies of the pope or the Vatican.

Nor is the church in Cuba directly criticized any longer, except implicitly for its past sins. José Felipe Carneado, head of the party's religious affairs office, put the officialist view succinctly when asked recently about the changed church-state relationship: "The church has adjusted its positions to the new socio-historic context, and we are perfectly in agreement with the changes this has brought about."[49]

Rather than the church having at long last come around, thereby enabling the state to deal with it more cooperatively, one has to look elsewhere to explain the new relationship. The single most important factor is certainly the Cuban church itself, mainly its consistent, if frustrated, attempt, more visible since the early 1980s, to effect a dialogue at the highest levels.

At a gathering of the Cuban clergy in July 1979 to discuss the recently concluded Puebla conference, the idea of a "Puebla in Cuba" was proposed and accepted, out of which came the several-year-long national church renewal and reflection process known as the Reflexión Eclesial Cubana (REC), culminating in the historic 1986 Encuentro Nacional Eclesial Cubano. The process involved an assessment of the church's past and present state and an analysis of the present Cuban society; the strengths and weaknesses of both were presented frankly.

Well before the results of those reflections began circulating as working drafts for the ENEC, the bishops presented a confidential document to the president that repeated their reasons for wanting to initiate a process of sustained dialogue. They wanted to talk about a number of things, the least of which were the practical problems that Carneado's office was available to deal with—getting materials to repair a church roof, importing motor vehicles, and such. They wanted to "dialogue" about such themes as the Christian roots of the Cuban nation, the problems affecting contemporary Cuban society, and the contribution that religion and the church—once freed from its second-class status—could make in helping construct a better Cuba. They suggested that the hostilities of the past could only be truly overcome by looking anew at the conditions that caused them. Their efforts went essentially unanswered from 1983 to 1985; a foreign churchman was told by Castro that the bishops' position was "very harsh," but finally, after the U.S. bishops' visit, Castro agreed to meet with the Cuban bishops. He did so on two occasions.

A sustained dialogue, as the church has used the word, has not yet truly developed, despite the tendency of outside observers to credit the present state of reduced tension to some ubiquitous dialogue. It seems even less accurate to assert that the concessions made by the state that lighten the burden of discrimination borne by believers are "indicative of this new attempt at dialogue by the revolutionary government."[50] The government has indeed made important changes, but it has not sought—it seems fair to say that it has shunned—the kind of dialogue that the church has been looking for.

Curiously, President Castro is uncomfortable with the very word itself, seeming to equate it with arbitration or conflict resolution. He objected to interviewer Miná's use of the term, "given the fact that there has been no conflict . . . nor anything to negotiate, so there is no need for dialogue. I would say that contacts, exchanges of views, meetings to solve particular problems are what's appropriate. . . . One would think that there was a conflict and that we were aiming to resolve it by a dialogue."[51]

Despite the lack of sustained, high-level exchanges of views on major issues (which is what the bishops seem to want, whether it is called dialogue or not) a rapprochement is, in fact, occurring. The church's reasons for desiring it seem clear: it seeks, in the first place, to secure the full freedom and participation in the society of practicing believers, and it also seeks to enable the church to have some social presence, to bring its ethical and moral perspective to the task of addressing some of the acknowledged problems of today's society. At the moment the church appears to be the more consistent suitor. Speaking in 1987, Havana's archbishop Jaime Ortega said that people outside Cuba used to think that the church was the obstacle in the 1960s and 1970s to better relations with the government, but now it is the government that needs to explain why an improved relationship is so slow. "It seems that the church wants it and can follow through, and it seems that the state wants it—but can the state follow through?"[52]

Whether it can follow through fully, that is, whether it can reverse the psychological orientation of three decades of militant atheism and persuade the thousands of committees for the defense of the revolution to stop regarding religious behavior as deviant, does remain to be seen. Castro himself has commented to more than one visiting bishop that the still persistent "subtle discrimination" has its roots at the local cadre level, not in the leadership echelons of the party.

But such rapprochement as has occurred is also, and obviously, due to the personal will of President Castro. External as well as internal factors help account for the improved relationship. The continued restrictions imposed on the church have clearly become an unnecessary liability hampering improved relations, with the rest of Latin America as well as with Western Europe and North America. Certain prominent Central and South American visitors, considered friends of the revolution, have expressed dismay both at the physical deterioration of some of the country's older churches (several have now been repaired and restored) and the failure to treat the local church seriously.

For exiled critics like Juan Clark, the apparent thaw is just a tactical maneuver: The church is no threat, and concessions or goodwill gestures will have little internal effect and may be advantageous abroad. The church was allowed to survive, in his view, only for tactical reasons, in deference to world public opinion.[53]

Even less-skeptical observers also grant the driving influence of world—especially Latin American—public opinion. A European diplomat in Cuba told a reporter that "Castro's overtures towards the church have cost him little, but they have greatly enhanced his image";[54] and journalist Joseph Treaster writes that Castro has sought more cordial relations with the church "as an element in his successful effort to rekindle relations with the rest of Latin America and that the church's embrace of the poor and the adoption of liberation theology by some priests had helped blur the ideological differences."[55] In sum, as Dominguez puts it, "the Cuban government came to recognize that its behavior toward the church in Cuba had repercussions for its foreign policy and this opened some political space for the church in Cuba."[56]

More elusive are the internal influences upon the thaw. Cuba is today a society in which the young majority have neither known the excesses of the Batista era nor fully shared the revolutionary fervor of the early days. Motivation, particularly when material incentives are ruled out, becomes an increasing problem. The church, like the party, strongly emphasizes moral motivation and values traits such as austerity, self-sacrifice, and solidarity. It is possible that the church could now be viewed as socially helpful, rather than as an obstacle, in exemplifying certain shared ideals. The nuns working in social assistance programs, for example, are frequently held up as models. It is now policy for personnel working in state-managed facilities for the elderly to intern in the homes run by the sisters, where, by all accounts, better care is provided at lower cost.[57]

On the broader level of social morality and the health of the society, some see Castro as concerned with "motivating Cuban youth toward integrity and concern for the common good"[58] in the face of growing problems no longer so different from Cuba's more decadent neighbors. A much-discussed homily delivered in November 1988 by the church's best known spokesman, Msgr. Carlos Manuel de Céspedes, identified publicly certain of the internal problems, especially among the young: apathy and indifference, lack of identification with the struggles of the past, dishonesty, and fascination with things foreign. Others have commented on the high rates of divorce and abortion, alcohol abuse and sexual promiscuity, all the more noteworthy in a social order that outsiders once described as puritan. The church or religion in general cannot be expected to have any beneficial effect on more than its own faithful, at least in the near term, but the state may well consider an improved status for religion today an investment in tomorrow's strengthened moral fabric. The ENEC final document is replete with affirmations of the desire of Christians to contribute fully, as believers, to the building of an ever-improving social order.

Conclusion

More than the Catholic church is moving into a new stage in Cuba today. Indeed, while the church is at pains to peel back the very un-Cuban overlay of official irreligion, thereby revealing the Catholic substratum of nearly five centuries, the fact remains that the popular religion of Cuba can be called Catholic only by considerable extension of the term. The traditional Afro-Cuban religious systems generally referred to as *santería*, or spiritism, have not only not disappeared with thirty years of "scientific socialism" but appear to be stronger than ever and far from the exclusive preserve of Cubans of African heritage.

As in other parts of Latin America where the spiritist or traditional religious forms are mixed together with aspects of Christian faith, the church in Cuba has only lately begun to pay serious attention to the growing phenomena of popular religiosity. But it has begun, and the ENEC document notes that religious syncretism today should be an area of heightened pastoral attention. The church acknowledges that popular religion contributes both to the development of the church and to the unity of the civil society.[59] The officially atheist state, obviously concerned for civil unity, is having also to tread new paths as it confronts today's church and religion in Cuba.

FACT SHEET

The Catholic Church in Cuba

Current strength of the church (1989)
- 4,141,600 faithful (total population: 10,667,000)
- 220 priests (138 diocesan; 82 religious)
- 37 religious brothers

7 bishops (active)
247 nuns
20 seminarians

Number of churches and church facilities
231 parishes
387 churches/chapels (auxiliary parishes, many of them rural, without resident clergy, served by one or more of the above parishes)
6 church-run hospitals (1 hospital, 2 sanatoria, 1 clinic, 2 old-age homes)
2 seminaries (minor seminary in Santiago de Cuba, major seminary in Havana)

Underground religious periodicals

There are no samizdat publications in Cuba and few religious publications of any kind. Until recently the state controlled all printing. During the early 1970s the official Catholic directory ("Almanaque de la caridad") was printed on government presses; at present, two or three minor Protestant publications (e.g., *Heraldo Cristiano*) are printed on state presses, although there are evangelical printing facilities at Matanzas which print, e.g., *Tribuna Ecumenica*. The Catholic church received permission in 1988 to import a printing press from Germany. The principal Catholic press formerly conducted by the Franciscans, publisher of the widely read *La Quincena*, was closed down and taken over by the government in 1966.

Primates since 1959

Manuel Cardinal Arteaga y Betancourt (1941–63), archbishop of Havana, made cardinal 1945 (died March 20, 1965)
Evelio Diaz Cia (1959–63), coadjutor archbishop *sedi datus* and apostolic administrator *sede plena;* (1963–70) archbishop of Havana (died July 21, 1984)
Francisco Ricardo Oves Fernandez (1970–81), archbishop of Havana (retired March 28, 1981)
Jaime Lucas Ortega y Alamino (1981–present), archbishop of Havana

14

The Catholic Church in Sandinista Nicaragua

Humberto Belli

Hope, more than apprehension, seems to have characterized the state of mind of the vast majority of the segments that composed the Nicaraguan Catholic church when the Sandinista guerrillas paraded in triumph down the streets of Managua on July 19, 1979. The Catholic church in Nicaragua had played a crucial role in the overall revolutionary upheaval, a circumstance acknowledged by the victorious Sandinista Front.[1]

Some individual priests and members of religious orders had joined the struggle as secret collaborators of the guerrillas. Some had joined as combatants, even shedding their blood for the cause, as did the Spanish-born priest Garcia Laviana, who was killed in action in 1978. Priests such as Maryknoll Miguel D'Escoto, the Jesuit Fernando Cardenal, and his brother Ernesto, a well-known poet, had been part of the Sandinistas' diplomatic entourage that successfully toured Western nations during the Nicaraguan civil war.

Although guarded in voicing official support for the revolutionaries, the church hierarchy had nonetheless contributed greatly to undermining the legitimacy of the embattled dictatorship of General Anastasio Somoza. In the early 1970s a set of pastoral letters had denounced the regime's violations of human rights and deplored its social policies. They also had referred to the then embryonic Marxist guerrillas as "the irrepressible cry of a whole people that has become conscious of its situation and seeks ways to break the molds that imprison it."[2]

On June 2, 1979, in the climax of the war, the Nicaraguan Bishops' Conference, at the initiative of Bishop Salazar y Espinoza of Leon, issued a pastoral letter in which Pope Paul VI was quoted as saying that the church could not "deny the moral . . . legitimacy [of revolutionary insurrections] in the case of evident and prolonged tyranny."[3]

Vatican II and Medellín's Influence

To understand how these stands and outlooks came to prevail in the Nicaraguan church, we need to go back to the Second Vatican Council (1962–65) and to the Latin American Bishops' Conference at Medellín, Colombia (1968). These two landmark events had a profound influence on the Latin American church, particularly in the realms of faith and politics.

One of the greatest achievements of Vatican II, according to Nicaraguan writer Pablo A. Cuadra, was the recovery of the church's independence from civil or political power, "the loosening of the ties that, since Constantine, still remained between Church and State (or as it was called earlier, between Throne and Altar)."[4]

Vatican II also opened some significant doors to pluralism and espoused an attitude of openness and understanding toward non-Christians, including Marxists. The attitudes of Catholics in this regard ranged from those of the conservatives, who retained either the preconciliar, unambiguous rejection of communism, to the moderates, who advocated understanding and dialogue—though still warning about potential dangers and incompatibilities—to the liberals and the radicals, who, with varying emphasis, implicitly or explicitly defended the use of Marxist analysis. Riding high on the expectations created by Vatican II, Medellín issued strong calls on behalf of the church's commitment for social justice.

That echoes of these developments were to be strongly welcomed in Nicaragua was partially a consequence of the four long decades of authoritarian rule by the Somozas. Increasingly corrupt and uninspiring, the ruling dynasty was perceived by many as the stumbling block for extending the benefits of progress to the poor and for opening the doors to democratization. Many anti-Somoza Catholics, including a good share of conservatives (the main civic opposition group in Nicaragua was the Conservative party), felt very uncomfortable before the relative compliance, if not manifest alliance, that the church's hierarchy had exhibited in regard to the Somoza family. For them, the new winds brought about by Vatican II and Medellín were a refreshing breeze insofar as they seemed to herald a church purified from its complicity with earthly powers. It is thus plausible to speculate that the theological conservatism of a large portion of Nicaraguan Catholics may have been softened or modified, at least in some respects, by their peculiar political situation.

Conservatives and Modernizers: A Complex Picture

For some other Catholics, however, mostly those identified with Somoza's dictatorship or with the prevailing status quo, the changes seemed like a dark, threatening cloud. For lack of a better label these can be categorized as right-wing Catholics, although they were not a homogeneous group. Some of them rejected most of the postconciliar changes, including changes in the liturgy. Some others of a more modernizing bent (Somoza's ruling party—the Liberal party—was mildly anticlerical and in some respects pro-modern) welcomed the liturgical changes and even theological pluralism. Where most of the right-wing group tended to coincide was in their rejection of the sociopolitical role that the more progressive Catholics were advocating for the church. Their motto could have been Do Not Mix Religion with Politics. Yet there were still others among the right-wing Catholics who wanted to see the church as a bulwark of law and order, and as such, an institution blessing the authorities.

The Catholics making up this cluster of groups included many members of the Catholic hierarchy who had taken office before the 1970s and some leaders of religious institutions, such as the Jesuit priest Leon Pallais. He was a personal friend of Somoza as well as a chaplain of the national guard and the president of the Catholic Central American University.

These men lost most of their influence within the institutional church during the early 1970s. A key element in this change was the appointment of new bishops, a process probably undertaken by the Vatican in opposition to some members of the old—and aging—hierarchy, although with the support of some anti-Somoza Catholics. Another important event was a strike in 1970 at the Central American University, where students and faculty, backed by the relatively modernist opposition newspaper *La Prensa* and other political forces, managed to remove Fr. Leon Pallais from office and bring in more liberal-minded Jesuits.

A similar reshuffling of leaders also took place among some religious orders. Thus, in the early 1970s the Nicaraguan Catholic church was solidly in the hands of "progressives," or "moderates." The label encompasses those who tended to embrace the reforms of Vatican II and Medellín's call for greater involvement in sociopolitical affairs, but who also stressed continuity with the past and the primacy of the church's hierarchy. In social and political matters they stood for the "prophetic" ministry of the church, meaning its readiness to denounce injustices and to pass moral judgment on systems of power and their corresponding policies. But they insisted, on the other hand, that it was not the church's role to offer specific sociopolitical solutions or take up partisan positions. In line with traditional social teachings of the church, they rejected both individualistic liberalism and collectivistic Marxism, favoring some vaguely defined forms of social democracy (or "bourgeois reformism," from the perspective of the Left).

These Catholics differed among themselves, however, in the degree to which they distanced themselves from the prevailing political models—capitalism and socialism—and in regard to the emphasis that they gave to this-worldly concerns. While some emphasized the church's participation in social projects and community development, others were more concerned with more traditional aspects of Catholic religiosity: prayers, devotions, and sacramental life. These relatively more modern segments of the church eventually came under the leadership of Miguel Obando y Bravo, who was ordained archbishop of Managua in 1970. A man of Indian and mulatto ancestry, Archbishop Obando came to embody the Catholic church's break with its record of political aloofness and mild compliance with secular rulers. He refused Somoza's efforts to win him with gifts and soon became the strongest voice in the church denouncing the regime's violation of human rights. Together with the other Nicaraguan bishops he coauthored a set of pastoral letters criticizing the government and the sociopolitical outlines of Nicaraguan society. He also took the lead, in conjunction with some priests and religious, in organizing the first grass-roots communities and unions in the Nicaraguan countryside and in promoting Christian base communities (CEBS).

Archbishop Obando's stands earned him the enmity of the Somoza regime, whose media suggested that he was a communist sympathizer and a secret *comandante* (Sandinista leader). The attacks increased his popularity and drew many Catholics, including those of more liberal convictions, to close ranks in his defense.

Yet in spite of his outspoken criticism of the regime, the archbishop of Managua retained the traditional religious outlook that many Nicaraguans cherished—he was devoted to Mary, the rosary, and the Eucharist. His uncommon mix of modern social activism and religious traditionalism furthered his appeal to the more conservative lower classes and peasants.

Radicals within the church and politicians of all convictions had to reckon with the archbishop's popularity. Even the Sandinista guerrillas, who were aware of the archbishop's more traditional theological outlook—including his distrust for communism—called him to act as an intermediary between themselves and the government on a couple of occasions when the guerrillas kidnapped Somocista officials.

Radical Christians

Nonetheless, there was mute but mounting disagreement between the positions represented by the archbishop and those gradually promoted by people who were identified more with the radical side of the Catholic spectrum. These radical Catholics originally were made up of a small but influential group of foreign-educated priests and laypersons who were deeply influenced by the radical currents flowing from the University of Louvain in Belgium and from other European centers. One of the first organizers in Nicaragua was the Franciscan priest Uriel Molina, who was educated in Europe and a participant in the 1972 Christians for Socialism Conference that took place in Chile. Other important figures were the upper-class Nicaraguan priests Ernesto and Fernando Cardenal.

Father Molina founded one of the first radical CEBS in Managua in early 1972, made up of twelve upper- and middle-class college students. They called themselves "revolutionary Christians" and considered "Marxist analysis" a very important intellectual tool. "We had study sessions to analyze the Nicaraguan reality making use of the Marxist method," recalled Fr. Molina.[5]

Father Ernesto Cardenal founded another community in the archipelago of Solentiname in Lake Nicaragua. It consisted of some local peasants plus a growing stream of visiting poets, intellectuals, and artists, who flocked to the site after Cardenal's book *The Gospel in Solentiname* brought it international notoriety. Cardenal represented the most radical subvariant in the group. In very explicit terms he equated communism with the Kingdom of God and claimed that acceptance of Marx was essential for living up to the Gospels.[6]

The radical, or "revolutionary," Christians in Nicaragua share in common their belief in liberation theology as espoused by its most notorious founder, Gustavo Gutierrez. Although allowances can be made for a certain diversity of positions among the liberationists, a key feature they all share, and which the Nicaraguan radical Christians fully embrace, is "the centrality of revolution"—a belief that revolutionary political action against the ruling socioeconomic order is the way to make Christian love for the poor truly effective. In this regard they are strongly this-worldly: They tend to devalue traditional piety and the supernatural while overemphasizing the duty of political activism, including partisan political militancy.

Liberationists are usually hostile to capitalism (and to the United States), which they view as the main force oppressing the Latin American poor. They also tend to favor socialism and often share, with different degrees of expressiveness, a corresponding sympathy for Cuba and, sometimes, for the Soviet Union.

These versions of liberationism had a good deal of resonance within some of the religious orders working in Nicaragua, especially among those which, like the Jesuits, were staffed with a large share of foreign-born religious who had been more exposed to liberalizing trends. By the late 1970s their strongest following was in three Jesuit-led organizations: Instituto Juan XXIII, Instituto Histórico Centroamericano (IHCA), and the Centro de Promocion Agraria (CEPA), which centered its work on the creation of peasant organizations that could engage in political action.

Liberationist priests and lay leaders intended to spread their influence through the CEBS and through the Delegates of the Word, a program started by the hierarchy to provide lay religious leadership in rural areas not regularly served by priests. They were partially successful in provinces such as Esteli and in some rural areas on the Atlantic coast, although the extent to which their rather intellectual approach permeated the minds of the humble, traditionalist peasants is unknown. Many of their members, particularly the young and those with urban, middle-class backgrounds, became involved with the Sandinista guerrillas.

As the country entered a period of tremendous upheaval following the 1978 assassination of Pedro J. Chamorro, Nicaragua's most influential political opposition leader, a measure of unity, albeit superficial, seemed to emerge between the hierarchy and the revolutionary Christians. The mounting antagonism toward the Somoza regime drew many elements together and tended to blur other fundamental issues. This was also a time when many Nicaraguan Catholics who did not share the neo-Marxist theological positions of priests such as Ernesto Cardenal but were open to collaboration with the Marxists gave their support to the Sandinista Front.

Catholics Divide on the Sandinista Regime

When the revolution finally triumphed in 1979, most Nicaraguan Catholics welcomed it. The possible exceptions—the right-wing sectors described previously—almost disappeared from sight as most of their leaders went into exile, while those remaining in the country were practically ostracized. Among those Catholics welcoming the revolution a difference in tone could soon be discerned, and, on a closer analysis, a profound difference in the content of their pronouncements was evident.

The Catholic hierarchy issued its first postrevolution pastoral letter on July 13, 1979. It thanked the "brother countries who have helped us in our liberation,"[7] and it expressed the bishops' confidence "in the high ideals that have encouraged our liberation movement."[8]

On November 17, 1979, the bishops issued a second pastoral document, greeting the end of the civil war as an "exceptional opportunity for announcing and bearing witness to God's Kingdom" and calling on the Nicaraguan church to face the future with confidence and determination, warning, "If through fear and mistrust . . . we neglect this crucial opportunity to commit ourselves to the poor . . . we would be in serious violation of the Gospel's teaching."[9] In this document the bishops even indicated their readiness to accept some type of socialism—hinting that they suspected that some variety of this system was in the private agenda of the revolutionary leadership.

Liberals and radicals inside and outside Nicaragua hailed the pastoral letter as a very progressive piece of church thought in sociopolitical matters. And so it was. Yet the Nicaraguan bishops were not offering unconditional support to the new rulers. Their tone was one of guarded confidence. In their first postrevolution pastoral letter the bishops had already expressed their concern for safeguarding the church's independence: "As a Church we must remain free . . . before any system, to opt always for man, for the oppressed, and for man's right to organize his own society."[10] In their November pastoral they also had offered a set of provisos in regard to the acceptable type of socialism, and they warned Nicaraguans, "Our commitment to the revolutionary process cannot mean naïveté or blind enthusiasm, much less the creation of a new idol before which there is a duty to bow down unconditionally."[11]

The bishops as a whole, like so many other Nicaraguans, were aware that the leadership of the Sandinista movement, itself in control of the coalition of forces that toppled the Somoza dictatorship, was in the hands of men with Marxist-Leninist backgrounds. Individual members of the hierarchy differed, however, in their perceptions of the degree to which the comandantes' communistic ideology was of the pragmatic or rigid variety, and the extent to which non-Marxist influences could modify their policies. Bishop Lopez Ardon from Esteli was among the most optimistic, while Bishop Salazar from Leon was among the least optimistic. The documents of revolutionary Christians and the host of Catholics of more liberal persuasions showed great enthusiasm, including, at times, militant calls for what amounted to unconditional support for the revolution. Their distinctive approach was no doubt connected to their theological presuppositions. A March 20, 1980, document endorsed by a majority of the individual leaders and organizations identified with the revolutionary Christians claimed: "The only way to love God, whom we do not see, is by contributing to the advancement of this revolutionary process. . . . Only then shall we be loving our brothers, whom we do see. Therefore, we say that to be a Christian is to be a revolutionary."[12]

A significant catch here is that for the radical Christians, being a revolutionary was synonymous with being a Sandinista. They made the connection more explicit a few lines later, adding, "Preference for and solidarity with the poor in Nicaragua today means to work under the guidance of the Sandinista Front."[13] The thread of their argument, soon to be repeated by the Sandinista leaders, was that being a Christian demanded that one be a supporter of the Sandinista party, for the party was the revolution's vanguard as well as the representative of the poor. The duty of supporting the revolution was extended to the church. Seeming to echo Gutierrez's statement in regard to the option for the poor,[14] Fr. Teofilo Cabestrero, a Spanish theologian who came to Nicaragua after the revolution, wrote in *Amanecer*, one of Nicaragua's liberationist publications: "In Nicaragua the revolutionary process asks the Church to make its option for the poor concrete. Here one chooses either for the poor people (supporting the radical changes of the revolution), or for the entrepreneurial class, supporting (either directly or indirectly) its political project."[15] Failure to support the revolution, said to be represented by the Sandinista party, was thus tantamount to making an option for the rich, or the oppressors.

The argument was not new. A standard practice among Marxist regimes has been to brand its dissidents as allies of the bourgeoisie or the oppressors. The relative newness of this situation was in the theological weight given to such a claim. With the input of this radical theology, the alleged and real adversaries of the socialist state could be typecast as enemies not only of the proletariat but of Christ as well, with the added advantage that such a charge was being made not by the political authorities alone but by a vocal section of the Catholic community as well.

The Catholic hierarchy saw in these positions a challenge to its understanding of Christian faith and practice. It also saw an invitation to revert to preconciliar Constantinism and its tradition of turning the church into a subservient branch of a secular state.

In fact, some of the revolutionary Christians' most renowned leaders went so far as to claim that their commitment to the revolutionary process had to be unconditional.[16] Underlying this claim was their tendency to see in the revolution and in its leaders the highest expressions of Christian practices—in themselves products of their rather secularized religious views. If the Sandinistas were the most revolutionary, would they not be more Christian than the other Christians? Amando Lopez, S.J., president of Central American University, said: "If I were to put in concrete terms, what Christians would expect from the FSLN [Sandinista Front], I would say—and not as a literary expression—what Christians expect from the FSLN is that they make us Christians."[17] The expression was indeed more than a literary or an emotional outburst. It carried with it a whole theological approach, one that fit the political aspirations of the ruling Sandinistas in a very remarkable way.

The Sandinistas' Religious Policies

As soon as the old regime collapsed, the Sandinistas moved quickly to secure their place as the indisputable "vanguard" of the Nicaraguan revolution. In most regards they followed old patterns: identification of state and party; widespread confiscation of the news media; creation of revolutionary block committees entrusted with keeping track of neighbors' activities; and creation of party mass organizations meant to absorb and channel most aspects of people's lives. Pressure and intimidation against those who were unwilling to join became common.

But in other ways, particularly in regard to the church, the Nicaraguan revolution had some distinct features. Private schools were allowed to operate and even received state subsidies—although with increasingly rigid controls on the curricula. The government also moved slowly in confiscating businesses and allowed many of its opponents, at least for a few years, to actively coexist. But most significantly the Sandinista Front did not declare itself Marxist-Leninist, nor has it officially announced that it intends to promote atheistic education or views.

On the other hand, many internal documents of the party, together with many semiprivate confessions of top-ranking Sandinista leaders, revealed their allegiance to classic Marxist-Leninist ideology.[18] The most likely hypothesis for these discrepancies is that the Sandinistas' concessions to private organizations and individuals, as well as their reluctance to publicize their adherence to communism's basic ideals or policies, have been mostly a matter of strategy, not of ideological differences.

Regardless of its origins, the payoffs of such a low-key approach are obvious: It not only created a considerable and lengthy controversy about the nature of the regime but also allowed the Sandinistas to arouse and keep an amount of support from the international Christian community, which would have been unthinkable had they declared themselves atheist communists.

It is precisely the Sandinistas' understanding of the international circumstances, coupled with their awareness of the deep-seated religiosity of vast segments of the Nicaraguan population, that in all probability led them to outline their relatively distinctive approach to the church. In discussing the Sandinistas' goals in religious matters, some scholars get entangled in whether or not the Sandinistas are hostile to religion or the church. It may be more in tune with the complexities of the situation to ask what type of church and religiosity the Sandinistas may wish to see existing, and how willing they may be to let churches departing from their ideal type conduct "business as usual."

Documents and concrete policies of the party reveal that the Sandinistas, committed as they are to a secular political ideology, are ready to allow, and even patronize, churches willing to endorse their particular revolutionary perspectives. But they also reveal that the Sandinistas are ready to curtail, by means ranging from subtle to direct, the influence of other churches.

A statement in this regard is found in a government manual used for the 1980 literacy campaign. In lesson 22, which speaks about religion in the new Nicaragua, we read: "There will be freedom of religion for those churches willing to protect the interest of the people."[19] This conditional declaration of freedom is itself a repetition of similar statements found in party documents predating the triumph of the revolution.[20]

Yet the documents also reveal the Sandinistas' awareness of the power of the church and the dangers of confronting nonrevolutionary, religious elements in direct ways. A private memorandum of the Sandinista party leaked to the press in late 1979 is revealing. The document, signed by Julio Lopez, head of the Sandinista Front's Department of Propaganda and Political Education, addressed the regional leaders of the party on how to approach the upcoming celebration of Christmas. It calls the militants to "rescue" the celebration for the revolution, by giving it a "new, fundamentally political content." The memorandum warns party members about the imprudence of proceeding otherwise:

> Only five months after the triumph of the revolution, it would be rather foolish to directly confront a tradition of more than 1979 years, because it would entail political conflicts and the inevitable loss of confidence of our people. . . .
>
> Sixty-two years of revolution in the Soviet Union have not been enough to completely eradicate this religious tradition. Therefore to pretend to uproot such a tradition from our people in such a short time could only constitute a petit-bourgeois revolutionary attitude.[21]

The Sandinistas thus have chosen to emphasize, perhaps more than most Marxist regimes on record, the politicization and manipulation of religious symbols and meanings. And in their initially careful and rather indirect approach, they found an invaluable ally in the radical Christians.

The liberationists indeed provided a theological way to politicize the main contents of the Christian faith by depicting Christmas as the advent of the new, revolutionary man: Christ as the subversive of Nazareth; sin as the capitalist system; and socialism as the Kingdom of God. They also made a conscientious effort to dispel the fear of communism among traditional Catholics and to present Marxism as a neutral tool of social analysis compatible with Christian beliefs.[22] The government was able to promote these viewpoints in the powerful state media without immediately seeming hypocritical because it could point to the revolutionary priests and say, "They are the ones who are making these claims."

Spokesmen for the revolutionary Christians also provided the Sandinistas with the additional, and very significant, service of denying, before a rather puzzled international audience, the Marxist-Leninist character of the revolution's leadership and goals.

The liberationists also contributed by echoing, in theological terms, the Sandinista contention tersely expressed by the government junta in 1981: True, sincere Christians in Nicaragua embrace the option for the poor as represented by the Sandinista Front.[23] This claim became a useful ideological tool in confronting those Christians who hesitated or refused to support the government, who usually were portrayed as Christians unworthy of the name.

The first targets of such criticisms were the Catholic bishops and their lay supporters who had aligned themselves with Archbishop Obando. Although the Nicaraguan hierarchy, as exemplified by its first pastoral documents, had taken a rather positive attitude before the newly installed regime, some radical Catholics resented the hierarchy's provisos and cautionary statements. Visiting liberation theologian Jon Sobrino regretted the church's fear of Marxism and atheism, saying, "Deep down the Church is afraid of God."[24]

As time wore on, the revolutionary Christians' charges against the progressive and moderate Christians grew bitter, portraying the bishops—especially Obando—as leaders of the church of the rich. The government reacted by providing its allies within the churches with access to the state-controlled media and by only gradually curtailing the freedom of expression of all other Christians. Cristophe Batasch, writing in *Le Monde Diplomatique*, commented on the sagacity of the Sandinistas in "letting the leftist Christians take care of combatting the bishops."[25]

The radical and liberal pro-Sandinista Christians explained away the growing confrontation between the Catholic hierarchy and the revolutionary Christians and government, using jointly, or separately, a neo-Marxist frame of reference and a variant of the traditional-modern dichotomy. According to the first approach, the clash was occurring because the Catholic church refused to see in the mounting tensions of Nicaraguan society a class conflict between rich and poor, and because it failed to identify the Sandinista Front as the poor's defender. According to the second approach, the hierarchy was still trapped in preconciliar categories and concerns and was unable to embrace the concerns for social justice and democratic pluralism.

The Nicaraguan government compounded this picture by appointing four Catholic priests to cabinet positions: Miguel D'Escoto, minister of foreign affairs; Ernesto Cardenal, minister of culture; Fernando Cardenal, director of Sandinista youth (a constitutive section of the Sandinista party); and Edgard Parrales, minister of social welfare.

The fact was indeed unprecedented in the modern history of the region. To some observers it seemed the best evidence of an appreciative and understanding relationship between the government and the church—an outstanding sign of the Nicaraguan revolutionaries' novel openness to religion. But for most of the Nicaraguan bishops, as well as for other analysts, the move was a direct blow, "ably concealed, at the church's independence." Pablo A. Cuadra, who as editor of *La Prensa* had enthusiastically welcomed the changes of Vatican II, put it this way: "It was the return to the politicized curate: it obliged the Church to serve one party and thus to renounce its independence and cease being a luminous sign of Christ's love for all."[26]

The dispute over having priests in the government led to one of the first and most open confrontations between the church and the government. The Nicaraguan bishops first tried to persuade the four priests involved to return to their pastoral duties, claiming that their political roles were incompatible with their priestly ministry. The priests argued that by occupying those positions they were serving the Nicaraguan people at a time when a national emergency and the shortage of qualified personnel made it almost imperative. When the dialogue yielded no fruit, the bishops issued a statement on June 4, 1981, publicly demanding that the priests resign from their posts.

The revolutionary Christians responded with an agitation campaign against the bishops that involved sit-ins and the takeover of some Catholic churches. Tomas Borge, minister of the interior, applauded these actions and accused the bishops of persecuting their own church members.

The four priests responded with a defiant document which ended, "Finally we declare our unbreakable commitment to the people's Sandinista revolution, in loyalty to our people, which is the same as saying, in loyalty to the will of God."[27]

The echo of the debate reached the Vatican. Agostino Cardinal Casaroli, as head of the Vatican's Secretariat of State, apparently had told the Nicaraguan bishops to take the steps they deemed necessary. But Archbishop Obando, perhaps sensing the dangers of direct confrontation, wanted the Holy See—not him—to initiate and assume the imposition of stern disciplinary measures.[28] The Sandinistas, in the meantime, hurriedly sent a delegation to Rome to reassure the Vatican of their good intentions toward the church. Finally, Cardinal Casaroli recommended imposing limited restrictions for as long as the priests remained in office. Basically, they were not to perform any of the sacraments.

Sandinista spokesman Tomas Borge welcomed the resolution and termed it "wise." In fact, the obvious political advantages of keeping four priests in government would not be jeopardized by their inability to participate in the sacramental life of the church.

Direct Curtailments

In the wake of this confrontation the policy of indirect curtailment of the church's activities gradually ceded ground to more direct measures, resulting in open conflict. Part of this shift may have been by government design. Most probably it resulted from a profound incompatibility between a state that aspires to a hegemonic role in the political as well as in the moral-cultural realm and a church determined to retain its autonomy and its capacity to pass moral judgment on the actions of the state.

Some conflicts started with the church criticizing a particular governmental policy and ended with the authorities retaliating. At other times the government initiated the action either by demanding from the church the endorsement of some specific position or by unilaterally depriving the church of some of its rights.

As the record shows, the policies of the Sandinista government have led to a steady imposition of important restrictions on the institutional church. Particularly poignant has been the gradual process of silencing the church. In July 1981 the government "recommended" that Archbishop Obando, who had been conducting a televised Sunday mass since the last decade of the Somoza dictatorship, limit his appearances to once a month and let the other three Sunday masses rotate among "popular" priests. The archbishop interpreted this proposal as an attempt by the government to interfere in the internal affairs of the church, and refused. The Sandinistas then canceled his program.

Governmental decrees limiting freedom of expression hit the church in 1982 when Radio Católica, the hierarchy's radio station, was suspended for one month. The imposition in March 1982 of a nationwide state of emergency also meant further curtailments of the church's freedom. *La Prensa*, a strong mouthpiece for the church hierarchy, fell under a rather severe censorship, and with it the remaining independent radio stations. Although the government allowed *La Prensa* to print the archbishop's Sunday homily for a few years more, articles defending the hierarchy from government attacks were commonly censored. Not even the pope escaped this treatment. A letter he sent to the Nicaraguan bishops in the summer of 1982 was barred from publication. Only after a month of vigorous protests, involving three closings of *La Prensa*, was the ban lifted.[29] By Easter 1983 the government had decreed that sermons and homilies by church leaders had to be censored as a precondition for broadcasting. The apex of these restrictions was reached in October 1985, when in a sudden move the government decreed a new and more sweeping state of emergency. Officially meant to neutralize the creation of a "counterrevolutionary internal front," the crackdown affected the church and independent labor far more.

Sandinista troops took over the printing facilities of the church, confiscated the first and only issue of the weekly publication *Iglesia*, shut down the offices of COPROSA (the Catholic church's social relief organization), and dismantled the church's newly created human rights office. The government charged that *Iglesia* carried antistate propaganda and used the fact that COPROSA had received funds from USAID (United States Agency for International Development) to argue that the church was carrying out plans developed by the CIA.

The silencing of the church was practically completed on January 1, 1986, when Radio Católica was shut down indefinitely after failing to broadcast a full speech of Nicaragua's president Daniel Ortega.

The round of peace negotiations that followed the signing of the so-called Esquipulas Accord in August 1987 meant an eleven-month reopening of outlets such as Radio Católica and *La Prensa*. On July 11, 1988, arguing that both institutions were inciting to subversion, the government shut them down, only to reopen them again later, but with restrictions. Radio Católica, in particular, was curtailed in its capacity to broadcast news. At no point in time has the church recovered its printing facilities or COPROSA, and even if it does, the ongoing events suggest that governmental concessions may be shaky or short-lived.

Restrictions on the church's free expression are one side of the coin. The other side is made up of a continuous defamation campaign against its most outstanding leaders. Charges against church leaders have ranged from subtle innuendos to grotesque caricatures (some with sexual overtones) and from sophisticated political criticisms to slanderous accusations and insults. Severely limited in their access to the media, the Nicaraguan bishops and their supporters often have found themselves unable to counter the allegations of their accusers.

In this regard, the Central American peace talks, started in August 1987 and known as the Esquipulas agreements, produced a letup in the attacks. By September 1988, however, the Sandinistas were organizing weekly demonstrations outside the cardinal's office, and on October 15 President Ortega publicly denounced him and the other Nicaraguan bishops as being "instruments of Ronald Reagan's politics of death."[30] This sudden reversal was attributed to the Sandinistas' discomfiture over the role played by Cardinal Obando as a member of a verification commission set up in 1988 to monitor compliance with the terms of the peace agreements.

Crippling the Leadership

Attacks against religious leaders have sometimes involved attempts to discredit the moral character of the victims or to implicate them in counterrevolutionary conspiracies.

An instance of the first case was that of Fr. Bismarck Carballo, assistant of the archbishop of Managua and director of Radio Católica. The Sandinista media claimed that he had been caught in a tryst with a woman and showed pictures of the naked priest in the process of being arrested. The fact that cameras of Sandinista television and reporters of the Sandinista newspapers were at the scene of the "affair" lent credence to Carballo's and the archbishop's allegations that it had been a Sandinista setup. A Sandinista defector, Miguel Bolanos, later accused Tomas Borge of masterminding the incident.[31]

Another case involved Fr. Amado Peña. The government showed a film in which the priest was seen allegedly conspiring with a counterrevolutionary. Flaws in the film, together with the coincidental, videotaped capture of Fr. Peña's explosives-filled luggage, made the government's claims look disingenuous in this case also.

The Sandinistas have, however, avoided arresting priests for long periods. Even in the case of Fr. Peña, where (according to the interior police) there was irrefutable evidence of his conspiracy, the authorities allowed him to take refuge at the Managua seminary before "pardoning" him a year later.

Arrests were short term even during the crackdown of October 1985, which led to the detention of nearly fifty priests—close to 20 percent of the Nicaraguan clergy—and hundreds of Catholic lay activists, including leaders of Catholic charismatic renewal and other lay movements. The priests were fingerprinted, photographed, and admonished—with varying degrees of verbal and, sometimes, physical roughness—and then released.

Much more effective in "neutralizing" undesirable members of the church has been the expulsion of priests, affecting twenty foreign-born priests and two native Nicaraguans. The analysis of these incidents suggests a very careful selection by the Sandinista authorities. The most climactic year in terms of expulsions was 1984, when in a single stroke the government expelled ten foreign-born priests without any legal procedure on the charge that they had unduly participated in a demonstration in support of Fr. Peña. In fact, only five of them participated in the march. One of the priests who did not march, Fr. Santiago Anitua, S.J., attributes their expulsion not to their participation in politics but to the fact that they were all working in areas that the government regards as key and sensitive.[32]

Father Anitua, a leader in the Catholic charismatic renewal and the spiritual director of Managua's major seminary, provides the following (abridged) description of the other expelled priests:

> Fr. Mario Madriz, director of the large Don Bosco High School, which educates thousands of poor young people in the Indian neighborhood of Monimbó, in Masaya. Fr. Feliciano Montero, director of the even

> larger Don Bosco Youth Center of Managua. Fr. Mario Friandi, in charge of Catholic youth sports in Managua, an organization that on Sundays rallied some 10,000 young people. Fr. Benito Le Plant, founder of 352 peasant communities and several cooperatives, also leader of the Delegates of the Word. Fr. Benito Pitito, Fr. Vicente Gaudelli as well as Fr. Peña and myself [Fr. Anitua], [were] priests of the four largest and adjacent working-class districts in Managua, the ones that played an important role in the insurrection against Somoza. Fr. Huerta, parish priest of the Indian Monimbó barrio in Masaya—also key in sparking the anti-Somoza revolt in 1978. Fr. Francisco San Martin, shepherd of the Cursillo movement and other influential lay organizations.[33]

Until 1986 the expulsions of priests and religious had affected only foreign-born citizens. The forced exile of Bishop Pablo Vega and Monsignor Bismarck Carballo during the summer of 1986 marked the first time that Nicaraguan prelates were expelled. In this regard, as in others, the peace negotiations that followed the Esquipulas Accord provided for the return of some, but not all, expelled priests. Monsignor Carballo and Fr. Pitito returned in 1987. Bishop Vega, who was given permission to return, chose to remain in Honduras.

Another category of direct governmental actions against the church has involved mob attacks. The first of these attacks against church members occurred in November 1981, when a Sandinista mob threw stones at the bishop of Juigalpa, Pablo Vega. Archbishop Obando was attacked three times during the following two years. The worst round took place in October 1983, when twenty-six Catholic churches were assaulted simultaneously, disrupting mass and injuring several parishioners and a few priests. The last mob attack reported against the church took place in 1984.

Thorny Issues

This type of action, whether mob attacks, the expulsion of priests, or the closing down of church facilities, has often been tied to specific disputes between the church and the government. The proper role of the church in the revolution, together with the participation of priests in government, remains a divisive issue. Father Escoto and the Cardenal brothers have now completed a decade in the service of the Sandinista Front.

The church's insistence on acting as the "voice of the voiceless"—using in this regard a parlance common among liberation theologians—and on denouncing violations of human rights also continues to pit church against state. The church's first official human rights action under the revolutionary regime was in February 1982, when in a pastoral letter the hierarchy denounced the forced relocation of thousands of Miskito Indians, a process that involved burning several of their villages and mistreating and killing some Indians. The government accused the bishops of lying and of betraying Nicaragua's national interest. Information released two years later by the Organization of American States's Human Rights Commission[34] and the Sandinistas' own admissions in the following years confirmed the accuracy of the bishops' charges. What angered the Sandinistas was, of course, the fact that those denunciations were made in the midst of renewed Contra activity and at a time when the debate about Nicaragua was heating up in the U.S. Congress. The debate has remained hot for many years since then, and any charges of human rights violations have been interpreted by the government as attempts to bolster its enemies and as unpatriotic acts bordering on treason.

The educational policies of the Sandinistas also have been a thorny issue in their relations with the church. A superficial look at Nicaragua could suggest that the government is more a friend than a foe of private Catholic education. The government, in fact, did not interrupt a prerevolutionary policy of public aid for private schools. Several years after the revolution, most of those schools continued receiving some form of governmental subsidies, while many religious men and women continued teaching. The promotion of atheism has not been publicly announced as a goal of the government's educational policies. On the other hand, governmental control of the schools' curricula is considerable, and curriculum content shows a pronounced reliance on Marxist philosophy, a pervasive exaltation of militarism, and plain party propaganda.[35] Religious courses cannot be taught during ordinary hours, and the government effectively interferes in the hiring policies of Catholic institutions. Subsidies are often coupled with tight restrictions on tuition increases, a policy that, given the hyperinflation of the Nicaraguan economy, puts private schools in a very stressful situation.

In December 1982 the bishops issued a pastoral letter praising some progress made in the field of education but criticizing its increasingly atheistic content.[36] The government responded with its customary round of verbal attacks and with the vow that in Nicaragua, "there would be no parallel education, never"—meaning that there would be no education at variance with the official education mandated by the state.[37]

An even more acute conflict between church and state erupted in regard to the law of compulsory military service enacted by the government in 1983. The bishops' objection was that the law forced all young Nicaraguans to join an essentially partisan—as opposed to national—army. (In Nicaragua the army is officially a branch of the Sandinista party.) This time the church stand gave rise not only to the usual verbal onslaught but to the worst wave of mob attacks so far.

Even more acute was the confrontation that occurred when the church issued a call for dialogue and reconciliation between Sandinistas and Contras in April 1984. The bishops' call brought down the most bitter reaction of the Sandinistas, who called their proposal "criminal."[38] The government's move against Fr. Peña and the consequent expulsion of ten priests may be seen as part of the Sandinistas' response to a stand that, at that time, was taboo.

The authorities also have tried to put the church on the defensive by demanding from the hierarchy a public condemnation of U.S. support for the Contras. Archbishop Obando and the Nicaraguan Episcopal Conference have steadfastly rejected this demand. The archbishop contended that the government, in its pursuit of a church pronouncement in this matter, was not at all seeking the church's moral guidance but rather the production of a statement that can be manipulated for political purposes.[39] His position, which deeply irritated the government, was that there ought to be a dialogue between the Sandinistas and the Contras.

Roughly two years later, the government partially reversed its stand on this issue. In summer 1987 the Sandinistas took the surprising step of naming Archbishop Obando as one of a three-member reconciliation committee, created to help carry out the agreement of Esquipulas. And on March 23, 1988, a high-ranking Sandinista delegation engaged in face-to-face talks with Contra leaders in the southern Nicaraguan town of Sapoa. As mentioned, the cardinal emerged from these talks as one of the two members of the Verification Commission created to supervise compliance with the cease-fire. But then, in October, he was subjected to a particularly virulent campaign after the government, in defiance of the Sapoa agreements, confiscated a shipment of eighteen jeeps to the cardinal that were to be used by him to carry out his verification duties. According to unidentified church officials quoted by the Associated Press, the aim of this new wave of attacks was to force the cardinal to step down from the Verification Commission, inasmuch as it was gathering material harmful to the government.[40]

A Divided Catholic Community

The controversial issues pitting church and state in Nicaragua have brought polarization to the Nicaraguan Catholic community. On the one hand stood the hierarchy and its host of lay and clerical supporters—from progressive to conservative Catholics—and on the other stood the so-called revolutionary Christians—from ultraradical Catholics like Ernesto Cardenal to less extremist liberals.

The split in the Nicaraguan Catholic community cut across class lines, producing a complex and at times ironic picture. With few exceptions the lower Nicaraguan clergy tended to band around the hierarchy. Most Catholic support for the government and the radical liberationist positions came from foreign-staffed religious orders, in particular the Jesuits and some contingents of Dominicans and Capuchins.

In terms of the laity, there has been a tendency among businessmen and significant segments of the middle- and upper-middle-class professionals to join with peasants and lower-class urban dwellers—especially those who belonged to what is known as the "informal sector" of the economy—in supporting the non-Sandinista bishops. The case was particularly strong in regard to Archbishop Obando. *New York Times* journalist Stephen Kinzer, who traveled with the prelate through some Nicaraguan villages in 1984, testified to this effect: "Archbishop Obando can draw an instant crowd anywhere in Nicaragua. . . . Anyone who follows Obando in his trips in the countryside can see that he is venerated even more emotionally among the poor."[41] Kinzer's insight has been confirmed repeatedly by the size of the crowds who accompany the archbishop in the holy day processions and by the massive welcome he received on returning from Rome after his ordination as cardinal.

The progressive-moderate Catholics also have been active in the development of CEBs, and most lay renewal movements count them among their organized membership.

In contrast with these Catholics, and in spite of their efforts to develop a lower-class constituency, those identified with the revolutionary Christians (at times referred to as the "people's church") have found themselves confined to an elite with a high percentage of middle- and upper-middle-class intellectuals and clergy. A foreign observer, Peruvian novelist Mario Vargas Llosa, agrees: "Its name notwithstanding, the 'people's church' is largely composed of members of the religious elite—priests and laymen whose intellectual disquisitions and sociopolitical work lie beyond the scope of most of the Catholic poor. The efforts of the leaders of the 'people's church' to combine politics and religion have only found a response in the intellectually militant members of the middle class, many of whom are already converts."[42]

The revolutionary Christians' failure to build a popular base of support has been corroborated by several other indicators. When demonstrating on behalf of the government or staging sit-ins against the Catholic hierarchy, the revolutionary Christians usually have to mobilize people from distant locations and fill out the crowd with Sandinista militants. A 1986 demonstration led by Fr. Miguel D'Escoto at the closing of Holy Week gathered a few thousand supporters in Managua. But it was nearly impossible to distinguish between Catholics and the scores of Sandinista militants mobilized by the party.

The close identification between revolutionary political activism and pastoral church activity has been one of the possible reasons for the radical Christians' failure to create large, grass-roots bases of support. When traditional Catholics convert to liberationism, they commonly become deeply involved in partisan political work. Michael Dodson described the problem in the following terms: "Some Christians who sought initially to maintain active roles of leadership in their CEBS while taking on the political and organizational tasks of reconstruction found the political tasks eclipsing their work in the church. Even though they might see political work to be a part of the work of the church they were sometimes forced to neglect their spiritual and pastoral tasks."[43]

A further reason for the revolutionary Christians' elitism is the fact, already hinted at by Vargas Llosa, that their secularized, intellectualized religious views do not hold much appeal for traditional-minded people. As is often the case even in developed societies, liberal Christian denominations lose membership before the rapid growth of conservative fundamentalist ones.

Indeed, the revolutionary Christians' real influence has been international rather than national, a fact which in Nicaragua's case takes on a crucial significance. Nicaragua's liberationist centers have been printing multilingual publications for overseas distribution, and they are very active in hosting foreign tourists. The fact that many of their members speak English and other languages enables them to interact with groups of mostly Anglo-Saxon Westerners in a way that is often off limits for the predominantly native Catholic hierarchy and clergy.

Funds for these centers and their publications mostly come from North American and European sources, particularly the World Council of Churches and some mainline Protestant denominations.[44] The Catholic church's capacity for receiving foreign funds has been curtailed drastically by state regulations that demand prior approval of foreign grants benefiting private organizations. More than once such funds have been denied.

The Vatican and the Pope

The Vatican's first reaction to the Nicaraguan revolution is still not clear. It seems clearer, however, that until the middle of 1982 the Nicaraguan bishops were weathering the gathering storms in relative isolation. Delegations of revolutionary Christians visiting Cardinal Casaroli had been instrumental in depicting the archbishop of Managua as the stumbling block for smoother relations between church and state.

It seems that more liberal-minded people in the Secretariat of State harbored some misgivings about Archbishop Obando. They wanted to reduce Obando's profile, thus lending more weight to the rest of the bishops. The conservatives, by contrast, saw strengthening Obando and capitalizing on his charisma and popularity as the best way to secure the church's unity.

The Holy See's apostolic delegate to Nicaragua since 1981, Msgr. Andrea de Montezemolo, seems to have shared the liberals' outlook. It was no secret in Nicaragua at that time that Archbishop Obando was not happy with him, and that his reports to the Vatican failed to communicate the concerns of a good segment of the Nicaraguan hierarchy.

When those concerns reached the pope, seemingly through unofficial lay Catholic envoys, the pope decided to strengthen the archbishop's hand and bypass the cautions of the secretary of state. The letter John Paul II sent to the Nicaraguan bishops in July 1982 signaled his growing concern for what was happening in Nicaragua and his explicit desire to bolster the stand of the bishops who shared the views of Archbishop Obando. The pope called the faithful to obedience and unity with their bishops, upholding the hierarchy's role as the authority of the church. He explicitly criticized the pretense of the "people's church" directly or indirectly advocated by most liberationists as unacceptable and contrary to Catholic tradition.

The pope's visit to Nicaragua in March 1983 brought him into closer identification with Archbishop Obando and the progressive-moderate Catholics, and put him on a collision course with the Sandinistas and their most fervent radical Catholic supporters. From the very start the pope's visit was marred by tensions. The Vatican had requested the exclusion of the priests in government from the public ceremonies, offering to reciprocate by assuring a low profile for the archbishop of Managua. The understanding was that the pope's visit would be strictly pastoral and that both the government and the local church would make every effort to prevent the politicization of the event. As one of these measures, no partisan banners or slogans were to be displayed.[45]

When the pope arrived at the Managua airport, he did not find Archbishop Obando in the entourage but instead, amidst a sea of Sandinista Front flags, Fr. Ernesto Cardenal, Nicaraguan minister of culture. The pope refused to allow Cardenal to kiss his ring and visibly admonished him.

He celebrated mass at night, in Managua, before a crowd roughly estimated at half a million people. The Sandinistas had stuffed the first rows of the plaza with their own flag-waving militants. Some of them had powerful megaphones and, as members of the Vatican delegation discovered to their dismay, they also had microphones connected to the main loudspeaker system, including television. Heckling and interruptions took place during the pope's homily and then for the remainder of the mass. Although the pope avoided any criticism of the government, he repeated in his homily many of the concepts about the unity of the church that he had expressed in his 1982 letter to the Nicaraguan bishops.

The heckling crowd near the altar was demanding that the pope pray for the "martyrs of the revolution" (those killed by the Contras) and gave shouts of "We want peace" and "People's power." The pope interrupted his homily to say: "The first one who wants peace is the church." The shouting and the interruptions, some of them very defiant, continued until the end of the mass. While the pope distributed communion, a female agitator cried through the loudspeaker systems: "Holy Father, if you are truly the representative of Christ on earth, we demand (*te exigimos*) that you side with us."[46]

According to the Sandinistas, what angered them was the pope's failure to pray for their "martyrs." Nicaraguan minister of the interior Tomas Borge put it this way: "I think the message of the Pope in Nicaragua was full of great omissions. The problem is not so much what he said but what he failed to say."[47] In this regard it is important to note that in some earlier conflicts between the state and the Nicaraguan hierarchy, church leaders were liable to commit sins of omission by abstaining from showing support for either the revolution or some of its policies or stands.

What happened in Nicaragua during the pope's visit strengthened the more traditional elements in the Vatican and gave more weight to the voices demanding more support for Archbishop Obando. Both Vatican Radio and *L'Osservatore Romano*, which had kept a rather guarded stance toward Nicaragua, openly voiced criticism of the Nicaraguan government.

In April 1985 the pope resolved to ordain Archbishop Obando as cardinal. When news of the appointment reached Nicaragua, President Ortega, possibly in an attempt to save face, hurriedly went to salute the archbishop amidst great publicity.

On his return trip from Rome, Cardinal Obando made an overnight stay in Miami, where he celebrated a mass for the large Nicaraguan exile community. Among those attending the ceremony were some top leaders of the anti-Sandinista insurgency, who managed to secure places in the front rows. These circumstances kindled the fires of the Sandinista media, who accused the cardinal of having celebrated a mass for the "counterrevolutionaries."

The welcome of the cardinal at Managua is comparable only to the one offered to the pope in 1983. Hundreds of thousand of Nicaraguans showed up. The government acted cautiously, and only a few clashes between the police and Catholic marchers were reported.

His promotion to the College of Cardinals gave Archbishop Obando the long-sought opportunity to request the appointment of a new, exclusive papal nuncio for Nicaragua. The current nuncio, Msgr. de Montezemolo, was also serving Honduras. In addition to their differences in outlooks, the archbishop had resented the fact that in 1984 the nuncio had apparently intrigued in Rome to have a liberal prelate, the American Pablo Smith, appointed as auxiliary bishop of the diocese of Bluefields—one classified as mission territory and, as such, dependent on the Vatican's Congregation for the Propagation of the Faith.[48] Father Smith's first act upon being ordained as bishop was to invite President Ortega to his inaugural mass.

With Archbishop Obando now a cardinal, the relations with the government became more strained, possibly because of the triumphant pastoral visits that he conducted throughout several Nicaraguan dioceses following his ordination. Everywhere he went, huge crowds greeted him. Their enthusiasm was partly religious and partly political, for the cardinal had already become a powerful symbol of resistance to the state. By October 1985 the government had decided not to tolerate such rallies any more. It required difficult-to-get permissions to have religious marches, and on various occasions sent the army to forcibly prevent country dwellers from gathering. Members of the welcoming committees were punished with arrests.

Things became bleaker in 1986 with the indefinite shutdown of Radio Católica on January 1, the expulsions of Bishops Vega and Carballo in early summer, and the indefinite shutdown of *La Prensa*, the only remaining independent newspaper. In an attempt to bring some relief to the Nicaraguan church, a combination of ecclesiastical efforts involving the Vatican, the local hierarchy, and some episcopal conferences staged the International Eucharistic Congress from November 16 to November 23, 1986. This event brought renowned Catholic personalities like Mother Theresa and Boston's Bernard Cardinal Law to Nicaragua.

This time the government gave some positive signs. President Ortega received Cardinal Law and other Vatican envoys. He also reversed an earlier government decision to bar Mother Theresa's Sisters of Charity from working in Nicaragua. A new and well-publicized round of church-state dialogue followed these overtures. The talks, however, failed to produce significant results. While the government insisted that the national episcopate condemn U.S. aid to the Nicaraguan rebels, Cardinal Obando insisted on the return of Bishops Vega and Carballo.

The Vatican's position in these issues is a matter of speculation. The government and its friends in the radical Catholic community presented the new papal nuncio, Msgr. Paolo Giglio, as interested in dialogue and mutual understanding with the government. At the same time it was rumored that the Sandinistas were seeking a concordat with the church that would confine it to strictly spiritual matters.[49] In fact, from the end of 1986 through the beginning of 1987, Cardinal Obando, perhaps at the urging of Casaroli, had indeed taken a more conciliatory approach, avoiding direct references to the government in his homilies. In the meantime, the government had stepped up the intimidation of lay leaders throughout the country and increased its control over the curricula of Catholic schools.[50]

Conclusion

When the Sandinistas came to power in 1979, one hope among many Christians was that the very visible participation of Catholics in the Nicaraguan revolutionary process could open a new and less antagonistic chapter in the history of church-state relations in Marxist regimes. As it stands today, developments in Nicaragua have disappointed those hopes, although there is still some controversy about what may have caused the repetition of the typical cycle of confrontations.

The modernization of large segments of the Catholic church has not seemed to alter this reality. If anything, the wedge that separates traditional Catholics from radicals has provided the Sandinista government with a relatively effective strategy to confront the institutional church—one that is supplemented by the tendency among liberal-leaning Westerners to read into this type of conflict an overly simplified collision between "modernizers" and "conservatives."

The examination of the nearly completed decade of church-state disputes in revolutionary Nicaragua lends credence to the notion that the width and range of conflicts between the two institutions is so deeply ingrained that no easy accommodation is in sight. The institutional church may become much more cautious in its public expressions and more skillful in its use of diplomatic means, but it is unlikely to provide the Sandinistas with the type of endorsements that they have sought.

As for the possibility that the Sandinistas might become more liberal in their treatment of the church, the round of peace talks started in Central America in August 1987 may have increased the ranks of the skeptical. Although the process led to some early significant concessions, many of them were short term and paled before some other hardenings—such as the ongoing hypermilitarization of the Sandinista state,[51] the renewed role of the mobs, further shutdowns of Radio Católica and *La Prensa*, and a new wave of harassment of the archbishop of Managua.

A closer analysis of these apparent contradictions suggests that the Sandinistas' tolerance of dissent, including that represented by the Catholic church, is a function of the perceived threats to their power. The peace talks may have started because the Sandinistas felt cornered by the increased military capability of the rebels in early 1987 and the possibility of more U.S. aid to them. The talks may have stalled because the rebels became besieged by internal rifts and because there were more indications—by the middle of 1988—that Congress had grown more reluctant to fund them.

Yet the equation of forces brought to bear on the behavior of the Nicaraguan government is more complex. The dismal state of the economy and the action of other diplomatic pressures may still play a significant role. These other forces may be acting at a time when the Sandinistas are approaching the end of the mobilization phase of the revolution. A decade in power may have a sobering impact on some leaders, weary, perhaps, of grand plans to refashion society and besieged by more prosaic concerns. In time, and provided that the right kind of influences are brought to bear, they may become genuinely interested in long-term accommodation with the church—which, ironically, may lead to some muting of the most vociferous elements among the radical Christians.

In the tortuous history of church-state relations, the Sandinistas have shown more than once that they are susceptible to the reactions of the international Catholic community. Nothing precludes this from continuing to be the case.

FACT SHEET

The Catholic Church in Nicaragua

Current strength of the church
- 2,400,000 faithful
- 398 priests and monks
- 9 bishops
- 450 nuns
- 40 seminarians

Number of churches and church facilities (1987)
- approx. 400 churches
- 2 seminaries
- 10 convents
- 0 monasteries
- 68 church-run schools (20 high schools, 48 elementary or technical schools)
- 0 church-run hospitals

Chief news organs
- None: all banned

Underground religious periodicals
None: only photocopies of pastoral letters and church documents

Primate since 1970
Miguel Cardinal Obando y Bravo (1970–present)

IV

PAPAL POLICY

15

Papal Eastern Diplomacy and the Vatican Apparatus

Hansjakob Stehle

With the demise of the medieval church kingdom (the Papal States) in 1870, diplomacy ceased to be an instrument for furthering the secular power pretensions of the Roman Catholic church. Since then, papal policy also has lacked material, let alone military, means to further its religious goals. The formation of a sovereign ministate in the Vatican (1929) did not alter this situation, although in the age of powerful anticlerical and atheist dictatorships, the policy of the popes, including their Eastern policy, has been oriented exclusively toward pastoral goals, i.e., toward the preservation and protection of religious observance and freedom of worship and maintaining the church structures necessary for those purposes. Since every type of conflict makes this task more difficult, Vatican diplomacy always has tried to promote both domestic and international understanding, and even in cases where no formal modus vivendi or concordat agreement was realizable, to stay in contact and in communication. "If it were a question of saving a few souls, of preventing greater evil, we would have the courage to deal even with the devil in person," said Pope Pius XI as early as 1929.[1] In the conviction that "truth does not allow us to despair of our opponents,"[2] John Paul II has continued the course set by his predecessors in Vatican pastoral diplomacy: "The Holy See remains open to relations with every country and system, whereby it basically seeks the good, which is simply the welfare of humanity. . . . We are convinced that such a dialogue cannot be easy, since it starts from diametrically opposed worldviews, but it must be possible and effective."[3]

The Papal Diplomatic Apparatus

The objective and personal continuity of this pastoral diplomacy is guaranteed in the hierarchically organized administrative apparatus of the Vatican —the Roman Curia—and above all by the secretary of state, Agostino Cardinal Casaroli (born 1914). In the diplomatic service since 1940, Casaroli played an essential part in the first phase of Vatican relations with the communist regimes in Eastern Europe during the pontificates of John XXIII and Paul VI (discussed later in this chapter). Between 1961 and 1979 he was secretary of the Council for the Public Affairs of the Church—in practical terms, the Vatican foreign minister. In 1979 John Paul II named him cardinal-state secretary. This post embraces three functions: governmental chief of the Vatican state (as the pope's deputy); highest administrative officer and coordinator of all Vatican "ministries" (congregations, councils, commissions, and committees) which concern themselves with the internal affairs of the church, including those of local churches (including those in communist-ruled states); and prefect of the Council for Public Negotiations of the Church (since June 1988 the Department for General Affairs), which is responsible for all political and ecclesiastical negotiations and for diplomatic relations with states and their governments. Almost all contacts with communist regimes are handled by this body, which in practical terms corresponds to a ministry for foreign affairs. Of the mere thirty-seven persons (including typists) who work in this "foreign ministry," ten diplomats concern themselves with communist states—eight of them exclusively. In 1979 Achille Silvestrini (born 1923), a close collaborator of Casaroli, was named to succeed Casaroli as secretary of the council. He held the post until June 1988, when he was succeeded by Angelo Sodano (born 1927). The deputy secretary is a monsignor of Lithuanian origin, Andrys Backis. Silvestrini and Sodano have represented the Vatican at international conferences, above all at the follow-up conferences of the signatories of the Helsinki Accords. But it is not only on these occasions that the secretary comes into contact with communist diplomats. In Rome the secretary of the Department for General Affairs has fairly regular meetings with the Vatican expert at the Soviet embassy to the Italian government;[4] the Soviet ambassador to Italy also meets with Cardinal-Secretary Casaroli several times a year, upon request. Such meetings are set up by Monsignor Muñoz Faustino Sainz, a Spaniard and the department's expert on the Soviet Union (with whom Fr. Stanisław Slowieniec, a Jesuit of Belorussian descent, collaborates, mainly as translator).

Casaroli visited Moscow on February 25, 1971, to append the Vatican signature to the Non-proliferation Treaty and to conduct a short discussion in the Soviet Council for Religious Affairs. After that, no papal diplomat journeyed to the Soviet Union until June 1988, when Casaroli took part in the celebration of the millennium of the Christianization of Kievan Rus. Aside from reliance on correspondence, the Vatican is able to maintain legal contact with Catholics in the Baltic republics only through the rather infrequent trips to Rome which the Lithuanian and Latvian bishops have been allowed to make since the early 1960s.[5] The religious ties with the Orthodox Moscow Patriarchate are above all fostered by the papal Secretariat for the Unity of Christians and its president, Dutch Cardinal Johannes Willebrands, who has traveled to Moscow several times. Fr. Pierre Duprey, secretary of the Secretariat for Ecumenical Cooperation, Ukrainian curial archbishop Miroslav Marusyn (secretary of the Congregation for the Eastern Churches), Edward Cassidy (Casaroli's deputy), and "Foreign Minister" Sodano, collectively constitute the Papal Commission for Russia, which was established in 1930. Since 1934 this commission has been responsible for Catholics of the Latin rite in the (long-vacant) bishoprics of Mohilew, Minsk, Kamieniec-Podolsk, Tiraspol, and Zytomir. This commission, which lay dormant for decades, was resuscitated in 1985 and, reinforced by the addition of several experts, now includes a study group which meets several times a year. Without administrative authority, though with an advisory function, this body quietly purveys decisive assistance in the difficult, uninstitutionalized relations of the Vatican with the Soviet Union.

The Vatican maintains full, normalized diplomatic relations with only two communist-ruled states: Yugoslavia, which resumed ties in 1970 after an eighteen-year hiatus, and Cuba, with whom, in contrast to all the states of Eastern Europe, relations have never been broken, despite recurrent tensions. The Vatican was able to restore seminormalized diplomatic relations with Poland in 1974, four years before the election of Karol Wojtyła to the papacy. A diplomat with the rank of ambassador but with the title of chief of the governmental delegation of the People's Republic of Poland for permanent working contacts with the Holy See was accredited to the Vatican at that time. Out of consideration for the strength of the church in Poland and its primate, the Vatican desisted from naming a corresponding papal nuncio in Warsaw. Only in 1978 did the pope announce, in the course of his third visit to Poland, that a papal nuncio would be assigned to Warsaw—in effect establishing formal diplomatic relations between the Vatican and Poland. Prior to the naming of the papal nuncio, this function was performed through regular visits to Warsaw and trips throughout Poland undertaken by an apostolic nuncio for special assignments. He lives in Rome and works in the papal "Foreign Ministry" (the Council for Public Affairs), though he has an office reserved for his use in Warsaw, in the building of the old nunciate.

From 1973 to 1986 Archbishop Luigi Poggi (born 1917) was nuncio-at-large for Eastern Europe. In 1986 this function was taken over by Archbishop Francesco Colasuonno (born 1925), who had served as papal representative in Washington, D.C., New Delhi, Taipei, Mozambique, and finally, for a year, in Belgrade. In his new post he is concerned with all of Eastern Europe except the Soviet Union. In this task he has two assistants: Monsignor Janusz Bolonek, who is concerned exclusively with Polish affairs,[6] and Fr. John Bukovsky, an American of Slovak descent who is solely responsible for five countries: Hungary, Czechoslovakia, Romania, Bulgaria, and Albania.

Only with Hungary are there regular, formal contacts, based on "partial agreements"[7] signed in 1964 and similar in nature to a treaty. Once a year the chief of the Budapest Office for Church Affairs (since 1963, Imre Miklós) travels to the Vatican, and once a year the Vatican special nuncio (Poggi, now Colasuonno) travels to Budapest. Problems between church and state which are not soluble in negotiations between the Hungarian bishops and the regime are discussed at this level and usually are resolved by mutual agreement.

Vatican diplomacy with other Eastern bloc states is much more laborious. Only after difficult preparatory discussions with the respective embassies accredited to Italy, and often with long intervals, can the special nuncio (almost always accompanied by Fr. Bukovsky) travel to Czechoslovakia, Romania, and Bulgaria to gather personal impressions of the clergy and the believers (though often amid obstructions by party functionaries and police); the Vatican also has been able to settle some problems in direct discussions with regime representatives, whether formally or informally.

For decades there have been no contacts with Albania, the only communist state to ban all forms of religious practice. On the other hand, Monsignor Claudio Celli, the Asia specialist in the Department for General Affairs, has been able to obtain at least sporadic reports from the isolated Catholics in China, Vietnam, and North Korea.

The German Democratic Republic (GDR) presents a special case for papal Eastern diplomacy. Matters relating to the GDR are handled by Monsignor Giovanni Lajolo, who is also responsible for the Federal Republic of Germany. Here Vatican diplomacy confines itself to opportune attempts to assure formal-legal guarantees for a relatively bearable situation (few obstructions of religious life and no state interference in church structures and the nomination of bishops).

Compared to the foreign policy apparatuses of modern states, the apparatus of the Vatican State Secretariat and its Department for General Affairs is modestly staffed and organizationally cumbersome. To be sure, there is a division of labor, but there are no job descriptions as such, and even the competencies of the country/regional specialists are not entirely precisely set down. All its working papers (reports, proposals, etc.) are forwarded by its secretary to Cardinal-Secretary Casaroli, and most of them are not released even by him. He sends about 90 percent of these papers, with commentary or advice, to the pope, who, as absolute monarch of the Apostolic See and of the Roman church, alone has the final word.

Pope John Paul II has his own style of governance. On the one hand, he often protracts his decisions—some papers return to the responsible officials with decisions only after several weeks. On the other hand, he obtains advice in most unbureaucratic ways: He regularly invites not only cardinals and bishops but also specialists of lower ecclesiastical stature to take lunch or dinner with him, in order to be informed in direct conversation about their areas of work. The current bishops from the Eastern bloc states are also invited when in Rome, giving them the opportunity to speak with the pope informally as well as with the specialists responsible for their countries. At the same time they can report on their talks with other officials of the Vatican congregations who are responsible for specific areas of church life in their countries—above all, with the Congregations of the Doctrine of the Faith (under Joseph Cardinal Ratzinger), the Bishops (Bernardin Cardinal Gantin), Sacraments and Rites (Eduardo Martinez Somalo), the Clergy (Antonio Cardinal Innocenti), the Orders (Jean Cardinal Hamer), Evangelization and Missions (Jozef Tomko), and Catholic Education (William Wakefield Cardinal Baum).

Dialogue in Practice and Theory

The church's pastoral-diplomatic endeavors in Eastern Europe are coordinated by the cardinal-secretary and draw upon all channels of the Vatican apparatus. The extent to which this happens depends on the particular religious situation of the country. In a country like Poland, with a strong church whose bishops are in permanent working contact with the regime, more modest efforts are required on the part of the Vatican than in the case of a local church which finds itself in an extremely weak condition, whether because of decades of persecution (as in Czechoslovakia) or because of the slightness of its numerical presence (as in Bulgaria). The prospects for success of this Vatican Ostpolitik are in any event smallest where there is the greatest need. For this reason the Vatican also has recourse to institutions which have no direct significance in church policy but serve to create an atmosphere of cooperation on a theological-philosophical basis, which in turn promotes dialogue.

The Vatican Secretariat for Non-believers, established by Pope Paul VI in 1965 and led for two decades by Franz Cardinal Kőnig of Vienna, has served this purpose. Since 1985 the French curial cardinal, Paul Poupard (born 1930), has been president of this secretariat, whose members include, among others, Franjo Cardinal Kuharić (of Zagreb), Franciszek Macharski (of Kraków), Joachim Meisner (of East Berlin), Myroslav Ivan Lubachivsky (of Lvov), and Cardinal-Secretary Casaroli. The decree establishing this institution assigned it the task of "studying the phenomenon of atheism in order to fathom its deeper motivations and establish a dialogue with non-believers." On this basis the Vatican cosponsored a Marxist-Catholic colloquium on the theme "science and faith" in Ljubljana in 1984. A second symposium, which was held in Budapest in October 1986, was a "first" in that it enjoyed official church and state patronage (being organized, respectively, by the Vatican Secretariat for Non-believers and the Hungarian Academy of Sciences). The theme of this meeting, "society and ethical values," unavoidably also touched on the problem of political and religious freedom, permitting recognition of the changes of climate that confirm Cardinal Poupard's declaration that "dialogue is the only possible way to assuage tense situations and to eliminate ideological discrimination."[8]

In this way the Vatican has pursued its Ostpolitik cautiously, flexibly, and patiently for more than forty years. "Here, years and decades do not count," said Cardinal-Secretary Casaroli, recalling the Roman tradition of thinking in terms of centuries.[9] This tradition answers the question "success or failure?" with reference to criteria other than those of usual politics. The principle of hope permits a patient realism which, as Casaroli said, "weighs the bearable and the unbearable, that which may be renounced and that which may not be renounced, with Christian prudence."[10] In practice, this means that the classical concordats of the 1920s—when they were the usual practice—are not valid models for agreements with a communist regime. Partial solutions, even on an informal basis, have been and continue to be the goal; a modus vivendi, the reciprocal practical tolerance assured in a specific domain, is preferred to "global" settlements. In this way "the policy of 'all or nothing' or of 'now or never' is avoided."[11]

But why does the Vatican decline to break off dialogue even with extremely inflexible partners? The answer lies in the Roman Catholic view —not shared by Protestants—that the hierarchical structures are indispensable. Without the pope there can be no bishops; without the bishops, no priests; without priests, no sacraments (except baptism by desire or by blood); and without the sacraments (which could be validly dispensed even by unworthy priests) there is no salvation of souls. These principles of dogma make the installation of bishops and general guarantees for the institutions a central problem for all Vatican Ostpolitik. Because the Catholic church, in its self-image, is a public organization, not a secret cult, it needs the "legal possibility to fulfill its mission in freedom under every regime."

This is how Cardinal Casaroli formulated it in a programmatic letter that he sent to Prague's Cardinal Tomášek on February 14, 1983, on behalf of the pope. Even here the "hierarchical structure" of the church was placed at the center, and the conclusion was drawn that in order to guarantee it, "the Holy See is ever prepared, and wishes, to negotiate with the secular authorities."

Papal Ostpolitik since 1917

Shortly after the Russian October Revolution of 1917, which was the first revolution to make a militant atheist doctrine its state policy, the Vatican began to try to soften the religious consequences of the event.[12] Whereas the first contacts in 1919 (an exchange of telegrams between the cardinal-secretary of Pope Benedict XV and Lenin in favor of persecuted believers) were published,[13] for more than half a century a veil of secrecy lay over the Vatican-Soviet negotiations that took place in the 1920s. The famine in Russia in 1920–21 presented the first occasion for such negotiations. After month-long discussions between Wacław Worowski, chief of the first Soviet trade mission in Rome, and Cardinal-Secretary Pietro Gasparri, the two sides signed the first (and to date only) written agreement between Moscow and the Vatican, on March 12, 1922, "regarding the dispatch of agents of the Holy See to Russia, who, with the exclusion of any kind of political propaganda, enjoy full freedom to devote themselves to the relief of the people by distributing foodstuffs to the hungry."[14]

With this treaty, the text of which was published for the first time in 1975,[15] the Vatican joined ranks with the American Relief Administration (administered by Herbert Hoover). The thirteen members of religious orders of the Papal Assistance Mission, led by the American Jesuit Edmund Walsh, were supposed to furnish not merely material but also moral-religious sustenance to the roughly one million persecuted Catholics of Soviet Russia. Shortly before this mission traveled to Russia in summer 1922, the Vatican used the World Economic Conference in Genoa to give it a kind of diplomatic backing: Through the mediation of German Chancellor Josef Wirth, a Catholic who in the course of the Genoa Conference had signed a controversial treaty with the Soviets at Rapallo, a lengthy discussion between Soviet Foreign Minister Georgi V. Chicherin and Vatican Undersecretary Giuseppe Pizzardo came about on May 9, 1922, likewise in Rapallo. In the discussion, which lasted several hours, not only religious freedom but also the problem of confiscated church property was discussed. For the young Soviet regime, the prospect that its recognition under international law might be advanced through the prestige of the Vatican was more important than the mission's relatively modest material assistance.

On the other hand, the Vatican tried diplomatic means to overcome the increasing difficulties which confronted Fr. Walsh's mission in Russia. To this end the German embassy in Moscow served as mediator and thus spun a thread of conversation which the papal nuncio in Berlin, Eugenio Pacelli (later to become Pope Pius XII), would take up in February 1924 with the Soviet ambassador, Nikolai Krestinskii.

Twice—on October 6, 1925, and on June 14, 1927—Pacelli met with Foreign Minister Chicherin in a private apartment in Berlin (owned by the German ambassador in Moscow). During these meetings the possibility of a Soviet "decree concerning the legal status of the Catholic religion and its hierarchy"—though not a concordat as such—was taken up.[16] A languid exchange of notes on this subject between 1925 and 1927 was impeded by the well-known duality of Vatican strategy. Because the expulsion and imprisonment of bishops threatened to leave the Catholic bishoprics of Russia without leadership, Pope Pius XI sent the French Jesuit Fr. Michel d'Herbigny to the Soviet Union several times in the course of 1923–26 with the assignment of consecrating secret bishops, even while Pacelli was conducting official negotiations in Berlin for the legal installation of bishops. D'Herbigny knew nothing of these negotiations, though Pacelli (who himself had secretly consecrated d'Herbigny a bishop in the Berlin nunciate) was precisely informed about the Jesuit's assignment. Since neither d'Herbigny's action nor the two-track strategy could remain hidden from the Soviets for long, this action could achieve only short-term success. The secret hierarchy would soon be wiped out by the secret police. One of the most important demands of the Vatican—sanction of catechistic instruction for children—had been rejected at once by Moscow. Even so, without substantial concessions of this nature the Vatican was not prepared to satisfy the albeit ever-dwindling Soviet interest in "recognition" through the dispatch of an apostolic delegate to Moscow.

On October 6, 1927, Nuncio Pacelli presented Soviet Ambassador Krestinskii in Berlin with the last, already scaled-down, Vatican proposal, to wit, that "the Holy See is prepared to take into account objections of a political nature that the Russian government may have against candidates for the office of bishops and requests permission to open seminaries, to send Russia clergymen agreeable to the government, and to support these clerics and their works."[17]

The Soviets never replied to this proposal. With the Fifteenth Party Congress in December 1927 began the period of "intensified class struggle" and increasing Stalinist terrors against religious communities. On December 16, 1927, Pius XI instructed Cardinal-Secretary Gasparri: "As long as the persecution continues in Russia, we can no longer negotiate with the Soviets."[18]

Undoubtedly the Vatican continued to use every diplomatic and political opportunity to achieve a minimal pastoral presence in the Soviet Union. Thus, with the assumption of diplomatic relations between the United States and the Soviet Union in 1933, Fr. Leopold Braun was allowed to set up an office in the American embassy in Moscow and could simultaneously serve as vicar in Moscow's Catholic church. Since the French pastor of this church, Fr. Pie Eugene Neveu, whom d'Herbigny had secretly consecrated a bishop, had to leave the Soviet Union, the Vatican used the new climate fostered by the Franco-Soviet Assistance Pact (1935) to establish Fr. Michel Florent as pastor in Leningrad, where he remained until 1941. While the 1930s remained characterized by a climate of terror, the papal encyclical *Divini redemptoris* (1937) condemned communism more sharply than ever before or later, not merely as an atheist ideology but as a Moscow world organization and as a system—whereby Pius XI at the same time affirmed his devotion to the peoples of the Soviet Union.

Only during World War II were there again fainthearted contacts. A courtesy visit of Soviet Ambassador Dekanossow (in Berlin) to the papal nuncio in January 1941 remained without consequence, as was the case with the visit of the apostolic delegate in Turkey, Angelo Roncalli (later Pope John XXIII) to Ambassador Nikolai Ivanov on March 22, 1943, with a request for information about Italian prisoners of war. The wartime softening of Stalin's religious policy (most detectable where the Orthodox church was concerned) was in accord with the Vatican's refusal to bless Hitler's war of enslavement against the Soviet Union as a "crusade." Indeed, the Vatican allowed the American bishops to let it be known confidentially that the warnings in *Divini redemptoris* about cooperation with communists did not apply to American war assistance to the Soviet Union, though the Vatican would not have anything to do with the advice offered by its Moscow delegate, Fr. Braun, in October 1941 (in a letter to the American representative at the Vatican, Myron Taylor) that the Roman Curia should "make hay while the sun shines . . . and negotiate about a *modus vivendi* between the Church and the [Soviet] regime."[19]

After 1946, the Sovietization of Eastern Europe crippled any possibility of an "Eastern" initiative on the part of the Vatican. Pius XII's personal recollections of the abortive attempts at dialogue in the 1920s contributed to the mood at the Vatican. Only in Poland and Hungary did the chairmen of the episcopal conferences, respectively Stefan Wyszyński and Jószef Grősz, attempt, in vain, in 1950 to achieve a modus vivendi with the communist regimes, through agreements negotiated without consulting the Vatican. Only when signs of thaw became evident after Stalin's death were there also signs of relaxation on the Vatican's part. A study trip to the Soviet Union by a Catholic professor of theology, Marcel Reding, served also as a reconnaissance to determine "whether a modus vivendi is basically possible" (as Reding put it in a conversation with Soviet Vice Premier Anastas Mikoyan on December 28, 1955). The Soviet answer was evasive. The church would "seek ways, under all conditions, of assuring a minimum of pastoral care, and of saving what could be saved,"[20] as one of Pius XII's closest advisers, Fr. Gustav Gundlach, put it on September 12, 1956. He added that this did not amount to a desertion to communism.

A new phase in Vatican Ostpolitik began with the pontificate of John XXIII and the Second Vatican Council he convened. When the new pope, in his encyclical *Pacem in terris* (April 11, 1963), distinguished between error and those falling into error and between ideologies and their variable implementation, thus opening up the possibility of a dialogue or even a practical cooperation, it was not, however, a matter of a new Catholic doctrine. What was new was that these ideas were expressed in a phase of relative East-West relaxation and intrachurch openness. The Vatican and the pope, portrayed for decades in communist propaganda as devils, were now suddenly depicted in a milder light.

First Secretary Khrushchev's message of congratulation to the pope on his eightieth birthday (on November 27, 1961) opened contact. This was facilitated by the newly established Vatican Secretariat for the Unity of Christians. Its secretary, Monsignor Jan Willebrands, took up contact with the Russian Orthodox church, made his first trip to Moscow on September 27, 1962, and reached an agreement on the participation of observers from the Moscow Patriarchate at the ecumenical council. With his second Moscow trip in early February 1963, Willebrands obtained the release of the Ukrainian-Catholic metropolitan, Josef Slipyi, who had been imprisoned since 1945 and who now returned to Rome with Willebrands, albeit with the understanding that he would not be allowed to return to his episcopal seat in Lvov. In the meantime, the pope became involved in a dramatic mediation between Washington and Moscow in the Cuban missile crisis. On October 26, 1962, when Khrushchev declared himself prepared to withdraw the Soviet missiles from Cuba, *Pravda* published the pope's appeal for peace, praising his "realism."

This by no means ushered in any radical change. Soviet religious policy showed only a few signs of softening, e.g., in the release of clergy from Siberian labor camps and in the installation of bishops in the Baltic republics. But the change of climate spread to other communist-ruled states. Eighty-nine Catholic bishops from communist-ruled countries (aside from China and Albania) were allowed to come to Rome for sessions of the ecumenical council, most of them seeing Rome for the first time since the end of World War II. And the Vatican, supplied in this way with essential personal information which it had lacked for years, now began to become diplomatically active in Eastern Europe. On May 9, 1963, Agostino Casaroli, then Vatican "foreign minister," traveled to Budapest for the first of five rounds of talks, which led to the signing on September 15, 1964, of a "partial agreement." This partial agreement made possible the nomination—for the first time in fourteen years—of five bishops in Hungary who were acceptable to both the Vatican and the regime, as well as other improvements in conditions for the church.[21]

Pope John XXIII died while these negotiations were in progress, and in June 1963 Cardinal Montini was elected his successor, taking the name Paul VI. The new pope stood closer to the diplomatic tradition of the Vatican and let it be known that the Holy See was open to "honorable negotiations in good faith, where it finds effective signs of good will."[22] So Casaroli began the first of four rounds of negotiations with Yugoslavia on June 26, 1964, which led eventually to the signing of a protocol after thirty-eight negotiation sessions over two years.[23] The protocol guaranteed regime recognition of freedom of faith and conscience and the jurisdiction of the Vatican over Yugoslav Catholics and their hierarchy, and underlined the separation of church and state. The Vatican, in turn, confirmed the principle that religion should not be misused for political purposes. Each of the signatories "noted" the standpoint of the other side. That was the cautious formula of a normalization confirmed almost five years later when Yugoslav President Josip Broz Tito was received by Paul VI in the Vatican on March 29, 1971, on an official visit with all the appurtenances of protocol.

It proved difficult to make the Yugoslav form of agreement acceptable to other communist regimes, because in all the countries of the Soviet bloc, with the exception of Poland and the GDR, underground hierarchies (with secret bishops) had arisen in the first two decades after 1945. The legalization of this situation came up against psychological and political obstacles as well as historical prejudices and ideological constraints. This was illustrated especially in Czechoslovakia, where Casaroli was able to obtain the release of Josef Cardinal Beran of Prague from prison on February 19, 1965, bringing him to Rome, and to install František Tomášek as his successor in the archbishopric of Prague. But only after eight more years of constantly stagnating negotiations were four new bishops installed on March 3, 1973, with Casaroli himself consecrating them (in Nitra and Olmouz). Since then, contacts between Prague and the Vatican have never completely broken off, but all negotiations remained almost without fruition for the next fifteen years. On August 9, 1985, Cardinal-Secretary Casaroli went to the Moravian town of Velehrad to celebrate a festive liturgy before tens of thousands of believers on the 1,100th anniversary of the death of the Apostle to the Slavs, Bishop Saint Methodius. He was able to conduct talks with functionaries in Prague on that occasion, but the talks did nothing to relax religious policy in Czechoslovakia.

Vatican diplomacy also made little progress in Romania. Although Romanian Prime Minister Ion Gheorghe Maurer (on January 24, 1964) and party chief Nicolae Ceauşescu (on May 26, 1973) both visited Pope Paul VI during their respective trips to Italy, Special Nuncio Poggi was able to undertake the first fact-finding trip to Romania, accompanied by Fr. Bukovsky, only in January 1975. During his subsequent two visits, in July 1977 and July 1979, Poggi succeeded in working out a draft "statute" for Romania's Catholic church with church functionaries in Bucharest. But contacts stagnated in the following years, not least because of the question of the suppressed Greek Rite Catholic church. Even Franz Cardinal König of Vienna, who as president of the Vatican's Secretariat for Non-believers had been able to work out some difficulties during trips to Prague, Budapest, and Belgrade, was not able to get anywhere in Bucharest in the face of opposition from the Orthodox patriarch.

In Bulgaria party chief Todor Zhivkov quite unexpectedly and without negotiations opened up the possibility of installing bishops in two long-vacant dioceses during a visit to Paul VI on June 27, 1975. Casaroli was able to visit Bulgaria's Catholics (who number about sixty thousand) November 4–8, 1976. Their small number made it simpler for the regime to ease the pressure in the post-Stalin phase. Indeed, in contrast to Ukraine, Romania, and Czechoslovakia, Bulgaria had never outlawed the Greek Rite Uniates, who had retained an exarchate in Sofia. So Bulgarian Foreign Minister Petar Mladenov could declare, when he visited Pope John Paul II on December 14, 1979, that "the progress already achieved" gives the Catholic church of Bulgaria "the opportunity to fulfill its mission."[24] Even the shadow cast on Bulgaria during the trial of Mehmet Ali Agca for his attempt on the pope's life in 1981, of suspected but inadequately documentable Bulgarian complicity, did not affect the relatively relaxed relations. Every year on May 24, the feast day of Saint Cyril (who is buried in Rome), a delegation of the Bulgarian Ministry of Culture visits the Vatican.

After the first visit of Soviet Foreign Minister Andrei Gromyko to the Vatican (April 27, 1966), followed on January 30, 1967, by a formal audience with Soviet President Nikolai Podgorny, Gromyko returned again on November 14, 1970, and February 21, 1974, for talks with Paul VI, though Gromyko tried to dodge the subject of church and religion by claiming "incompetence" in this area. This excuse served him less well when he was received by Pope John Paul II on January 24, 1979, for a two-hour discussion.

The election of a pope from Poland had awakened Moscow's interest in the Vatican, but also—for historical and ideological reasons—Soviet worries and prejudices. Until then, Poland had been an area where the strong Polish episcopate and Cardinal-Primate Wyszyński had required almost no help from Rome; for that reason Vatican activities were never viewed without a certain jealousy. That also could be observed during Agostino Casaroli's three fact-finding trips through Polish dioceses in 1967. One result of Casaroli's subsequent report was the naming of the archbishop of Kraków, Karol Wojtyła, to the Sacred College of Cardinals in 1967, setting the stage for his election to the papacy in 1978.

Despite the establishment of a permanent working group for Polish-Vatican contacts in 1974, there was no formal agreement between the Vatican and the Polish government. Polish state president Edvard Ochab had even avoided visiting Pope Paul VI when he had come to Rome in April 1967 (in contrast to Podgorny two months before). Party chief Edvard Gierek corrected this omission ten years later (December 1, 1977) and told the pope of "the historical imperative of a patriotic unity beyond the difference of doctrines."[25] When, another ten years later (on January 13, 1987), party chief General Wojciech Jaruzelski paid a "historic visit" (as the pope described it) to the Vatican, this "unity" was exposed to a difficult trial. In the meantime, a trip by John Paul II to his Polish homeland in 1979—"an act of clear courage on both sides"[26]—had set in motion a domestic political revolution and had encouraged the great expectations unleashed by Solidarnośc in 1980–81, which, after the movement's dramatic defeat, were followed by deep disappointment. The essential function of the subsequent visit of the pope to Poland in 1983 was to console the Polish people. But the pope's third visit, in June 1987, discrepant in its sentimental and diplomatic challenge, could have unforeseen consequences.

Pope John Paul II's frequent travels throughout the world have enhanced the international weight of Vatican diplomacy, even in the eyes of communist regimes. This is expressed in more than the disciplinary actions and theological steps adopted within the church that struck at the political sensitivity of communist regimes, as, for example, a 1982 decree banning clerical membership in politically oriented priests' organizations or a 1984 instruction of the Congregation for Faith and Doctrine regarding liberation theology. The augmented attention East European regimes have paid to the Catholic church—in a negative sense, but also in a positive sense—confirms the growing prestige the Vatican won through its activity in the international arena in the 1980s.

A Vatican delegation led by Casaroli made substantial contributions to the contents of the Final Act of the Conference on Security and Cooperation in Europe (CSCE) in Helsinki in 1975. The delegation had insisted above all on the formulations on human rights which are contained in the so-called Basket 4. Afterward, when there was no further progress in making human rights obligations more precise at the First CSCE Verification Conference in Belgrade (1977–78), John Paul II, who had already come before the UN General Assembly in New York in this connection, made a personal appeal, on September 1, 1980, to all those assembled at the Second CSCE Verification Conference in Madrid: "Religious freedom guaranteed by law will serve to assure tranquility and the common welfare of every country and of every society."[27] After five sessions in three years, in which the Vatican collaborated and presented concrete problems (such as that of the suppressed Uniate church in the USSR and Romania), the Madrid conference arrived at a common closing document, which observed that "the participant states confirm that they recognize, respect, and will guarantee through appropriate measures, the freedom of the individual to confess a religion or a conviction in accord with the imperative of his conscience and to practise it—whether alone or in a community."[28] The states promised also to review the demands of religious communities for a legal statute "with benevolence."

Encouraged by this small success, the pope had Vatican Deputy "Foreign Minister" Backis introduce a new ten-point proposal before the Third CSCE Verification Conference in Vienna on January 30, 1987. The proposal names concrete means by which religious freedom may be expressed: the right of parents and families to religious education; the right of religious communities to train priests, build churches, print religious publications, enjoy access to the media, administer their own affairs, and maintain contact with their cobelievers and ecclesiastical superiors both domestically and abroad; and the right of all believers to equal status as citizens, without discrimination.[29] At a subsequent CSCE conference (Venice, February 2–6, 1988) Soviet representative Yuri Kashlev openly declared, for the first time, that the Leninist norms observed in religious policy over the previous seventy years will no longer be followed, while Vatican diplomat Faustino Sainz expressed the hope that a change in Moscow's religious policy will also benefit the 1.5 million Catholics living *outside* the Baltic republics, who have neither a bishop nor a seminary.

Insofar as the Vatican has made itself the spokesman for the interests of *all* religions,[30] and not merely of its own church, its Ostpolitik has assumed a wider dimension and a stronger underpinning. "If [military] security is indivisible, then so too is détente indivisible,"[31] which would include domestic peace and consequently détente between church and state. That also signifies that the flexibility and chance of success of Vatican pastoral diplomacy vis-à-vis communist states depend on the more general international situation. Lacking their own power resources, the popes can summon only their moral prestige and their proven ability to resist and adapt.

The wisdom of the Vatican's attitude in this regard was confirmed during Cardinal Casaroli's 1988 trip to Moscow. Not only did his talks with the Soviets clearly benefit from the new climate created by Gorbachev's *perestroika*, but Casaroli could openly express, in a public talk at Moscow's Bolshoi Theater, the pope's expectation "that the Soviet state's entire relationship toward religion will be infused in general by a new breath of air." The cardinal cited Gorbachev's announcement that Soviet legislation on religion would be changed,[32] and he recalled, in a diplomatically subtle way, that the modern world no longer accepts the principle *cuius regio eius religio* under which princes once arrogated to themselves the right to determine the faith of their peoples. Casaroli called on the Soviets to respect the "fact" of religion. "The realism of state demands it, and respect for humanity urges it." The cardinal delivered a memorandum to Gorbachev with the Vatican's wishes (which Gorbachev promised to review) and, on his return to Rome, described his Moscow trip as "a bridge across seventy years."[33]

16

Karol Wojtyła and Marxism

George H. Williams

It is at first puzzling to find that Karol Wojtyła's prepapal writings contain few explicit allusions to Marxism. Although he was already the author of some 1,490 items in seven languages at the time he was elected pope, there is not a single Marxist name or even an entry like "state," "society," "communism," or "collectivism" in the analytical index to his published prepapal bibliography.[1] Of course, there is much to recount of his action as prelate in a communist country, and it is possible in some of his works to peer through to the inner contours of Karol Wojtyła's thought as he came to grips with the communist disturbance of the Christian fabric of Polish society after it had already been tattered and slashed by the Nazis.

Student Days

Karol Wojtyła, son of an officer in the Austro-Hungarian army in World War I (the father's military record is still in the military archives in Vienna), knew some German even as a boy living in his native town of Wadowice. There he chose, on his own, to go not to the Catholic high school but to the municipal high school (*gimnazjum*), which still carried on the classical Austrian-German tradition. In the last year in the *gimnazjum* (the equivalent of education through freshman year in an American college), students in interwar Poland studied philosophy and other subjects that are spread out over four years in American colleges. A *gimnazjum* student was almost by definition one preparing for the university. In that thirteenth year of preuniversity instruction in Wadowice, Wojtyła read all of Immanuel Kant's *Critique of Pure Reason* in the original German. His class was presumably assigned only selections of it, but he chose to read the whole, and in German, as it had not yet been translated into Polish.[2]

When he matriculated at the Jagiellonian University in Kraków, it was in the Department of Slavic Languages and Literature. His studies required a knowledge of Old Church Slavonic, roughly the equivalent of studying Beowulf in Anglo-Saxon, except that this archaic Slavic is still the common liturgical language of the Byzantine rite of all Slavic peoples, Orthodox and Uniate. That is as near as he came to religion and philosophy in his single year as a university student in Kraków, which was brought to an end by the Nazis. The record does not reveal any more than his roles in the student theater and then in several underground theaters, notably in the Kraków Theater of the Living Word. This underground troupe had something of a religious component. Its dramaturgical theorist and director had a sense of the *mysterium tremendum et fascinosum*. Director Mieczysław Kotlarczyk had encountered that concept in Rudolf Otto's book *The Idea of the Holy* (published in German in 1917), and subsequently the leading actor in that troupe would use the words of Otto as prelate and as supreme pontiff.[3]

As a secret seminarian, still sleeping in his apartment by night and working by day in the Solvay Chemical Works in industrial Kraków, Wojtyła first encountered Thomism in a manual of metaphysics in the Neothomist, or transcendental Thomist, tradition of the school of Louvain, published at Lwów (now Lvov, part of the Soviet Ukraine). The author was the Reverend Professor Kazimierz Wais; his book, *Metafizyka* (published in 1924).[4] The pope himself, in a 1980 book-length interview with a French convert, Andrew Froissard, entitled *N'ayez pas peur*,[5] recollected this first encounter with metaphysics. His own words are precious reminiscences as he describes how he coped with the study of Thomism, central to even an underground seminary curriculum with scanty means and removed from normal accoutrements of study:

> From the beginning this was the obstacle. My literary education, centered in the humanities, absolutely did not prepare me for the scholastic theses and formulas that the Manual set before me from start to finish. I had to beat a trail through thick briars of concepts, of analyses and axioms, without even being able to identify the terrain over which I was making my way. After having hacked away for two months in the vegetation, there was a clearing, a discovery of the profound reasons for what I had as yet only experienced and felt intimations of. Presented for examination, I said to my examiner that in my opinion the vision of the world that I had made my own *conquise* in the Manual of metaphysics, body to body as it were, was much more precious than the mark which I had gotten. I was not ex-

> aggerating. What intuition and sensibility had taught me up to then about the world had been solidly confirmed.
>
> That discovery, which is at the basis of the structures of thought which are still mine to this day, is at the basis also of my essentially pastoral calling. Circumstances have never left me much time for study. By temperament I prefer thought to erudition. I was enabled to take account of that during my later career as professor at Kraków and Lublin. My conception of the person, "unique" in his identity, and of man as such at the center of the universe, was born of the experience and of sharing with others much more than with reading. Books, study, reflection, and discussion—that I do not flee as you know—help in formulating what experience teaches. In these two dimensions of my life and activity, the pastoral vocation carried the day over that of the professor and man of studies. This showed itself gradually ever more profoundly and more strongly but if the two vocations have distanced themselves from each other, there has never been a rupture between them.[6]

The pope returned to that manual in the same dialogue with Froissard in describing his opposition to positivism as a school of philosophy reduced to the common stance in much university life, in his Poland no less than in America. He continued,

> Important results have been obtained by the philosophy of religion on the level of the intellectual knowledge of God. This philosophy [specifically, phenomenology] uses another method than the philosophy of being. It grounds itself in the analysis of religious experience, thus taking account of human subjectivity. This type of analysis is particularly close to my thought. Here it concerns directly the knowledge of *God* and not only of *the Absolute* as in the purely metaphysical perspective proper to the philosophy of being. That does not prevent me from being convinced that the opening toward being and existence (more precisely toward being in the aspect of existence) remains an essential basis for the knowledge of God through reason.[7]

Karol Wojtyła's habilitation thesis was written to qualify him to be a seminary or university professor.[8] He always felt that he was primarily a pastor concerned with his flock, and the topic assigned to him was meant to appeal to his pastoral proclivities, his concern for ethical behavior, and possibly to make the most of his clear mastery of German. He was asked to write an assessment of the ethical system of the phenomenologist Max Scheler (1874–1928), a convert to Catholicism whose effort to establish the objective status of value and moral obligation represented for Catholics a possible improvement over Kant, while still taking seriously the Kantian *Critiques*[9] and ethical achievement.

To write the thesis Fr. Wojtyła read the whole of Scheler's principal works on ethics against the formal system of Kant. Kant interiorized ethics in the realm of consciousness, ordered by the internal forms or a priori principles. Scheler, an associate of Edmund Husserl, sought to establish the reliably objective status of value as "experienced" in the new epistemological procedure (in *Der Formalismus in der Ethik und die materiale Wertethik*, 1913/1916). Scheler's *Formalismus* was important in shaping Wojtyła's thought in that it presented ethics in the context of the emerging sociologies, in particular the sociologies of religion, in Hohenzollern Germany. In this book, which Wojtyła is said to have translated for his own use into Polish, there is much about the social context of ethics. Terms in the emerging discipline of sociology, itself influenced by Marxist categories for classes, society, community, association, group, caste, ethos, vocation, and so forth, abound in Scheler. Wojtyła's usage of these terms may reflect something of their specific Schelerian resonance or definition before they became standardized by the discipline (and possibly of Scheler's contemporary, Ferdinand Tönnies).

As is common with doctoral students, Wojtyła shared some of his inchoate thoughts with his students at Kraków and at the Catholic University in Lublin (KUL) in advance of the publication of his thesis. By chance, we get the best idea of what he was premising and then presupposing in most of his philosophical and ethical writings in a communist environment by overhearing his lectures as now published. KUL occupies a unique place among the universities of the People's Republic of Poland. This republic lost two cities with a long university tradition: Vilna and Lwów; and the theological faculties of the universities that survived within the Poland displaced westward by losses in the East and by annexations from Germany in the West were severed from the state universities by the new regime. This was in accordance with the principle of the full separation of church and state embodied in the Constitution of July 22, 1952. In Kraków and Warsaw a successful effort was made to establish self-subsistent faculties of theology. The only intact university in Poland with a faculty of theology and a faculty of canon law was the one established in Lublin in 1918. Its charter and basic library represent the displacement from Saint Petersburg of the faculty of a major center for Poles under tsarist Russia. This library has been so far expanded that it is generally regarded as the richest in humanistic holdings of any university in Poland; and it is the only university where, as once everywhere in Europe, the faculties still elect their own rector, His Magnificence, as he is ceremonially called, with the robe of a medieval prince of academe. Given the origin of KUL in what is now

Leningrad, its faculties could have felt, especially after the liberation of Lublin by Soviet armies in 1944, a special responsibility to engage in discreet dialogue with Marxism, since all students would have been obliged to study it in their equivalent of high school. Moreover, a state university dedicated to Marie Curie-Sklodowska was established in Lublin within sight of KUL with its own department of philosophy and subdepartment of Marxist philosophy. It is possible that Stefan Wyszyński, when he was bishop of Lublin, was wary of dialogue.[10]

Since Marxist-Leninist dialectial materialism was also a reaction to the philosophical idealism engendered by Kant, who had denied the accessibility of the mind to "things in themselves," Thomism at KUL could not but be conscious of its quite different assignment of also undoing Kant, but in the direction of upholding the possibility of objective truth and even with a new understanding of the *human act* (*actio hominis*) as distinguished from the involuntary or instinctive acts of man.[11] The redefinition of act, praxis, and hence of the person as sovereign was thus inevitably the center of concern in the philosophy and ethics of a Catholic university now holding out in a Poland that was officially Marxist. Even though Karol Wojtyła never expressly mentioned Marxism-Leninism, it would seem plausible that the agenda of transcendental Thomism at KUL was in polemical parallelism to the ambient dialectical materialism.

Wojtyła as Professor

In this remarkable setting in Lublin (the basic building is appropriately a former Dominican cloister with an ancient and beautiful chapel), Wojtyła was active from 1955 to 1957 as docent and eventually incumbent of the chair of ethics, although never with the title of professor ordinarius, at first because he had not completed his second thesis, and then, after becoming ordinary of Kraków, because he could only be present in Lublin part time. Recently we have come into possession of his three courses of lectures, not in the original Polish but in German translation.[12] The course titles in the three successive terms served are Act and Experience, The Good and Value, Norm and Happiness. On reading them, one would scarcely know that they were delivered to students in the faculty of arts and sciences, as we would say (actually the division [*widział*] of Christian philosophy) in a communist country. One would know only that the lecturer is a Catholic concerned with the demonstration of objective values, universal norms of behavior, and that the sovereign person is the instigator of responsible action, however much external forces are factored in to explain behavior. The name of Karl Marx is not heard, nor even some code name for communism. Yet here in these lectures we have the soil and the seeds out of which came the six papal encyclicals and several apostolic instructions to date of the pope from Poland. The three now accessible KUL courses also explain how the pope could in his pronouncements, and particularly in the encyclical on work, be almost evenhanded in his criticism of both capitalism and communism, the latter scrupulously called only "collectivism," although in his writings before becoming pope Karol Wojtyła also used "totalism," seldom "totalitarianism"—(*totalitario* as an adjective was first used by Benito Mussolini in 1925)—almost never "Marxism," and again never either "socialism" or "communism."

As a Catholic docent in the Poland of Primate Wyszyński, Karol Wojtyła had deep reasons for eschewing both "socialism" and "communism," in a tactic perhaps agreed upon by KUL in order to avoid co-optation in the course of dialogue. The Communist party in Poland is officially the United Workers' party. The older socialist parties were either eliminated or co-opted under communist hegemony, and the few Catholic deputies in the Polish Sejm became scarcely more than tokens. The distinction between socialism and communism had collapsed in Poland under Stalinist pressure.

Docent Wojtyła, avoiding "socialism" and "communism" as having in Poland the same sense, appears to have located in the term *utilitarianism* the roots both of Soviet-style materialist communism and of the materialist consumerist capitalism of the West.

In an early article concerning ethics, Wojtyła discussed the aspiration to perfection, an aspiration he called "perfectiorism," which, he said, has nothing of "normativism" in it.[13] He defined "perfectiorism" as progressively becoming better through every act, in contrast to the usual perfectionism, which suggests an attainment, a state of moral completeness. It is an ethical formulation related to the philosophy of being. In this article Wojtyła took Aristotle and Aquinas as representatives of the philosophy of being, the latter modifying the former with elements from Plato and Augustine, which makes possible a readier understanding of realistic participation in an ontological good by virtue of a personal decision and hence as conducive to perfectiorism. Against these two main figures are Kant and Scheler. In the article the author gave no hint that Scheler was the subject of the habilitation thesis to appear in published form in 1959. Clearly the article represented the author's effort to place the achievement and the deficiency of Scheler in a broad historical context. Scheler, according to Wojtyła, found in the subjective apriorism of Kant only a faint trace of the possibility of perfectiorism: in the categorical imperative and the sense of ought and duty. Although Scheler intended to uphold the objectivity of value outside consciousness over and against Kant, Wojtyła held that both represented a "philosophy of consciousness" rather than of being, and hence that perfectiorism was fully internalized in Kant and emotionalized, and hence confused, in Scheler without a *compelling* objective norm. In Scheler the act was so much more the effort of the will sustained by the emotion of love that there was in his system a positive rejection of Kant's duty as promotive of what Scheler pilloried as "Pharisaism"; but the Schelerian system remained defective, according to Wojtyła, precisely in not moving from the perception or intuition of the good in some winsome embodiment of it to the performance of a succession of good deeds that would be for Wojtyła the desirable perfectiorism.

Wojtyła's lectures on the British philosophers David Hume (1711–76) and Jeremy Bentham (1748–1832) stressed that they were exponents of a philosophy of consciousness and not of being and objective value. Their utilitarianism, which stressed the search for pleasure (Hume) and the achievement of "the greatest good for the greatest number" (Bentham), provided, according to Wojtyła, the theoretical underpinning for the practical materialism in free-enterprise economies and the seedbed for the dialectical materialism of Karl Marx and Friedrich Engels.[14] In this analysis Wojtyła agreed with Scheler.

But in pointing this out, one must note also that the young docent of ethics at KUL had so fully taken on the individualism of British liberalism, defined by him philosophically and politically as the sanction of laissez-faire capitalism, that in the midst of a society living under the canopy and by the directives of the same kind of materialism collectivized, he found himself engaged almost wholly in the reconception of individualism on a Thomist/Schelerian basis as phenomenological personalism. He defined this personalism as the sovereignty of each human *suppositum* (the language of Aquinas), that is, of each individual as substance or subject capable of responding to good or evil responsibly. This responsible personalism, in which the transcendent person is understood in a palpable succession of voluntary acts, whether internal or external, was inherently Christian and not solely phenomenological because it presupposed as given in experience that man, whether he knows why or not, has sufficient free will intact despite the Fall. It presupposed the restoration of the divine image in man through the Incarnation of the Eternal Word of God and hence also of a responsible will and the capability of heeding objective norms. The consequence of Wojtyła's affirmation of the sovereign person as liberated from the worst in his genesis or environment, whether in collectivist, capitalist, or primitive society, was that Wojtyła as ethicist seldom turned to the larger structures of society, except family and church.

He has not left us in his *prepapal* writings a social ethic, a social gospel derived from the Old Testament, an analysis of moral man and immoral society, reflections on the ironies of history and the ambiguities of the human condition, or an analysis of corporate or institutional guilt and a presentation of distinctive strategies for approximating public righteousness. He no doubt sympathized with Primate Wyszyński's spirited articulation of Catholic social thought and policy energized for the difficult situation of the church in Poland, but he does not appear to have reflected extensively on social policy as an ethicist. He ascetically adjusted to his wracked society as restructured by the party and stressed rather the perfectiorism of the sovereign person within the smaller collectivities, which he called communions or fellowships, the largest being the nation. The last, as a Pole of the People's Republic, he thought of primarily in terms of a racially, culturally, religiously, and by then also linguistically homogeneous community. For the multiracial and multiconfessional societies of the New World, like Brazil and the United States, "nation" (in the sense of a natural community of which one is a member) is less apposite; and in the case of states like Canada, South Africa, or East Germany, though for different reasons, almost invalid. In any case, the most frequently cited social grouping in the prepapal Wojtyła is the family.

The habilitation thesis on Scheler (published in Lublin in 1959) does not in itself belong to the account of Wojtyła's interpretation of communism. But a year later, in *Love and Responsibility* (published in Polish in 1960, in English in 1981), Wojtyła dealt expressly with the communities of married love (families) and of communities of ascetic nuptial or bridal love (monasteries and convents, and also other fellowships and households of celibate clerics). Turning from the basic ideas of the book, universally familiar in the pope's communications on sexual ethics,[15] one notes only that in the appendix to the book, "A Clarification of a Few Philosophical Terms," he included utilitarianism and several other terms and names, all with negative significance for the author. Several British movements, such as Puritanism and Malthusianism, figured conspicuously in the selection.

Wojtyła as Prelate

During the Second Vatican Council (1962–65), Karol Wojtyła, first auxiliary bishop and later archbishop of Kraków, was an ever more prominent participant. Because of his sonorous voice, with its now familiar cadence, he was chosen to bespeak the collective judgment of the Polish episcopate in the basilica. From near the start of the council it was agreed by all not to speak of communism by that name. There evolved various circumlocutions, depending on whether the fathers had in mind Marxism-atheism and the theory of religion as an epiphenomenon of class interest or Marxist economy and political policy. During the third period of the council,

Archbishop Wojtyła spoke on religious liberty in a way that anticipated his later focus (as pope) in his direct dealings with authoritarian states. On September 25, 1964, for instance, he said,

> This principle [of liberty] constitutes a fundamental right of religious man in society, which ought to be observed by all most strictly and especially by those who govern states. . . . For religion consists in the free adherence of the human mind to God, which is in all respects personal and conscientious: it arises from the desire for truth. . . . And with this relation the secular arm may not interfere, because religion itself by its nature transcends all things secular.[16]

Under the impact of the council and his interchange with the bishops from throughout the world over the four-year period, Archbishop Wojtyła published his major philosophical work, *Osoba i Czyn* (Kraków, 1969), published in English as *The Acting Person*, two years after his elevation to cardinal.[17] In the last chapter of this work, as well as in certain related articles, Wojtyła refined his distinction between the person as "a member of a community" and the person as "a neighbor." In his analysis, characteristically very spare in examples, he meant by "member" a participant in a natural or in a grace-ordered community, for example, the family, the parish, the nation. Wojtyła did not expressly mention the parable of the Good Samaritan, unique to Luke, because his analysis of the human act came in the context of a phenomenological inquiry. But it is clearly in this chapter that the future pope first set forth his idea of the global neighbor who acts humanely and even at risk to himself, reaching beyond his own community to a person or persons in need in another community. Wojtyła as ethicist, adhering to the incarnate Word revealed in the decisive earthly teacher of the ways of God, found in the neighbor of the Dominical parable something universal and profound about human nature, the savior person who, moved by natural grace, assumes responsibility for others. Although this elevation of the neighbor above the member of a community is only incidentally developed as a section of what the author seems to have regarded as an appendage to the main book, the idea would grow and mingle with his emphasis on one's being "a man for others," to impart to his Christian humanism or incarnational universalism a heightened individualism. The sovereign person converges in the servant, the man for others. The Good Samaritan, whom he called simply "the neighbor," was in *Osoba i Czyn* the authentic person over and against the blinding collectivities of class, caste, status, race, ideology, public opinion, and partisan loyalty.

At Vatican II the archbishop of Kraków was especially active in drafting the constitution on the church in the modern world, *Gaudium et spes*, and the decree on religious liberty. These and the other documents he came to interpret in book form for the implementation of them in his metropolitical province. Already in 1970, in an article for priests on a single section of *Gaudium et spes*, namely, section 2, one can see interesting evidence of the continuity of his pre- and postconciliar thought. The core of section 2 is as follows: "The *world* which the Council has in mind is the whole human family seen in the context of everything which envelops it: it is the world as the theater of human history, bearing the marks of its travails, its triumphs and failures, the world, which in the Christian vision has been created and is sustained by the love of its maker, which has been freed from the slavery of sin by Christ, who was crucified and rose again in order to break the stranglehold of *the Evil One*, so that it might be fashioned anew."[18] Without direct concern about censorship but with a view to tactful communication to priests, Wojtyła employed, evidently in reference to both the Anglo-American and the Marxist variant of materialism, the British philosophical term *utilitarianism*. He began his commentary on the passage in *Gaudium et spes*, section 2, with an allusion to 1 John 2: 15–17 about the three lusts (*concupiscentiae*): of the flesh, of the eyes, and the pride of life, all potentially within the front lines of the Evil One. He clearly made the second concupiscence, of the eyes, pride in, or lust for, knowledge; and it is very likely that he had in mind the scholastic systematization of these lusts as the *libido sentiendi, libido sciendi*, and *libido dominandi*. He insisted in his small piece that priests must persist in teaching about the *bonum in se*, which he acknowledged is easier for Catholics to discuss in theory than to promote in practice. He went on:

> Every good makes its appearance in the world not only through a variegated state of being ranked with respect to manifold strivings and needs but also it experiences—as a consequence of this correct ranking [a Schelerian motif]—its own alienation in relation to it. The essence of this alienation expresses itself *in all forms of utilitarianism*. It is by no means an abstraction but also an expression of real attitudes which man has at his disposition, as individual, and as a society. Utilitarianism denies the deepest objective value of everything in order, in place of the *bonum in se* [the good in and for itself], to leave only need and utility as the measure of value. [Utilitarianism asks] not what is kind or good in a given thing in its own right, but rather what its use is, what application can it have. Utilitarianism is a symptom of an attitude.[19]

Although he may well have lectured on one or two British utilitarians in KUL, Wojtyła would have known that the priests for whom he was writing in 1970 were not preoccupied with the rise of a British school of philosophy but rather with its materialistic consequences; and as long as he was addressing his fellow Polish priests in Polish, we must assume that he was using utilitarianism to refer both to the communist ethos and to the consumerist mentality he would soon so deplore on several visits to the West. The article of 1970 preserves a valuable testimony to the continuity in his thought between Lublin and Rome.

When he came to publish his systematic study of Vatican II in 1972, he no longer used the term *utilitarianism*. In *U podstaw Odnowy*,[20] an account of all the conciliar constitutions and decrees for the faithful living in a society structured by communism, the only allusion to the oppressive party and government is in his comment on *Lumen gentium*, section 13, where in reference to "the kingdoms of this world" the cardinal evokes the massive celebration in 1966 of the millenium of Christianity under Mary Queen of Poland.[21] Nor does he call for dialogue. In *Gaudium et spes* the council had encouraged dialogue with atheists, whether persons who had come to this position for want of the gift of faith or those who espoused systematic or organized atheism as an extension of ideological policy. Where Wyszyński was dead set against any dialogue except at the very top—i.e., between the hierarchy and the highest officers of the state—Wojtyła merely ends the relevant chapter in *U podstaw Odnowy* with the conciliar call to dialogue, without appending any comment of his own.

In any case, Cardinal Wojtyła had fully appropriated Wyszyński's tactics, which were based on the primate's conviction that in the long run Catholicism in Poland could escape dismemberment in the grip of communist ideology only by keeping intellectuals, workers, and farmers united, by keeping priests out of politics, and by avoiding the dissipation of Catholic strength and solidarity in Poland that would allegedly issue from dialogue with Marxist theorists of social justice. This was no doubt one reason for the primate's discontinuance of the Polish edition of *Concilium*, with its many Third World and ecumenical articles sometimes open to Marxist critique of the institutional church. In a siege situation only the duly authorized were permitted to parley with the foe, not clubs of Catholic intellectuals, and not parish priests.[22]

In the synod of bishops in 1974, which was devoted to the theme "Evangelization of the World," Wojtyła was responsible for a major address on that subject. In this he devoted a whole section to "The Notion of the World," citing again *Gaudium et spes*, section 2. Herein he distinguished three meanings of "world," noting right off that this constitution on the church *in* the modern world had a different preposition from that in the theme of the synod, "*of* the world."[23] He acknowledged that both meanings were valid. One meaning was that of the world potentially restored in what has been called the incarnational universalism of the council. This incarnational universalism was based ultimately on St. Irenaeus of Lyons and his doctrine of the recapitulation of the race by the second Adam in the incarnation of the Eternal Word and in the teachings and example of Jesus Christ.

Then the cardinal distinguished a third meaning, the world as human flesh, overweening technology, and ideological *superbia*, a "world" still partially in the grip or under the temptation of the Evil One. He developed at some length his idea of "the anti-Gospel," of "anti-evangelization," and spoke of Christ, perhaps for the first time, anticipating his later Lenten retreat theme and book, as "the sign of contradiction" (Luke 2:34) coming into this world of the three *libidines* (cf. 1 John 2:16). He named in a general way one form of the anti-Gospel—the "anthropocentrism" that puts man in the place of God and the existentialism of Jean-Paul Sartre.

In mentioning Sartre, the cardinal knew that he was dealing with a particularly attractive form of sophisticated atheism which had something in common with Marxism. Sartre had written *Existentialism Is a Humanism* (1946),[24] only to abandon that humanist view later, in growing pessimism about the human condition, underlining life's utter meaninglessness. Subsequently, Sartre wrote his *Critique of Dialectical Reason* (1960),[25] an attempt to reconcile existentialism and Marxism; but in the end he perceived the inevitability of ongoing conflict among men even in "classless society." His erstwhile existentialist ally, Merleau-Ponty, a phenomenologist, eventually broke with Sartre. Merleau-Ponty wrote a critique of Marxist theory and the policy of the French Communist party in particular. Wojtyła's own interest in phenomenology made him appreciate Merleau-Ponty's critique of Sartre and the current of Marxism among French intellectuals.[26]

In the aforementioned synodal address of 1974, Wojtyła subsumed Sartrean existentialism and Marxism under the generic label *atheistic anthropocentrism*. This was in exegeting a conciliar text (*Gaudium et spes*) at the very place where in 1970 he still used utilitarianism (above at note 19). Although the latter term had for the cardinal already lost much of its philosophical resonance, still such a precise point for its disappearance and its studied replacement serves as a marker in the evolving stages of his social critique.

Wojtyła had at least three occasions in 1976 to set forth in other contexts his idea of the anti-Gospel in an ever more explicitly eschatological framework. In the Lenten retreat before Pope Paul VI and the curial prelates, Wojtyła made the already noted passage in Luke 2 the basis of his meditations that come to us in book form as *Sign of Contradiction*. In it he evoked the sequence of Easter Sunday about the "wondrous duel between life and death" in the world and referred to the struggle against Christ on the part of the anti-Word and the anti-gospel.[27] He mentioned Marxists by name only three times.

In the first statement he said that "today one cannot understand [the radical denials of] Sartre or Marx without having read and pondered very deeply the first three chapters of Genesis." The other two references were in meditations where he brought out the sharing in the *munus regale* of Christ, not only by priests but also by laypersons, their kingly character of office as set forth in *Gaudium et spes*, section 36. His comment followed: "It is a superb text! It certainly deserves to be read and interpreted in the light of contemporary anthropology, social ethics, and economics. Any analysis of it must take into account the whole philosophical tradition, beginning with Aristotle. . . . Marxist philosophy especially . . . puts 'praxis' before 'theory' and deduces all its explanations of reality—especially the reality of man—from that 'praxis,' i.e., to say from the work by which man 'created himself within nature.'" Already in reference to the same council text he had said earlier in the retreat:

> The Anti-Word does not stop there [with the forgetfulness of God]. It goes further still. . . . The concept of alienation as formulated by Marx . . . has been applied to religion: . . . religion has an alienating function. To alienate means, here, to de-humanize. By professing and practising religion, man deprives himself of his own right to this humanity and ascribes all prerogative to God, that is to say to a concept of his own devising—thus subordinating himself to one of his own products![28]

Of course, Wojtyła's view during the retreat was that Marxist collectivism subordinates man to his work in general and deprives him of freedom. We see here the seed of a whole section of the later encyclical on work.

Although this is the only direct reference to the ideology of his native land—one could scarcely expect more at a Lenten retreat—the cardinal persevered in reproducing his more comprehensive thought about utilitarianism as the common basis of both capitalist consumerism and communist collectivism. In his conclusion he dealt in succession with "the program of consumerism" without "transcendental ends," which desires "to reshape" Christ, opposing him while "paying him lip-service." Then he moved to the other form of materialism and noted that it springs from the same philosophical roots, which, without the knowledge of what we have been pursuing in his thought, might escape notice:

> Yet that [consumerism] is not the only form of contradiction of Christ. Alongside what can be called "indirect contradiction"—and inciden-

> tally there are many variations on it, many shades and blends—alongside that there is another form of contradiction *probably* arising out of the same historical basis as the first one—and therefore more or less a result of that first one. It is a form of direct opposition to Christ, an undisguised rejection of the Gospel, a flat denial of the truth about God, man and the world as proclaimed by the Gospel. This denial sometimes takes on a brutal character.[29]

In the Lenten retreat before Paul VI, Wojtyła thus continued the thematic approach of his KUL lectures: capitalism and Marxism have a common philosophical root—utilitarianism.

Wojtyła attended the World Eucharistic Congress in Philadelphia in 1976. At the end of his extended visit, during which he worked on the American edition of his *The Acting Person*, he spoke at Harvard University on alienation, and in New York, in a farewell address, he spoke to combined representatives of the Polish American Congress and the Polish American Clergy Association. The theme we have been pursuing in his thought became in New York sharper and more eschatological in urgency: "We are now standing in the face of the greatest historical confrontation between the Church and the Anti-Church, of the Gospel versus the Anti-Gospel." He intimated, however, that the New World was perhaps almost as much "the new Babylon" as the Marxist empire of the proletariat.[30]

Earlier he had been phenomenological rather than eschatological in his lecture "Participation or Alienation?" in Emerson Hall at Harvard University, on July 27, 1976.[31] This communication did not have any reference to the common roots of two kinds of materialism in the modern world, as in the Lenten retreat, nor any of the eschatological language of Gospel and anti-Gospel of both the Lenten retreat and the New York farewell to Polish Americans. But it did have the distinction of employing in the title the term "alienation" and of dealing substantially with a term and concept (*Entfremdung*) that, while as old as the Greek and Latin of Christian civilization, had acquired its special significance in relation to class alienation as progressively defined in the writings of Karl Marx during the years 1843–46 against the Young Hegelians, the French Socialists, and the British utilitarians and the economists of classical liberalism. The lecture had, moreover, the distinction of actually citing a contemporary Polish Marxist writer, Adam Schaff, with specific pagination.[32]

As in so much of the writing of the prepapal Wojtyła, the center of discussion was the person as sovereign from the Thomist-phenomenological point of view. "Personalism" is a major entry in the index of his cited *Scritti*. I might add that in this lecture Wojtyła in fact presupposed what he had worked out in his *Osoba i Czyn*, which would not become available in

English until February 1979. He proceeded on the basis of the free will of the sovereign person. But this person is not best understood as an isolated individual with sovereignty thus described and located. For such a person, "participation" in "the other I" is "a duty."[33] He contrasted this "impulse from within" in spontaneity, here following Scheler, to the "closing of the subject concerning 'the others.'" These others are neighbors in Wojtyła's high sense, based upon Christ's parable (Luke 10:29–37) and the related injunction ("love thy neighbor as thyself," Matthew 19:19), which one's partner in dialogue acknowledges naturally, though he may not acknowledge the source.[34] Wojtyła again expressly singled out Sartre. For Wojtyła, alienation was (in his Harvard lecture) the isolation of one nonparticipatory in the immediate community and in the global neighborhood. He turned from this rather specialized modern formulation to sum up the Marxist view rather clearly:

> According to Marxist philosophy, man is alienated by his own creations: the economic and political systems, property ownership, and labor. Marx had included religion in that concept, too. And so, a conclusion is drawn that it suffices to transform the world on the level of those creations, to change the economic and political system, undertake the struggle against religion—and the era of alienation will end, and there will come "the kingdom of liberty," that is, a full self-realization for everyone and all together. However, some contemporary Marxists rightly draw attention to the fact that various forms of alienation are not overcome in that way, and in fact, new ones arise, which in turn need to be overcome.[35]

On the level of personal relations, the lecturer deplored the unnecessarily individualistic ultimate pessimism and nonparticipation of Sartre and the wholly collectivist alienation of Marx and asserted that in its most fundamental meaning, as in classical usage, alienation is a personal experience, not that primarily of a collectivity or class of such a community: "Alienation is the negation of participation. It cannot [in its most profound sense] be linked to the world of human creations, production of structures."[36]

One need not follow parallels to, and slight developments of, the distinctively Wojtyłan fusion of Western and communist social and experiential malaise, whether individual or group alienation, except to mention in passing a program he initiated to cope with the sense of nonparticipation, especially of the young in the hostile environment of an officially communist land. At the synod of bishops in Rome in 1977, with its theme of catechizing, he described in considerable detail a project that had all the marks of having also originated with him in Poland, though it was of universal scope. This was the movement Light and Life as an instrument for the renewal and maintenance of the faith in Poland. The development of what were called "oases," transcending parochial lines, suggested the idea of nurture and solidarity for young people growing up in the desert of communism, drawing living waters with the aid of youth leaders under the direction of priests in the stony wilderness of Marxist materialism.

In 1977 Wojtyła was in Milan to deliver a lecture, by implication critical of the Marxist theory of culture—"The Problem of Culture Constituting Itself through Human Praxis"—in which, distinguishing between the transitive and the intransitive in the human act,[37] he sought to safeguard a large degree of autonomy and freedom of input of the person precisely in the realm of labor and the means of production, all suggested by the term *praxis* prominent in Marxist social theory. He sought to lay bare the springs of human creativity in the realm of economic toil and to interpret civilization as the accumulation of acts of individual initiative and culture as a common legacy, at least partly independent of politicoeconomic structures.

Supreme Pontiff

There is a remarkable continuity in the thought and policy of Wojtyła as cardinal and of Wojtyła as pope. But now, as supreme pontiff, he is obliged to deal with communist states throughout the world, from North Korea to Nicaragua, and to come to grips with revolutionary movements. In his inaugural encyclical, *Redemptor hominis*,[38] Pope John Paul II addressed the issue of personal and ideological atheism, once more linking the two kinds of materialism with their common root. "The map of the world's religions," he observed, "has superimposed on it, in previously unknown layers typical of our time, the phenomenon of atheism in its various forms, beginning with atheism that is programmed, organized and structured as a political system." In this section (no. 11), which is devoted to intrafaith ecumenism and to dialogue with atheists, the conciliar word "dialogue" is not used.

Turning from Europe, of which the pope feels more self-consciously a part than perhaps any of his Italian predecessors, we see him dealing with an extraordinary problem in China, where religions were recently given a new lease on life, but where the party compelled local Catholics to break off ties with the Vatican. On his visit to Manila in February 1981, while nominally addressing Filipino Catholics of Chinese extraction, he declared all of China to be under Mary as Queen of Heaven.[39] John Paul II has been watchful of the church in Vietnam; its independence is threatened as in China. Yet he also has called fervently for the reunification of the two Koreas, and his visit there may have helped in the subsequent relaxation of tension between the North and the South. From the French Revolution through the Russian Revolution to the Maoist Revolution and the revolutions in Central America and elsewhere, again it is not primarily the legitimate social and economic changes the pope opposes as much as the programmatic displacement of theology by ideology and the resort to violence. As much as his three immediate predecessors, John Paul II is concerned with peace on earth and the progress of nations. Deeply committed to rapid social change with justice for all, he probably acknowledges that his revulsion from violence is visceral as well as ethical and theological. He lived too long in Kraków within range of the screams of terror by night and then by day, himself personally a victim of violence at the hands of Nazi ideology. And his close watch from within the People's Republic of Poland as prelate, and from without as pope, of day-to-day communism, with its sometimes refined but enervating coercions, makes him by profession an ethicist, by papal office *doctor omnius* on universal moral norms, a heeded authority on personhood and violence. His encyclical on the divine richness of mercy, *Dives in misericordia* (November 1980), is one of his fresh approaches to the phenomenon that he knows so well in human nature and human collectivities. So cognizant is he of violence against his own person, of violence everywhere engendering violence, that he may well become the supreme interpreter in some future communication on the psychology, the sociology, and even the theology of violence, that grave manifestation of original sin that prompted Cain out of resentment to slay even his brother Abel. The pope is not a social or political restorationist in the European sense of the word.

The near-fatal attempt on the pope's life in Rome by Mehmet Ali Agca on May 13, 1981, was widely considered at the time to be the indirect work of the secret police in Bulgaria, heeding a higher authority. But neither this attempt on his life nor the second attempt by a disgruntled priest in Portugal exactly a year later has deflected John Paul II from seeking to reconcile peoples and classes.

The linkage of the two kinds of materialism (capitalist/consumerist and communist/collectivist) becomes explicit in the third encyclical, *Laborem exercens* (September 14, 1981). Here, the pope stressed the "error of economism," "an error of materialism" that developed in "the economic and social practice . . . of the time of the birth and rapid development of industrialization" within "the philosophy and economic theories of the eighteenth century."[40] The pope therewith made clear the time but not the place, which was, of course, Great Britain, scene of the first stages of the Industrial Revolution. The philosophers he most clearly had in mind were, as we know from his KUL lectures, Hume and Bentham. The pope's presupposed but never fully stated view of the common root error of both economic systems and the ethos and the ethics of the two kinds of societies explains how it is possible in *Laborem exercens*[41] for him to write about the errors of economism in such a way that it is not always certain whether the references are to the East or the West or even to the Southern Hemisphere. What emerges could even be construed as theoretical approval of the pragmatic mixed economy and federal political structure in Yugoslavia across the Adriatic from where the pope penned, initially in Polish, this third encyclical. But surely he was thinking very much of Solidarity, which the first pilgrimage to his native land in 1979 had called forth. The twenty-one points of the Program of Solidarity of August 1980 were undoubtedly close to his ideal for countries of the degree of industrialization and general culture of his native land, even to his point that workers should not be identified with any one party.[42]

Within the historical context set forth by the pope, and also within the known ideobiographical context of the author himself, it is evident that the pope feels that Britain was the first country to break with the *traditional* collectivity of European society, the first to permit the closing off of the commons for the benefit of the agricultural entrepreneurs, the first to legitimate the deracination and exploitation of workers, including children, in the even more complicated and strenuous concentrations of labor in mines and factories. As he used to say in the classroom, utilitarianism sanctioned the conceptual distance between this labor and the capital, defined not only as the money but also as the physical means of production. No papal document has ever stated so clearly as *Laborem exercens* what Karl Marx and Friedrich Engels thought out; namely, that capital is congealed labor. The pope took cognizance of the fact that the polarization of the two became the foundation both for the economic acerbation of the plight of the working classes and the eventual political assuagement of this by the Liberal (and eventually the Labour) party in Britain. These first mitigations had not concealed for Marx the evidence of class conflict and of what he considered the evidence of culture and religion as the epiphenomena of class control of capital. The pope, in any case, was quite forthright in speaking of "the ethically just social reaction" to "the error of materialism," to "practical materialism"[43] on the part of workingmen organized eventually in their own party in Britain, and to "the ethically motivated reaction" even on the part of fundamental theorists like Marx and Engels.

But the failure of Marxism, or collectivism, as the pope continues to call it, is that the management of capital in collectivization represents simply the replacement of exploitative owners by scarcely less demanding and callous state-appointed managers. The Soviet system and its replications amount only to state capitalism that further exacerbates social alienation and inhibits authentic participation. At the same time, evolved (managerial) capitalism, which on a small scale and in certain countries is indeed susceptible of amelioration of working conditions, of the enlistment of worker participation in ideas, techniques, and benefits, can end up on a large scale with indifference to domestic workers and the unfair exploitation of the whole citizenry of developing countries by keeping their chief raw materials artificially cheap. This trend toward the disadvantagement of both domestic workers in the "home" country and unfair exploitation of the common heritage of foreign peoples is especially true of the supranational corporations. In any case, common to both collectivism and capitalism is the assumption of the priority of capital over work, of products over people. The whole encyclical is a stirring call to reinstate the priority of labor over capital and to reaffirm the priority of the working person—broadly defined to include almost every adult in society—over his or her work, all together participating "at the common workbench."

John Paul II is inclined to write greater proportions of his encyclicals and other communications on faith and morals than did his predecessors, who in general indicated the broad lines of what was desired and left it to staffs of specialists to draft the actual document, to be reviewed and modified by the pontiff in question, before ultimately being translated into Latin. John Paul II, who is interested in the natural sciences and the implications of technology for peace and war, and who has given a wide range of themes to his Pontifical Academy of Sciences to work over, does nevertheless more openly seek out assistance in the natural sciences from specialists, in recognition of his having been exposed as a youth, seminarian, and professor primarily to the humanistic, philosophical, and theological disciplines. In ethics, where he was long an academic professional, he still tends to be more personalist than structuralist or institutionalist. Insight into institutional racism, institutional sexism, and other problems built into North American corporate life and Latin American societies may not yield to his more personalistic and individualistic approach, which was grounded in incarnational universalism and given specificity in his moving appeals to regeneration and conversion away from oppressive collectivity of all kinds. His repeated summons to redress, on a large scale, the economic imbalance between the Northern and the Southern hemispheres testify to the fact that he is earnest and hopeful in this personalistic approach to social injustice.

John Paul II knows that in dealing with communism as the established ideology and political economy of a given state, he must act by diplomacy and thereby attempt to mitigate the policies of the given authorities in such societies. As for such states in Europe, we may take note of the pope's reiterated concern for "the unity of the continent of Europe."

Although geographically this continent from Ireland to the Urals is a modern conceptualization, John Paul II, as a native of Poland, does attach unusual importance to it. One of his first enunciations of the ideal occurred in Gniezno in June 1979, and his fullest articulation of it was his address before the king of Spain and the European Episcopal Conference assembled in Santiago de Compostela in November 1982. In the meantime, on December 30, 1980, he had elevated Saints Cyril and Methodius to the rank of copatrons of Europe with Saint Benedict.[44] This preoccupation with a spiritually united Europe does have bearing on his thought, particularly his policy with respect to communist states and Eurocommunist parties.

The pope, facing the Kremlin, is ever aware that the Polish-Lithuanian commonwealth once stretched from Kraków to far beyond Kiev. By the Synod of Brest-Litovsk of 1596, a large percentage of the Orthodox of the eastern two-thirds of that vast realm, ruled first from Kraków and then from Warsaw, had become Uniates. In a Uniate sobor in Soviet Lvov (formerly Polish Lwów, where in the Catholic cathedral in 1648 King John Casimir, a former cardinal, made his vows to the Black Madonna as the queen of Poland amidst war and treason), Josef Stalin imposed a decision in 1946 that all Uniates within the territories annexed from eastern Poland submit to the jurisdiction of the Orthodox patriarch of Moscow. John Paul II longs for a united, Christian Europe, united in spirit and united through a pan-European episcopal conference with a permanent office in Switzerland. It would appear that he has something different in mind from the old Uniate formula. Perhaps he is interested in helping to breathe life into the Patriarchal church of Moscow-Zagorsk and in encouraging it by example and otherwise to act less subserviently toward the state apparatus. He knows that even seventy years after the revolution millions in the Soviet Union are still Christians. His would appear to be an ecumenical Ostpolitik.

There has been further evolution of the diplomatic Ostpolitik under John Paul II, with intense concern for world peace, nuclear freeze, and nuclear disarmament, as well as for concordats with Poland and Hungary. The pope sent a distinguished papal delegation headed by a layman to confer with Leonid Brezhnev on nuclear peace. Brezhnev received the delegation for two hours and urged that there be more exchanges of this kind. The pope also sent two personal representatives each time to the state funerals of Leonid I. Brezhnev (1982), Yuri V. Andropov (1984), and Konstantin Chernenko (1985).

As primate of Italy, the pope has special responsibilities in the republic. He fully dissociated himself from the Christian Democratic party, the special ally of his predecessors. He speaks out on moral issues in the Republic of Italy as any primate would, but he also is friendly with the many communist mayors and provincial governors of the republic. His restraint and even occasional humor when dealing with Eurocommunist leaders reflects not only prudence but also civil respect. His deeply held conviction about incarnational universalism makes it possible for him to address communist officials, whether Italian or French or from the diplomatic corps, with a humaneness and sense of our common humanity and without the slightest compromise of his deeply held view that Marxism-Leninism is oppressive to the human spirit.

John Paul II picked up his theme of the unity of Europe on a February 1984 visit to Bari in Apulia, where the relics of Saint Nicholas of Myra are preserved in the basilica, accompanied by the Orthodox incumbent of that see. Noting that Saint Nicholas had been revered "throughout the centuries also among the people of Russia," he declared that "Europe, Eastern Europe as well as Western Europe, cannot understand itself—hence, cannot understand the meaning of its history, the importance and significance of the revolutions that have upset it and of the ideologies that have left their marks in the wake of its history—if it prescinds from the tragedy of the mutual estrangement between Rome and Constantinople."[45]

As the Reformation and revolutionary Marxism rose first in the heartland of Europe, so did the first adumbration of liberation theology, although it is now widely associated with the Third World, particularly with Latin America. The Vatican came to grips with Marxism in Catholic accoutrements in a document prepared by the prefect of the Sacred Congregation for the Doctrine of the Faith, Josef Cardinal Ratzinger, previously archbishop of Munich, entitled *Instruction on Certain Aspects of the Theology of Liberation* (August 6, 1984).[46] Besides citing addresses from John Paul II in Latin America, it draws upon several of the most important of Wojtyła's works that were written while he was archbishop of Kraków. In the case of the *Instruction*, to be sure, the pope delegated the composition to Cardinal Ratzinger and his twelve fellow cardinals (among them the conservative Alfonso Trujillo Lopez, archbishop of Medellín). But Wojtyła's initiative and even vocabulary and cadence must have been already part of the original drafts. The liveliness of direct discourse still pulsates through the document.

The *Instruction* has the monitory urgency of Cardinal Cajetan in dealing with Luther in Augsburg in 1518. It reminds one too of the first papal encyclical in a vernacular language, also addressed to totalitarianism, *Mit brennender Sorge* (With burning concern), directed by Pius XI to be read from all pulpits in Nazi Germany on Palm Sunday in 1937, two years before Germany's invasion of Poland. The *Instruction* is drafted in a forceful style that is also elevated and sophisticated, often cast in the future tense with anguish and alarm. It registers the degree to which the Sacred Congregation for the Doctrine of the Faith regards Latin America, which holds nearly half of the population of the Catholic world, as in the throes of a possible *triple* revolution.

In a pan-Christian context the *Instruction* clearly expresses fear that the unnamed leadership of the different liberation theologies, and specifically that theology called "a system," with its own evolving institutions and vocabulary,[47] while professing to be scriptural and Catholic, is on the point of promoting something analogous to the Protestant revolt of the sixteenth century, this time belatedly in the Hispanic world, which had earlier escaped the Reformation. Liberation theology now threatens to move in a radical Protestant direction reminiscent of Puritanism, that is, laic, congregational, and even communitarian but under the estimable banners of the church of the poor, of the church as the ongoing people of God in history, of the people's church, seen by the South American theological leadership as liberating. This, however, is seen by the *Instruction* as eventuating in the co-optation and absorption of the Christian impulse for social service by the revolutionary leadership in Latin America (and elsewhere) and hence in a renewed ideological servitude of the masses.

With the analogy of a Protestant revolt in Hispanic Christendom, the drafters of the *Instruction* are nevertheless confident, without any allusion to non-Catholics, that Luther's proclamation of salvation by faith and freedom from the Law, recovered from St. Paul, is today the common ground of all Christians. In fact, "the Law" now becomes, in this intensely argued document, "the scientific principles of Marxism": (1) the "law of history," (2) the "law of the struggle of the classes," and (3) "the relativization and contextualization of truth."[48]

Against this allegedly inexorable law of class conflict the *Instruction* interposes canon law and the authority of the universal Magisterium in spirited assertion of the divine Transcendence. But whereas Luther pointed to that transcending above all institutions, including the church, in his programmatic distinction between justification by faith and the follow-up sanctification ("righteous works"), an unacceptable distinction to Catholic theologians in his time, the *Instruction* seeks to take the lead in the ecumenical struggle to preserve the essentials of the common Christian heritage.

The *Instruction* is also, though not expressly, set against any Latin American replication of the Protestant social gospel of North America of the late nineteenth and early twentieth centuries, which, mitigating the excesses of capitalism, also cast its message sometimes in fervid messianic, millennialist, and progressivist-utopian terms and with optimism about the advent of the Kingdom, an eschatological note absent from the great papal encyclicals on social distributive justice. The document fully acknowledges that theologians of liberation "deserve credit in Latin America [and elsewhere] for restoring to a place of honor the great texts of the prophets and of the Gospel in the defense of the poor" and makes an authentic acknowledgment of corporate and collective sin—the first in magisterial teaching since Marx and Freud drew attention to the many religious disguises of class interests and many rationalizations, personal and collective, of fundamental human drives—in such phrases as "structures which conceal poverty and which are themselves forms of violence [and] generate violence."[49] At the same time the *Instruction* puts the emphasis on personal sin. Indeed, phrasing in the introduction perpetuates a distinction between "liberation from servitude" and "liberation from sin," the latter said to be given secondary importance by liberation theologians.

The *Instruction* holds that the extremists in liberation theology have turned the church of the poor into a congregation of the proletariat (as that class was once defined by Marx, in a capitalist rather than in a precapitalist society, as in most of the Third World), and thus have sought to turn the church of the people of God into the church of a spurious class.[50] Thus the *Instruction* sets itself against the penetration into the very interior of the church of the syntax, terminology, and even the social perceptions of Marxism, of an utterly alien system of inevitable totalitarianism, though this word is eschewed in the document. This is perhaps the most spirited Vatican directive to appear in the twentieth century.

In celebration of the eleventh centenary of the death of Methodius, who, together with his brother Cyril, set out from Thessalonica to begin the Christian mission among the Moravian Slavs, John Paul II issued his fourth encyclical, *Slavorum apostoli* (Apostles of the Slavs) in July 1985. Already declared copatrons of Europe with Saint Benedict, they were seen by the Slavic pope as precursors of ecumenism, embodiments of Christian unity, and models for the process of Christian inculturation. Although he called Constantinople and Rome in the ninth century "sister Churches," he made it clear that then, as now, Rome was "the visible center of the Church's unity." Although in the encyclical there is much in praise of the way in which the Slavic missionaries "adapted to the mentality and customs of the new peoples" and "unceasingly promoted and extended" the indigenous culture, as well as awareness of the fact that linguistically and culturally "the heritage of the brothers from Salonika . . . remains for the Slavs [Latin, Uniate, and Orthodox] deeper and stronger than any division," there is little suggesting how by analogy Christians East and West can cope with the secular and the Marxist presuppositions in their societies. But, perhaps for the first time, the pope went beyond confessional, cultural, and economic concepts of the unity of Europe when he concluded:

"By exercising their own charism, Cyril and Methodius made a decisive contribution to the building of Europe not only in a Christian religious communion but also to its *civil* and cultural union. Not even today does there exist any other way of overcoming and repairing the divisions and antagonisms both in Europe and in the world."[51]

John Paul addressed himself directly, though not centrally, to Marxism in his fifth encyclical. In *Dominum et vivificantem* (The Lord and Giver of Life), issued for the feast of Pentecost in 1986, the pope had in mind primarily the preparation of Christians and the world for the jubilee year 2000. This great theological disquisition on the Holy Spirit (declared consubstantial with the Father and the Son at the ecumenical council of Constantinople in 381) passes by the once-vexed issue between the East and the West, the *filioque*—the Latin addendum to the Creed of Nicaea as strengthened by Constantinople—in order to place the teaching at the highest ecumenical level. Within this very broad context the pope turned to criticize that form of philosophical and ideological materialism that is most opposed to all that is said elsewhere in the teaching:

> The system which has developed most and carried to extreme practical consequences this form of thought, ideology and praxis is dialectical and historical materialism, which is still recognized as the essential core of Marxism. Though it sometimes also speaks of the "spirit" and of "questions of the spirit," as for example in the fields of culture and morality, it does so only insofar as it considers certain facts as derived from matter (epiphenomena), since according to this system, matter is the one and only form of being. It follows . . . that religion can only be understood as a kind of "idealistic illusion" *to be fought* with the most suitable means and methods according to circumstances of time and place, in order to eliminate it from society and from man's very heart.[52]

In no other pronouncement at such a level of authority has John Paul II warned so severely and explicitly against Marxism and all its guises and embodiments, while in this encyclical, in contrast to his inaugural encyclical, he refrained from directly identifying the utilitarian materialism that in his mind is associated with secularism and consumerism. The sixth encyclical, *Redemptoris mater* (The Mother of the Redeemer), promulgated for Pentecost 1987 to mark the beginning of the Marian Year, is not wholly an intra-Christian teaching, for in it Mary is described in the language of Vatican II as the one who always "precedes" the church and may prepare non-Christian peoples for Christian teaching. In an expressly ecumenical invitation, the pope addressed himself to the Russian Orthodox, observing that during the Marian Year, "there will occur the millennium of the baptism of Saint Vladimir, grand duke of Kiev (988)." And tracing briefly the spread of Christianity as a result of that conversion "as far as the northern territories of the Asian continent," he expressed the intention of joining "in prayer with all those who are celebrating . . . both Orthodox and Catholics."[53]

Although *L'Osservatore Romano* had editorialized favorably on the accession of Mikhail Gorbachev as general secretary of the CPSU,[54] and although the pope is known to have wanted to celebrate the millennium with the patriarch, if not in once-Polish Kiev then at least in Zagorsk or in the Danilovsky monastery in Moscow, splendidly refurbished as the patriarchal seat, the reaction to the allusion to the millennium in the Soviet press was prompt and negative.[55] John Paul II, like all his pontifical predecessors since the Marian epiphany in Fatima at the time of the Russian Revolution, has on several occasions considered the public and solemn dedication of Russia to the Immaculate Heart of Mary.[56] Although he has made progressively more specific embraces of the Soviet people, such a dedication has always seemed in the end politically imprudent, and ecumenical sensibility and diffidence also impose themselves, as the pope is aware of the millions of Christians—Orthodox, but also Lutheran, Baptist, and others—stretching from Vilnius to Vladivostok. The scope, depth, and passion of the Marian encyclical can thus be seen as a powerful initiative of John Paul II in rallying Christians everywhere to the proletariats of the world, to the poor, and to the poor in spirit.

The pope's Ostpolitik is in effect a continuation of Pope Paul's efforts to come to terms with the governments of communist states and obtain religious freedom among them by negotiation and exhortation without concession. It is part of the pope's more general view that the church is the principal defender of the fundamental rights of man, which he expressed in May 1985 in a speech marking the ninth centenary of the death of Pope Gregory VII Hildebrand, defender of the independence of the universal church against the claims of Emperor Henry IV. He said that the church requires from the state "the right to preach the faith in complete freedom" and "to give its own moral judgment about political realities when the issues of fundamental human rights or the salvation of souls is at stake."[57]

The pope has continued to espouse the need for a spiritually united Europe, appealing in May 1987 for cultural and religious unity from "the Atlantic to the Urals," and condemning curbs on the practice of religion everywhere.[58] For John Paul II, the polarization between those states which oppress religion and those which permit religious organizations to operate freely is more fundamental than divisions between political blocs, economic groupings, or other collectivities.[59] He is a restorationist in the civil realm of global neighbors of the ideals of the Charter of the United Nations. He calls all sides to think what they really mean, to mean what they say, and to be respectful, however forthright, when they speak the language of social change and implement their professed intention of peace among nations.

Notes

1 Introduction

I am deeply indebted to Janice Broun, Margaret E. Crahan, Michael Dodson, Eric O. Hanson, Joseph A. Komonchak, Arthur F. McGovern, and William M. Shea for comments on earlier drafts of this chapter.

1. Daniel H. Levine, *Religion and Politics in Latin America: The Catholic Church in Venezuela and Colombia* (Princeton, N.J.: Princeton University Press, 1981), pp. 20–21.

2. Avery Dulles, S.J., *The Resilient Church: The Necessity and Limits of Adaptation* (Garden City, N.Y.: Doubleday, 1977), pp. 29–30, 38.

3. Hans Küng, *The Church*, trans. from German by Ray Ockenden and Rosaleen Ockenden (New York: Sheed and Ward, 1967), p. 5.

4. Alfred Loisy, *The Gospel and the Church*, trans. from French by Christopher Home (New York: Charles Scribner's Sons, 1912).

5. Richard P. McBrien, *Catholicism*, Study edition (San Francisco: Harper and Row, 1981), p. 1172.

6. Ibid., p. 685.

7. Imposed on traditionalist philosopher Auguste Bonnetty (and implicitly on other philosophers and theologians) by the Congregation of the Index in 1855, and sanctioned as the single legitimate Catholic theology in Pope Leo XIII's encyclical *Aeterni patris* in 1879, neoscholasticism held that there was no conflict between faith and reason, provided a metaphysical basis for arguing that civil authority had an obligation to support right religion, and provided a unified theological credo around which the increasingly ultramontane bishops would participate in building up the centralized authority of the Holy See. Gerald A. McCool, *Catholic Theology in the Nineteenth Century* (New York: Seabury Press, 1977), pp. 129–30, 134–35, 161, 227–28. The text of *Aeterni patris* (August 4, 1879) is reprinted in *One Hundred Years of Thomism: Aeterni Patris and Afterwards*, ed. Victor B. Brezik (Houston, Texas: Center for Thomistic Studies, 1981), pp. 173–97.

8. McCool, *Catholic Theology*, p. 169.

9. Adam Nowotny (pseud.), "Fortress Catholicism: Wojtyła's Polish Roots," in *The Church*

in Anguish: Has the Vatican Betrayed Vatican II?, ed. Hans Küng and Leonard Swidler (San Francisco: Harper and Row, 1987).

10. Rama P. Coomaraswamy, *The Destruction of the Christian Tradition* (London: Perennial Books, 1981), p. 66.

11. McCool, *Catholic Theology*, chap. 2.

12. Summarized in McBrien, *Catholicism*, pp. 659–61.

13. Joseph Cardinal Ratzinger [in interview] with Vittorio Messori, *The Ratzinger Report*, trans. from German by Salvator Attanasio and Graham Harrison (San Francisco: Ignatius Press, 1985), pp. 61–62.

14. Quoted in *New York Times*, December 24, 1986, p. A-13. The pope himself told a group of American bishops in September 1987: "It is sometimes claimed that dissent from the Magisterium is totally compatible with being a 'good Catholic' and poses no obstacles to the reception of the sacraments. This is a grave error." *New York Times*, September 17, 1987, p. 1.

15. *Encyclical Letter of Pope Pius XI on Atheistic Communism* (March 19, 1937), Official Vatican text. (Boston: St. Paul Editions), p. 21.

16. Peter Nichols, *The Pope's Divisions: The Roman Catholic Church Today* (New York: Holt, Rinehart and Winston, 1981), p. 240.

17. Joseph A. Komonchak, "The Ecclesial and Cultural Roles of Theology," *Proceedings of the Catholic Theological Society of America* 40 (1985): 23, as cited in Patrick Granfield, *The Limits of the Papacy: Authority and Autonomy in the Church* (New York: Crossroad, 1987), p. 5.

18. Ronald Modras, "A Man of Contradictions? The Early Writings of Karol Wojtyła," in Küng and Swidler, *Church in Anguish*, pp. 47–48.

19. E.g., William M. Shea, "The Pope, Our Brother," *Commonweal*, November 7, 1986, pp. 587–88.

20. *Dignitatis humanae* (Declaration on religious liberty; December 7, 1965), reprinted in *Vatican Council II: The Conciliar and Post Conciliar Documents*, ed. Austin Flannery (Boston: St. Paul Editions, 1980), pp. 799–812. See also Pope John Paul II, *The Freedom of Conscience and of Religion* (letter sent to heads of state of nations who signed the 1975 Helsinki Accords, September 1, 1980), reprinted from *L'Osservatore Romano*, English edition, by St. Paul Editions.

21. McBrien, *Catholicism*, p. 678.

22. Loisy, *Gospel and the Church*, p. 195.

23. Avery Dulles, *The Catholicity of the Church* (Oxford: Clarendon Press, 1985), p. 98.

24. Summarized in Avery Dulles, *The Survival of Dogma* (Garden City, N.Y.: Doubleday, 1971), p. 117.

25. Ibid., pp. 114, 190–94.

26. Hans Küng, "Cardinal Ratzinger, Pope Wojtyła, and Fear at the Vatican: An Open Word after a Long Silence," in Küng and Swidler, *Church in Anguish*, pp. 59, 63–65.

27. Hermann Häring, "Joseph Ratzinger's 'Nightmare Theology,'" in Küng and Swidler, *Church in Anguish*, pp. 75–76.

28. Norbert Greinacher, "'Liberation' from Liberation Theology? Motives and Aims of the Antagonists and Defamers of Liberation Theology," in Küng and Swidler, *Church in Anguish*, p. 151.

29. Küng, "Cardinal Ratzinger," p. 59.

30. Dulles, *Resilient Church*, p. 67.

31. Quoted in Levine, *Religion and Politics in Latin America*, p. 42.

32. Quoted in James Hitchcock, *Catholicism and Modernity: Confrontation or Capitulation?* (New York: Seabury Press, 1979), pp. 135–36.

33. Ivan Illich, *Celebration of Awareness: A Call for Institutional Revolution* (Garden City, N.Y.: Doubleday, 1970), pp. 98, 100.

34. Greinacher, " 'Liberation' from Liberation Theology," p. 150.

35. Sacred Congregation for the Doctrine of the Faith, *Instruction on Certain Aspects of the "Theology of Liberation"* (Boston: St. Paul Editions, 1984), p. 26.

36. Dulles, *Survival of Dogma*, pp. 190–94.

37. Hitchcock, *Catholicism and Modernity*, p. 31.

38. Ibid., p. 9.

39. Ibid., p. 203.

40. Ibid., pp. 177–78.

41. Ibid., p. 48.

42. Romano Guardini, *The Church and the Catholic and the Spirit of the Liturgy*, trans. by Ada Lane (New York: Sheed and Ward, 1953), p. 205, quoted in Hitchcock, *Catholicism and Modernity*, p. 215.

43. Gerard Noel, *The Anatomy of the Catholic Church* (London: Hodder and Stoughton, 1980), pp. 105–7; *New York Times*, October 18, 1987, p. 5; and *Süddeutsche Zeitung* (Munich), November 14–15, 1987, p. 8.

44. Noel, *Anatomy*, p. 110.

45. *New York Times*, October 18, 1987, p. 5; *Neue Zürcher Zeitung*, October 31, 1987, p. 4; *Herder Korrespondenz* 41, no. 12 (December 1987): 561; and *Süddeutsche Zeitung*, April 9–10, 1988, p. 8. For further discussion of Léfebvre, see Eric O. Hanson, *The Catholic Church in World Politics* (Princeton, N.J.: Princeton University Press, 1987), pp. 102–4.

46. *Frankfurter Allgemeine*, June 18, 1988, p. 6, June 20, 1988, p. 4, and July 1, 1988, p. 5; *Die Welt* (Bonn) June 20, 1988, pp. 1–2; *Frankfurter Rundschau*, July 1, 1988, p. 2; *Neue Zürcher Zeitung*, July 12, 1988, p. 1; and *Die Zeit*, July 15, 1988, p. 4.

47. Coomaraswamy, *Destruction*, p. 67.

48. *Ratzinger Report*, p. 79.

49. Coomaraswamy, *Destruction*, p. 29; Dulles, *Resilient Church*, p. 101; and *New York Times*, January 29, 1988, p. 7.

50. *Ratzinger Report*, p. 52.

51. E.g., Rev. Leonardo Boff of Brazil and Rev. Gustavo Gutierrez. See Boff's *Church: Charism and Power—Liberation Theology and the Institutional Church*, trans. from Spanish by John W. Diercksmeier (New York: Crossroad, 1986).

52. C. Rene Padilla, "Liberation Theology Is Remarkably Protestant," *Christianity Today*, May 15, 1987, p. 12.

53. George Gallup, Jr., and Jim Castelli, *The American Catholic People: Their Beliefs, Practices, and Values* (Garden City, N.Y.: Doubleday, 1987), pp. 25, 34–35.

54. Ibid., pp. 14, 24–25.

55. Hansjakob Stehle, *Eastern Politics of the Vatican, 1917–1979*, trans. from German by Sandra Smith (Athens: Ohio University Press, 1981), p. 13.

56. *L'Osservatore Romano*, March 13, 1933, quoted in Stehle, *Eastern Politics*, p. 151.

57. See Stehle, *Eastern Politics*, pp. 170–71.

58. *Encyclical Letter on Atheistic Communism*, pp. 4, 12.

59. Quoted in ibid., p. 212.

60. Quoted in Nichols, *Pope's Divisions*, p. 51.

61. Karol Cardinal Wojtyła (Pope John Paul II), *Sources of Renewal: The Implementation of*

the Second Vatican Council, trans. from Polish by P. S. Falla (San Francisco: Harper and Row, 1980), p. 411.

62. Quoted in Nichols, *Pope's Divisions*, p. 341.

63. Ibid., p. 409.

64. Excerpts from *Sollicitudo rei socialis*, in *New York Times*, February 20, 1988, p. 4. See also *Süddeutsche Zeitung*, February 20–21, 1988, pp. 1, 2. The pope's fifth encyclical, *Dominum et vivificantem* (May 30, 1986), was devoted to a criticism of Marxism and other forms of philosophical materialism. Excerpts printed in *New York Times*, May 31, 1986, p. 4.

65. George Weigel, *Tranquillitas Ordinis: The Present Failure and Future Promise of American Catholic Thought on War and Peace* (Oxford: Oxford University Press, 1987), p. 43.

66. Stehle, *Eastern Politics*, p. 259.

67. Tomislav Šagi-Bunić, *Katolička crkva i hrvatski narod* (Zagreb: Kršćanska sadašnjost, 1983), p. 11.

68. Quoted in Bogdan Szajkowski, *Next to God . . . Poland: Politics and Religion in Contemporary Poland* (New York: St. Martin's Press, 1983), p. 223.

69. *Ratzinger Report*, p. 156; see also p. 83.

70. William M. Shea, "Protestant Fundamentalism and Catholic Integralism: Who Is the Enemy?" (Paper presented at the Woodrow Wilson Center for International Scholars, Washington, D.C., December 11, 1986).

71. Juan Clark, *Religious Repression in Cuba* (Coral Gables, Fla.: University of Miami Press, 1986), p. 31. For a general study of Castro's policy toward all denominations, see Margaret E. Crahan, "Salvation through Christ or Marx: Religion in Revolutionary Cuba," *Journal of Interamerican Studies* 21, no. 1 (February 1979).

72. Humberto Belli, *Breaking Faith: The Sandinista Revolution and Its Impact on Freedom and Christian Faith in Nicaragua* (Westchester, Ill.: Crossway Books, 1985), p. 142.

73. See Christel Lane, *Christian Religion in the Soviet Union* (London: George Allen and Unwin, 1978).

74. Granfield, *Limits of the Papacy*, p. 19.

75. Quoted in Stehle, *Eastern Politics*, p. 164.

76. Avery, *Survival of Dogma*, p. 24; also argued by Johann Sebastian Drey, founder of the Catholic Tübingen school, as cited in Dulles, *Catholicity of the Church*, pp. 151–52. See also Coomaraswamy, *Destruction*, pp. 21–25.

77. Quoted in Stehle, *Eastern Politics*, p. 236.

78. Quoted in ibid., p. 269.

79. J. N. D. Kelly, *The Oxford Dictionary of Popes* (Oxford: Oxford University Press, 1986), pp. 6–10; and "Papacy," in *New Catholic Encyclopedia* (New York: McGraw Hill, 1967), 10: 952.

80. Dulles, *Resilient Church*, p. 117.

81. Quoted in Granfield, *Limits of the Papacy*, p. 35. Also see Kelly, *Oxford Dictionary*, pp. 154–55; and Walter Ullmann, *A Short History of the Papacy in the Middle Ages* (London: Methuen, 1972), chap. 7.

82. Granfield, *Limits of the Papacy*, p. 35; Eric John, ed., *The Popes: A Concise Biographical History* (New York: Hawthorn Books, 1964), pp. 223–26; "Innocent III, Pope," in *New Catholic Encyclopedia* (New York: McGraw-Hill, 1967), 7:521–23; and Kelly, *Oxford Dictionary*, pp. 186–88.

83. Quoted in Granfield, *Limits of the Papacy*, p. 32.

84. McBrien, *Catholicism*, p. 833.

85. Quoted in Francis Oakley, *The Western Church in the Later Middle Ages* (Ithaca, N.Y.: Cornell University Press, 1979), p. 165.

86. Granfield, *Limits of the Papacy*, pp. 52–55.

87. "Papacy," p. 968.

88. Quoted in Granfield, *Limits of the Papacy*, pp. 37–38.

89. Dulles, *Resilient Church*, p. 115.

90. Wojtyła, *Sources of Renewal*, p. 151.

91. See Eric O. Hanson, *Catholic Politics in China and Korea* (Maryknoll, N.Y.: Orbis Books, 1980), pp. 66–67.

92. Viz., Albania, Czechoslovakia, Hungary, Poland, Romania, and Yugoslavia. See Pedro Ramet, *Cross and Commissar: The Politics of Religion in Eastern Europe and the USSR* (Bloomington: Indiana University Press, 1987), chap. 2.

93. The approach was made to Iosyp Terelya. See Reuter Press Agency, February 13, 1983; and Roman Solchanyk, "Ukrainian Catholic Activist Iosyp Terelya Sentenced," *Radio Liberty Research*, September 3, 1985, pp. 1–2.

94. Peter Fleming, S.J., with Ismael Zuloaga, S.J., "The Catholic Church in China: A New Chapter," *Religion in Communist Lands* 14, no. 2 (Summer 1986): 126–27. For further discussion of Catholicism in China, see Richard C. Bush, Jr., *Religion in Communist China* (Nashville: Abingdon Press, 1970); and Angelo S. Lazzarotto, *La Chiesa cattolica in Cina—La "politica di liberta religiosa" dopo Mao* (Milan: Jaca Book, 1982).

95. Stehle, *Eastern Politics*, p. 299.

96. See chapter 12 in this volume.

97. An "Instruction on Christian Freedom and Liberation" issued by the Vatican's Congregation for the Doctrine of the Faith on April 5, 1986, held that "it is not for the pastors of the Church to intervene directly in the political construction and organization of social life. This task forms part of the vocation of the laity acting on their own initiative with their fellow citizens." Excerpts in *New York Times*, April 6, 1986, p. 10. See also *Ratzinger Report*, pp. 175–83.

98. Belli, *Breaking Faith*, pp. 156–57.

99. Ibid., p. 160.

100. For more detailed discussion, see Ramet, *Cross and Commissar*, chap. 6.

101. *Ratzinger Report*, p. 74.

102. Nichols, *Pope's Divisions*, p. 203.

103. *New York Times*, April 12, 1987, sec. 4, p. E-3.

104. Levine, *Religion and Politics in Latin America*, pp. 307, 310.

105. Klaus Nientiedt, "Eine neue Form des Kircheseins—Basisgemeinden in der Weltkirche," *Herder Korrespondenz* 38, no. 9 (September 1984): 424–28.

106. Janós Wildmann, "Hungary: From the Ruling Church to the 'Church of the People,'" *Religion in Communist Lands* 14, no. 2 (Summer 1986): 167. See also "'The Hope of the Church': Basis Groups in Hungary," *Frontier* (March–April 1987): 18.

107. Diethild Treffert, "Ungarn: Einigkeit—das Schlüsselproblem der Kirche," *Herder Korrespondenz* 35, no. 3 (March 1981): 154; and Emmerich András, "Offene Konflikte in Ungarns Kirche," *Herder Korrespondenz* 36, no. 4 (April 1982): 170.

108. *Keston News Service*, no. 248 (April 17, 1986): 15. For further discussion see Ramet, *Cross and Commissar*, chap. 8.

109. Quoted in Hanson, *Catholic Church in World Politics*, p. 219.

110. Edith Markos, "Hungarian Catholic Hierarchy Publicizes Vatican Criticism of Bulányi," *Radio Free Europe Research*, June 30, 1987, pp. 25–26.

111. Lawrence S. Cunningham, *The Catholic Experience* (New York: Crossroad, 1985), p. 227. This is confirmed for the Nicaraguan context by Michael Dodson, "Nicaragua: The Struggle for the Church," in *Religion and Political Conflict in Latin America*, ed. Daniel Levine

(Chapel Hill: University of North Carolina Press, 1986), p. 91; and by Hanson, *Catholic Church in World Politics*, p. 275.

112. Arthur L. Greil and David Kowalewski, "Church-State Relations in Russia and Nicaragua: Early Revolutionary Years," *Journal for the Scientific Study of Religion* 26, no. 1 (March 1987): 97.

113. *Die Welt* (Bonn), February 6, 1987, p. 3.

114. Belli, *Breaking Faith*, pp. 153–54.

115. Juan Hernandez Pico, "The Experience of Nicaragua's Revolutionary Christians," in *The Challenge of Basic Christian Communities*, ed. Sergio Torres and John Eagleson (Maryknoll, N.Y.: Orbis Books, 1981), pp. 64, 68. For an effective rebuttal of liberation theology, see Michael Novak, *Will It Liberate? Questions about Liberation Theology* (New York: Paulist Press, 1986).

116. John Paul II, "Opening Address at Puebla," reprinted in *The Pope and Revolution: John Paul II Confronts Liberation Theology*, ed. Quentin L. Quade (Washington, D.C.: Ethics and Public Policy Center, 1982), pp. 53–54.

117. Padilla, "Liberation Theology," p. 12.

118. Dodson, "Nicaragua: The Struggle for the Church," pp. 87–89. See also Michael Dodson and Laura Nuzzi O'Shaughnessy, "Religion and Politics," in *Nicaragua: The First Five Years*, ed. Thomas W. Walker (New York: Praeger, 1985). There is a growing literature on church-state relations in Sandinista Nicaragua, including the following: Bahman Bakhtiari, "Revolution and the Church in Nicaragua and El Salvador," *Journal of Church and State* 28, no. 1 (Winter 1986); Betsy Cohn and Patricia Hynds, "The Manipulation of Religion Issue," in *Reagan vs. the Sandinistas*, ed. Thomas W. Walker (Boulder, Colo.: Westview Press, 1987); and Michael Dodson, "The Politics of Religion in Revolutionary Nicaragua," *Annals of the American Academy of Political and Social Science* 483 (January 1986).

119. Quoted in Thomas G. Sanders, "The Puebla Conference," *American Universities Field Staff Reports*, no. 30 (1979): 7. One observer wrote, "Even when they might continue to say in their declarations that they will obey the bishops and the Pope, their actions demonstrate the contrary. In fact they not only do not agree with the bishops, as in the case of Nicaragua, but they support their enemies. They have developed a community of free thinkers, obeying their local leader instead of the central authority. Each base community is capable of being a small 'church.'" See Geraldine Macias, "Christian Base Communities: Spiritual Renewal or Political Manipulation?" *Catholicism in Crisis* (May 1985): 12.

120. Fr. John Bukovsky, an American of Slovak descent, as cited in Stehle, *Eastern Politics*, pp. 340–41.

121. Gerhard Simon, *Die katholische Kirche in Litauen* (Cologne: Bundesinstitut für ostwissenschaftliche und internationale Studien, 1982), no. 13, pp. 11–12; and Saulius Girnius, "Religious Trends in Eastern Europe—Lithuania," *Radio Free Europe Research*, October 1, 1986, p. 41.

122. Quoted in *New York Times*, November 13, 1986, p. A-20.

123. Interviews, Vatican City, June 1987.

124. Quoted in Hanson, *Catholic Church in World Politics*, pp. 75–76.

125. Quoted in Nichols, *Pope's Divisions*, pp. 124–25.

126. There is, of course, a difference between the attitudes of the pre–World War II governments and those of the communist regimes. The former were generally proreligious governments, and their negotiations were conducted in a spirit of mutual benefit. The latter are antireligious, and hence negotiations with them have had an entirely different character.

127. Stehle, *Eastern Politics*, pp. 101, 253.

128. Ibid., p. 265.

129. Ibid., pp. 324–25. See also Zdenko Roter, *Katoliška cerkev in država v Jugoslaviji 1945–1973* (Ljubljana: Cankarjeva založba, 1976), pp. 203–6.

130. Stehle, *Eastern Politics*, p. 279.

131. Ibid., pp. 276–77.

132. Quoted in Szajkowski, *Next to God*, p. 18.

133. Ronald C. Monticone, *The Catholic Church in Communist Poland, 1945–1985* (Boulder, Colo.: East European Monographs, 1986), p. 34.

134. Ibid., p. 153.

135. Scot J. Paltrow, "Poland and the Pope: The Vatican's Relations with Poland, 1978 to the Present," *Millennium* 15, no. 1 (Spring 1986): 7–8; and Monticone, *Catholic Church*, p. 163.

136. Cited in E. J. Dionne, Jr., "Determined to Lead," *New York Times Magazine*, May 12, 1985, p. 23.

137. See Reinhard Henkys, "Kirche in der Deutschen Demokratischen Republic," in *Religionsfreiheit und Menschenrechte*, ed. Paul Lendvai (Graz: Verlag Styria, 1983).

138. Stehle, *Eastern Politics*, p. 333.

139. Quoted in Monticone, *Catholic Church*, p. 42.

140. *Keston News Service*, no. 33a (July 20, 1989), p. 2.

2 Catholic Social Teachings

1. My own work, *Marxism: An American Christian Perspective* (Maryknoll, N.Y.: Orbis Books, 1980), chap. 3, contains a fuller treatment on historical background and more bibliographical references. Jean-Yves Calvez, S.J., and Jacques Perrin, S.J., *The Church and Social Justice, The Social Teachings of the Popes from Leo XIII to Pius XII, 1878–1958* (Chicago: Regnery, 1961), remains a classic study of church social teachings. For two recent and strongly contrasting interpretations of church social teachings, see Donal Dorr, *Option for the Poor. A Hundred Years of Vatican Social Teaching* (Maryknoll, N.Y.: Orbis, 1983); and Michael Novak, *Freedom with Justice* (San Francisco: Harper and Row, 1984). Closer to Novak's more conservative view and rich in historical detail is Francis H. Mueller, *The Church and the Social Question* (Washington, D.C.: American Enterprise Institute, 1984). For an excellent set of commentaries on Catholic social doctrines viewed from different perspectives, see *Readings in Moral Theology*. No. 5, *Official Catholic Social Teaching*, ed. Charles E. Curran and Richard A. McCormick, S.J. (New York: Paulist Press, 1986).

2. For a study of nineteenth-century Catholic social thinkers, see Alec R. Vidler, *A Century of Social Catholicism, 1820–1920* (London: SPCK, 1964).

3. Leo XIII, *Rerum novarum*, n. 1, published in *Five Great Encyclicals* (New York: Paulist Press, 1955). The church teachings cited in this chapter are cited by the paragraph numbers used in all translations and editions.

4. Ibid., n. 2.

5. Ibid., n. 13.

6. Ibid., n. 16.

7. Ibid., n. 22.

8. Ibid., nn. 2, 36.

9. Ibid., n. 22.

10. Ibid., nn. 23–24.

11. Ibid., n. 16.

12. For a fuller discussion of this worldview, see William Dych, "The Dualism in the Faith of the Church," in *The Faith that Does Justice*, ed. John C. Haughey, S.J. (New York:

Paulist Press, 1977). For ideas on the changes that have affected this tradition, I am also indebted to Peter Bernardi, S.J., "Catholic Social Teachings: Continuity and Development," (Unpublished MS, Cambridge, Mass., 1984).

13. Leo XIII, *Rerum novarum*, n. 18, in *Five Great Encyclicals*.

14. Ibid., n. 15.

15. Ibid., n. 20.

16. Ibid., nn. 3–12, 30.

17. Ibid., nn. 3, 14.

18. Ibid., n. 15.

19. Ibid., nn. 3, 6, 11, 28.

20. Ibid., n. 5.

21. Ibid., nn. 5–11.

22. Ibid., n. 2.

23. Ibid., n. 17.

24. Ibid., n. 34.

25. Ibid., n. 36.

26. Ibid., n. 28.

27. Ibid., nn. 26–33.

28. Dorr, *Option for the Poor*, sees a need for the church to go beyond moral appeals and to animate the poor to demand their rights, pp. 19 and passim.

29. See Mueller, *Church and the Social Question*, pp. 89–96, 101–107; and Novak, *Freedom with Justice*, on Pesch, pp. 69ff.

30. Pius XI, *Quadragesimo anno*, nn. 41–44, in *Five Great Encyclicals*.

31. Ibid., nn. 105ff.

32. Ibid., nn. 78, 97.

33. Ibid., n. 45.

34. Ibid., nn. 59–60.

35. Ibid., n. 105.

36. Ibid., n. 109.

37. Ibid., n. 120.

38. Ibid., n. 119.

39. Ibid., n. 114.

40. Ibid., nn. 46, 88.

41. Ibid., nn. 81–97.

42. Ibid., nn. 64–65.

43. Ibid., n. 79.

44. Ibid., nn. 57–58, 71–74, 88, 110.

45. For a study of the concept of "social justice" see David Hollenbach, S.J., *Claims in Conflict* (New York: Paulist Press, 1979), pp. 54–56, 152–55, 179–80.

46. Pius XI, *Divini redemptoris*, n. 7, in *Five Great Encyclicals*.

47. Ibid., nn. 8–14.

48. Ibid., n. 58.

49. Pius XII, "The Anniversary of Rerum Novarum" (June 1941), in *The Major Addresses of Pope Pius XII*, vol. 1, ed. Vincent A. Yzermans (St. Paul, Minn.: North Central, 1961), p. 30.

50. Calvez and Perrin, *Church and Social Justice*, pp. 194ff.

51. Pius XII, "The Anniversary of Rerum Novarum," pp. 32–33.

52. Benjamin Masse, S.J., ed., *The Church and Social Progress* (Milwaukee: Bruce, 1966), in his own chapter on "Pius XII and the Social Order," claims that this focus on personalized

labor was one of the two major concerns in Pius XII's socioeconomic teachings. The other major concern was to establish a new "corporative" type of society; see pp. 39–43.

53. Pius XII, "The Anniversary of Rerum Novarum," pp. 33–34.

54. Pius XII, "The Social Problem," in *Major Addresses*, 1:131.

55. Pius XII, Christmas Address 1942, in *Major Addresses*, 2:161.

56. Pius XII, "The Social Problem," p. 130.

57. Pius XII, "The Catholic Employer" (June 1955), in *Major Addresses*, 1:338.

58. Pius XII, "Automation" (June 1957), in *Major Addresses*, 1:414.

59. See Masse, *Church and Social Progress*, p. 40.

60. Pius XII, "The Church and Labor" (June 1943), in *Major Addresses*, 1:53.

61. See Henri Chambre, *Christianity and Communism*. Volume 96 of *Twentieth Century Encyclopedia of Catholicism* (New York: Hawthorn, 1960), p. 29.

62. For a fuller development of Pius XII's views on a "corporative society" see Calvez and Perrin, *Church and Social Justice*, pp. 427ff.

63. The texts of John XXIII's encyclicals can be found in *The Gospel of Peace and Justice*, ed. Joseph Gremillion (Maryknoll, N.Y.: Orbis Books, 1976).

64. Novak, *Freedom with Justice*, pp. 128–29.

65. Dorr, *Option for the Poor*, pp. 105–16.

66. John XXIII, *Pacem in terris*, n. 11, in Gremillion, *Gospel of Peace and Justice*.

67. John XXIII, *Mater et magistra*, nn. 19, 30, 109, in Gremillion, *Gospel of Peace and Justice*.

68. Ibid., n. 43.

69. Vatican II, *Gaudium et spes*, n. 69, in Gremillion, *Gospel of Peace and Justice*.

70. Ibid., n. 70.

71. Ibid., nn. 3, 11.

72. Ibid., n. 40.

73. Ibid., n. 2.

74. Ibid., n. 55.

75. Ibid., n. 34.

76. Ibid., n. 39.

77. Ibid., n. 10.

78. Ibid., n. 42.

79. Ibid., n. 76.

80. Ibid., n. 39.

81. On the unity of the spiritual and the temporal, see *Gaudium et spes*, nn. 11, 35, 59, 63. Also see Charles Curran, "Catholic Social Ethics: A New Approach?" *Clergy Review* (February and March 1985), esp. p. 87 in the March (pt. 2) issue.

82. 1971 Bishops' Synod, "Justice in the World," n. 6, in Gremillion, *The Gospel of Peace and Justice*. For a commentary on this document and discussion over the controversy surrounding the expression "constitutive dimension," see Dorr, *Option for the Poor*, chap. 9.

83. In "Review and Outlook," *Wall Street Journal*, March 30, 1967, p. 14.

84. Paul VI, *Populorum progressio*, nn. 7–10, in Gremillion, *Gospel of Peace and Justice*.

85. Ibid., nn. 58–60.

86. Ibid., n. 26.

87. Conference of Latin American Bishops at Medellín, document on "Justice," no. 1, in Gremillion, *Gospel of Peace and Justice*, p. 445.

88. Ibid., document on "Peace," no. 9, p. 457.

89. Ibid., document on "Justice," no. 3, p. 446.

90. Paul VI, *Octogesima adveniens*, nn. 31, 33, in Gremillion, *Gospel of Peace and Justice*.

91. 1971 Bishops' Synod, "Justice in the World," nn. 4, 30–35, 77.

92. Ibid., nn. 5, 10, 13, 16, 17, 31, 39–48, 49–58, 76. (These numbers correspond, in sequence, to the various points noted in the chapter.)

93. Gustavo Gutierrez, *A Theology of Liberation*, trans. and ed. Sister Caridad Inda and John Eagleson (Maryknoll, N.Y.: Orbis Books, 1973). See also chap. 5, "Liberation Theology in Latin America," in McGovern, *Marxism*.

94. *Christians and Socialism*, ed. John Eagleson, trans. John Drury (Maryknoll, N.Y.: Orbis Books, 1975), doc. 19. See also McGovern, *Marxism*, chap. 6 on Chile, pp. 231–32.

95. Dorr, *Option for the Poor*, pp. 196–201.

96. See the introductory essays by Penny Lernoux and Moises Sandoval in *Puebla and Beyond*, ed. John Eagleson and Philip Scharper (Maryknoll, N.Y.: Orbis Books, 1979).

97. John Paul II, *Laborem exercens*, from the opening paragraph. The text of *Laborem exercens*, along with a commentary, can be found in Gregory Baum, *The Priority of Labor* (New York: Paulist Press, 1982).

98. Ibid., n. 3.

99. Ibid., n. 4.

100. Ibid., n. 9.

101. Ibid., n. 6.

102. Ibid., n. 12.

103. Ibid., n. 7.

104. Ibid., n. 11.

105. Ibid., nn. 4–5.

106. Ibid., nn. 14, 17.

107. Ibid., n. 20.

108. Ibid., nn. 14–15.

109. Ibid., n. 14.

110. Ibid., n. 17.

111. Ibid., n. 13.

112. *Instruction on Certain Aspects of the Theology of Liberation*, published in *National Catholic Reporter*, September 21, 1984.

113. Congregation for the Doctrine of the Faith, *Instruction on Christian Freedom and Liberation* (Vatican City: Libreria Editrice Vaticana, 1986). In response to criticisms, the *Instruction* argues that the hierarchical structure of the church is not opposed to equality, nor is church authority opposed to freedom of thought; nn. 20–24.

114. Ibid., n. 3.

115. Ibid., nn. 10–19.

116. Ibid., n. 31.

117. Ibid., nn. 44–45.

118. Ibid., n. 47.

119. Ibid., nn. 52–53.

120. Ibid., n. 63.

121. Ibid.

122. Ibid., n. 64.

123. Ibid., n. 75.

124. Ibid., n. 68.

125. Ibid., nn. 68, 77.

126. Ibid., nn. 46–48.

127. Ibid., n. 68.

128. Ibid., n. 75; also n. 60.

129. Ibid., n. 75.

130. Ibid., n. 79.

131. John Paul II, *Sollicitudo rei socialis*; reprinted in *Origins*, March 3, 1988, paragraph nos. 14–15, 20–24, and 36–40, especially.

132. John Paul II's letter to the Brazilian bishops was published in part in the *National Catholic Reporter*, May 9, 1986. The statement by the CELAM representative, Msgr. Enrique Castillo Morales, is cited in *Vida Nueva* (Madrid), February 13, 1988, p. 373.

3 Soviet Union

The authors would like to express their gratitude to Kestutis Girnius and Valdis Labinskis of Radio Free Europe's Lithuanian and Latvian services, respectively; to Saulius Girnius of Radio Free Europe Research; and to Oxana Antic of Radio Liberty Research for providing a number of sources and offering their consultation and support.

1. *Prawo i Zycie* (Warsaw), February 8, 1986.

2. *L'Unita*, January 25, 1987. For purposes of comparison, it may be noted that the number of Russian Orthodox believers is estimated to be fifty million. See Eugen Voss, ed., *Die Religionsfreiheit in Osteuropa* (Zollikon: G2W-Verlag, 1984), p. 167.

3. V. A. Kuroedov, *Religiia i tserkov' v Sovetskom gosudarstve* (Moscow: Izdatel'stvo politicheskoi literatury, 1981), p. 140; Igor Trojanowski, *Katholische Kirche in der UdSSR* (Moscow: APN Verlag, 1984), p. 14; and *USSR Yearbook '88* (Moscow: Novosti Press Agency, 1988), p. 307. According to Vatican sources, there are 1,200 registered Catholic communities in the Soviet Union. See Hansjakob Stehle in *Die Zeit*, August 4, 1988.

4. The nexus of religion and nationalism in various contexts is treated in Pedro Ramet, ed., *Religion and Nationalism in Soviet and East European Politics*, rev. and exp. ed. (Durham, N.C.: Duke University Press, 1989). See especially the contributions by Ramet, Kestutis K. Girnius, and Vasyl Markus. See also Bohdan R. Bociurkiw, "Religion and Nationalism in the Contemporary Ukraine," in *Nationalism in the USSR and Eastern Europe in the Era of Brezhnev and Kosygin*, ed. George W. Simmonds (Detroit: University of Detroit Press, 1977), pp. 81–93; David Kowalewski, "The Religious-National Interlock: Faith and Ethnicity in the Soviet Union," *Canadian Review of Studies in Nationalism* 9, no. 1 (Spring 1982): 97–111; and Bohdan R. Bociurkiw, Dennis J. Dunn, and Pedro Ramet, *Eastern Europe: Religion and Nationalism*, with an introduction by George W. Hoffman (Washington, D.C.: The Wilson Center, European Institute, East European Program, Occasional Paper no. 3, 1985).

5. *Entsiklopedicheskii slovar'*, vol. 14a (St. Peterburg: F. A. Brokgauz and I. A. Efron, 1895), p. 745; and Albert Galter, *The Red Book of the Persecuted Church* (Dublin: M. H. Gill and Son, 1957), p. 39.

6. For details on the establishment of the Russian Catholic exarchate, see Andrei Sheptitskii, "Russkii katolicheskii ekzarkhat v Rossii," in *Ex Oriente: Religiöse und philosophische Probleme des Ostens und des Westens*, ed. Ludwig Berg (Mainz: Matthias-Grünewald-Verlag, 1927), pp. 66–77.

7. The survey in this section is based on several standard works on the subject, including Galter, *Red Book*, pp. 31–53; Walter Kolarz, *Religion in the Soviet Union* (London: Macmillan, 1961), pp. 181–88, 197–204, and 218–26; James J. Zatko, *Descent into Darkness: The Destruction of the Roman Catholic Church in Russia, 1917–1923* (Notre Dame: University of Notre Dame Press, 1965); and Hansjakob Stehle, *Eastern Politics of the Vatican 1917–1979*, trans. by Sandra Smith (Athens: Ohio University Press, 1981), pp. 11–195.

8. For the table of organization, see Stehle, *Eastern Politics of the Vatican*, p. 105.

9. Galter, *Red Book*, p. 50.

10. For details on the League of Militant Godless, see V. Shishakov, "Soiuz voinstvuiushchikh bezbozhnikov (1925–1931)," in *Voinstvuiushchee bezbozhie v SSSR za 15 let 1917–1932*, ed. M. Enisherlov, A. Lukashevskii, and M. Mitin (Moscow: Ogiz, 1932), pp. 323–39.

11. Stehle, *Eastern Politics of the Vatican*, p. 180; and Paul Mailleux, S.J., "Catholics in the Soviet Union," in *Aspects of Religion in the Soviet Union 1917–1967*, ed. Richard H. Marshall, Jr. (Chicago: University of Chicago Press, 1971), p. 364.

12. Galter, *Red Book*, pp. 56, 64; Bohdan R. Bociurkiw, "The Uniate Church in the Soviet Ukraine: A Case Study in Soviet Church Policy," *Canadian Slavonic Papers* 7 (1965): 89–90; and Dennis J. Dunn, *The Catholic Church and the Soviet Government, 1939–1949* (Boulder, Colo.: East European Quarterly, 1977), p. 51.

13. See Osyp Zinkewych and Taras R. Lonchyna, eds., *Martyrolohiia ukrains'kykh tserkov*. Vol. 2, *Ukrains'ka Katolyts'ka Tserkva: Dokumenty, materiialy, khrystyians'kyi samvydav Ukrainy* (Toronto: V. Symonenko Smoloskyp Publishers, 1985), p. 233.

14. Tadeusz Poleski (pseud.), "Pastoral Work by the Catholic Church in Belorussia (1917–1984)," *Religion in Communist Lands* 13, no. 3 (Winter 1985): 305.

15. Galter, *Red Book*, pp. 54ff.; Kolarz, *Religion in the Soviet Union*, p. 207; Dunn, *Catholic Church*, pp. 45–81; Karlis Rukis, "Die Verfolgung der katholischen Kirche in der Sowjetlettland," *Acta Baltica*, no. 1 (1960–61): 93–97; and V. Stanley Vardys, *The Catholic Church, Dissent and Nationality in Soviet Lithuania* (Boulder, Colo.: East European Quarterly, 1978), p. 51.

16. Two of the four returned to Lithuania in the mid-1950s but were not permitted to exercise their offices. See Kolarz, *Religion in the Soviet Union*, pp. 207–8.

17. Vardys, *Catholic Church*, pp. 77–82; and Casimir C. Gecys, "The Roman Catholic Church in the Lithuanian SSR," in *Religion in the USSR*, ed. Boris Iwanow (Munich: Institute for the Study of the USSR, 1960), p. 111.

18. Galter, *Red Book*, pp. 61–62; Kolarz, *Religion in the Soviet Union*, p. 208; World Federation of Free Latvians, *Report on the Implementation of the Helsinki Final Act of August 1, 1975 in Soviet Occupied Latvia* (Rockville, Md.: World Federation of Free Latvians, 1980), p. 36; and A. A. Podmazov, *Sovremennaia religioznost': Osobennosti, dinamika, krizisnye iavleniia (Na materiale Latviiskoi SSSR)* (Riga: Zinatne, 1985), pp. 10, 131.

19. Galter, *Red Book*, p. 54.

20. The liquidation of the Ukrainian Uniate church is treated in detail by Bociurkiw, "The Uniate Church in the Soviet Ukraine," pp. 89–113; *First Victims of Communism: White Book on the Religious Persecution in Ukraine* (Rome: Analecta O.S.B.M., 1953); and Ivan Hrynioch, *Die Zerstörung der Ukrainisch-Katholischen Kirche in der Sowjetunion* (Würzburg: Augustinus-Verlag, n.d.). See also Bohdan R. Bociurkiw, "The Suppression of the Ukrainian Greek Catholic Church in Postwar Soviet Union and Poland," in *Religion and Nationalism in Eastern Europe and the Soviet Union*, ed. Dennis J. Dunn (Boulder, Colo.: Lynne Rienner, 1987), pp. 97–104.

21. Ia. N. Marash, *Politika Vatikana i katolicheskoi tserkvi v Zapadnoi Belorussii (1918–1939)* (Minsk: Belarus', 1983), p. 15; and A. S. Maikhrovich and E. S. Prokoshina, eds., *Katolitsizm v Belorussii. Traditsionalizm i prisposoblenie* (Minsk: Nauka i Tekhnika, 1987), p. 49.

22. See Ivan Hvat, "The Moscow Patriarchate and the Liquidation of the Eastern-Rite Catholic Church in Ukraine," *Religion in Communist Lands* 13, no. 2 (Summer 1985): 182–88.

23. See *First Victims*, p. 56.

24. *Vospitivat' ubezhdennykh patriotov-internatsionalistov. Po materialam Vsesoiuznoi nauchno-prakticheskoi konferentsii "Razvitie natsional'nykh otnoshenii v usloviiakh zrelogo*

sotsializma. Opyt i problemy patrioticheskogo i internatsional'nogo vospitaniia" (Riga, 28–30 iiunia 1982 g.) (Moscow: Izdatel'stvo politicheskoi literatury, 1982), pp. 66, 75.

25. "Doklad chlena Politbiura TsK KPSS, sekretaria TsK KPSS E. K. Ligacheva," *Kommunist*, no. 15 (October 1986): 18.

26. Joshua Rothenberg, "The Legal Status of Religion in the Soviet Union," in Marshall, *Aspects of Religion*, pp. 84–85.

27. Bohdan R. Bociurkiw, "Church-State Relations in the USSR," in *Religion and the Soviet State: A Dilemma of Power*, ed. Max Hayward and William C. Fletcher (London: Pall Mall Press, 1969), pp. 96–99; Donald A. Lowrie and William C. Fletcher, "Khrushchev's Religious Policy, 1959–1964," in Marshall, *Aspects of Religion*, pp. 131–55; and R. P. Platonov, *Propaganda nauchnogo ateizma. Istoriko-sotsiologicheskoe issledovanie na materialakh Kompartii Belorusiii* (Minsk: Belarus', 1982), pp. 87–90.

28. For details, see Bohdan R. Bociurkiw, "Religion and Atheism in Soviet Society," in Marshall, *Aspects of Religion*, pp. 49–53.

29. The two remaining bishops that had been deported, Vincentas Borisevicius and Mecislovas Reinys, died in 1946 and 1953, respectively. It is assumed that Borisevicius was executed. See Vardys, *Catholic Church*, pp. 75–76.

30. Ibid., pp. 82–83; and *The Chronicle of the Catholic Church in Lithuania*, no. 2 [1972] in *The Chronicle of the Catholic Church in Lithuania: Underground Journal of Human Rights Violations*, Vol. 1, *Nos. 1–9 1972–1974*, trans. and ed. by Nijole Grazulis (Chicago: Loyola University Press and Society for the Publication of the Chronicle of the Catholic Church in Lithuania, 1981), pp. 58–63.

31. Vardys, *Catholic Church*, p. 86.

32. Ibid., pp. 127–49.

33. J. Rutkis, ed., *Latvia: Country and People* (Stockholm: Latvian National Foundation, 1967), p. 625; Kolarz, *Religion in the Soviet Union*, p. 209; Rukis, "Die Verfolgung der katholischen Kirche," p. 98; and Podmazov, *Sovremennaia religioznost'*, p. 131.

34. Stehle, *Eastern Politics of the Vatican*, p. 363.

35. Bohdan R. Bociurkiw, "Religious Situation in Soviet Ukraine," in *Ukraine in a Changing World*, ed. Walter Dushnyck (New York: Ukrainian Congress Committee of America, 1977), p. 175.

36. Bohdan R. Bociurkiw, "The Catacomb Church: Ukrainian Greek Catholics in the USSR," *Religion in Communist Lands* 5, no. 1 (Spring 1977): 5.

37. Kolarz, *Religion in the Soviet Union*, p. 242.

38. Bociurkiw, "The Catacomb Church," p. 7.

39. Bociurkiw, "The Uniate Church in the Soviet Ukraine," p. 109.

40. I. I. Migovich, *Klerikal'nyi natsionalizm na sluzhbe antisovetizma (Na primere uniatsko-natsionalisticheskogo al'iansa)* (Moscow: Izdatel'stvo Znanie, 1987), p. 31. On Velychkovs'kyi, see also the Ukrainian samizdat journal *Ukrains'kyi visnyk*, no. 1 (January 1970), in *Ukrains'kyi visnyk. Vypusk I–II. Sichen' 1970-traven' 1970* (Paris: Ukrains'ke Vydavnytstvo Smoloskyp im. V. Symonenka, 1971), pp. 59–61.

41. Ibid., p. 59.

42. Bociurkiw, "The Catacomb Church," p. 11.

43. The "miracle of Serednia" is noted by Kolarz, *Religion in the Soviet Union*, p. 241. For a more detailed discussion of the Pokutnyky, see Vasyl Markus, "Religion and Nationalism in Ukraine," in Ramet, *Religion and Nationalism*, pp. 156–57; and Bohdan R. Bociurkiw, "Institutional Religion and Nationality in the Soviet Union," in *Soviet Nationalities in Strategic Perspective*, ed. S. Enders Wimbush (London: Croom Helm, 1985), pp. 195–96.

44. *Arkhiv Samizdata* no. 5371 (*Khronika katolicheskoi tserkvi na Ukraine*, no. 1), p. 3 (hereinafter cited as *AS* followed by the appropriate number); and *AS* no. 5406 (*Khronika katolicheskoi tserkvi na Ukraine*, no. 5), p. 15.

45. "Administratio Metropoliae Rigensis" (Unpublished typescript, Riga, September 1987), pp. 15–20.

46. Kolarz, *Religion in the Soviet Union*, p. 206; P. Lida, "Polacy, Litwini, Bialorusini," *Kultura* (Paris), nos. 1–2 (January–February 1980): 50–51; and Vitalis Karov (pseud.), "Doswiadczenia katolikow w ZSRS," *Libertas* (Paris), no. 5 (1986): 83.

47. "The Situation of the Roman Catholic Church in Belorussia," *Religion in Communist Lands* 10, no. 2 (Autumn 1982): 178; and *Svoboda sovesti* (Minsk: Belarus', 1986), p. 44.

48. "The Situation of the Roman Catholic Church," p. 184.

49. *L'Unitá*, January 27, 1987; APN, September 14, 1988; and "Administratio Metropoliae Rigensis," pp. 16–19.

50. Maikhrovich and Prokoshina, *Katolitsizm v Belorussii*, p. 214.

51. "The Situation of the Roman Catholic Church," p. 182; and Lida, "Polacy, Litwini, Bialorusini," p. 59.

52. *Keston News Service*, no. 70 (April 26, 1979): 2. The 1979 Soviet census lists only 6,993 Lithuanians in Belorussia.

53. See, for example, Jonas Papartis, "Fifteenth Report of the Lithuanian *Chronicle* on Catholics in the USSR (Belorussia)," *Radio Liberty Research*, 338/83, September 7, 1983.

54. Maikhrovich and Prokoshina, *Katolitsizm v Belorussii*, p. 172.

55. Ibid., p. 200.

56. TASS, September 6, 1988; and *Keston News Service*, no. 311 (October 20, 1988): 13.

57. *Tygodnik Powszechny*, September 1988.

58. See Roman Solchanyk, "Belorussian Informal Groups Criticized for Nationalism," *Radio Liberty Research*, November 3, 1988.

59. *L'Osservatore Romano* (English weekly edition), July 31, 1989 (emphasis in the original); Charles Robertiello, *RFE-RL* Special/FF-036, August 7, 1989.

60. Bohdan R. Bociurkiw, "Catholics in the Soviet Union Today" (Paper presented at the symposium on Religion in the USSR, 1975, held at Radio Liberty in Munich, April 16–18, 1975), p. 13.

61. *Radyans'ka Ukraina*, March 27, 1988; and *Lad*, May 8, 1988.

62. Mailleux, "Catholics in the Soviet Union," p. 366; and Trojanowski, *Katholische Kirche*, p. 15.

63. *Visti z Ukrainy*, no. 47 (November 1987). See also *Lad*, May 8, 1988, which also gives the figure of forty-one parishes.

64. *Keston News Service*, no. 284 (September 24, 1987): 7; and *Keston News Service*, no. 294 (February 18, 1988): 10.

65. *Magyar Tavirati Iroda* (Hungarian News Agency), May 25, 1989; and *Keston News Service*, no. 327 (June 8, 1989): 7.

66. *AS* no. 3324, p. 4.

67. *A Chronicle of Current Events* (November 30, 1977) (London: Amnesty International Publications, 1978), no. 47, p. 56.

68. *AS* no. 3323, pp. 1–3; Jonas Papartis, "The Eighth Report of the Lithuanian *Chronicle* on Catholics in the USSR (Moldavia)," *Radio Liberty Research*, June 20, 1980; and *The Times*, September 5, 1980. The harassment of Catholics in Moldavia is also described in *AS* no. 3325, pp. 1–4; and *AS* no. 3326, pp. 1–3.

69. Fyodor Angeli and Georgi Stoylik, *Moldavia* (Moscow: Novosti Press Agency Publishing House, 1982), p. 64; and Karov, "Doswiadczenia katolikow," p. 84.

70. The text is not dated, but it refers to the May 31, 1986, issue of *Izvestiia*. The document is not yet registered by *Arkhiv Samizdata* in Munich.

71. TASS, April 28, 1989.

72. *Deutsche Tagespost* (Würzburg), July 28, 1987; *Russkaia mysl'*, September 15, 1989; and TASS, December 25, 1989.

73. Velo Salo, "The Struggle between the State and the Churches," in *A Case Study of a Soviet Republic: The Estonian SSR*, ed. Tonu Parming and Elmar Jarvesoo (Boulder, Colo.: Westview Press, 1978), p. 208; *Soviet Estonia: Land, People, Culture* (Tallinn: Valgus Publishers, 1980), p. 262; Sergiusz Bankowski, *Die Katholiken in der Sowjetunion* (Zollikon: Glaube in der 2. Welt, 1981), p. 214; and *Keston News Service*, no. 289 (December 3, 1987): 20.

74. "Kosciol katolicki w ZSSR," *Kultura* (Paris) 5 (May 1978): 46–47; and "Administratio Metropoliae Rigensis," p. 15.

75. *Le Quotidien* (Paris), February 13, 1985; Agence France Presse (AFP), June 28, 1985; *Le Monde*, June 28, 1985; and *Keston News Service*, no. 274 (April 30, 1987): 2. See also the appeal to Prime Minister Margaret Thatcher on behalf of Swidnicki and other arrested members of the Christian Ecumenical Group, in *AS* no. 6003, pp. 1–2.

76. *Rheinischer Merkur*, October 7, 1977; and *Die Welt*, September, 1978. The church in Frunze is referred to in an article in *Sovetskaia Kirgiziia*, May 8, 1980.

77. Pastoral work in Central Asia is described in the memoirs of Fr. Wladyslaw Bukowinski, *Wspomnenia z Kazachstanu* (London: Spotkania, 1979). See also the recent report by Gerd Stricker, "Zwischen Identitätskrise und Ausreisewunsch: Zu Besuch bei deutschen Gemeinden in Mittelasien," *Glaube in der 2. Welt* 16, no. 9 (September 1988): 25–27.

78. Trojanowski, *Katholische Kirche*, pp. 36–38; and *Przeglad Katolicki*, March 19–26, 1987.

79. Bohdan R. Bociurkiw, "Religious Dissent in the U.S.S.R.: Lithuanian Catholics," in *Marxism and Religion in Eastern Europe: Papers Presented at the Banff International Slavic Conference, September 4–7, 1974*, ed. Richard T. DeGeorge and James P. Scanlan (Dordrecht-Boston: D. Reidel, 1976), pp. 146–75; and V. Stanley Vardys, "Lithuania's Catholic Movement Reappraised," *Survey* 25, no. 3 (Summer 1980): 56.

80. *Lithuania: An Encyclopedic Survey* (Vilnius: Encyclopedia Publishers, 1986), p. 413.

81. Saulius Girnius, "Fifteen Years of the Lithuanian *Chronicle of the Lithuanian Catholic Church*," *Radio Free Europe Research*, May 8, 1987.

82. For a detailed analysis, see Vardys, "Lithuania's Catholic Movement," pp. 65–73. The relationship between Catholics and the national opposition movement in Lithuania is discussed by Kestutis K. Girnius, "Catholicism and Nationalism in Lithuania," in Ramet, *Religion and Nationalism*, pp. 109–37.

83. For the text, see *Religion in Communist Lands* 7, no. 2 (Summer 1979): pp. 88–89.

84. Kestutis Girnius and Saulius Girnius, "Five Years of the Catholic Committee in Lithuania: Its Achievements and Dispersal," *Radio Liberty Research*, November 11, 1983.

85. Ibid.; and Saulius Girnius, "Lithuanian Priest Sentenced for 'Anti-Soviet Activity,'" *Radio Liberty Research*, December 6, 1983. In the summer of 1984 it was announced that an "underground group" was formed to carry on the committee's activities. See Pedro Ramet, "Religious Ferment in Eastern Europe," *Survey* 28, no. 4 (Winter 1984): 107.

86. For the text see *Religion in Communist Lands* 7, no. 2 (Summer 1979): 89–90.

87. Roman Solchanyk, "Poland and the Soviet West," in Wimbush, *Soviet Nationalities*, p. 174. The impact of developments in Poland on Lithuania is also treated by V. Stanley Vardys, "Polish Echoes in the Baltic," *Problems of Communism* 32, no. 4 (July–August 1983): 21–34.

88. *Chronicle of the Catholic Church in Lithuania*, no. 54, August 15, 1982 (Brooklyn:

Lithuanian R.C. Priests' League of America, 1983), pp. 4–16. See also Kestutis Girnius, "Apostolic Administrators Appointed to Lithuania Dioceses," *Radio Liberty Research*, July 16, 1982.

89. Reuter, Associated Press (AP), and Deutsche Presse Agentur (DPA), November 28, 1986; and United Press International (UPI), December 7, 1986.

90. Kestutis Girnius, "The Uneven Struggle Continued: Catholic Dissent since 1978" (Unpublished manuscript), p. 20.

91. Saulius Girnius, "The Catholic Church in 1988," *Radio Free Europe Research*, October 5, 1988; and idem, "Lithuania," *Radio Free Europe Research*, December 30, 1988.

92. Saulius Girnius, "Religious Societies in Lithuania," *Radio Free Europe Research*, June 7, 1985.

93. *Lithuania*, p. 49; APN, April 9, 1982; APN, September 4, 1985; *Slowo Powszechne*, May 15, 1986; and TASS, October 5, 1986.

94. TASS, July 23, 1987; and Saulius Girnius, "Possible Return of Confiscated Church," *Radio Free Europe Research*, June 15, 1987. For the text of the petition, see *AS* no. 5946, pp. 1–3.

95. Saulius Girnius, "Deaths of Catholic Priests," *Radio Free Europe Research*, December 4, 1984; and idem, "Religious Trends in Eastern Europe: Lithuania," *Radio Free Europe Research*, October 1, 1986.

96. *Keston News Service*, no. 281 (August 6, 1987): 15.

97. AP, January 27, 1984; and UPI, March 1, 1984.

98. *The Times*, August 27, 1984. For a report on the anniversary celebrations in Lithuania, see Marite Sapiets, "The Five Hundredth Anniversary of St. Casimir's Death in Lithuania," *Religion in Communist Lands* 13, no. 2 (Summer 1985): 213–15.

99. *Los Angeles Times*, November 19, 1986.

100. Jan B. de Weydenthal, "The Pope's Visit to Poland," *Radio Free Europe Research* June 26, 1987.

101. For details see Marite Sapiets, "The Anniversaries of Christianity in the Baltic Republics," *Religion in Communist Lands* 15, no. 2 (Summer 1987): 200–203.

102. *Moskovskie novosti*, July 26, 1987.

103. The transcript of the press conference is published in *Rzeczpospolita*, September 7, 1987. See also AFP, September 1, 1987; and Radio Vatican, September 2, 1987.

104. Radio Warsaw, October 25, 1987; *Frankfurter Allgemeine Zeitung*, October 29, 1987; and *The Times*, October 31, 1987.

105. Girnius, "The Uneven Struggle," pp. 4–5.

106. Vardys, *Catholic Church*, p. 212.

107. Gerhard Simon, "Die katholische Kirche in der Sowjetunion," in *Religionsfreiheit und Menschenrechte: Bilanz und Aussicht*, ed. Paul Lendvai (Graz: Verlag Styria, 1983), p. 95.

108. Kestutis Girnius, "Some Soviet Statistics on the Number of Catholics in Lithuania," *Radio Liberty Research*, October 18, 1979.

109. Ibid.

110. Girnius, "The Uneven Struggle," p. 4.

111. Podmazov, *Sovremennaia religioznost'*, pp. 127–28.

112. Reuter, March 1, 1986.

113. *L'Osservatore Romano*, May 3, 1985; "Administratio Metropoliae Rigensis," pp. 1–7; and "Elenchus alumnorum Seminarii Rigensis anno 1987/1988" (Unpublished typescript), pp. 1–3.

114. *AS* no. 2412, pp. 1–2. See also Dzintra Bungs, "Roman Catholics in Latvia Petition USSR Government," *Radio Liberty Research*, February 11, 1976.

115. Dzintra Bungs, "The Deaths of Two Priests Still Unexplained," *Radio Free Europe Research*, December 4, 1984.

116. *AS* no. 4203, pp. 1–2; and Katholische Nachrichten Agentur, December 11, 1981.

117. *Chronicle of the Catholic Church in Lithuania*, no. 28, June 29, 1977 (Brooklyn: Lithuanian R.C. Priests' League of America, 1978), p. 11.

118. Podmazov, *Sovremennaia religioznost'*, p. 138; and *Keston News Service*, no. 273 (April 16, 1987): 7.

119. Viktors Krasts, "Cardinal Julijans Vaivods and the Catholic Church in Latvia," *Radio Liberty Research*, February 2, 1983; and Trojanowski, *Katholische Kirche*, p. 37.

120. *Frankfurter Allgemeine Zeitung*, November 16, 1982.

121. Reuter, January 8, 1983; and *New York Times*, January 9, 1983.

122. UPI, January 28, 1983. See also "An Interview with the New Latvian Cardinal," *Religion in Communist Lands* 11, no. 2 (Summer 1983): 207–9.

123. Katholische Nachrichten Agentur, August 21, 1986; *Keston News Service*, no. 258 (September 4, 1986): 4; and Rudolf Grulich, "Lettland—ein Marienland: Wallfahrt nach Aglona," *Glaube in der 2. Welt* 15, nos. 7–8 (July–August 1987): 42–44.

124. Marite Sapiets, "The Anniversaries of the Christianity in the Baltic Republics," *Religion in Communist Lands*, 15, no. 2 (Summer 1987): 200–203.

125. Gerd Stricker, *Die Kirchen in der Sowjetunion 1975–1985* (Cologne: Berichte des Bundesinstituts für ostwissenschaftliche und internationale Studien, 1986), no. 18, p. 29, citing an unnamed personal source.

126. *Keston News Service*, no. 280 (July 23, 1987): 6–7.

127. Podmazov, *Sovremennaia religioznost'*, pp. 132–33.

128. Ibid., p. 127.

129. Ibid., pp. 100, 127.

130. Ibid., p. 138.

131. Ibid., p. 22.

132. See *Chronicle of the Catholic Church in Lithuania*, no. 49, September 8, 1981 (Brooklyn: Lithuanian R.C. Priests' League of America, 1982), pp. 69–73.

133. *AS* no. 4625, pp. 1–20.

134. *AS* no. 4897, p. 1 (emphasis in the original).

135. *AS* no. 4898, pp. 1–3.

136. Roman Solchanyk, "Ukrainian Catholic Activist Arrested," *Radio Liberty Research*, February 14, 1983.

137. *AS* no. 5405 (*Khronika katolicheskoi tserkvi na Ukraine*, no. 4), p. 20.

138. For an analysis of the first nine issues of the Ukrainian *Chronicle*, see Andrew Sorokowski, "The Chronicle of the Catholic Church in Ukraine," *Religion in Communist Lands* 13, no. 3 (Winter 1985): 292–97.

139. Roman Solchanyk, "Authorities Move against Ukrainian Catholic (Uniate) Activists," *Radio Liberty Research*, May 22, 1985.

140. *Ukrains'kyi visnyk*, no. 8, September 1987 (New York: Zakordonne Predstavnytstvo Ukrains'koi Hel'sins'koi Spilku, 1988), p. 180. Radio Liberty's *Arkhiv Samizdata* in Munich also received and issued an unnumbered "special issue" of the *Chronicle* (*AS* no. 5515, pp. 1–14) and one issue of the *Ukrainian Catholic Herald* dated 1984 (*AS* no. 5414, pp. 1–46). See Roman Solchanyk, "Special Issue of *The Chronicle of the Catholic Church in the Ukraine* Reaches the West," *Radio Liberty Research*, September 18, 1975; and idem, "First Issue of New *Samizdat* Journal Put Out by Ukrainian Catholics (Uniates)," *Radio Liberty Research* March 26, 1985.

141. See Philip Walters, "Cardinal Slipyj: The Man and His Church," *Religion in Com-*

munist Lands 13, no. 1 (Spring 1985): 91–93. The Vatican's first public high-level defense of Ukrainian Catholics, although without specifically naming them, came in the speech of Msgr. Achille Silvestrini at the Belgrade conference reviewing the Helsinki Final Act in October 1977. See the *Sun* (Baltimore), October 8, 1977.

142. Hansjakob Stehle, "The Ostpolitik of the Vatican and the Polish Pope," *Religion in Communist Lands* 8, no. 1 (Spring 1980): 18. Similar sentiments were expressed in a statement issued by Slipyi's secretariat directly after John Paul II's election. See UPI, October 19, 1978.

143. For an English translation of the letter, see *Letter of His Holiness Pope John Paul II to Josyf Cardinal Slipyj* (Cambridge, Mass.: Harvard University Ukrainian Studies Fund, n.d.).

144. Oxana Antic, "The Pope's Letter to Cardinal Slipyi," *Radio Liberty Research*, June 18, 1979.

145. See Ivan Hvat, "The Ukrainian Catholic Church, the Vatican, and the Soviet Union during the Pontificate of Pope John Paul II," *Religion in Communist Lands* 11, no. 3 (Winter 1983): 270.

146. I. V. Poluk, "O praktike rabote po protivodeistviiu katolicheskoi i uniatskoi propagande," *Voprosy nauchnogo ateizma*, no. 28 (Moscow: Mysl', 1981), p. 203.

147. For the texts of the four documents see "Zur Lage der ukrainischen Katholiken: Eine Dokumentation," *Informationen und Berichte: Digest des Ostens* (Königstein), no. 7 (July 1981): 1–9. The correspondence between Patriarch Pimen and Pope John Paul II was published in *Zhurnal Moskovskoi Partriarkhii*, no. 4 (April 1981): 6–7.

148. *Spotkania* (Warsaw-Lublin), no. 16 (1981): 84–87 (photocopy of original). For a German translation of the text see "Zur Lage der ukrainischen Katholiken in der UdSSR und in Polen," *Glaube in der 2. Welt* 10, no. 4 (April 1982): 127–30.

149. See the speech by Leonid Kravchuk, head of the Propaganda and Agitation Department of the Central Committee of the Ukrainian party, at the 1982 Riga conference on national relations, in *Neprimirimost'k burzhuaznoi ideologii, perezhitkam natsionalizma. Po materialam Vsesoiuznoi nauchno-prakticheskoi konferentsii "Razvitie natsional'nykh otnoshenii v usloviiakh zrelogo sotsializma. Opyt i problemy patrioticheskogo i internatsional'nogo vospitaniia" (Riga, 28–30 iiunia 1982 g.)* (Moscow: Mezhdunarodnye Otnosheniia, 1982), p. 41.

150. *Stanovlennia i rozvytok masovoho ateizmu v zakhidnykh oblastiakh Ukrains'koi RSR* (Kiev: Naukova Dumka, 1981), pp. 51–52.

151. Ibid., p. 183.

152. *Bericht über die Bistumswallfahrt der Diözese Augsburg in die Ukraine und nach Russland anlässlich der Tausendjahrfeier der Taufe der Rus' vom 2. bis 15. September 1988* ([Augsburg]: n.p., n.d.), p. 33.

153. For a biography of Vinnyts'kyi see *AS* no. 5337, pp. 1–3.

154. Jonas Papartis, "The Tenth Report of the Lithuanian *Chronicle* on Catholics in the USSR (Belorussia and the Ukraine)," *Radio Liberty Research*, November 6, 1980.

155. *AS* no. 4852, pp. 1–4. The "ideologically subversive activities" of Kavats'kyi and Iesyp are described by Migovich, *Klerikal'nyi natsionalizm*, p. 32. According to *Keston News Service*, no. 282 (August 20, 1987): 13, Iesyp has been released from internal exile prior to the expiration of his term.

156. *AS* no. 5591 (Biulleten' "+26"), p. 3; and *Keston News Service*, no. 290 (December 17, 1987): 7. The same issue of *Keston News Service* reported that Vinnyts'kyi was released early and returned to Lvov.

157. Poluk, "O praktike rabote," pp. 202–3.

158. L. F. Shevtsova, *Sotsializm i katolitsizm (Vzaimootnosheniia gosudarstva i katolicheskoi tserkvi v sotsialisticheskikh stranakh)* (Moscow: Izdatel'stvo Nauka, 1982), p. 9.

159. Ibid., p. 39.

160. *Neprimirimost' k burzhuaznoi ideologii*, pp. 41–42.

161. A. Babiichuk, "Molodezhi—ideinuiu zakalku," *Nauka i religiia*, no. 1 (1985): 10.

162. See, for example, the short reports in *Ukrains'kyi istorychnyi zhurnal*, no. 2 (1983): 155; and *Nauka i religiia*, no. 11 (1985): 34, on conferences held in Kiev in 1982 and Lvov in 1985, respectively.

163. O. V. Shuba, *Relihiini viruvannia i natsional'ni vidnosyny* (Kiev: Vydavnytstvo politychnoi literatury Ukrainy, 1985), pp. 36–37. See also his *Religiia i natsional'nye otnosheniia* (Kiev: Izdatel'stvo pri Kievskom gosudarstvennom universitete izdatel'skogo ob"edinennia Vyshcha Shkola, 1983).

164. *Neprimirimost' k burzhuaznoi ideologii*, p. 37.

165. *Sovershenstvovanie razvitogo sotsializma i ideologicheskaia rabota partii v svete reshenii iiun'skogo (1983 g.) plenuma TsK KPSS. Materialy Vsesoiuznoi nauchno-prakticheskoi konferentsii. Moskva, 10–11 dekabria 1984 g.* (Moscow: Izdatel'stvo Politicheskoi Literatury, 1985), p. 105.

166. See *Keston News Service*, no. 265 (December 11, 1986): 9.

167. *Prawo i Zycie*, February 8, 1986.

168. S. Tsvigun, "O proiskakh imperialisticheskikh razvedok," *Kommunist*, no. 14 (September 1981): 98.

169. *Los Angeles Times*, February 28, 1985.

170. *L'Unitá*, March 20, 1985. The February 21 date is provided in the Russian-language version of the interview published in *Zhurnal Moskovskoi Patriarkhii*, no. 6 (1985): 3.

171. *L'Osservatore Romano* (Polish monthly edition), 6, no. 8 (August 1985): 32. At the 1986 review conference in Vienna Silvestrini recalled the "painful situation that has continued without interruption for forty years, namely, a religious community that has been deprived of all legal existence." See *L'Osservatore Romano* (Polish monthly edition), 7, nos. 11–12 (November–December 1986): 8.

172. The pope's address was published in Ukrainian in *L'Osservatore Romano*, October 7–8, 1985.

173. *L'Unitá*, September 10, 1986.

174. "La 'via della pazienza ragionevole,' " *Il Regno* 32, no. 565 (January 15, 1987): 3.

175. See "Torzhestvennyi akt, posviashchennyi prazdnovaniiu 40-letiia L'vovskogo Tserkovnogo Sobora, L'vov, 17–19 maia 1986 goda," *Zhurnal Moskovskoi Patriarkhii*, no. 8 (1986): 5–23.

176. *News from Ukraine*, no. 18 (April 1986): 7.

177. *New York Times*, April 18, 1987.

178. See Oxana Antic, "Religious Policy under Gorbachev," *Radio Liberty Research*, September 28, 1987.

179. AP, September 1, 1987.

180. *Literaturnaia gazeta*, February 4, 1987.

181. International Society for Human Rights (Frankfurt) Press Release, February 24, 1987; and *Keston News Service*, no. 284 (September 24, 1987): 6.

182. Igor' Klimenko, "Predlagaiu skrestit' shpagi," *Sobesednik*, no. 24 (July 1987): 11.

183. *Literaturnaia gazeta*, August 19, 1987; *Moskovskie novosti*, September 13, 1987; and Serhii Mykolaienko, "Shcho dali?" *Pamiatky Ukrainy*, no. 2 (April–June 1988): 64.

184. An English translation of the text is published in *Ukrainian Press Service* (Paris), no. 6 (June 1987): 2–5.

185. *AS* no. 6097, pp. 1–6. See also *Frankfurter Allgemeine Zeitung*, August 12, 1987; *Le Monde*, August 21, 1987; and *Keston News Service*, no. 283 (September 10, 1987): 6–7.

186. *AS* no. 6038, pp. 1–3; and *Informatsionnyi Biulleten' Glasnost'*, no. 9 (September 1987): 6 (supplement to *Russkaia mysl'*, January 29, 1988).

187. "Khrystyians'kyi holos. Zhurnal Katolyts'koi Tserkvy v Ukraini," no. 1 (31) (Unpublished typescript, Lvov, 1988), p. 45.

188. Reuter, January 26, 1988; *Keston News Service*, no. 293 (February 4, 1988): p. 4; and Radio Kiev, October 4, 1987.

189. "Khrystyians'kyi holos," no. 1, pp. 57–59. See also Reuter, December 22, 1987; and the *Daily Telegraph*, December 23, 1987.

190. *Izvestiia*, December 23, 1987; and *Sotsialisticheskaia industriia*, January 7, 1988.

191. Radio Vatican, February 21, 1988; and Katholische Nachrichten Agentur, February 21, 1988.

192. AP, Reuter, and UPI, September 29, 1987.

193. *The Times*, January 19, 1988; and Reuter and DPA, March 2, 1988.

194. *Radians'ka Ukraina*, March 27, 1988.

195. See *Message "Magnum Baptismi Donum" of the Supreme Pontiff John Paul II to the Ukrainian Catholics on the Occasion of the Millennium of the Baptism of Kievan Rus'* (Vatican City: Libreria Editrice Vaticana, n.d.).

196. *Filosofs'ka dumka*, no. 5 (September–October 1988): 62. See also *Pid praporom leninizmu*, no. 6 (March 1988): 54; and *Visnyk Akademii nauk Ukrains'koi RSR*, no. 9 (1988): 95–98 for reports on similar conferences in Lvov.

197. AP, June 13, 1988; and UPI, June 14, 1988.

198. Interview with Achille Cardinal Silvestrini in *Il Tempo*, August 4, 1988.

199. Saulis Girnius, "Lithuanian Government Officials Meet Church Leaders," *Radio Free Europe Research*, October 28, 1987; and *Sovetskaia Litva*, February 10 and May 15, 1988.

200. Kestutis Girnius, "Bishop Steponavicius Allowed to Resume His Duties," *Radio Free Europe Research*, January 5, 1989.

201. See the report on the meeting between Cardinal Sladkevicius and party and government leaders in *Sovetskaia Litva*, October 13, 1988.

202. Saulius Girnius, "The Church Hierarcy Restored," *Radio Free Europe Research*, March 16, 1989.

203. Radio Vilnius, January 10, 1989; and *Kataliku pasaulis*, no. 1 (February 5, 1989): 24.

204. *Sovetskaia Litva*, Nov. 10, 1989; ELTA and TASS, December 1, 1989. For the text of the announcement on religious instruction, signed by the minister of education and Cardinal Skladkevicius, see *Tevynes sviesa*, December 1, 1989.

205. Charles Robertiello, *RFE-RL* Special/FF-070, January 25, 1989.

206. *New York Times*, June 11, 1988; and *Ukrainian Press Service* (Paris), nos. 7–8 (July–August 1988): 8–9.

207. Bohdan Nahaylo, "Ukrainian Catholic Issue Overshadows Start of Moscow Patriarchate's Millennial Celebrations," *Radio Libert Research*, June 6, 1988; *Avvenire*, July 9, 1988; and *Frankfurter Allgemeine Zeitung*, August 3, 1988.

208. *Izvestiia*, April 9, 1988. See also Metropolitan Filaret of Kiev, in *News from Ukraine*, no. 22 (May 1988); and Metropolitan Nikodim of Lvov and Ternopil', in *Golos Rodiny*, no. 20 (May 1988).

209. *Argumenty i fakty*, no. 1 (January 6–12, 1989).

210. Nahaylo, "Ukrainian Catholic Issue"; *Die Welt*, January 6, 1989; *Russkaia mysl'*, February 17, 1989; and AP, UPI, and Reuter, February 6, 1989.

211. "Dialog vo blago otechestva," *Vek XX i mir*, no. 7 (1988): 48; and *Moskovskie novosti*, October 30, 1988.

212. *Moskovskie novosti*, August 13, 1989; and Georgii Rozhnov, " 'Eto my, Gospodi!';"

Ogonek, no. 38 (September 16–23, 1989): 6–8. On the role of Soviet security organs in the liquidation of the church, see also the interview with M. Odintsov in *Argumenty i fakty*, no. 40 (October 7–13, 1989).

213. V. Grigorenko, "Esli bez predvziatosti...," *Nauka i religiia*, no. 12 (1987): 19; *Molod' Ukrainy*, May 17, 1988; and P. L. Iarots'kyi and O. I. Utkin, "Uniats'ka tserkva: Pravda istorii i suchasnist'," *Pid praporom leninizmu*, no. 23 (December 1988): 74–75.

214. Roman Solchanyk, "Ukrainian Atheist Journal Condemns 'Vulgar Atheism,' Proposes Religious Reforms," *Radio Liberty Research*, March 2, 1988. See also the *New York Times*, January 22, 1989.

215. See *Bericht über die Bistumswallfahrt*, p. 16.

216. *Izvestiia*, February 1, 1989; *Slowo Powszechne*, December 16–18, 1988; and *Keston News Service*, no. 295 (March 3, 1988).

217. Roman Solchanyk, "Ukrainian Catholics in the USSR: Towards Legalization," *Report on the USSR* 1, no. 50 (December 15, 1989): 28. According to Leonid Kolesnikov, the chairman of the Council for Religious Affairs of the RSFSR, during the same period only 600 new parishes encompassing *all* religions were registered in the RSFSR. See *Literaturnaia Rossiia*, December 22, 1989.

218. *Washington Post*, September 18, 1989; *Moskovskie novosti*, September 24, 1989; and *Keston News Service*, no. 339 (November 30, 1989): 4–5.

219. TASS, December 27, 1989.

220. Solchanyk, "Ukrainian Catholics in the USSR," p. 27.

221. *Moskovskie novosti*, July 30, 1989; Reuter, November 20, 1989.

222. Leonid Mlechin, "Osennii variant," *Novoe vremia*, no. 41 (October 6, 1989): 35–36. For an analysis of Russian Orthodox views of Ukrainian Catholics, see Myroslaw Tataryn, "Russian Orthodox Attitudes Towards the Ukrainian Catholic Church," *Religion in Communist Lands* 17, no. 4 (Winter 1989): 313–31.

223. See the remarks of Volodymyr Hryhorenko, the head of the Ideology Department of the Lvov party Oblast' Committee, as cited by Rozhnov, *op. cit.*, and the interview with Leonid Kravchuk, the Ukrainian party's new ideological secretary, in *Molod' Ukrainy*, November 29, 1989.

224. *Robitnycha hazeta*, August 20, 1989. See also the attack on the Ukrainian Catholic church in *Pravda*, Oct. 17, 1989.

225. See Solchanyk, "Ukrainian Catholics in the USSR," pp. 27–28; and idem, "Church and State Split on Ukrainian Catholic Issue," *Report on the USSR* 2, no. 1 (January 5, 1990): 10–12.

4 East Germany

1. Martin Höllen, *Heinrich Wienken, der "unpolitische" Kirchenpolitiker* (Mainz: Grünewald Verlag, 1981), p. 129.

2. Ernst-Alfred Jauch and Gisela Helwig, "Katholische Kirche," in *Kirche und Gesellschaft in beiden deutschen Staaten*, ed. Gisela Helwig and Detlef Urban (Cologne: Verlag Wissenschaft und Politik, 1987), p. 12.

3. Höllen, *Heinrich Wienken*, pp. 124–30.

4. Walter Adolph, *Kardinal Preysing und zwei Diktaturen* (West Berlin: Morus Verlag, 1971), p. 221.

5. Höllen, *Heinrich Wienken*, p. 136.

6. Jauch and Helwig, "Katholische Kirche," p. 17.

7. Adolph, *Kardinal Preysing*, pp. 214–19.

8. Ibid., p. 237.

9. Höllen, *Heinrich Wienken*, p. 133.

10. Adolph, *Kardinal Preysing*, p. 255.

11. Ibid., pp. 254–57.

12. Höllen, *Heinrich Wienken*, pp. 140–41.

13. Wolfgang Knauft, "Die katholische Kirche in der DDR 1945–1976," *Stimmen der Zeit*, no. 195 (February 1977): 91; Hansjakob Stehle, *Eastern Politics of the Vatican 1917–1979* (Athens: Ohio University Press, 1981), pp. 261–62.

14. Wolfgang Knauft, *Katholische Kirche in der DDR. Gemeinden in der Bewährung 1945–1980* (Mainz: Grünewald Verlag, 1980), p. 65.

15. Stehle, *Eastern Policy*, pp. 161–62; Höllen, *Heinrich Wienken*, p. 132; Knauft, *Katholische Kirche*, pp. 50–56.

16. Höllen, *Heinrich Wienken*, p. 130.

17. *Herder Korrespondenz* 13, no. 11 (August 1959): 552; Knauft, *Katholische Kirche*, pp. 68–72.

18. Knauft, *Katholische Kirche*, pp. 66–67.

19. Ibid., pp. 60–61, 103–5.

20. Adolph, *Kardinal Preysing*, pp. 238–42, 234–45; Klemens Richter, "Katholische Kirche in der DDR," *Jahrbuch für christlische Sozialwissenschaften* 13 (1972): 223; Knauft, "Die katholische Kirche," p. 89.

21. Knauft, *Katholische Kirche*, p. 79.

22. Knauft, "Die katholische Kirche," p. 92; Jauch and Helwig, "Katholische Kirche," p. 17.

23. "Fastenhirtenbrief 1959," *Herder Korrespondenz* 13, no. 6 (March 1959): 293–94; "Die Gewissensnot der Christen in der DDR," *Herder Korrespondenz* 12, no. 9 (June 1958): 425.

24. Knauft, *Katholische Kirche*, pp. 76–77.

25. Ibid., p. 82.

26. Ibid., pp. 89–90, 106–7; "Die Terrorprozesse gegen Laien und Priester in der Sowjetzone," *Herder Korrespondenz* 13, no. 5 (February 1959): 218–20.

27. Already in 1956 the churches' missions in railroad stations had been closed on grounds of alleged spying. See Knauft, *Katholische Kirche*, pp. 83–84, 113; Friedhelm Baukloh, "Die katholische Kirche in der Sowjetzone," *SBZ Archiv* 12, no. 20 (October 1961): 314–17.

28. Knauft, *Katholische Kirche*, p. 88.

29. Ibid., pp. 124–25.

30. Richter, "Katholische Kirche," pp. 228–29.

31. Knauft, *Katholische Kirche*, p. 120.

32. The Commissariats of Schwerin (Mecklenburg), Magdeburg (Saxony-Anhalt), Erfurt (Thuringia), and Meiningen (south Thüringen) belong legally to the dioceses of Osnabruck, Paderborn, Fulda, and Würzburg, respectively. Until 1972 Goerlitz was the seat of the vicar capitular for the East German portion of the archdiocese of Wrocław in Poland.

33. *Neues Deutschland*, December 24, 1965; E. A., "Katholische Bischöfe im Kreuzfeuer," *SBZ Archiv* 17, no. 3 (February 1966): 36–38.

34. "Zur 'Auswertung' des Konzils durch die SED," *Herder Korrespondenz* 20, no. 4 (April 1966): 166–67.

35. "Kirchenpolitische Entwicklung in der DDR," *Herder Korrespondenz* 23, no. 5 (May 1969): 224.

36. "Protokoll, Gespräch Seigewasser-Bengsch vom 15. März 1973," Archives of Christian Democratic Union Deutschlands, March 16, 1973; Knauft, *Katholische Kirche*, p. 170.

37. Friedrich Baukloh, " 'Pacem in terris' und die SED," *SBZ Archiv* 14, no. 15 (August 1963): 228–30; see discussion of Herman Matern's 1969 policy speech in "Kirchenpolitische Vorstellungen in der DDR," *Herder Korrespondenz* 24, no. 4 (April 1970): 152.

38. Knauft, *Katholische Kirche*, p. 143.

39. See Stehle, *Eastern Politics*.

40. "Kirchenpolitische Vorstellung," pp. 151–52; Klemens Richter, "Zum Verhältnis von Staat und Kirche in der DDR," *Deutschland Archiv* 6, no. 2 (February 1973): 140.

41. Richter, "Zum Verhältnis," p. 141; Klemens Richter, "Erste Pastoralsynode der katholischen Kirche in der DDR," *Deutschland Archiv* 6, no. 3 (March 1973): 349.

42. "Kirchenpolitische Probleme—Aussprache CDU Vorsitzender Gerald Götting mit Staatssekretär Hans Seigewasser, Mitglieder der Sekretariat des Zentralkommittees Kurt Hüttner und Rudi Bellman vom 22 June 1970," Aktenvermerk, June 30, 1970, CDU Archives.

43. Knauft, "Die katholische Kirche," pp. 102–4.

44. Klemens Richter, "Die vatikanische Ostpolitik und die DDR," *Deutschland Archiv* 12, no. 7 (July 1979): 747; Jauch and Helwig, "Katholische Kirche," p. 31.

45. Knauft, *Katholische Kirche*, p. 86.

46. Klemens Richter, "Haben wir als Christen noch eine Chance?" *Deutschland Archiv* 14, no. 5 (May 1981): 459.

47. Alfred Cardinal Bengsch, "Remarks to Central Commission for the Preparation of the Second Vatican Council, May 4, 1962," in Stehle, *Eastern Policy*, pp. 443–45.

48. Stehle, *Eastern Policy*, pp. 357–58.

49. "Pastoralbrief der DDR-Bischöfe zur Jugendweihe," *Herder Korrespondenz* 26, no. 6 (June 1972): 268–70.

50. "Wahl zur ortliche Volksvertretung. Einschätzung Staatssekretariats," October 23, 1965; and "Zur Wahlbeteiligung kirchlichen Amtsträger und Theologen," May 28, 1974, CDU Archives.

51. Regarding Bengsch's own political abstinence, see "Aktenvermerk betrachtens Beteiligung von kirchlichen Amtsträger an Volksentschied," April 16, 1968; and letter, Bengsch to Götting, May 10, 1972, in CDU Archives.

52. Knauft, *Katholische Kirche*, pp. 181–82; Klemens Richter, "Kein Beitrag zur Ökumene in der DDR," *Deutschland Archiv* 11, no. 10 (October 1978): 1039–41.

53. This 1.5 percent membership rate of Catholic priests, reflecting the Preysing decree against participation, contrasts with the 4 percent rate among Lutheran clergy and 5 percent among the so-called free churches (e.g., Methodists, etc.). See "Zur Wahlbeteiligung."

54. Knauft, *Katholische Kirche*, p. 165.

55. "Kurzinformationen," *Herder Korrespondenz* 24, no. 7 (July 1970): 340–41.

56. "Ostberliner Tagung 'fortschrittlicher' Katholiken," *Herder Korrenspondenz* 20, no. 5 (May 1966): 212.

57. "Aktuelle Aspekte kommunistischer Kirchenpolitik in der 'DDR,' " *Herder Korrespondenz* 19, no. 6 (March 1965): 259.

58. "Kurzinformationen," p. 341.

59. Richter, "Katholische Kirche," p. 239.

60. Klemens Richter, "Aufbruch oder Resignation? Zur Situation der Katholischen Kirchen in der DDR," *Deutschland Archiv* 4, no. 10 (October 1971): 973–74; Richter, "Kein Beitrag," pp. 1102–3.

61. Richter, "Katholische Kirche," p. 241.

62. Knauft, *Katholische Kirche*, p. 134; "Flexiblere Kirchenpolitik der Bischöfe der DDR?" *Herder Korrespondenz* 24, no. 1 (January 1970): 24.

63. Knauft, *Katholische Kirche*, p. 153; "Zur Vorbereitung der Synode in der DDR," *Herder Korrespondenz* 25, no. 11 (November 1971): 547.

64. "Diskussion auf begrenztem Spielraum," *Herder Korrespondenz* 26, no. 8 (August 1972): 407–8; Richter, "Erste Pastoralsynode," p. 350.

65. " 'Progressive Katholiken' der DDR fordern neue Standortbestimmung der Kirche,"

Herder Korrespondenz 26, no. 9 (September 1972): 423–24; Knauft, *Katholische Kirche*, p. 155; Klemens Richter, "Zur Situation der Kirchen in der DDR. Die katholische Kirche," *Deutschland Archiv* 6, no. 12 (December 1973): 1255.

66. Knauft, "Die katholische Kirche," p. 102; "Zur Vorbereitung," pp. 545–48; "DDR Synode unter Systemzwang," *Herder Korrespondenz* 27, no. 1 (January 1973): 48–51; Richter, "Erste Pastoralsynode," pp. 349–52.

67. Knauft, *Katholische Kirche*, pp. 158–59.

68. A number of sources exist on the peace movement in the GDR, including Pedro Ramet, "Church and Peace in the GDR," *Problems of Communism* 33, no. 4 (July–August 1984): 44–56; and Ronald D. Asmus, "Is There a Peace Movement in the GDR?" *Orbis* 27, no. 2 (Summer 1983): 301–41.

69. Klemens Richter, "Kirchen und Wehrdienstverweigerung in der DDR," *Deutschland Archiv* 12, no. 1 (January 1979): 43–44.

70. Richter, "Kirchen und Wehrdienstverweigerung," p. 44; Klemens Richter, "Katholische Kirche in der DDR und Friedensbewegung," *Deutschland Archiv* 15, no. 7 (August 1982): 685.

71. Richter, "Katholische Kirche und Friedensbewegung," pp. 686–87; Jauch and Helwig, "Katholische Kirche," p. 35; "Kirche in der DDR gegen Wehrerziehung," *Herder Korrespondenz* 32, no. 8 (August 1978): 376–79.

72. Cordelia Rambacher, "Friedensbewegung in der DDR," *Herder Korrespondenz* 36, no. 5 (May 1982): 220; Ernst-Alfred Jauch, "Neue Akzente nach langer Zurückhaltung?" *Herder Korrespondenz* 36, no. 9 (September 1982): 425–26; Horst Glassl, "Zur Situation der katholischen Kirche in der DDR," *Kirche in Not*, no. 31 (1983): 120; Richter, "Katholische Kirche und Friedensbewegung," p. 685.

73. "Hirtenwort der Bischöfe der DDR zur Busszeit 1981," *Herder Korrespondenz* 35, no. 5 (May 1981): 241.

74. Glassl, "Zur Situation," pp. 121–23; Jauch, "Neue Akzente," pp. 425–28; Richter, "Katholische Kirche und Friedensbewegung," p. 688.

75. "Kurzinformation," *Herder Korrespondenz* 36, no. 12 (December 1982): 621; Jauch and Helwig, "Katholische Kirche," p. 37.

76. Glassl, "Zur Situation," pp. 122–23; Jauch and Helwig, "Katholische Kirche," p. 38; "Hirtenwort der Katholischen Bischöfe in der DDR zum Frieden," *Deutschland Archiv* 16, no. 3 (March 1983): 326–29.

77. Klemens Richter, "Veränderte Haltung der DDR-Katholiken," *Deutschland Archiv* 16, no. 5 (May 1983): 454–58; Ernst-Alfred Jauch, "DDR-Friedenshirtenbrief: Ende eines selbstverordneten Gettos?" *Herder Korrespondenz* 37, no. 2 (February 1983): 55–57.

78. Beatus Brenner, "Kurskorrektur," *Materialdienst des konfessionskundlichen Instituts Bensheim* 38, no. 1 (January–February 1987): 16–17.

79. "Die Kirche hat die Wirklichkeit Gottes zu bezeugen," *Herder Korrespondenz* 36, no. 9 (September 1982): 436–42.

80. "Auf dieses Land ist Gottes Wort gefallen," *Herder Korrespondenz* 41, no. 8 (August 1987): 380.

81. "Kurzinformationen," *Herder Korrespondenz* 42, no. 1 (January 1988): 47–48.

82. Horst Dähn, *Konfrontation oder Kooperation? Das Verhältnis von Staat und Kirche in der SBZ/DDR, 1945–1980* (Opladen: Westdeutscher Verlag, 1982), pp. 174, 181–82.

83. "Kurzinformationen," *Herder Korrespondenz* 42, no. 1 (January 1988): 47–48; Brenner, "Kurskorrektur," pp. 16–17.

84. "Auf dieses Land," pp. 367–68.

85. Knauft, "Die katholische Kirche," pp. 98, 100; Jauch and Helwig, "Katholische Kirche," p. 24.

86. Richter, "Katholische Kirche," p. 232; Knauft, *Katholische Kirche*, pp. 149–52; Jauch and Helwig, "Katholische Kirche," p. 24.

87. Gottlob Hild, "Humanae Vitae (II)," *Materialdienst des konfessionskundlichen Instituts Bensheim* 19, no. 6 (November–December 1968): 99.

88. Richter, "Kein Beitrag," pp. 1100–1101.

5 Poland

1. Józef Sułowski, "Poland's Entry into the Family of Christian States," in *Poland in Christian Civilization*, ed. Jerzy Braun (London: Veritas, 1985), pp. 67–90.

2. Witold Sawicki, "Sprawa świętego Stanisława, biskupa," in *Historia Kościoła w Polsce*, ed. Bolestaw Kumor and Zdzisław Obertyński (Poznań: Pallotinum, 1974–79), 1(1): 74–80.

3. Norman Davies, *God's Playground: A History of Poland* (New York: Columbia University Press, 1982), 1:166.

4. Hanna Dylągowa, "Od upadku państwa polskiego do Powstania Listopadowego, 1795–1831," in *Chrześcijaństwo w Polsce. Zarys przemian, 966–1945*, ed. Jerzy Kłoczowski (Lublin: Towarzystwo Naukowe KUL, 1980), pp. 203–18.

5. Davies, *God's Playground*, 2:213.

6. Kazimierz Gołab, "Concordats between Poland and the Holy See," in Braun, *Poland in Christian Civilization*, pp. 581–88.

7. E.g., Stanisław Markiewicz, *Państwo i Kościół w Polsce* (Warsaw: Krajowa Agencja Wydawnicza, 1984), p. 6.

8. Davies, *God's Playground*, 2:213.

9. Wiesław Mysłek, *Kościół katolicki w Polsce w latach 1918–1939. Zarys historyczny* (Warsaw: Książka i Wiedza, 1966), pp. 582–85.

10. Zenon Fijałkowski, *Kościół katolicki na ziemiach polskich w latach okupacii hitlerowskiej* (Warsaw: Książka i Wiedza, 1983), p. 74.

11. E.g., Tadeusz M. Jaroszewski, *Laicyzacja* (Warsaw: Iskry, 1966), p. 74.

12. "Tezy Komitetu Centralnego Polskiej Partii Robotniczej, 1974" (Mimeograph).

13. Michał Pietrzak, *Prawo wyznaniowe* (Warsaw: Państwowe Wydawnictwo Naukowe, 1982), pp. 75–107.

14. Constitution of July 22, 1952, Articles 70 and 80.

15. Maciej Pomian-Srzednicki, *Religious Change in Contemporary Poland: Secularization and Politics* (London: Routledge and Kegan Paul, 1982).

16. E.g., exemption of church lands from the agrarian reform, participation of high officials in religious ceremonies, etc.

17. Infatuated with a dream of sharing power with the rulers and conquering the system from within, Piasecki persistently cooperated with the communists in their antichurch machinations. (For details see Andrzej Micewski, *Współrządzic czy nie kłamać?* [Paris: Libella, 1978].) But in 1980 the new leadership, with Ryszard Reiff at its head, gave support to the Solidarity movement. After the Jaruzelski coup of December 13, 1981, however, Pax fell again into the hands of a reactionary group led by Zenon Komender. The full story can be found in "Pax po 13 grudnia," *Spotkania* (Paris), nos. 21–22 (1984): 112–17.

18. *Tygodnik Powszechny* (Kraków), February 15, 1987, pp. 1–2.

19. Ibid., January 26, 1986, p. 3.

20. Quoted in Bogdan Szajkowski, *Next to God . . . Poland* (New York: St. Martin's Press, 1983), p. 42.

21. E.g., Archbishop of Kraków Adam Sapieha; see Jacek Majchrowski and Stefan Nawrot, *Niektóre elementy stosunków kościelno-państwowych w Polsce lat 1945–50* (Kraków: Uniwersytet Jagielloński, Instytut Religioznawstwa, 1984), p. 11.

22. Edward D. Wynot, Jr., "Reluctant Bedfellows: The Catholic Church and the Polish State, 1918–1939," in *Marxism and Religion in Eastern Europe*, ed. Richard T. DeGeorge and James P. Scanlan (Dordrecht, Holland: D. Reidel, 1976), pp. 93–105.

23. Majchrowski and Nawrot, *Niektóre elementy*, pp. 11–12.

24. *Listy pasterskie Episkopatu Polski, 1945–1974* (Paris: Editions du Dialogue, 1975), p. 42.

25. Majchrowski and Nawrot, *Niektóre elementy*, p. 18.

26. *Tygodnik Powszechny*, March 24, 1985, p. 1.

27. Stefan Cardinal Wyszyński, *Zapiski więzienne* (Paris: Editions du Dialogue, 1982), p. 23. Also published as *A Freedom Within: The Prison Notes of Stefan Cardinal Wyszyński* (New York: Harcourt, Brace, Jovanovich, 1984).

28. Andrzej Micewski, *Kardynał Stefan Wyszyński, Prymas i mąż stanu* (Paris: Editions du Dialogue, 1982).

29. Kazimierz Kąkol, *Kardynał Stefan Wyszyński jakim go znałem* (Warsaw: Instytut Wydawniczy Związków Zawodowych, 1985).

30. Wyszyński, *Zapiski*, p. 20.

31. Ewa Jabłońska-Deptuła, "W dobie Wiosny Ludów i Powstania Styczniowego," in Kłoczowski, *Chrześcijaństwo*, pp. 224–33.

32. Ryszard Bender, "I Wojna Swiatowa i Polska niepodległa, 1914–1939," in Ibid., pp. 284–85.

33. Józef Tischner, *Polski kształt dialogu* (Paris: Editions Spotkania, 1981), p. 11.

34. Józef Majka, "Historyczno-kulturowe uwarunkowania katolicyzmu polskiego," *Colloquium Salutis* (Wrocław), no. 12 (1980): 251–68.

35. For details see Pomian-Srzednicki, *Religious Change*, chap. 4.

36. Piotr Szydłowski, *Kryzys kultury w polskieg mysli katolickiej, 1918–1939* (Warsaw: Państwowe Wydawnictwo Naukowe, 1984), p. 80.

37. Leszek Kolakowski and Stuart Hampshire, eds., *The Socialist Idea: A Reappraisal* (New York: Basic Books, 1974), p. 7.

38. Tadeusz Mazowiecki, "Chrześcijaństwo a prawa człowieka," in *Chrześcijanie wobec praw człowieka* (Paris: Editions du Dialogue, 1980), p. 11.

39. *Listy pasterskie*, pp. 38–39.

40. Adam Michnik, *Kościół, Lewica, Dialog* (Paris: Instytut Literacki, 1977).

41. Edward Ciupak, *Religijność młodego Polaka* (Warsaw: Państwowe Wydawnictwo Naukowe, 1984).

42. For more details see Vincent C. Chrypinski, "Church and Nationality in Post-War Poland," in *Religion and Nationalism in Soviet and East European Politics*, ed. Pedro Ramet. Rev. and exp. ed. (Durham, N.C.: Duke University Press, 1989), pp. 259–62.

43. Ibid., pp. 260–61.

44. Recently the government permitted the formation of several new clubs.

45. For an incisive view on its editor-in-chief, Jerzy Turowicz, see Justine De Lacy, "Someone from Cracow," *Atlantic Monthly* (November 1986): 95–105.

46. Józef Grudzień, ed., *Wybrane problemy marksistowskiego religioznawstwa* (Warsaw: Książka i Wiedza, 1972), pp. 19–29.

47. Witold Zdaniewicz, "Religiousness in Poland, 1979–1980," in *Religiousness in the Polish Society Life*, ed. Witold Zdaniewicz (Warsaw: Pallotinum, 1981), pp. 35–64.

48. Rev. Władysław Piwowarski, "Blaski i cienie polskiej religijności," in *Oblicza katolicyzmu w Polsce*, ed. Józef Wołkowski (Warsaw: Augustinum, 1984), p. 30.

49. Wołkowski, *Oblicza*, p. 35.

50. The following information, if not marked otherwise, is derived from Witold Zdaniewicz, *Kościół katolicki w Polsce, 1945–1982* (Poznań: Pallotinum, 1982).

51. *Niedziela* (Częstochowa), nos. 13, 17, and 19 (1985).

52. Marian Radwan, "Ile kościolów brakuje w miastach?" (Lublin: Biblioteka Spotkań, 1981, Mimeographed), p. 4.

53. Ibid., p. 7.

54. *Tygodnik Powszechny*, February 9, 1986, pp. 1–2.

55. Zdaniewicz, *Kościół Katolicki*, p. 33.

56. *Polityka* (Warsaw), November 23, 1985, pp. 3–4.

57. In fact, the shortages result primarily from the lack of building supplies used for equipping of houses rather than church structures.

58. Wyszyński, *Zapiski*, p. 245.

59. Stanisław Barańczak, "The Cardinal and Communism," *New Republic*, February 4, 1985, pp. 34–36.

60. *Tygodnik Powszechny*, January 17, 1988, p. 7.

61. Witold Zdaniewicz, *The Catholic Church in Poland, 1945–1978* (Poznań: Pallotinum, 1979), pp. 35–36.

62. Zdaniewicz, *Kościoł Katolicki*, p. 44.

63. Ibid., pp. 45–56.

64. *Tygodnik Powszechny*, January 17, 1988.

65. Adam Ciechanowski, *Socjologiczne problemy powolań kapłańskich w Polsce w latach 1944–1964* (Warsaw: Centralny Osrodek Doskonalenia Kadr Laickich, 1969).

66. Jan Nowak, *Wojna w eterze* (London: Odnowa, 1985), p. 195.

67. Radosław Piszczek, *Księża Caritas* (Warsaw: Caritas, 1984).

68. *Dziennik Polski* (Detroit), December 17–18, 1982.

69. Czesław Strzeszewski et al., eds., *Historia katolicyzmu społecznego w Polsce* (Warsaw: ODISS, 1981), pp. 31–34, 167–76.

70. Grzegorz Polak and Jan Turnau, "Duszpasterstwo w Polsce," *Więź* (Warsaw), nos. 4–6 (1985): 29–36.

71. Andrzej Święcicki et al., "Kościół w Polsce" pp. 30, 33.

72. E.g., Rev. Władysław Piwowarski, as cited in Wołkowski, *Oblicza*, p. 41.

73. Zdaniewicz, *Kościół Katolicki*, pp. 69–71, 78–83.

74. Władysław Piwowarski, "Kościół ludowy wobec potrzeb i problemów duszpasterstwa," in *Religijność ludowa*, ed. Władysław Piwowarski (Wrocław: Księgarnia Archidiecezjalna, 1983), pp. 333–67.

6 Czechoslovakia

1. For a brief historical overview see Zdenek Kalista, "Katolictvi v ceskych dejinach" (Catholicism in Czech history), *Studie*, no. 79 (1982): 1–28. An earlier work by Ludvík Němec, *Church and State in Czechoslovakia* (New York: Vantage Press, 1955), is an engaged treatment of Czechoslovak church-state history to 1954.

2. See Vratislav Busek and Nicolas Spulber, eds. *Czechoslovakia* (New York: Praeger, 1957), p. 141.

3. "Die Situation der Kirche in der CSSR" (Studiengesellschaft für Fragen mittel-und-osteuropäischer Partnerschaft, Bonn, 1974, Mimeographed), p. 4.

4. See Milan J. Reban, "Czechoslovakia: The New Federation," in *The Politics of Ethnicity in Eastern Europe*, ed. George Klein and Milan J. Reban (Boulder, Colo.: East European Monographs, 1981).

5. Pedro Ramet, *Cross and Commissar: The Politics of Religion in Eastern Europe and the USSR* (Bloomington: Indiana University Press, 1987), pp. 75–76.

6. See especially Karel Kaplan, "Komuniste a cirkev—konflikt v polovine 1949" (Communists and the church—conflict in mid-1949), *Studie*, no. 62 (1979): 89–102.

7. "While the character of the aggressor and defender intermingle and merge, the opposing forces tend to balance each other. They take the same forms to meet and neutralize each other more completely." Eugene Dupreel's theorem, quoted in Jan F. Triska and David D. Finley, *Soviet Foreign Policy* (New York: Macmillan, 1968), p. 284.

8. For a detailed review with considerable documentation see Karel Kaplan, "Church and State in Czechoslovakia from 1948 to 1956," parts 1 and 2, *Religion in Communist Lands* 14, no. 1 (Spring 1986): 59–72; 14, no. 2 (Summer 1986): 180–93.

9. Kaplan's account, utilizing internal documents, gives A. Čepička's view (Čepička was the general secretary of the National Front and the person in charge of religious matters) of May 4. See "Church and State, Part 1," p. 63.

10. Kaplan, "Church and State, Part 1," p. 65.

11. Kaplan, "Komuniste a cirkev," pp. 92–93. According to Slanský's notation, the Soviets gave their assent.

12. See Kaplan, "Church and State, Part 1," p. 70.

13. See Kaplan, "Church and State, Part 1," p. 72.

14. For a brief account see Josef Rabas, "The Roman Catholic Church in Czechoslovakia," *Occasional Papers on Religion in Eastern Europe* 2, no. 6 (September 1982): 1–17. I am indebted to his summary of the pertinent laws.

15. See Ivan Marianov, "Grecko-katolicka cirkev v CSSR" (The Greek Catholic church in the CSSR), *Obroda*, no. 3 (January 29, 1969): 15.

16. See Kaplan, "Church and State, Part 2," pp. 186–87.

17. Kaplan, "Church and State, Part 2," p. 188.

18. Josef Rabas recounts what transpired: "In this manner, Archbishops Vojtaššak, Gojdic, Hopko, Buzálka, Zela and Trochta were given long sentences. Archbishop Beran remained under police guard until he was permitted to leave for Rome, but never again to return to his native country. Bishops Hlouch and Soukup were also banned. The Suffragan bishop Dr. Matousek . . . was allowed only to serve a Prague parish. . . . The bishops who had been secretly ordained on instructions from Pope Pius XII, Bishops Tomášek, Hlad and Otcenasek, were soon discovered; Hlad and Otcenasek were given prison sentences. . . . The Greek Catholic Bishops, Diocesan Bishop Gojdic and Suffragan Bishop Hopko, were both incarcerated for long periods. Bishop Gojdic died in the concentration camp of Leopoldov; his Suffragan Bishop was released from jail in the early sixties, but then was not permitted to perform his pastoral duties" (Rabas, "Roman Catholic Church," p. 9).

19. See Karel Kaplan, "Church and State in Czechoslovakia from 1948 to 1956," *Religion in Communist Lands* 14, no. 3 (Winter 1986): 273–82.

20. See Kaplan, "Church and State in Czechoslovakia," p. 282.

21. *New York Times*, October 18, 1967.

22. See Peter A. Toma and Milan J. Reban, "Church-State Schism in Czechoslovakia," in *Religion and Atheism in the U.S.S.R. and Eastern Europe*, ed. Bohdan R. Bociurkiw and John W. Strong (London: Macmillan, 1975), pp. 273–91.

23. See B. Kuchar, "Nabozenstvo podporuje deformacije vo vyvine emocii" (Religion aids deformation of emotional development), *Pravda*, February 2, 1972; as well as *Pravda* articles of February 1 and 3, 1972.

24. *Frankfurter Allgemeine*, February 20, 1986. Hrůza's figures were reported in a samizdat source, *Informace o Cirkví* (Information about the church), no. 9, 1985, and in Radio Free Europe/Radio Liberty, *Soviet East European Report* 3, no. 18 (April 1, 1986).

25. *Kurier* (Vienna), July 30, 1986.

26. See *Frankfurter Allgemeine*, February 20, 1986.

27. *Kurier*, July 30, 1986.

28. Austrian television interview, July 11, 1986.

29. P. Matuska, "Czechoslovakia," *Radio Free Europe Research*, October 1, 1986, p. 18.

30. The amended law on abortion went into effect on January 1, 1987.

31. Vasil Bejda, "Kam jde Vatikan?" (Whither goes Vatican?), *Otazky miru a socialismu* (Questions of peace and socialism), no. 9 (1985): 76–80.

32. Karel Hrůza, *Tvorba*, August 11, 1982, pp. 4–5.

33. Many samizdat documents, petitions, trials, and the religious matters taken up by Charter 77 members testify to this.

34. For example, Slovak-born Cardinal Jozef Tomko is serving as prefect of the Congregation for the Evangelization of the Peoples. In October 1986 he offered a denunciation of Marxism, later somewhat muted in *L'Osservatore Romano*, October 16, 1986.

7 Hungary

1. It should be noted that besides the predominant Catholic church there are also important Protestant churches in Hungary. Their situation will be examined in a future volume of studies. In 1949, the last time the census contained information about religion, 70 percent of the population was Catholic, 22 percent Calvinist, 6 percent Lutheran, and just over 1 percent Jewish. The remaining 1 percent consisted of Eastern Orthodox, Unitarians, Baptists, Methodists, and a small number of nonbelievers.

2. See Imre Kovács, *Im Schatten der Sowjets* (Zurich: Thomas Verlag, 1948), pp. 245–52.

3. This illusion, in retrospect incredibly naïve, was shared by many at the time. Ferenc Nagy, premier of Hungary between 1945 and 1947, based his entire policy on the same expectation. See his memoirs, *The Struggle behind the Iron Curtain* (New York: Macmillan, 1948).

4. Rákosi even toyed with the idea of separating the Hungarian Catholic church from Rome and creating a schismatic "Hungarian National church." (Information received from Mr. István Barankovics, leader of the Democratic People's Party of Hungary.)

5. See my "The Agreement between the Government of the Hungarian People's Republic and the Roman Catholic Bench of Bishops" (M.A. thesis, Columbia University, 1958).

6. The English version of the texts of the agreements with the churches are published in Vladimir Gsovski, ed., *Church and State Behind the Iron Curtain* (New York: Praeger, 1955), pp. 134–41.

7. The deadline for ending state subsidies has been postponed repeatedly, the last time in 1984. The money is paid directly to the individual priest and can be withheld at the discretion of the authorities. Thus state subsidies are used as a means of reward and punishment.

8. A good summary of church-state relations in the 1950s is given by K. Z., "Egy elhallgatott évforduló" (An anniversary passed over in silence), *Katolikus Szemle* (Rome) 37, no. 3, (Fall 1985): 266–68; see also Emeric András and Julius Morel, *Hungarian Catholicism: A Handbook* (Toronto: St. Elizabeth of Hungary Parish, 1983), pp. 19–25.

9. Act I of 1951. Text in András and Morel, *Hungarian Catholicism*, pp. 168–69.

10. Legal Regulation no. 20/1951 of the Presidential Council of the People's Republic. Text in ibid., p. 175.

11. It is interesting to see that a contemporary Marxist historian, Jenő Gergely, in his *A katolikus egyház Magyarországon 1944–1971* (The Catholic church in Hungary 1944–1971) (Budapest: Kossuth, 1985), pp. 132–33, not only describes, disapprovingly, these shameful practices, but also cites police reports on the hostile reaction to them on the part of the clergy and the faithful.

12. See my "Towards Normalization of Church-State Relations in Hungary," in *Religion*

and Atheism in the USSR and Eastern Europe, ed. Bohdan R. Bociurkiw and John Strong (London: Macmillan, 1975), pp. 291–313.

13. February 12, 1976.

14. May 24, 1976.

15. This is the theme of the official publication *Staat und Kirchen in Ungarn* (State and churches in Hungary) (Vienna: Ungarisches Pressebüro Wien, 1977). See also the article of Politburo member and Deputy Prime Minister György Aczél, "The Socialist State and the Churches in Hungary," *The New Hungarian Quarterly* 18, no. 66 (Summer 1977): 49–62.

16. *Társadalmi Szemle* 19 (November 1964): 14–15.

17. The study first appeared in the January 1977 issue of *Világosság* (Light), the monthly for the propagation of the "materialist worldview"; it was reprinted under the title "Beziehungen Neuen Typus" (New type of relations) as the lead article in the above-mentioned government publication, *Staat und Kirchen in Ungarn*, pp. 5–13. Quotations on p. 9.

18. In the following five sections I draw heavily on my earlier study "Religion in a Communist Consumer Society: The Case of Kádár's Hungary," *Occasional Papers on Religion in Eastern Europe* 1, no. 5 (September 1981): 1–10.

19. Béla Csanád, "A katolikus vallásosság mérése hazánkban" (Measuring the degree of Catholic religiosity in our country), *Vigilia* 41 (May 1976): 294–99.

20. Jenő Bangó, "Vallásszociológiai kollókvium Budapesten" (Colloquium on the sociology of religion in Budapest), *Katolikus Szemle* 20, no. 3 (Fall 1968): 274.

21. To the already large body of literature dealing with the many ills of Hungarian society some startling revelations have been added in recent years about the existence of widespread prostitution and a large and growing lumpenproletariat of jobless drifters. These subjects were taboo in the past because neither group is supposed to exist in socialist countries. Reports on prostitution are from time to time published in the press destined for the general public, e.g., *Hétfői Hírek*, July 31, 1978; *Magyar Hirlap*, August 5, 1978; *Élet és Irodalom*, May 5, 1979. A dramatic report on alcoholism, vagrancy, and people on skid row appeared in *Élet és Irodalom*, February 4, 1978.

22. The essay by Aczél and three articles by Cserháti, of which the last one was an answer to Aczél, were reprinted (in German translation) in *Staat und Kirchen in Ungarn*, pp. 15–67. Cserháti's contention that religious believers do follow moral precepts to a higher degree than nonbelievers is supported by a study carried out by a team from the Catholic Theological Academy in Budapest. By taking the number of suicides, divorces, abortions, and the incidence of the use of oral contraceptives, and correlating these figures with the intensity of Catholic practice in each city and county, the researchers were able to establish a significant negative correlation throughout the country, without exception, between these two sets of data. In a nutshell, their findings show that where Catholicism is stronger, the rates of suicide, divorce, and abortion are definitely and significantly lower. See Csanád, "Measuring the Degree," pp. 300–303.

23. *Népszabadság*, June 13, 1979, pp. 4–5.

24. Jenő Bangó, "Vallásszociológia Magyarországon" (Sociology of religion in Hungary), *Katolikus Szemle* 22, no. 2 (Summer 1970): 143–55. See also Tamás Nyíri, "Világi keresztények" (Secular Christians), *Vigilia* 41 (May 1976): 303–4.

25. Ibid., pp. 304–7.

26. See "Juvenile Delinquency an Increasing Problem," Radio Free Europe, *Hungarian Situation Report/32* (December 20, 1978): 6–10. Cf. *Statistical Pocket Book of Hungary 1977*, p. 209.

27. Quoted by Ernst Kux in "Growing Tensions in Eastern Europe," *Problems of Communism* 29, no. 2 (March–April 1980): 35.

28. For example, in 1980 only 40 young men were ordained, while in the same year 89 priests died. The number of seminarians preparing for the priesthood fell from an all-time high of 1,079 in 1948 to 130 in 1983. See "Die Kirche in Ungarn," *Pro Mundi Vita: Dossiers* (Brussels, 1984), pp. 21–22. It is interesting to note that the Uniate bishopric of Hajdúdorog, where the priests are not bound by the oath of celibacy but are free to marry, is the only diocese in Hungary which has no problem attracting young men to the priestly vocation.

29. He died of a heart attack on June 30, 1986.

30. "Enlightened" Emperor Josef II (1780–90) treated the church as an institution in the service of the state and the clergy as civil servants. According to some observers, "Josephi-ism" still influences the thinking of both state and church officials in all lands which were part of the Habsburg Empire. See Imre András, "Nehézségek a lelkipásztori munkában Magyarországon" (Difficulties in the pastoral work in Hungary), *Katolikus Szemle* 35, no. 1 (Winter 1983): 64.

31. The 1958 Vatican decree excommunicating the Hungarian "peace priest" parliamentarians was quietly shelved, and since 1971 priests need only the permission of the local bishop to stand for election and accept political office.

32. See the frank assessment about the Communists' lack of trust of the "peace priests" in Gergely, *A katolikus egyház Magyarországon*, p. 133.

33. Cardinal Lékai's achievements are flatteringly described in a richly illustrated book based on a documentary film shown on Hungarian television. The book's title is the Hungarian translation of the primate's motto (*Succisa Virescit*), *"A megnyesett fa kizöldül": Portré Dr. Lékai Lászlóról* (Pruning stimulates growth: A portrait of Dr. László Lékai) (Budapest: Közgazdasági és Jogi Könyvkiadó, 1984).

34. See my "The Base Community—A Challenge to the Peaceful Co-existence between Church and State in Hungary," *Occasional Papers on Religion in Eastern Europe* 1, no. 6 (November 1981): 1–9.

35. See "Bázisközösségek és hitoktatás: vatikáni levél Lékai László biborosérseknek" (Base communities and religious instruction: A letter from the Vatican to Archbishop László Cardinal Lékai), *Katolikus Szemle* 35, no. 2 (Summer 1983): 165–66; Imre András, "Kompromisszumos javaslat a bázisközösségek ügyében" (Proposal for compromise in the affair of the base communities), *Katolikus Szemle* 35, no. 3 (Fall 1983): 288–90.

36. See, for example, Gergely, *A katolikus egyház Magyarországon*, pp. 196–97.

37. In addition to the Catholic periodicals (a weekly and a biweekly newspaper, plus a monthly and a quarterly journal), the publication figures of which remained steady for the last two decades, the number of books published by the two Catholic publishers increased from four in 1954 to twenty-seven in 1980. This trend seems to continue. Moreover, a considerable amount of religious material in Hungarian published abroad is reaching Hungary with relative ease. The churches are given half an hour each Sunday morning for radio broadcasting of religious services, including sermons. Of this allotment, the Catholic church receives about fifteen to twenty half hours per year. However, the churches are denied access to the most influential mass medium of our times, television.

38. See, for example *Staat und Kirchen in Ungarn*, pp. 105–9.

39. See József Cserháti, "Az egyházi kisközösségek teológiája" (The theology of the small church communities), *Vigilia* 46, no. 3 (March 1981): 145–53; András Szennay, "Az egyházi kisközösségek" (The small church communities), *Vigilia* 46, no. 6 (June 1981): 367–76.

40. Ferenc Szabó, "II János Pál pápa beszéde a magyar főpásztorokhoz" (Pope John Paul II's address to the Hungarian episcopate), *Katolikus Szemle* 34, no. 4 (Winter 1982): 369–72.

41. András, "Difficulties in Pastoral Work," pp. 64–66.

42. *The State and the Churches in Hungary* (Budapest: Buda Press, 1987).

43. "Good Relations between the State and the Churches," in *The State and the Churches in Hungary* (Budapest: Buda Press, 1987), pp. 1–23.

44. *Kathpress* (Vienna), February 3, 1988.

45. Ibid., April 14, 1988.

46. A former Franciscan friar and professor of philosophy, László Paskai (born 1927) was rector of the Budapest Central Seminary from 1973 to 1978, when Pope Paul VI appointed him bishop and apostolic administrator of the diocese of Veszprém. In 1982 Paskai was named coadjutor archbishop of Kalocsa. A week after Lékai's death, Paskai was elected chairman of the Catholic Bishops' Conference. On March 6, 1987, the Vatican and the Hungarian government simultaneously announced that, with the preliminary consent of Hungary's Presidential Council, Pope John Paul II had appointed László Paskai as the eighty-first archbishop of Esztergom, primate of Hungary. Paskai seems to be a fortunate choice for a difficult job. He is highly intelligent and articulate, open-minded, forceful yet tactful, a born statesman and diplomat.

47. Interview with László Cardinal Paskai in Montreal, Canada, September 25, 1988.

48. *Kathpress*, April 14, 1988. Primate Paskai published his recommendations in an article in the Catholic weekly *Új Ember*, May 15, 1988. These were essentially the same as Bishop Szendi's demands, only in a less bellicose, more diplomatic language.

49. Grósz resigned from the prime ministership on November 23, 1988. This will in no way diminish his power, since in the communist system the party dominates the government. The new prime minister is Miklós Németh.

50. *Kathpress*, August 26, 1988, attributed the letter to HSWP General Secretary and Prime Minister Károly Grósz. According to Edith Markos, Hungarian church sources say that the letter was signed by State Secretary Imre Miklós, the chairman of the Office for Church Affairs. My account follows closely the article by Edith Markos, "The Government Promises the Church More Religious Freedom," *Radio Free Europe Research* (September 23, 1988): 13–14.

51. The incident was reported by the Budapest correspondent of the Viennese daily *Die Presse*, July 20, 1988.

52. *Keston News Service*, no. 308 (September 8, 1988): 13.

53. See, e.g., "Pázmány Péter emlékezete" (Commemorating Péter Pázmány), *Magyar Hirlap* 41, no. 8 (April 22, 1988): 4.

54. *Keston News Service*, no. 308 (September 8, 1988), p. 14, and no. 323 (April 13, 1989), p. 13; and *Glas Koncila* (Zagreb, August 13, 1989), p. 1.

55. *Markos*, p. 16.

56. *Magyar Kurir* (Hungarian Catholic Press Agency) (French edition), September 12, 1988, p. 4.

57. The numerous guests included Archbishop Francesco Colasuonno, apostolic nuncio in charge of extraordinary affairs and personal legate of the pope; Józef Cardinal Glemp, primate of Poland; bishops from Austria, Germany, and Yugoslavia, and the Orthodox Metropolitan Simeon of Bulgaria.

58. The date of the papal visit to Hungary had not been fixed. It should be noted that earlier in the summer, on June 24, 1988, over 50,000 Hungarian pilgrims attended the papal mass in Trausdorf, which lies just across the border in Austria. The Hungarian authorities, in cooperation with their Austrian counterparts, did everything to facilitate the smooth transport of this unprecedented number of people crossing the Iron Curtain twice in a single day.

59. *Markos*, p. 16.

60. The superiors of the religious orders which operate the eight Catholic schools were notified a year ago that the limits on the number of students would no longer be enforced;

however, because of shortage of staff and funds, they were unable to take advantage of the change. As in past years, hundreds of applicants again had to be turned away. (Interview with László Cardinal Paskai, Montreal, September 25, 1988).

61. Death and retirement necessitated the recent renewal of practically the entire hierarchy. All three archbishops and six diocesan bishops were appointed in 1987. Rome chose men who excelled in pastoral work, with scant regard to their administrative experience. For example, István Seregély, pastor of a small-town parish, was appointed archbishop of Eger, the largest diocese in Hungary. The government gave unprecedented swift approval to these nominations.

62. The issue that lies closest to the heart of all Hungarians and grieves them most is Romania's treatment of its Hungarian minority in Transylvania. The Catholic church, alongside the other churches of Hungary, has repeatedly protested against the violation of human rights in Romania and is actively engaged in aiding the Transylvanian refugees entering Hungary in great numbers. In his public appearances both at home and abroad, Cardinal Primate Paskai never misses an opportunity to call attention to the plight of the Transylvanians. For the close connection between religion and nationalism in Hungary, see my chapter in *Religion and Nationalism in Soviet and East European Politics*, ed. Pedro Ramet, rev. and exp. ed. (Durham, N.C.: Duke University Press, 1989), pp. 286–98; 473–77.

63. The July 9, 1988, issue of the official organ of the HSWP, *Népszabadság*, contained a report of a roundtable conference on the topic "Is the Influence of Religion Increasing in Hungary?" State Secretary Imre Miklós, as well as the leaders of the KISZ, the Federation of Young Communists, had to concede that there was indeed a resurgence of interest in religion among the young people of Hungary. *Magyar Kurir* (French edition), August 3, 1988, pp. 16–19.

8 Yugoslavia

I am grateful to Stella Alexander and Ivo Banac for their helpful comments on earlier drafts of this chapter.

1. Zlatko Markus, "Sadašnji trenutak crkve u Hrvatskoj," *Hrvatska revija* (Buenos Aires), 25, no. 2 (June 1975): 223–24.

2. Frane Franić, *Putovi dijaloga* (Split: Crkva u svijetu, 1973), quoted in Markus, "Sadašnji trenutak," p. 219.

3. Čiril Petešić, *Katoličko svećenstvo u NOB-u 1941–1945* (Zagreb: VPA, 1982), p. 130.

4. Ibid., p. 55.

5. AVNOJ is the Antifascist Council of the People's Liberation of Yugoslavia.

6. Petešić, *Katoličko svećenstvo*, pp. 32, 36.

7. See Ivo Banac, *The National Question in Yugoslavia: Origins, History, Politics* (Ithaca, N.Y.: Cornell University Press, 1984).

8. Fikreta Jelić-Butić, *Ustaše i NDH* (Zagreb: S. N. Liber and Školska Knjiga, 1977), p. 214.

9. Petešić, *Katoličko svećenstvo*, p. 95.

10. Richard Pattee, *The Case of Cardinal Aloysius Stepinac* (Milwaukee: Bruce Publishing, 1953), pp. 114, 276–81, 300–305. Stepinac's efforts on behalf of the Orthodox are noted in Ivan Cvitković's generally unsympathetic biography, *Ko je bio Alojzije Stepinac*, 2d ed. (Sarajevo: Oslobodjenje, 1986), p. 209.

11. Quoted in Branko Bošnjak and Štefica Bahtijarević, *Socijalističko društvo, crkva and religija* (Zagreb: Institut za društvena istraživanja Sveučilišta u Zagrebu, 1969), p. 159.

12. O. Aleksa Benigar, *Alojzije Stepinac, Hrvatski Kardinal* (Rome: Ziral, 1974), p. 492.

13. Quoted in ibid., pp. 502–3.

14. See Pedro Ramet, *Cross and Commissar: The Politics of Religion in Eastern Europe and the USSR* (Bloomington: Indiana University Press, 1987), p. 29.

15. Rastko Vidić, *The Position of the Church in Yugoslavia* (Belgrade: Jugoslavija, 1962), pp. 69–70.

16. Giuseppe Masucci, *Misija u Hrvatskoj 1941–1946* (diary) (Madrid: Drina, 1967), pp. 204–5.

17. Benigar, *Alojzije Stepinac*, p. 508.

18. See article by Dragoljub Petrović in *Književne novine*, October 15, 1985.

19. Quoted in Benigar, *Alojzije Stepinac*, p. 536.

20. Ibid., pp. 540–41.

21. Ibid., pp. 519, 542–43.

22. Ibid., p. 555; confirmed in *New York Times*, September 20, 1946, p. 9.

23. *New York Times*, September 24, 1946, p. 11.

24. Ibid., September 28, 1946, p. 5.

25. Benigar, *Alojzije Stepinac*, p. 578; and *New York Times*, September 26, 1946, p. 7.

26. Jakov Blažević, *Mač a ne mir. Za pravnu sigurnost gradjana*, 4 vols. (Zagreb/Belgrade/Sarajevo: Mladost/Prosveta/Svjetlost, 1980), 3:208–9.

27. Benigar, *Alojzije Stepinac*, p. 601.

28. Blažević, *Mač a ne mir*, 3:211, 234–36.

29. Ibid., 3:237–38. Pattee (*Case*, p. 129) estimates that some 200,000 former Catholics who had been pressured into Orthodoxy were among those converting to Catholicism during the war.

30. Blažević, *Mač a ne mir*, 3:360, 284–85.

31. *L'Osservatore Romano*, September 30, 1946, summarized in *New York Times*, October 1, 1946, p. 15.

32. Blažević, *Mač a ne mir*, 3:210–11.

33. Ibid., 3:374.

34. Stella Alexander, *The Triple Myth: A Life of Archbishop Alojzije Stepinac* (Boulder, Colo.: East European Monographs, 1987), p. 178.

35. *L'Osservatore Romano*, October 12, 1946, translated into Croatian in Benigar, *Alojzije Stepinac*, pp. 635–38; and *L'Osservatore Romano*, October 31, 1946, excerpted in *New York Times*, November 1, 1946, p. 17.

36. Quoted in Benigar, *Alojzije Stepinac*, p. 639.

37. *Polet*, February 8 and 15, 1985, as quoted in *Glas koncila*, February 24, 1985, p. 3.

38. *Borba*, October 24, 1945, p. 3.

39. This latter story seems to have been a complete fabrication, however, since on December 10, 1945, twenty priests from the Bar Archdiocese sent a letter to Stepinac objecting that Archbishop Dobrecić had made no such statements to the press. See Benigar, *Alojzije Stepinac*, p. 546.

40. Stella Alexander, *Church and State in Yugoslavia since 1945* (Cambridge: Cambridge University Press, 1979), p. 126.

41. Report in *Borba*, December 18, 1952, reprinted in *Dokumenti 1948*, vol. 3, ed. Vladimir Dedijer (Belgrade: Rad, 1979), pp. 466–68.

42. Fra Ignacije Gavran, *Lucerna Lucens? Odnos vrhbosanskog ordinarijata prema bosanskim Franjevcima (1881–1975)* (Visoko: n.p., 1978), p. 155.

43. Rudolf Grulich, *Kreuz, Halbmond und Roter Stern: Zur Situation der katholischen Kirche in Jugoslawien* (Munich: Aktion West-Ost, 1979), p. 62.

44. E.g., Gavran, *Lucerna Lucens*, pp. 158–59; and Grulich, *Kreuz, Halbmond*, p. 62.

45. Quoted in Gavran, *Lucerna Lucens*, p. 158n.

46. *Vjesnik*, July 15, 1978, trans. in Joint Publications Research Service (JPRS), *East Europe Report*, no. 72058 (October 17, 1978).

47. *NIN*, no. 1900 (March 22, 1987): 32.

48. Interview, Ljubljana, July 1982.

49. Quoted in Alexander, *Church and State*, p. 229.

50. Paul Mojzes, "Religious Liberty in Yugoslavia: A Study in Ambiguity," in *Religious Liberty and Human Rights in Nations and in Religions*, ed. Leonard Swidler (Philadelphia: Ecumenical Press, 1986), pp. 25–26.

51. Quoted in Zdenko Roter, "Relations between the State and the Catholic Church in Yugoslavia," *Socialist Thought and Practice* 18, no. 11 (November 1974): 69.

52. *New York Times*, June 26, 1966, p. 4.

53. Quoted in Zdenko Roter, *Katoliška cerkev in država v Jugoslaviji 1945–1973* (Ljubljana: Cankarjeva založba, 1976), p. 203.

54. Ibid., p. 206.

55. For details see Pedro Ramet, "Catholicism and Politics in Socialist Yugoslavia," *Religion in Communist Lands* 10, no. 3 (Winter 1982): 261–62.

56. *Borba*, October 9, 1970, p. 6. For further discussion of the Catholic church's association with Croatian nationalism, see Pedro Ramet, "Religion and Nationalism in Yugoslavia," in *Religion and Nationalism in Soviet and East European Politics*, ed. Pedro Ramet, rev. and exp. ed. (Durham, N.C.: Duke University Press, 1989).

57. "Vjernost Alojziju Stepincu—za reviziju sudskog procesa i kanonizaciju!" *Hrvatska revija* 20, no. 1 (March 1970): 85–87.

58. *Borba*, January 14, 1973, p. 7, trans. in JPRS, *Translations on Eastern Europe*, no. 58221 (February 13, 1973).

59. *Nedjeljna Dalmacija* (Varazdin), December 9, 1972, quoted in *Glas koncila*, January 7, 1973, p. 12, trans. in JPRS, *Translations on Eastern Europe*, no. 58479 (March 14, 1973).

60. *Glas koncila*, December 25, 1980.

61. *Frankfurter Allgemeine*, November 2, 1987, p. 4.

62. Tanjug, November 15, 1987, quoted in *Keston News Service*, no. 290 (December 17, 1987): 14.

63. *Glas koncila*, December 6, 1987, p. 2, and December 13, 1987, p. 2; and *AKSA Bulletin* (Catholic news summary translation service edited by Stella Alexander with Muriel Heppell and Kresimir Šidor), January 26, 1988, pp. 5–6.

64. *Družina*, August 1, 1971, cited in *Borba*, August 1, 1971, p. 5.

65. Interview with Franjo Cardinal Kuharić, in *Veritas* (March 1987), excerpted in *Glas koncila*, March 8, 1987, p. 3.

66. Dionisie Ghermani, "Die katholische Kirche in Kroatien/Slowenien," *Kirche in Not* 27 (1979): 93; *Glas koncila*, February 19, 1984, p. 4, and June 16, 1985, p. 3.

67. *Delo* (Ljubljana), February 20, 1988, as reported in *AKSA Bulletin*, April 14, 1988, p. 4.

68. *Keston News Service*, no. 274 (April 30, 1987): 16–17.

69. *Glas koncila*, October 25, 1981, p. 3.

70. Interview with Archbishop of Belgrade Dr. Franc Perko, in *Danas*, no. 260 (February 10, 1987): p. 26; and source listed in n. 65.

71. Drago Šimundža, "Ustavni i stvarni položaj vjernika u društvu," *Crkva u svijetu*, no. 4, 1987, reprinted in *Glas koncila*, December 25, 1987, p. 5; *Frankfurter Allgemeine*, March 17, 1988, p. 1; and *Glas koncila*, April 3, 1988, p. 5.

72. *Glas koncila*, January 7, 1973, p. 12.

73. Ibid., January 22, 1978, p. 3, trans. in JPRS, *East Europe Report*, no. 70836 (March 24, 1978).

74. See Pedro Ramet, "Factionalism in Church-State Interaction: The Croatian Catholic Church in the 1980s," *Slavic Review* 44, no. 2 (Summer 1985); reprinted as chap. 6 of Ramet, *Cross and Commissar*.

75. Fr. Živko Kustić, chief editor of *Glas koncila*, in interview with the author in Zagreb, June 25, 1987.

76. *Vjesnik*, April 5, 1987, summarized in *Glas koncila*, April 12, 1987, p. 2.

77. Zlatko Frid, *Religija u samoupravnom socijalizmu* (Zagreb: Centar za društvene djelatnosti omladine RK SOH, 1971), p. 118.

78. Ibid., pp. 109–13. Yet there are churches in the diocese of Kotor that even today continue to be used by both Catholics and Orthodox.

79. Viktor Novak, *Velika optužba*, 3 vols. (Sarajevo: Svjetlost, 1960), 1: 20–34; and *Glas koncila*, March 27, 1983, p. 8.

80. *Glas koncila*, December 15, 1985, p. 6.

81. *Frankfurter Allgemeine*, July 23, 1980, p. 5; and *Vjesnik: Sedam dana*, April 24, 1982, p. 17.

82. *Glas koncila*, April 19, 1981, pp. 7, 9.

83. *Vjesnik: Sedam dana*, April 30, 1982, p. 10; and *Frankfurter Allgemeine*, February 8, 1983, p. 10, July 5, 1983, p. 8, and February 21, 1985, p. 12.

84. *Vjesnik: Sedam dana*, July 31, 1982, p. 14.

85. Rudolf Grulich, *Die Katholische Kirche in der Sozialistischen Föderativen Republik Jugoslawien* (Zollikon: Glaube in der 2. Welt, 1980), p. 11.

86. *Vjesnik u srijedu*, May 6, 1970, pp. 10–11. See also Berislav Gavranović, *Uspostava redovite katoličke hijerarhije u Bosni i Hercegovini 1881 godine* (Belgrade: Filosofski fakultet, 1935).

87. Gavran, *Lucerna Lucens*, p. 152.

88. Ibid., p. 146.

89. See ibid., pp. 146–51.

90. Rene Laurentin and Ljudevit Rupčić, *Is the Virgin Mary Appearing at Medjugorje?* (Washington, D.C.: Word Among Us Press, 1984), pp. 113–14.

91. *Sveta Baština* (March 1987), as summarized in *Aktualnosti Krscanske Sadasnjosti* (AKSA), April 3, 1987, translated in *AKSA Bulletin*, June 14, 1987, p. 7.

92. *Duga*, August 25, 1984, in *AKSA Bulletin*, November 28, 1984, p. 5.

93. Manojlo Bročić, "The Position and Activities of the Religious Communities in Yugoslavia with Special Attention to the Serbian Orthodox Church," in *Religion and Atheism in the USSR and Eastern Europe*, ed. Bohdan R. Baciurkiw and John W. Strong (London: Macmillan, 1975), pp. 364–65.

94. Srdjan Vrcan, "Omladina osamdesetih godina, religija i crkva," in *Položaj, svest i ponašanje mlade generacije Jugoslavije: Preliminarna analiza rezultata istraživanja*, ed. S. Vrcan et al. (Zagreb: IDIS, 1986), p. 159.

95. AKSA, February 22, 1985, as extracted in *AKSA Bulletin*, April 17, 1985, p. 5.

96. *Nedeljna Dalmacija*, April 21, 1985, reported in AKSA, April 26, 1985, as extracted in *AKSA Bulletin*, July 25, 1985, p. 5.

97. AKSA, June 6, 1986, in *AKSA Bulletin*, August 5, 1986, p. 4; and *Keston News Service*, no. 257 (August 21, 1986): 12.

98. *Borba* (Zagreb edition), February 6, 1986, p. 3.

99. Grulich, *Kreuz, Halbmond*, pp. 58–59.

100. Bošnjak and Bahtijarević, *Socijalističko društvo*, p. 33.

101. Ibid., p. 134.

102. Ibid., p. 83.

103. Ibid., pp. 83–84.

104. Ibid., p. 63.

105. *Nedjeljna borba* (Zagreb), February 14–15, 1987, summarized in *AKSA Bulletin*, May 26, 1987, p. 2.

106. Quoted in Bošnjak and Bahtijarević, *Socijalističko društvo*, p. 133.

107. Zagreb Domestic Service, May 16, 1986, trans. in FBIS, *Daily Report* (Eastern Europe), May 20, 1986, p. 114. See also *Vjesnik*, November 25, 1985, summarized in AKSA, November 28, 1985, as reported in *AKSA Bulletin*, January 31, 1986, p. 5.

108. Radio Vatican in Serbo-Croatian, April 19, 1985, trans. in JPRS, *East Europe Report*, no. EPS-85-057 (May 17, 1985): 156–58.

109. *Glas koncila*, May 11, 1986, p. 2.

110. *AKSA Bulletin*, August 16, 1985, p. 8, quoting *Danas*, July 2, 1985.

111. *Frankfurter Allgemeine*, January 8, 1985, p. 3. See also *Glas koncila*, November 25, 1984, p. 2.

112. *NIN*, no. 1879 (January 4, 1987): 15–16; and *Frankfurter Allgemeine*, January 2, 1987, p. 4.

113. Interview, Ljubljana, July 1987; and *Keston News Service*, no. 336 (October 19, 1989), p. 14. See AKSA, December 30, 1988, and January 6, 1989, as reported in *AKSA Bulletin*, March 6, 1989, pp. 3–4.

114. *Borba* (Zagreb edition), October 31–November 1, 1987, p. 3; *Dnevnik* (Novi Sad), November 13, 1987, summarized in AKSA, November 13, 1987, as reported in *AKSA Bulletin*, January 26, 1988, p. 7; and *Glas koncila*, January 3, 1988, p. 3.

115. *Delo*, January 6, 1988, reported in *AKSA Bulletin*, March 9, 1988, p. 10; and *Ilustrovana politika* (Belgrade), February 2, 1988, reported in *AKSA Bulletin*, April 14, 1988, p. 8.

116. For discussion, see *Glas koncila*, August 17, 1986, p. 3.

9 Romania

1. The material on the historical background is mostly from R. W. Seton Watson, *The History of the Romanians* (Cambridge: Cambridge University Press, 1934); and Pierre Gherman, *Pensée Romaine; Peuple Roumain* (Paris: Spes, 1967). Since they overlap and complement each other I have generally avoided specific references. Gherman writes from the Catholic standpoint. Likewise, there is much overlapping in the main sources for the more recent history of the Eastern Rite Catholic church, as provided by Gherman, *Pensée Romaine*; Lino Gussoni and Aristede Brunello, *The Silent Church* (New York: Veritas, 1954); Flavio Popan, *Il Martirio della Chiesa di Romania* (Urbania, Pesaro: La Chiesa del Silenzio, 1976); *L'Église Roumaine unie*, No. 19, 3rd Qtr. (Mareil-Marly: Aide à l'Église en détresse, 1975); Alexander Ratiu and William Virtue, *Stolen Church* (Huntington, Ind.: Our Sunday Visitor, 1979).

2. Seton Watson, *History*, p. 174. The 1766 census of Transylvania listed 140,000 Reformed (Calvinists, mostly Hungarians), 1,300,000 Lutherans (mostly Saxons), 93,000 Roman Catholics (both), and 28,000 Unitarians (mostly Saxons). The number of Romanians was 547,243.

3. Popan, *Il Martirio*, pp. 13–16. The Calvinist-dominated Diet challenged it, arguing that it had taken place under duress, and some priests were pressurized to renounce the union; Athanasius called another synod in 1699, which ratified the agreement.

4. Gherman, *Pensée Romaine*, pp. 62–63.

5. Seton Watson, *History*, pp. 178–79. He protested on behalf of a people "wounded to the marrow." When other members of the Diet retorted that "the Wallachs are vagabonds

. . . brigands, lazy thieves," he replied, "It cannot be otherwise since they are so bloodily persecuted; . . . to the poor you leave nothing but their skins, on which you live. Do the Romanians not work the salt and iron and gold mines for you?"

6. Gherman, *Pensée Romaine*, pp. 78–80, 83–84, 94. When in 1842 the Diet decreed that only Hungarian could be used in church and school, the Blaj cathedral chapter declared that Hungarian would never be introduced into their schools; later, Bishop Basil Suciu refused subsidies in order to maintain their independence. Toward the end of the century the church had to resist an attempt to attach it to the new Eastern Rite Diocese of Hajdudorogh and counter the introduction of services in Magyar. In 1912 the Papal bull *Christi fideles graeci* actually detached eighty-three parishes and transferred them to Hajdudorogh, though this was partially reversed after Romania became independent.

7. Gherman, *Pensée Romaine*, pp. 189–90.

8. Gussoni and Brunello, *Silent Church*, pp. 111, 144. Before the communist takeover there were 376 secondary schools with 51,000 students.

9. Gussoni and Brunello, *Silent Church*, p. 109.

10. In "Il pastore è morto, ma la chiesa vive," *CSEO Documentazione* (Bologna, Italy) (November 1977): 301; the anonymous author, a priest or priests, refers to Latin Rite dioceses in Moldavia from the Middle Ages onward.

11. Gherman, *Pensée Romaine*, pp. 207–8, 237.

12. Ion Ratiu, "Uniates in Romania," *Tablet*, February 27, 1982, p. 199.

13. Popan, *Il Martirio*, pp. 22–23.

14. For greater detail see Janice Broun, "The Latin-Rite Roman Catholic Church of Romania," *Religion in Communist Lands* 12 no. 2 (1984): 168–69.

15. Popan, *Il Martirio*, p. 70.

16. Ion Ratiu, "Romanian Catholics," *Tablet*, September 2, 1978.

17. "Le Cri d'une Église martyrisée," in *Aide à l'Église en détresse*, no. 31, 1981.

18. Anna Halja, "Ukrainische unierte in Rumänien," *Informationen und Berichte, Digest des Ostens* (Haus der Begegnung, Königstein), no. 3 (1982).

19. One, Ion Chertes, bishop of Cluj-Gherda, is now a "vegetable" (private source).

20. See appeal from the Committee for the Restitution of the Romanian Catholic Church to UNO, August 1977, in *CSEO* (January 1978): 35–36: "We are not just a Catholic Church; we are the Romanian Catholic Church united to the Catholic Church but with our own rite. We do not wish to be forced into a Church with an alien rite. We are born Romanians. We are not just a cult; we are a Romanian cultural institution."

21. For instance, see *Keston News Service*, no. 254 (July 10, 1986): 10–11 for a spurious document planted by the authorities to stir up anti-Hungarian feeling.

22. Ratiu, "Romanian Catholics."

23. *CSEO* (January 1978): 35–36. In a memorandum to Ceauşescu they claimed to have been the most devout church and the most faithful to the Romanian nation. "We would faithfully defend the unity and sovereignty of the Romanian people and oppose the interference of other states in national life. We would work in an ecumenical spirit with our sister Orthodox Church and the other cults. The possibility of staunching innumerable bleeding wounds is in your hands. Our cause is holy and just."

24. "Les Évêques Gréco-Catholiques s'adressent à la Conférence de Madrid," *Catacombes* (Paris) (November 1980): 10.

25. The source, corroborated by others, is Fr. Petru Mareş, who became the most outspoken Catholic priest in the late 1970s and was forced into exile in the West. Corrborated in Dina Campana, ed., *Luci nelle tenebre* (Rome: La Chiesa del Silenzio, 1980), 2: 208–9.

26. Hansjakob Stehle, *Eastern Politics of the Vatican 1917–1979*, trans. from German by

Sandra Smith (Athens: Ohio University Press, 1981), pp. 263–68. Stehle thinks that Pius XII was too ready to plunge the church into a catacomb situation.

27. Information supplied in 1965 by a Frenchman who had lived in Romania; see "Un regard porté sur la vie de l'Église Catholique en Roumanie: Mission en Tourisme et Loisir" (Keston College Archives); Daniel Madden, "Romania's Illegal Catholics," *Columbia* (USA) (December 1969): 8–18, provides valuable, well-researched information and revealing interviews with clergy approved by the state. Significantly, Madden was not allowed to meet Marton. For an excellent inside account of the sufferings of those years, particularly in Moldavia, see "Il pastore è morto."

28. Report of a private conversation with Rudolf Grulich. *Aid to the Church in Need Report* (Königstein, 1977).

29. Broun, "Latin Rite Roman Catholic Church," p. 172.

30. Pierre Gherman, *Le bienheureux Jérémie, humble disciple valaque de St. François* (Brussels: Van Ruys, 1983).

31. Statistics in the *Annuario Pontificio* were often incomplete, showing some odd discrepancies; and in some years only out-of-date figures were given. Letter from Aid to the Church in Need, August 25, 1980, in Keston College Archives.

32. A conference center built around 1980 is the only new building apart from Iaşi seminary. The few remaining religious, survivors from 1949, are too old to be providing care for retired priests!

33. Mareş reported that in 1978 newly ordained priests often went directly to their parish with only a breviary. For years they had no manuals, only cyclostyled, almost illegible texts. Most teaching was done by dictation, with every book shared.

34. *Keston News Service*, no. 247 (April 3, 1986): 11, quoting *Kathpress*.

35. Reported by Mareş.

36. Broun, "Latin Rite Roman Catholic Church," p. 176, summarizing scanty information.

37. *Kathpress*, January 2, 1981.

38. Letter to pope from a group of Romanian Catholics, December 1978, in Keston College Archives.

39. There are, however, many people still haunted by remembrance of past persecution and families where parents are afraid to pass on their beliefs to their children. There are others who are simply too exhausted by the relentless demands of daily life (queueing for hours to obtain the most basic foods, often unobtainable during the present crisis, which seems likely to continue) to take their children to church. It is amazing that mass attendance is as high as it is.

40. "Les Évêques Gréco-Catholiques s'adressent à la Conférence de Madrid."

41. "Il pastore è morto"; and letter to pope, 1978. The latter is an outspoken collective appeal which also systematically lists the overall disabilities suffered by Romanian Catholics and their demands.

42. In Augustin's favor it should be noted that he seems to have been a good pastor, instructing children well. On a visit to Italy he made the point that Catholic churches in Bucharest were better attended than those in Rome!

43. According to Augustin in an interview with Francesco Strazzari, in *Messenger of St. Anthony of Padua* (Padua) (July 1980): 5, corroborated by Mareş's testimony.

44. "They are on firm ground. Our new Pope has laboured and suffered and struggled. He's so secure; why? Because for him faith is real; it's not something to discuss or debate; it's not some thing. It's all!" (Mareş).

45. In neighboring Hungary, Christians of various denominations are now taking greater interest in their conationals in Transylvania. A group calling itself the Committee for Rec-

onciliation circulated a petition in Budapest on behalf of Hungarian Christians in Romania. About a thousand believers signed the petition. The Hungarian Catholic Bishops' Conference also addressed this subject in late 1986.

10 Albania

1. *Albanian Catholic Bulletin* 2 (1981).

2. Romans 15, 19.

3. Edgar Hösch, *The Balkans. A Short History from Greek Times to the Present Day* (London: Faber and Faber, 1972), pp. 23–27.

4. Peter R. Prifti, *Socialist Albania since 1944* (Cambridge, Mass.: MIT Press, 1978), pp. 5–6.

5. Gjon Sinishta, *The Fulfilled Promise* (Santa Clara, Calif.: n.p., 1976), pp. 190–91.

6. Marmullaku, *Albania and the Albanians* (London: Hurst, 1975), pp. 30–39.

7. Anton Logoreci, *The Albanians. Europe's Forgotten Survivors* (London: Victor Gollancz, 1977), p. 16.

8. This came under the administration of the archbishop of Durres and had about 4,000 Catholics. Its aim was primarily missionary, seeking to create a favorable atmosphere for the union of Orthodox and Catholics. Sinishta, *The Fulfilled Promise*, pp. 38–44.

9. Bernard Tönnes, "Religious Persecution in Albania," *Religion in Communist Lands* 10, no. 3 (Winter 1982): 16.

10. Further theological study was pursued usually in Italy or in Croatia. The Albanians had better relations with Croats than with other Slavs.

11. They included Fr. Gjergj Fishta (1871–1940), a Franciscan widely recognised as Albania's greatest poet; Archbishop Vincenz Prendushi (1885–1949), provincial of the Franciscans, a poet; Fr. Lazar Shantoja (1892–1945), poet and journalist; Fr. Bernadin Palaj (1894–1947), poet; and Fr. Anton Harapi, a Franciscan (1888–1946). Harapi was an educator, lecturer, and writer who had been indefatigable in his missionary work, especially during the cholera epidemic of 1916. He had become Catholic representative on the High Regency, the ruling body set up by the Nazis, in order to try to put an end to the civil war. Sinishta, *The Fulfilled Promise*, pp. 79–90, 99–103, 111–17, 181–82.

12. *Kisha Dhe Historia e Saj* (Ferizaj, Yugoslavia: Drita, 1982). Taken from English translation of Albanian history section, in the author's possession.

13. Most of the material for this section is from Edith Durham, *High Albania* (Arnold 1909; reprint, London: Virago, 1985); and Marmullaku, *Albania and the Albanians*. In one Catholic village Edith Durham was told: "We are in blood with the Jews for they slew our Christ. We are in blood with the Turks because they insult him. We are in blood with the Orthodox because they do not pray to him properly." A man who had killed a Muslim at the age of twelve claimed to be an excellent Christian but added, "When the Last Day comes we shall have the most awful fight with Christ!"

14. Perpetuators of blood feuds were usually summarily executed and the families involved were settled far apart from one another in order to preclude any attempt to continue the feud. Marmullaku, *Albania and the Albanians*, pp. 82–91.

15. Ann Bridge, *Singing Waters* (New York: Harold Matson, 1946).

16. The Catholic orphanage in Shkodra, with about a thousand orphans, was left open until 1950.

17. Interestingly, the primate, Archbishop Kristofor Kisi, was deposed on August 28, 1949, for the crime of "trying to detach the church from the Eastern Orthodox faith and surrender it to the Vatican." Prifti, *Socialist Albania*, pp. 152–53.

18. Professor Jeh Vala, "Bishop Fran Gjini—Dignified Defender of his Flock," in Sinishta, *The Fulfilled Promise*, pp. 91–94.

19. A very active person who had shown considerable bravery in defending Albanians from the Germans, the National Liberation Front, and the Communists. Anton Gaspi, "A Testimony to Bishop Volaj of Sappa," in Sinishta, *The Fulfilled Promise*, pp. 95–98.

20. Most of the information in this section is from Sinishta, *The Fulfilled Promise*.

21. Michael Marku, "Profile of a Young Martyr," in Sinishta, *The Fulfilled Promise*, pp. 138–40.

22. Jak Gardin, S.J., quoted in Sinishta, *The Fulfilled Promise*, p. 55.

23. Nika Stajka, *The Last Days of Freedom* (New York: Vantage Press, 1980), pp. 67–84. Stajka also gives a graphic account of life and death in the labor camps.

24. One, at least, Martin Shkurti, was allowed to run a (prosperous) parish after his ordination in 1963. In 1968 he and his family escaped to Yugoslavia, only to be returned to the Albanian authorities. He was executed before a large crowd in Shkodra. Sinishta, *The Fulfilled Promise*, p. 70.

25. The party was bitterly critical of Gromyko's audience with Paul VI in 1966 and subsequent contacts between the Soviet leaders and the pope. They reminded the Kremlin of the many sins committed by the Vatican against communism, including attempts by the Catholic church to mobilize "crusades" against the Soviet Union following the October Revolution and the part played by Cardinal Mindszenty in "organizing" the Hungarian counterrevolution. They further charged the Soviet Union with fostering a revival of religion! Prifti, *Socialist Albania*, p. 160.

26. Dilaver Sadikaj, "The Revolutionary Movement against Religion in the Sixties," *Studine Historik: University of Tirana Quarterly Journal* 4 (1981), as translated in *Albanian Catholic Bulletin* 4 (1983): 20–34.

27. Prifti, *Socialist Albania*, p. 161.

28. Sadikaj's figures are 2,035 buildings, including 740 mosques, 608 Orthodox churches, and only 157 Catholic churches ("Revolutionary Movement," p. 23). The figure 327 is from the Tirana monthly, *Mendori* (September 1967).

29. For instance, in Shkodra the cathedral was converted into a sports center, complete with swimming pool. St. Nicholas Church became an apartment building. A former convent became the headquarters of the Sigurini (the secret police). Other churches became clubs, cinemas, dance halls, barns, and latrines.

30. Sadikaj, "Revolutionary Movement," pp. 27, 28.

31. Ibid., pp. 26, 28.

32. *Albanian Catholic Bulletin* 1 (1980), 2 (1981): 10.

33. *Keston News Service*, no. 161 (November 4, 1982): 2–3.

34. *Albanian Catholic Bulletin* 4 (1983): 10.

35. Ibid., 7 (1986): 34.

36. Gjon Sinishta, "Albania: The World's First Godless State," *Homiletic and Pastoral Review* (November 1980); and Gjon Sinishta, "Grave Violations of Religious Rights in Albania," *Occasional Papers on Religion in Eastern Europe* 3, no. 5 (July 1983): 15. Among these were Fr. Mark Hasi (20 years), Fr. Zef Bllumbi (15 years), Fr. Gege Lumaj (15 years), Fr. Injaj Gjoka, Fr. Rrok Gjuraj, Fr. Anton Luli, S.J. (reported to have been very active), Fr. Gjergj Vata, S.J., Fr. Simon Jubana and his elder brother, Lazar, and two Franciscans.

37. *Keston News Service*, no. 120 (March 26, 1981): 11–12, and no. 159 (October 7, 1982): 4.

38. *Albanian Catholic Bulletin* 9 (1988): 30–31.

39. Ibid., 1 (1980): 1–2.

40. It had an icon of Mary, said to have been miraculously transported to Genazzano in Italy in 1467 when Albanians were fleeing from the Turks. *Keston News Service*, no. 108 (October 20, 1988): 9.

41. *Rruga e partisse*, March 1, 1984, as quoted in Louis Zanga, "Albania: The World's First Atheist State but with Deeply Rooted Religious Feelings," *Radio Free Europe Research*, May 23, 1984, p. 5.

42. *Albanian Catholic Bulletin* 2 (1981): 32.

43. Tönnes, "Religious Persecution in Albania," pp. 254–55.

44. *Documentation on Central Europe* (Louvain), no. 4 (1980).

45. *Keston News Service*, no. 159 (October 7, 1982): 3.

46. Ibid., no. 247 (April 3, 1986): 11.

47. Speech by Pope Paul VI, as reported in the *Tablet*, May 13, 1973, p. 43.

48. *Keston News Service*, no. 159 (October 7, 1982): 7.

11 China

1. For a discussion of the role of political culture in Catholic politics see Eric O. Hanson, *The Catholic Church in World Politics* (Princeton: Princeton University Press, 1987). Political culture is defined as "that unique amalgamation of historical memory, types of social organizations, and traditional modes of thought that provides the contemporary environment for political and economic institutions" (p. 361).

2. The term comes from Ivan Vallier, "The Roman Catholic Church: A Transnational Actor," in *Transnational Relations and World Politics*, ed. Robert O. Keohane and Joseph F. Nye, Jr. (Cambridge: Harvard University Press, 1972), pp. 129–52.

3. See David S. G. Goodman, "The Sixth Plenum of the 11th Central Committee of the CCP: Look Back in Anger?" *China Quarterly* 87 (September 1981): 518–27.

4. Eric O. Hanson, *Catholic Politics in China and Korea* (Maryknoll, N.Y.: Orbis Books, 1980). The summary cited below can be found on p. 113, with additions from other parts of the book.

5. The papal rites decision (1715) declared that Catholics could no longer follow Confucian ritual. In 1704 the Roman Inquisition obtained the first papal condemnation of the rites. Then a papal legate, Maillard de Tournon, spent five years in discussions in China. Chinese state proscription (1736) drove Catholics underground.

6. Despite notable exceptions (e.g., the French Jesuits in Shanghai), this statement is true for non-Christian Asia in general. The Chinese rites decision constituted a major hindrance to native Catholic intellectual activity in Asia into the twentieth century.

7. Bob Whyte, *Unfinished Encounter: China and Christianity* (London: Fount, 1988), pp. 448–49. The center of Chinese Catholic intellectual life is Shanghai, where the Association of Catholic Intellectuals was formed in June 1986.

8. "Self-government, self-support, and self-propagation." See Hanson, *Catholic Politics*, pp. 60–61, for the Catholic Three Self Movement of 1950–51.

9. In May 1988 six hundred major seminarians were reported studying in fifteen government-approved seminaries: national (Beijing); regional (Beijing, Chengdu, Sheshan, Shenyang, Xian, and Wuhan); provincial (Hohot, Jinan, Shijiazhuang, Taiyuan); and semi-officially recognized diocesan (Hankou, Jilin, Kunming, Xianxian).

10. See, for example, the document "In Dialogue with China" (Manila, September 8, 1986), which, while always respecting the conscience of the faithful, advises priests to teach at state-approved seminaries and laity to attend state-approved churches if they consider the priest "a good pastor."

11. The Religious Affairs Bureau (RAB) was established in 1951 as the Religious Affairs Office of the Committee on Cultural and Educational Affairs of the Government Administration Council, a state organization. For its history and operation see Hanson, *Catholic Politics*, pp. 60–71.

12. For an interview with Monsignor Paolo Giglio, chargé in Taiwan 1978–86 and now archbishop and nuncio in Nicaragua, see *Asia Focus* 2 (May 9, 1986).

13. For the pope's text and documentation on Casaroli's visit to Bishop Deng, see *Religion in the People's Republic of China* [hereinafter *RPRC*] 5 (May 1981): 10–15.

14. *RPRC* 5 (May 1981): 14.

15. For the seventy-nine-year-old archbishop's discussion of the meaning of the appointment, see *Asia Focus* 3 (June 12, 1987).

16. Chinese reaction to Deng's appointment can be found in *RPRC* 6 (October 1981): 7–12.

17. So, according to Tong, the bishop was not even accorded the hearing given to the nefarious Gang of Four. Angelo Lazzarotto, *The Catholic Church in Post-Mao China* (Hong Kong: Holy Spirit Study Centre, 1982), pp. 143–45.

18. Wei received a sentence of fifteen years on October 16. The *dazibao* (large-character poster) movement began in Beijing in November 1978. For a detailed chronology and fine analysis of the democracy movement, see Kjeld Erik Brodsgaard, "The Democracy Movement in China, 1978–1979: Opposition Movements, Wall Poster Campaigns, and Underground Journals," *Asian Survey* 21 (July 1981): 747–74.

19. For analysis of Chinese religious policy toward the Catholic church in 1979–82, the following three sources are recommended: *China News Analysis*, no. 1156 (June 8, 1979); *China News Analysis*, no. 1186 (August 1, 1980); and Angelo Lazarrotto, "The Chinese Communist Party and Religion," *Missiology* 9 (July 1983): 267–90.

20. *China News Analysis*, no. 1156, p. 5.

21. The New China News Agency (NCNA) releases can be found in *RPRC* 2–3 (July 1980): 43–46.

22. See Richard Madsen, *Morality and Power in a Chinese Village* (Berkeley: University of California Press, 1985). In his last chapter Madsen shows how the period affected his four main types of local officials. In summary he writes: "When Maoism exploded into absurdity, the moral basis of Chinese culture disintegrated into its diverse themes. The Communist gentry, the Communist rebel, the moralistic revolutionary, and the peasant technocrat emerged in all their one-sided, incompatible purity. Being thus one-dimensionally moral as persons, they became immoral as politicians. And thus Chinese political culture became demoralized —an ironic, tragic end for Mao's attempt at moral revolution" (p. 262).

23. *Guanxixue* means "the manipulation of relationships." See John Wilson Lewis, "Political Networks and the Chinese Policy Process," an occasional paper of the Northeast Asia–United States Forum on International Policy, Stanford University, March 1986. On the CCP's attempt to deal with the problem, see "Trust and Rituals: Party Rectification 1984," *China News Analysis*, no. 1269 (September 10, 1984). Bo Yibo's May 26, 1987, report summing up the campaign received little attention. Less than .1 percent of party cadres were expelled.

24. For an excellent summary of this politically crucial year see Stanley Rosen, "China in 1987: The Year of the Thirteenth Party Congress," *Asian Survey* 28 (January 1988): 35–51.

25. Bishop Jin, a respected Shanghai Jesuit, said he had prayed for six months before he had decided to accept his former position as rector of Sheshan. Jin became an auxiliary bishop of Shanghai in the following January and succeeded Shanghai bishop Zhang Jiashu when the latter died in February 1988.

26. The relative openness and policy agenda of the current Shanghai situation is represented by the position of PRC officials like Yang Zengnian, former director of the Shanghai

RAB and now vice director of the Shanghai Province United Front Department. For an interview with Yang at the dedication of new facilities for Sheshan Regional Seminary, see *Asia Focus* 2 (October 10, 1986).

27. Of the seven Western economic powers, Catholics constitute a majority in France and Italy and a plurality in Canada, West Germany, and the United States.

28. *New York Times*, July 4 and 5, 1985. For a summary of Catholic events in China during 1985 see *Asia Focus* 2 (January 10, 1986).

29. *Asia Focus* 2 (February 7, 1986).

30. *Asia Focus* 4 (June 4, 1988).

31. *Asia Focus* 4 (November 12, 1988).

32. *Asia Focus* 4 (April 16, 1988).

33. For the brief story of his family, see Hanson, *Catholic Politics*, pp. 50–51.

34. *New York Times*, May 2, 1983. Amnesty International has taken up the case of the four Jesuits, as it had of that of Bishop Gong. An NCNA release indicated that Roman Catholics had been arrested for "following the wishes of the Roman Curia" and "trying to undermine the independence of Chinese churches." Union of Catholic Asian News from Hong Kong, in *Hong Kong Sunday Examiner*, January 8, 1982.

35. "Premier Zhao Ziyang indirectly confirmed that something was in the air, at a press conference on 23 May 1984, in which he said that he had noticed that the Pope's recent remarks during his ten-day Asian tour in May had shown some change in position" (Whyte, *Unfinished Encounter*, p. 441).

36. See Orville Schell, "China's Andre Sakharov," *Atlantic Monthly* (May 1988): 35–52.

37. See Kenneth Lieberthal, "Domestic Politics and Foreign Policy," in *China's Foreign Relations in the 1980s*, ed. Harry Harding (New Haven, Conn.: Yale University Press, 1984), pp. 43–70.

38. For example, in April 1986 the Reagan administration announced that it planned to sell $550 million worth of aviation electronics to the PRC. In November 1986 three U.S. Navy warships visited Qingdao for the first time since 1949.

39. See Bishop Jin's explicit denial of this position in *Asia Focus* 2 (April 18, 1986).

40. See, for example, Hanson, *Catholic Politics*, pp. 15–31.

41. *Asia Focus* 2 (November 28, December 5, 1986).

42. Whyte, *Unfinished Encounter*, p. 450.

43. *Asia Focus* 4 (August 27, 1988).

44. *National Catholic Reporter*, June 3, 1988. Bishop Jin did not say if those bishops include the eight still publicly recognized by the Vatican.

45. For example, see Reuter from Rome, March 6, 1984, in *New York Times*, March 7, 1984.

46. *Asia Focus* 2 (December 19, 1986).

47. *Asia Focus* 4 (November 5, 1988).

12 Vietnam

1. Piero Gheddo, *The Cross and the Bo-Tree: Catholics and Buddhists in Vietnam* (New York: Sheed and Ward, 1970), p. 4.

2. Ibid.

3. "Vietnam," in *New Catholic Encyclopedia* (New York: McGraw-Hill, 1967), 14:661–62.

4. Gheddo, *Cross*, pp. 71, 99.

5. "The Catholics and the National Movement," in *Vietnamese Studies*, no. 53 (Hanoi: Xunhasaba, 1979), pp. 76–77.

6. Tom Dooley, *Deliver Us from Evil*, pp. 97–105, in *Dr. Tom Dooley's Three Great Books* (New York: Farrar, Straus and Cudahy, 1960).

7. Text of letter published in *Vietnamese Studies*, no. 53, p. 198.

8. "Un document du P.C. vietnamien concernant l'Église catholique," *Échange France-Asie* (Paris), no. 72 (February 1982): 5–7; see also Pham Quang Hieu, "Several Ideas on Vigorously Developing the Democratic Rights of Religious Compatriots," *Hoc Tap* (Hanoi) (July 1970): 22–26, translated in Foreign Broadcast Information Service (FBIS) *Daily Report* (Asia-Pacific), August 26, 1970, pp. K15–K19.

9. Pham Quang Hieu, "Several Ideas," pp. K15–K19.

10. *Vietnamese Studies*, no. 53, p. 123.

11. Ibid., p. 200.

12. Ibid., p. 123.

13. Gheddo, *Cross*, p. 85.

14. Text of decree published in *Vietnamese Studies*, no. 53, pp. 192–96.

15. Gheddo, *Cross*, p. 81; *L'Osservatore Romano*, August 13, 1955.

16. Bernard Fall, *The Two Vietnams* (New York: Praeger, 1963), p. 156. There was much controversy during the war over the number of people killed during this campaign, with estimates ranging from fifteen hundred to several hundred thousand.

17. The Hung, "The Church with Respect to the Building of the North and the Struggle for National Reunification," *Hoc Tap* (February 1962). Translated version at the Indochina Archive, University of California, Berkeley, DRV/SM/Rel/February 1962.

18. *Asia* (Hong Kong) (January 1960): 17.

19. Gheddo, *Cross*, p. 88.

20. The Hung, "The Church." Translation on file at Indochina Archive, DRV/SM/Rel/February 1962.

21. Gheddo, *Cross*, pp. 88–89.

22. François Houtart and Genevieve Lemercinier, *Hai Van: Life in a Vietnamese Commune* (London: Zed Books, 1984), p. 170.

23. The Hung, "The Church"; Houtart and Lemercinier, *Hai Van*, p. 169.

24. Houtart and Lemercinier, *Hai Van*, p. 169.

25. *Vietnamese Studies*, no. 53, p. 130.

26. *Le Monde*, June 9, 1971.

27. See, for example, P. Chan Ly, "Political Activity," *Chinh Nghia* (Hanoi), October 30, 1966. Translation on file at Indochina Archive, DRV/SM/Rel/October 1962.

28. Gheddo, *Cross*, pp. 94–95.

29. *Vietnamese Studies*, no. 53, p. 128.

30. Ibid., p. 133.

31. *Échange France-Asie*, no. 72 (February 1982): A–D (introduction to a translated document), includes detailed commentary on these three languages.

32. Text of resolution published in *Chinh Nghia*, December 20, 1977, translated by the Joint Publications Research Service (JPRS), *Vietnam Report*, no. 70556, February 17, 1978, pp. 6–10.

33. Internal document of the Communist party, undated but apparently written sometime between September 2, 1978, and September 2, 1979; translated into French by *Échange France-Asie* (February 1982).

34. "The Catholic Church in South Vietnam—May 1972," unclassified report (no source listed) at the Indochina Archive, VN/Rel/1972.

35. Tiziano Terzani, *Giai Phong: The Fall and Liberation of Saigon* (New York: St. Martin's Press, 1976), pp. 269–71.

36. "Controls by the SRV on Catholic Church Activities," refugee interview summary (no source listed), U.C. Indochina Archive, SRV/SM/Rel/November 1980.

37. Ibid.; also confidential refugee interview, 1986.

38. Vu Luong, "The Answer," *Chinh Nghia*, March 13, 1975; trans. in JPRS, no. 64913, *Translations on North Vietnam*, June 4, 1975, pp. 22–23.

39. Fr. Sesto Quercetti, "The Vietnam Church: Conflict and Change," *America*, September 18, 1976, p. 142. SRV spokesmen maintain that priests and nuns are arrested for political and not religious activities; yet the line between political and religious dissent is rather thin, as indicated by Article 81 of the 1985 Penal Code, which prohibits "causing divisions between the religious and nonreligious and separating religious followers from the people's government and social organizations," punishable by up to fifteen years in prison. The Criminal Code was published in *Nhan Dan*, July 12, 15, 16, 17, 1985, trans. in JPRS *Southeast Asia Report*, no. 85–135 (September 3, 1985): 1–92.

40. *Asia Focus*, February 27, 1987, p. 6. On September 13, 1987, Vietnam announced that 6,685 prisoners would be released from reeducation camps and sentences would be reduced for 5,320 others. It is possible that a number of priests are among those released, but at this writing (September 1987) there has been no such news.

41. *Bangkok Post*, November 23, 1987, p. 2.

42. Claude Lange, "Controverses sur la 'Liberte Religieuse' au Vietnam," *Monde Asiatiques*, no. 12 (Winter 1977): 329–30; reprinted from *Échange France-Asie*, no. 31 (January 1978).

43. *Vietnamese Studies*, no. 53, p. 136.

44. See Archbishop Binh's 1977 speech to the Vatican. English text in *Religion in Communist Lands* 10, no. 1 (Spring 1982): 66–68.

45. Ibid.

46. *Vietnam Courier* (January 1979). French translation of the text of Archbishop Binh's letter describing purpose of retreat published in *Lien Lac* (Philippines) (January 1979): 1–10.

47. Vietnam News Agency (VNA), May 3; FBIS *Daily Report* (Asia and Pacific), May 6, 1980, p. K4.

48. French translation of the text of the circular letter was published in *Lien Lac* (October 1980): 74–81. See also *Lien Lac* (August 1980): 354–56; and VNA, May 3, 1980, in FBIS *Daily Report* (Asia and Pacific), May 6, 1980, p. K4.

49. *Lien Lac* (November 1980): 96. See also Rev. John Emanuel, "The Church in Vietnam Today: Three Perspectives," *Worldmission* (Spring 1981): 50–58.

50. See, for example, *Vietnamese Studies*, no. 53, pp. 142–52.

51. Refugee interview summary, SRV/SM/Rel/May 1980 file, U.C. Indochina Archive.

52. Private letter published in *Lien Lac* (May 1978): 3.

53. Refugee interview summary, DRV/SM/Rel/May 1976, Indochina Archive. Ho Nai consists primarily of Catholics who fled the North in 1954.

54. Refugee interview summary, on file at U.C. Indochina Archive, SRV/SM/Rel/1981.

55. *Lien Lac* (February 1981).

56. Jean Mais, "Church-State Relations in Vietnam," *Pro Mundi Vita: Dossiers* (Brussels), no. 4 (Asia-Australasia Dossier, no. 35) (1985): 25. It seems ironic that the leading author of this bishops' letter, which was welcomed by SRV spokesmen and cited by them on subsequent occasions as a basis for church-state dialogue, would be arrested the same year and accused of plotting to overthrow the government.

57. *The Times* (London), February 14, 1984. Amnesty International, "Arrest and Trial of Priests and Lay Catholics in Viet Nam," external A.I. document, London, August 1983.

58. *Keston News Service*, no. 264 (November 27, 1986): 14.

59. VNA, May 29, 1987; FBIS, June 3, 1987, p. N2.

60. *Asiaweek*, November 20, 1987.

61. *Asia Focus*, October 29, 1988, pp. 1, 7.

62. Statement of Fr. Thanh Long made at a meeting organized by the Fatherland Front in Ho Chi Minh City, March 11–12, 1988; *Indochina Journal* (Fall 1988): 15–16.

63. *Saigon Giai Phong*, July 15, 1987, p. 2; FBIS, August 7, 1987, pp. N5–N8; see also *Asia Focus*, August 8 and 15, 1987, p. 1, which includes a summary of Fr. Thu's letter.

64. *Far Eastern Economic Review*, July 30, 1987, p. 7 ("Intelligence" section).

65. *Asia Focus*, June 25, 1988.

66. Text of this statement, along with a longer statement made by Archbishop Dien one week later, was published in *Religion in Communist Lands* 10, no. 1 (Spring 1982): 61–66.

67. Lange, "Controverses," pp. 329–41.

68. "Flashes sur le Vietnam," no. 4, Paris 1980, cited by Jean Mais in "Le Comite d'Union des Catholiques Patriotes du Vietnam," *Échange France-Asie*, Dossier no. 10/84-1/85 (December 1984–January 1985); *Vietnam News Agency*, January 20.

69. Jean Mais, "Le Comite d'Union" (December 1984–January 1985). This article is by far the most comprehensive account of the formation of the CSPVC and the reaction of the church hierarchy, including several important documents. For Archbishop Binh's meeting with the preparatory congress, see also Hanoi Domestic Service, August 28, 1983, trans. in *Summary of World Broadcasts/BBC: Far East*, August 31, 1983.

70. Ibid.

71. Ibid. Carries text of statutes.

72. Ibid.

73. See the *Far Eastern Economic Review*, March 15, 1984, pp. 27–28, for an interesting report on the fluctuating fortunes of some prominent southern "progressive" Catholics. Fr. Chan Tin's decline in status may be related to a letter he wrote to the Fatherland Front in 1982 urging an end to the reeducation camps and restrictions on religious liberty. The English translation of his letter was published in *Vietnam Today*, a document distributed in April 1985 by a Vietnamese émigré magazine in France, *Que Me*.

74. *Échange France-Asie* (December 1984–January 1985): 25–45.

75. *Asia Focus*, January 4, 1985, pp. 1, 4.

76. *Asia Focus*, July 26, 1986, p. 4.

77. *Échange France-Asie* (December 1984–January 1985): 30–31.

78. English translation of letter published in *Indochina Journal* (Fall 1984): 22–25.

79. *Échange France-Asie* (December 1984–January 1985): 36–38, carries French translation of Archbishop Dien's letter to members of his diocese describing his treatment. See also *Sunday Examiner* (Hong Kong), October 12, 1984.

80. Text of Msgr. Dien's letter, along with commentary, in *France Catholique* (Paris), September 20, 1986, pp. 10–12. See also *Keston News Service*, no. 260 (October 2, 1986).

81. *Asia Focus*, May 8, 1987, p. 1.

82. English translation published in *Indochina Journal* (Fall 1988): 16.

83. *Échange France-Asie* (December 1984–January 1985): 32–35, carries large extracts of Fr. Trinh's letter, which were distributed at a press conference of foreign journalists by CSPVC member Fr. Vuong Dinh Bich.

84. *Asia Focus*, May 10, 1985, p. 5.

85. *Vietnam Courier* (July 1987): 24.

86. Houtart and Lemercinier, *Hai Van*, p. 163.

87. Ibid., p. 179.

88. Some of these articles were discussed by P. J. Honey in "Roman Catholicism in the DRV," *China News Analysis*, June 14, 1963.

89. *Asia Focus*, March 14, 1986, pp. 1, 3; Mais, "Church-State Relations in Vietnam," pp. 15–18.

90. Ibid.; and David Jenkins, "The Nervous Co-existence of Catholicism and Communism," *Far Eastern Economic Review*, November 1, 1984, pp. 42–45.

91. "Trip Report of Disciples of Christ Delegation to Vietnam, April 2–17, 1986" (Unpublished), a project of the People-to-People Program of the Division of Overseas Ministry of the Christian Church (Disciples of Christ). The trip was led by Bill Herod of Church World Service and Rev. Barbara Fuller.

92. *Asia Focus*, March 14, 1986, p. 1.

93. *Asia Focus*, February 27, 1987, p. 1; see also Barbara Crossette, "For Vietnam's Catholic Church, a Modest Revival," *New York Times*, August 29, 1987.

94. *Asia Focus*, October 29, 1988, pp. 1, 7.

95. *Sunday Examiner* (Hong Kong), November 22, 1985.

96. Refugee interview summary, Indochina Archive, SRV/SM/Rel/1981 file.

97. Confidential interview and refugee interview summary, SRV/SM/Rel/1981 file, Indochina Archive.

98. Agence-France Press (Gilles Campion), June 5, 1988, FBIS-EAS 88-110, June 8, 1988.

99. The text of his statement, at a meeting on January 18, 1988, organized by the Fatherland Front in Ho Chi Minh City, was published in *Indochina Journal* (Fall 1988): 12–14.

100. *Asia Focus*, September 10, 1988, p. 10, October 1, p. 1.

101. *Asia Focus*, May 10, 1985, p. 5.

102. *Asia Focus*, September 12, 1987, p. 1.

103. *Asia Focus*, November 15 and 23, 1985, p. 1.

104. *Asiaweek*, March 2, 1986, p. 24.

105. *Asia Focus*, September 10, 1988, p. 1.

13 Cuba

1. The first of these episcopal visits occurred in May 1984 with Archbishop Jean Vilnet of Lille, president of the French episcopal conference. Other U.S. bishops have included Archbishop Flores of San Antonio (February 1986), John Cardinal O'Connor of New York (April 1981), and Bernard Cardinal Law of Boston (February 1989). A delegation of the German Bishops' Conference visited in December 1988, as did Roger Cardinal Etchegaray of the Pontifical Commission Justitia et Pax. Another Vatican figure, Archbishop Fiorenzo Angelini, president of the Pontifical Commission for Health Care Workers, was in Cuba the previous month.

2. Frei Betto, *Fidel y la Religión* (Havana: Oficina de Publicaciones del Consejo de Estado, 1985). English translation published as *Fidel and Religion: Castro Talks on Religion and Revolution with Frei Betto* (New York: Simon and Schuster, 1987).

3. The meeting took place February 17–23, 1986, following over six years of meetings in all the parishes. The 266-page report issued by the assembly has been published as *Documento Final e Instrucción Pastoral de los Obispos* (Rome: Tipografia Don Bosco, 1987).

4. Pierre de Charentenay, "Chiesa é Stato a Cuba," *La Civiltá Cattolica*, December 17, 1988, p. 602.

5. Leslie Dewart, *Christianity and Revolution: The Lesson of Cuba* (New York: Herder and Herder, 1963), p. 95.

6. J. Lloyd Mecham, *Church and State in Latin America* (Chapel Hill: University of North Carolina Press, 1966), pp. 305–6.

7. Manuel P. Maza, "The Cuban Catholic Church: True Struggles and False Dilemmas" (Master's thesis, Georgetown University 1982), p. 62.

8. Hugh Thomas, *Cuba: Or the Pursuit of Freedom* (London: Eyre and Spottiswoode, 1971), p. 1100.

9. Thomas, *Cuba*, p. 497.

10. Herbert L. Matthews, *Revolution in Cuba* (New York: Charles Scribner's Sons, 1975), p. 353.

11. Raul Gómez Treto, *The Church and Socialism* (Maryknoll, N.Y.: Orbis Books, 1988), p. 37.

12. John M. Kirk, "Church in Revolutionary Cuba," *The Ecumenist* 26, no. 6 (September–October 1988): 81.

13. Frei Betto, *Fidel y la Religión*, p. 145; see also, e.g., Gianni Miná, *Un Encuentro con Fidel* (Havana: Oficina de Publicaciones del Consejo de Estado, 1987), p. 253.

14. Jorge Dominguez, "International and National Aspects of the Experience of the Roman Catholic Church in Cuba," *Cuban Studies* 19 (1989): 46.

15. Manuel Fernandez, *Religión y Revolución en Cuba* (Miami: Saeta Ediciones, 1984), p. 112.

16. Maza, "Cuban Catholic Church," p. 59.

17. Harvey Cox, "Thoughts on the Church and Cuba," *Nation* 244, no. 18 (May 9, 1987): 612.

18. François Houtart and Emil Pin, *The Church and the Latin American Revolution* (New York: Sheed and Ward, 1965), p. 46. Data from the UN Economic Commission for Latin America (ECLA) put Cuba's 1960 urban population at 54.6 percent.

19. Thomas, *Cuba*, p. 1093.

20. Pedro A. Sánchez, *Cuba and the CGIAR Centers* (Washington, D.C.: World Bank, 1986), p. 14.

21. See Fernandez, *Religión*, p. 108, for the text. Also Pablo M. Alfonso, *Cuba, Castro y los Católicos* (Miami: Ediciones Hispanamerican Books, 1985), pp. 102–5; Gómez Treto, *Church and Socialism*, pp. 39–42.

22. For example, Gómez Treto, *Church and Socialism*, pp. 35–40.

23. Betto, *Fidel y la Religión*, p. 216.

24. "Open Letter from the Cuban Bishops to the Prime Minister," December 4, 1960, in *Religion in Cuba Today*, ed. Alice L. Hageman and Philip E. Wheaton (New York: Association Press, 1971), p. 275.

25. Betto, *Fidel y la Religión*, p. 136. In 1960 he repeatedly denounced the Catholic schools as "a plague of cassocked bullies and mercenary teachers," and worse. See Fernandez, *Religión*, pp. 102–10, for numerous instances.

26. Maza, "Cuban Catholic Church," p. 60.

27. Mercedes García Tudurí, "Resumen de la historia de la Educación en Cuba," *Exilio* 3, nos. 3–4, 4, no. 1 (1969–70): 121. The Federation of Cuban Catholic Secondary Schools, which encompassed primary and special schools as well, had 245 institutional members, while the Federation of Cuban Private Schools numbered thirty-six, in addition to which a "cierto numero de colegios" were unaffiliated with either. Mecham, *Church and State*, p. 302, noted 338 Catholic schools, almost certainly an overcount, possibly (given his sources) inadvertently including the Protestant schools. Aldo Büntig (in *Religion in Cuba Today*, p. 313) also wrote of "324 Catholic high schools." Gómez Treto, *Church and Socialism*, p. 13, found only 212 Catholic schools in 1955 and seems to have converted two of the most important second-

ary schools, LaSalle and Belén, into universities; Kirk, "Church in Cuba," p. 84, listed only 112, divided between 24 schools for boys and 88 for girls, while the former dictator Batista (in his 1964 book *The Growth and Decline of the Cuban Republic*, cited in Maza, "Cuban Catholic Church," p. 111) reported 130 Catholic boys' schools and 194 for girls, a total of 324.

28. Tudurí, "Resumen," pp. 131–32; and Lourdes Casal, "Comentario a García Turdurí," *Exilio* 3, nos. 3–4, vol. 4, no. 1 (1969–70) pp. 293–94. See also Sánchez, *Cuba*, p. 17.

29. Sánchez, *Cuba*, pp. 16–17.

30. ENEC, no. 560.

31. ENEC, no. 51.

32. The Communist party, Partido Socialista Popular, like most of its Latin American counterparts, favored the political road to power and considered the July 26 movement adventurist and naïve.

33. Fernandez, *Religión*, pp. 161–62; Gómez Treto, *Church and Socialism*, pp. 28–29.

34. A still controversial historian of the Cuban church, Ismael Testé, believes there was a frustrated attempt to found a national church on the China model, but as careful a student of the period as Fernandez doubts this and finds no corroborating evidence. See Fernandez, *Religión*, p. 122.

35. See, e.g., Fernandez, *Religión*, pp. 161–73, on the shortcomings of the rhetoric typical of the Christian revolutionaries of the time.

36. Alfonso, *Cuba*, pp. 185–88.

37. Fernandez, *Religión*, p. 120.

38. Fernandez, *Religión*, p. 121.

39. Juan Clark, *Religious Repression in Cuba* (Coral Gables: University of Miami Press, 1986), pp. 21–22, 65.

40. Fernandez, *Religión*, p. 126.

41. Loredo was accused of harboring a failed hijacker who shot the pilot of the plane he had sought to commandeer and sought refuge in the Iglesia San Francisco in Old Havana, a Franciscan church particularly identified with the anti-Batista struggle and the home of Cuba's most progressive Catholic publication, *La Quincena*. When Loredo was arrested in April 1966, the entire church compound, including the magazine, was taken over; the church was returned October 4, 1987.

42. Fernandez, *Religión*, p. 123. In private communications Cuban church figures have confided that Zacchi, and later they themselves, did intervene in numerous instances involving other political prisoners, but they were always careful to maintain the confidentiality of their exchanges.

43. Dominguez, "International and National Aspects," p. 48.

44. See Hageman and Wheaton, *Religion in Cuba Today*, pp. 288–94, 298–308, for texts.

45. Alfonso, *Cuba*, p. 174.

46. Betto, *Fidel y la Religión*, p. 11.

47. *Granma Weekly Review* (Havana), May 1, 1988.

48. Miná, *Encuentro*, pp. 261–63.

49. José F. Carneado, "Una Cuestión de Principios," *Cuba Internacional*, no. 225 (September 1988): 26.

50. Kirk, "Church in Cuba," p. 82.

51. Miná, *Encuentro*, pp. 258–59.

52. Dominguez, "International and National Aspects," p. 57.

53. Juan Clark, *Religious Repression*, p. 494.

54. Gilles Trequesser, Reuter news release, July 21, 1988.

55. Joseph B. Treaster, "Man and God in Cuba: A Castro-Church Détente?" *New York Times*, May 15, 1987.

56. Dominguez, "International and National Aspects," p. 53.

57. Ibid.

58. Tennant C. Wright, S.J., "Cuba: The Church is Open," *America* 157, no. 11 (October 24, 1987): 267.

59. ENEC, no. 514.

14 Nicaragua

1. FSLN, "Comunicado de la Direccion Nacional del FSLN sobre la Religion," *Nicarauac*, no. 5 (April–June 1981): 95.

2. Nicaraguan Bishops' Conference, "Sobre los Principios que Rigen la Actividad Politica de Toda la Iglesia como Tal," Managua, Episcopal Conference, March 19, 1972.

3. Nicaraguan Bishops' Conference, "Mensaje al Pueblo Nicaraguense," Managua, Episcopal Conference, June 2, 1979, p. 2.

4. Pablo A. Cuadra, "Responsibilities of the Church in Central America," *Crisis* (September 1986): 9.

5. Uriel Molina, in "El Sendero de una Experiencia," *Nicarauac*, no. 5 (April–June 1981): 23.

6. Ernesto Cardenal, "El Evangelio me Hizo Marxista," *Sabado Grafico* (Madrid) (October 1978).

7. Nicaraguan Bishops' Conference, "Mensaje de la Conferencia Episcopal al Pueblo Católico y a todos los Nicaraguenses," Managua, Episcopal Conference, July 31, 1979, p. 2.

8. Ibid., p. 3.

9. Nicaraguan Bishops' Conference, "Compromiso Cristiano para una Nicaragua Nueva," Managua, Episcopal Conference, November 17, 1979, p. 12.

10. Nicaraguan Bishops' Conference, "Mensaje," p. 7.

11. Nicaraguan Bishops' Conference, "Compromiso," p. 11.

12. *Los Cristianos estan con la Revolucion* (Costa Rica: Departamento Ecumenico de Investigaciones, 1980), p. 3.

13. Ibid.

14. Gustavo Gutierrez, "Liberation Praxis and Christian Faith," in *Frontiers of Theology in Latin America*, ed. Rosino Gibellini (Maryknoll, N.Y.: Orbis Books, 1979), p. 9.

15. Teofilo Cabestrero, "Mision de la Iglesia en un Pueblo en Revolucion," *Amanecer*, no. 1 (May 1981): 13.

16. Juan Hernandez Pico, S.J., "Para Acercar el Reino: Compromiso Absoluto con un Proyecto Relativo," *Cristianos Revolucionarios*, no. 3 (Managua: Instituto Historico Centroamericano, 1980), p. 28.

17. Amando Lopez, S.J., in *Fe Cristiana y Revolucion Sandinista* (Managua: Instituto Historico Centroamericano, 1980), p. 347.

18. In this regard see David Nolan *The Ideology of the Sandinistas and the Nicaraguan Revolution* (Coral Gables, Fla.: Institute of Interamerican Studies, 1984). It offers the most comprehensive set of documents revealing the ideology of the Sandinista movement.

19. Ministry of Education, *El Amanecer del Pueblo* (Managua: 1980), lesson 22.

20. 1969 FSLN Program of Government, clause 9. In Nolan, *Ideology*, p. 37.

21. FSLN, Departamento de Propaganda y Educacion Politica, "Memorandum a los Responsables Regionales," quoted in Humberto Belli, *Breaking Faith: The Sandinista Revolution and Its Impact on Freedom and Christian Faith in Nicaragua* (Westchester, Ill.: Crossways, 1985), p. 141.

22. See, for instance, *Marxismo, Socialismo, Comunismo; yo le tengo miedo y vos?* (Managua: Instituto Historico Centroamericano, 1979).

23. *Barricada* (Managua), January 1, 1981, p. 1.

24. Jon Sobrino, "Dios y los Procesos Revolucionarios," in *Apuntes para una Teologia Nicaraguense*, ed. CAV-IHCA (San Jose, Costa Rica: Departamento Ecumenico de Investigaciones, 1981), pp. 107–8.

25. Quoted in Carlos Corsi et al., *Centroamerica en Llamas* (Bogota: CONFE, 1980).

26. Cuadra, "Responsibilities," p. 10.

27. Departamento Ecumenico de Investigaciones, *Sacerdotes en el Gobierno Nicaraguense: Poder o Servicio?* (San Jose, Costa Rica: DEI, 1981), p. 12.

28. Private interview with the author.

29. *La Prensa* (Managua), August 13, 1982, pp. 1–6.

30. In *The First Freedom* (Puebla Institute newsletter) (November–December 1988): 5.

31. Quoted in Belli, *Breaking Faith*, p. 199.

32. Fr. Santiago Anitua, S.J., "The Expelling of Ten Catholic Priests from Nicaragua," in *The Puebla Institute, Occasional Bulletins*, no. 4 (October 1984): 3.

33. Ibid.

34. OAS-CIDH, *Report on the Situation of Human Rights of a Segment of the Nicaraguan Population of Miskito Origin* (Washington, D.C.: OAS, 1984), pp. 129–30.

35. Barbara E. Joe, "Revolutionary Education in Nicaragua," in *Nicaragua in Focus* (Puebla Institute) (April 1988): 4–9.

36. Nicaraguan Bishops' Conference, *Carta Pastoral del Episcopado de Nicaragua Sobre la Educacion Católica* (Managua: Episcopal Conference, 1982), 8.

37. Quoted in *El Nuevo Diario* (Managua), December 16, 1982, p. 10.

38. *Barricada*, April 30, 1984, p. 3.

39. Quoted in Humberto Belli, "Revolutionary Love," in *Nicaragua in Focus* (April 1988): 48.

40. *The First Freedom* (November–December 1988): 5.

41. Stephen Kinzer, "Nicaragua's Combative Archbishop," *New York Times Magazine*, November 18, 1984, pp. 90, 93.

42. Mario Vargas Llosa, "In Nicaragua," in *New York Times Magazine* (April 28, 1985), p. 46.

43. Michael Dodson and Laura Nuzzi O'Shaughnessy, "Religion and Politics," in *Nicaragua: The First Five Years*, ed. Thomas Walker (New York: Praeger, 1985), pp. 128–29.

44. A detailed source of information in this regard is provided by the Institute on Religion and Democracy, *Church Support for Pro-Sandinista Network* (Washington, D.C.: IRD, 1984), p. 14.

45. SEDAC [Episcopal Secretariat of Central America], *Juan Pablo II en America Central* (Costa Rica, 1984), p. 142.

46. "The Papal Mass in Managua, Nicaragua, March 4, 1983," excerpts taped from the official Sandinista television broadcast, distributed by the Nicaraguan Information Center, San Charles, Missouri, 1983.

47. Tomas Borge, as quoted by Agence France Presse (March 2, 1983) in *Diario las Americas* (Miami), March 4, 1983, p. 6.

48. Version privately provided to the author by Vatican officials in November 1983.

49. Joan Frawley, "A New Line in Nicaragua," *National Catholic Register*, January 11, 1987, pp. 1–7.

50. Ibid.

51. The military buildup was further confirmed by the declarations of high-ranking Sandinista defector Major Roger Miranda in October 1987.

15 Papal Eastern Diplomacy

This chapter was translated from German by Pedro Ramet.

1. Speech to theology students in Rome, March 12, 1929.

2. Message of peace, January 1, 1980.

3. Speech before the Polish Episcopal Conference, in *Acta Apostolicae Sedis* (1978): 70.

4. The embassy expert on the Vatican has for years been Yuri Bogomasov.

5. Archbishop Liudas Povilonis, apostolic administrator of Kaunas (Lithuania), travels most frequently to Rome. Moscow seems to ignore the fact that a representative of the Lithuanian government-in-exile is accredited to the Holy See.

6. Common reports notwithstanding, the number of Vatican officials of Polish descent has scarcely increased at all under John Paul II. Monsignor Janusz Bolonek is the only Pole in the department, while the only Poles in the State Secretariat, viz., Monsignors Jozef Kowalczyk and Tadeusz Rakoczy, are preoccupied above all with translation work.

7. His text was never published.

8. See *Atheism and Dialogue*, no. 4 (1986). This journal, published by the Secretariat for Non-believers, appears in English, French, and Spanish.

9. See Casaroli's interview with *Die Presse* (Vienna), December 21, 1974.

10. Ibid.

11. Ibid. See also his lecture in Vienna, November 18, 1977, German text in *Österreichische Zeitschrift für Aussenpolitik* 6 (1977).

12. See Hansjakob Stehle, *Eastern Politics of the Vatican, 1917–1979*, trans. from German by Sandra Smith (Athens: Ohio University Press, 1981).

13. See *L'Osservatore Romano*, April 2, 1919, p. 1.

14. Stehle, *Eastern Politics*, p. 435.

15. The full text is published in ibid.

16. See the Flynn Memorandum, included as an appendix in the papers of Myron Taylor, cited in Ennio di Nolfo, *Vaticano e Stati Uniti, 1939–1952* (Milan: Franco Augeli Editore, 1978), p. 438.

17. Private disclosure by the archivist of the Secret Archive of the State Secretariat, Fr. Angelo Martini, S.J., December 2, 1973.

18. Ibid.

19. See di Nolfo, *Vaticano*, p. 159.

20. Text of the Gundlach report. See minutes of the Congress in *Kirche in Not*, Vol. 1 (Königstein-Taunus, 1957), p. 11.

21. On June 9, 1977, Hungarian party chief János Kádár was received by Pope Paul VI in a private audience. The pope called this an " 'endpoint' after a long period of distance and tension 'whose echo has not yet quite died away.' " *L'Osservatore Romano*, June 10–11, 1977, p. 2.

22. Speech, September 12, 1965.

23. The complete text in an authorized English translation is published in *The Legal Status of Religious Communities in Yugoslavia* (Belgrade: Medjunarodna štampa Interpress, 1967), pp. 84–86.

24. *L'Osservatore Romano*, December 15, 1978, p. 1.

25. Ibid., December 2, 1977, p. 1.

26. Pope John Paul II on June 9, 1979, in Kraków.

27. *L'Osservatore Romano*, September 2, 1980, p. 1.

28. See *Europa Archiv*, no. 20 (1983): D540.

29. See *L'Osservatore Romano*, no. 26, 1987, p. 2.

30. Such an alliance became visible, for the first time in history, with the organization of the peace meetings of all religions of the world in Assisi, Italy, on October 27, 1986. Even the Moscow Patriarchate was represented there by its metropolitan of Kiev.

31. Silvestrini at the Madrid conference, November 13, 1980, as quoted in *L'Osservatore Romano* (Polish edition), no. 10, 1980, p. 7.

32. See Gorbachev's declaration to Orthodox Patriarch Pimen on April 29, 1988; reported in *Novosti*, no. 41 (May 6, 1988).

33. See *L'Osservatore Romano*, June 15, 1988, p. 1. The original French text of Casaroli's talk in Moscow was published in *L'Osservatore Romano*, June 11, 1988.

16 Karol Wojtyła and Marxism

This chapter is an adapted version of an essay that was originally published in the *Pope John Paul II Lecture Series* (St. Paul, Minn.: St. John Vianney Seminary, 1985). Reprinted by permission of the author and of St. John Vianney Seminary.

1. *Scritti* (Vatican City: Libreria Editrice, 1980).

2. George H. Williams, *The Mind of John Paul II: Origins of His Thought and Action* (New York: Seabury Press, 1981), p. 124; and George Blazynski, *John Paul II* (London: Weidenfeld and Nicolson, 1979), pp. 33, 35.

3. See Williams, *The Mind*, p. 405; and Karol Wojtyła, *Sign of Contradiction*, trans. from Polish (New York: Seabury Press, 1979), p. 39.

4. Williams, *The Mind*, pp. 86ff.

5. André Frossart, ed., *N'ayez pas peur: Dialogues avec Jean-Paul II* (Paris: Laffont, 1982), pp. 20, 51, 74. I have not checked my translation of the original against the authorized translation (published by St. Martin's Press in 1984).

6. Ibid., p. 51.

7. Ibid., p. 74.

8. Williams, *The Mind*, pp. 115–40.

9. Immanuel Kant, *The Critique of Pure Reason* (1787); trans. by J. M. D. Meiklejohn (London: Dent, 1934); and Immanuel Kant, *The Critique of Practical Reason* (1788), trans. by Lewis White Beck (New York: Liberal Arts Press, 1956).

10. Williams, *The Mind*, pp. 141–50.

11. In informal remarks after an April 5, 1986, plenary address to the American Catholic Philosophical Association, Mieczysław A. Krąpiec, O.P., then rector of the Catholic University of Lublin, indicated that the Lublin philosophers wished to avoid, in their thought, any kind of subjectivism, which they considered to have been a cause of the horrors of the Second World War.

12. Karol Wojtyła (John Paul II), *Lubliner Vorlesungen*, ed. Juliusz Stroynowski with foreword by Tadeusz Styczen (Stuttgart-Degerloch: Seewald, 1980).

13. "W poszukaniu podstaw perfekcjoryzmu w etice," *Roczniki Filosoficzne* 4 (1955–57): 303–17, trans. in *Primat des Geistes: Philosophische Schriften*, ed. Juliusz Stroynowski with foreword by Andrzej Połtawski (Stuttgart-Degerloch: Seewald, 1979), pp. 311–28. The term *perfekcjoryzm* is not found in the multivolume Polish dictionary by Jan Karlowicz et al. (Warsaw, 1909), nor its equivalent in other languages of more recent date, nor in the analytical index of the multivolume *Dictionnaire de Théologie Catholique*, tables generales (Paris, 1968). Wojtyła's use of the term "normativism" in this early essay as a label for something to be avoided seems to represent an early, groping expression of his desire to regard ethical norms as based on an insight into objective good and evil, universally valid, not as a "heteronomous" legalism imposed from without.

14. Jeremy Bentham's *Plan for an Universal and Perpetual Peace* (1789) (London: Sweet and Maxwell, 1927), along with Kant's *Zum ewigen Frieden* (1795) (Leipzig: P. Reclam, Jr., 1932) entered the general current of utopian thought, including the Marxist ideal of a classless and hence peaceful society.

15. Karol Wojtyła's marked stress on personal ethics (in distinction from social ethics) is underscored by the prominence given by him to his teaching on sexual ethics and marriage, most recently in the collection of his Wednesday audience communications, *Feast of Love: On Human Intimacy*, ed. Mary Durkin (Chicago: Loyola Press, 1984). Already available in Italian and French, this is the first instance of a *papal book* made up wholly of the words of a reigning pontiff. Its magisterial status or authority is undefined among the many prepapal books and papal documents coming to us in abundance.

16. Quoted in *Acta Synodalia Sacrosancti Concilii Oecumenici, Vaticani II* (Vatican City: Polyglot Press, 1970–78), 2:532.

17. Karol Wojtyła, *The Acting Person* (Dordrecht, Holland: Analecta Husserliana, 1979). This major work is dealt with in its two basic editions in my *The Mind*, chap. 8. Better than my own treatment are the reflections of Josef Seifert, "Karol Cardinal Wojtyła (Pope John Paul II) as Philosopher and the Cracow/Lublin School of Philosophy," *Aletheia* 2 (1981): 130–99. See also Rocco Buttiglione, *Il pensiero di Karol Wojtyła* (Milan: Jaca Book, 1982), who, however, deals with *Osoba i Czyn* as though it had been written even in its definitive form before Wojtyła's participation in Vatican II. For variants in the work in other languages, see my bibliographical remarks in R. William Franklin, ed., *The Law of Nations and the Book of Nature* (Collegeville, Minn.: Christian Humanism Project, 1984).

18. "Notatki na marginesie konstytucji Gaudium et spes, 2," *Ateneum Kaplańskie* 74, no. 1 (1970): 3–6, trans. into German in *Von der Königswürde des Menschen*, ed. Juliusz Stroynowski with foreword by Franz Cardinal König (Stuttgart-Dergloch: Seewald, 1979), pp. 143–46.

19. Ibid., pp. 1, 144.

20. Karol Wojtyła, *U podstaw Odnowy: Studium o realizacji Vaticanum II* (Kraków: Polskie Towarzystwo Teologiczne, 1972).

21. Ibid., p. 142; and Karol Wojtyła, *Sources of Renewal: The Implementation of the Second Vatican Council*, trans. from Polish by P. S. Falla (San Francisco: Harper and Row, 1980), p. 162. The English version adds the explanatory date in parentheses.

22. See Williams, *The Mind*, pp. 233–34.

23. *Karol Wojtyła e il Sinodo dei Vescovi* (Vatican City: Libreria Editrice, 1980), pp. 204–8.

24. Jean-Paul Sartre, *L'existentialisme est un humanisme* (Paris: Nagel, 1946).

25. Jean-Paul Sartre, *Critique de la raison dialectique* (Paris: Gallimard, 1960).

26. No doubt also important here would be Gabriel Marcel's well-known criticism of Sartre, as in his *Les Hommes contre l'humain* (Paris: La Colombe, 1951).

27. Wojtyła, *Sign*, pp. 94, 29.

28. Ibid., pp. 24, 34, 138ff., 140.

29. Ibid., pp. 199ff.

30. The whole of the September 4, 1976, speech is quoted in my "The Ecumenical Intentions of John Paul II," *Harvard Theological Review* 72, no. 2 (April 1982): 141–76, specifically p. 147. The starkly eschatological section of the Dudleian lecture is not included in the other and, in several other ways distinctive, version of the lecture published as "The Ecumenism of John Paul II," *Journal of Ecumenical Studies* 19, no. 4 (Fall 1982): 681–718.

31. *Analecta Husserliana* 6 (1977): 61–73. The cardinal's paper had originally been delivered for him in French at a colloquium in Fribourg, Switzerland. The editor, Dr. Anna-Teresa Tymieniecka, chose to print the English translation of the French original without notice of

its delivery at Harvard. But except for the introductory reference to Fribourg, the text is exactly what was delivered in the presence of the late Humberto Cardinal Medeiros and other dignitaries in Emerson Hall.

32. See *Analecta Husserliana* 6 (1977): 72.

33. Ibid., p. 66.

34. Ibid., p. 64. I developed this theme in an unpublished lecture at the Catholic University of America, "The Distinctiveness of John Paul II," Washington, D.C., November 19, 1983.

35. *Analecta Husserliana* 6 (1977): 72. Here he refers to Adam Schaff, *Marksizm i jednostka ludska* (Warsaw: PAN, 1965), pp. 176–95.

36. Ibid., p. 72.

37. "Il problema del constituirsi della cultura attraverso la 'praxis' umana," *Rivista de Filosofia Neo-Scolastica* 69 (1977): 513–24. See also Pierluigi Pollini, "Il problema della filosofia della prassi in Marx e Wojtyła," in *La filosofia di Karol Wojtyła*, ed. Stanisław Grygiel et al. (Bologna: CSEO, 1983), pp. 61–73; and Williams, *The Mind*, pp. 252ff.

38. I did not see this so clearly when I wrote about *Redemptoris hominis* in *The Mind*, chap. 10, but I did anticipate correctly some of his themes in *Laborem exercens*.

39. See George H. Williams, *Contours of Church and State in the Thought of John Paul II* (Waco, Texas: Baylor University Press, 1983), p. 38. This booklet brings together, with an added bibliography, two articles of similar titles which appeared originally in *Journal of Church and State* 24, no. 3 (Autumn 1982): 463–96, and 25, no. 1 (Winter 1983): 13–55.

40. *Laborem exercens*, sect. 12.

41. Ibid., sect. 11.

42. Ibid., sect. 20.

43. Ibid., sect. 13.

44. I have dealt with the theme of the cultural unity of Europe in the thought of John Paul II in Franklin, *The Law of Nations*. The lecture in commemoration of the 1,500th anniversary of the birth of St. Benedict, given in 1982, was editorally divided into two amplifications, with updating "bibliographical reflections," pp. 38–58.

45. See *L'Osservatore Romano*, November 10, 1984, p. 1 (my italics).

46. *Instruction*, English version (Vatican City: Polyglot Press, 1984), printed in *Origins* 14, no. 13 (September 13, 1984). The following section on the *Instruction* is an adaptation of my "Postscript on Liberation Theology and Humanism," in *Law of Nations*, pp. 54–58.

47. *Instruction*, English version, pp. 29, 33.

48. Ibid., pp. 22, 29, 21.

49. Ibid., pp. 24, 31, 32.

50. Ibid., p. 30.

51. *Slavorum apostoli* (Vatican City: Polyglot Press, 1985); *L'Osservatore Romano*, July 2, 1985, p. 1; and *Origins* 15, no. 8 (July 18, 1985) (my emphasis).

52. *Dominum et vivificantem* (Vatican City: Polyglot Press, 1986); *L'Osservatore Romano*, May 30, 1986, p. 1; and *Origins* 16, no. 4 (June 12, 1986) (my emphasis).

53. *Redemptoris mater* (Vatican City: Polyglot Press, 1987); and *Origins* 16, no. 43 (April 9, 1987).

54. *L'Osservatore Romano*, March 13, 1985, p. 1.

55. TASS, March 28, 1987.

56. Because of the special devotion of John Paul II to Mary of Fatima, he may for a long time have felt under some personal spiritual restraint. I have suggested a connection between certain eschatological and Marian views of the pope in my "Ecumenical Intentions of John Paul," pp. 144–52, esp. n. 21. In now appealing to the Orthodox throughout the Soviet Union

and elsewhere in *Redemptoris mater*, he clearly opted for sustained diplomatic and ecumenical dialogue with the Soviet government and the patriarchal church, despite setbacks and repeated expressions of reserve on the other sides.

57. Commemorative address given in Salerno, reported in *L'Osservatore Romano*, May 26, 1985, p. 3.

58. *L'Osservatore Romano*, May 7, 1987, p. 1.

59. This is an expression modeled on Luther's *simul justus simul peccator*.

Index

Ablewicz, Jerzy, 134
Aczél, György, 165
Aftenie, Bishop Vasile, 214
Agca, Mehmet Ali, 372
Albania, 232–50, 344
Albanian Orthodox church, 237, 240, 244
Alia, Ramiz, 247, 249
Amnesty International, 233
Andropov, Yuri V., 375
Angola, 26
Anitua, Fr. Santiago, 327
Aquinas, St. Thomas, 31, 362
Aquino, Cory, 262
Arapăs, Patriarch Teoçtist (Romanian Orthodox), 218
Aristotle, 368
Artuković, Andrija, 183
Athanasius, Bishop, 209
Augustin, Bishop Franz, 219, 220, 226

Backis, Andrys, 342, 354
Bakarić, Vladimir, 184–85
Balan, Bishop Ion, 215
Balint, Auxiliary Bishop Lajos, 220
Base communities: in Nicaragua, 316
Batasch, Cristophe, 323
Batista, Fulgencio, 310
Baum, William Wakefield Cardinal, 345
Bautain, Louis, 5
Belorussia, 53, 61, 62, 85
Benedict XV (pope), 347
Bengsch, Alfred Cardinal (of Berlin), 96, 100, 101, 102, 103, 104, 106, 107, 108, 110, 112
Bentham, Jeremy, 362, 372
Beran, Josef Cardinal, 145, 146, 150, 351
Berecz, János, 176
Berlin Conference of European Catholics, 104–5
Bertram, Cardinal, 95
Betto, Frei, 296, 302, 307, 308
Bibles, import and printing, 222
Bich, Fr. Vuong Dinh, 288
Bici, Fr. Zef, 244
Bien, Fr. Ho Thanh, 273
Binh, Archbishop Nguyen Van, 280, 281–82, 283, 285, 288, 289, 293–94
von Bismarck, Otto, 30
Blachnicki, Fr. Franciszek, 130
Blaj, schools of, 209–10
Blanco, Luis Amado, 305
Blažević, Jakov, 187–89
Boff, Leonardo, 43
Bolanos, Miguel, 327
Bolonek, Msgr. Janusz, 344
Boniface VIII (pope), 16

Borge, Tomas, 324, 327, 334
Bouillard, Henri, 7
Boza Masvida, Bishop Eduardo, 298
Braun, Fr. Leopold, 349
Brezhnev, Leonid I., 59, 66, 76, 375
Bridge, Ann, 240
Budkiewicz, Msgr. Constantine, 52
Bukatko, Archbishop Gabrijel, 197
Bukovsky, Fr. John, 344, 352
Bulányi, Fr. György, 20–21, 170–71
Bulgaria, 345, 352, 372
Buttiglione, Rocco, 6

Cabestrero, Fr. Teofilo, 320
Cajetan, Cardinal, 376
Cakuls, Bishop Janis, 73
Calvez, Fr. Jean-Yves, 35
Calvinists, 209
Can, Trinh Van Cardinal, 278, 295
Can, Fr. Truong Ba, 279, 288
Cao Jinru, 263
Capuchins, 331
Carballo, Fr. Bismarck, 327, 328, 335
Cardenal, Fr. Ernesto, 317, 323, 328, 333
Cardenal, Fernando, 313, 328
Caritas: in Poland, 136; in Yugoslavia, 185
Carneado, José Felipe, 308
Casaroli, Agostino Cardinal, 20, 25, 85, 102, 161, 254, 258, 324, 342–43, 345, 346, 351, 355
Cassidy, Edward, 343
Castro, Fidel, 21, 298, 299, 302, 306–9
Ceauşescu, Nicolae, 216, 217, 229
Čekada, Archbishop Smiljan, 182, 197–98
Celli, Msgr. Claudio, 344
Centoz, Archbishop Luigi, 303
Chamorro, Pedro J., 318
Charnets'kyi, Bishop Mykola, 55, 60
Chernenko, Konstantin, 375
Chi, Bishop Pham Ngoc, 271, 280, 287
Chicherin, Georgi V., 345–46
China, 18, 241, 251–67, 344
Chinese Buddhist Association, 263
Chinese Catholic Patriotic Association, 256, 260, 261, 265
Chodanenko, Fr. Bronislaw, 64
Chon, Dang Thanh, 284
Christianity Today Theological Society (Zagreb), 182, 197, 198–99
Chronicle of the Catholic Church in Lithuania, 59, 62, 66, 69, 72, 74, 77
Chronicle of the Catholic Church in Ukraine, 75
Cieplak, Jan, 52
Clark, Juan, 310
Clement, St. (pope), 15
Coba, Bishop Ernest, 242, 244, 245
Colasuonno, Archbishop Francesco, 176
Committee for Solidarity of Patriotic Vietnamese Catholics, 273, 286
Committee for the Defense of Religious Rights (Romania), 218
Committee for the Defense of the Rights of Believers (Catholic, Lithuania), 22, 66, 69
Committee for the Restoration of the Church (Romania), 218
Committee in Defense of the Ukrainian Catholic Church, 83
Concordat: in Poland (1925), 120; in Romania (1927), 211
Conservatives, 5–6
Coomaraswamy, Rama, 10
Council for Religious Affairs (USSR), 49, 73
Councils: First Vatican (1869–70), 17; Second Vatican (1962–65), 4, 6, 9, 17, 18, 23, 36, 37–38, 41, 58, 106, 111, 121, 122, 123, 128, 156, 160, 167, 181–82, 197–98, 254, 276–78, 297, 307, 314, 363–64
Cox, Harvey, 300
Crisan, Bishop Traian, 218
Cristea, Bishop Miron, 210
Croatian Peasant Party, 185, 187
Cserháti, Bishop Jozsef, 20, 165, 172, 178
Csibi, Fr. János, 226–27
Csilik, Fr. János, 226
Cuadra, Pablo A., 324
Cuba, 24, 296–312, 343
Čule, Bishop Petar, 199
Cunningham, Lawrence, 21
Curie-Sklodowska, Marie, 360
Czapik, Archbishop Gyula, 159, 160
Czechoslovakia, 18, 22, 27, 103, 142–55, 344, 345, 351
Czerniak, Bishop Jan, 134

Dąbrowski, Bronisław, 134

Dang, Tranh Bach, 282
Daszkal, Bishop Stefan, 220
Davidek, Felix, 22
de Bonald, Louis, 5
Dedi, Bishop Nikol, 241
Dekanossow, Ambassador, 349
de Lubac, Henri, 7
Dema, Fr. Benedict, 244
de Maistre, Joseph, 5
de Montezemolo, Msgr. Andrea, 333, 335
Deng Xiaoping, 259, 260, 261, 262, 265
Deng Yiming, Bishop, 254, 257–59
de Rhodes, Fr. Alexandre, 270
D'Escoto, Fr. Miguel, 313, 323, 328, 331
Dewart, Leslie, 9, 298
d'Herbigny, Fr. Michel, 52, 348–49
Dickens, Charles, 29
Diem, Ngo Dinh, 272, 277, 281
Dien, Archbishop Philippe Nguyen Kim, 282, 286, 288–89
Dives in misericordia (1980), 372
Divini redemptoris (1937), 11, 34, 53, 300, 349
Djilas, Milovan, 189
Doan, Fr. Nguyen Cong, 284
Dobrecić, Archbishop Nikola, 189
Dodson, Michael, 22, 332
Doepfner, Julius Cardinal (of Berlin), 96, 99, 100
Domin, Auxiliary Bishop Czesław, 138
Dominguez, Jorge, 306, 310
Dominicans, 331
Dominum et vivificantem (1986), 379
Dong, Pham Van, 283
Dong Guangqing, Bishop, 267
Dooley, John, 272
Dorr, Donal, 37, 40
Dragomir, Bishop Ion, 218
Dubček, Alexander, 151
Duc, Ngo Cong, 279
Dulbinskis, Bishop Kazimirs, 54, 59, 86
Dulles, Avery, 4, 7
Duprey, Fr. Pierre, 343
Durcovici, Bishop Anton, 219
Durham, Edith, 240

Ecsy, Fr. Ion, 226
Edel'shtein, Fr. Georgii, 87
Eggerath, Werner, 99
Einaudi, Giulio, 307
Engels, Friedrich, 362, 373
Estonia, 54, 61
Evangelical Christians, 227

Fall, Bernard, 274
False Decretals of Pseudo-Isidore, 16
Fang Lizhi, 264
Fan Xueyuan, Bishop Peter Joseph, 264
Farkas, Mihály, 158
Fedorov, Fr. Leonid, 51
Feranec, Bishop Jozef, 153
Ferdinand, Emperor, 210
Filaret, Metropolitan (of Kiev and Halych), 71, 80, 84, 87
Filaret, Metropolitan (of Minsk), 63, 80, 84, 87
Fishta, Bishop Antonin, 242, 245
Florent, Fr. Michel, 349
Frančetić, Colonel Jure, 188
Franco, Francisco, 299
Franciscans: in Albania, 235, 238, 240, 241, 244; in Bosnia, 187, 188, 190–91, 193, 194, 199–200
Franić, Archbishop Frane, 182, 191, 197–99
Frentiu, Bishop Traian, 214
Friandi, Fr. Mario, 328
Frison, Bishop Alexander, 52
Fuchs, Otto Hartmut, 105
Fu Tieshan, Archbishop Michael, 266

Gabris, Bishop, 153
Gantin, Bernadin Cardinal, 345
Garaj, Bishop Stefan, 153
Gardin, Fr. Jak, 241
Gasparri, Pietro Cardinal, 347, 348
Gaudelli, Fr. Vicente, 326
Gaudium et spes, 37–38, 364–65, 368
Gerasimov, Gennadii, 70
German Democratic Republic, 26, 93–115, 344, 350
Germany, West, 96, 113, 114, 229
Gerő, Ernő, 158
Gheddo, Pierro, 274
Gheorghiu-Dej, Gheorghe, 213
Gherghel, Bishop Petru, 220
Gierek, Edvard, 25, 121
Giglio, Msgr. Paolo, 335
Gilkey, Langdon, 7

Girnius, Kestutis, 71
Gjalaj, Fr. Konrad, 243
Gjini, Bishop Fran, 241
Gjoni, Fr. Fran Mark, 245
Glagolitic alphabet, 183
Glemp, Józef Cardinal, 63, 81, 134, 135, 136
Godo, Fr. Michael, 223
Gojdic, Bishop Paul, 148
Gómez Treto, Raul, 297, 302
Gomułka, Władysław, 25, 26
Gong Pinmei, Bishop, 261, 262
Gorbachev, Mikhail, 27, 83, 85, 89, 172, 263, 355, 380
Gottwald, Klement, 144
Greek Rite Catholics: in Romania, 209–10, 211, 212, 213–17, 219, 224, 229. *See also* Ukrainian Greek Rite Catholics
Gregory VII, St. (pope), 15, 117, 380
Greil, Arthur L., 21
Greinacher, Norbert, 7
Grmič, Bishop Vekoslav, 197
Gromyko, Andrei, 352
Grösz, Archbishop József, 18, 24, 159, 160, 349
Grósz, Károly, 173, 174
Grotewohl, Otto, 96
Guardini, Romano, 9
Gudava, Eduard, 64
Gudava, Tengiz, 64
Guevara, Ernesto "Che," 21
Gulbinowicz, Archbishop Henryk, 134
Gundlach, Fr. Gustav, 350
Gutierrez, Gustavo, 40, 43, 317, 320
Gysi, Klaus, 102
Gyulay, Bishop Endre, 174–75

Haki, Hulusi, 248
Hamer, Jean Cardinal, 345
Harapi, Fr. Anton, 241
Harapi, Fr. Mark, 244
Häring, Hermann, 7
Hart, Armando, 307
Hel', Ivan, 83
Henry IV, Emperor, 380
Hernández Pico, Juan, 21
Hien, Nguyen Van, 284
Hien, Phong, 277, 278
Hiep, Fr. Tran Thai, 292
Hierarchy, 15–23, 346
Hirka, Bishop Jan, 153
Hitchcock, James, 9
Hitler, Adolf, 349
Hlond, August Cardinal-Primate, 24, 122
Hoa, Bishop Nguyen Van, 288
Honecker, Erich, 102, 103, 111, 113
Hoover, Herbert, 347
Hopko, Bishop Basil, 148
Horthy, Admiral Mïklós Hung, 157
Hossu, Bishop Iulius, 210, 215, 217
Houtart, François, 290–91
Hoxha, Enver, 234, 237, 239, 240–41, 242, 243
Hrushiv, Miraculous apparition of the Madonna at, 82
Hrůza, Karel, 152, 154
Hugo, Victor, 29
Hume, David, 362, 372
Hung, The, 276
Hungary, 18, 20, 26, 27, 150, 156–80, 344, 375
Husák, Gustáv, 148
Husserl, Edmund, 359
Hu Yaobang, 261
Hyginus, St. (pope), 15

Iesyp, Fr. Roman, 77
Iglesia (Nicaraguan religious publication), 326
Illich, Ivan, 8
Immaculate conception, 17
Innocent III (pope), 16
Innocenti, Antonio Cardinal, 345
Integralists, 9–10
Iuvenalii, Metropolitan (Russian Orthodox), 76
Ivanov, Ambassador Nikolai, 349

Jakab, Bishop Antal, 220
Jakova, Tut, 242
Janku, Vladimir, 153
Jaroszewski, Tadeusz M., 135
Jaruzelski, Wojciech, 121, 136, 353
Jedretić, Archbishop Kuzma, 182
Jehovah's Witnesses, 200, 306
Jelačić, Fr. Bonaventura, 188

Jerome of Wallachia, 220
Jesuits, 8, 149, 199, 235, 241, 255, 270, 298–300
Jin Luxian, Bishop, 261, 262, 265
John XXIII (pope), 34, 37, 101, 161, 256, 349, 350, 351
John Paul II (pope), 6, 10, 12, 13, 15, 17, 20, 21, 35, 41, 43, 66, 68, 70, 73, 75, 76, 80, 82, 85, 102, 134, 139, 172, 176, 177, 197, 218, 220, 228, 248, 257, 258, 263, 294, 333, 341, 342, 343, 345, 353, 356–81
Jugendweihe, 98, 103, 106–7, 110
Justinian Marina, Patriarch (Romanian Orthodox), 213–14

Kádár, János, 160, 162, 166, 170, 174
Kąkol, Kazimierz, 121
Kant, Immanuel, 356, 359, 360, 361
Kaplan, Karel, 146, 147, 149
Kapto, Oleksandr, 56, 79
Kashlev, Yuri, 354
Kastrioti, Gjerje, 234
Kavatsiv, Fr. Vasyl', 77
Kelly, Bishop Thomas C., 12
von Ketteler, Bishop Wilhelm Emmanuel, 30
Kharchev, Konstantin, 49, 81
Khira, Bishop Oleksander, 56
Khmara, Stepan, 83
Khomyshyn, Bishop Hryhorii, 55
Khrushchev, Nikita, 5, 55, 57, 58, 243, 350
Khue, Archbishop Trinh Nhu, 274, 277, 278
Kinzer, Stephen, 331
Kirill, Archbishop, 88, 89
Kirk, John, 299
Kleutgen, Josef, 4
Kobryn, Vasyl', 75
Kołakowski, Leszek, 127
Kolarz, Walter, 60, 61
Kolesnyk, Mykola, 87
Komonchak, Joseph A., 6
Kondrusiewicz, Rev. Tadeusz, 63
König, Franz Cardinal, 219–20, 345, 352
Korea, North, 344, 371
Kostel'nyk, Fr. Hryhorii, 55
Kosygin, Aleksei, 59
Kotlarczyk, Mieczysław, 357
Kotsylovs'kyi, Bishop Iosafat, 55
Kowalewski, David, 21
Krauter, Bishop Sebastian, 220
Kravchuk, Leonid, 78
Krestinskii, Ambassador Nikolai, 348
Kriksciunas, Bishop Romualdas, 58, 68, 85
Krusche, Bishop Werner, 113
Kuharić, Franjo Cardinal, 195, 204, 346
Küng, Hans, 3, 7
Kuroedov, Vladimir, 66
Kurti, Fr. Shtjefen Jak, 244, 245, 248
Kustić, Fr. Živko, 196
Kvaternik, General Slavko, 186–87
Ky, Fr. Vu Xuan, 273

Laborem exercens (1981), 41–42, 45, 122, 372–73
Lach, Bishop Josip, 183
Laigueglia, Giuseppe, 306
Lajolo, Msgr. Giovanni, 344
Lakota, Bishop Hryhorii, 55
Lalić, Ivan, 204
Lan, Fr. Nguyen Ngoc, 279, 281, 288
Lan, Bishop Nguyen Van, 286
Laramani Christians, 234
Latvia, 49, 53, 54, 59, 61, 72–74, 85
Laurinavicius, Bronius, 69
Laviana, Garcia, 313
League of Militant Godless, 52
Léfebvre, Archbishop Marcel, 9–10
Lékai, László Cardinal, 20, 162, 167, 168, 170, 172
Lek Dukahjini, Prince, 238
Lemaitre, Henri, 280
Lemercinier, Genevieve, 290–91
Lenin, V. I., 347
Leo XIII (pope), 28, 29, 30–32, 33, 34, 41, 185
Leopold I (Habsburg), 209
Le Plant, Fr. Benito, 326
Liaison Committee of Patriotic and Peace-Loving Catholics (Vietnam), 273, 274, 287–88
Liatyshevs'kyi, Bishop Ivan, 55, 60
Liberals, 7
Liberation theology, 10, 21, 39, 40–45, 377–78

Lieu, Fr. Tuong Van, 277
Ligachev, Egor, 56
Linh, Nguyen Van, 285, 289
Lithuania, 22, 27, 49, 50, 53, 54, 57, 58–59, 61, 65–67, 69, 70–71, 85
Ljevar, Bosiljko, 182
Loisy, Abbé Alfred, 4, 7
Lopez, Amando, 320
Lopez Ardon, Bishop, 317
Lopez Trujillo, Archbishop Alfonso, 41, 374
Lord's Army (Romania), 218
Loredo, Fr. Miguel Angel, 306
Luan, Chau Tam, 279
Luan, Fr. Tran The, 279
Lubachivs'kyi, Archbishop Myroslav Ivan, 76, 80, 87, 346
Lukács, József, 165
Luli, Fr. Ndoc, 245
Lutheran Church, 72, 73–74, 93, 94, 98, 99, 100, 103, 104, 107, 108, 109, 110, 111, 112–13, 114, 209
Luther year (1983), 111
Ly, Fr. Nguyen Van, 289

McBrien, Richard P., 4, 6, 16
Maček, Vladko, 187
Macharski, Archbishop Franciszek, 134, 346
Madonna. *See* Hrushiv; Medjugorje
Madriz, Fr. Mario, 327
Mai, Bishop Nguyen Huy, 288
Majka, Józef, 126, 135
Makarii, Archbishop (of Ivano-Frankivs'k and Kolomyia), 80
Malaj, Fr. Ded, 243
Mao Zedong, 253
Marcone, Abbot Ramito, 184
Mareş, Fr. Petru, 216, 224
Maritain, Jacques, 34
Markus, Zlatko, 182
Marton, Bishop Aron, 219, 220
Marusyn, Archbishop Miroslav, 343
Marx, Karl, 362, 368, 369, 370, 373
Masucci, Don Giuseppe, 184
Mater et magistra (1961), 26, 37
Matthews, Herbert, 301
Matulaitis, Bishop Juozapas, 86
Matulionis, Fr. Jonas Kastytis, 69, 70
Matulionis, Bishop Teofilius, 58
Maurer, Ion Gheorghe, 352
Maza, Manuel, 300
Mazelis, Bishop Petras, 58
Mazrreku, Fr. Filip, 245
Medellín Conference (1968), 39, 44, 300, 307, 314
Medjugorje, miraculous apparition of Madonna at, 200
Meisner, Joachim Cardinal (of Berlin), 110, 346
Meshkella, Fr. Pjeter, 245
Micewski, Andrzej, 124
Micu (Klein), Bishop John Innocent, 210
Mieszko, Prince, 117
Miklós, Imre, 163, 173, 175, 344
Mikołajczyk, Stanisław, 122
Mikoyan, Anastas, 350
Milanović, Božo, 190
Millennium of Kievan Rus', 343
Mina, Gianni, 308
Mindszenty, József Cardinal, 13, 157, 158, 160, 162
Minh, Ho Chi, 271, 275
Minh, Fr. Huynh Cong, 279, 292
Mišić, Bishop Alojzije, 183
Miskito Indians, 328–29
Mit brennender Sorge (1937), 11, 376
Miziołek, Bishop Władysław, 137
Mladenov, Petar, 352
Moldavia, 64
Molina, Fr. Uriel, 21, 317
Montero, Fr. Feliciano, 327
Mounier, Emmanuel, 34
Muslims, 200, 218, 233–34, 235, 240, 243
Mussolini, Benito, 238

Ndocaj, Marc, 246
Nell-Breuning, Oswald, 32
Nemanjić, Sava, 183
Neoscholastics, 5–6
Nestor, Bishop, 56
Neveu, Bishop Pie Eugen, 24, 52, 349
Newman, John Henry Cardinal, 4
Nghi, Bishop Nicholas Huynh Van, 294
Nhien, Msgr. Nguyen Dinh, 277
Nhuan, Ho Ngoc, 279

Nicaragua, 14, 18, 21–22, 24, 26, 313–38
Nicholas, St., 376
Nichols, Peter, 6
Nigris, Archbishop Leone, 241
Noli, Bishop Fan, 237
Novak, Michael, 37
Novotný, Antonin, 150
Nukss, Bishop Wilhelms, 86
Nuschke, Otto, 97, 99
Nyers, Rezsö, 174

Oasis (Poland), 130
Obando y Bravo, Archbishop Miguel, 316, 323, 324, 325, 328, 330, 331, 333, 334, 335, 336
O'Connor, John J. Cardinal, 308
Octogesima adveniens (1971), 39
Ogden, Schubert, 7
Ogorodnikov, Alexander, 87
O'Hara, Archbishop Gerald, 212
Opus Pacis movement (Hungary), 160–61, 168
Orszulik, Rev. Alojzy, 22
Ortega, Daniel, 326, 334
Ortega, Archbishop Jaime, 309

Pacem in terris (Czechoslovak priests' organization), 18, 153, 199
Pacem in terris (1963), 26, 37, 256, 350
Pacifism: in East Germany, 108–10
Palfi, Fr. Géza, 226
Pallais, Fr. Leon, 315
Paltarokas, Bishop Kazimieras, 54
Paraga, Dobroslav, 195
Pasha, Vaso, 236
Paskai, László Cardinal, 21, 64, 177, 179, 229
Pasztor, Bishop Jan, 153
Patriotic Priests (Peace Committee of the Catholic Clergy in Czechoslovakia), 150, 151
Paul I (pope), 234
Paul VI (pope), 11, 23, 26, 38–40, 102, 104, 114, 121, 161, 162, 217, 220, 248, 277, 313, 342, 345, 351, 352, 353, 369
Pavelić, Ante, 182, 186, 187
Pax Association (Poland), 120
Pázmány, Péter Cardinal, 175–76
Peace Committee of the Catholic Clergy in Czechoslovakia, 150, 151
Peña, Fr. Amado, 327, 330
Pesch, Heinrich, 32
Peter, St., 4
Peterca, Vladimir, 222
Philby, Kim, 237
Phuoc, Fr. Pham Quang, 288
Piasecki, Bolesław, 120
Pichler, Bishop Alfred, 197
Picura, Bishop Ion (Romanian Orthodox), 216
Pimen, Patriarch (Russian Orthodox), 83
Pipa, Mustafer, 241
Pius I, St. (pope), 15
Pius IX (pope), 16–17
Pius X Brotherhood, 9
Pius XI (pope), 6, 11, 29, 32–34, 36, 52–53, 300, 340, 348, 349, 376
Pius XII (pope), 11, 15, 34–36, 122, 183, 213, 219, 242, 348, 349, 350
Pizzardo, Giuseppe, 347
Plesca, Bishop Petru, 220
Pletkus, Bishop Juozas, 58
Plojhar, Fr. Josef, 145, 150
Ploscariu, Bishop Ioan, 218
Podgorny, Nikolai, 352, 353
Poggi, Archbishop Luigi, 220, 344, 352
Pokutnyky, 60–61
Poland, 24–25, 26, 102, 110, 117–41, 150, 284, 343, 345, 351, 353, 359, 370–71, 375
Popiełuszko, Fr. Jerzy, 26, 121
Populorum progressio (1967), 39
Poresh, Vladimir, 87
Pos, Fr. Franjo, 182
Potochniak, Fr. Antin, 61
Poupard, Paul Cardinal, 346
Povilonis, Bishop Liudvikas, 58, 68, 85
Prendushi, Archbishop Vincenz, 241
von Preysing, Konrad Cardinal (of Berlin), 95, 104
Preysing Decree, 96
Priests' associations: Yugoslavia, 189–92
Prusina, Ivan, 200
Pseudo-Isidore. See *False Decretals*
Puebla Conference (1979), 15, 20, 22, 41, 44, 307, 308

Quadragesimo Anno (1931), 32–34
Quercetti, Fr. Sesto, 280
Quy, Fr. Tran Van, 289

Radek, Karl, 51
Radicals, 7–9
Rákosi, Mátyás, 158
Ramanauskas, Bishop Pranas, 58
Ratzinger, Joseph Cardinal, 5–6, 7, 10, 21, 42–43, 112, 345, 376
Redemptoris mater (1987), 379
Reding, Marcel, 349–50
Ren Wuzhi, 261
Rerum novarum (1891), 28, 30–31, 35, 41
Revolutionary Popular Action Movement (Cuba), 305
Ribičič, Mitja, 205
Ricci, Mateo, 255
Rittig, Msgr. Svetozar, 182–83, 184
Robu, Msgr. Ioan, 220, 225
Romania, 207–31, 344, 352
Romanian Orthodox Church, 213–17
Romzha, Bishop, 56
von der Ropp, Archbishop Eduard, 51
Russian Orthodox Church, 73, 74, 88, 148, 350
Rusu, Bishop Alexandre, 215
Ryan, John A., 32

Šagi-Bunić, Fr. Tomislav, 13, 203
Sainz, Msgr. Muñoz Faustino, 342
Sajudis (Lithuanian Popular Front), 86
Sakharov, Andrei, 87
Sakić, Viktor, 182
Salaverri, Joachim, 5
Salazar y Espinoza, Bishop, 313
Salis-Seewis, Bishop Franjo, 184
Sang, Bishop François-Xavier Nguyen Van, 285
Sardiñas, Fr. Guillermo, 297
Šarić, Archbishop Ivan, 183
Sartre, Jean-Paul, 368, 370
Scanderbeg. *See* Kastrioti, Gjerje
Schaff, Adam, 369
Scheler, Max, 358–59, 360–63, 370
Schönherr, Bishop Albrecht, 113
Schools: in Cuba, 302–3
Ściegienny, Piotr, 137
Seigewasser, Hans, 108
Senderov, Valerii, 87
Šeper, Franjo Cardinal, 193, 197–98
Seventh Day Adventists, 200
Shehu, Mehmet, 246
Sheptyts'kyi, Metropolitan Andrei, 51, 53–54
Shevchenko, Taras, 88
Shevchenko, Vitalii, 83
Shllaku, Bishop Bernadin, 241, 242
Shuba, Oleksii, 79
Shu-Park Chan, 262
Silvestrini, Achille, 342
Simons, Bishop Francis, 9
Simrak, Bishop Janko, 185
Sin, Jaime Cardinal, 261, 262, 264, 265
Sinishta, Gjon, 248
Široki Brijeg monastery, 184, 188
Skucha, Auxiliary Bishop Piotr, 134
Sladkevicius, Bishop Vincentas, 58, 65, 68, 85
Slanský, Rudolf, 144
Slavorum apostoli (1985), 378
Slipyi, Metropolitan Iosyf, 55, 60, 75, 76, 80, 216, 350
Sloskans, Boleslavs, 52
Slovenia, 27
Slowieniec, Fr. Stanisław, 342
Smith, Fr. Pablo, 335
Sodano, Angelo, 342, 343
Solidarity (trade union), 123, 353
Sollicitudo rei socialis (1988), 12–13, 45
Soltys, Ihnatii, 61
Somalo, Bishop Eduardo Martinez, 345
Somoza, General Anastasio, 313, 316
Soviet Union, 14, 26, 49–90
Spain, 299
Spiljak, Mika, 203
Springovics, Archbishop Antonijs, 54
Spülbeck, Bishop Otto (of Meissen), 103, 110
Stajka, Nika, 242
Stalin, Josef, 52, 57, 215, 243, 349, 375
Stanisław, St. (of Szczepanów), 117
Stanojević, Branimir, 203
Stehle, Hansjakob, 27
Stephen I, King (of Hungary), 176–77

Stepinac, Alojzije Cardinal, 181, 183, 185, 186–89, 191, 193, 203–4
Steponavicius, Bishop Julijonas, 58, 65, 85, 86
Sterniuk, Archbishop Volodymyr, 87
Stojałowski, Stanisław, 137
Straub, Brúnó, 176–77
Stroba, Archbishop Jerzy, 134
Strods, Bishop Peteris, 54
Strossmayer, Bishop Josip Juraj, 181, 183, 185, 190, 204
Suciu, Bishop Ion, 214
Šuštar, Archbishop Alojzij, 204
Svarinskas, Fr. Alfonsas, 67, 70, 86
Svete, Zdenko, 204
Swidnicki, Fr. Jozef, 64–65
Syllabus of 1864, 11
Szendi, Bishop József, 173

Tagliaferri, Mario, 306
Tamkevicius, Fr. Sigitas, 67, 70, 87
Tancher, Volodymyr, 87
Taylor, Myron, 349
Telesphorus, St. (pope), 15
Terelia, Iosyp, 74–75, 83
Thanh, Fr. Le Tan, 292
Tho, Nguyen Huu, 289
Thu, Bishop Le Huu, 271
Thu, Fr. Tran Van, 285–86
Thuan, Bishop Nguyen Van, 281, 282, 293
Tin, Fr. Chan, 279, 281, 288, 293
Tischner, Józef, 126
Tiso, Msgr. Josef, 143
Tito, Josip Broz, 5, 184–85, 189, 351
Todea, Bishop Alexander, 218
Tokarczuk, Bishop Ignacy, 131
Tomášek, František Cardinal, 22, 152, 153, 347, 351
Tomko, Bishop Josef, 345
Tönnies, Ferdinand, 359
Torres, Camilo, 8, 304
Tracy, David, 7
Traditionalists, 5
Trinh, Fr. Vo Thanh, 273, 287, 288, 289
Troshani, Bishop Nikoll, 242, 245
Trung, Ly Chanh, 279
Trung, Nguyen Van, 279
Tu, Fr. Phan Khac, 279, 288, 290
Tuan, Bishop Bui, 288

Ukrainian Greek Rite Catholics, 18, 27, 49, 53–55, 59–61, 74–75, 78–84, 148
Ulanfu, 260
Ulbricht, Walter, 98, 99–100, 101
Urban, Jerzy, 22
Ustaše (fascists), 181, 182–83, 185, 186–87

Vaicius, Bishop, 68
Vaivods, Bishop Julijans, 59, 86, 88
Vargas Llosa, Mario, 329, 330
Vas, Zoltán, 158
Vata, Gjergj, 241
Vatican Councils. *See* Councils
Vega, Bishop Pablo, 328, 335
Vego, Ivica, 200
Velychkovs'kyi, Bishop Vasyl', 60
Verhun, Msgr. Petro, 55
Vichku, Ivan, 64
Viet, Hoang Quoc, 283
Viet Minh, 271–73
Vietnam, 18, 270–95, 344
Vinh, Fr. Nguyen The, 273, 287
Vinnyts'kyi, Fr. Mykhailo, 77
Volaz, Bishop Gjergj, 241
Vosykevych, Fr. Ievhen, 77
Vrana, Bishop Josef, 153
Vrcan, Srdjan, 193

Walsh, Fr. Edmund, 347–48
Wanke, Bishop Joachim (of Erfurt), 109, 110, 111
Wei Jingsheng, 264
Whyte, Bob, 264
Wienken, Heinrich, 95, 96, 97
Willebrands, Johannes Cardinal, 76, 87, 343, 350
Wirth, Josef, 347
Witos, Wincenty, 125
Wojtyła, Karol Cardinal. *See* John Paul II
World Bank, 301
Wu Cheng-chung, Bishop John Baptist, 262, 263, 265
Wyszyński, Stefan Cardinal, 24–25, 121, 124, 128, 134–35, 349, 361, 363

Xiao Xianfa, 260

Yakunin, Gleb, 87
Yang Gaojian, Bishop Michael, 258
Yang Zengnian, 261, 263
Young Hegelians, 369
Yu Bin, Archbishop Paul, 266
Yugoslavia, 5, 14, 18–19, 26, 181–206, 239, 243, 246, 343, 351

Zacchi, Archbishop Cesare, 305–6
Žanić, Bishop Pavao, 200
Zaval'niuk, Vladyslav, 64, 72
Zdebskis, Fr. Juozas, 67, 69
Zemaitis, Bishop Juozas, 86
Zerr, Bishop, 52
Zhang Jiashu, Bishop, 261
Zhao Puchu, 263–64
Zhao Ziyang, 261, 262, 264, 265
Zhivkov, Todor, 352
Zhu Hongshen, Fr., 264
Zigliari, Francesco Cardinal, 30
Znak movement (Poland), 128
Zog, King (of Albania), 236, 238
Zogu, Ahmet. *See* Zog, King
Zondaks, Auxiliary Bishop Valerijans, 59, 73
Zong, Huaide Bishop, 261

About the Contributors

Humberto Belli is Associate Professor of Sociology at the Franciscan University of Steubenville, and chair of the Puebla Institute. A former Sandinista (1969–74), he later joined the staff of *La Prensa*, the only opposition newspaper in Nicaragua. He is the author of *Nicaragua: Christians under Fire* (1983) and *Breaking Faith: The Sandinista Revolution and Its Impact on Freedom and Christian Faith in Nicaragua* (1985), and coeditor (with Carlos Corsi) of *Centro America en Llamas* (1982). He has contributed chapters to *Is Capitalism Christian?* (1985), *Voices against the State* (1988), and *Liberation Theology* (1988). His articles have appeared in *America*, *Catholicism in Crisis*, *Policy Review*, and other periodicals.

Janice Broun is a free-lance journalist specializing in religion under communism. She is the author of the Pro Mundi Vita dossier *The Church in Bulgaria* (1986) and *Conscience and Captivity: Religion in Eastern Europe* (1989), and coeditor (with Anna Tapay) of *Prague Winter* (1988). Her articles have appeared in *America*, *Commonweal*, *Religion in Communist Lands*, and other periodicals. She is now East European correspondent for News Network International.

Vincent C. Chrypinski is Professor Emeritus of Political Science at the University of Windsor, Canada. He has contributed chapters to *Religion and Atheism in the USSR and Eastern Europe* (1975), *Sisyphus and Poland: Reflections on Martial Law* (1986), and *Religion and Nationalism in Soviet and East European Politics* (revised and expanded edition, 1989). His articles have appeared in *Canadian Slavonic Papers*, *International Journal*, *Slavic Review*, and other journals.

Stephen Denney is Library Assistant at the Indochina Archive of the Institute of East Asian Studies, University of California, Berkeley. He is coauthor (with Ginetta Sagan) of *Violations of Human Rights in the Socialist Republic of Vietnam: April 30, 1975, to April 30, 1983* (1983) and editor, since 1979, of the *Indochina Journal*. His articles have appeared in *Buddhist Peace Fellowship Newsletter* and *Reconciliation International*.

Robert F. Goeckel is Assistant Professor of Political Science at the State University of New York, Geneseo. He is the author of *Lenin and Luther: The Role of the Lutheran Church in East Germany since 1945* (in press). He has contributed chapters to *East Germany, West Germany, and the Soviet Union: The Changing Relationship* (1986), *Quality of Life in the German Democratic Republic* (1988), and *East Germany in Comparative Perspective* (1989). His articles have appeared in *Deutschland Archiv*, *International Journal of Sociology*, and *World Politics*.

Eric O. Hanson is Associate Professor of Political Science at Santa Clara University and a member of the Stanford University Center for International Security and Arms Control. He is the author of *Catholic Politics in China and Korea* (1980) and *The Catholic Church in World Politics* (1987). He lived in East Asia for five years in the 1960s and 1970s and was a television analyst on John Paul II's trip to the United States in 1987.

Ivan Hvat is Program Specialist in the Ukrainian Service at Radio Liberty, Munich. His articles on Soviet and East European religious affairs have been published in *Religion in Communist Lands* and other journals. He contributed a chapter to *The Lemko Land: Territory, People, History, Culture* (1988).

Leslie László is Professor of Political Science at Concordia University, Canada, and the author of *Resistance of the Spirit: The Churches in Hungary During the Second World War* (in Hungarian, 1980). He has contributed chapters to *Religion and Atheism in the USSR and Eastern Europe* (1975), *Eastern Christianity and Politics in the Twentieth Century* (1988), and *Religion and Nationalism in Soviet and East European Politics* (revised and expanded edition, 1989). His articles have appeared in *East European Quarterly*, *Occasional Papers on Religion in Eastern Europe*, *East Central Europe*, and other journals.

Arthur F. McGovern, S.J., is Professor of Philosophy at the University of Detroit and faculty director of the university's Honors Program. He is the author of *Marxism: An American Christian Perspective* (1980) and *Liberation Theology and Its Critics* (1989). He is coauthor of *Ethical Dilemmas in the Modern Corporation* (1988) and has contributed chapters to several other books. His articles have appeared in *America*, *Commonweal*, *Journal of Ecumenical Studies*, and other periodicals and journals.

Thomas E. Quigley is the adviser on Latin American issues at the United States Catholic Conference, the secretariat of the American Catholic hierarchy. He is the editor of *Freedom and Unfreedom in the Americas* (1971) and *American Catholics and Vietnam* (1968). He has contributed chapters to *The Word in the Third World* (1968), *The Church and Society in Latin America* (1984), and *Central America: Human Rights and U.S. Foreign Policy* (1985). His articles have appeared in *America*, *Christianity and Crisis*, *Commonweal*, and other journals.

Pedro Ramet is Associate Professor of International Studies at the University of Washington. He is the author of *Nationalism and Federalism in Yugoslavia, 1963–1983* (1984), *Cross and Commissar: The Politics of Religion in Eastern Europe and the USSR* (1987), and *The Soviet-Syrian Relationship since 1955: A Troubled Alliance* (forthcoming), and editor of *Yugoslavia in the 1980s* (1985), *Eastern Christianity and Politics in the Twentieth Century* (1988), and *Religion and Nationalism in Soviet and East European Politics* (revised and expanded edition, 1989). He contributed chapters to *Gorbachev and the Soviet Future* (1988), *Die Muslime in der Sowjetunion und Jugoslawien* (1989), and *Candle in the Wind* (1989). His articles have appeared in *Problems of Communism*, *World Politics*, and *Political Science Quarterly*.

Milan J. Reban is Associate Professor of Political Science at North Texas State University. He is the coeditor (with George Klein) of *The Politics of Ethnicity in Eastern Europe* (1981). He is coauthor (with Peter Toma) of a chapter in *Religion and Atheism in the USSR and Eastern Europe* (1975).

Roman Solchanyk is Director of Program Research and Development at Radio Liberty, Munich. He is coauthor of *Ukraine Under Gorbachev* (forthcoming) and coeditor of *Ukrainian Socio-Political Thought in the Twentieth Century: Documents and Source Materials*, 3 vols. (1983). His articles have appeared in *Slavic Review*, *Soviet Studies*, *Canadian Slavonic Papers*, and other journals.

Hansjakob Stehle has been correspondent in Rome for West German radio and *Die Zeit* since 1970. From 1955 to 1963 he was editor and correspondent in Poland for the *Frankfurter Allgemeine*. He is the author of *Deutschlands Osten—Polens Westen* (1965), *The Independent Satellite: Society and Politics in Poland* (1965), *Nachbarn im Osten* (1971), and *Eastern Politics of the Vatican, 1917–1979* (1981). He has contributed chapters to *Communism in Europe* (1964), *Die Ostbeziehungen der Europaischen Gemeinschaft* (1977), *Religionsfreiheit und Menschenrechte* (1983), and *Morality and Reality: The*

Life and Times of Andrei Sheptytskyi (1988). He also periodically writes for *The World Today*.

George Huntston Pease Williams is Hollis Professor of Divinity Emeritus at Harvard University. He is the author of *The Radical Reformation* (1962; Spanish ed., 1983), *The Polish Brethren*, 2 vols. (1980), *The Mind of John Paul II* (1981), and other books. He is the coeditor (with Angel M. Mergal) of *Anabaptist and Spiritual Writers* (1957) and (with Norman Pettit) of *The Writings of Thomas Hooker* (1975). He has received honorary doctorates from six universities, most recently from the University of Edinburgh (1987), and was honored with a festschrift in 1980: *Continuity and Discontinuity in Church History: Essays in Honor of George Huntston Williams*, edited by F. Forrester Church and Timothy George. In 1980 he was decorated as a Knight of St. Gregory the Great. In 1989 he brought out an annotated edition of Stanislaw Lubiniecki's 1685 classic *Historia Reformationis Polonicae* (originally published in Amsterdam).